SECURITY IN THE GULF

The Adelphi Library

Security in the Gulf

THE ADELPHI LIBRARY 7

SHAHRAM CHUBIN
ROBERT LITWAK
AVI PLASCOV

Published for
THE INTERNATIONAL INSTITUTE FOR
STRATEGIC STUDIES
by
Gower

Published by

Gower Publishing Company Limited,
Gower House,
Croft Road,
Aldershot, Hants GU11 3HR, England

British Library Cataloguing in Publication Data

Chubin, Shahram
  Security in the Gulf — (The Adelphi library; 7)
  1. Security, International
  2. Persian Gulf region — Strategic aspects
  I. Title   II. Litwak, Robert
  III. Plascov, Avi   IV. Series
  327.1'16   DS326
  ISBN 0-566-00452-6

ISBN 0 566 00452 6

Contents

Contributors

John Duke Anthony	:	Professor at School for Advanced International Studies (SAIS) John Hopkins University, Washington DC
Michael Field	:	Freelance writer formerly with the *Financial Times*
Allan G. Hill	:	Senior Research Fellow London School of Hygiene and Tropical Medicine
Arnold Hottinger	:	Correspondent for the *Neue Zuricher Zeitung*, Zurich

Introduction

Shahram Chubin

These papers were originally presented at an international conference in November 1979. They have been amended in the light of conference discussions as well as subsequent events.

The Institute has embarked on a major study of security in the Gulf. These conference topics were intended to serve as a launching point for the wider project, but were consciously framed to address the dynamics of political forces inside the littoral states. It may appear in the light of the Soviet invasion of Afghanistan, and of developments in Iran, which have concentrated superpower attention on this region, that this is too narrow a focus. I do not believe that this is the case. In the Gulf threats to security come from many sources. For the foreseeable future—for the next decade at least—OECD dependency will continue (if it does not increase) on the Gulf for oil supplies, for 40 per cent of world oil is located here. Although a common interest, Alliance members have differential dependencies and vulnerabilities. Soviet interest in the region has also grown as the Soviet Union has acquired most of the attributes of a global power, and that interest may increase in the 1980s with the need to secure oil for Eastern Europe and possibly a direct need for oil imports to the Soviet Union.

Together with a growing and overlapping interest by the superpowers there has occurred a shift in the military balance of power in the region. This is in part a consequence of Britain's winding down of imperial commitment and American reluctance to substitute for it; in part a result of growing Soviet military power; and in part an outgrowth of the regional political environment in which local states are more assertive about their own priorities, goals and interests. The military imbalance—

reflecting geopolitical asymmetries—has not yet had a decisive effect on the politics of the region but on the level of political perceptions it has a marked and (presumably given the trends) a growing one. The challenge for the two blocs in the next decade will be to work out rules of engagement that protect their interests but do not unduly disturb their existing relationships with regional states. A major obstacle to such an agreement on mutual access is likely to be the unstable regional political environment which will provide tempting opportunities for the exploitation and enhancement of one side's interests, whilst administering a setback to the other. The test will be to devise a sufficiently discriminating policy that will be able both to distinguish between and to address separately instabilities that have regional origins and instabilities that are clear threats to Western interests fostered by the opposing bloc.

For the West, dependency on the Persian Gulf extends beyond the mere flow of oil. The issues of price and rate of production are also important. The notion that oil producing states cannot 'drink their oil' has been disproved by recent history; for the producer, limiting production can be a very economical way of raising prices. The foreign orientation of the producing states is therefore of consequence; policy changes can affect the oil flow. If oil embargoes (or reduced production) are one possibility, another is interruption from loss of control. Revolutions (as in Iran), or major inter-state warfare illustrate this.

For better or worse, therefore, the economic and political wellbeing of the OECD will be progressively entangled with the destiny of the Gulf states. Yet this region is unlike any other in which the West has vital security interests. It is not, and cannot be, covered by a traditional security guarantee—like NATO. It is culturally separate. It is undergoing a period of rapid change which creates strains on existing societies and forms of government whose ultimate shape is of necessity uncertain. These three elements in combination underscore the delicacy of the relationship between the West and the oil producers. Regional politics prevent an alliance with the West because of the West's support for Israel. The cultural divide inhibits an intimate relationship and the stresses of 'modernization' make a sound analysis of the region's 'stability' difficult.

Despite the military 'overhang' problem and superpower rivalry, the major threats to the region are only partly external. Inter-state rivalries and conflicts arising from ideological, dynastic or historical and territorial differences are another—and fertile—source of instability. More important still are the range of forces unleashed by the rapid embrace of new technology and new ideas, made possible by oil wealth.

What then are the local instabilities and are they evenly distributed? The conference papers look at their domestic origins and focus on the differences among the least studied states. Iran and Iraq have been excluded on the grounds that they are already relatively well studied.

Their collective aim is to identify various aspects of the modernization process, economic development, the politicization of populations, and urbanization, and to discuss their varying impact on the Gulf states, with reference to their (indigenous) capacity to deal with them. The question of the adaptability of existing institutions (formal and informal) and procedures is thus addressed.

The challenges faced by the states are broadly comparable:

1 Rapid rates of population growth with a large proportion of restive young.

2 Movement from rural areas into towns and cities which entails urbanization, and the decline of traditional society, etc.

3 The adaptation of political institutions to the need for more political participation.

4 The diversification of economies away from a single resource.

5 Manpower shortages, immigrants and their political implications.

6 The reconciliation and synthesis of traditional moral values with new norms and social organization.

In addressing these and other questions, two papers are organized around specific countries and two along functional lines. The first two compare political forces at work in Saudi Arabia, Kuwait, Bahrain and the UAE; the latter two discuss the problems of states endowed with adequate but finite material resources, but lacking human and other requisites for their optimum use. The Gulf states are all clearly undergoing a similar process and face parallel predicaments but neither the pressures nor their means for coping with them are identical. This is the result of different social structures and political institutions and an outgrowth of differential oil income. Bahrain, one of the earliest and now a declining oil producer, was perhaps least affected by the price explosion of the 1970s; it has now lived with an urban and relatively politicized population for two decades. Bahrain is also less affected by immigrant populations which Kutait and Saudi Arabia witness in different forms. Similarly, economic development has had differential impact on Kuwait and Saudi Arabia; the former has managed the task of distribution better than the latter where a major cleavage exists (according to Arnold Hottinger) between the small stratum of very rich and the majority, very poor.

In the UAE the problems are different as John Duke Anthony shows. The federation of seven unequally endowed shaikhdoms has lasted a decade and survived periodic crises. In practice, rivalries have persisted in the distribution of key portfolios, in differences in the pace and degree of integration and especially in the composition and control of the union versus the individual shaikhly armed forces. Rivalry also persists in the tendency toward the competition in prestige projects rather than in a rationalized co-ordination of industrialization. The UAE has survived despite inequalities in wealth, traditional rivalries, and reliance on foreign immigrants; three-quarters of the population are foreigners (mainly non-Arabs; Indians, Pakistanis, Iranians and Baluchis). Differences between the two core states—Dubai and Abu Dhabi—reflect historical rivalries but these have nevertheless been submerged enough to allow the union to survive.

Policies which have encouraged the spreading of wealth among the emirates have given the union a stronger foundation. Saudi Arabia, the most influential outside power, has lent its support to this. As a result the UAE appears more stable than the more homogenous Saudi Arabia.

The modernization process is inherently stressful; the leadership embarks upon a path whose destination is uncertain. It loosens its bonds with its traditional constituency in the expectation of receiving support and loyalty from the new, transformed, populace. In so doing it runs the risk of alienating its power base without compensating gains elsewhere. As in Iran, for diametrically opposed reasons, the left and right might become dissatisfied and unite to replace the government, in the guise of a 'traditional backlash'.

The economic 'problems' of oil rich states may be much more serious than they are conspicuous. Oil revenues distort economic development in a profound way. Oil revenues serve to cover and hence foster mistakes. They encourage a fundamental attitude toward planning that lacks measurable criteria, that is uneconomic, and which promotes wastefulness and 'white elephants'. To be sure, oil revenues are a great asset and Michael Field's somewhat optimistic paper describes the economic benefits associated with them. If states suffer from small markets, small or a poorly trained labour pool or inadequate infrastructure, these can be rectified by oil revenues. States can provide a complete spectrum of services to their citizens—free education and health care, food and housing subsidies and no taxes. But the political costs of such policies are perhaps less obvious. As Allan Hill notes, the importation of labour creates its own problems. Immigrants are discriminated against. Whether emboldened or thoroughly alienated they pose potential political problems for they may combine to further 'their interests at the expense of the host country'. In some states the proportion of the population that are native citizens is less than half—as in Kuwait and the UAE. In others, such as Saudi Arabia, they are the dominant element in the workforce. According to some calculations, the number of immigrants in the Gulf will number five million by 1985 (as against three million in 1980). The political consequences of this will vary but almost everywhere a two class system will be perpetuated differentiating in favour of the native citizens and against the often more productive immigrant.

Michael Field's paper strengthens the case for those who argue that while an economic opportunity exists—and a unique one among less developed countries—oil revenues are as much a political liability as an economic asset. The welfare state and rentier mentality create economic problems in the longer run when citizens see the state's task as one of providing them with benefits but with little commensurate responsibility of their own. But it also creates political problems for governments which are burdened with demands that they can scarcely be expected to bear. The purely financial consequences of the enrichment mentality which may encourage corruption and speculation may not be totally without value; it may, for example, assist in the spreading of wealth. Again, politically, the costs are high as materialism—and the social disruption attendant on rapid change—comes to be seen as an alien, intrusive force.

A further problem is created by surplus income and its productive use. Invested locally it tends after a certain point to strain the infrastructure and increase inflation. Invested overseas it is protected against neither inflation nor seizure. The economic incentives for conserving oil production appear to be strong and growing. This reinforces other conclusions: that problems arise not from too little but from too much growth; that rapid change increases inequalities; and that the process of modernization is inherently unpredictable in its outcome. The risks of not moving on the political front, however, may be higher in the storing up of tensions. In Bahrain and Kuwait there have been indications of an interest in reviving the limited constitutional experiments, the National Assemblies that were dissolved in 1975 and 1976. Even in Saudi Arabia, long opposed to these experiments, there is a new urgency since the November Mecca Mosque episode of creating a Consultative Council. Iraq too, although not the subject of this study, is also, in mid 1980, moving towards elections. Few societies can absorb the massive concentrated infusion of money without consequent strains on their value systems, pattern of social organization and resultant stability. Yet from the Western viewpoint the overriding need is for an orderly 'process' of development that leaves intact those mechanisms most conducive to the management of the transition. If it is not to be disruptive and disorderly, it will require a degree of continuity with past experience and the retention of the authentically valuable rather than indiscriminate acceptance of change for its own sake.

For the West, the 'security of oil supplies' has tended to have a circumscribed meaning unrelated to its political context. The extraordinary social and political pressures released by the wrenching of the states of the Gulf from their traditional patterns of existence has immensely complicated their governance. To these, as the region's geopolitical importance has risen, regional and external pressures have been added. An understanding of these pressures is the first step toward a policy that can be responsive to them.

As the West's interest in the Persian Gulf has shifted from denying the region to the USSR to securing access to the flow of oil on acceptable terms, the purely military dimension of her influence has declined. As part of this project a separate paper on the Limitations and Scope of outside Power Influence will be forthcoming. Increased dependence has been occurring at a time of decreased influence. Internal instabilities are only one of several sources of threat to the security of oil supplies and they are perhaps the least amenable to Western influence. The others are: superpower rivalry; local conflicts; terrorist activities and regional political pressures. Nevertheless, given the multiple threats to its interests, the West has had to become more entangled in the affairs of the Gulf. The challenge for the West will be in defining security in a region where stability is precarious. Although limited, Western power is not inconsequential. At the least it should demonstrate more sensitivity to regional politics and local priorities and avoid exacerbating existing instabilities—by unbridled commercialism, for example. More positively, the power that appears militarily dependable and genuinely committed to the region's welfare will be in a position to benefit. It may not influence events directly but it will influence—through the perceptions of local states—their choices as they weigh the balance of risks involved in potential policies.

1 Political institutions in Saudi Arabia, Kuwait and Bahrain

Arnold Hottinger

The leadership tradition in the Arab world

The governments of Kuwait, Bahrain and Saudi Arabia have all grown out of what can be termed the Arab tribal tradition of government. This is characterised by the rule of one man, a shaikh, usually tempered by some kind of informal mechanism of consultation, a tribal council. The shaikh or ruler can be 'elected' but this is no formal election—rather a *de facto* nomination arrived at by a process of internal struggles, alliances and consultations which eventually leads to the most powerful, rich, prestigious and influential head of clan becoming tribal boss. Once firmly entrenched, there is a tendency for the leader to keep the position within his clan and family. This is often possible because the shaikh or ruler can use his position to further increase his pre-eminent standing by gaining more riches, prestige, influence, etc. over other possible rivals.

A change of ruling clan and family usually occurs if the shaikh fails in his undertakings. In that case his prestige is diminished and possible rivals are given a chance to replace him. They will normally belong to a different clan or even tribe because the disaster befalling the previous shaikh is normally of a collective nature such as defeat in a tribal war. This invariably means that the whole clan or tribe loses power thus allowing a new clan or tribe to take over the leadership.

No hereditary rule

If there is no disaster, the leadership will remain within the ruling family—but it is not a hereditary leadership. Children or even young men cannot lead a clan or tribe. The leadership usually then goes to some relative of the previous ruler, and the family council speaks an authoritative word when the decision is made. The deceased ruler or shaikh, particularly if he has been powerful and successful, may also indicate the choice of his successor, frequently by associating him with his rule while he still remains the supreme authority. Money and other forms of fortune also play an important part in achieving and maintaining rule. The classical tribal shaikh has to be rich enough to offer lavish hospitality to his followers and to outside dignitaries. He is also a war leader and obtains an important part of the spoils of war. But essentially he remains *primus inter pares,* and a symbol of this position is the fact that all tribal subjects or colleagues—both qualifications apply—have free access to the shaikh and can come to him to present grievances or requests either at any time or, if the standing of the ruler increases, at certain hours in the evening when a *Majlis* is held.

Titulation

A major tribal leader is given the title *amir,* commander, and this is the title officially translated as 'ruler' which is still held by those who rule Kuwait and Bahrain. The passage between shaikh and amir is fluid (as are most things within this traditional concept of tribal leadership); in current language, but not in official titulation, both rulers are still known as the shaikh. *Malik,* or 'king', which has been the title of the ruler of Saudi Arabia since Malik Abdul Aziz Ibn Sa'ud, implies a greater distance between the ruler and the ruled. However, it is not really a Bedouin title and it can even imply a negative shade of meaning, denoting a 'foreign' ruler from the city tradition of non-desert lands. It is not precisely clear when Abdul Aziz assumed the title of Malik, but it was probably when he started preparing the conquest of Mecca and came into competition with the other *Muluk* (kings) created by the colonial powers, basically Great Britain. Abdul Aziz could not afford to be inferior to his rival 'king' Hussain, the Sharif of Mecca, or later his sons Faisal, the 'king' of Iraq and Abdullah, 'king' of Jordan.

It is evident that many of the characteristics of this traditional tribal leadership concept have remained in all three countries. They were only slightly modified as they emerged as rich, very rich or immensely rich oil states and began affording themselves cities and more or less modern economies, development plans, bureaucrats, welfare institutions, schools and universities, standing armies, air forces, overseas representatives, immigrant populations and so forth.

From clan to government

The different members of the ruler's family in all three countries took over the newly formed ministries, particularly the key ones of finance, security (internally and externally), sometimes oil, sometimes foreign affairs, and almost always inter-Arab relations. Technicians were recruited to run those ministries under 'Royal' direction. In some less sensitive and more technical ministries and state agencies so-called commoners, i.e. people who did not belong to the ruling families, were used as ministers, particularly when technicians were needed.

Many of the other institutions remained. The ruler, or amir, consulted with his family when important decisions had to be taken or appointments made. Part of the state income went into his private treasury from which his own expenses and many of the necessary prestige payments were met. Budgets were introduced in order to administer the rest of the state money. In Bahrain a fixed proportion of the state income, one quarter (which in 1975 equalled seven million dollars), goes to the family, and the internal distribution of that money is decided by the ruler and his informal family council. Similar flexible rules or division apply in the other two states, but the amounts are, of course, much more substantial. The *Majlis* with theoretical free access for all 'subjects' has remained, although in a rudimentary, formalized way. The principle of heredity has not been introduced, and the succession is still managed by the former ruler and the family council. It has been stabilized to some degree by introducing the concept of successor to the 'throne' who, in all three countries, is given the office of prime minister, and who is generally recognized as the heir. But until the actual succession takes place there is always the possibility of upset.

The flexibility of one man rule

In all these three countries the government structures have changed much less than their economic and social features. The latter have been changed by oil and oil money, and subsequently by the amenities which those riches brought—hospitals, schools, building activities encompassing whole cities and a totally new infrastructure for the entire country in each case. The nature of the leadership, particularly at the highest level, has remained essentially unchanged since Bedouin times, although it has been expanded enormously in the middle and lower tiers by the creation of large bureaucracies. The fact that the type of top leadership could be preserved shows the flexibility and adaptability of the traditional system of tribal rule. The simplicity of the system has proved as adaptable as the members of the top family themselves, limited only by their ability to learn to adapt themselves to the new circumstances.

Removal of unfit rulers

There have been some failures in learning; the most notable example was that of King Sa'ud Ibn Abdul Aziz, who increased the sumptious expenses expected from a Bedouin chief in proportion to the growth of his oil income without much consideration for the other needs of the kingdom, from defence to development. In consequence, he spent most of the country's money and his own energy in building expensive palaces and in other conspicuous and unproductive efforts to consume the oil millions. As at the same time Abdel Nasser was making a determined attempt to subvert Saudi Arabia and to bring the royal family down, a crisis developed. It was most dangerous at the period after the fall of the Yemeni *Imam* as a result of an internal revolution strongly sustained by Egyptian troops. The crisis was finally mastered by King Faisal, the second brother of Sa'ud, after the family council had decided that the King had to remit his powers to him and—at a latter stage—deposed the King altogether. This was probably the most severe crisis the Saudi kingdom has so far had to face. Its danger came from the combination of interior weaknesses and exterior, pan-Arab, threat. The shadow of Nasserism hung over the kingdom from 1962, the beginning of the Yemeni war, up to 1967 when the threat disappeared as a result of the defeat of the Egyptians in the Six Day War. At one time, Nasser had even formed a Saudi government-in-exile and some Saudi princes, together with several pilots and their airplanes, defected to him. His frugal standard of living soon helped to rectify the precarious state finances, he appealed to tribal loyalty and he built up the Saudi army and tribal forces (White army). Saudi Arabia fostered countersubversion in the Yemen by aiding the deposed Imam Badr against the pro-Egyptian revolution and appealed for American aid via diplomatic channels. Finally, Faisal promoted a pan-Islamic policy designed to counter the pan-Arab appeal of Nasser and an Arab policy designed to keep Egypt in check by discreetly aiding all enemies of Egypt.

Another conspicuous case of failing to evolve with the times was that of Shaikh Shakhbut of Abu Dhabi, who was unwilling to develop his country as quickly as his new oil fortune would have permitted. He was called a miser and eventually in 1966 was replaced by his more generous brother Zaid in a palace coup aided, if not actually engineered, by the British, at that time the protecting power. A comparable situation arose in Oman where, in 1970, Sultan Said Bin Taimour was deposed (again with British intervention) in favour of his son. Taimour's excessively tyrannical rule was considered especially dangerous in the context of the subversive guerrilla activity initiated by PFLOAG (Peoples Front for the Liberation of Oman and the Arab Gulf—now known as PFLO as its Arab Gulf aspirations have been provisionally suspended), a marxist front aided by revolutionary South Yemen. His son, Sultan Qabus, was able to defeat the rebellion. Said Bin Taimur had been anchored deep in a medieval past and had been incapable of meeting the rising aspirations of his subjects. Similarily, the Amir of Qatar was replaced in 1972

4

by a more 'modern' relative when the family council decided that the old amir no longer met the needs of the day.

The tribal system therefore clearly possesses corrective mechanisms which can be brought into play when the ruling family becomes aware of a collective danger and of the incapacity of the ruling amir to master it. In the past such corrections have naturally been accompanied by violence with the amir often being killed either by a relative or as a result of a conspiracy of relatives. The fact that deposition and exile have now taken the place of physical elimination is partly due to the availability of friendly powers willing to smooth over the process and to provide exile,[1] and also due to the fact that, as in many other aspects of present day social and political life, the availability of large amounts of money helps to 'humanize' this process.

Within the common framework of leadership derived from the traditional system of rule of the tribes, the three countries considered here have had their individual characteristics, diverging fortunes and developments and differing difficulties which in each case have tended to modify the style and details of leadership and rule.

Bahrain

In a sense, Bahrain has gone through the most gradual and least turbulent development due to the fact that oil has been produced for a relatively long time (since 1932) and in relatively small quantities (only 19.9 million barrels a year in 1977 and declining by 4 per cent in recent years). This has meant a modest but steady influx of money into the state treasury and into the amir's personal exchequer (as mentioned above, three-quarters for the state, one quarter for the amir and his family). The relatively small trickle of money combined with the fact that Bahrain had been an urban horticultural community of settled nature for centuries, also aided by sober British supervision of the administration up to 1971, has given rise to the gradual development of the Bahraini community. Initially, oil royalties were used for sanitation, schooling, infrastructure (including housing and security) and the continuity of such investments over the decades has permitted the development of Bahrain as a centre of the service industries for the whole Gulf region. Air transport, communications, a hotel industry and some industrialization were added to the main staple industries of the past—date cultivation, shipbuilding, pearling, commerce, fishing and sea transport.

1 Ex-King Said retired to exile in Cairo and Sultan Taimour found exile in London.

The urban nature of much of Bahrain has meant a quick politicization of the populace and the rather rapid penetration of ideas such as Nasser's pan-Arabism and the Movement of Arab Nationalists (Haraka). This has posed a security threat to the regime. There have been serious riots particularly in times of general pan-Arab agitation, and the Protectorate authorities have taken severe action against actual and potential subversive elements who belonged mostly to the educated and partially educated lower classes. A typical example was the agitation of 1956 (the year of Suez) against the protective power and the ruling house. It was followed by the exile of leading Nasserites and Harakis to Saint Helena (lasting in some cases until 1961), and later, after more trouble, by a permanent state of emergency which lasted from 1961 to 1971 (when independence was granted). But this state of emergency was discreetly managed. It served basically as an instrument to keep the known political opposition under the menace of incarceration. A very tough but apparently capable British police specialist was brought in by the Protectorate authority and was later kept on by the amir in the quality of an adviser to the independent state. He had served before against the Mau Mau insurrection in Kenya. It seems to be principally due to him that the opposition was contained and, with the decline of the general pan-Arab fortunes of Narrerism, of the Haraka and later the PFLOAG mentioned above, the opposition appears to have become rather quiescent.

No viable parliament

In the atmosphere of relatively mild but persistent and systematically managed policy repression it proved impossible to introduce a parliament. This was attempted in 1973 but it was dissolved after twenty months. Saudi Arabia, an influential neighbour of Bahrain, never looked with favour on this experiment, because Riyadh never intended to have a parliament and disliked the precedents created in Bahrain and Kuwait. But a still more decisive reason for the abolition of the assembly was the fact that a vocal minority of deputies began questioning in public the prerogatives of the amir and his family. They had some success among their parliamentary colleagues who had been elected on more conservative tickets, because of the natural tendency of such assemblies to seek to widen and affirm their sovereignty and independence. Thus the interests of the amir and the assembly clashed. The press played its usual role of publicizing and amplifying the claims of the opposition deputies, and the assembly was dissolved. Government continued under the management of different ministers with the key portfolios being retained by the ruling house and the attention of the community was shifted, by a carefully controlled press, onto the essentially technical tasks of development which have become increasingly more complex as the sophistication of the services rendered increased, and ever more urgent as the oil royalties declined due to the exhaustion of the local oil wells.

A post-oil economy?

Bahrain has been the first oil state to face the transition from an oil to a post-oil economy. But this transition has been relatively easy for the island state. Because the oil revenues were always reasonably limited, a non-oil economy had always been maintained and was added to over the years. Moreover, Bahrain can take advantage of the other oil countries around the Gulf, who are still extraordinarily rich, by offering them its services. This service role will be much more difficult to build up and sustain once the revenues of the big oil producers begin to decline. Being forced to develop its services at a relatively early stage, while there is still plenty of excess money all over the Gulf, Bahrain will have a distinct advantage over the purely oil producing countries whose economies will have to adapt as their revenues begin to decline.

The Shi'i threat

Bahrain has become preoccupied with the Shi'i revolution in Iran, and the apparent intention of part of the ruling Shi'i establishment there to 'export the revolution', This is hardly surprising when it is remembered that Iranian claims to sovereignty over the islands were only dropped by the Shah in 1970.

In August 1979 about 1,500 Shi'is demonstrated in the bazaar centre of old Bahrain and such demonstrations were repeated several times on a minor scale. The Shi'is comprise the poorer part of the population. The ruling family and most wealthy merchants are Sunni. Five out of seventeen ministers are Shi'i, although in the less important ministries. The Shi'i community is divided between native Shi'is who speak Arabic, and foreign labourers who happen to be Shi'ites—Iranians, Pakistanis or Shi'i Iraqis. This is an advantage to the ruling Sunnis, but it can also be a source of concern because of the danger that a revolutionary attitude could spread from the native Shi'is to the foreign Shi'is and from them to all foreign workers. The latter, as in all Gulf oil states, constitute a somewhat underprivileged class of strangers admitted provisionally and with limited rights in Bahrain.

The authorities decided to cut to the root of Shi'i troubles and, in October 1979, expelled a Shi'i shaikh who called himself the representative of 'imam' Khomeiny in Bahrain. Since then the Shi'is have been quiescent. Iraq seized the occasion to emphasize repeatedly that its army would be at the disposal of Bahrain and any other Arab Gulf state to defend the Arab nature of the Gulf, but the Bahrainis replied that such aid was not needed at the present time. It is very doubtful that the rulers would welcome the thought of Iraqi armed forces landing on their islands, because Iraqi ambitions to play an increased political role in the Gulf are well known, and so far all the Gulf states have collaborated informally but firmly to keep such ambitions in check. If need be, Bahrain would probably first call for Saudi aid. Informal collaboration of the interior ministers and security chiefs between Saudi Arabia, Kuwait, Bahrain and other Gulf states has been established for many years and was reinforced after the Iranian revolution, and again after the latest Shi'i demonstrations.

Kuwait

Kuwait had a constitution and a parliament from 1963 to 1976. There were regular elections, but after each four-year period the size and influence of the opposition increased. Although it remained a minority in the chamber, the influence of the parliament was much greater than was indicated by mere members, in part because it found an important echo among the Palestinians who constitute an important and active minority in Kuwait, notwithstanding the fact that they have no civic rights such as the Kuwaiti citizens enjoy.

Furthermore, the opposition in parliament managed to champion generally popular causes and sometimes obtained the backing of significant section of the pro-government deputies. This was the case in a famous debate in 1972 when the chamber forced the government to nationalize the Kuwait Oil Company in its entirety and not just 75 per cent of it, as the government had proposed.

In private, some of the opposition deputies—perhaps most clearly and convincingly Dr Ahmed al-Khatib (one of the heads of a branch of the pro-Haraka groupings)—posed a whole range of questions relating to the position of privilege enjoyed by the ruling family and, more generally, by all Kuwaiti citizens as compared to Arab immigrants and to foreigners as a whole. According to the Haraka, Arab oil riches ought to profit all Arabs (including the Palestinians and Palestine) and not just a few 'feudal' families and some privileged small groups. They maintained that the Arab states, as they exist today, do not have a right to exist and to act as sovereign states, according to Haraka, because their frontiers are artificial and were imposed by 'colonialism' on an Arab nation which really ought to form one whole. It is easy to see that for anybody holding such beliefs the case of Kuwait, detached from the rest of the Arab territories in 1913 by British colonial action (basically at that time in context of growing German influence immediately before the First World War), and later maintained and consolidated as a 'state' due to its oil riches, represents an especially glaring case of the 'colonialist' *divide et impera* policy applied to the Arab world and which persists thanks to 'feudal' interests implanted and fostered by those same colonialists.

Such criticisms struck at the heart of royal rule and called into question the very existence of Kuwait. Citizenship policies are also especially sensitive for many of the same reasons.

The end of the Kuwaiti parliament

On 29 August 1976 parliament in Kuwait was finally suspended for a period of four years. Those parts of the constitution which had guaranteed freedom of the press and postulated new elections after each dissolution of parliament also went into suspension. The reasons for the step were never made quite clear. The press was forbidden to write about them. However, it was hinted officially that the dissolution had something to do with the Palestinians who were said (in presumably inspired press reports outside of Kuwait) to have been in a dangerous mood of despair and radicalism induced by the battles and troubles in Lebanon and then by their culmination. One frequently voiced explanation for the suspension of parliament was that the Palestinians had lost their provisional homes in Lebanon and that it was feared they could try to turn Kuwait into a new provisional home for themselves.

This may have been in part, but it was certainly not the whole truth. It seems most likely that the Palestinians living in Kuwait were blamed because they were close to the opposition (in fact they had amalgamated with it) and at the same time it was easier to attack them than the elected Kuwaiti deputies.

Another part of the truth was that Saudi Arabia had always been unhappy about the establishment of parliaments on the Arabian peninsula. The Kuwaiti parliament, where the most lively debates took place (some of them about such sensitive issues as the privileges of the ruling house) had been the most conspicuous. (Bahrain had by then already abolished its assembly.)

The central issue, however, which led to the dissolution and to the subsequent silencing of the opposition press was almost certainly the clash of wills and of interests which had developed between opposition and government. The government basically consisted of representatives of the ruling family who held all the key positions. It was presided over by the successor to the throne, acting as prime minister. There had been attacks on some of the ministers who belonged to the ruling house on the unwritten law which assured them of key positions. There was a still distant but not impossible danger of the government being brought down by the chamber, as the assembly came more and more under the influence of the opposition groupings. This would have been an intolerable blow to the ruling house. The ruler and his councillors obviously preferred to prevent such developments by ending the parliamentarian experiment quickly.

A revised constitution has been promised for 1980. An assembly of experts is to rewrite it 'in harmony with the spirit of our islamic law and our traditions' and 'in order to safeguard the unity of our homeland its stability and a democratic power', as the dissolution order of 1976 had put it. The new text has not yet been revealed but it will probably contain devices which make it impossible for the chamber to overthrow the government, thus reducing the assembly to a consultative role.

Professional groups closed down

When the Kuwaiti parliament was dissolved in 1976 the professional associations of the Kuwaiti lawyers and journalists were also closed. This happened because they had become the meeting grounds of professionals from Kuwait with those of other Arab countries and, above all, with the Palestinians. These groups short-circuited to some extent the superimposed pyramidal system and helped the circulation of ideas. Such ideas probably subverted the existing order of things. Questioning of the privileges of the Kuwaiti ruling class was justified in the eyes of other Arab groups who were on the whole more qualified than themselves in their professional skills.

In the following year the authorities also closed the Patriotic Club of Kuwait (an-Nadi al-Watani). This had been the most significant meeting ground of the Palestinians and the Kuwaitis who felt inclined towards pan-Arabism (calling itself Arab Nationalism) or towards the Palestinian struggle for their home country which is generally considered a duty incumbent on all Arabs. The closure of this club has been the clearest indication given by the authorities so far that they are watching closely the growing links between the Palestinian minority (close to 25 per cent of the total population of Kuwait) and the Kuwaiti professionals and leaders of the emerging bourgeoisie. The reasons are clear. Any amalgamation between those two influential groups could prove dangerous for the ruling stratum of Kuwaiti shaikhs. They would have the capacity to rule the country and they are open to the basically Palestinian or pan-Arab argument that Kuwait ought to abolish 'feudalism' and place itself at the unconditional service of Arab Nationalism and the Palestine cause, not just by giving aid (which is what the present regime does) but by founding a new regime, basically nationalist oriented (i.e. pan-Arabic) and much more closely allied both to pan-Arab and Palestinian aspirations. When the government acts against the meeting grounds of those two strata of Kuwaiti society it makes clear its awareness of the dangers such interactions can bring for itself and it underlines its will to keep separate from the Kuwaiti citizens what can be classed as 'foreign' Palestinians and other Arabs.

Procedures are much more direct against non-Arab foreigners. According to Kuwait police department records, 18,000 persons were expelled from Kuwait in the last three months of 1979, i.e. between

200 and 250 every day. They were mostly simple people who came as labourers. Some were Iraqis but most were non-Arab and they were expelled because their papers were not in order. However, there are many more whose papers are also not in order but who manage to stay on—partly because they prove useful in their jobs and thus gain the protection of their bosses, Kuwaiti or otherwise, who help them to regularize their situation, and partly because they do not make themsleves conspicuous by political or trade union activities.

The Kuwaiti pyramid

In the meantime a certain amount of stability in Kuwait is induced by the complex and finely graded pyramid of privilege and power on which the state rests. From top to bottom it is structured as follows: ruler, key ministers from the ruling house, other ministers, Kuwaiti citizens, Palestinians, other Arab immigrants and, at the bottom, non-Arab immigrants. The Kuwaiti citizens can be subdivided into native Kuwaitis and other Arabs and foreigners who have been admitted to citizenship. All those ranks correspond to positions of privilege relative to the one immediately below, and it is clear that in the vast majority of cases each rank concentrates on preserving its own privileges and excluding the one underneath from ascending. This makes for enough internal antagonisms, finely differentiated from layer to layer, to ensure security for the leadership.

The case of the Palestinians provides an illustration of the kind of issue involved. For the moderate Palestinian groups, Fatah above all, Kuwait represents a reservoir of money. Important financial contributions to the movement come from the government directly and even more from 'taxes' the PLO is allowed to collect—or even helped by the government to collect—from Palestinians residing in Kuwait. If they were to quarrel with the government the Palestinians would lose those advantages. There are some groups amongst them who would care little, even as the more radical minorities—the Popular Front (Habash) or the Popular Democratic Front (Hawatmeh—but they are kept in check by their own Palestinian majority following Fatah and wanting to avoid what the Palestinians call 'secondary issues' (such as internal fights in the Arab countries outside Palestine). The rulers of Kuwait can thus rely on the Palestinians policing themselves as long as they obtain financial contributions of substance from the country.

For other groups it is similarly the risk of losing their relatively comfortable position which makes them keep their own 'class' and the 'class' below themselves in order. This is even true of the non-Arab immigrant workers who are badly paid and enjoy few of the privileges of social welfare reserved for the Kuwaitis and the immigrant Arabs (at least those who have regular papers, which is not always the case) but

11

who risk expulsion to their homeland where they would be considerably worse off.

Since the owners of privilege in the top ranks of the pyramidal structure do not owe their position to any special skill or efficiency, the whole structure is dependent on oil money permeating it from top to bottom. The top layers, not being especially productive, keep their position by appropriating a relatively large part of that money, either directly via the treasury of the ruler or indirectly via more or less ample sinecures in the state bureaucracies. Even those lower classes who generally work for their money live ultimately on the reminder of the oil royalties since without them there would be very little true productivity. Looking to the still fairly distant future when there will be little oil left, there is an attempt to make Kuwaiti society more productive and less dependent on oil money but it is unlikely that it can be replaced by any other productive activity. Basically, the whole social structure such as it is today has been produced by oil wealth and seems to be dependent on it for its maintenance and inner cohesion, and the top ranks are occupied by essentially non-productive people. However, as long as the oil flows and the wealth trickles down, it will probably remain stable—at least so long as it is not disturbed from the outside.

The decisive question of 'gradation'

The principal characteristic of Kuwaiti pyramid of privilege as compared to that of Saudi Arabia seems to be its fine gradation. This means that the different layers of privilege have preserved some contact with members of the lower half of each level being aware of the danger of dropping down or being engulfed by the stratum below. Each layer, therefore, has a considerable interest in keeping its own group in order, so as to avoid the danger of collapse of the whole, and to keep those below in their place, to avoid losing its own position.

There are no large gaps between the strata as in Saudi Arabia where society tends to split itself more and more into the super-rich able to profit immensely from the oil money and the degraded and proletarianized poor who are victims of inflation, deracination and loss of their traditional ways of life and means of subsistence. The fine gradation in Kuwait is no doubt the fruit of careful policies to raise up the Kuwaiti poor and unskilled (through housing, free building sites, obligatory Kuwaiti participation in foreign businesses, etc.) and to give the immigrants reasonable rewards through salaries, while keeping away undesirables and superfluous foreign elements. Nevertheless, an administration is needed with some skill and Kuwait acquired this early on, thanks to the Palestinian immigrants who have filled the middle ranks of an administration headed by Kuwaitis. Even the size of the small city state has made for transparency in administrative and social affairs and this has helped greatly. Social differences in absolute terms from top to bottom may be as great or nearly as great as they are in Saudi Arabia, but the difference lies in the presence of many middle strata between these extremes which are in close touch with each other and form one coherent whole. Because everybody participates (although quite unequally) it is a structure which retains its cohesion to a considerable degree. Only when the upper strata are completely divorced from the lower ranks is there a danger that they will neglect the needs of the lower ranks.

The Kuwaiti army

The Kuwaiti army today has 10,000 men and is very well armed. In March 1977 the purchase of Russian SAM rockets created something of a sensation. Military expenses between 1973 and 1976 were $4,300 million and, by 1978, they had risen by a further $1,500 million. The army grew out of the bodyguard of the ruling house. Its officers have been trained by the British, and it has always been commanded by members of the ruling family itself. It has been expanded primarily against the Iraqi threat, a fact well known although little talked about in Kuwait. At various times Iraq has exerted claims either for the complete annexation of Kuwait or for some parts of its territory. The most recent of these claims were in connection with the building of a big Iraqi naval base close to Kuwaiti shores. There have been periodic military invasions and some occupation of Kuwaiti territory. The Kuwaiti army, therefore, primarily has a tripwire function—it is there to fight against any renewed Iraqi danger with sufficient vigour to enable Kuwaiti diplomacy to mobilize support in the other Arab countries and, if need be, in the rest of the world. A mixture of Arab and world support has in the past proved sufficient to moderate Iraqi claims but the Kuwaitis are well aware that such support is much more likely to materialize if Kuwait itself shows signs of resistance.

The fact that the Kuwaiti army has one clearly defined potential enemy is presumably the main reason for the loyalty of the army. There is no evidence of unrest within their ranks or of any anti-government conspiracies. In fact, it would be against all their interests to conspire against the present regime because its breakdown would inevitably mean a new bid for possession by Iraq. Nor would it be to the advantage of the Kuwaiti professional soldiers (most of whom are of Kuwaiti Bedouin stock) to be overrun by the Iraqi army and incorporated into it on conditions much less attractive then those prevailing at present in Kuwait.

Saudi Arabia

Saudi Arabia is clearly differentiated from the two other regimes by the physical size of the country and by the use which the Saudi system makes of religion. The religious connotation has been with the Wahhabis from their beginnings and it is still very much alive. 'The Koran is our constitution' was a favourite maxim of King Faisal. The Wahhabi current in the regime has been reinforced since 1924, the year of the conquest of Mecca, by the assumption of the role of guardian of the sacred places. But for a great many years the fact that the different provinces of Arabia had been united under one dynasty was also an element of inner tension since each province had its own local traditions and dignitaries. Abdul Aziz, who resigned from 1953 to 1964, had to keep all those tendencies in balance; the most serious challenges to his rule came from his own followers, the Wahhabi Eastern Arabs, when they rose against him. The much maligned policy of multiple marriages of the king to women of all sections of the tribes and regions of his vast realm had to be understood in this context.

Even when the oil money started to come in it was many decades before the essential structures of the vast desert empire were changed. In the city states of Bahrain and Kuwait the influence of new wealth was bound to be much more immediate. The real transformation in Saudi Arabia has begun only recently—in the cities during the reigns of Sa'ud Ibn Abdul Aziz (1953–64) and of Faisal (1964–75), and in the desert and in the villages only after the quadrupling of the oil revenues in 1973. This explains the apparent stability so far enjoyed by the regime. Although the city population has been volatile and accessible to such ideas as Arab Nationalism, Ba'athism, Arab Socialism, etc. for quite a long time, the real power basis of the regime has been the Bedouin, or White army, whose task has been to counterbalance the regular army. The latter has been inclined to undertake coups during the last twenty years and apparently remains so inclined. Many of these attempts have been aborted by the Americans and by the different Arab secret services who have infiltrated the army, but it has been the Bedouin army, until recently loyal to the ruling house and the throne, which has been the main protector of the monarchy. It lives on the bounty of the rulers and is commanded directly by some of them.

Immigration started on a large scale with the Yemen war of 1962–67; much later than in Kuwait. It has been Palestinian only in the cities, but Yemeni all over the country for the Yemenis have become the real labour force of Saudi Arabia. Because of the vastness of the country and its many different sections and divisions, a finely gradated pyramid comparable to that of Kuwait has not come into existence. The gaps between the different layers of the society are correspondingly much wider.

Because religion has been used much too blatantly as an instrument of power by the ruling classes for many centuries, a force of cohesion is becoming a divisive influence. The religious laws are officially enforced for the ruled but they are increasingly flaunted by the rulers who seem to imagine—quite wrongly—that their subjects are unaware of their drinking and fornicating as long as it is done in the privacy of their mansions. In the last few years a double standard has evolved and it is spreading and deepening. It separates the ruling class, who use their fortunes to avoid strict obedience to the religious laws by travel abroad and seclusion at home, from the people even though they impose strict laws on their subjects and sometimes enforce them by the cruel punishments prescribed by the Islamic code. As one taxi driver in Riyadh put it recently, 'I agree with cutting off the hands of thieves. But in that case the men of the royal family ought to have no hands left!'

Awareness of the existence of this double standard has spread slowly, in part because Faisal in his lifetime kept the worst abuses in check and because he lived an austere life. But the recent jockeying for power and position inside the ruling house, which is destined to go on for some time, has allowed many of the privileged to escape the constraints of strict supervision by their superiors and elders. In the cities two district societies have evolved. The first is a Muslim one and consists of those subjects whose way of life continues to be controlled by strict application of the law. The second is a 'Westernized', hedonistic, materialistic society essentially preoccupied with making money by whatever means and using it for conspicuous consumption. Instead of the cohesion between the different layers of society evident in Kuwait, the chasms in Saudi Arabia are growing wider and deeper. Religion has thus become an element of division in Saudi society rather than a unifying factor.

There is some awareness among the rulers about this development. It is brought home to them by the numerous military conspiracies which are taking place more or less continuously. Details are always kept secret but there is a continuing trickle of news about officers escaping to seek refuge in Iraq, pilots absconding with their aircraft or about units being punished or investigated because of rebellious movements. None of this news can be checked, but it amounts to considerable evidence of disaffection. The rulers have reacted by imposing very strict controls on foreign workers. There are waves of periodic checks and any foreigner caught without documents on his person is expelled.

The impact of development on the native Saudis is creating a more difficult problem. The rulers seem to believe that it would help if they were to settle the Bedouins and to transform them into labourers. Why they should believe this is inexplicable since it could equally well tend to increase instability, but so great is the pressure of new money that the rulers, in their urge to spend it profitably, seem to feel that settlement is a proper thing for the Bedouin to want. Combined with this is the pressure of well-meaning but financially interested foreigners, mainly American and European, who want to sell Saudi Arabia their particular 'development model' because it is the only one they know and it promotes their desire to sell appliances and furnishings.

Plans appear to be in hand to impose general conscription on the Saudi population and thus to form a 'national army'. If this comes about it will probably spell the end of the regime for an army of this kind is likely to overthrow it. That the need for a national army is felt by the rulers can be seen as a sign of their current deep concern caused, among other things, by the downfall of the Shah. But the remedy which they have been persuaded to adopt is likely to carry with it the worst dangers of all.

The mosque occupation

On 4 November 1979 the Great Mosque of Mecca was occupied and held by a group of armed insurrectionists for several weeks. The authorities did what they could to minimize the significance of the event and have attributed the seizure to 'purely religious' fanatics whom they termed 'Khawarij', taking advantage of the double sense of this term which means both a specific religious sect (Kharijiya) and 'people who have left the consensus of the believers'. In reality there can be no doubt that the action represented a mixed religio-sociological and political protest against the regime and its corrupt and impious behaviour (made worse in the eyes of the believers by its lip service to Islam) and as such was typical of traditional Islam. At the same time the old regional tensions between the Hijaz and Najd provinces seem to have played a role. Perhaps also the old opposition of the time of Abdul Nasser (Arabian Peoples Popular Front) played a part as was claimed in Beirut by an old opponent of the regime (and one time head of government in exile), Nasser as Sayyid. Undoubtedly elements of the army and of the National Guard were also involved.

The event was extremely serious. This was shown by the fact that all army and security commanders were dismissed and replaced by new men once the danger was over. Also there has been an incipient political reaction. Prince Fahd has promised a kind of consultative assembly to channel the discontent which obviously abounds in the kingdom but which has no outlet.

In the past there was a physical link between the tribes and the royal house arising from the systematic policy of King Abdul Aziz who married and then divorced the daughters of the tribal heads. They went home with their babies and received alimony for themselves and the princes. No stigma was attached to this, according to the tradition of the Bedouins, and the consequence of the policy was that some member of the royal house and son of the king grew up in each tribe in physical contact with the tribesmen whose natural spokesman he became at court. This system broke down as the princes left their tribes either in the desert or in the slums accumulating around the big cities and became playboys. Yet the archaic system did function well and it has not been replaced by anything else. The princes, the members of the royal house and the businessmen are thus in danger of isolating themselves more and more from the rest of the country and of losing any sense of what is going on in the unprivileged strata of the kingdom. There are attempts to replace the missing connection by secret service activities but Iran has shown the dangers inherent in such a 'security' approach. The ruling class becomes trapped by their own security services into increasing isolation from reality and at the same time they are detested because of the methods used by the 'security' services. Their power has not yet reached that of Savak in Iran but the danger is there and is bound to increase as long as the channels of communication between the rulers and the ruled are blocked.

The regimes compared

Of the three countries considered here, Saudi Arabia is the most unstable. Money has here dissolved order and social cohesion based on the clan. In the city states of Bahrain and Kuwait a more or less stable society has evolved, characterized by comparatively close contact and interaction between the different layers and strata of the society. These societies are unlikely to change violently as long as they are undisturbed from the outside and so long as oil keeps bringing in money—in big streams in the case of Kuwait, in small but vital trickles at Bahrain.

Stability in Saudi Arabia seems much more precarious. The kingdom has been held together essentially by Bedouin loyalties reinforced by a religious bond, and both are being eroded by money. The process of erosion has already gone quite far, and there is probably little that can be done about it at this stage. Liberalization would be fatal, because it will only quicken decay. More and tighter security may help in the short run, but in the long run it will increase the probability of a military coup because the officers and men of the regular and of the Bedouin army are bound to resent the presence and operation of security men in their midst, particularly if they are, as is the case in Saudi Arabia, foreigners or foreign trained. The increased size and technology of the army coupled with renunciation of the principles on which the Bedouin army has built, can only have disastrous consequences for the Saudi regime.

Saudi society will inevitably develop in directions which will foster instability and multiply reasons for resentment, because the country is already split between rich and poor. The ruling class is deeply corrupt and they preach one thing to their subjects and do the opposite. Yet further development means even more money and power for these ruling groups and more corruption. For the subjects it primarily means inflation and alienation. There are no Mullahs in Saudi Arabia independent enough of government supervision and finance to articulate these resentments. This means that it will probably be the army around which opposition elements will coalesce and which will one day liquidate the Saudi regime.

This also in all probability will be the end of stability for the smaller Gulf countries, and it will very probably open up an era of Saudi–Iraqi Arab nationalist and anti-American rivalry and *surenchere*. It is not easy to suggest ways of averting the impending disaster for Saudi society is too opaque for the outsider to perceive anything but the mere outlines. Perhaps the projected consultative assembly is a step in the right direction, but it may already be too late and pressures are such that a loosening of the controls and opening the channels of communication may only accelerate the break up of the regime. It would be advisable to have a small tribally loyal elite army but the rulers seem to be heading towards a policy of general conscription and of dissolving the White or Bedouin army. This is almost certainly a step towards a *coup d'etat*. Generally the political structures are such that there is little chance of reasonable advice from whatever source reaches the rulers. The ruling family itself is at cross purposes and whatever one faction wants to do will probably be checked by the opposite group. This stalemate makes it unlikely that the little time available to counteract the pressures outlined will be used profitably by the Saudi leadership.

2 Transformation amidst tradition: the UAE in transition

John Duke Anthony

The United Arab Emirates—the Middle East's longest and most successful experiment to date in regional political integration—is nearing completion of its first decade of existence. The fact that the seven previously independent shaikhdoms which agreed to form a loose confederation on 2 December 1971 are still together is, by any standard, a remarkable achievement; Only a minority of observers present at the UAE's creation were confident of the fledgling union's ability to survive the first six months, let alone half a decade. Having come this far despite numerous problems, it is appropriate to consider not only the principal forces and factors affecting the union's development since its inception but also, in the face of an uncertain future, its prospects until 1981 when the provisional constitution expires.

Integrative factors

The removal of external threats

At its birth, the UAE was faced with several thorny territorial and external security problems. On the day before the federation came into being, Iran occupied three islands in the Gulf claimed by Ra's al-Khaymah and Sharjah. Moreover, to the south, leftist guerrillas were seeking to topple the dynasty in neighbouring Oman and carry their revolutionary ideology to the Gulf; Iraq was lending support to various dissident groups seeking to unseat the emirates' governments; and a longstanding border dispute between Abu Dhabi and Saudi Arabia prevented the union from establishing diplomatic relations with its most powerful Arab neighbour.

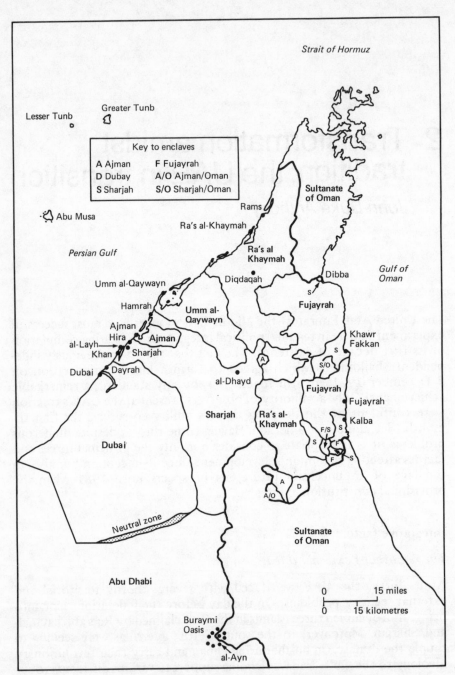

Internal frontiers of the United Arab Emirates

By 1976, however, all of these problems had been solved or appeared manageable. Relations between the UAE and its two largest neighbours, Iran and Saudi Arabia, had improved markedly; political contacts and economic ties between Iran and individual UAE states, especially Dubai and Abu Dhabi, had grown considerably; boundary and other disputes between Saudi Arabia and Abu Dhabi were settled in August 1974, leading to the establishment of diplomatic relations; the Dhofar rebellion in neighbouring Oman was officially brought to an end in December 1975; [1] and the cause for concern about Iraqi intentions toward the emirates had also subsided.[2]

There is growing consensus among the elites of the member states that the federation, as it now exists, does not impinge upon their collective interests as much as some had supposed. It is a truism that not all UAE citizens understand fully what their rulers agreed to upon joining the union. Yet in their daily affairs, most of the politically aware citizens are increasingly cognizant of the relatively few powers that were taken from the individual states and accorded the federation. Equally important, most of the rulers and their supporters remain satisfied with the several constitutional provisions that protect the right of each state to administer its domestic affairs—and a significant portion of its external economic affairs—with a minimum of interference from federal authorities.

The rulers of the poorer, non-oil producing states of 'Ajman, Umm al-Qaywayn, Ra's al-Khaymah and Fujayrah remain the most dependent on the existing framework, in as much as it is the principal if not the sole means whereby they have been able to obtain the economic assistance necessary for developing their societies without having to make major concessions of their individual sovereignty. More specifically, these states have for some time been dependent upon Abu Dhabi's aid. An added inducement to their acceptance of the framework was the fact that this was what Abu Dhabi wanted and indeed stipulated as the *sine qua non* for its continued assistance.

1 The insurrection never directly affected the emirates. Although the war lasted for ten years, most of the conflict was waged nearly 600 miles away from the UAE in Dhofar, Oman's southernmost province. Only once, in early 1973, when arms caches were discovered in Abu Dhabi and local members of the rebel movement were arrested, was the rebellion ever considered an immediate threat to the union itself.

2 Iraq and the UAE exchanged ambassadors within a year after the union was founded. Following the signing of the Algiers Accord between Iran and Iraq in March 1975, Baghdad ceased its assistance to the rebels fighting in Oman and to Ba'athist cells previously active in the emirates. Subsequently, relations between Iraq and all the Lower Gulf states, including the UAE, improved considerably, reaching their zenith in the wake of the Camp David accords when all of these states endorsed the 'Camp Baghdad Accords' in opposition to the Egyptian-Israeli peace treaty of March 1979. This is not to say, of course, that relations between these states and Iraq thereafter became or are likely to become cordial. Still fresh in the minds of most emirate leaders is the fact that Iraq was the principal stumbling block preventing the signing of a regional security agreement during the Gulf foreign ministers' meeting in Muscat in late November 1976. In addition, along with post-Shah Iran, Iraq continues to be considered a major external security threat by several Gulf states.

These poor emirates' choices are in any case limited. Their lack of oil denies them any meaningful prospect of either increasing their political position within the UAE or improving their chances for survival outside the union. There are those in each emirate who believe that an augmented population base might, if coupled with the eventual discovery of petroleum, be parlayed into a more powerful bargaining position within the union. Ra's al-Khaymah and Sharjah are two emirates which have, at times, pursued policies (such as liberal land purchasing schemes for immigrants) in accordance with this assumption. On the other hand, there are those who contend, with somewhat greater persuasiveness in recent years, that increasing population remains questionable due to the fact that it has not yet been proven successful. These people would argue that, for the present, the problems attendant on a swollen population in terms of the stress thereby put on the still somewhat limited infrastructure (i.e. schools, electricity, water, housing, etc.) can be viewed as net liabilities regardless of the security and economic gains accorded to the military elites and development planners. There also remains a consideration that has less to do with political and economic development *per se* than with questions related to ethnicity, religion and nationalism. To wit: with this area priding itself on being adjacent to the epicentre of the Arab and Islamic worlds, there have always been citizens who have argued that the number of people from other non-Arab and/or non-Muslim countries in their midst should be restricted. Those who argue this point retain an attentive audience for their views.

The three wealthiest emirates—Abu Dhabi, Dubai and Sharjah—have from time to time viewed the federation quite differently. Shaikh Zayid, ruler of Abu Dhabi and president of the UAE, has consistently sought more powers for the federal government, which is funded primarily by Abu Dhabi. Shaikh Rashid, ruler of Dubai, has at times expressed somewhat less than wholehearted support for the federation. For several years in succession, Dubai was a source of considerable irritation to UAE officials in Abu Dhabi and elsewhere owing to charges that it did not pay its share of the budget. Dubai's rival, Sharjah, has from the outset been greatly interested in obtaining a larger voice in federal circles not only for reasons of enhancing its overall position in regional affairs, but also out of an abiding concern for the union itself.

For some time now, each of these states, on balance, has seen its interests being met more readily by remaining in, rather than withdrawing from, the UAE. Of added importance, in the sense that it has served to reinforce this view, have been outside pressures. External influences in favour of unity, emanating especially from Saudi Arabia, and also from the USA and Great Britain, have been a consistent factor inducing Dubai and Ra's al-Khaymah—emirates led by two of the most independent minded rulers in all Arabia—to remain in the union. Conversely, no strong outside encouragement for secession has developed.[1]

There also remains a generation gap in political attitudes towards the federation. The older leaders, whose original loyalties grew out of experiences that predated the union and which were heavily rooted in the more narrowly contrived interests of their particular emirate, tribe, or extended family, continue to find it much more difficult to establish federal loyalties than do members of the younger generation. The latter are much more ready and willing to declare openly their belief in its ongoing validity and viability. It is to this second group, comprising nearly half of the citizenry and cutting politically, socially and economically across all segments of the population, including the ruling households and other families and tribes, that most of the positions of prestige and influence in the UAE—and also in many cases those of real power—are increasingly being transferred.

Because of the shortage of qualified personnel, many high positions have traditionally been held by expatriates or by ruling family members, the latter often lacking sufficient technical training. However, with free education for nationals up to university and post-graduate levels having been available for some years, the educational system has been greatly expanded and improved. Thus, in the longer run (and as happens everywhere when old people die), the balance of leadership will shift even more in favour of the younger generation. Even in the relatively short span of less than a decade, the record of achievement in this regard has been impressive. And there is reason to expect that this trend will be accelerated in the near future owing to the likelihood of the aging rulers of 'Ajman and Umm al-Qaywayn, who came to power in 1928 and 1929 respectively, either passing on or yielding to pressures in favour of their abdication.

Integration of the armed forces of the member states

When the UAE was established, each shaikhdom was assured that its own defence establishment could be retained and, if necessary, expanded. As a consequence, the Abu Dhabi Defence Force (ADDF) quickly grew to a size five times greater than the federal Union Defence Force (UDF). This gave cause for concern among the other members and began to fuel internal arms rivalries that might otherwise have been avoided. In May 1976, however, the flags of each of the emirate armies were run down and federal banners hoisted in their place as they became units of a re-unified federal defence force. The creation of a single defence force with

---

1 During the period prior to the overthrow of the Pahlavi dynasty in Iran, however, it was widely believed that Dubai's less than wholehearted support for the union's programmes and policies—and periodic reports that Dubai might consider 'going it alone'—enjoyed the personal endorsement of the Shah.

both internal and external security responsibilities for the UAE as a whole as well as the individual emirates is perhaps the most impressive example to date of the growth of integrative forces within the federation.[1]

Integration of information policies

From the beginning of the federation's existence, union authorities were bedevilled by the persistence of an unco-ordinated network of media outlets and policies among the emirates. The establishment of separate, and often competing, news stations throughout the UAE frequently resulted in the dissemination of knowledge relating to UAE affairs that was either misinformed, inaccurate or, in some cases, in direct opposition to stated union policies. Some of the more embarrassing episodes related to the different positions taken by several of the emirates on foreign oil concessions. For example, during delicate negotiations over Abu Dhabi's acquiring 60 per cent equity participation in its own oil industry, Dubai Radio announced without Abu Dhabi's prior knowledge that Dubai had just successfully achieved 100 per cent equity participation (even if it was more a 'paper' 100 per cent than a real one) in Dubai Petroleum Company.

This kind of lack of co-operation has been reduced since 1976, when co-ordination of the media was placed under a federal broadcasting agency. The morale of federal spokesmen subsequently rose noticeably as opportunities for individual emirates to use the media to undermine union-wide policies were thereby decreased considerably. This development received an unexpected impetus in mid 1979 when the ruler of Dubai, who along with his counterpart in Ra's al-Khaymah had frequently pursued policies in his own emirate that were at odds with UAE goals, agreed to become the federation's prime minister.

Diminishing dependence on expatriates in key sectors

The primary force that first brought the emirates together and kept them united was the expatriate, largely British, presence. This group was also the backbone of local administrations in many of the emirates. There were less than forty UAE citizens with university degrees at the time—not a single lawyer or judge, and probably no more than a dozen individuals among the indigenous inhabitants with advanced training in petroleum economics, financial management or development planning.

---

1 Control of the military command structure, as opposed to the integration of its constituent units, however, has been a more controversial issue. The matter occasioned a minor political crisis when Shaikh Zayid appointed his second eldest son, Sandhurst trained Shaikh Sultan, as Commander of the UAE Defence Force in 1978. Shaikh Muhammad, third son of the ruler of Dubai (and UAE Vice-President) Shaikh Rashid, however, has held the important post of Minister of Defence since the UAE's inception.

In order to get the federation to work, therefore, it was necessary to retain or place skilled expatriates at all levels of the administrative, economic and defence structures. Fortunately for the union, the sizeable body of foreign specialists already present was willing to remain, permitting a much smoother transition to independence than might otherwise have been possible.

The day is fast approaching, however, when UAE citizens, with the help of foreign Arabs, will be able to take over completely from the non-Arab expatriates and administer the federation by themselves. Native expertise has been and continues to be demonstrated with impressive frequency in many fields. Oil, finance and foreign affairs remain in the forefront as the UAE has repeatedly provided evidence of an ability to act with independence of mind and purpose in regional matters affecting the wider Arab and Islamic worlds. The union's stand with Saudi Arabia in December 1976 against the rest of OPEC on the issue of oil prices is perhaps the best known case in point. Some observers give greater credit for this development to the self-assurance of Shaikh Zayid and the great improvement in Saudi–Abu Dhabi relations. Even so, no one since has gainsayed the thesis that it was also the product of a growing spirit of confidence within the UAE government itself.

In sum, evidence of a diverse and diffuse nature continues to mount which would indicate that favourable attitudes toward continuing the federation for the foreseeable future have indeed taken root throughout the UAE. In assessing that future, however, these signs of progress must be weighed against a number of shortcomings which, all along, have sapped the union's vitality and which could, unless somehow checked, easily undermine the logic of its unity, both now and in the future.

Disintegrative forces

The perpetuation of rivalries and jealousies

No one expected that these seven previously separate shaikhdoms would, upon joining the union, bury overnight their longstanding rivalries. Indeed, one reason why it took more than three years to establish the UAE was the deeply embedded tensions existing among them.

The better part of a decade is by no means to be construed as an insignificant span of time. Yet in this case it has been too limited a period to allay the suspicions and distrusts of a century. In recent years, moreover, the discovery of oil has served as much to exacerbate as to ameliorate intra-UAE rivalries. Recognizing their inability to stand alone without an adequate economic base, every ruling house in the UAE has been and to this day remains titillated with dreams of grandeur by the existence or possibility of the discovery of oil. None of them, however, has a chance to fulfill such hopes without oil, and none of those who have it can benefit so well if their respective sovereignties are submerged in the federation.

The calibre of UAE government personnel

When the federal experiment began, many senior policy positions were awarded to members of the various ruling families and others with little or no regard for their qualifications. Competition for such jobs was fierce. Moreover, the difficulty was compounded by the necessity of maintaining at least a semblance of balance in positions among the emirates, the smaller of which have until recently had very few university graduates available. This shortcoming was mitigated by the appointment of deputy ministers and permanent secretaries who were selected more on the basis of merit. Even so, the ministers themselves retained ultimate decision making authority. Thus, despite sound advice by expatriates and a growing number of qualified local bureaucrats, there have been numerous cases of incompetence, particularly in approving unsound projects. The problem has at times been exacerbated as expatriates and local citizens have attempted to promote the interests of individual contracting and consulting firms.

Moreover, even as an increasing number of citizens return from abroad with a higher education, the services of many who might otherwise opt for a UAE government career are more often than not recruited instead by the private sector, owing to the more lucrative opportunities to be had in business, or, as has happened in some instances, by the local government of their native emirate. This internal 'brain drain', should it persist, will continue to retard the development and efficiency of federal government institutions for some time to come.[1]

Unresolved border disputes

The political map of the union demonstrates graphically the complexity of boundary arrangements among the UAE member states. All but Abu Dhabi and Umm al-Qaywayn lay claim to sovereignty over non-contiguous territories, generally determined by tribal affiliation. As a result, the existence of numerous border disputes has long been a barrier to co-operation among the member states of the UAE. Although oil exploration provided a catalyst for settling some two dozen contested areas in the 1950s, close to a dozen disputes remain.

---

1 Even at the time of writing, nearly every single professional, technical and managerial position in the UAE in such administratively, militarily and economically critical areas of endeavour as utilities and communications is still staffed by foreigners.

Even some of the 'settled' disputes, however, still rankle. For example, the offshore boundary dispute between Umm al-Qaywayn and Sharjah was settled in a formula whereby Sharjah pays Umm al-Qaywayn a percentage of the revenues from oil produced in the area formerly claimed by the latter, but only after total revenues from production have been first shared with Iran. Having, in effect, to stand third in line remains as humiliating for the people of Umm al-Qaywayn in 1979 as it was in 1971 when they lost control of the area to Sharjah in the first place. Moreover, declining production in the Abu Musa field means that Umm al-Qaywayn's income from this source will also decline unless Sharjah agrees to a new sharing formula.

A territorial dispute on the UAE's east coast developed in May 1972 when Fujayran and Sharjan tribesmen fought a violent series of battles in which two dozen died. The presence there of UAE military units has been required ever since. A third boundary conflict, between Dubai and Sharjah, was one reason why Shaikh Zayid threatened in August 1976 not to run for re-election as president of the UAE for another five year term. This boundary dispute is complicated further by the fact that important economic issues have been involved. The land in contention was to have been the site of Sharjah's Charles de Gaulle Financial Centre, which the commercial elites of neighbouring Dubai perceived as a bid by their counterparts in Sharjah to lure away business firms that were already located in, or were contemplating moving to, Dubai.

The question of succession in key states

The question of rulership succession in the UAE states has historically been surrounded by intrigue and, on occasion, murder. This persisted even during the period of British protection. In the past, the absence of a clearly agreed upon successor has provided fertile ground for dynastic intrigue among relatives of the various rulers and, on more than one occasion, has resulted in the premature removal of a ruler from power. It is still too early to tell, however, how much the creation of the federation will mitigate this violent and stormy tradition, particularly in view of the fact that the individuals who would fill the post of heir apparent have not yet been selected in several UAE states.

The impact of geography and changing technology on the economic fortunes of key UAE states

For many years Abu Dhabi and Sharjah have been intensely jealous of neighbouring Dubai. Abu Dhabi's jealousy of Dubai's phenomenal commercial success has been reinforced by its ongoing dependence on Dubai's merchants for a substantial portion of its supplies. Some members of the ruling family also still resent the fact that Dubai's success is in part attributable to its having seceded from Abu Dhabi during the last century and that Dubai fought an inconclusive war with Abu Dhabi as recently as 1947. Most of all, Dubai, although much smaller, poorer and militarily weaker than Abu Dhabi, managed not only to achieve a position of *de jure* political parity with Abu Dhabi in the UAE at its founding but also was able to place a more impressive group of spokesmen for its interests into the union government than was Abu Dhabi. All of these jealousies and resentments have tended to strengthen the desire of many in Abu Dhabi to put their emirate ahead of Dubai in practically every field imaginable even, in the view of some extremists, at the price of undermining the still fragile federal framework of which both are key members.

Sharjah, for its part, has had equal if not greater reason to be jealous of Dubai. Until the 1950s, when Dubai became the political centre of the former Trucial States, political pre-eminence belonged to Sharjah owing mainly to its position as headquarters for the British Political Agency and the site of a Royal Air Force base. It was partially because of British irritation at Sharjah's ruler (the same one who was deposed in 1965, only to return and murder his cousin, who succeeded him, in the abortive coup of 1972) that Dubai attained commercial pre-eminence over Sharjah during this period. In addition, the two states were at war with one another as recently as the late 1930s and early 1940s and, unlike Abu Dhabi and Dubai, significant territorial disputes—as noted above—still exist between them. The al-Qasimi rulers of Sharjah and Ra's al-Khaymah have also tended to look down on the al-Maktum dynasty of Dubai. It was therefore doubly galling to Sharjah to take a back seat to Dubai and Abu Dhabi at independence, being denied the right, which the other two have, to veto any proposal put forth in the federation.

Abu Dhabi city, as the capital of the UAE, has already eclipsed Dubai politically. Dubai's commercial pre-eminence could also be undercut, although hardly eclipsed, as the result of two recent developments. The first is the road which lies inward from the shoreline between Abu Dhabi and Qatar that will link the UAE directly to Europe, the source of a substantial proportion of the country's imports. Construction of the road has proceeded slowly over the past five years, but it is expected to be completed some time in 1980.

Since the road will reach Abu Dhabi first, it remains to be seen whether much of the traditional transhipment of goods bound for Abu Dhabi through the port of Dubai will be as necessary as before, and whether, as overland transit from Europe begins to compete with shipping, Abu Dhabi merchants can become more competitive with Dubai merchants than has hitherto been the case.

At the same time, Sharjah has continued to develop port facilities at Khor Fakkan on the Gulf of Oman. Although relatively close by road to the rest of the UAE it is considerably closer by sea from outside the Gulf and, as Lloyds of London took note in 1979, has the added advantage of obviating the need to traverse the heavily sailed Straits of Hormuz, thus lowering insurance rates. The shorter distance would also mean savings on travel time, fuel and personnel costs for shippers.

Khor Fakkan's prospects have increased markedly in the past few years with the ongoing problems of port congestion and shipping delays plaguing many Arabian Peninsula ports. There is also a growing interest among shipping firms in containerization, for which Khor Fakkan, with its ability to handle ships of forty foot draught (i.e. ten feet more than any other port in the UAE) is regarded as the most convenient location for the modern roll-on, roll-off method of discharging cargo. In addition, Sharjah has persisted in its efforts to provide a system of rapid transit of cargo through co-ordinated air and sea port facilities. For these reasons, Sharjah merchants also stand to become more competitive with Dubai's merchants.

None of this need be interpreted as an imminent death knell to Dubai's string of astounding commercial achievements to date. It does, however, underscore the limits regarding the use to which even a highly developed sense of commercial acumen, for which Dubai is renowned, can be put when apolitical geographic and technological forces, over which neither Dubai nor anyone else has control, are introduced into the situation. How and whether Dubai will be able to cope with these new developments will deserve close watching. (Should the emirate ultimately prove unable to meet this challenge—unlike any other it has encountered so far—demands from .Sharjah for a fundamental realignment of UAE political power would appear almost certain.) Whether Dubai would be willing to acquiesce in such demands or whether, to avoid confrontation, it would move to secure its interests by seceding from the union, is questionable. Equally uncertain is whether Sharjah could or would permit such a realignment to be vetoed or otherwise prohibited by Dubai. The acceptance of the post of UAE premier by Dubai ruler Shaikh Rashid in July 1979 served to some extent to lessen the apprehensions of insiders and outsiders alike as to the first scenario, even though it shed little if any light on the likely outcome of the second one.

The lack of effective industrial co-ordination

Dating from the period prior to the union's establishment, a pattern of ostentatious expenditure has frequently characterized some of the investment and development projects launched by the various emirates. First, various emirates wanted their own 'international' airport, then an 'international' harbour, then cement factories, then container ports, then petro-chemical plants, then skyscraper hotels and, most recently, 'international' trade centres. These highly visible, costly and often duplicatory schemes were launched in accordance with decisions made not by federal agencies responsible for development on a regional basis, but by the rulers of the individual emirates. The impetus for these projects continues to be 'one-upmanship' and inter-emirate competition for commercial pre-eminence and regional prestige. For most of the life of the UAE so far, relatively little thought and even less in the way of serious discussion and debate appears to have been given as to how the interests of the union as a whole might be affected.

Outsiders, anxious to win lucrative contracts, have consistently taken advantage of these features of competitive one-upmanship among the UAE member states. Numerous foreign consultants, not to mention ambitious local entrepreneurs, have encouraged the various ruling house-holds to believe that they can successfully develop separately from their neighbours and, in certain fields, even from the UAE. Various members of the political elites of Dubai, Ra's al-Khaymah, and to a lesser extent Sharjah, have consistently entertained ambitions of independent state-hood or relative autonomy within the UAE. For this reason alone, the continued existence of the UAE remains uncertain.

Intra-UAE competition has been persistent. As a consequence, there is reason to wonder whether a union of the emirates, however loosely organized, might be expected to survive and, if so, for how long. The question mark remains so long as individual rulers are permitted to pursue unchecked the more parochial interests of their respective emirates, regardless of whether these serve federal interests. The failure to date of federal ministries to act as a screening, checking—and, where necessary, blocking—device on projects of a 'showpiece' nature has permitted a number of ill-planned expenditures on programmes that have had a negative effect on the UAE's regional and international image. (Unfortunately for the cause of federation in the UAE, the fact that the union ministries lack both legal and practical authority, as well as funds, to control most of these projects, would seem to indicate that this situation is likely to continue for some time to come.)

Immigration

Immigration as an issue pertinent to federal and emirate development goals continues to be a subject of widespread discussion and debate throughout the UAE. In terms of its political and socio-economic implications, it remains one of the two or three most important ques-tions confronting union decision makers. While British officials involved with development planning were mindful of the issue as early as the mid 1960s, public admission of serious concern in the highest echelons of UAE officialdom dates mainly from the formation of a revised

Council of Ministers in 1977. Since then the youngest ministers—most of whom enjoy support on immigration matters from a wide strata of the citizenry—have kept the issue at the forefront. Their concerns, all of which are shared by the older generation, are rooted in a tangled web that links such questions as ethnicity, social change, and internal security to the federation's prospects for economic wellbeing and long term political stability.

An early sign of progress in coming to grips with the matter was the publication, even before the 1977 cabinet came into being, of a Ministry of Labour and Social Affairs requirement for all aliens without valid work permits to come forth and register or re-register as foreign workers. A period of grace was proclaimed from August to November 1976, during which time an amnesty would apply to all those whose documents contained irregularities. The most astonishing result was that some 100,000 foreigners took advantage of the offer. In so doing, they tacitly acknowledged that their presence in the UAE had been 'illegal'.

In the process of obtaining such data, however, the problem became not only one of imposing order and efficiency on a previously near chaotic situation. It also reflected a larger, much more pervasive concern of a philosophical nature, and served to raise a wide variety of humanistic questions for which conventional wisdom offers no easy answers. Moving the immigration issue to centre stage, in short, has revealed an immense amount of societal anxiety about how UAE citizens should go about confronting the outside world and the future.

The basis for UAE officialdom's concern remains unassailable. The children of senior government officials are a distinct minority in classrooms averaging 55 students. These officials view a situation in which the overwhelming majority of the pupils are foreigners as one that warrants their legitimate concern. Their fear is that their children will not be inculcated with a sufficient sense of 'UAE-ness' in the course of their education.

The immigration problem in the classroom is different from the one at the working class level. The latter, an almost exclusively adult male phenomenon, can be viewed daily and most dramatically among the thousands of aliens engaged in port or construction work or among those, from Oman and elsewhere, who bear the union's weaponry—but not its passport. In its cultural and civilizational context, the educational dimension of the difficulty is twofold. First, the local students are taught not by their fellow citizens but by Egyptians, Jordanians, Palestinians, Indians and Pakistanis. These and other expatriate teachers have little knowledge or appreciation of the indigenous culture of the UAE area. Worse, on such occasions when some of them deign to speak of the country as a whole or its governmental establishment in particular, it is often in patronizing or negative terms.

Secondly, the immigration problem manifests itself in terms of the nature and orientation of the local student's peer groups. The latter, who in every instance are mainly foreigners, have become an important source of much that a UAE student is learning nowadays in terms of attitudes, behaviour and values. The effect on large numbers of UAE youth of being awash, as it were, in a sea of aliens has been to leave them confused and disoriented as to the ultimate source of administration and authority in their country. More troubling, in terms of educational and economic efficiency, it has contributed to the blurred view of many as to the locus of control over some of the union's most basic institutions.

Other UAE citizens are concerned about the immigration issue not only from the perspective of the classroom or the corps of construction workers or foreign mercenaries but equally from that of the enormous costs which the immigration issue entails by the provision of a growing range of health and other social services to the UAE population as a whole. With three-quarters of the nearly 800,000 inhabitants being foreigners, the costs of what some analysts estimate to be 80 per cent of the health facilities allocated to their use represents an inordinately high proportion of the sums involved. Some officials are increasingly finding that such expenditures, whether in absolute or relative terms, are difficult to justify. Their frame of reference is the growing feeling among the citizenry—admittedly based more on emotions and ethnicity than economics—that the majority of the beneficiaries are foreigners who contributed little, if anything, to the expenditures which brought such facilities and services into existence.

What is rapidly emerging from the discussions and debates surrounding the immigration issue, in short, is a rather pronounced 'we—they' consciousness. Such sentiments are particularly noticeable among the politically aware members of the citizenry in Abu Dhabi, Dubai and the other emirates. Neither the phenomenon itself nor its causes, however, are new to the Gulf. What is occurring on an increasingly broad scale in the emirates is nothing less than that which has existed in Kuwait for quite some time: namely a chauvinistic all of 'the UAE for the UAE-ans only'. And, as happened earlier in Kuwait, the issue has increasingly begun to affect the political dynamics of the federal government. If nothing else, the proponents within UAE officialdom of tighter restrictions on the immigrant community are being strengthened daily by the growing incidence of crimes of violence committed by foreigners, not to mention the continuing controversy to which the latter also contribute by virtue of their considerably different lifestyles and values.

As has been the case for much of the past decade, and reflective of a nearly identical situation in this regard in Kuwait, Qatar, Bahrain and Oman, the great majority of the foreign labour force continues to be engaged in the construction sector of the local economies. Abu Dhabi,

Dubai and Sharjah are most affected. Most if not all of these workers are expected to and actually do return to their native countries when the project for which their services were contracted is completed. Once the basic infrastructural boom is over, it is anticipated that this hitherto almost amorphous sea of aliens will have departed for other lands.

What is especially troubling to federal and emirate decision makers, however, has little to do with this group of immigrant workers. On the contrary, their presence, although never uncontroversial, has been acknowledged by most groups throughout the history of the UAE as having been indispensable to such economic development as has occurred or is being considered. Their concern, rather, is mainly for the kind of permanent foreign labour force that, of necessity, will need to be imported to Dubai, Abu Dhabi and elsewhere in the UAE to run the aluminium smelter, gas liquefaction plants and other industrial ventures already under way or being contemplated. Unlike the first group, this latter element is conservatively estimated to number in the high tens of thousands. The industrial units, in short, will require a stable labour force, even more schools and health facilities than have already been built, plus housing and, eventually, permission and provision for their families to join them, all of which are certain to spell continued stress on an already strained social system as the UAE persists in its efforts to modernize in the fastest possible time.

A related concern is the lack to date of a comprehensive labour law covering the UAE as a whole or, failing that, one which would up-date and give weight to the sole existing labour laws (Dubai, 1965 and Abu Dhabi, 1966). Neither of the latter pieces of legislation is enforceable in practice due to the absence of a corps of trained inspectors in the Ministry of Labour. Adequate legislation or a greater corpus of federal regulation than presently exists is needed not only to facilitate a more co-ordinated approach to the entire range of labour questions on a union-wide basis, but also to contribute to the goal of enhancing internal security. The assassination of Seif Ghobash in the autumn of 1977, the universally revered and exceptionally gifted Minister of State for Foreign Affairs, occasioned great public anguish over a situation—the regulation of foreign labour—which had clearly become out of hand.[1]

The immigration issue also lies at the heart of what is one of the most basic of all developmental questions posed for the union: namely, the kinds of skills that will be needed if Abu Dhabi, Dubai and the other emirates—and indeed, the UAE as a whole—are not only to survive but

---

1 Within UAE officialdom, no one seemed to know anything at all about the background or whereabouts of the assassin until the moment he was apprehended, even though in the course of his interrogation it was revealed that he had been living and working in Abu Dhabi uninterruptedly for five months prior to the event. Throughout that period of time the individual, a Palestinian, had been working as a low level painter while waiting for instructions from abroad on when to kill 'Abd al-Halim al-Kaddam (the Syrian Foreign Minister) for whom the shots were intended but missed.

33

prosper and flourish in the process. In Abu Dhabi, the situation is especially acute and can perhaps be illustrated most dramatically in terms of the military, the ranks of which are filled mostly by foreigners. Indeed, 85 per cent of rank and file are Omani, the remainder being mainly Arab, including local UAE citizens, some Jordanians, plus a considerable number of Baluchis. At the officer level most are UAE citizens, some of whom are naturalized having previously held Jordanian citizenship. There are still a few British military personnel who are retained informally in more or less ex-officio advisory capacities, although none are in uniform or associated with those in command positions.

The task of finding and retaining local citizens already in the military for the purpose of sending them to be trained abroad is more difficult than one might imagine. The problem is to get such individuals out of the country and embarked on their foreign training courses before they resign and succumb to the lucrative inducements pressed on them by relatives and others who persuade them to go into business. The difficulty of instilling and maintaining military discipline in the armed forces—by traditional standards as honourable as any other profession—thus continues to elude an early or easy resolution. An unintended consequence of parallel significance is that, for the same reasons, there is even less hope of instilling and maintaining discipline in a local working class that would be expected in the course of performing whatever manual, casual or other labour required, to serve the industrial sector or the professions.

The problem has emerged in large measure out of the boom which continues to characterize much of contemporary Abu Dhabi, Dubai and most of the other emirates. For many citizens, in short, there seems little reason why they should choose a career as an industrial worker, a soldier or as a member of one of the white collar professions when they can go into business and make, if not a billion dollars, then in any case a great many dirhams. The number of local inhabitants in the military and the professions who have already left and are contemplating leaving their jobs to enter the business sector is alarming. Yet the trend appears certain to continue. That is, the pattern depicted here seems bound to persist so long as the situation remains one in which most, if not all, of the socially repugnant or physically arduous work performed in the UAE is carried out not by the local citizenry but by members of a foreign servant class.

Conclusion

In conclusion, it is clear that the UAE's chances for long run success, and indeed even its prospects for the next few years, are mixed. Despite a growing cohesiveness within the union as a whole, there are many factors—conflicting federal, national, parochial, tribal and dynastic sentiments and competing economic development programmes—that are and will remain beyond the capacity of the union government, as currently structured, to control. Even so, that the seven rulers have elected for the time being to remain in rather than withdraw from the union is evidence enough that the UAE's strengths exceed its weaknesses so far. To be sure, the exact nature of the concessions for strengthening federal authority that the rulers made to Shaikh Zayid during the last half of 1976 is unknown. Moreover, equally unknown is what private agreements may have been negotiated when Shaikh Rashid agreed to become the federation's prime minister. What is most significant would appear to be the fact that Zayid was persuaded to serve for another five year term as UAE president and that Rashid agreed for the first time to accept a degree of personal responsibility for the administration of federal affairs on a day to day basis.

In terms of the most important period ahead—i.e. the period until 1981 which coincides with the second terms of office of both Shaikh Zayid as UAE president and Shaikh Rashid as vice-president and with the extended life of the provisional constitution—it would seem that the UAE stands a good chance of surviving for at least two more years. The union's prospects beyond that point are understandably much more difficult to predict. What seems certain, however, is that many of the issues discussed in this paper that have negatively affected the UAE's prospects to date are likely to have come to a head by then.

Some of the more disquieting issues that will need to be resolved if the UAE is to continue beyond that point are those relating to the formal and actual distribution of authority within the union—issues that are intricately linked to a continuing debate over the federal constitution. The 1976 decision, following months of debate, to extend the life of the provisional constitution, merely postponed a number of fights over the issues of union powers versus emirate powers as these relate to such problems as economic co-ordination and integration and other issues discussed here. These can be expected to surface again, if not in the near future then certainly by 1981 when the provisional constitution must once more be extended or replaced and a new UAE president and vice-president elected.

A matter of concern in this regard is the potential for the constitutional issue itself to become the focus of all the rivalries, tensions and mutual distrust that threaten the continued cohesiveness of the UAE. For example, failure to adopt a permanent constitution or to adopt one giving the UAE greater executive powers might lead Shaikh Zayid to resign as president or even pull Abu Dhabi (and perhaps 'Ajman, Fujayrah and Umm al-Qaywayn along with it) out of the UAE. Conversely, a constitution that strengthened the central government at the emirates' expense or gave Sharjah equality with Dubai might lead Shaikh Rashid to pull Dubai out of the union.[1]

In short, the acid test of whether the other rulers are prepared to accommodate Shaikh Zayid over the long run—and, if so, to what extent and, also quite possibly, on what terms—is still to come. To be sure, a truer indication than verbal commitments to this effect will be the degree to which the other rulers do in fact permit central authority to become commensurate with central responsibility. In this regard, Abu Dhabi, Sharjah, 'Ajman, Umm al-Qaywayn and Fujayrah, for the time being at least, will not prove stumbling blocks.

Before Shaikh Rashid became prime minister, conventional wisdom used to hold that the likely course of action in Dubai and Ra's al-Khaymah would be far less certain. In those two states, barring a change in the leadership or a turnabout in the attitudes of their respective rulers, pundits used to say that the continued prevalence of parochial sentiments and policies at the expense of federalist goals seemed probable. Yet Rashid's acceptance of an appointment to the premiership stunned most analysts. In itself, that act raised as much confusion as certainty in the minds of those who ponder the meaning of its ultimate significance.

Most observers—UAE citizens and outsiders alike—have little difficulty identifying with the determination of the rulers of Dubai and Ra's al-Khaymah to develop their societies as rapidly as possible. Nearly everyone is impressed by the remarkable degree of achievement which Dubai, in particular, has registered in this regard. Equally, many if not all of these same observers view positively the integrative aspirations of the federal apparatus in Abu Dhabi.

Yet a continuing dilemma in the UAE emerges from a basic incompatibility here. It stems from what, in essence, are two very different—some would say contradictory—courses of development. It is not so much, if at all, a matter of saying that both cannot prevail, that one must yield to the other. More accurate perhaps would be the view that there is room for existence between the two extremes: an in-between (not necessarily to be equated with middle) ground between the continued existence of seven independent emirates surviving in what in some fields could become an increasingly strong federation.

---

1 A set of scenarios in which disintegrative forces existing more in one emirate than in the rest, might affect the union as a whole, would include: a possible situation in which Sharjah, failing to obtain veto powers in the Supreme Council of Rulers, might seek to withdraw from the union; a possible growth of 'Abu Dhabi First' sentiment in the UAE capital, which might foster a move by leading segments in that emirate to withdraw from the union; or a situation in Dubai whereby the merchant community, in reaction to the federal machinery in Abu Dhabi, might press Shaikh Rashid to secede.

At the time of the UAE's founding this problem was not so much solved as pushed aside. Yet more than any other difficulty, it was this that returned repeatedly throughout the first eight years to haunt and hamper the federation's efforts to achieve success. Lacking an early resolution, it will continue to pose immense—in some cases insurmountable—difficulties for emirate and federal leaders in the period ahead. The situation, in short, remains one of a majority of the emirates being willing to permit the federation to play a dominant role, versus some that clearly are interested in exposing whatever other alternatives might exist[1] of seven rulers unable as yet to determine as a group whether, as they proceed with the task of developing their societies, the union—whether as pre-eminent power, helpful collaborator or unwelcomed irritant—is to be in front of, alongside or behind them. Only on a more satisfactory resolution of this question in favour of the federalists than has occurred to date—and not before such a resolution—will the UAE's chances for long run survival be enhanced.

---

1 Alternative approaches to confronting the future that have been mooted from time to time have usually postulated the creation of a unitary state at such time in the future when a significant portion of the population would come to take the view that the federal structure was no longer viable. Such a hypothesis has usually positioned Abu Dhabi town at the political, administrative and economic centre of any new edifice. Beyond the geographic confines of the federal union, the possibilities become at once more numerous and ingenious. Among the various proposals discussed over the years have been: a 'greater Oman', which would entail a fusing of one or more of the present UAE states with the Sultanate; a revival of the original nine state federation idea for which Bahrain and Qatar were candidates for membership during the 1968–71 period prior to the British withdrawal; the establishment of an interlocking network of relationships just short of a federal apparatus between Kuwait and Bahrain; and a virtual plethora of functional co-operative relationships among all the states of the area, e.g. customs unions, currency standardization, homogenization of health services delivery systems, uniform weights and measures, postal systems, passports, educational curricula, shipping, refining, regional security, etc.

3 Economic problems of Arabian Peninsula oil states

Michael Field

Introduction: a diminishing asset

Every one of the Arabian oil states is deeply concerned with the knowledge that oil is a diminishing resource. They are equally aware that oil is more or less the only natural resource they have. Together, these thoughts have led to an intense preoccupation with the value of oil reserves, with extracting the highest possible price for them and conserving them for as long as possible. It is standard producer rhetoric—particularly in Kuwait where the art has reached its most sophisticated form—to talk of managing the national asset as 'a trust for the generations yet unborn'. These feelings are matched by an equally obsessive concern with oil income accounting for nearly all of the Arabian governments' revenues and all but a fraction of the countries' foreign exchange receipts.

It goes without saying that the first and biggest economic problem for the producers must be the question of how long the oil will last, or more precisely how long it will be before their oil income drops below the level of their spending. This question underlies the first tentative moves being made towards levying domestic taxes, which most Arabians would now regard as an unjust intrustion on their fundamental rights. It underlies the new idea of disabusing citizens of their view of the state as a source of perpetual enrichment, this being a theme occasionally taken up by Abdel-Rahman Atiqi, the Finance Minister of Kuwait. It also dictates the pace at which industrialization programmes are being pushed ahead in the different states. It is certainly seen as being the vital factor in the region's future internal stability.

To date, the massive chanelling of wealth into private hands has been a major force for social contentment in the Gulf—any state would be content if 70 per cent of its nationals had their own private incomes from rents, as is the case in Kuwait. There must be a question of whether this stability will continue if and when the injections of wealth have to stop. At present it is impossible to imagine a more destabilizing problem than the oil producing governments finding themselves running out of money. On the other hand, while the money lasts the Arabian Peninsula oil producers are free of most of the classic afflictions of other developing countries. This is not to say that the producers do not suffer from some of the usual anxieties of reliance on a single resource, or that they have not experienced bottlenecks or high rates of inflation in their efforts to develop fast, or that there are no problems in having very small populations who are unwilling to take up the technical professions or do manual labour. But it does mean that the producers have no balance of payments or budgetary problems, that failures of early diversification projects do not matter in fiscal or export terms, and that the states can buy themselves out of many of their social problems.

To try to suggest dates when the oil producers might find their oil incomes insufficient for their spending would be a fruitless exercise. It would involve too many diverse factors, such as the level of economic growth in the Western economies, and it would have to incorporate a whole range of different 'bases' embracing a time span of up to half a century. Furthermore, it would be irrelevant because there will not be particular dates when individual producers will slide into deficit once and for all. Rather than thinking in terms of this simple 'dividing line' pattern, it would be better to think of a graph in which the two lines representing income and spending draw gradually closer together and then begin continually crossing over each other. As a result of oil price rises the income line will move above the spending line, then as spending rises and production falls (it is already falling in Bahrain and Oman and on the point of falling in Qatar) the income line will dip below the spending line until such time as a crisis in a producer state, a surge in demand in the consumer countries or the drop in supply itself leads to another price rise. The first signs of this pattern have already been visible in the last two or three years: in exceptional circumstances in 1978 even Saudi Arabia ran a small deficit, although now there seems little prospect of the deficit reappearing for a year or two.

The mixed pattern of surpluses and deficits will probably run on until the end of this century or longer. With regard to the income side of their accounts, the producers seem increasingly determined to spin out their reserves for as long as possible, and whatever this may mean for the Western economies it will certainly be beneficial for their own security. The three producers with spare capacity, Saudi Arabia, Kuwait and Abu Dhabi, have all set official ceilings on their output. Kuwait has indeed cut its output to a point where in 1978 it achieved a reserves-production ratio of 97 years. Barring breakthroughs in the development of alternative sources of energy, it also seems fair to assume that as Middle Eastern production falls, for geological or policy reasons, the drop in volume will be more than offset by rises in price. This at least should be the pattern in the early years. On such occasions as income does fall temporarily below spending, the producers will be able to draw on their considerable financial reserves.

On the spending side it is clear that the producers now seem concerned to moderate their expenditure in order to avoid the disruptive social consequences of high inflation and boom-bust cycles. In this context it might be wise in future for the consumers to acquiesce in bigger petro-dollar surpluses and put less emphasis on encouraging the producers to spend their revenues. There is no doubt that Western encouragement was partly to blame for the massive spending plans of the Shah of Iran and his deluded opinion that his country could be transformed into a major industrial power by the end of this century.

On the other hand, nobody should persuade himself that now that the producers have embarked upon programmes of massive development it will be possible to cut spending permanently once the initial capital expenditure has been completed. There obviously will be a fall in spending for a time; this can be seen in the consistent surpluses returned by Kuwait, which had installed much of its infrastructure and industry before the 1973—74 oil price rises. However, in the longer term, the current budget will tend to increase with an expanding population and the necessity of staffing and maintaining an ever larger number of social amenities, hospitals, ports, roads, airports and schools. As with amenities anywhere else in the world, the older structures become the higher will be the cost of maintaining them, and in the Arabian Peninsula the harsh climate ages buildings and machinery much faster than in most of the industrialized world.

In spite of this last proviso, the overall prospects for the Arabian oil producers continuing to receive an adequate supply of revenues for a generation seem quite good. Some states are better placed than others. Saudi Arabia, Kuwait and Abu Dhabi are the most secure. Bahrain, Oman and Qatar are in less happy positions, but all are relatively small consumers of revenues and they can rely on receiving help from the others, especially Saudi Arabia. Indeed, Bahrain and Oman are already receiving large amounts of direct and indirect Saudi aid, although they have found it does not come entirely without social and political strings. The important point is that the adequacy of the incomes of these 'poorer' states will be determined not so much by their own oil production as by the production of Saudi Arabia.

Diversification

The development priority of all the oil producers has been infra-structure—roads, ports, airports, telecommunications, seawater desalina-tion, electric power and sewerage. By the time of the oil price explosion of 1973—74, these projects were more or less complete in Kuwait and Bahrain, although they have had to be expanded since, and now, in mid 1980, the infrastructural work is nearly complete in Qatar, Abu Dhabi and Dubai. It is only in the northern emirates, Oman and Saudi Arabia, because of their vast size and much bigger populations, that there are significant numbers of infrastructural contracts still to be awarded.

After infrastructure has come diversification. The producers' aware-ness of the diminishing nature of their asset has meant that after an early flush of wild spending, all governments have conceived the major long term economic ambition of developing supplementary sources of income. Typically, the pattern has been for major diversification projects to be started about 15—20 years after the beginning of oil production—the intervening years having been marked partly by social and infra-structural spending and partly by sheer waste. It was in the first half of the 1960s that Saudi Arabia and Kuwait planned their original heavy industries, after beginning significant oil production in both cases in 1946.

The decision to diversify was almost inevitable. The most obvious alternative—building a massive portfolio of foreign investments—pro-vides a politically insecure souce of income, as Iran's recent experience with its US assets has shown, and seems not to be acceptable to the countries that would receive the investments. To be safe from inflation as well as providing a source of income, a large proportion of the foreign holdings would have to be in real estate and direct investments in industry, agriculture or large blocks of shares in major companies. So far there has been no evidence that the recipient countries would be prepared to make these investments available to the producers on anything like the scale that would be required if the producers were eventually to live off them. Taken as a group, the producers' present investments are mostly in paper assets, although the smaller investors—Kuwait, Abu Dhabi and Qatar—do have a large part of their reserves in more substan-tial forms of holdings. (For the reasons already mentioned, it is probably only these smaller investors that have the option of trying to put a significant part of their funds into direct investments. The West will tolerate receiving in direct investments a fair part of a $40—50 billion portfolio, which is what Kuwait, Abu Dhabi and Qatar own between them, but it might not tolerate having a similar proportion of assets invested direct from a $110—120 billion portfolio, which is the total of Arabian oil producer governments' foreign holdings if Saudi Arabia is added in.) In almost all cases—Kuwait being the partial exception—

foreign investments are seen as a means of making up periodic shortfalls of revenue and at a later stage as a supplement to new sources of domestic income: not as the major source of income on which the states will rely when their oil revenues decline.

Another option for the producers would be conservation, which in a sense only postpones the evil day when oil revenues will be inadequate for spending, coupled with slower spending at home. These ideas now seem to be being given greater weight in the producers' planning, but they have to be just one aspect in a multi-pronged approach to the future. All of the producers feel that they have to diversify their sources of income at home, notwithstanding the problems of industrial pollution, the social and security costs of importing large numbers of foreigners, and the dangers of investing in 'white elephants', some of which are inevitable in the early stages of development. (In Arabia the cost of a white elephant is not so much the waste of capital as the labour opportunity cost.) As much as anything else, the producers' decision to diversify is motivated by the pride that comes from self-sufficiency.

Obviously one can count as diversification practically any economic activity that earns new export revenues or saves the import of foreign goods or services and the Arabian Peninsula oil producers have indeed developed a vast range of businesses running from dry docks to irrigated agriculture to an embryonic movie industry. The main emphases, however, seem to have been in heavy process plant industry, light industry, the development of associated and unassociated gas, banking and foreign investment services (mainly in Kuwait and Bahrain) and, in Bahrain, the development of a role as a regional communications, leisure and service centre in which many of the foreign companies operating in the Gulf have established their bases. Dubai, meanwhile, has continued the entrepot trade it built up in the 1950s and 1960s, before its oil came on stream, although the last five years have seen a change in the nature of its business. Whereas it used to be a base for smuggling and legitimate export trade activity, it is now more of a vast shopping emporium in which the bulk of its goods are sold within the state and taken out by the buyers.

The diversification into service industries in Kuwait, Bahrain and Dubai is already an established success—at least in economic terms. There could possibly be problems stemming from Bahrain's role if the indigenous population becomes unhappy with the enormous Western cultural influence that comes from having so many Americans and Europeans on the island, but this is more a political and social issue that lies outside the scope of this paper. As far as Kuwait is concerned, the development of financial institutions has the unqualified advantage of requiring relatively few expatriates and offering careers which Kuwaiti nationals seem to find attractive.

The problems with diversification lie mainly with the development of industry and gas resources, which in revenue supplement terms could make a much bigger contribution than financial services. These industries are examined below.

Heavy industry

The major capital intensive process plants, loosely referred to as 'heavy industries', involve refining, liquified natural gas (frozen mains gas), natural gas liquids (for bottled fuel and chemical feedstocks), petro-chemicals, fertilisers, aluminium and steel. Most of these projects are planned to earn export revenues rather than produce import substi-tutes (the only partial exceptions being steel mills) and all of them have the advantage in the eyes of Middle Eastern planners of making use of the region's abundant resources of 'associated' natural gas (produced with oil), while yielding a large revenue for the size of the labour force employed. The attraction of the projects is increased by the fact that most of the associated gas now produced has to be flared, and would be impracticable to export on a large scale. At present the consumer countries do not have the receiving and distribution facilities to take the gas; the trade in liquified natural gas (LNG) is normally run as a 'service' between a particular liquifaction plant and a particular receiving terminal. Furthermore, given that gas is no more abundant globally than oil, the consumers may prefer to limit the contribution of natural gas to their energy consumption and buy from the Gulf as their present supplies run low in 10 or 15 years time. For the Middle Eastern planners in this case it does not matter if they make gas available to their indus-tries for as little as 20 per cent of the price being paid by the American consumer or 10 per cent of the price received by Algeria for gas exports. There is no opportunity cost in such a pricing policy.

For most of the time that the 'heavy' industrial projects have been under discussion since 1973 they have met with a very sceptical response from economists and journalists in the industrialized world. The main criticisms at the start were that they would encounter operating costs 60—80 per cent above normal Western levels and capital costs of any-thing from 35—100 per cent above Western levels. There were severe doubts whether these costs could be offset by hidden subsidies in cheap gas, electricity, water and land rental. There were also fears that the severe environment of the Arabian Peninsula, with extreme heat, dust, humidity and saline water supplies, would cause breakdowns leading to long periods of closure and financial losses. Worse still were the market-ing prospects. The natural gas liquids (NGL) facilities under construction in Saudi Arabia alone are big enough to double the present NGL capacity of the entire free world outside North America, which has made even the Arabian planners themselves admit that their plant is likely to be underutilized. The refineries and petrochemical plants , in contrast, will account for quite minor proportions (2 or 3 per cent) of world capacity in the 1980s even if all those planned are built, but they will be operating in markets already plagued by huge surpluses. In putting forward all these grounds for scepticism, the Western critics of Arabian industrial plans were able to point to the performance of the existing Arabian heavy industries. With the exception of Aluminium Bahrain (ALBA) and the NGL plants and refineries which were originally owned by oil concessionaires and tied in with their own corporate requirements, the performance of the early Arabian industries has been disastrous. Apart from very high running costs, there have been successions of breakdowns (in its first seven years of operations the Saudi fertiliser plant never ran for a full year at more than 55 per cent of capacity), and marketing operations seem to have had more than their share of bad luck, caused by cyclical slumps and exacerbated by the distance of Arabian plants from the main consumers.

In the last 12 to 18 months, however, a somewhat more optimistic climate has surrounded the Arabian industrialization plans. The established plants in the last two or three years have begun to overcome their technical problems, which suggests that although teething troubles in the Middle East may go on for longer than in the Western world, they are not permanent and can be solved by experience and modifications in design. At the same time, as inflation rates have fallen and bottle-necks have disappeared, estimates of additional capital and operating costs in the Middle East have been reduced to plus 25—40 per cent—levels which probably can be offset by supplies of cheap gas.

Another positive development has been the more rigorous approach towards their projects adopted in the last two years by the producers, who seem to have become more determined to see that the projects they build are really the most competitive they can find. Since 1974 there has been an enormous thinning out of numbers of candidate projects, accompanied by a growing awareness of the need to avoid duplication of projects within the region. To assist regional co-ordination, the Arabian industry ministers at a conference in Qatar in 1976 established the Gulf Organization for Industrial Consulting—although it is not yet clear how much authority this body will wield. As with all organizations of its type, much will depend on the forcefulness of the personalities at the top.

The most important change in the outlook for the heavy industries, however, has been in marketing. Since the Iranian revolution and the new oil crisis the prospects for sales of large quantities of NGL, which can be absorbed into the market much more easily than LNG, must have improved. There have been reports of European petrochemical producers looking at NGL—and buying it—as a feedstock in preference to naphtha refined from crude oil, and it is no doubt significant that Kuwait, the first oil exporter to bring on stream one of the new generation of NGL plants, has this year been raising its NGL prices. Similarly, at a time of crisis when the companies and consumer governments are anxious to secure crude oil supplies, there must be better prospects for sales of Middle Eastern refinery products and petrochemicals tied to crude oil allocations. This linkage is not something the Arabian governments like to talk about openly, but it is certainly an option available to them in their negotiations with individual purchasers and, in a more general sense, it will also affect the willingness of consumer governments to open their markets to Arabian industrial products in the face of inevitable opposition from unions and established producers at home.

Yet even with this general upturn in the prospects for Arabian heavy industry, it must be emphasized that heavy industrial revenues will never look very impressive financially as a supplement to oil incomes. At present oil and chemicals prices, the six Saudi petrochemical projects now at the advanced planning stage might not yield a revenue greater than that from 250,000 barrels a day of oil production—which is about 1/40th of current Saudi output.

Light industry

Most of the smaller manufacturing projects in the oil producing states in the last ten years have been set up by private investors, either through public companies or through private companies or partnerships. Although since 1976 there has been considerable government encouragement given through the cheap loans of the industrial development banks in Kuwait and Saudi Arabia, which account for almost all the region's light industry, the degree of private sector enthusiasm shown for industrial investment has been one of the surprises of Arabian development since the 1973—74 oil price explosion. By far the most popular type of project has been in building materials, although there have also been a number of investments in steel fabrication yards, simple food industries (notably flour milling) and industrial maintenance operations. In virtually every case the projects are designed to produce import substitutes rather than generate export revenues, although a few projects are now being built to cater for regional markets.

It seems likely that a fair number of the new industries, especially in Saudi Arabia, will go bankrupt. The Saudi policy has been to encourage the private sector to invest and not to be too strict about the economics of the projects to which it gives loans (at 2 per cent) through the Saudi Industrial Development Fund (SIDF). The idea is that even if quite a lot of projects do collapse a good number will succeed, and meanwhile the government does not have to worry too much about the money it may lose. As long as a project is regarded as being 'appropriate' for the kingdom—in other words not requiring too many imported labourers and standing at least a chance of being competitive with imports—it is more or less entitled to an SIDF loan as of right. (Occasionally SIDF loans have eventually been given to less competitive projects of which the government does not approve—a well known example being the Juffali-Daimler Benz plant for the assembly of Mercedes trucks.) Where the government is less prepared to offer support is with protection by tariffs which, if levied at all on industrial products coming into Saudi Arabia, are normally set at 20 per cent. Tariffs are unavoidably inflationary, and so protection will only be given if an otherwise desirable industry really needs it and is going to account for the greater proportion of the kingdom's demand for the product it manufactures.

The Arabian Peninsula is an unfavourable environment for light industry. There are all the extra capital and operating costs that afflict the heavy industries, including the need to house expatriate managers and technicians, pay them large salaries, fly them home once or twice a year and possibly pay for their children to be privately educated. Breakdowns occur more frequently, and take longer and cost more to repair, and there is always the possibility that the high rate of inflation in the oil states will make a project uncompetitive with imports between the time it is conceived and the time it is brought to fruition.

The problems are well illustrated by a notably successful company, Kirby Industries, originally a Houston firm which was bought outright by the Alghanim family in 1975 and which established its headquarters and a plant in Kuwait. The company had the built in advantage of manufacturing a product which could hardly help competing with imports: the steel frame building systems it makes, if imported from the USA, would have half of their cost accounted for by freight. From the first year the company made a profit, although since then its profits have grown more slowly than was hoped, and it has been particularly successful at penetrating export markets—it has even been considering exporting to China. And yet the profits earned in Kuwait have been substantially less than those from Kirby's continuing (and expanding) US operations, even though in America the company has to pay tax. Management has cost double what it costs in the USA, the inventory has to cover nine months compared to two weeks, the scrap factor is nine times as high because of a less able labour force, the Indian clerks at the middle and junior management levels have made expensive mistakes in every area of operations and, whereas in the USA the company could sell through hundreds of established outlets, in the Middle East it has had to develop a sales network of its own from scratch.

Kirby is saved by the huge freight cost of importing steel buildings and, as a general rule in the Middle East, it is the industries that save the customer paying freight to import by air that have been the most competitive. A good example of this has been SAPPCO, which manufactures plastic pipes in Riyadh and has been phenomenally profitable from the start. It also helps if the industry is technically very simple, as are many building products industries. (Kirby's problems, of course, stem from its being a relatively complicated factory.) The relationship between freight advantage and complexity of manufacture is well illustrated by the experience of SAFAMI, a loss making fabricator of pipe systems for the oil and gas industries in Saudi Arabia. As a fairly rigid rule, SAFAMI has found that it has won contracts where the technical problems have been small and the freight costs high, but lost any contract where high quality work has been necessary. It is not that it cannot provide high quality, complicated work—it has imported welders from Texas—it just cannot do so competitively.

Although the experience of these companies presents a rather pessimistic picture overall, it does seem that conditions for light industry are gradually improving. Encouraged by industrial banks and the Gulf Organisation for Industrial Consulting, investors are now thinking of aiming their plants at the regional market rather than simply at their domestic markets. Now that the most obvious and most competitive industries, producing products for which there will be the biggest demand, have mostly been built, this regional orientation will be virtually a matter of necessity if new plants are to take advantage of economies of scale. It also seems likely that Arabian management and other Arab and Indian labour are gradually becoming more used to the demands of industry, and are therefore more efficient—particularly in their ability to avoid and repair breakdowns. And, as more and more industries and supporting service businesses are started up, there must be less need for each new plant to integrate vertically. Hitherto it has had to provide, at great expense to itself, its own service departments, its own repair tools, its own export sales outlets, etc., all of which have unavoidably spent much of their time lying idle. In future, in a more diverse economy, an industrial plant should be able to buy these services locally as and when it needs them.

Intermediate development stage

Neither light nor heavy industries in Arabia can be thought of as successes in the terms by which economic performance is normally judged. If the Arabian Peninsula were in imminent danger of running out of oil, or of finding its oil revenues inadequate for its spending, the poor performance of its industries would be a serious matter. As it is, the governments can afford to take a long term view: they believe that there is a clear logic in starting diversification early. There is the obvious pride in developing self-sufficiency and, meanwhile, what revenues are earned are not unwelcome. The present industries can be a training ground for the people who will launch the next phase of Arabian industrial development. As Dr Ghazi Algosaibi, the Saudi Industry Minister, has said, part of the purpose of the present generation of industries is to accustom some of the Saudi population to the routine of industrial life. Also the oil producers have to spend, and be seen to be spending, their money somehow—and although the pace of development may be considerably slowed following the social and religious troubles of the last year, this motive may still be as important as any other. Even if the projects are not perfect, what else can the producers do with their money except channel more and more into private hands, as discussed later?

Another aspect of the present diversification programmes is that there are just two cases where the new manufacturing and service industries are already playing, or soon might play, a genuinely important role in the national economy. The Bahrain government now draws some 40 per cent of its revenues from non-oil sources, while the net foreign income of ALBA and the offshore banking units alone are reckoned to contribute nearly a third as much foreign exchange as the state's oil revenues from all sources. (Bahrain not only has its own small field, it refines Saudi oil and receives half the revenues from a small offshore Saudi field.) If one includes invisible foreign exchange earnings from the dry dock, hotels and the whole leisure service centre business, it seems likely that over a third of Bahrain's total foreign exchange income is now being derived from sources other than oil.

The other country where diversification has an immediate relevance is Qatar. This state is at present perhaps more dependent on its oil income than any Arabian producer apart from Abu Dhabi, but clearly it is also going to be the next producer (after Bahrain) to find its oil income becoming inadequate for its spending. The day may be postponed by oil price rises, but meanwhile there is no doubt that the Qatar government is taking its heavy industry programme very seriously. The evidence shows in the state signing contracts, starting construction and bringing its post-1974 batch of industries to completion much more quickly than any other producer. As the Qataris see it, there is a risk that the alternative to their earning a significant industrial income ten years hence could be financial dependence on Saudi Arabia, which they would rather avoid.

But neither the Qatar nor the Bahrain cases alters the fact that for the Arabian oil producers as a whole revenue from diversification programmes is not going to be significant in volume or really essential for many years to come. (Bahrain and Qatar are also exceptional in being small states with relatively small needs for revenue, which means that income from diversification there has a better chance of making an impact than it does elsewhere.) The producers are realistic about their position. Although one often hears talk about building industries and developing the service side of the economy 'for the day when oil runs out', all of the present phase of diversification involves projects which run off oil or the disposal of oil income. The heavy industries use oil or associated natural gas as their feedstock and fuel; the light industries built so far are mostly intended to provide building materials for the oil financed development boom and depend on the cheap loans that oil revenues make possible; and the banking and foreign investment businesses that have grown up in Bahrain and Kuwait are geared either to financing imports and construction or disposing of private and government surpluses that stem from oil revenues. Apart from the badly mismanaged fishing business, and agricultural production in the major Saudi cases, there is very little economic activity in the Arabian Peninsula which would continue to make sense without oil. One must see the diversification schemes so far as being an intermediate stage, on the foundations of which governments hope there will eventually grow a new economy, of a shape as yet undefined, which will sustain Arabia in the post-oil era.

Unassociated gas

The only important exception to these comments may be natural gas. All of the gas being exploited in Arabia at present is associated gas, dissolved in oil or found as a cap on top of oil reservoirs, and this obviously has a life as long as the life of the oilfields; but recently there have been discoveries of unassociated gas. This gas, found on its own at depths much greater than oil in the Middle East, is still something of an unknown quantity, although the drilling done so far gives grounds for optimism. Major fields have been discovered, although not yet fully appraised, in Iran, Abu Dhabi and Qatar, while Aramco says that whereever it has done deep drilling it has struck gas. The company's employees are prepared to suggest unofficially that wherever there is a suitable reservoir formation at the deep Khuff levels where gas has been found so far, there will indeed turn out to be a gasfield. This applies in the major Saudi oil producing area from south Ghawar to Qatif. Nowhere is the development of these gasfields being pushed ahead as yet, mainly because there is no financial urgency to do so and no very big established trade in LNG into which the new fields could be fitted without difficulty. When the unassociated gas is developed it will not necessarily be possible to substitute it for associated gas in the present gas based heavy industries such as petrochemicals and fertilizers; both the calorific value and the content of unassociated gas (in terms of proportions of methane, ethane and NGL) is generally different from that of associated gases. Nor may it be that unassociated gas reserves will last very much longer than oil. However, the development of these reserves would count as an industrial diversification (of a sort) which right from the start would yield a revenue entirely independent from that of oil production.

The super-rich society

Ironically, at the same time as the Arabian oil producers have been trying to diversify their sources of income over the last ten or twenty years, they have been pursuing another policy which can only make diversifications more difficult and put off the day when their economies might be self-sufficient without oil revenues. This has been the whole-sale enrichment of their own citizens. The richer the population become the more dependent they must be on a high oil income to maintain the standard of living to which they have made themselves accustomed, and the less prepared they are to forsake the easy lives of landlord or driver for the more demanding routine of manager or industrial shift worker. One might say that the oil producers have set themselves the almost impossible task of not only diversifying, but diversifying while maintaining their people as some of the richest in the world.

The people of the Arabian oil states, or at least some of the Arabian oil states, are rich not only in the technical statistical sense of appearing to have the highest per capita incomes when their states' oil revenues are divided by numbers of population. They are rich in the real personal sense of having the world's highest disposable incomes and living in the world's most generous welfare states.

Per capita income as normally calculated is a rather meaningless figure because it gives all residents of the state the same average income, whereas in practice there is no averagely wealthy person in Arabia: in Kuwait, Qatar and Abu Dhabi especially there are rich nationals and mostly poor immigrants. In Bahrain, Saudi Arabia and Oman the picture is slightly different in so far as these states have some relatively poor nationals as well as poor foreigners. Bahrain and Oman both have had oil revenues too small to enable them to embark on the wholesale enrichment of their people, and Saudi Arabia was in much the same position up to 1973. In its first twenty-five years of oil production, Saudi Arabia's cumulative revenues came to no more than Kuwait's, although they had to be spread over a vastly greater country and much bigger population. In Saudi Arabia there has also been an ideological objection to making the enrichment of citizens an end in itself. This was certainly the view held in King Faisal's day and embodied in the Second Five Year Plan, which states that its principle social objective would be to assure all Saudis '. . . an adequate dignified minimum standard of living. Levels above this minimum will continue to be the reward of individual effort and achievement.' Under the pressure of raised popular expectations, however, the present Saudi rulers seem to have allowed themselves to slide towards the enrichment philosophy, probably without making a formal decision for or against it.

Although the philosophy may not be pursued with equal thoroughness in all countries, there are a number of spending policies and pieces of business and social legislation which one comes to recognize as being peculiarly 'Arabian oil state' in character. They are ingeniously designed to pump real personal wealth into the hands of citizens while giving non-citizens enough to induce them to stay and perform their useful work but no more.

In Kuwait, which has the most comprehensive enrichment policies and is therefore the most commonly quoted example, the major means of distributing wealth has been through the purchase of land at inflated prices. The exact mechanics of land buying have varied from area to area according to time and circumstances. Typically, the state buys land at the market price or slightly over, zones it, installs services and infrastructure and then leases it or sells it off for further development or private houses for only slightly more than it paid in the first place. From the point of view of the relatively 'poor' Kuwaiti, this may involve his selling land in one area at a high price and then being sold land with services provided in a lower price area elsewhere—at the same time as being given a cheap loan with which to build a house. (His capital profit on the land transaction he can invest.) In fact, government sales of land are relatively uncommon. Normally the government leases back the land, which means that the state now owns about 90 per cent of the land in Kuwait City and ensures that the flow of capital is mostly one way. In other countries, and particularly in Saudi Arabia where the modern state has grown out of a less settled community, most of the land has been vested from the start in the hands of the ruling family, and has been used for gifts to subjects whom the family has wanted to reward. In all countries urban land prices and rents are extremely high because the expansion of the economy and the growth of population seems to have outstripped the rate at which services have been provided for new land. In all countries, too, only nationals may own land or buildings, which gives them a monopoly of rent income from expatriates, and in most countries there are housing banks which provide house-holders and developers with very cheap building loans. Occasionally there have been cases of all outstanding loans being written off by governments that are anxious for political or economic reasons to make a gesture of goodwill towards their people. There are free housing schemes almost everywhere for the 'poorest' citizens.

To complement these policies, Arabian governments pay extremely generous salaries for jobs that often require nominal effort or perfunctory attendance, although traditionally the Saudis have been less generous than the Kuwaitis. There are virtually no taxes or social security contributions to be paid. Among the few exceptions applied to non-foreigners are the religious tax, zakat, which is a semi-optional levy of 2½ per cent on the increase in a man's assets over a year, a few indirect taxes levied on imports to protect local manufacturers, and a small Kuwaiti corporation tax which companies have to pay to a fund for scientific advancement. Income tax and purchase taxes of any sort so far have been unthinkable.

Education is free everywhere, with governments paying the tuition fees and (extremely generous) pocket money of students who qualify to go to university abroad. Health services likewise are mostly free— although the much publicised King Faisal Hospital in Riyadh is a private establishment. Once again, governments pay for patients who need specialist treatment to be sent to hospital abroad, and they also pay the expenses of the relations who accompany the patient. In most states internal telephone calls are free, although water can be quite expensive. Most of this particular category of welfare policies benefits the whole community, although foreigners do not get paid for when they go abroad to university or to hospital.

In commerce, the oil states help their citizens by confining to them alone the ownership of shares in public companies, and in most cases insisting that nationals have at least 51 per cent of any private business. As with housing, cheap loans are provided for industrialists and contractors, although in Saudi Arabia foreign partners are also eligible for loans as long as their share in a business is below a certain level. In the emirates, Saudi Arabia and Qatar the state also seems reasonably happy to tolerate huge commissions being paid by foreign companies to agents who help them win government contracts—even though commissions on occasions have put up contract prices by over 20 per cent. Kuwait seems to suffer less from this sort of practice, although it has often been prepared to bale out private sector businessmen who have run into trouble—giving them loans or buying the shares of the companies they have launched. The most recent example of this policy in operation came at the end of 1977 when the Kuwait government launched a buying operation to support prices on the Kuwaiti stock exchange.

Taken as a whole the enriching policies have made the Arabians addicted to a type of life which only oil revenues on a vast scale (which fortunately is likely to continue) can make possible. They have also made them much more dependent on immigrants than they would have been in societies with less generous spending policies; it was calculated recently in Kuwait that every Kuwaiti national born is going to need two and a half immigrants to run the economy off which he lives. It is often said that immigrants are necessary for their technical and managerial skills and because the indigenous populations of the oil states have been simply too small in numbers to operate a modern economy. In reality, this is only half of the story. The fact that the enriching policies have been easiest to focus on two areas of activity—trade and land—has meant that those eligible for enrichment, i.e. citizens, have gravitated to these two activities. Many Arabians are perfectly capable and well enough educated to pursue careers in the professions, government service, state corporations or industrial management. Others—the driver, doorman, tea boy class—are quite capable of working as labourers or learning a skill. The fact that only a very few of either class chooses to take up these options is partly a matter of cultural tradition, but also a matter of the rewards being greater, or the life being easier for the same reward elsewhere.

Two questions have emerged from the enrichment policies over the last five years. The first, broadly speaking, has been how effective are they? And the second has been, should they be continued?

In Kuwait the enrichment policies have been so thorough, and have been in operation for so long, that the first question does not arise. But elsewhere, governments have been worried by the feeling that high rates of inflation, caused by overspending producing bottlenecks, may have made their established policies inadequate. There has been no doubt at all that the gap between the richest and the 'poorest' has widened and there are fears that the high expectations created among all citizens by the oil price explosion may not have been fulfilled. In Saudi Arabia there has been a drift from the villages into the big towns, and those who have not made a success of their new lives as drivers, lorry owners or minor contractors must be disillusioned. Their jealousies must have been sharpened by the nature of the Arabian market place, where the 'buyer beware' philosophy is unchallenged and where merchants will exploit any temporary monopoly or tightness in the market to the greatest possible degree. In Arabia there is not the constraint that there is on Western corporations of exposure of excessive profits or racketeering damaging a company's image.

In all the Arabian oil producers these strains have been added to the normal social strains of fast growth in the region. The governments' spending programmes have led to an influx of Arab and non-Arab immigrants and visitors, who may or may not represent a security risk but who certainly do introduce alien cultural influences. Governments' spending also changes the jobs, lives and routines of their citizens, it enables them to go abroad, and the cash it puts in their pockets gives them Western material aspirations. Originally it was feared that these changes would lead to demands for greater political participation and the erosion of the family, now the fear is of parts of the population rejecting the Western influence to which they have been exposed and becoming involved in the 'Muslim revival' which produced the occupation of the Mecca mosque and the riots in the Saudi Eastern Province and in Bahrain.

Even before the economies settled down to more modest rates of growth in the last year or so, the economic malaise in Arabian society never reached anything like the intensity that it did in Iran. The economic mismanagement had been less serious, the rural—urban drift had taken place on a smaller scale, slower down spending did not not seem to cause unemployment (and certainly not unemployment among the people who mattered—the citizens) and, most important, the governments had the money directly to alleviate their peoples' problems on a scale that the Iranians could not match. It was in their response to inflation and their fears of a disillusioned citizenry that the Saudis moved towards the 'absolute welfare' enrichment policies of the richer Gulf states. All Arabian oil state governments began subsidizing staple foods, either by setting price controls and paying subsidies to the traditional importers, or by setting up their own loss making 'supply companies' and issuing all residents (not just citizens) with ration books. They also raised salaries in government service and the armed forces, set profit controls on non-food consumer imports (although these were widely ignored), passed legislation on permissable commissions for agents negotiating any sort of contract (also ineffective) and fixed prices for the output of local industries and utilities. In Saudi Arabia at one point the government decreed a 60 per cent cut in the electricity tariff and subsidized the producers' losses. In Bahrain, where such lavish subsidies have been beyond the government's means, the state has introduced compulsory employers' social security contributions.

In future it seems likely that Arabian governments will spend more slowly so as to control inflation and restrain the growth of excessive expectations. In Saudi Arabia there will probably be more emphasis put on rural spending, including the development of agriculture, in order to half the drift to the towns and keep people more insulated from modern cultural influences. (There are also directly social, as opposed to economic, considerations dictating slower spending, but these fall slightly outside the scope of this chapter.)

The other question sometimes heard in Arabia recently—concerning whether the enrichment policies should be continued—may seem at first to be a direct contradiction of the governments' concern with preventing the economic disillusionment of their subjects. (In fact, the question applies mainly to policies which actively enrich citizens, rather than to the alleviation of the effects of inflation.) Furthermore, it is being asked mainly in Kuwait, whose citizens are in a different league of wealth from most of the other Arabians, and it must be admitted that even in Kuwait the question is only raised occasionally and in a fairly tentative form.

The main questioner so far as been Abdel-Rahman Atiqi, the Finance Minister, who has spoken against the government's tendency to always bale out public and private sector 'lame ducks', and has even mentioned once or twice that eventually citizens will themselves have to play a role in supporting their government by paying taxes, as people do elsewhere in the world. (Most of Atiqi's motives in making his occasional remarks have been to prepare Kuwaitis psychologically for the day when they will have to pay tax.) In practical terms, all that has happened in Kuwait has been a tightening up on the payment of tax by foreign companies in joint ventures and the introduction of a 5 per cent corporate profits tax, paid to the Fund for Scientific Advancement. This tax is not part of the law but in practice it seems to be compulsory. In Bahrain there has been the social security contributions law, which is gradually being extended to embrace smaller companies.

Arabian businessmen would be quite right in seeing these new rules as the thin end of a wedge. It will be done very gradually but governments will want to establish the principle of tax well in advance of their actually needing internal finance to supplement their oil revenues. For social reasons they will also want increasingly to regulate profits and the brutal code of Arabian business practice. Commercial life will become more and more subject to the type of regulation that is taken for granted in the West. The business community may resist the changes, as the Bahrain merchants resisted the introduction of a commercial registration fee early in 1977 and got the amount halved from $10,000 annually to $5,000, but slowly the Arabians will be asked to undertake a big adjustment of their view of the state. Instead of thinking of it as a provider of all things, they will have to see it as an institution that they themselves have a duty partially to support.

Basic data on oil producers

Saudi Arabia: *Oil revenues 1978:* $37 billion
Oil reserves: 166 billion barrels
Production 1978: 8.3 million barrels a day
Reserves/production ratio: 55 years
Start of production: 1939, restarted 1946
Population: 6.5 million (2 million immigrants)

Kuwait: *Oil revenues 1978:* $9.5 billion
Oil reserves: 66 billion barrels
Production 1978: 1.9 million barrels a day
Reserves/production ratio: 97 years
Start of oil production: 1946
Population: 1.5 million (0.8 million immigrants)

Bahrain: *Oil revenues 1978:* $0.4 billion
Oil reserves: 0.25 billion barrels
Production 1978: 0.06 million barrels a day
Reserves/production ratio: 12 years
Start of oil production: mid 1930s
Population: 300,000 (100,000 immigrants)

NOTE: Bahrain already draws some 40 per cent of its state revenues from sources other than oil. Unlike the highly affluent people of the other Arabian oil states, its relatively well educated citizens are prepared to take industrial and junior management jobs: at times the government has had to pursue formal job creating policies because it has been unable to adopt the enrichment policies of other Arabian countries. Many Bahrainis wear Western dress rather than the *thobe*, which has become tne self-conscious distinguishing uniform of the other Arabians.

To help Bahrain's sources of income other Arabian countries, notably Saudi Arabia, appear to have avoided competing with some of Bahrain's development schemes. The Saudis share the revenues of an offshore oilfield with Bahrain and have held back on their own aluminium project, while the Kuwaitis have avoided competing with Bahrain's offshore banking units. OAPEC has located its dry dock in Bahrain, and the island has long been the headquarters of Gulf Air (owned by all the lower Gulf states and Oman)—not that there would have been any competitors for the base when the airline was set up. However, there have been some exceptions to this pattern of good neighbourliness. Dubai has its own dry dock and aluminium smelter, and the UAE's equivalent of offshore banking units have had their development held back not by government policy but by the lack of international confidence in the UAE banking system.

Qatar:	*Oil revenues 1978:* $2.2 billion
	Oil reserves: 4 billion barrels
	Production 1978: 0.48 million barrels a day
	Reserves/production ratio: 23 years
	Start of oil production: 1949
	Population: 170,000 (120,000 immigrants)

Abu Dhabi:	*Oil revenues 1978:* $7 billion
	Oil reserves: 30 billion barrels
	Production 1978: 1.45 million barrels a day
	Reserves/production ratio: 57 years
	Start of oil production: 1962 (development began 1966)
	Population: 280,000 (230,000 immigrants)

Dubai:	*Oil revenues 1978:* $1.7 billion
	Oil reserves: 1.3 billion barrels
	Production 1978: 0.36 million barrels a day
	Reserves/production ratio: 10 years
	Start of oil production: 1969
	Population: 280,000 (220,000 immigrants)

Oman:	*Oil revenues 1978:* $1.7 billion
	Oil reserves: 2.5 billion barrels
	Production 1978: 0.32 million barrels a day
	Reserves/production ratio: 22 years
	Start of oil production: 1958
	Population: 1 million (200,000 immigrants)

4 Population, migration and development in the Gulf states

Allan G. Hill

Introduction

Between the five 'city states' of the Gulf (Kuwait, Qatar, the United Arab Emirates, Bahrain and Oman) and the three larger units (Iran, Iraq and Saudi Arabia) there are obviously significant differences in size, in wealth, in type of economic development and hence in population characteristics.[1] The oil dominated economies of the smaller states have expanded rapidly in the post-1945 period using imported labour principally from the other Arab countries but also from Asia (the Indian sub-continent), Europe and North America. At present, the main period of immigration, at least of the 'semi-permanent' kind where dependants accompany the workers and remain there for many years, appears to be over and more of the growth of the immigrant populations in the city states is now due to natural increase rather than to immigration. These natural increase rates for citizens and aliens alike have now reached very high levels due to a combination of rapidly reduced mortality and almost unaltered levels of fertility. In the larger oil states, immigration has never been as important politically or socially as elsewhere in the Gulf simply because the immigrants, although numerous, amount to only a smaller fraction of the total population. Natural increase rates in Iran, Iraq and Saudi Arabia are a little lower than in the smaller oil states due to a slower decline in mortality but the growth rates of these larger populations are still high, producing a substantial numerical increase in the total population each year.

---

1 All eight countries are subsequently referred to as 'Gulf countries'; the five smaller units including Saudi Arabia are referred to as 'Gulf states'.

There are thus two different sets of population based problems faced by the two groups of Gulf countries. The five smaller countries and Saudi Arabia have to find ways of continuing their past economic expansion, based as it is on the use of substantial amounts of expatriate labour. In addition to arranging the continuous supply of new foreign labour, they have to supervise the composition and growth of the existing immigrant communities which, because of their now quite long established position in the Gulf states, are growing at high rates of natural increase. Their own national populations are also expanding very rapidly and creating an annual addition of youngsters which even rich oil states are finding difficulty in absorbing, especially when compounded by the growing numbers of children of immigrants with similar needs for schooling, health care and the like. The larger oil states, by comparison, have a much smaller problem of immigration although Saudi Arabia, despite its larger population and area, still experiences many of the immigration problems faced by the smaller states. Even Iraq and Iran are dependent on skilled foreign workers in certain key sectors of the economy, notably oil. The problems in these larger countries are basically the conventional ones faced by most developing countries—rapid population growth running ahead of balanced economic growth and of service provision for the expanding populations. In the oil states, of course, the level of service provision desired or considered acceptable is very much higher than in most non-oil developing countries and this sector is an extensive user of labour. An additional problem in the larger states is that the indigenous populations are not homogeneous in religion, language and ethnic background. Hence, problems related to the geographic distribution and national aspirations of the minorities are as important as the balance between the citizens and the immigrants which is of major concern to the smaller countries of the Gulf.

This paper concentrates principally on the demographic and related economic and political problems faced by the oil states of Arabia, but some specific population problems facing Iraq and Iran are also considered.

The demographic situation in the late 1970s

Whilst there is considerable variation in the size of the populations of the Gulf countries (Table 4.1), all are part of the high fertility region of south-west Asia. With the exception of Iran, there appears to be no well established downward trend in fertility in any of the other seven countries either amongst the nationals or among the resident alien populations. The combination of falling mortality and almost unchanged fertility results in very high rates of natural increase.

Table 4.1
Population size and growth rates in the states surrounding the Gulf

	Area ('000 KM²)	Estimated mid 1979 population ('000)	Proportion of total population foreigners (%)	Estimated annual population growth rate (%)	Proportion of total population urban (%)
Bahrain	.6	285	13.9	3.4	80
Iran	1,648.0	46,462	0.5	3.0	44
Iraq	434.9	12,812	4.0	3.1	62
Kuwait	17.8	1,262	52.5	5.9	89
Oman	212.4	867	25.0	3.2	5
Qatar	11.0	239	61.8	8.5	88
Saudi Arabia	2,149.7	8,396	21.0	3.6	21
United Arab Emirates	83.6	883	70.0	11.4	84

Note: The population totals have been estimated by projecting forwards from the last census year using known rates of growth. These growth rates are not well established in Qatar, the UAE and Oman; in Oman, with no complete census, the figures are very approximate.

There appears to be a well established pattern of demographic evolution to which all the Gulf states tend to conform. It begins during the time that oil is first discovered with high mortality conditions and quite high levels of fertility associated with early and almost universal marriage. Following the beginning of work on the first major development plan, heavy investments are usually made in the health sector with the result that adult mortality begins to decline. Next the problem of infant and childhood mortality is tackled and special efforts are made to improve the conditions of childbearing and then to ensure that more of the newborn survive by improving feeding practices and by dealing with the most common causes of childhood death. This point has been reached by all the Gulf countries but at different times. Kuwait and Bahrain are probably the most advanced because of a combination of their small size and the early discovery and development of oil. Iran and Saudi Arabia are taking longer to pass through the same stages simply because of their larger size.

At a later stage a few elite families start to reduce their high fertility levels by a combination of later marriage and the deliberate control of marital fertility. This lower level of fertility prevails amongst women with a secondary level of education or above and so the onset of a more general fertility decline is related to the productivity of the educational system. An important question is therefore whether the education system can do more than keep pace with larger cohorts so that the educational levels of the female population as a whole rise steadily in the future.

It is possible to plot the progress of the Gulf states through these stages. It is interesting to note that there is a kind of 'wave' effect sweeping down the Gulf roughly in step with the first export of significant amounts of oil.

The rates of natural increase for the immigrant communities of the Gulf are more difficult to fit into this overall pattern simply because the immigrants themselves come from a very diverse set of origins. Certainly, many young male migrants from surrounding Middle Eastern countries migrate to save money with marriage in mind but it is much harder to see a simple connection between income and fertility for those already married who live and work in the Gulf. An obvious key factor affecting the fertility of the immigrants is whether they are unaccompanied males or not. The well established immigrant groups have fertility and mortality levels which match the levels of the nationals although, in some cases, fertility amongst the immigrants appears to be even higher than that of the nationals (e.g. the Palestinians in Kuwait). With much reduced levels of net immigration in recent years in most Gulf states, the growth of the immigrant populations due to natural increase assumes a much greater numerical significance.

Immigration itself has also passed through a number of states in the

Gulf countries as the economies of each have grown and matured. At the outset, soon after the discovery of oil, the kind of labour needed was a small number of highly skilled engineers and technicians and a larger number of semi-skilled workers primarily in the oil sector. To meet these needs, expatriates from the West were imported to fill the first category and, for the second, workers were brought from India and Pakistan. At least one oil company had a recruiting station in Bombay to provide a supply of foremen and clerks.

Unskilled labour came from the local population or from the Arab countries nearby. Persian workers crossed the Gulf in large numbers at an early stage to work in Arabia. As the development of the country got under way, the demands for unskilled labour increased dramatically since the expansion of each country's economy invariably began with a dramatic growth in construction activity. At about this time (the early 1950s in Kuwait, later in the lower Gulf) the refugees from Palestine provided a ready source of unskilled and semi-skilled labour. Some Arabs from the northern Arab countries quickly established strong business footholds and others became influential in government or in the professions. Both the refugees and others in the professions had good reasons for bringing their dependants with them—the first group had no choice apart from leaving them in refugee camps and the second group had the resources and the established position which made them feel comfortable with their new life in the Gulf. Thus, the migrant flow from the Arab countries quickly changed from being a purely male flow to one in which children and women were present in significant proportions. On the other hand, the immigrants from the Yemens, Iran, Oman, Sudan and other poor countries to the south has remained a largely male influx. The turnover of this last group of migrants is very high since they return home at not more than annual intervals and they are replaced by migrants from the same origins with approximately the same characteristics.

The most recent development has been for the oil states to move away from the traditional sources of labour and turn to Asians in increasing numbers. The advantages of Asian labour is first that it is cheaper; the introduction of Asians into Saudi Arabia (Pakistanis and workers from south east Asia including the Philippines) has driven down wage rates and led to the return migration of some North Yemeni workers as a result. An additional attraction of the labour from Asia is that workers generally leave their dependants at home so that there is less pressure to provide social and other services for immigrants. The males can therefore be accommodated in rather frugal 'work camps'. Finally, it seems that Asian contractors are offering contracts which include the import, use and then the export of labour at the end of the contract. The South Koreans encourage this way of working since it helps to recapture a larger fraction of the workers's remittances in the domestic economy as the workers are paid in Korea in local currency. Several major projects in the Gulf, including the OAPEC dry dock in Bahrain have been built in this way, usually ahead of schedule.

Urbanization and its consequences

The cities of the Middle East have always been dominant in the economic, political and religious life of the region. Recently, they have also come to dominate numerically because of rapid rates of natural increase of the urban populations combined with substantial migration into the cities from rural areas. In general, about half of the recent population growth of Middle Eastern cities is due to migration and half to the excess of births over deaths. Between 1970 and 1975, the urban population of the region grew at an average of 5.2 per cent per annum and many individual cities grew much more rapidly. Between 1963 and 1974, for example, Riyadh's population jumped from 159,000 to 667,000, Jeddah grew from 147,000 to 561,000 and smaller towns like Taif, Medina and Hofuf at least doubled in size. As a result, well over half of all Middle Easterners now live in towns and cities and this fraction is increasing steadily, leading to a clear reduction in the numbers working in the agricultural sector. The already heavy reliance of the Gulf countries on imported meat, grains and even dairy produce is increasing further as a result; even tastes have changed, moving away from domestic-ally produced foodstuffs in favour of the imported substitutes.

The bulk of urban employment in the Gulf countries is in the service sector, especially in professional and personal services. High wages have attracted labour from other sectors and driven up the price of labour in agriculture and industry. Finding skilled and semi-skilled production workers from within the domestic labour markets in the Gulf is very difficult which means that long term plans for industrial development and diversification even in the larger countries (Iraq, Iran and Saudi Arabia) look rather bleak.

The cities themselves now consist of a heterogeneous mix of peoples frequently living in separate quarters from one another. The restrictions on foreigners owning land and property in most Gulf countries have produced a fairly strict system of residential segregation between citizens and immigrants. This may be one factor responsible for the almost negligible amount of intercommunal violence in the Gulf states. But in Iraq and Iran especially, the flood of rural—urban migrants has produced large areas of squatter housing which form a marked contrast to the smart villas and apartments of the established urban middle class. The juxtaposition of rich and poor in the city appears to have brought about comparatively little class resentment on the part of the 'have nots', possibly because large inequalities in income distribution have always been a feature of the region or because the inequalities are not expressed in class terms. Nevertheless, the immigrant from Khuzistan in Tehran or from Amara in Baghdad does feel some antipathy to a system which apparently looks after him so badly. The half-finished land reform process in Iraq and Iran forced many peasants into cities and any suggestion that those in power support these erstwhile landlords and shaikhs inevitably produces feelings of bitterness. The neglect of the rural areas where daily wages for a labourer can still be less than one-tenth of those in Baghdad or Tehran contributes to the continuing rural exodus and to the growing potential problem of large numbers of disaffected people in the major cities.

It is remarkable that despite the concentration of people in urban areas social change and modernization have not proceeded more rapidly. (Even today, very few urban women work outside the house and attitudes to women and children appear to have changed very little.) High fertility seems as important a goal as any even amongst the lower classes, a group one would expect to be most constrained by resources in an urban setting. It is especially hard to explain this effect in the Gulf states where the higher status immigrants (Europeans and northern area Arabs) have displayed 'modern' attitudes and behaviour. Perhaps it is because the modern mercantile type of economy does not require a drastic break from the past, being essentially based on family and kinship as before, or perhaps the Gulf nationals are retreating behind their traditional values to avoid total absorption by the imported variety. Whatever the explanation, the economic and political consequences of retaining the older values include an increased dependence on foreign labour (if women are not in the labour force) and a lack of capacity in certain areas (the less pleasant maintenance jobs in engineering, for example). A possibly offsetting political consideration is that by adopting a traditional posture on social and religious matters, the ruling elites are less likely to be identified with the West if there is a backlash from the disgruntled masses in the shantytowns of the major cities.

Immigration

During the search for oil and thereafter when oil exporting began, important differences emerged between the Gulf states which considerably affected the character and volume of the immigrant flows. First, the timing of the oil discoveries had a bearing on subsequent developments; for example, the decision by the allies to focus production, export and refining efforts on Bahrain during the Second World War meant that Bahrain got an early start at the expense of countries like Kuwait—despite the former's meagre total reserves. The pattern of discovery also affected the timing of oil developments for it took some time to appreciate that the whole Gulf region was a massive oil reservoir after the early discoveries had been made in the Zagros mountains in Iran around 1908. Thus, we find that in the 1970s the lower Gulf states shared many of the attributes of Kuwait in the 1950s. Whereas the Kuwaitis were looking for skilled immigrants in the 1970s, since one of their several construction booms had been completed, the lower Gulf states were still demanding large numbers of construction workers and unskilled labour.

Secondly, the magnitude of the oil reserves discovered has had a profound affect on the character of subsequent developments. Compare the neighbouring countries of Bahrain and Qatar; the Bahrainis, because of their small oil reserves, quickly turned to oil and gas processing industries which gave them an introduction to the engineering industry in general. This led to Bahrain becoming a service and repair centre for the whole of the Gulf region, especially for companies operating in the offshore zone. Qatar, on the other hand, after oil exporting began in 1949, discovered and produced more and more oil as time went by and concern about seeking alternative sources of revenue evaporated when the ageing Dukhan field was supplemented by new discoveries offshore.

Thirdly, some countries in the Gulf had developed longstanding ties with countries outside the Gulf prior to the discovery of oil. Political responsibility for the Gulf states was passed from the government of India to the British Foreign Office as recently as 1949 and the connections with the Indian sub-continent have been preserved by the lower Gulf states through trade and exchange of people. Each of these factors helps to explain the different nationality 'mix' found in each of the labour importing countries.

Another factor of considerable importance affecting the character and direction of the migrant stream was the establishment of the state of Israel. This coincided with the beginning of a period of very rapid economic growth in the Gulf (especially Kuwait) so that the obvious place where the displaced Palestinians could find work was the Gulf. Many migrated on a temporary basis but soon found that return to Palestine was impossible. In 1970, for example, 33 per cent of the Jordanians and Palestinians in Kuwait had been there for ten years or more. Other states in the Gulf were slower to develop and were in any case wary of the political implications of admitting Palestinians. The lower Gulf states had access to the pool of cheap labour from India and Pakistan and so admitted very few Palestinians. It seems that Saudi Arabia also preferred Asians to Palestinians although the reasons for this preference are not clear.

Considering the length of the unpatrolled boundaries and the attractiveness of the wage rates in the Gulf countries, the surprising thing is that the influx of migrants, both workers and dependants, has not been larger. The principal reason whey the flow has not swamped the smaller countries is the emergence of a strong system of regional co-operation between the labour exporters and the labour importers. As part of a system of control, most of the oil states introduced nationality and labour laws which first defined the native national population in terms which excluded the post-oil immigrants and then gave preference to nationals in employment and in a host of other fields. Only nationals can own property and businesses in the oil states, for example, and immigrants are excluded from certain grades in the civil service and are discriminated against in the provision of social welfare benefits and the supply of other services.

Nonetheless, the post-1973 oil price rises started another boom in the economies of the oil states which meant increased demands for imported labour and it was the result of this boom which has led many labour exporting countries to become seriously worried about skilled manpower shortages in their own economies. The oil states themselves have begun to turn to Asian sources of labour due to a combination of high prices and shortage of supply from the usual Arab labour sending countries. Use of Asian labour may introduce a new set of problems for the control of immigration in the oil states but, in the short term, the use of indentured labour brought in by contractors from east Asia relieves the labour importers from some of the worries they have over the control of, for example, Yemeni and Pakistani workers and their dependants.

Every labour importing country in the Gulf requires migrants to obtain a visa and a work permit prior to immigration. This entails production of a document from an employer offering a migrant a job and assuming legal responsibility for that person. The migrants' immediate dependants are usually granted visitor or residence permits on application once the migrant is established in his or her new place of work. There are some parts of the economy where these rules cannot be so strictly applied, e.g. domestic servants and day labourers in the ports or in the construction industry. From time to time, illegal migrants are deported in considerable numbers but, in most cases, the illegal immigration of male unskilled labourers does not pose any threat to the security of the national economy since these workers are highly mobile and are unlikely to become a major charge on the public services because they are unaccompanied men and also because they do not use these services as they are nervous about being detected as illegal entrants.

In general, then, a system for the control of regional movements of people has grown up which is quite efficient at curtailing the enormous numbers of migrants who would undoubtedly otherwise enter the oil producing states. The system is based on the self-interest of labour exporters and of labour importers which appear to broadly coincide at present although there are signs of friction both in the labour exporting and in the labour importing countries. The importers are concerned about the size of their immigrant communities and at the way some national groups have a hold on certain sectors of the economy (see p. (see p.   ). The labour exporters feel that their own development plans are suffering from the loss of skilled workers abroad and they are also aware of some of the problems their workers are facing in the oil exporting states. Recent moves by the Egyptians to restrict the movement of single women to Arabia and growing complaints about the systems of discrimination between citizens and immigrants are signs of growing disenchantment with the existing arrangements. At the core of the difficulties is the issue of the very restrictive nationality laws enacted by all the Gulf states.

Nationality quotas

None of the labour importing countries have explicit nationality quotas except that in most countries, Iran excluded, Arab workers and migrants are given preference over non-Arabs by the labour and nationality laws. In practice, every country watches very closely the total numbers and composition of its foreign population and from time to time takes steps to control further immigration from one or more sources, or even to allow the numbers from one country to decline by repatriation or by reducing the number of new entry permits. External political events (e.g. the threatened takeover of Kuwait by Iraq in 1961 and the 1967 Arab-Israeli war) affect both the flow and return of migrants and official attitudes to migrants from a single source. Palestinians have suffered from systematic discrimination in almost every Arab country except Kuwait. The Palestinian communities in Abu Dhabi and Saudi Arabia are newly established and have yet to acquire the same dominant status as they have in Kuwait.

A problem faced by all Gulf countries is that some immigrants from the northern Arab countries, once established, introduce their dependants and start behaving like a settled population by having children, demanding housing, education and other services. Other nationalities have a much higher turnover rate since they may specialize in the supply of certain grades of labour. Thus, it is relatively easy to predict the future composition of the immigrant community given a certain amount of information about future development projects. For a large construction programme, for example, Kuwait knows that it will need labour normally supplied by Oman, Yemen and Egypt for the heavy manual tasks. To staff a new hospital, some Arab doctors and nurses may be found but it will probably be necessary to turn to India or Pakistan or even to recruit from the Philippines. To expand the education system, on the other hand, teachers will probably be recruited from Jordan, Palestine, Egypt, Syria and Lebanon.

The result of this policy of controlling immigration and the immigrants very closely is that 'enclaves' build up. Suburbs in Kuwait have become almost independent units in which the residents are supported by work carried out for Kuwaitis, but in their offices and in their homes live separate lives from the national population. The same can be said of some of the major new industrial cities developing elsewhere in Saudi Arabia. Yenbo and Jubail, for example, will be industrial enclaves built and operated by expatriates but with presumably Saudi managers in key positions.

Naturalization

A key part of the legislation developed in the Gulf states to control migration is the law on naturalization. At an early stage in each country's development, a decision was taken not to offer nationality to new immigrants. In Kuwait, for example, legislation was introduced in 1948, just two years after the start of oil exporting. In part, the rulers of the Gulf states made this decision out of a genuine fear that they would be overwhelmed by a flood of immigrants from the more populous Arab countries and from India and Pakistan. However, there were other components in the decision. One of them was the Arab League decision that the Palestinian refugees would not be naturalized and absorbed by other Arab countries. Another seems to have been an early acceptance that they would rather employ foreigners to do the manual, technical and non-administrative jobs in the economy despite the dependence on outsiders which this would produce. Only if the new arrivals could be effectively identified and dominated would the system be acceptable and reasonably secure. Thus the policy which has emerged of discrimination against the immigrants in every walk of life has to be seen as an essential part of the development of every Gulf state. Without the security brought about by 'separate development' of the native and immigrant communities in the Gulf, the political independence and stability of each of the small Gulf states would be seriously threatened. However, there are vested interests on both sides in maintaining stability and prosperity in the Gulf so that the injustices inherent in the system are rarely fully aired or translated into sustained demands for improvement or serious political activity.

Most Arab countries will allow foreigners, especially Arabs, to apply for nationality after four to five years of residence but in the Gulf the conditions attached to naturalization are much more severe. Kuwait, for example, requires fifteen years of continuous residence and, even on naturalization, excludes the newly naturalized from having certain political rights. The Kuwaiti law only permits a maximum of fifty naturalizations in any one year although, in practice, *Badu* (Bedouin) and others from the bordering countries are given passports following a period of service in the army or the police force. The new nationals carry distinct identity cards.

In the UAE, Arabs from Qatar, Oman and Bahrain are granted citizenship after only three years of residence (ten years for Arabs from other countries). Again, the newly naturalized are excluded from full rights of citizenship for the first seven years after naturalization. Of all the Gulf countries, the UAE seems the most willing to offer immigrants citizenship. Elsewhere, nationality legally acquired, remains a closely guarded reward only offered for outstanding service to the state or to key political figures or exiles.

Dependence on migrants

Although the proportions of foreigners in the labour forces of the Gulf countries (Table 4.2) are an indication of a high degree of reliance on outside labour, the reciprocal relations which have developed between labour exporting and labour importing countries plus the diversity of sources of supply of labour mean that the Gulf countries are not as vulnerable to external forces as the employment figures would suggest. For many Middle Eastern countries the loss of workers' remittances would be a very serious problem (Table 4.3) so that there is a strong interest on the side of the labour exporters not to interfere dramatically with the supply of labour. In addition, when the Gulf countries have indicated that they can and will recruit workers, skilled and unskilled, from almost anywhere around the world, the chances of a sudden serious labour shortage developing are probably remote, although short term bottlenecks in the supply of particular grades of labour are more likely.

The real danger in depending on outside labour is not that the whole supply may suddenly dry up but that the workers themselves may cease to identify their interests with those of the state employing them and may combine or form associations aimed at furthering their own interests at the expense of the host country. This has not happened so far partly because of the prohibition of trade unions, and indeed almost all kinds of political activity in the Gulf, but also because of the high turnover rates of the immigrant labour forces. Only the longer established, semi-stable populations such as the Palestinians in Kuwait are at all likely to try to air their collective grievances but the external and internal policies in every Gulf state are strongly influenced by the need to prevent this kind of event happening. The strongly pro-PLO international stance of Kuwait is a direct outgrowth of the powerful position occupied by the Palestinians in the state. The balance is not an easy one to strike but the lack of major protests against the immigration or naturalization policies of the labour importers and the discrimination system within the Gulf countries is an indication that the governments have become skillful at managing the situation. It is also a measure of the strength of the self-interest shared by all immigrant workers in the Gulf who generally want to continue earning money at existing rates in preference to trying to change the system and possibly losing all. Quite deliberately, the Gulf states set out to protect themselves by diversifying their sources of labour supply so that difficulties with one country or group of countries need not be a catastrophic blow. The trend towards the use of Asian labour is notable in this context for the size of the pool from which the Gulf countries can draw is virtually inexhaustible once the principle of using non-Arab labour is established.

Table 4.2

Employment in selected Gulf countries around 1975

	Economically active nationals ('000)	Crude labour force participation rate (%)	Economically active aliens ('000)	Labour force aliens (%)
Bahrain	45.8	21.4	30.0	39.6
Kuwait	91.8	19.4	211.4	69.7
Oman	141.5	25.0	73.5	34.0
Qatar	12.5	18.4	53.8	81.1
Saudi Arabia	1,326.1	22.3	391.2	49.4
UAE	45.0	22.5	296.5	86.8

Source: Birks and Sinclair (1978, 1979)

Table 4.3

Flow of workers' remittances and its share in total imports and exports of goods in selected labour exporting countries

Country	1974 Remittances*	1974 As percentage of Exports	1974 As percentage of Imports	1975 Remittances	1975 As percentage of Exports	1975 As percentage of Imports	1976 Remittances	1976 As percentage of Exports	1976 As percentage of Imports	1977 Remittances	1977 As percentage of Exports	1977 As percentage of Imports
Algeria	390	9	9	466	11	7	245	5	4	246	4	3
Bangladesh ***	36	13	2	35	9	1	36	10	1	83	18	9
Egypt	189	11	5	367	23	7	754	47	18	1,425	66	27
India ***	276	8	5	490	12	8	750**	17	12	–	–	–
Jordan	75	48	12	167	109	18	396	198	34	425	186	38
Morocco	356	21	17	533	35	18	548	43	18	577	44	18
Pakistan ***	151	15	6	230	22	8	353	31	12	1,118	88	40
Syrian Arab Republic	62	8	4	55	6	3	51**	5	2	–	–	–
Tunisia	118	13	9	146	17	8	135	17	8	142	16	8
Turkey	1,425	93	33	1,317	94	25	982	50	17	982	56	17
Yemen Arab Republic***	159	1,325	69	221	1,556	72	525	4,269	137	1,013	5,449	139
Yemen PDR	41	410	23	56	373	32	115	261	40	179****	352	49

Sources: IMF consolidated balance of payments and World Bank Reports

–   Data not available
*   In current prices, million dollars, gross figures
**   Estimate
*** Fiscal year ending June of the indicated year
**** Preliminary

It is possible for the pact between immigrants and nationals to break down. For example, a series of unfairly restrictive policies might force all migrant workers to combine against the government to obtain better working conditions and basic rights. Importation of cheaper Asian labour could create unrest amongst the traditional Arab sources of labour. These difficulties are never far below the surface; the replacement in recent months of Yemeni workers in Saudi Arabia by Asian, especially Pakistani labour, has led to return migration to North Yemen and to feelings of resentment on both sides. Clearly, it is only the constant monitoring and manipulation of the situation by the Gulf countries coupled with the vested interests of the workers which stands between order and chaos in the Gulf labour markets.

There is a secondary aspect of dependency which in the short run may be more important. This is the tendency to rely on a few sending countries for labour of a certain quality since, generally speaking, the labour exporting countries each specialize in the supply of migrants with particular levels of education and skills. Certain key sectors of the economy of each of the Gulf states are dominated by expatriates from just a few countries. In Kuwait, for example, 30 per cent of the school teachers in 1975 were from Jordan and Palestine and 32 per cent were from Egypt, although steps are being taken to reduce this dependency. Over two-thirds of all doctors and dentists were from the same two countries whereas almost half of all the tailors in Kuwait were from Pakistan. In Qatar, the civil service is heavily dependent on the northern Arab countries and Egypt, whereas almost all the traders and labourers in the private sector came from India, Pakistan and Iran. In Oman there is an especially heavy reliance on Asian labour in the building trades— carpenters, bricklayers, electricians, and also foremen and supervisors. In Saudi Arabia it is again the construction industry which uses the highest proportions of Asian labour plus dwindling numbers from North Yemen, but the commerce and personal services sector of the economy is also heavily dependent on Asians and to a lesser extent on northern area Arabs.

Despite all this foreign labour, the key policy decisions are still taken by nationals. In most Gulf countries an inner group of able and well educated nationals, often related to the ruling family, operate as an oligarchy and ensure that the running of the state remains firmly under the control of its citizens. It is this group of men who decide immigration and indeed all other policies. In the smaller states there is no well organized opposition to this 'junta' type of administration and the little that has emerged in the past (e.g. in the prorogued Kuwait National Assembly) has been suppressed. It seems that massive improvements in material welfare are sufficient at least to mute political opposition in the smaller Gulf states where divisions within the natural population are not as significant as in Iraq, Iran or even Saudi Arabia.

The Kuwait experience

The growth and change of the immigrant community is most fully documented in Kuwait where non-Kuwaitis (immigrants) grew from just 93,000 in 1957 to a total of 523,000 in 1975. Kuwait began its post-oil experience with an immigrant community drawn very largely from neighbouring countries—Iraq, Iran, Saudi Arabia and, to a lesser extent, from Oman and the Indian sub-continent. Initially a population of young unaccompanied males, the immigrant population has matured and changed until it has become more like the native population in age and sex composition (Table 4.4).

Table 4.4

Selected attributes of the immigrant population of Kuwait 1957—75

	Total non-Kuwaitis ('000)	Sex ratio	Under age 5 (%)	Males 10+ illiterate (%)
1957	92.8	365	7	43
1961	159.7	267	12	–
1965	247.3	236	15	33
1970	391.3	166	17	32
1975	522.7	143	17	27

Source: 1957, 1961, 1965, 1970 and 1975 censuses

Some of these compositional changes were due to the changing nationality structure of the non-Kuwaiti population (Table 4.5). In recent years the immigrants from the Gulf region have declined in proportional importance (although increasing in number) while the northern area Arabs (especially Jordanians and Palestinians) constitute an enlarged proportion of the total. The 'socio-economic status scale' groups together immigrants with similar levels of education, employment status and socio-economic activity. Thus, at one extreme, we find the Iranis, Omanis and Yemenis, over 83 per cent of whom have no schooling, with sex ratios over 555 and working in manual jobs or in sales and service activities. By contrast, Egyptians, Indians and Pakistanis are better educated, have more balanced sex ratios (133—179), work in professional, technical and clerical posts and are frequently accompanied by their wives and families. Other nationalities have intermediate positions on the simple typology which nevertheless captures some of the considerable variety within the non-Kuwaiti population.

Table 4.5

The national composition of the non-Kuwaiti population 1957—75

Nationality	1957 (%)	1965 (%)	1970 (%)	1975 (%)
Iraqi	28	10	10	9
Iranian	21	12	10	8
Jordanian and Palestinian	16	31	38	39
Lebanese	7	8	6	5
Omani	7	8	4	1
Indian	4	5	4	6
Pakistani	3	5	4	4
Saudi	2	4	2	2
Syrian	2	7	7	8
Egyptian	2	4	8	12
Others	8	9	7	6
Total (%'s)	100	100	100	100
Total numbers of non-Kuwaitis	92,851	247,280	391,266	522,749

Sources: Censuses of population 1957, 1965, 1970 and 1975, various tables

An additional point is that the number of non-Kuwaiti women in the labour force is very small (17 per cent) for an immigrant community and most of this proportion is accounted for by the Egyptian community which supplies Kuwait with most of its female school teachers (girls and boys are taught separately in Kuwait). Thus it seems that the attraction of Kuwait for potential migrants is twofold. Firstly, for young men it offers well paid employment together with some additional benefits like free medical care, some subsidized foodstuffs and sanitary housing. Secondly, for dependants, the attractions also include the availability of free schooling, cheap public utilities and access to a selection of goods (such as radios, clothing and cars) often unavailable or inaccessible because of their price or their scarcity in the home country.

Saudi Arabia, North Yemen and the Asian connection

Some estimates of the volume of Arab workers in the oil states have been collected by Birks and Sinclair and a summary of their findings is shown as Table 4.6. The importance of Saudi Arabia as a labour importer shows up clearly, but apart from some data on the nationality composition of the labour force (Table 4.7), we know very little about the size and recent changes in the non-Saudi population.

The country most affected by Saudi policies on immigration is North Yemen since Yemenis still constitute about one-third of the total labour force (over one-third of all foreign workers) in the kingdom. The effect of emigration and remittances on the North Yemeni economy is far reaching because of the size of the numbers involved and because almost all parts of the country have been touched by the exodus. Accurate meaurement of the number of Yemenis in Saudi Arabia is not easy but, by early 1980, we can estimate the total numbers of Yemenis abroad on a short term basis at about 575,000 (about 550,000 employed workers) with possibly another 175,000 longer term migrants. Not all work in Saudi Arabia but, using the same proportions by country as for the February 1975 census, we obtain a figure for all long and short term emigrants from Yemen in Saudi Arabia of just under 600,000. Of this total about 540,000 would be male workers.

These are crude estimates based on a revision of published statistics known to understate illegal cross border movements. Since 1975, several developments have occurred which will probably reduce the inflow of new migrants from Yemen. Firstly, the Yemeni government prohibited further emigration and restricted the issue of new passports. In 1978 Saudi Arabia also insisted on passports and work permits for Yemenis as for other nationalities. These slowed the rate of immigration but the determined migrant can simply walk across an unpatrolled section of the border or enter using a *hajj* visa. In November 1979 the raid on Mecca in which a North Yemeni tribal group near the Saudi border were heavily implicated resulted in deportations of Yemenis and Egyptians plus some other nationals.

The Yemeni community in Saudi Arabia is as varied in origin and experience as the Yemeni population itself. Many of the early Yemeni migrants to Saudi obtained experience in commerce, domestic service and other trades in Aden before 1967. This probably explains the very heavy out migration from the southern governorates of Ta'izz and Ibb where in certain districts 10—20 per cent of the total population or up to one-third of all men are working abroad. Men from Asir in the north find it easy to cross into the southern part of Sa'nosi where they are often seen as taxi drivers and construction workers. Some significant minorities from South Yemen are also part of the Yemeni community in Saudi—a good example are the religious leaders and goldsmiths from

Table 4.6

Arab migrant workers in the Middle East in 1975

Country of origin	Country of work								Total
	Bahrain	Iraq	Jordan	Kuwait	Libyan Arab Jamahiriya	Qatar	Saudi Arabia	United Arab Emirates	
Egypt	1,200	7,000	5,300	37,600	229,500	2,900	95,000	12,500	391,000
Iraq	100	–	–	18,000	–	–	2,000	500	20,600
Jordan (including Palestine)	600	5,000	–	47,700	14,200	6,000	175,000	14,500	263,000
Lebanon	100	3,000	7,500	5,700	500	20,000	20,000	4,500	48,500
Oman	1,400	–	–	3,700	–	1,500	17,500	14,000	38,100
People's Democratic Republic of Yemen	1,100	–	–	8,700	–	1,300	55,000	4,500	70,600
Somalia	–	–	–	200	–	–	5,000	1,000	6,200
Sudan	400	200	–	900	7,000	400	35,000	1,500	45,400
Syrian Arab Republic	100	–	20,000	16,500	13,000	800	15,000	4,500	69,000
Yemen Arab Republic	1,100	–	–	2,800	–	1,300	280,400	4,500	290,100
Maghreb	–	–	–	100	41,000	–	–	–	41,100
Total	6,100	15,200	32,800	143,400	310,400	14,700	699,900	62,000	1,284,500

– Indicates no migrants of this nationality recorded
Figures may not add due to rounding

Table 2.7

Employment by nationality in Saudi Arabia 1975

Nationality	Number ('000)	(%)
Saudi	1,026	57.1
N.Yemen	280	15.6
Jordanian and Palestinian	175	9.7
Egyptian	95	5.3
PDR Yemen	55	3.1
Sudan	35	1.9
Lebanese	20	1.1
Omani	17	0.9
Syrian	15	0.8
Somali	5	0.3
Iraqi	2	0.1
Non-Saudi Arabs	700	38.9
Pakistani	15	0.8
Indian	15	0.8
Other Asian	8	0.4
Asians	38	2.1
Others	35	1.9
Total non-Saudi	773	43.0
Total	1,798	100.0

Sources: Labour Force Survey of Saudi Arabia and estimates by Birks and Sinclair (1979)

the Hadhramaut.

Certainly, any further tightening of Saudi controls on immigration and immigrants would affect North Yemen very profoundly. With only 2−3 per cent of imports covered by exports, Yemen's economy is kept afloat primarily by remittances, secondarily by aid. Private remittances quadrupled between 1972−73 and 1976−77 and further leaps more recently have sustained the development boom in more recent years. Despite the distorting affects of currently rapid inflation, Yemen would be in dire straits if remittances or Saudi aid were to be significantly reduced.

Recent estimates[1] suggest that in early 1979 there were probably 800,000 Asians in the Middle East of whom the majority were from India (300,000) and Pakistan (350,000). Bangladesh, Korea and the Phillipines were the other major labour exporters. These numbers are increasing steadily especially in the Gulf and Saudi Arabia as a result of the Mecca raid. Clearly, Saudi policy on import of labour is of central importance to a large number of Arab countries and to an increasingly large number of countries in Asia.

1 Keely, (1980), *Far Eastern Economic Review*, 1979.

Migrants and minorities in the larger Gulf countries

In Iraq and Iran temporary migrants have never been a major threat to the stability and independence of either country. In fact, it is very hard to see any link between demographic processes and the political fortunes of one or more of the tribal or religious groups which are so important in determining the longevity of the regimes in power. One can certainly imagine circumstances in which tensions could rise dangerously; the Gulf states, for example, could choose to exacerbate regional strains in Iran through these long established connections with Iranian immigrants from Baluchistan and Khuzistan. More likely is the possibility of further Iraq—Iran disagreement over Kurdistan and over the possibility of an 'Arabistan' in the south west of Iran. But these kinds of pressures are the result of foreign policy and not demography.

It may be useful to review briefly the main religious and ethnic groups present in each of the larger Gulf countries. Iraq has possibly the most heterogeneous native born population on the Arab side of the Gulf. The major split between Sunni and Shi'ia Islam was based on events which took place in what is now Iraq and so it is not surprising to find that about 55 per cent of the total population (three-quarters of the Arabs) are Shi'i Muslims. Despite attempts to overcome these sectarian differences by the 1958 Revolution and the 1964 Interim Constitution, the Shi'i heartland in Kut and Amara provinces in the south maintains its characteristic outlook. The 1958 land reform proved unsuccessful in the south, resulting in the 1961 Amara Laws which in some ways protected the rights of the Shi'i shaikhs. As a result, migration to Baghdad from the poverty stricken marsh area has been very significant and the largely illiterate Shi'i peasantry forms the bulk of the shanty-town population of eastern Baghdad.

North of Baghdad, the population is largely Sunni and this includes the dwindling Badu. By far the largest Sunni group are the Kurds who probably constitute 15—20 per cent of the total Iraqi population. As a group, the Kurds also spread over Syria, Turkey and Iran and probably number eight million in all, of whom about two million each are in Iraq and Iran. Far from unified, divided into three distinct linguistic and tribal groups (Badinan, Suran and Baban), the history of Kurdish resistance to central control is long and well studied. Again, the issue is how strongly one or more outside forces encourage the Kurds in the pursuit of the Kurdistan ideal.

Without introducing the less important minorities such as the Turko-mans, the Persians, Lurs, Yezidis, Christians and Mandeans, it is plain that the oil wealth of Iraq has not made the government or development of this complicated country any easier. Despite investment by the state in agriculture and heavy industry, substantial parts of the Iraqi population are not part of the modern economy and it is inevitable that some groups will want to redistribute the national cake in their favour, particularly as the cake is seen as not only large and tempting but also as unequally sliced.

Saudi society is by contrast much more homogeneous although the tide of immigration has swept in a largely Arab population of 'wage slaves'. For most political purposes, these non-Saudis are not seen as a major threat to the regime since they are 'disenfranchised' and have vested interests compatible with those of the Saudi rulers. Much more of a threat are the immigrants from neighbouring countries in which one or more revolutions have politicized the population. Some immigrants from both Yemens, Somalia, Sudan and even Egypt fall into this category, and the Shi'i oil workers of Iranian descent in eastern Arabia may be added to this list. The vulnerability of the regime to irredentism, especially with a religious twist, was demonstrated in November 1979 when the Shi'ia population became politically restive and were dealt with firmly by the Saudi authorities.

Of all the Gulf countries, Iran is probably the most complex and much of this complexity stems from the tribal and ethnic variety within its borders. From a demographic standpoint all that can be done here is to indicate the magnitude of the differentials in population growth and welfare which exist in Iran. Whilst in urban areas fertility was falling and infant mortality was no more than 60 per thousand, in rural areas fertility was virtually unchanged (crude birth rates of around 50 per thousand) and infant mortality at least 120 per thousand in the mid 1970s. Much wider differentials can be found within a single city but perhaps the most useful conclusion from the available statistics is that different groups and different parts of the country have had very different experiences under the Shah. As in most developing countries, income and welfare differentials initially widen before closing again as the state machinery for redistribution improves. The strains during the critical middle phase can be disastrous for the ruling authorities.

The political response to immigration and rapid population growth

Several of the well established immigrant groups in Arabia assert quite accurately that without their help the Arab oil exporting countries would not be where they are today. It is remarkable that this sentiment has received little political expression and that the host populations have managed to preserve their dominant position despite, in many cases, being a minority group in their own country. Some of the reasons for this have been explained above but it may be valuable to summarize here the main features of the system which allows the nationals to continue to exercise a considerable degree of control over their immigrant populations.

Legal provisions for control of entry

The six Arabian oil exporters have enacted very similar legislation which provides for:

1 Entry visas required for all visitors.

2 The sponsorship and responsibility for workers being assumed by employers.

3 The issue of work permits and entry visas outside the country of immigration.

4 Annual renewal of all work permits and visas.

5 Deportation by administrative order rather than by legal proceedings.

Nationality laws

In most states, these provide for:

1 Witholding of naturalization from most immigrants, even long established residents, and those born in the country of residence.

2 Witholding of full rights of citizenship for some period of years or forever from those newly naturalized.

Labour laws

The preference system for nationals is protected by laws stating:

1 Nationals must be offered a job opening first, followed by other Arabs and lastly all other foreigners.

2 Certain kinds of job, e.g. senior civil service positions, jobs in the army and police and even jobs such as driving a taxi, are reserved for nationals.

3 immigrants are not paid fully for some of the welfare benefits due to nationals (benefits include cash payments for family support, rent subsidies, pensions, etc.).

Property and business laws

The laws on these topics are extensive and complex but in general they state that:

1 Only citizens can own outright land, buildings and businesses.

2 Foreign participation in a businessmust be less than a majority shareholding.

3 Immigrants are excluded from the subsidized housing which is a feature of all the Gulf states and also from the property compensation schemes through which governments pass huge sums of money to the people.

4 Commercial licences for trade including importing all restricted to nationals.

Political activities

The governments generally prohibit:

1 Most forms of criticism of the government and its policies.

2 All parties, organizations or trade unions are prohibited unless especially approved (e.g. the Bahrain Family Planning Association had to obtain special permission to open more than a headquarters office).

3 Public demonstrations, strikes, political protests, etc.

This very general summary indicates the nature of the legal controls at the disposal of the governments of the region to control immigration and the immigrants, but there are in addition a number of standard practices which further circumscribe the rights of foreign workers. One of the implications of the laws on ownership of property and businesses is that only certain residential areas contain accommodation for renting. Thus a system of residential segregation exists in most cities. As a corollary, the services in the immigrant areas are less well developed and facilities such as the health clinics and the co-operative shopping centres in the housing areas designed for nationals are not accessible to non-residents. The immigrant housing areas are often crowded and dirty compared to the luxurious living conditions of the national population. In their daily life, therefore, immigrants of all nationalities are constantly reminded of their inferior status.

A second implication of the laws on immigration is that it is possible to discriminate against certain nationalities by simply refusing them entry and work permits. Thus, groups who might be inclined to settle with their dependants can be prevented from entering or even forced to leave at the annual review of permits. At any time a national can insist on obtaining the job of an immigrant, resulting in the displacement of that immigrant. Thus, when the school system finds it difficult to keep up the provision of teachers and classrooms, it is the immigrant children who are excluded from public schools and whose parents may face increasing difficulty in renewing their work and residence permits.

Viewed *in toto,* the collection of laws coupled with extensions to the laws by 'usual practice' amounts to a comprehensive set of controls designed to make full use of immigrant labour whilst conceding only the bare minimum to the immigrants in the way of civil rights, welfare benefits and naturalization possibilities. Clearly, the attractive salaries offered and the self-interest and conservatism they engender are the prime factors preventing political pressures for the improvement in the position of the foreign workers from developing a powerful momentum.

Conclusion

The main population related problem faced by the oil exporting countries of Arabia is the control of immigration and the immigrant communities they employ. Over the years the governments of the Gulf states have considered proposals for the naturalization of many of the long stay immigrants but this seems an unlikely policy change in present circumstances. One of the results of very rapid natural increase rates of the national populations is that the nationals feel slightly more secure now that their numbers are at least into six figures and approaching seven. The Kuwaitis, for example, were quite pleased to find they had at least a million people in the state by the time the 1975 census results were announced.

Since wholesale naturalization of sizeable parts of the immigrant communities is unlikely in the foreseeable future, it is fair to ask about the meaning of the kinds of development now under way in the Gulf states. Some figures from Kuwait illustrate this point very well: taking the book values of the assets of ten joint stock companies in Kuwait and their employment of Kuwaitis, we find that each Kuwaiti job represents an investment of at least £75,000. Admittedly, the Kuwaitis were probably the senior management but this kind of development of capital intensive, high technology industries often connected to the downstream end of the oil industry provide very few employment prospects for the bulk of the Kuwaiti population, not all of whom are millionaires. In these circumstances, and despite the regional benefits which flow from the remittance income of migrants, it is difficult to escape the conclusion that for the long term stability of the Gulf countries and for the improvement of the quality of life of all the national populations, not just the well educated elites, it is necessary for them to re-think their investment and development programmes and at the same time to encourage more of their nationals to participate at all levels in operating their own economies.

Notes

The majority of the demographic estimates were derived from original sources but the following sources were also referred to and quoted in places:

Benham, D. and Amani, M., *La Population de l'Iran,* CICRED Monographic Series, 1974.

Courbage, Y. and Kjurciev, A., 'Alternative population projections and analysis of the essential data in Bahrain', *ECWA Population Bulletin,* 6, January 1974.

Hill, A.G., 'The demography of the population in Kuwait', *Demography,* 12, 3, 537–548, 1975.

Levels and Trends in Fertility and Mortality in Kuwait, University of Jordan and the US National Academy of Sciences, 1979.

Iran, Plan and Budget Organization, *Population Growth of Iran, First Survey Year 1973–74,* 1976.

UN ECWA (Beirut) (Annual) *Population Data Sheets.*

Many of the statistics on immigration come from a series produced by Birks, J.S. and Sinclair, C.A. as part of their international migration study at Durham University. The main country reports are:

Kuwait 1977, Oman 1977, Qatar 1978, UEA 1978, Bahrain 1978, Saudi Arabia 1979.

The laws on international migration in the region have been reviewed by Georges Dib:

Migration and naturalization laws in the Arab Republic of Egypt, the Hashemite Kingdom of Jordan, Kuwait, Lebanon, the Syrian Arab Republic and the United Arab Emirates, paper for the UN ECWA Seminar on Population and Development, Amman, 18–30 November 1978, E/ECWA/POP/WG.12/BP.5 and in a paper on the same topic for a seminar in Washington DC in 1979.

Many of the ideas on international migration in the Middle East were discussed at a study group sponsored by the Population Council at the Jordanian Royal Scientific Society in December 1978. The key paper was presented by Charles B. Keely. See *Report on the Study Group on Migration Abroad,* Amman, Population Council WANA Regional Paper, 2–3 December 1978. The information on North Yemen comes from an anthropology fieldworker there, Ms Cynthia Myntti of the London School of Economics. The two stage model of immigration is evaluated in:

Hill, A.G., 'Les travailleurs etrangers dans les pays du Golf', *Tiers-Monde,* 18, 69, 115–13, 1977.

See also Charles B. Keely's paper on 'Asian Worker Migration to the Middle East', Population Council, Centre for Policy Studies, Working Paper 52, 1980.

Index

Abdul Aziz, Sa'ud Ibn, 2, 4, 14, 16

Abu Dhabi: armed forces of, 23, 24; assistance to other members of UAE, 21; basis data on, 57; coup of 1966, 4; distribution of wealth in, 50; conflict with Dubai, xi; jealousy of Dubai, 27—8; equity participation in oil industry, 24; gas industry of, 49; infrastructure development of, 41—3; investments of, 41—2; and Iran, 21; oil industry participation, 24; oil output ceiling, 39; Palestinians in, 67; Shakhbut deposed, 4; dispute with Saudi Arabia, 19, 21; and UAE federal powers, 22; possible withdrawal from UAE, 35

Abu Dhabi city, 28

Afghanistan: invaded by USSR, viii

agents: limit on commission of, 52

agriculture: decline in, 63

'Ajman, 21, 23, 35

al-Khatib, Dr Ahmed, 8

Algeria: workers' remittances to, 71

Algiers Accord, 21n

amir (commander): evolution of role of, 3; as title, 2

Atiqu, Abdel-Rahman, 38, 54

Bahrain: basic data on, 56, 76; budget introduced in, 3; constitutional development of, xii, 1—5, 6—7; distribution of wealth in, 50; diversification in 42, 48, 65; employment data, 70; government in, 1—5, 6—7; Haraka in, 6; immigrant population of, 7, 76; infrastructure development in, 41—3; Nasserism in, 6; national economy of, 48; oil production decline, 7, 39; oil production and societal change, x, 39, 64—5; parliament in, 6—7; as regional centre, 42, 65; religious riots in, 53; service industries in, 48; Shi'i threat to, 7—8; social security contributions in, 54, 55; structure of society in, 5—8, 17

Bangladesh: migrants from to Middle East, 77; workers' remittances to, 71

banks: and industrial development, 45

Bedouin: naturalisation of, 68—9; role of in Saudi Arabia, 14, 15, 17

business ethic: absence of, 53, 55

'Camp Baghdad Accords', 21n
Camp David, 21n
children: attitudes to, 64
civil rights: of immigrants, 82
climate: and type of buildings, 40
colonialism: and Arab states, 8
commission: limit on agents', 52
constitutional development: in Bahrain, xii, 1—5, 6—7; in Iraq, xii; in Kuwait, xii, 1—5, 9—10; in Saudi Arabia, xii, 1—5; from tribal tradition, 2—3; in UAE, 21

cultural influences, 53, 54

demographics, see population
discrimination: policy re. immigrants, 68—9

Dubai: conflict with Abu Dhabi, xi; basic data on, 57; commercial success of, 27—8, 42; diversification in, 42; and independent statehood, 30; infrastructure development in, 41—3; and Iran, 21; oil industry equity participation, 24; dispute with Sharjah, 27; and UAE, 22; withdrawal from UAE, 36

economic development, x
education: finance for, 52; and immigrants, 31—2, 33, 81; in Kuwait, 74; and population levels, 61; recruitment of teachers for, 67, 72, 74; in UAE, 23, 24—5, 26, 31—2, 33

Egypt: migrant workers of, 67, 74, 76; attempt to subvert Saudi Arabia, 4; sending teachers to Kuwait, 67, 74; workers' remittances to, 71

elections: in Kuwait, 9
electricity: tariff cut in Saudi Arabia, 54

expatriates: role of, 61—2, 72

family: role of, 53, 64
fertility: and population size, 58, 59, 60, 61

Fujayrah: dependence on UAE, 21; dispute with Sharjah, 27; withdrawal from UAE, 35

gas industry: associated with oil, 43—4; unassociated, 49

Ghobash, Seif, 33
government, see constitutional development

Great Britain: and balance of power in Gulf states, viii; creating Kuwait, 8; creating kings in Gulf states, 2; and deposing of Shakjbut of Abu Dhabi, 4; and deposing of Taimour of Oman, 4; training Kuwaiti army, 13; political responsibility of for Gulf states, 65; and immigration in UAE, 30; support for UAE, 22

Great Mosque of Mecca: occupied, 16, 75, 77, 79

Gulf Organisation for Industrial Consulting, 44, 47

Haraka (Movement of Arab Nationalists): in Bahrain, 6; in Kuwait, 8; on privilege, 8

health and social services: finance for, 52; and immigrants, 32, 33

housing: differences in, 63–4; segregation of citizens and immigrants, 63; schemes, 51

ideology: as source of conflict, ix

immigrants: amnesty for, 31; Asian, 62–3, 70, 72; in Bahrain, 7; as cause of conflict, x, xi; control of, 66, 67–8, 79–82; data for each oil producing state, 56–7; discrimination policy against, 68–9, 80–1; economic function of, 43–4, 52–3, 59, 64, 69–72, 75–6, 79; education of, 31–2, 33, 79; fertility of, 61; health and social services for, 32, 80, 81; illegal, 31, 66, 75; increase in, 58, 61–2; in Kuwait, x, xi, 8, 10–11, 11, 56, 68, 69–70, 70, 72, 73–4; Palestinian, 11; pattern of and oil development, 64–5, 66; as proportion of labour force, 69, 70; quotas on, 67–8; remittances from, 71; residential segregation of, 63–4, 81; in Saudi Arabia, x, xi, 14, 15; and Saudi Arabian industrial development, 43–4, 59, 64; in structure of society, 11, 79–82; transient or permanent, 32–3; in UAE, xi, 30–4

imports, reliance on, 63

India: migrants to Middle East from, 77; political responsibility for Gulf states, 65; workers' remittances to, 71

industrialisation, 38

industry: and environment, 46; heavy, 43–5; and labour supply, 63; light, 45–7; loans for, 45, 52; service, 42

infrastructure: development of, 41–3

investment, 41–2, 82

Iran: claims to Bahrain, 7; economic malaise in, 53–4; foreign workers in, 59; gas in, 49; housing conditions in, 63–4; immigrants from, 62; investments of, 41; land reform in, 64; migrants in, 76–7; modernisation of, xi; population decline in, 59; religious and ethnic groups of, 79; revolution in, ix, xi, 7; secret service in, 17; and Sharjah, 27; and UAE, 19, 21, 21n

Iraq: offered support to Bahrain against Iran, 7; constitutional development in, xii; foreign workers in, 59; housing conditions in, 63–4; immigrant population of, 76; and Kuwait, 13; and land reform in, 64; migrant workers of, 76, 78–9; religious and ethnic groups of, 79–80; and UAE, 19, 21, 21n

Islamic code: rules of in Saudi Arabian society, 15

Israel: as factor in migration pattern to Gulf states, 65; Western support for and Gulf states, ix

Jordan: immigrant population of, 76; migrant workers of, 76; workers' remittances to, 71

Khawarij, 16

Khor Fakkan, 28–9

Kuwait: army of, 13; basic data on, 56, 73–4, constitutional

development, xii, 1—5; corporation tax, 51—2; data on non-Kuwaiti population, 73—4, 76; distribution of wealth in, 50, 51, 52—3, 54; diversification in, 42; employment data, 72; expatriates in, 72; government, 1—5; history of, 8—13, immigrants, x, xi, 8, 10—11, 56, 68, 68—9, 70, 72, 73—4; infrastructure developed in, 41 —3; investments of, 41—2; Iraqi threat, 13; loans to light industry in, 45; military expenses of, 13; nationalisation of Kuwait Oil Co., 8; naturalisation policy, 68—9; oil production and society in, x; oil output ceiling, 39—40; Palestinians in, 8, 9, 12, 61, 65, 67, 69; parliament in, 8, 9—10; professional groups in, 10—11; social welfare in, 11—12; structure of society in, 11—13, 17; teachers in, 72, 74
Kuwait Oil Co: nationalised, 8

labour force: Asians in, 62—3, 70; control of flow of, 66, 67—8; make-up of, 69—70; remittances of immigrants, 71; in Saudi Arabia, 48; source of, 62, 69, 70; in UAE, 33—4; and women, 64
land: as means of distributing wealth in Kuwait, 51; as gift in Saudi Arabia, 51; ownership restrictions, 51, 63, 66, 80; reform, 64
Lebabon: migrant workers of, 78
Libyan Arab Jamahiriya: immigrant population of, 76

Majlis, 2, 3
Maghreb: migrant workers of, 76

Malik, (King), 2
manual labour: aversion to, 34, 39, 48
marriage: role of multiple in Saudi Arabian society, 14
Mecca: conquest of by Abdul Aziz, 2; Great Mosque occupied, 16, 53
modernisation: as source of conflict, x, xi
Morocco: workers'remittances to 71
mortality, 58
Moslem religion: role of in Saudi Arabian society, 14—15, 17, see also Shi'i, Sunni
'Muslim revival', 53

Nasser, Abdul, 4, 16
Nasserism: in Bahrain, 6; in Saudi Arabia, 4
naturalisation, 68—9, 80, 82

OAPEC (Organisation of Arab Petroleum Exporting Countries): dry dock, 63
OECD (Organisation for Economic and Cultural Development): dependency on Gulf oil, xiii, ix
OPEC (Organisation of Petroleum Exporting Countries): UAE versus Saudi Arabia in 1976, 25
oil: Arab states dependence on, 38—40; conservation of, 42; data for each oil producing state, 56—7; development of society, ix, 12; embargoes, ix; government participation in industry, 24; income versus spending, 39; OECD dependency on Gulf for, viii; output ceilings on, 39—40; population growth and, 61, 64—5;

price, ix, 39—40; rate of production, ix; security of supply and politicisation, xii—xiii, 12

Oman: basic data, 57; coup of 1970, 4; distribution of wealth in, 50; Dhofar rebellion, 21; employment data, 70; expatriates in, 72; immigrants from, 62; infrastructure development in, 41—3; migrant workers of, 76; oil production decline, 39; Taimour deposed, 4; and UAE, 19

PDRY (Peoples Democratic Republic of Yemen); migrant workers of, 76; return of migrants to, 62, 72; workers' remittances to, 71

PFLOAG (Peoples Front for the Liberation of Oman and the Arab Gulf), 4

Pakistan: migrants from to Middle East, 77; workers' remittances to, 71; workers in Saudi Arabia, 72

Palestinians: in Abu Dhabi, 67; Arab League decision on naturalisation of, 68; fertility levels of, 61; in Kuwait, 8, 9, 10, 11, 12, 67, 69; naturalisation of, 68; in Saudi Arabia, 14, 67; as source of labour, 62, 65

Patriotic Club of Kuwait, 10

politicisation: and outside cultural influences, 53; and security of oil supply, xii—xiii

Popular Democratic Front (Hawatmeh), 11

Popular Front (Habash), 11

population: data for each oil producing state, 56—7; and development of oil industry, 61; female education and control of increases in, 61; growth of, x, 58, 59, 60; mix and political alignments, 65; political use of in emirates, 22; problems of, 59; in urban areas, 63; *see also* immigrants

prime minister: as successor to 'throne', 3

professional classes: in Kuwait, 10

profit controls, 54, 55

Qatar: basic data on, 57; constitutional development, 4—5; distribution of wealth in, 50; diversification in, 48, 65; employment data, 70; expatriates in, 72; gas, 49; immigrant population of, 76; infrastructure development in, 41—3; investments of, 41—2; oil production decline, 39, 48; road to Europe, 12

Ra's al-Khaymah, 19, 21, 22, 30

Rashid, Shaikh: accepts UAE premiership, 29, 36; extends term of office, 35; support for UAE, 22

religion: as cause of conflict, 59

rents: as source of private income, 39

rural—urban drift, 53—4, 54, 65, 66

Saudi Arabia: dispute with Abu Dhabi, 19, 21; agricultural development in, 54; aid to other UAE states, 40; army of, 18; Asian immigrants in, 65; Bahraini parliament, 6; basic data on, 56; role of Bedouin of, 14, 15, 17; constitutional development, xii, 1—5; distribution of wealth, 50, 51—2; electricity

constitutional provisions of, 21; creation of, 19; education and federal government, 23, 24—5, 26, 31; employment data, 70; ethnicity in, 32; expatriates in, 24—5, 32; future of, 35—7; immigrant population, x, xi, 32—3, 76; immigration, 30—4, industrial co-ordination in, 29 —30; information policies, 24; internal frontiers of, 20; and Iran, 21, 21n; and Iraq, 19, 21, 21n; naturalisation policy, 69; oil production and societal change, x—xi; population augmentation in poor emirates, 22; realignment of, 29; and Saudi Arabia, xi, 21; students view of, 32; succession in, 27; teachers in, 31; technology in, 27—9; territorial problems, 19

US: and Gulf states, viii; support for UAE, 22

USSR: invasion of Afghanistan, viii; interest in Gulf states, viii; oil needs of, viii

Umm al-Qaywayn: dispute with Sharjah, 27; leadership in 23; and UAE, 21, 35

urbanisation, x, 65—6

violence: and immigrants in UAE, 32

Wahhabis, 14
water, cost of, 52
welfare policies, 52, 82
women: attitudes to, 64; education of and control of population, 61; role of, 64

YAR (Yemeni Arab Republic): economy, 75, 77; migrant workers of, 14, 75, 76; prohibition of emigration, 75; return of migrants, 62, 72; workers' remittances to, 71

zakat, 51
Zayid, Shaikh, 22, 24n, 25, 27, 35

SECURITY IN THE PERSIAN GULF   2

SECURITY IN THE PERSIAN GULF

Security in the Persian Gulf 2:

Sources of Inter-State Conflict

ROBERT LITWAK
Research Associate
International Institute for Strategic Studies

Published for
THE INTERNATIONAL INSTITUTE
FOR STRATEGIC STUDIES
by
GOWER

Published by

Gower Publishing Company Limited,
Gower House, Croft Road,
Aldershot, Hants GU11 3HR, England

British Library Cataloguing in Publication Data

Litwak, Robert
    Sources of inter-state conflict. — (Security in the Persian Gulf, 2)
    1. Security, International
    2. Persian Gulf — Foreign relations
    I. Title. II. Litwak, Robert. III. Series.
327'.166'0953   DS49.7

ISBN 0-566-00451-8

Printed and bound in Great Britain by
Biddles Ltd, Guildford and King's Lynn

Contents

Maps

Introduction

With some fifty-seven per cent of the world's oil trade originatiñg from the littoral states of the Persian Gulf, the paramount importance of this region within the international system is self-evident. Yet the turbulent events of the last eighteen months — both in the southern tip of the Arabian Peninsula and, more recently, at the head of the Gulf — have underscored once again the ominously fragile bases of stability in the area. Even the most cursory survey of these current developments reveals a veritable mosaic of domestically and regionally based security threats. Moreover, the multiple and often contradictory demands of rapid modernization, the revival of sectarianism, and the heightened strategic importance accorded to the region by external powers, *inter alia*, are powerful new forces militating in favour of the Gulf's continuing political volatility. It is within this context that a serious reappraisal of security in the Persian Gulf has become an imperative.

The central purpose of this paper is to examine both the traditional and novel sources of *inter-state* conflict which threaten the stability of the area. In so doing, it seeks to provide a comprehensive inventory of these cases — whether actual or potential — together with an analysis of their background and present status. Here, it must be borne in mind that, given the non-legalistic tradition of the area, disputes are rarely settled *per se*. Rather, owing to the perceived interest of the parties involved, they remain dormant or deferred — yet always bearing the potential to re-emerge as a catalyst of inter-state conflict under the appropriate conditions. Hence, the discussion will focus upon the various political and economic conditions — both regional and domestic — under which specific disputes (or indeed, to the extent that generalization is possible, a specific type of conflict) could become salient in the coming period.[1] To a large degree, this analysis is premised upon the interaction between the trends which are at present manifest in the sub-region with those that one believes could develop.

Having set out the principal questions to which this monograph is addressed, a short outline of its structure might prove useful. For the sake of clarity as well as the book's internal coherence, a geographical framework is employed. Chapter 1[2] focuses upon the set of bilateral differences — territorial, sectarian and ideological — which have aggravated relations between Iraq and Iran in the past — and which, as evidenced in the recent onset of hostilities along their common frontier, remain of an ongoing nature. The next chapter deals both with the land frontier disputes of northern Arabia and the demarcation of continental shelf boundaries in the Upper Gulf. Similar attention is accorded the states of the Lower Gulf (i.e. those stretching east from Bahrain along both littorals to the Strait of Hormuz) in Chapter 3. The fourth geographical sub-division centres upon the politically pivotal — and historically volatile — set of relations between Saudi Arabia, the Yemens, and Oman. The concluding section of this book seeks to briefly explore the discernible *patterns* of inter-state conflict in the region as well as the conditions under which disputes are 'managed' or manipulated by various actors.

---

1 At the outset of this projective analysis, it should be explicitly stated that the interest here extends only insofar as these conditions militate in favour of or against the outbreak of inter-state conflict; their impact both on the domestic level and with respect to relations between various local states and extra-regional powers will be examined within the other books of this project.

2 The phrase 'Northern Tier' was coined in the late 1950s to denote the original signatories of the Baghdad Pact — Turkey, Iraq, Iran and Pakistan. In this book, it is used to characterize the Iraqi-Iranian relationship in its regional political setting.

The author would like to acknowledge gratefully the assistance of Ms Mahnaz Ispahani in the researching of this study.

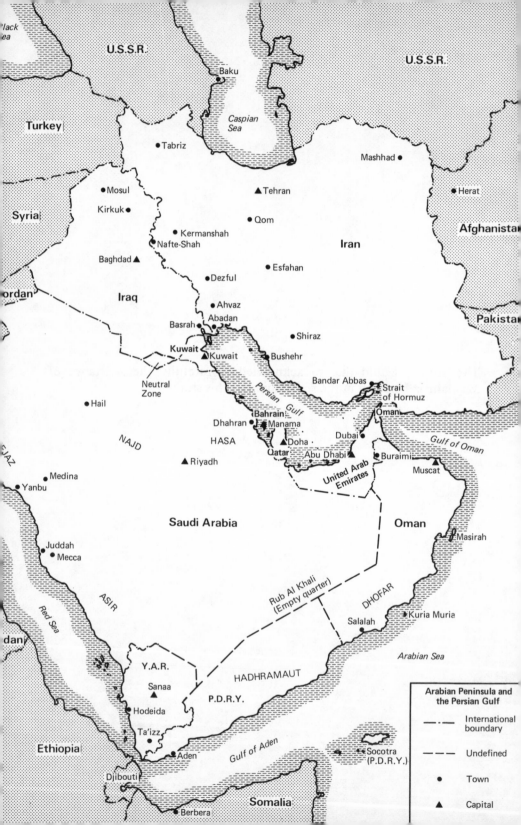

1 The 'Northern Tier'

Territorial disputes and resource questions

The Shatt al-Arab dispute

The Shatt al-Arab waterway is formed by the confluence of the Tigris and Euphrates Rivers with that of the Iranian River Karum. Stretching for 120 miles before emptying into the Gulf, it has been the principal focal point of the intermittently activated dispute between Iran and Iraq over the demarcation of their common border. With historical roots dating to the Ottoman period, the issue remained largely dormant for more than two decades following the conclusion of the Iraqi-Persian Treaty on 4 July 1937.[1] That agreement contained two major provisions: first, in designating the low water-mark on the eastern bank of the Shatt al-Arab as the frontier, it conferred to Iraq control over the waterway with the exception of the area adjacent to the Iranian ports of Abadan, Khorramshar and Khosrowabad where it was fixed at the *thalweg* (median line); and second, as a result of that demarcation, it provided that vessels on the Shatt should employ Iraqi pilots and fly the Iraqi flag (again with the exception of those three areas in which the boundary was determined at the *thalweg*).[2]

1 The 1937 agreement was preceded by two treaties concerning the status of the Shatt al-Arab: the Erzurum Treaty of 1847 between Iran and the Ottoman Empire; and the 1914 Constantinople Protocol between Iran, the Ottoman Empire, Great Britain and Russia.

2 Though no action was taken to that effect, the 1937 treaty did envisage a follow-on agreement which was to have established a joint commission for the administration of the waterway.

Though Iran did not fully comply with the unequal provisions of the 1937 agreement, relations between the two dynastic states remained close throughout the period until the 1958 revolution in Iraq. That relationship was grounded upon the similarities in both their domestic structures as well as the gradual convergence of their security perspectives. The latter was manifested in their joint active participation in the Baghdad Pact upon its founding in 1955. Membership in the alliance had the net effect not only of determining the manner in which their armed forces were configured (i.e. to meet any prospective Soviet threat) but also militated in favour of the deferral of bilateral problems, including the Shatt al-Arab controversy.

The bases of this relationship were fundamentally altered by the events of July 1958 in Baghdad.[1] The behaviour and expressed priorities of the Qasim regime reflected the advent not just of a new government, but of a wholly new set of circumstances. In these terms, the decision which it took in March 1959 to terminate its membership of the Baghdad Pact (thereafter CENTO) was nothing less than an explicit eschewal of the security perspective of the former monarchical regime. At the same time, the fundamental change in the domestic structure of Iraq was to have a profound impact on the nature of its relationship with Iran. Given the increasingly *ideological* tenor of the dispute between the two countries, there was a marked tendency for differences in one area — such as the Shatt al-Arab dispute — to call into question previous understandings dealing with the entire range of issues in their relationship.[2]

In November 1959-January 1960, the Shatt al-Arab issue emerged as the major point of contention between the two states. The crisis was triggered when Iraq began to interfere with Iranian vessels in an attempt to assert the prerogatives ostensibly conferred to it by way of the 1937 treaty.[3] A hardening in the Iranian position, as expressed in its declaratory policy, prompted Qasim to reassert Iraq's claim to the three mile territorial waters around Abadan which had been conferred to the Tehran government in one of the provisions of the 1937 agreement. This escalation in the level of rhetoric was accompanied by practical

---

1 For an extended discussion of the Shatt al-Arab question see Shahram Chubin and Sepehr Zabih, *The Foreign Relations of Iran*, University of California Press, Berkeley, 1974, p 171 ff.

2 *Ibid.*

3 Of course, Iraq ignored that provision of the treaty which required the eventual creation of a joint commission to administer the waterway.

measures on both sides to increase their military preparedness in the event of an outbreak of hostilities. Like Qasim's subsequent manipulation of the Kuwaiti frontier dispute (see p. 25), it could be argued that the Iraqi moves were timed, at least in part, so as to deflect public attention away from the nation's chronic domestic problems and the failure of the post-revolutionary regime to adequately address them. Again, it is significant to note that during this initial flare-up of the Shatt al-Arab dispute, other aspects of the Iraqi-Iranian relationship were also called into question.[1]

The 1959-60 episode was followed on 16 February 1961 by the Iranian announcement that vessels leaving or entering its ports would henceforth be guided by Iranian rather than Iraqi pilots. This move was motivated by the Iranian desire to frustrate Iraq's attempt to exercise exclusive rights over the waterway and to prompt strict compliance with the terms of the 1937 accord (i.e. the establishment of a joint commission to administer the waterway).[2] In an officially sanctioned response to the Iranian announcement, the Iraqi pilots from the Basrah port authority went on strike, thereby paralyzing the Iranian port of Abadan. This stemmed from the fact that ships bound for Abadan had first to traverse some forty miles of Iraqi territorial waters on the Shatt al-Arab. With Iraq unwilling to contemplate any departure from the *status quo ante*, the Iranian government was forced to accede to the Iraqi position in the face of the economic consequences of the strike action upon the port and refinery of Abadan.

Intermittent diplomatic exchanges between the two countries in the years following the second flare-up of the Shatt al-Arab question — although fostering a modest, if somewhat artificial, improvement in political atmosphere — failed to move the issue any closer to resolution. The return to power of the Ba'ath Party in 1968 produced a hardening in the Iraqi diplomatic posture *via-a-vis* the entire set of its bilateral differences with Iran. This stemmed not solely from the ideological predisposition of the Ba'ath. An important contributing factor was the problem of factionalism within the party. For under such conditions of internal power jockeying, various elements of the Ba'ath leadership sought to derive political utility — both on the domestic and inter-Arab political levels — through the adoption of a hardline attitude towards Iran as a demonstration of their 'Arabness'.

---

1 Iraq, for example, laid claim to the oil-rich Iranian province of Khuzestan on the grounds that its ethnic composition was primarily Arab. The question of Khuzestan (or 'Arabistan' as Baghdad prefers to call it) is considered on pp 13-15.

2 Chubin, *op.cit.*, pp 174-76.

The dispute over navigation rights in the Shatt al-Arab was revived on 15 April 1969 when, according to the Tehran daily, *Keyhan International*, the Iraqi Foreign Minister informed the Iranian Ambassador in Baghdad that Iraq intended to enforce 'its territorial rights' in the area.[1] It was asserted that, henceforth, Iranian vessels utilizing the waterway would be required to strike their colours and forbidden from carrying Iranian Imperial Navy personnel. The Iranian response came four days later when the Tehran government declared the 1937 treaty 'null and void' and asserted that it would take 'all necessary steps to safeguard its interests'. Invoking the principle *rebus sic stantibus*, Iran abrogated the treaty on the grounds that Iraq had violated the terms of the 1937 agreement in not equally sharing the tolls collected on the Shatt al-Arab.[2] Moreover, Tehran charged that its adoption had been largely imposed on both parties at the instigation of the British. In renouncing the 1937 treaty, Iran sought to shift the border with Iraq from the eastern bank of the Shatt al-Arab to the waterway's *thalweg*. While placing its forces on alert, Iraq let it be known that it did not wish to be drawn into conflict with Iran.

The dramatic improvement in the Iranian military position *vis-à-vis* Iraq during the 1960's was clearly one of the determining factors in its actions of April 1969. Iranian jet aircraft and naval vessels were able to provide ample cover for its ships as they defied the Iraqi restrictions noted in the diplomatic exchange of 15 April. On the regional political level, the crisis occurred little more than a year following the British announcement of its intention to withdraw from the Gulf area by the end of 1971. An additional source of tension between the two states, therefore, centred upon the evolution of a new regional security regime in the wake of this move. There is no doubt that Iraq felt compelled during this period to demonstrably oppose the Iranian attempt, as reflected in its declaratory policy and as tacitly countenanced by Washington, to supersede Britain as the 'stabilizing' power within the region. So as to be perceived as defending a much broader set of interests, Iraq seized upon Iran's irredentist claim to Bahrain (see p 41) in order to coalesce Arab diplomatic support for its position in the Shatt al-Arab dispute.[3]

---

1 *Arab Report and Record*, 16-30 April 1969.

2 For a discussion of the 1969 eruption of the Shatt al-Arab dispute and its aftermath see Majid Khadduri, *Socialist Iraq: A Study in Iraqi Politics since 1968*, Middle East Institute, Washington, D.C. 1978, pp 148-53.

3 Tehran endeavoured to out-manoeuvre this Iraqi attempt through the development of a relationship with Cairo following the withdrawal of Egyptian forces from Yemen in the autumn of 1967. During the 1969 crisis, Iranian officials were encouraged by the muted and impartial tenor of the Egyptian press (as contrasted with that of Syria). For an analysis of the development of relations between Iran and Egypt, see Chubin, *op.cit.*, chapter III.

Four border incidents in the first half of 1972[1] were accompanied by the large-scale deportation of Iranian nationals from the Iraqi border region, thereby creating a major social problem for the Tehran government.[2] This tense state of relations persisted during 1973 until the outbreak of the Yom Kippur war. At that time, Iraq, having transferred elements of its armed forces into Syria in order to project an image of itself as a confrontation state in the conflict with Israel, invited Iran to resume diplomatic relations. After a hiatus of two years, diplomatic ties were restored on 15 October 1973 with Iran pledging not to exploit Iraq's weakened military position along their border. Subsequent to the conclusion of the Arab-Israeli ceasefire on 24 October, Iraqi troops were recalled from Syria and redeployed along the Iranian frontier.

Although there was a certain congruence of Iraqi and Iranian interest *vis-à-vis* developments within OPEC during the period immediately following the fourth Middle East war, this was not reflected in their state-to-state relations. Border skirmishes resumed with increasing intensity in early 1974. On 10 February, the most serious frontier incident up to that time occurred with both sides sustaining heavy casualties. Whereas an Iraqi communiqué charged that the Iranians had provoked the fighting by shelling Badra and overflying its airspace, the Iranian government counterclaimed that hostilities had commenced with an Iraqi artillery attack, later followed by tanks and infantry, upon the Mehran frontier post.[3] At the request of the Iraqi Government, an urgent meeting of the Security Council was convened on 12 February to consider the border fighting between the two countries. With both sides reiterating their familiar negotiating positions, U.N. Secretary General Waldheim appointed a special representative to mediate in the dispute. Although further fighting broke out 100 miles north of Badra on 4 March, it was reported on 19 March that Iraq and Iran had agreed that 'a normal situation should prevail on the border between the two countries'.[4]

This was followed two days later by Waldheim's announcement that Iraq and Iran had agreed to the mutual reduction of force levels along the frontier and the early resumption of negotiations to address the entire range of their outstanding bilateral differences. In his report to the Security Council, the U.N. special representative stated that the border dispute arose in part from the use of different maps, and that

1 *Keesing's Contemporary Archives*, 1972, p 25514.

2 *Arab Report and Record*, 1-15 January 1972.

3 *Arab Report and Record*, 1-14 February 1974.

4 *Keesing's Contemporary Archives*, 1974, p 26465.

the two governments had indicated that they would accept the findings of a joint delimitation commission.[1] Despite the recurrence of border incidents, ministerial discussions took place between 13 August and 1 September 1974.

Though some progress towards the resolution of the Shatt al-Arab question appears to have been made in that round of negotiations, it was not until the March 1975 OPEC meeting in Algiers that final agreement was reached. On 6 March, the Algerian President, Houari Boumedienne, announced that after direct talks between the Shah and the then Iraqi Vice President, Saddam Hussein Takriti, they had concluded an agreement that 'completely eliminated the conflict between the two brotherly countries'.[2] The understanding included four main provisions:

1 Agreement to delimit their land frontier on the basis of the Protocol of Constantinople of 1913 and the verbal accord of 1914.

2 To demarcate the Shatt al-Arab waterway's boundary on the basis of the *thalweg* (i.e. median) line.

3 To 're-establish security and mutual confidence along their common frontiers' and undertake to exercise a strict and effective control with the aim of finally putting an end to 'all infiltrations of a subversive character from either side'.

4 The pledge of both parties to regard the provisions negotiated at the 1975 OPEC meeting as indivisible elements of a comprehensive settlement, such that a breach of any one would be considered a violation of the spirit of the Algiers Agreement.[3]

In political terms, the agreement embodied a straightforward *quid pro quo*. Whereas Iraq acceded to a revision of the 1937 treaty concerning the delimitation of the Shatt al-Arab, Iran was bound to cease its assistance to the Kurdish nationalist movement within Iraq (see pp 15-19). Nine days after the issuing of the Algiers Communiqué, the Iraqi and Iranian foreign ministers met in Tehran to discuss its implementation. On 15 March 1975, a protocol was signed establishing three committees to study the demarcation of the Shatt al-Arab, the land boundaries between Iraq and Iran, and ways of preventing infiltration across the border.[4]

Three months after the Tehran meeting, the foreign ministers met again in the Iraqi capital. This round of negotiations culminated in the

1 *Keesing's Contemporary Archives*, 1975, p 27053.

2 *Ibid.*

3 *Ibid.*

4 *Ibid.*, p 27054.

6

conclusion of the Baghdad Treaty on 13 June 1975 which codified the provisions of the Algiers Agreement. In addition to the implementation of the Algiers Communiqué and its protocol, the Baghdad Treaty established two commissions: the first, an Iraqi one, to consider the payment of compensation to the some 65,000 Iranian nationals expelled from the country by the Ba'athist regime; the second, an Iranian one, to assist Kurdish refugees, displaced by the war, who had chosen not to return to Iraq.[1]

From the Iraqi position, the improvement of relations with Iran, in conjunction with the moderation of its negotiating stance in the Kuwaiti dispute (see p 25), permitted it to assume a role in the deliberations on Persian Gulf security which no previous post-revolutionary regime had been able to adopt. While Iraq's dependence upon the Soviet Union as its major arms supplier persisted, there was a marked attempt on the part of Baghdad to distance itself somewhat from Moscow politically. During 1977-78 this new foreign policy orientation was reflected in strong Iraqi criticism of Soviet activities in both the Horn of Africa[2] and Afghanistan, in addition to the suppression of the Iraqi Communist Party on charges of creating illegal political cells within the nation's armed forces.[3]

Although many continued to query whether these Iraqi moves were merely tactical in nature, their net effect (particularly after the undermining of Egypt's regional political position after Camp David) was to permit Baghdad to re-enter not only the mainstream of inter-Arab politics but to participate in deliberations on Persian Gulf security questions. As will be discussed further below, the form which the latter assumed was a series of bilateral 'security consultations' between the Ba'athist leadership and Iran, Kuwait, and Saudi Arabia, amongst others. Indeed, given the expression of Iraqi concern over Soviet moves in the Horn of Africa and Afghanistan, there were those who discerned a growing convergence in the security perspectives of the three major Gulf powers. And yet, even though such trends within the strategic

---

1 Khadduri, *op.cit.*, p 152.

2 The Ba'ath Party's opposition to Soviet activities in Somalia-Ethiopia was registered in its official publication, *Ath Thawra* on 16 August 1977; see *Arab Report and Record*, 16-31 August 1977, pp 675-76. For a discussion of the Iraqi-Soviet relationship see Shahram Chubin, 'Soviet Policy Towards Iran and the Gulf', *Adelphi Papers*, no. 157, IISS, London, Spring 1980, pp 25-28.

3 In May 1978, twenty-one members of the CPI were hanged on these charges. While overtly anti-Soviet, the move was taken as a more general warning to the anti-Ba'ath forces. Baghdad's attempt — whether tactical or not — to distance itself from the Soviet Union was further reflected in its trade figures. After 1973, for example, the level of Iraqi imports from the Soviet bloc dropped from 25 per cent to nine per cent of the Iraqi total; June 1978: Moscow Narodny Bank, London; cited in David Lynn Price, 'Moscow and the Persian Gulf', *Problems of Communism*, March-April 1979, pp 1-13.

environment militated in favour of the modest Iraqi-Iranian *rapprochement* after the Algiers Agreement, the varied sources of their mutual antipathy — ethnic, sectarian, and, perhaps most importantly, ideological — remained the underlying reality of their relationship.

Whether purely tactical in nature or not, the fragile bases of the relationship into which they entered in 1975 collapsed with the political upheaval in Iran. As has generally been the case in Gulf politics, the assumption to power of a new regime brought with it a wholly new security perspective. Relations between Iraq and Iran steadily deteriorated following the February 1979 revolution for a number of reasons. The attitude of the new theocratic regime in Tehran was one of undisguised hostility towards the Ba'athist government, given the ostensibly cordial relations which existed between it and the Shah's regime in its final years. From the Iraqi perspective, there was the overriding fear that the Iranian post-revolutionary government would seek to foment unrest amongst its large Kurdish and Shi'ah communities.[1] An additional factor precipitating the open split between Iran and Iraq in the period following the events of January-February 1979 was the former's agitational activities in the Lower Gulf. Calls within the theocratic regime for the 'export' of Iran's revolution to other conservative monarchical states of the Gulf culminated in the revival of that nation's long-dormant claim to Bahrain (see pp 41-48). Seeking to preserve the regional balance of power, while concomitantly enhancing the credibility of its pan-Arabist posture, Iraq pledged to militarily repulse any such Iranian attempt.[2]

On 31 October 1979, Iraq for the first time declared the conditions under which an improvement in relations with Iran would be possible. In an interview apparently granted with the express approval of Baghdad, Iraq's Ambassador to Lebanon, engaging largely in polemics, outlined the ostensible prerequisites for a return to normal state-to-state relations: first, a revision of the 1975 Algiers Agreement regarding navigation rights on the Shatt al-Arab; second, the return of Abu Musa and the Tunb Islands to Arab sovereignty (for a discussion of the Shah's forcible seizure of these islands at the mouth of the Strait of Hormuz see p 56); and third, the provision of 'self-rule' to Iran's national minorities (i.e. the Kurds, the Baluchis, the Azerbaijani, and the Arabs of Khuzestan).[3]

1 In the past, much of Iraq's chronic political instability has derived from its sectarian and communal diversity: roughly 25 per cent of the population are Arab Sunni Moslems; 35 per cent are Arab Shi'ite Moslems; 20 per cent are Sunni Kurds.

2 *Financial Times*, 17 October 1979. Though Iraq was not a participant, the statement by Saddam Hussein coincided with the meeting of the Arab Foreign Ministers in Taif to discuss, amongst other topics, the implications of disturbances in the Shi'ite community in Bahrain.

3 *An-Nahar*, 31 October 1979; reported in *Financial Times*, 1 November 1979.

In spite of the radical change in circumstance between the 1969-75 and post-revolutionary periods of Iraqi-Iranian hostility, the *form* which the latter came to assume (prior to the conflict of autumn 1980) very much resembled that of the former. During both, the *ideological* nature of the struggle (i.e. mutual antipathy premised largely upon the incompatibility of their domestic structures)[1] had the net effect of allowing differences in one area (e.g. the Shatt al-Arab dispute) to spill over and destabilize the entire range of their relations. From the time of the Iraqi Ambassador's enunciation of Baghdad's maximalist demands — a clear exercise in domestic and inter-Arab politics — the frequency and intensity of skirmishes along the frontier increased. Though Iraq made no overt move on the Shatt al-Arab in contravention of the Algiers Agreement until September 1980, its pre-war strategy was to manipulate that issue (as with the question of sovereignty over the three islands at the mouth of the Strait of Hormuz[2] and the political status of the Arab population in Khuzestan) so as to weaken and diplomatically isolate Iran.[3] As suggested above, the concomitant gain to Iraq through this process was the enhancement of its position *vis-à-vis* inter-Arab politics. The projection of an ostensibly pan-Arabist political posture remains an important component of Iraqi regional policy. During the periods preceding and immediately following the initiation of renewed fighting along the Shatt al-Arab, Iraq sought, in part, to utilize the conflict with Iran as a political vehicle to foster the image of itself as the defender of the Arab nation.[4]

The onset of open hostilities between these ideologically hostile Gulf states came in mid-September 1980 following weeks of increasingly serious border incidents. On 17 September, Iraq took the formal

1 Ayatollah Khomeini, for example, has repeatedly called upon the Iraqi army to overthrow the 'corrupt' Ba'athist regime.

2 It is interesting to note that President Bani-Sadr has rationalized Iran's continuing occupation of Abu Musa and the Tunb Islands on the grounds that their relinquishment to any of the pro-Western Arab Gulf states would permit the United States to 'take charge of the Gulf'; *An-Nahar*, 24 March 1980; reported in the *Financial Times*, 25 March 1980.

3 In what was then taken as an important political signal, *Tass*, 10 April 1980, accused the Iraqi press of waging an 'anti-Iranian campaign' following major skirmishes along their frontier in the previous week. This stance might be attributed to the attempt by Iraq to distance itself politically from the Soviet Union. After the enunciation of Saddam Hussein's 'Pan-Arab Charter' (8 February 1980), Iraq explicitly endorsed efforts to overthrow the regime in Aden and expel Soviet military advisers from the PDRY; see *Financial Times*, 28 March 1980.

4 Iraqi declaratory policy, for example, continues to make repeated reference to historical Arab military victories over the Persians in order to coalesce popular support for the campaign against Iran. Syria, however, has bitterly criticized Saddam Hussein for going to war against Iraq and has directly challenged his characterization of the conflict in overtly racialist tones. Damascus maintains that the war is a diversion from the traditional Arab struggle against Israel and can only benefit the Americans.

step of abrogating the 1975 Algiers Agreement. Within four days, fighting spread to the Iranian port of Khorramshahr and to the area adjacent to Abadan airport. A major escalation in the conflict occurred on 22 September when Iraqi MiGs struck at air bases across Iran. This move was accompanied by the invasion of Ba'athist forces into Iran at four strategic points along the frontier. The important border town of Qasr-e-Shirin was quickly captured while the refinery city of Abadan was besieged.

Baghdad's war aims, as publicly enunciated during the first days of the conflict, closely conformed to the terms which the Iraqi Ambassador to Lebanon had previously advanced in his important interview of 31 October 1979 (i.e. the recognition of exclusive Iraqi navigational rights on the Shatt al-Arab, the return of Abu Musa and the Tunb Islands to Arab sovereignty, the provision of 'self-rule' to the Arab population of Khuzestan, etc.). Despite this official formulation of intent, however, it is evident that Iraq chose to strike against a militarily weakened and diplomatically isolated Iran because of the Islamic Republic's repeated efforts over the preceding eighteen months to topple the Ba'athist regime (as well as every other secular government in the region) through the export of its revolution. Hence, the real driving force behind Saddam Hussein's strategy was the desire, in turn, to trigger a major shift in the power structure within Iran by means of a rapid military victory at the expense of the Khomeini government. Though Ba'athist forces did score early territorial gains on the eastern bank of the Shatt al-Arab and in the northern frontier region, the Iraqi President seriously misjudged the impact of the conflict on the Iranian domestic situation. While the destruction of oil production and refinery facilities constitutes a severe economic loss to both regimes, the long-term political implications of the war remain uncertain. One of the immediate consequences of the conflict in the Iranian political context, however, was to narrow the scope for manoeuvre of the opposition operating both within (e.g. national minority movements) and outside the country. This has been evidenced in the attempt by the Khomeini regime to use the war as a means of revitalizing the revolution, while at the same time impugning the legitimacy of the opposition groups by publicly identifying them as internal instruments of Iraqi aggression.

The profound ideological hostility at the heart of the Iran-Iraq conflict continues to militate against the likelihood of a mediated settlement. The predominance of this characteristic of the dispute ensures that questions of territorial disposition — the ostensible focus of any prospective negotiations — remain distinct from the underlying political objectives of the combatants. A compounding problem attendant on any potential settlement is the mutual necessity for political face-saving devices. Having revived its claim to exclusive navigational rights on the Shatt al-Arab as, in part, the pretext for the war against Iran, it will be difficult for Baghdad to conclude an agreement which does not include that provision. Such an imposed, unequal settlement, however, would be virtually impossible for *any* Iranian regime to accept and, in any case, would most certainly lay the seeds for future conflict. Even the Khomeini regime, which has pointedly eschewed the Shah's security perspective, cannot be perceived as being incapable of defending the Iranian homeland. These practical considerations aside, the main factor precluding an early resolution of the conflict remains the inability of the warring parties to agree upon the political criteria of a settlement. In March 1975, the Shah and Saddam Hussein were able to achieve a *modus vivendi* on the basis of the principle of non-interference in one another's domestic affairs (e.g. the suspension of Iranian support for the Iraqi Kurds, etc.). The structural nature of the dispute between Iran and Iraq — that is, the conflict stemming from their contending notions of domestic legitimacy and national order — rules out the possibility of any such political accommodation in the current crisis. Under these circumstances, the prognosis would appear to be one of a continuing war of attrition until there occurs a decisive shift in the domestic power structure of either (or both) state(s).

The question of oilfields astride the Iran-Iraq border

Though the Shatt al-Arab question became the principal focal point of the dispute between Iraq and Iran after 1959, a secondary issue to emerge was that of the exploitation of oil reserves in the area adjacent to their common border. The question became a part of the public debate in April 1963 when the post-Qasim regime in Baghdad announced its intention to construct a twelve-inch oil pipeline from Khaneghain on the Iran-Iraq border to Baghdad. Though situated within Iraq, Khaneghain was part of a larger subterranean structure which included the Nafte-Shah and Khaneh oilfields on the Iranian side. In late July 1963, the Iraqi Minister of Petroleum visited Tehran as part of an effort to reach a negotiated settlement to the Khaneghain/Khaneh/Nafte-Shah dispute as well as differences over the delimitation of their territorial waters at the mouth of the Shatt al-Arab (see p 3). Though no progress was registered with respect to the latter issue, agreement was achieved on the joint exploitation of the oil resources in the border field. Specifically, the agreement established the precise volume which each state would be permitted to extract annually and provided for mutual inspection rights to assure strict adherence to the production quotas laid down.

It is significant to note that during both the 1969-75 and 1979-80 cycles of border skirmishing, the fighting — often in the form of heavy artillery exchanges — remained well away from this oil-rich border region. The dispute over the demarcation of this segment of the Iran-Iraq frontier again erupted into the open following Baghdad's unilateral abrogation of the 1975 Algiers Agreement in mid-September 1980.[1] In sharp contrast to the previous pattern of restraint, however, the onset of large-scale hostilities between Iran and Iraq has witnessed an end to the sanctuary status of the area encompassing the Khaneghain, Khaneh, and Nafte-Shah oilfields. This development is noteworthy in two respects: first, it reflects the limits of the contending parties to control the escalatory process once in an actual war situation; and, second, it again underscores the tendency, previously characterized, for Gulf conflicts stemming from ideological antipathy to expand in scope.

---

1 The Iraqis contend that the 1975 Treaty provided for the establishment of a joint border commission to review the question of Iranian sovereignty over some 200 square miles in the Nafte-Shah/Khaneh area.

National minority questions and sectarian disputes

The Khuzestan/'Arabistan' question

Though Khuzestan remains Iran's richest oil-producing province, its two million population is primarily Arab in ethnic composition. Between 1890 and 1925 the Khuzestanis enjoyed wide autonomy under one of the tribal shaikhs who managed to maintain close relations both with Tehran and the British. The latter were interested primarily in the security guarantee which he was able to provide for their developing oil industry. The question of sovereignty over Khuzestan was first raised in the aftermath of World War I when Iraq and Iran clashed over the demarcation of their border and the status of Iranian (Shi'ah) nationals in Iraq. In 1925, Reza Shah, having forcibly suppressed a move for autonomy in Khuzestan, began to settle the province with Persian speaking citizens so as to turn the Arab majority into a minority. In the period immediately following World War II, Khuzestan's Arab population renewed their drive for autonomy status. Though an appeal was made to Iraq and the Arab League to grant them Iraqi citizenship, the movement was again suppressed by the Iranian central government within a few months.

In terms of Iraqi policy, the real change in attitude came following the 1958 Revolution. Until that time, the Hashemite rulers in Baghdad had not pressed the issue out of their desire to maintain close relations with the dynastic leadership in Tehran. It was only within the context of the Shatt al-Arab crisis of 1959-60 that the Khuzestan/'Arabistan' issue again emerged as a major point of contention between Iraq and Iran. At that time, as will be recalled from the discussion above, the Qasim regime not only refused to implement the 1937 Treaty *vis-à-vis* the Shatt al-Arab, but, in a major departure from the pre-revolutionary government, laid claim to Khuzestan (or 'Arabistan' as Baghdad preferred to call it). During the 1969 crisis, Iraq again revived the 'Arabistan' issue as part of its campaign against Iran on the Shatt al-Arab and Kurdish questions. Although the Algiers Agreement of 1975 made no mention of the dispute over Khuzestan, it was widely acknowledged that one of its tacit provisions (in addition to the settlement of the Shatt al-Arab question and the termination of Iranian support for the Kurdish rebels in Iraq) was the renunciation of any Iraqi designs on 'Arabistan'.[1]

---

1 Indeed, in its aftermath, the Ba'athists cynically imprisoned Arabistan activists whom they had hitherto supported.

From the middle of 1978, strikes amongst the oil workers of Khuzestan played a major role in bringing about the Islamic Revolution.[1] With the rapid deterioration in relations between Iraq and Iran after February 1979, the Ba'athist regime began a conscious drive to aid and abet the resistance movement within Khuzestan. The inevitable results were the widespread disruption and sabotage of Iran's vulnerable oil industry. During the constitutional debate in 1979, the clerical authorities in Tehran maintained their vociferous opposition to any kind of meaningful regional devolution of power. At the same time, the escalating cycle of violence within Khuzestan threatened to deny them their primary source of revenue. Hoping to further foster the process of political fragmentation within Iran, the public articulation of Iraq's conditions for an improvement in bilateral relations[2] included the demand for the provision of self-rule in Khuzestan. Given the vital interest of the West in preserving a territorially integral Iranian state, it is significant to note that Iraq has not explicitly revived its own irredentist claim to 'Arabistan' (unlike the 1960 and 1969 crises). Regarded as untenable in international legal terms, Iraq has opted instead for the adoption of a more indirect, ostensibly pan-Arabist approach to the Khuzestan question during the current round of fighting with Iran. To be sure, however, its long-term goal (i.e., the elimination of Iran as a credible regional adversary through the political fragmentation of its periphery) remains unchanged. The adverse reaction of the Khuzestani population to the prospect of Iraqi occupation in the first week of the Autumn 1980 war — witness the exodus of urban dwellers to the Iranian interior — would suggest that Baghdad wrongly construed the military option as contributing toward that end.

The Kurdish question

With the exception of the Shatt al-Arab controversy, no other question has so dominated Iraqi-Iranian relations as that of the status of Kurdistan. Though active during World War II, the Kurdish resistance movement, under the leadership of Mullah Mostafa Barzani, was forced to retreat into Soviet Azerbaijan by a combined Iraqi-British military

---

1 Arab political consciousness within Khuzestan remains a coherent and potent force. In the immediate post-revolutionary period, previously disparate political and cultural societies coalesced to further their demands for autonomy through the creation of an umbrella organization — the Arab Political and Cultural Organization — under the leadership of Shaikh Mohammed Taher Shobeir Khaghani.

2 *An-Nahar*, 31 October 1979; reported in *Financial Times*, 1 November 1979.

force in the winter of 1947. During the period prior to the July 1958 revolution — one in which the Kurdish question remained relatively dormant — the major fear of the dynastic leaders in Tehran and Baghdad was that of Soviet inspired agitational activities in their respective Kurdish regions. Midway through 1961, Iranian and Iraqi Kurds joined in revolt against the Iraqi authorities though it is unlikely that this reflected a decision by Tehran to destabilize the Qasim regime.[1] At that time, Barzani was regarded by the Iranian government as little more than an agent of Iraqi and/or Soviet interests. Collaboration with Barzani against Iraq, however, was to become a major element of Iranian policy after 1965-66.[2]

The revival of the Shatt al-Arab dispute with Iran in April 1969 prompted the Ba'athist government to seek a negotiated settlement to the Kurdish question. Secret negotiations between Iraq and the Kurdish insurgents in Beirut culminated in the fifteen point Peace Agreement of 11 March 1970[3] which conferred nominal autonomy to that national region (i.e. the recognition of Kurdish as a national language, constitutional revisions to ensure the proportional representation of Kurds within government and the armed forces, the granting of a general amnesty to the Kurdish rebels by the central government, *inter alia*). Having previously attempted to manipulate the Kurdish issue so as to weaken the Iraqi position and enhance its own on such questions as the Shatt al-Arab dispute, the implications of the March 1970 settlement were not lost upon the Iranian government.

Differences between Baghdad and the Kurds over the implementation of the agreement, however, were to lead to an initial deterioration in relations, followed by the resumption of armed clashes. The 1972 Treaty of Friendship between the Soviet Union and Iraq was taken as a signal of Moscow's support for Iraq's forceful moves against the Kurdish insurgents. By 1973, Barzani was openly appealing for American, Iranian, and Israeli assistance. In what was to become a highly cynical exercise, Washington and Tehran regarded support for the Kurds as a means of weakening Iraq and, by implication, the Soviet Union. In August 1974, the Iraqi Army launched the biggest offensive against the Kurds since the beginning of the war in 1961. The result of this drive was to push the *Pesh Merga* guerrillas further into the mountains along the Turkish and Iranian frontiers.

1   Chubin, *op.cit.*, pp 178-81.

2   For an historical assessment of the Kurdish question during this period see Edgar O'Ballance, *The Kurdish Revolt, 1961-70*, Faber, London, 1973.

3   *Keesing's Contemporary Archives*, 1970, p 23916.

Kurdish resistance collapsed in the aftermath of the 6 March 1975 agreement reached in Algiers between the Shah and Saddam Hussein (see p 6). In return for Iraqi concessions on the Shatt al-Arab question, Iran tacitly pledged to cease its support for the Kurds. The practical implications of that move were the closure of the border to further military supplies and the withdrawal of Iranian forces operating within Iraq. By the end of March, the *Pesh Merga* rebels and the leadership of the Kurdish Democratic Party (KDP), including Barzani, were forced to retreat into Iran.[1] From Tehran, on 3 May, Barzani announced that the struggle for Kurdish autonomy had ended and would 'never be resumed'. The following July, however, it was reported that elements of the Kurdish resistance movement who wanted to continue the autonomy drive had, with the apparent backing of Syria, formed the Kurdistan National Union, later the Patriotic Union of Kurdistan (PUK), under the leadership of Jalal Talabani. Spearheaded by the PUK, the *Pesh Mergas* resumed hostilities against Iraqi forces in mid-1976.[2]

During the political period between the Algiers Agreement and the downfall of the Shah, the Iraqis pursued a two tiered policy in relation to the Kurdish question. In terms of its external relations, the period was one, as characterized above, in which Iraq consciously sought to project a more 'moderate' foreign policy orientation. Again, this was regarded as a prerequisite for re-entering the mainstream of inter-Arab politics and assuming some sort of regional security role. In terms of its relationship with Iran, the Kurdish question (as a potential source of state-to-state conflict) was dormant — though clearly only as a result of the kind of tactical *rapprochement* which emerged in the aftermath of the Algiers settlement. And yet, on the domestic plane, it was precisely that mutually advantageous, though largely cosmetic, improvement in the bilateral relationship which allowed the Iraqis to launch a major campaign against the Kurdish insurgents without fear of cross-border intervention.[3]

1 In early April 1975 it was reported that some 200,000 Kurds — both civilians and *Pesh Merga* guerrillas — had fled across the border into Iran. In the following weeks, however, at least half of these refugees were voluntarily repatriated to Iraq owing to the general amnesty offered by the Ba'athist government.

2 Formerly a left-wing opponent of Mullah Barzani within the KDP, Talabani's dependence upon Syrian assistance during this period was almost total. With the cessation of Syrian support for Talabani in the wake of the September 1978 *rapprochement* between the rival Ba'athist regimes in Damascus and Baghdad, PUK military operations within Iraq were brought to an end as well.

3 A major component of this programme has been a policy of forced resettlement of Kurdish refugees (i.e. to the southern and western provinces of Iraq). At the same time, some sixty Kurdish villages on the Iraqi frontier with Iran have been razed, thus transforming the border region into one large free-fire zone.

The Iranian revolution, and the ensuing political chaos within that country, has been accompanied by renewed demands for Kurdish autonomy. Despite the factional nature of the Tehran regime (i.e. the multiple decision-making centres reflecting the secular-theocratic schism) there is a consensus within the leadership that any form of regional devolution could set a dangerous precedent. It is this conviction which continues to provide the basis for official policy towards the ethnic minority areas.[1]

At present, the Iranian Kurdish movement comprises an uneasy coalition of two loose political groupings — the broader based of which is that under the direction of the Sunni Moslem leader, Shaikh Ezzedin Hosseini. Despite its religious core, Hosseini's support extends so far as to include such prominent left-wing Kurdish resistance groups as the avowedly Marxist-Leninist *Komala* party and the Kurdish *Fedayeen Khalq*. The second focal point of Kurdish political and military activities in the post-revolutionary period has been the Kurdish Democratic Party of Iran (KDPI), whose general secretary, Dr Abdul Rahman Kassemlou returned in 1978 after a twenty year exile. Though the relationship between Shaikh Hosseini and the KDPI remains ambiguous,[2] there is substantial agreement on a programme of autonomy amongst the various Kurdish factions under these umbrella organizations. That they are seeking such a political arrangement within the existing Iranian state structure (as opposed to the once mooted notion of a greater 'Kurdistan') is sustained by reports that the level of cross-border co-operation, specifically with the Kurdish groups operating within Iraq and Turkey, has been surprisingly low.

In the initial phase at least, the clerical authorities in Tehran appear to have embraced the view that a military solution to the Kurdish question was possible. Indeed, when the first Kurdish uprising was crushed in August 1979 by the Army and Revolutionary Guard (*Pasdaran*) it appeared as though Khomeini — desperately attempting to consolidate power at the centre amidst a fragmenting periphery — had succeeded in repressing the national minority group which posed the greatest immediate threat to the Tehran regime.[3] Only two months

---

1 Constituting some 50 per cent of Iran's total population, there are five main ethnic groups which are seeking greater autonomy within the existing state structure (i.e. the Kurds, Azerbaijanis, Arabs, Baluchis and Turkomans). Again, it should be reiterated that the primary focus of this work is on the conditions under which they might become a significant factor in *inter-state* relations.

2 For a discussion of the relationship between the different Kurdish political factions see Andrew Whitley, 'The Kurds: Pressures and Prospects', *Round Table*, pp 245-57.

3 Though the question of Soviet military assistance to the Kurdish insurgents remains a source of contention, there were reports that such aid was proffered in July/August 1979. For his part, Ayatollah Khomeini moved to ban the KDPI amidst repeated charges that the Kurds were 'communist-backed enemies of the revolution'. On 4 September, *TASS* denied allegations that it had supplied arms and supplies to the Kurdish resistance movement.

later, the turnabout in the military situation found government troops controlling little more than their garrisons and some urban areas.[1] During this round of fighting, the *Pesh Merga* guerrillas were estimated to number some 7,000 men while government forces — consisting of roughly equal *Pasdaran* and regular army contingents — were placed at 13,000. It is significant to note the subtle manner in which the Kurdish leadership sought to manipulate the uneasy relationship existing between the Revolutionary Guards and regular army units by drawing a sharp distinction between the two (i.e. harassing the former at every opportunity, while attacking the latter only in self-defence).[2]

The serious military setbacks sustained by government forces in October prompted the clerical authorities in Tehran to accede to a tactical shift in policy. In the ensuing period, the search for a rapid military solution to the Kurdish question was supplanted by the pursuit of negotiations. The despatch of a high-ranking government delegation to Mahabad on 2 November was accompanied by the institution of a *de facto* ceasefire. Shaikh Hosseini, acting in accord with the KDPI, the *Komala* and the *Fedayeen Khalq*, presented the government representatives with an eight point programme for autonomy which one report characterized as the 'most detailed and specific demands to have been made by the Kurds since their secessionist revolts began 30 years ago'.[3] Negotiations were temporarily suspended during the period immediately surrounding the referendum on the new Islamic Constitution (2-3 December) owing to the large-scale demonstrations within Kurdish urban areas in opposition to it. These acts of civil disobedience were used by the government as the occasion for augmenting their military presence in the region despite the tacit ceasefire.

At a press conference on 17 December, the then Minister of State, Dariush Foruhar, countered Hosseini's proposal with a draft outline of the government's own rather circumscribed plan for regional self-government. Though satisfying a number of the Kurdish leadership's basic demands, this proposal has failed to provide the basis for a negotiated settlement. A clear reflection of this impasse was the gradual breakdown of the ceasefire arrangements in the first quarter of 1980. Armed clashes, primarily between the *Pesh Mergas* and the *Pasdarans* (whose withdrawal from the region remains a persistent Kurdish demand) have occurred in particular around the towns of Bijar, Paveh, Sanandaj and Kamyaran. A new and politically significant element in

---

1 On 20 October, Mahabad, the traditional capital of Iran's five million Kurds, was retaken by the *Pesh Merga* guerrillas. For a detailed chronology of the military actions during this period see *Keesing's Contemporary Archives*, 1980, pp 30301-30304.

2 *Ibid.*, p 30304.

3 *Times*, 3 December 1979.

the current round of hostilities has been the commitment of leftist non-Kurdish forces to military activities.[1] These have been carried out in conjunction with local forces under the command of Shaikh Hosseini and Dr Kassemlou. This continued fighting adjacent to the Iraqi border has permitted the Tehran regime to maintain its claim that the Kurdish resistance movement is less an indigenous political phenomenon than a foreign insurgency abetted by Baghdad.

Iraqi support for the Kurdish rebellion in Iran coincided with the marked deterioration in relations between the rival Ba'athist and theocratic regimes. It should be underscored, however, that this assistance stemmed from Baghdad's desire to change the power structure *within* Iran, rather than to advance what from its perspective remains the dubious goal of Kurdish national identity. Following the onset of hostilities along the Iran-Iraq frontier in September 1980, fighting within Iranian Kurdistan quickly abated owing to the desire of the KDPI leadership not to be identified with Iraqi aggression. In sharp contrast, guerrillas under the direction of the Iraqi branch of the Kurdish Democratic Party have taken advantage of the absence of Ba'athist forces (who have joined the fighting against Iran further south) in order to renew their autonomy drive against the central government.

The Azerbaijani question

The Azeri Turks inhabit the region encompassing north-western Iran and the adjacent border area within the Soviet Union. In the former area, they constitute the largest ethnic minority with a population variously estimated at between five and ten million. Though retaining a separate linguistic and ethnic identity, they are, unlike the Kurds and Baluchis, adherents to the Shi'ah sect. The history of the Azeri Turks (or Azerbaijanis as they are more commonly called) has been a turbulent one. In 1907, when Persia was partitioned between the British and the Russians, Azerbaijan fell under the jurisdiction of the latter and remained within the Tsarist sphere until 1918. With the re-occupation of northern Iran by the Red Army in 1942, Iranian Azerbaijan was again brought under effective Russian (i.e. Soviet) political control.

---

1 The national organization of the *Fedayeen Khalq*, for example, has committed a non-Kurdish contingent of its members to fighting. At the same time, the KDPI is reported to have been infiltrated by individuals acting on the behest of the *Tudeh* party. See *Kurdistan News and Comment*, no. 2, London, September/October 1979; cited in Andrew Whitley, *op.cit.*, p 251. In the middle of 1980 there was speculation that the government's prior reluctance to strike at the KDPI's northern strongholds in Mahabad, Bukan and Sardasht stemmed from the desire to co-opt the more moderate elements of that organization into its struggle against *Komala* military concentrations in southern Kurdistan (*Times*, 12 August 1980).

The early establishment of an Azerbaijan SSR was regarded as providing at least some nominal expression to the claims of Azeri nationalism — albeit within the context of a Soviet state structure. In the Iranian sector, the indigenous resistance movements (which staged two abortive uprisings in 1920-21 and 1945-46) were unable to extract any major political concessions from the central government. During the latter period, the Soviet leadership abetted separatist movements both in Azerbaijan and Kurdistan as a means of directly pressuring the weakened Tehran regime into acceding to its programme of economic and political demands.[1] Clearly the most significant of these was the proposal to create a Soviet-Iranian oil consortium (with Moscow exercising 51 per cent control) for the exclusive exploration and extraction of oil in north-western Iran. In late 1945, a Soviet-backed Autonomous Republic of Azerbaijan was established amidst growing Western demands for implementation of the previously agreed scheme for the evacuation of Soviet troops from northern Iran six months after the cessation of hostilities in Europe (i.e. the Tripartite Treaty of 1942). A virtual ultimatum from President Truman, coupled with skilful diplomatic manoeuvrings on the part of the then Iranian Prime Minister,[2] provided the impetus which brought about the complete withdrawal of Soviet forces in 1946. The end of the crisis (i.e. the collapse of the separatist regime) came when elements of the Iranian Army were moved back into Azerbaijan and Kurdistan on the pretext of supervising the forthcoming round of parliamentary elections.

Under the Shah, the Azerbaijanis, many of whom had moved to the major urban centres of the south-central regions, appear to have encountered less socio-economic and administrative discrimination than did other ethnic groups. They were strongly represented in the military and the civil service, as well as within both the private sector and the professional classes. The fear of nationalist fragmentation, however, prompted the government to proscribe the use of the Azeri Turkish language in educational institutions and the media.

The revolution of 1979 served to sharpen the differences between the Azerbaijanis and the central government. Indeed, this rift may

---

1 See Sepehr Zabih, *The Communist Movement in Iran*, University of California Press, Berkeley, California, 1966, pp 71-122ff.

2 For a more detailed consideration of these events see Shahram Chubin and Sepehr Zabih, *The Foreign Relations of Iran: A Developing State in a Zone of Great-Power Conflict*, University of California Press, Berkeley, California, 1974, pp 38-42. Prime Minister Ahmad Ghavam, a senior Iranian statesman whose reputation dated back to the constitutional movement in the early 1900's, made tactical negotiating concessions on both the oil and Azerbaijan issues in order to attain the pre-eminent goal of a Soviet military withdrawal. This compromise was at the heart of the bilateral agreement concluded in Moscow on 4 April 1946. To the surprise of few observers, the nationwide parliamentary elections held following the Soviet evacuation produced a *Majlis* which refused to endorse the terms of the draft treaty. At that stage, however, the Soviet Union was not in a position to re-introduce its forces into the country without fear of a direct confrontation with the USA.

contain the most serious potential threat to the Khomeini regime for, as one observer has put it, the Azerbaijanis' dispute with the government is 'not just a question of regional rights or autonomy, although these enter into it, but a different view of the revolution and its future'.[1]

The focal points of opposition in Azerbaijan centre around Ayatollah Shariat-Madari and the political party which supports him — the MPRP (Muslim People's Republican party) — led by Abdolhassan Rostamkhani. The first eruption of this opposition movement came in December 1979 over the issue of the new Constitution. Unlike the Kurds or the Baluchis, Azerbaijani participation in the referendum boycott (2-3 December)[2] stemmed not primarily from the establishment of Shi'ism as the state religion (although Shariat-Madari did point out that the Constitution failed to acknowledge the fact that about half the Iranian population had different linguistic and/or religious inclinations). On one level, the heated, often violent, national debate over the final draft of the Constitution may be regarded as a stark reflection of the contending perspectives on 'the revolution and its future' as personified in Ayatollahs Khomeini and Shariat-Madari. Whereas the former has been the prime exponent of the avowed imperative of 'Islamic modernization', the latter has forcefully argued that a secular revival is the essential prerequisite for the rejuvenation of the Iranian economy. In terms of the mechanics of government, Shariat-Madari viewed the creation of the post of *Wali-Faqih* — presumably tailored to Khomeini's own envisaged role — as being irreconcilable with the constitutional assertion of the 'national sovereignty of the people'. In apparent retaliation for his participation in the anti-referendum campaign, Revolutionary Guards attacked the Qom home of Ayatollah Shariat-Madari on 5 December. This incident, in turn, precipitated a wave of demonstrations and violent clashes with Khomeini supporters in Tabriz, as well as renewed demands for regional autonomy.

Ayatollah Khomeini's subsequent attempt to dissolve all minority parties (beginning with the MPRP) prompted Shariat-Madari to accuse him openly of propelling Iran towards 'dictatorship'. In characteristic style, Khomeini responded by accusing the USA, Israel and other 'godless people who opposed Islam' of perpetrating the disruption in Tabriz. The dispatch of three high-level delegations to Azerbaijan in the first half of December, though unsuccessful, was a reflection of the priority accorded this ethnic minority question by the Tehran regime. On 13

---

1 *Guardian*, 10 December 1979.

2 It has been estimated that this MPRP-led boycott resulted in a voter turnout within Azerbaijan of little more than 20 per cent.

December 1979, 700,000 people marched through Tabriz in support of Shariat-Madari and the ten point programme drawn up by the MPRP.[1] The onset of the new year witnessed the eruption of yet another bout of escalating violence involving MPRP supporters and Revolutionary Guards. In rapid response, pressure on the MPRP by government forces was increased; on 11 January, *Pasdarans* raided party headquarters, killing four men on the spot with eleven subsequent executions. Little more than a week later, twenty-five Iranian Air Force personnel were arrested at their Tabriz base (four were later executed) on charges of supplying the MPRP with arms and planning a coup. A major political development in January was the apparent withdrawal of Shariat-Madari's support from the MPRP. Whether this action was taken in deference to Khomeini's wishes or in an effort to forestall further violence remains a point of contention. Though the withdrawal of Ayatollah Shariat-Madari served to defuse the immediate prospects of civil war, the trend towards greater nationalist fragmentation within Iran — exacerbating the danger of outside power manipulation and/or direct involvement — continues unabated. Given the recently more assertive nature of its policy towards areas adjacent to its frontier, the attitude of the Soviet Union towards this process will be considered more fully later.

The Baluchi question

The Baluchis are a Sunni Moslem ethnic group inhabiting some quarter million square miles within the territories of Iran, Pakistan and Afghanistan. In Iran, they constitute one of the five major ethnic minorities (numbering roughly 550,000) and occupy the south-eastern region of the country. Since the late nineteenth century, the Baluchis have pressed for an independent homeland with their most recent uprising occurring in Pakistan in 1974.

Under Pahlavi rule, the range of political activities open to the Baluchis was severely circumscribed, though attempts were made to incorporate them into the framework of socio-economic change through such mechanisms as road and infra-structural development. During the 1974 crisis in Pakistan, the Shah lent active military support to the Bhutto government in its successful suppression of the Baluchi separatist movement operating within its borders.

---

1 *Keesing's Contemporary Archives*, 1980, pp 30309-30310. At the time of this public unrest within Azerbaijan over the Constitutional referendum, Shaikh Ezzedin Hosseini, spiritual leader of the Kurdish Democratic Party, issued a statement supporting the 'legitimate demands' of the Azerbaijani people for national autonomy; *Observer*, 9 December 1979.

With the Iranian Revolution and the concomitant fragility of regional control exercised by the central government, the potential for Baluchi agitation has increased. This unrest has been manifest at both the provincial and national levels. A major source of provincial instability remains the long-standing rivalry between the Baluchis and the Sistanis. In contrast to the former, the latter are Shi'ah Persians with an overall population approximating 110,000. The special privileges which the Sistanis continue to enjoy under the theocratic (Shi'ah) regime in Tehran has been the precipitant of several violent incidents between the two ethnic minority groups. The most serious of these outbreaks occurred between 20-22 December 1979 in the provincial capital of Zahidan. On that occasion, the central government was prompted to dispatch forces to the area in order to restore control. Earlier in the same month, the Baluchis, as previously described, participated in the boycott of the new Islamic Constitution along with the Kurds and the Azerbaijanis.[1] Under the religious leadership of Mowlawi Abdul-Aziz Mollazadeh and his Ettehadol Moslemin Party, Baluchi opposition to the Draft Constitution stemmed from the document's pronounced hostility to any form of regional autonomy, in general, and its establishment of Shi'ism as the state religion, in particular. Relations with the Tehran regime remain tense owing to the failure of the revolutionaries to fulfil their earlier pledges of cultural equality and augmented financial assistance. As in Kurdistan and Azerbaijan, an additional factor exacerbating ties with the central government is the continued stationing of *Pasdarans* within the province.

At the rhetorical level, the response of the Khomeini regime to the unrest in Baluchistan has been to accuse 'foreigners and trouble-makers'[2] of intervening in Iranian affairs, while a Sistani leader has more explicitly laid blame on the USA and Soviet backed insurgents. Other internal opposition groups have been accused of fomenting civil disorder. In a statement apparently anticipating further disturbances in Baluchistan, Ayatollah Khomeini has alluded to the possibility of future interference by the *Mojahedin* and *Fedayeen Khalq* in Baluchi affairs.[3]

1 At the time of the referendum (2-3 December), Iranian officials in Baluchistan predicted a voter turnout as low as 3-4 per cent; reported in the *Guardian*, 3 December 1979.

2 *International Herald Tribune*, 28 December 1979.

3 *SWB* (ME/6455/i), 26 June 1980.

The problem of Baluchi secessionism, as previously noted, involves three frontiers. At present, an uprising in Iran or Pakistan would invite the co-operation of both governments in quelling the disturbance. Khomeini's interests, in this matter, parallel those of the Shah. Although it has recently moved to establish closer direct links with the Baluchi separatists,[1] the attitude of the Soviet Union towards such a prospective development — not to mention its desire to foster it — remains a major point of contention.

---

1 According to one source, these ties include the military training of over 3,000 men as well as the education of thousands of Baluchi students in the Soviet Union.

2 Northern Arabia and the Upper Gulf

Territorial disputes and irredentist claims

Iraq's claim to the Kuwaiti islands of Warbah and Bubiyan

On 19 June 1961, Kuwait became an independent sovereign state following the mutually agreed termination of the 1899 bilateral agreement which had established it as a British protectorate. Within a week, the then President of Iraq, Major-General Abdal-Karim Qasim, triggered a crisis when he unexpectedly laid claim to it at a press conference with the dramatic announcement that Kuwait constituted 'an integral part of Iraq'.[1] The basis of the Iraqi claim stemmed from the fact that Kuwait had been a district of the Ottoman Empire under the indirect administration of the governor of the Basrah *wilayat*. As a result, Qasim asserted that with the dissolution of that empire in the aftermath of World War I, Iraq had legally succeeded to the Turkish territorial sovereignty, or suzerainty, over Kuwait. Moreover, in an attempt to demonstrate that the Iraqi claim to sovereignty had been continuous since that time, it was noted that the Qasim announcement was not without precedent: it was observed that during the latter part of the inter-war period, King Ghazi had been moved to demand its outright annexation in various

---

1 For a more extended historical discussion of this period see Husain M. Al-Baharna, *The Legal Status of the Arabian Gulf States*, Manchester University Press, Manchester, 1968, pp 250-58; Majid Khadduri, *Republican Iraq: A Study in Iraqi Politics since the Revolution of 1958*, Oxford University Press, London, 1969, pp 166-73.

public statements. The Iraqi government's legal position in this dispute suffered from the fact that Turkey, both in the Treaties of Sèvres (1920) and Lausanne (1923), had renounced claim to any territories lying outside the frontiers established by those international agreements. As such, it proved increasingly difficult for Iraq to lay sovereign claim to a territorial possession which Turkey had not transferred to it. With that realization, the avowed basis of the Qasim government's spurious claim to Kuwait shifted from historical/legal to overtly political considerations.[1]

Rumours of an impending Iraqi military move prompted the Shaikh of Kuwait to invoke the bilateral defence pact concluded upon the termination of the 1899 agreement on 30 June 1961. Accordingly, the British government despatched a contingent of troops from Kenya to Kuwait on the following day. Though Britain and Kuwait appear to have been in accord that this deployment was necessary to deter any Iraqi military provocations on the border, it has been questioned whether the Qasim government in fact contemplated such action.[2] On 2 July, Kuwait, with British backing, approached the United Nations for membership and simultaneously asked that the Security Council consider the imminent threat which Iraq posed to its territorial integrity. The membership request was blocked by the Soviet Union on 7 July on the grounds that the 1961 defence agreement with Britain constituted undue foreign political influence in its internal affairs. Two weeks later, Kuwait was admitted to the Arab League in the face of vociferous Iraqi opposition. At that time, Kuwait asked the Secretary-General of the League for assistance so that the British force stationed on its borders could be replaced by an Arab one. Agreement on this was reached on 12 August with the completion of the withdrawal of British troops having been effected by 10 October. In their place, a 3,000-strong Arab League contingent composed of Saudi, Egyptian, Syrian and Jordanian forces was positioned in the country.

The motivations underlying Qasim's revival of this irredentist claim were twofold. Of primary significance was undoubtedly Kuwait's vast known and projected petroleum reserves; in 1960 its total oil production was already in excess of eighty million tons. With rumours circulating in the spring of 1961 that Kuwait intended to join the British Commonwealth upon her independence,[3] there was the feeling within Iraq (shared by Nasser) that Kuwait should break free from the British

1 *Ibid.*, p 168.

2 Edith and E.F. Penrose, *Iraq: International Relations and National Development*, Ernest Benn, London, 1978, pp 276, 293 (footnote 6).

3 Richard Gott, 'The Kuwait Incident', in D.C. Watt (ed.), *Survey of International Affairs, 1961*, Royal Institute of International Affairs, pp 522-23.

orbit and become part of some form of Arab regional union. As part of such a political alignment, it was argued that the large revenues derived from the exploitation of Kuwait's oil resources could be used to further the pan-Arabist cause in world politics. Of course the Qasim regime saw Baghdad rather than Cairo as the natural epicentre of such a political movement.

Apart from the consideration of control over Kuwaiti oil, it has been argued that Qasim was prompted to act owing to the state of Iraqi domestic politics in 1961. With increasing internal opposition being mounted to his regime, it is evident that the Kuwait incident was regarded, at least in part, as a means of shifting the focus of a politically fragmented nation from domestic to foreign affairs.[1]

In the aftermath of the so-called Ramadan Revolution of 8 February 1963, the newly-installed Iraqi government made clear its desire to ease tensions and normalize relations with Kuwait. Negotiations during the ensuing months culminated in the accord of 4 October 1963 whereby Iraq officially recognized the independence of Kuwait and confirmed the borders as defined in the 1932 Exchange of Letters[2] between the then Prime Minister of Iraq and the Ruler of Kuwait. This was done in return for the promise of Kuwaiti economic assistance. The 1963 agreement also included a provision for the creation of a joint commission to reach a final delimitation of their common frontier. During the course of those negotiations between 1964 and 1967 the terms of the discussion shifted significantly. The Iraqi delegation affirmed that the revolutionary government's recognition of Kuwait in 1963, though admittedly motivated by the desire to end the political isolation of Iraq through the renunciation of Qasim's maximalist demands, should not be construed as a blanket acceptance on Iraq's part of the territorial *status quo*.

Increasingly, the geographical focus of Iraqi attention, as evidenced in its declaratory policy, focussed upon Warbah and Bubiyan — two sparsely inhabited islands located little more than a kilometre from Iraq's ten nautical-mile stretch of coastline along the Persian Gulf. The question of jurisdictional rights over those islands had been the subject of discussions as early as 1951 when Iraq claimed that the protection of the port of Umm Qasr demanded that it exercise control over Warbah. Three years later, during the course of negotiations concerning plans to provide Kuwait with water from the Shatt al-Arab, the Iraqi claim was broadened to include the Kuwaiti coastal strip just south of Umm Qasr.

1   Khadduri, *op.cit.*, in note 1, p 168.

2   See al-Baharna, *loc.cit.*

28

Although the British government is reported to have suggested a *quid pro quo* arrangement (i.e. the provision of water from the Shatt al-Arab in return for the long-term leasing of Warbah to Iraq), Kuwait rejected the possibility of such a move in 1956.[1] It cited the fact that the 1932 Exchange of Letters had unequivocally designated Warbah, Bubiyan and several other islands in the northwest corner of the Gulf as being under Kuwaiti sovereignty. Given the suspicion surrounding Iraqi intentions any erosion of this position was deemed unacceptable. This line, though not always easy to sustain in practice, has been continuously pursued by the Kuwaiti government since that time.

Hopes for a negotiated settlement of this border dispute were raised with the return of the Ba'athists to power in 1968. It was recalled that during their brief tenure of office in 1963 they had been responsible both for according diplomatic recognition to Kuwait and repudiating Qasim's maximalist territorial demands. This belief was buttressed by Kuwait's evident willingness to diplomatically support Iraq in its dispute with Iran over the Shatt al-Arab.[2] Events took a rather different turn in April 1969, however, when Iraq took full advantage of the perception of a heightened Iranian threat to again press its request for the right to station its forces on Kuwaiti soil so as to protect the area adjacent to Umm Qasr.

A high-ranking diplomatic mission despatched to Kuwait under the direction of the Iraqi Defence and Interior Ministers placed the Kuwaiti government in a difficult position. Having been advised of a supposedly impending outbreak of hostilities between Iran and Iraq, Kuwait was now being asked to lend indirect assistance to a fellow member of the Arab League against an adversary whose declaratory policy (i.e. the Shah's characterization of Iran's incipient regional role in the wake of the 1968 British announcement) had raised serious questions as to its long-term aspirations and intentions in the Gulf. As with its staunch support of the Palestinian cause, the Kuwaiti leadership believed that at least the *perception* of its support for Iraq and this Iran-Arab dispute was important in order to maintain its credibility within the Arab world. An added consideration was the knowledge of what an alienated, ideologically antagonistic Iraq could attempt in the way of domestic destabilization (e.g. internal subversion via the Iraqi-oriented Palestinian factions) should Kuwait prove less forthcoming on this issue. The combination of these factors prompted it to accede to the Iraqi request during the ministerial meeting held at the height of the Shatt al-Arab crisis. The so-called 'unwritten agreement' which emerged from those

1 Majid Khadduri, *Socialist Iraq: A Study in Iraqi Politics Since 1968*, Middle East Institute, Washington, DC, 1978, p 154.

2 *Ibid.*, p 155.

discussions granted Iraq permission to temporarily station forces on the Kuwaiti side of the border so as to permit a forward defence of Umm Qasr.[1]

Although Kuwait's tacit approval of this scheme had been obtained at a moment of heightened border tension between Iraq and Iran, the Ba'athist regime in Baghdad sought to maintain Iraqi forces on Kuwaiti soil so long as the Shatt al-Arab dispute remained unresolved. Border skirmishing resulted from the Iraqi attempt on 20 March 1973 to augment their presence in the disputed area through the occupation of the Kuwaiti police post at al-Samtah. Though the immediate precipitant of this incident was control over the coastal area south of Umm Qasr, the underlying issue was clearly the question of jurisdiction over Warbah and Bubiyan Islands. Iraq's pursuit of this territorial claim was motivated by three inter-related sets of political and economic factors.

Of immediate concern to Baghdad was the necessity of obtaining a deep-water port through which its burgeoning oil exports could pass.[2] The expansion of the North Rumaila field in the southern part of the country during this period underscored the inadequacies of the existing Iraqi port system[3] as a conduit for this augmented export trade. Within this context, Iraq was determined to extend and consolidate control over the outlets for its oil exports. In particular, it sought a favourable resolution of the border dispute with Kuwait so that it might then construct a deep-water terminal off the shore of Bubiyan.[4] The development of such access routes — with their obvious commercial and political implications — was regarded in Baghdad as being wholly consonant with the emergence of Iraq as a major Gulf power. In various public statements, the Iraqi Foreign Minister made clear that one of the prerequisites for the assumption of such a role (i.e. thereby allowing it to mount a credible challenge to Iran for regional pre-eminence) was the extension of its coastline. Establishing such an extension of its

1 *Ibid.*, p 156.

2 With large areas of the country yet to be explored, Iraqi officials have speculated that actual reserves may be twice as large as those already proven. This would place Iraq second only to Saudi Arabia in total reserves within OPEC. In terms of production, Iraq supplanted Kuwait as OPEC's third largest producer in 1975 (behind Saudi Arabia and Iran). With a total volume approaching four million barrels/day, the Iranian crisis made Iraq the second largest producer within the organization.

3 The three main Iraqi ports are: Fao (situated at the swampy and alluvial mouth of the Shatt al-Arab); Basrah (located less than 100 kilometres from the Gulf on the Shatt, it is unable to accommodate vessels larger than 30,000 tons dead-weight); and Umm Qasr (the new port located on a tidal estuary commanded by Warbah and Bubiyan Islands).

4 Iraq's continuing pursuit of this goal is linked to its desire to reduce the country's dependence upon the pipeline through Syria for the export of its oil to the Mediterranean.

coastal area would, in turn, bolster Iraq's claim to a large share of the Gulf's undemarcated continental shelf (as shall be discussed below).

The border incident of 20 March was followed by the arrival of the Iraqi Foreign Minister in Kuwait on 6 April for discussions. Basing his argument on political rather than legal grounds, the Foreign Minister reiterated Iraq's claim to Bubiyan, Warbah and the coastal area adjacent to them. Though Kuwait continued to cling to the 1963 accord (ostensibly confirming the 1932 Exchange of Letters), Iraq maintained that neither was an internationally binding legal agreement. Indeed, the 1963 agreement was depicted as merely a recognition of Kuwait's independence rather than an acceptance of the territorial *status quo*. In response to an earlier Iraqi request for a deep-water terminal at the head of the Gulf, Kuwait is reported to have indicated that though the waters surrounding Bubiyan were too shallow to accommodate such an installation, it was prepared to allow Iraq pipeline passage rights across its territory for the eventual link-up to an offshore terminal.[1] With Iraq submitting an unacceptable counter-proposal, the three-day mission of the Iraqi Foreign Minister ended under the continuing shadow of deadlock.[2] A second round of negotiations the following August similarly foundered upon Iraq's demand that Kuwait should extend its long-term leases over both Bubiyan and Warbah.[3]

With the conclusion of the Algiers agreement in March 1975 ending the Shatt al-Arab dispute between Iraq and Iran, Iraq found it increasingly difficult to justify the continuing presence of its forces on the Kuwaiti coastal strip south of Umm Qasr. Following the visit of President Sadat to Kuwait and Baghdad on 12-16 May, it was reported that Kuwait had moderated her negotiating stance to the extent that she was now willing to discuss the leasing of certain territory in return for water-bearing Iraqi territory adjacent to its dry interior.[4]

Iraq's announcement in July 1977 of its intention to withdraw its forces from Kuwait was linked to its desire to assume a more active regional political role. Such a possibility had in the past been precluded by the pursuit of its territorial claim on Kuwait — and the suspicions as to the ultimate nature of Iraqi intentions which it had aroused amongst the other littoral states of the Gulf. Since the Sadat initiative and the conclusion of the Camp David accords, the primary focus of Baghdad's diplomatic offensive has been the attempt to establish Iraq as the undis-

1 *MEED*, 23 March 1973.

2 *Arab Report and Record*, 1973, p 157; *Economist*, 7 April 1973.

3 *MEED*, 24 August 1973.

4 *Keesing's Contemporary Archives*, 1975, p 27285.

puted leader of the Rejection Front. The political isolation of Egypt — the traditional centre of the Arab world — is viewed as a way of further enhancing Iraq's position within the region. The domestic complement to this policy has been the Ba'athist crackdown on the Iraqi Communist Party. This has served as a means of signalling to the Gulf's conservative monarchical regimes that Iraq is altering the nature of its relationship with the Soviet Union and that it shares the concern of the other regimes over this extra-regional ideological threat.[1]

In much the same way, its subsequent break with the post-revolutionary theocratic regime in Tehran has been politically manipulated by Iraq to underscore the mutuality of interest which the Arab Gulf states have in opposing this new ideological/sectarian threat. The revival of the Iranian claim to Bahrain (see p 41) was met by the Iraqi pledge to counter militarily any such attempt. The concomitant pursuit of 'security consultations' with other Gulf regimes have been motivated primarily by the Iraqi desire to minimize superpower and any other extra-regional involvement in Gulf politics as a new regional security regime begins to take shape. This places Iraq at odds both with Oman (which has recently been pushing its own proposal to guarantee the security of the Straits of Hormuz while at the same time being mooted as a possible host country for a direct American military presence) and Egypt, which now avowedly seeks to supersede Iran as the 'stabilizing' force in the region. Within this context, Iraq has sought to effect a modest *rapprochement* with the monarchical regimes south of it — Saudi Arabia and Kuwait. The dispute over Warbah and Bubiyan remains dormant as Iraq again faces the possibility of hostilities with Iran. Unlike 1969, it is interesting to note that during the current breach in relations Iraq has not requested permission to station its forces in Kuwait to defend Umm Qasr. Such a move would be sure to revive Kuwaiti fears of creeping annexation by Iraq.

Another indication of the improvement in relations between Baghdad and Kuwait — however transitory — was the report in late 1979 that the two parties had concluded an agreement giving Iraq access to the deep-water facilities at the Kuwait port of Mina Shuwaikh.[2] If actually implemented, this should go far in relieving the congestion at Umm Qasr and Basrah, a circumstance which Iraq has seized upon in the past to justify its claim to Bubiyan and Warbah.

---

1 In this regard, it is important to note Iraq's strong condemnation of Soviet behaviour in Afghanistan since the April 1978 coup, its recent split with the PDRY, and consistent support for Somalia in its differences with Ethiopia.

2 *MEED*, 9 November 1979.

Despite this turn of events, the primary long-term factor in Kuwaiti foreign and defence planning remains its unsettled border dispute with Iraq. In the final analysis, with total armed forces numbering only 11,100 servicemen,[1] Kuwait's security rests on the tacit assumption that none of its more powerful neighbours would allow any other country to militarily move against it. The immediate consequence of the Iranian Revolution has been to create a certain consonance of interests between Kuwait and Iraq. At the same time, the large-scale transfer of funds out of the country in the aftermath of the Iranian Revolution and the expulsion of the special representative of Ayatollah Khomeini on charges of fomenting unrest among the Shi'ah minority,[2] *inter alia*, are indicative of the fact that, within Kuwait, concern has again shifted to the problems of internal stability. Indeed, given the overlapping ethnic, tribal and sectarian cleavages within the country, fears have been expressed concerning the potential development of incidents of the type which have come to characterize the Lebanese Civil War. This new internal dimension further increases the Kuwaiti desire to be seen as co-operating with a 'moderated' Iraq. And yet, the factors which have brought about this new relationship are tempered by others (e.g. the Ba'athist ideological commitment to territorial and political amalgamation within the Arab world) which militate against its long-term viability.[3]

The Saudi-Iraqi border

The delimitation of the territorial boundary between Saudi Arabia and Iraq was accomplished by the Treaty of Muhammarah in May 1922. The protocol attached to the Treaty created a 2,500 square-mile Neutral Zone, similar to the one between Saudi Arabia and Kuwait, to ensure that the Bedouin tribes operating in that area would not be traversing international borders in their migratory movements.[4] According to this agreement, no military or permanent buildings were to be erected in the zone and the nomadic tribes of both countries were to have unimpeded access to its pastures and wells. This was followed in

1 *The Military Balance 1979-80*, IISS, London, 1979.

2 *Financial Times*, 28 September 1980.

3 The aftermath of the conflict with Iran, for example, may witness the revival of Iraq's claim to Bubiyan and Warbah under the rubric of pan-Arabism. Having consistently attempted to frame the nature of the conflagration with the Khomeini regime in these terms, Baghdad may attempt to legitimize the positioning of Iraqi forces on the islands by asserting that their presence at these strategic points is essential for the defence of the Arab nation.

4 Each Bedouin group claims a tribal *dira* or migratory route within which they enjoy access rights to pasturage and water. The area encompassing the Saudi-Iraqi Neutral Zone has in the past been under the control of the Shammar and Anazah tribes from Hail (Saudi Arabia).

May 1938 by an agreement which provided for the joint administration of the Neutral Zone. During this period, relations between Saudi Arabia and Iraq were strained owing to inter-dynastic competition and sectarian differences. Though the socialist revolution in July 1958 ousted the rival Hashemite regime in Baghdad, it created in the process a far more profound ideological threat from the Saudi perspective. Iraqi support for radical political movements in the Gulf, as well as its relationship with the Soviet Union, precluded the possibility of closer ties between the two countries throughout the 1960's and early 1970's.

As discussed above, the price which Iraq paid for the pursuit of such an ideologically inspired diplomatic posture was its political isolation within the Gulf. In these terms, the post-1975 moderation of Iraqi policy (as evidenced in the Algiers Agreement and the adoption of a more forthcoming attitude in its border talks with Kuwait) was clearly linked to its desire to assume a more active regional political role. The improvement of relations with Saudi Arabia was a major component of that process. On 2 July 1975 it was announced in Riyadh that agreement between Saudi Arabia and Iraq had been reached on the division of their Neutral Zone.[1] Under the agreement, the unexploited oil-rich zone was to be equally divided by a line drawn as straight as possible to the existing border.

Though Iraq broke out of its political isolation with these moves in 1975, it did not re-enter the mainstream of Arab politics until assuming leadership of the Rejection Front in the wake of the Camp David summit in 1978. The other component of this Iraqi diplomatic offensive was its participation in Gulf 'security consultations' with Iran and Saudi Arabia. The three day visit of the Saudi Defence and Aviation Minister, Prince Sultan Ibn Abd al Aziz, to Baghdad in early April 1978 was characterized by the Kuwaiti daily As-Siyassa as aimed at 'establishing some sort of co-operation in security among the three Gulf countries'.[2] In its discussions with Saudi Arabia after 1978, Iraq is reported to have urged that Riyadh should both adopt a more non-aligned diplomatic posture and move to limit the influx of non-Arab immigrant labour.[3] Bilateral consultations intensified in the volatile political atmosphere following the tumultuous events of January-February 1979 in Tehran. High level discussions between Iraq and Saudi Arabia on Gulf security (specifically, the implications of the Iranian crisis) were reported to have taken place in Riyadh around the time of the collapse of the short-lived Bakhtiar government.[4]

1   Keesing's Contemporary Archives, 1975, p 27285.

2   As-Siyassa, 19 April 1978; cited in Arab Report and Record, 1978, p 283.

3   The Baghdad Observer, 12 September 1978, accused the USA and its South Korean 'agents' of 'endeavouring to use a new form of indirect intervention through its world agents and tools' to maintain the flow of oil from the Gulf; cited in Arab Report and Record, 1978, p 636.

4   Financial Times, 5 February 1979.

The combined impact of the Camp David Accords and the Iranian Revolution (i.e. Tehran's call for the overthrow of the Saudi regime) have served to push Saudi Arabia into a loose tactical alliance with Iraq for the moment. In mid-September 1979 it was reported that the two countries had concluded a security agreement which included plans for intelligence co-ordination as well as possible extradition procedures. With large Shi'ah populations in southern Iraq and Saudi Arabia's Eastern province,[1] both governments share an interest in stemming the possibility of a sectarian resurgence under the direction of the year old theocratic Shi'ah regime in Tehran. An additional Saudi fear recently expressed is that, given the close relationship existing between the PLO and the Iranian government, the considerable Palestinian presence in the Arab Gulf states might be transformed into a major destabilizing force. This places an additional strain on the Saudi-American relationship — for it is accepted in Riyadh that only Washington can defuse the Palestinian issue by compelling Israel to make the requisite concessions. Arafat has presumably cultivated ties with the Khomeini regime, in part to ensure that Saudi Arabia continues to sense such pressure.

Within the Saudi-Iraqi 'security alliance' one finds each party trying to out-manoeuvre the other. The Saudis desire both to counterbalance Iran and moderate Iraqi behaviour through this relationship. And yet the Saudi ability to affect the latter might well demand that it distance itself from Washington (i.e. the adoption of a more overtly neutralist stance) or, at the very least, that the maintenance of its diverse links with the USA be placed on a more tacit footing. As with the new Iraqi relationship with Kuwait, the factors which have brought Riyadh and Baghdad together in the last eighteen months are tactical and perhaps of a shorter political half-life than is apparent at present. That said, however, having re-entered the mainstream of Arab Gulf politics after a decade and a half of relative isolation, and now attempting to coalesce regional diplomatic support in the conflict with Iran, it remains unlikely that Iraq will rashly move to alienate the conservative monarchical regimes to its south through the reversion to a more ideologically inspired foreign policy orientation.[2]

---

1 In late November 1979 there was a major clash between the Saudi National Guard and Shi'ah oil workers at Sayhat near Qatif; *MEED*, 7 December 1979.

2 President Saddam Husayn's recent 'Pan-Arab Declaration' is a further indication of Iraq's commitment to a more moderate diplomatic posture during the current period. In that address, he called for pan-Arab unity in the face of new threats and advanced a new 'charter' to regulate inter-Arab relations. Its two main principles are: the rejection of any foreign military presence in the Arab homeland and 'the banning of the use of armed force by any Arab state against any other Arab state and the solution of any disputes that may arise between the Arab countries by peaceful means . . . '; Baghdad Voice of the Masses (in Arabic), 8 February 1980 *SWB*; (ME/6343/A/1-4), 12 February 1980.

The land boundary between Saudi Arabia and Kuwait was delimited by the Treaty of 'Uqair in December 1922. One provision of this agreement established the Kuwait-Saudi Arabia Neutral Zone. Oil production started in this area of shared jurisdiction in 1954 with each side receiving revenues from its designated concessionaire. On 7 July 1965 Kuwait and Saudi Arabia agreed to terminate the temporary provision of the 1922 Treaty and equally partition the Neutral Zone.[1] While the agreement concluded on 18 December 1969 confirmed the demarcation of this land boundary, it was not extended to include their lateral offshore border (see p 39).

Relations between Saudi Arabia and Kuwait have been close since the emergence of the latter as a sovereign state in 1961. At that time, Saudi forces made up the majority of the 3,000 man Arab League contingent despatched to Kuwait to forestall a possible Iraqi military move. Underlying these close ties is the similarity of their domestic structures[2] (i.e. conservative monarchical regimes) and their compatible regional views. The last five years have witnessed only two occasions when there has been a real threat of a deterioration in Saudi-Kuwaiti relations, the first occurring in December 1976 when the Kuwaitis voted for a ten per cent increase in oil prices at the Doha OPEC Conference in opposition to the Saudi proposal for a five per cent increase. A second stressful episode took place in 1977 when Kuwait became the second Arab Gulf state to purchase arms from the Soviet Union.

While concern over developments in Iran since late 1977 has generally led to greater co-operation and consultation amongst the other littoral states of the Gulf, this has been particularly apparent in the attitudes of Saudi Arabia and Kuwait.[3] Like many of the other smaller states in the region (e.g. Dubai, Oman, North Yemen and Bahrain), the removal of Iran from its previous 'stabilizing' role has severely circumscribed Kuwait's long-term foreign policy options to the extent that it now figuratively has nowhere to go other than Saudi Arabia.[4]

---

1 See al-Baharna, *op.cit.*, pp 264-77.

2 This is notwithstanding the Kuwaiti parliamentary experiment of which the Saudis disapproved. Riyadh not only feared the unforeseen political consequences of such an attempt, but moreover, resented the bad light which it cast upon the centralized Saudi system.

3 Following the meeting between Crown Prince Fahd and the Kuwait Premier, Shaikh Saad Abdulla Salem as-Sabah in Riyadh on 2 December 1978, a communiqué was released in which the leaders expressed concern over the 'results that any change in the Iranian regime would have on neighbouring states'; *Arab Report and Record*, 1978, no. 22.

4 For the reasons suggested above, Kuwait's modest *rapprochement* with Iraq remains of a tactical nature.

Continental shelf boundaries

As codified at the 1958 Geneva Conference on the Law of the Sea, 'continental shelf' has been defined as land lying less than 100 fathoms beneath the sea and adjacent to the mainland. With depths rarely exceeding fifty fathoms (100 metres), the entire seabed of the Gulf is considered continental shelf by this legal doctrine.[1] The discovery and exploitation of offshore oil resources over the last quarter century in Gulf waters has added a novel dimension to the already thorny problem of boundary demarcation in the region. Indeed, many disputes over the delimitation of submarine boundaries have arisen as a direct result of overlapping oil concessions. Though none of the Gulf states is a signatory to the 1958 Convention on the Continental Shelf, it is striking when one reflects on the degree to which its central principles (most importantly the one regarding 'equidistance') have been accepted as customary law in the region. The principle of equidistance, as notably exercised in the cases of jurisdictional demarcation in the North Sea, provides for the delimitation of the continental shelf boundary between states according to a line running equidistant to the onshore territorial baseline of each. In the Gulf, owing to the presence of so many small islands, the major problem in implementing this approach has centred upon the determination of baselines. Many conflicts have involved attempts by various littoral states to claim that offshore islands (often themselves the subject of disputed sovereignty) should be given some weight in the determination of their baselines. When even a few additional kilometres could mean a fortune in additional revenues, it is evident that the states involved possess a powerful incentive to maintain their maximalist claims. With that as background, attention will now focus upon the negotiating history and current status of the specific continental shelf boundary lines in the Upper Gulf.

Kuwait-Iraq-Iran boundaries

The demarcation of the submarine boundaries in this northern triangle at the head of the Gulf has remained a continuing source of dispute.[2] Differences first arose in the early 1960s as the result of overlapping oil concessions. Since then, attempts to reach a favourable settlement have foundered in the face of Iraq's continuing claim to the Kuwaiti

---

1   For an extended consideration of the continental shelf concept and its specific application in the Gulf see Ali A. El-Hakim, *The Middle Eastern States and the Law of the Sea*, Manchester University Press, Manchester, 1979.

2   See Shahram Chubin and Sepehr Zabih, *The Foreign Relations of Iran*, University of California Press, Berkeley, California, 1974, pp 279-95.

islands of Bubiyan and Warbah and the intractable state of Iraqi-Iranian relations (until 1975 the focus of which was the Shatt al-Arab waterway dispute).

The establishment of a joint Kuwaiti-Iranian committee in June 1965 to determine their continental shelf boundary was followed in January 1968 by the initialling of an Accord between the two parties. During those deliberations, one of the main difficulties was the reaching of an understanding relating to the onshore baselines which would be used to determine equidistance. In the case of each country, it was argued that one of its prominent nearby islands (i.e. the Iranian island of Kharg and the Kuwaiti island of Failaka) should be considered part of its baseline for such purposes. A compromise on this point allowed both parties to confer to its island 'full effect' (i.e. to incorporate them into their respective baselines). Iraq angrily denounced the Kuwaiti-Iranian agreement on the grounds that it grossly infringed upon its own considerable continental shelf rights in the Gulf. This was reiterated in July 1970 by the Iraqi Foreign Minister following the issue of a joint Kuwaiti-Iranian communiqué which referred to an agreement to accelerate the work of the joint technical committee concerned with the demarcation of their common offshore boundary.[1] The failure to officially confirm the Iran-Kuwait agreement in treaty form has been due to uncertainty as to precisely where that continental shelf boundary line would intersect both the Iraq-Kuwait submarine border (given Iraq's claim to Bubiyan and Warbah) and the Kuwait-Saudi Arabia partitioned zone.

Though the 'Reconciliation' Treaty concluded between Iraq and Iran on the basis of the March 1975 Algiers Agreement contained no explicit mention of continental shelf delimitation, there was considerable hope that the favourable political environment engendered by the Treaty might produce some movement on this issue. The adoption by Iraq of a more 'moderate' foreign policy posture — a move, as already noted, reflecting its desire to re-enter the mainstream of Arab Gulf politics — was taken as further evidence to buttress this belief. With the concomitant improvement in trilateral relations during 1976-78 (e.g. Iraq's participation in 'security consultations') there was speculation that a joint continental shelf boundary agreement might be reached. Without an extension of its shoreline, however, Iraq had very little incentive to move the issue to resolution; indeed its interests lay quite to the contrary. Under these conditions, the issue remained dormant throughout the period between the Algiers Agreement and the Iranian Revolution. With Baghdad's unilateral abrogation of the 1975

---

1   El-Hakim, *op.cit.*, pp 112-13.

Accord[1] and the initiation of hostilities along the Iran-Iraq frontier, the continental shelf dispute has been revived under a wholly new set of political circumstances. Again, the ideological nature of the dispute between Iran and Iraq is such that when activated — as during the period preceding the Autumn 1980 conflict — it tends to encompass the entire range of their bilateral relations.

Iran-Saudi Arabia boundaries

The agreement concerning sovereignty over the islands of al-Arabiyah and Farsi and delimitation of the continental shelf between Saudi Arabia and Iran was concluded on 24 October 1968 and entered force on 29 January 1969.[2] The 1968 agreement is a modification of the median line agreement initialed by the two countries on 13 December 1965. The reluctance of the Iranian government to subsequently ratify this accord was reportedly related to the discovery of major new oil deposits in the Saudi northern zone immediately adjacent to the boundary line. While serving by and large to confirm the median line of 1965, the 1968 Treaty did mark an important variation on the equidistance principle insofar as it altered the former line to Iran's advantage to achieve a more equitable division of the seabed resources.[3]

This agreement is noteworthy in two additional respects. First, in an important precedent, it confirmed the 'half effect' given the Iranian island of Kharg in the determination of that state's baseline. (The 'half effect' principle is a compromise between considering the island as part of the mainland — 'full effect' — or wholly disregarding it for the purpose of continental shelf delimitation — 'no effect').[4] The 1968 Agreement's salient feature was a compromise granting jurisdiction over the islands of Farsi and al-Arabiyah to Iran and Saudi Arabia respectively. One provision conferred to each its own twelve mile territorial sea, a precedent which would subsequently be employed to resolve the status of Dayinnah island in the 1970 Agreement between Abu Dhabi and Qatar (see p 67).

1 *Financial Times*, 18 September 1980.

2 For an analysis of this agreement see Richard Young, 'Equitable Solutions for Offshore Boundaries: The 1968 Saudi Arabia-Iran Agreement', *American Journal of International Law*, 64, no. 1, January 1970, pp 152-57; US Department of State, Office of the Geographer, Bureau of Intelligence and Research, 'Continental Shelf Boundary: Iran-Saudi Arabia', *International Boundary Study: Limits in the Seas*, series A, no. 24, 6 July 1970.

3 *Ibid.*, pp 3-4, 7.

4 *Ibid.*, p 7.

Kuwait-Saudi Arabia boundaries

Though the Agreement of 18 December 1969 established a boundary line in the previously partitioned Neutral Zone between these states (i.e. with the provision of the equal sharing of revenue from oilfields split by it), it was not extended to encompass the adjoining continental shelf. The failure to achieve agreement on the delimitation of this submarine border primarily has been due to the ongoing jurisdictional dispute over the islands of Qaru and Umm al-Maradim. Though the length of this offshore lateral boundary line has yet to be determined, it has been recently reported that the segment which passes through the Safaniya and Khafji oilfields has been accorded *de facto* recognition for a number of years.[1]

With respect to the question of jurisdictional rights over Qaru and Umm al-Maradim,[2] Saudi Arabia apparently considers them to be subject to the same co-sovereignty status as that of the Neutral Zone. In June 1977, following the purchase by Kuwait of Soviet arms and its opposition to the Saudi line at the OPEC Conference in Doha, it was reported that Saudi forces had seized the islands. This assertion was dismissed by an official Kuwaiti source as 'fabricated and baseless'.[3] Nonetheless, it was followed on 17 August by a meeting between Prince Fahd and the Kuwaiti Interior and Defence Minister, Shaikh Saad Abdulla Salem as-Sabah, to 'define the continental shelf in the Partitioned Zone' shared by the two countries.[4]

As discussed above, relations between Saudi Arabia and Kuwait have been traditionally close. Though they suffered a clear setback in 1977, regional political trends (particularly the events in Iran) have since militated in favour of the resumption of the earlier pattern. Kuwait's previous ability to maintain a discrete equidistance from the Gulf's three major powers is clearly no longer possible. Given the profound differences between their domestic structures, Kuwait's *rapprochement* with Iraq arguably offers little more than the hope of a short-term, tactical alliance. This has the effect of accentuating Kuwaiti dependence on Saudi Arabia. Under these conditions of heightened political volatility within the region, both parties possess a powerful incentive to resolve or, at the very least, defer such outstanding bilateral issues as the demarcation of their continental shelf boundary.

1 El-Hakim, *op.cit.*, p 109.

2 Though previously a point of contention with Saudi Arabia, Kuwaiti sovereignty is now acknowledged over the island of Kubr.

3 *Qatar News Agency*, 19 and 21 June (monitored by BBC); cited in Colin Legum, (ed.) *Middle East Contemporary Survey 1976-77*, p 574.

4 *Ibid.*

40

3 The Lower Gulf States

Territorial disputes and irredentist claims

Iran's claim to Bahrain

The bases of Iran's intermittently voiced *revanchiste* claim to Bahrain are both historical and sectarian in origin. Yet it is significant to note that the emphasis accorded to either in Iranian declaratory policy has been largely a function of the nature and character of the Tehran regime at any given point. Thus, whereas the nation's dynastic rulers tended to highlight ancient Persian ties to the island as a justification for its position in the past, the present theocratic regime, swept to power in a wave of resurgent Islamic fundamentalism, has sought to frame the issue primarily in terms of the special affinity between Iran and the Bahrainian archipelago's Shi'ah majority. The timing and vehemence with which the claim has been pressed during various periods has been governed by the complex interplay between the constellation of contending internal political forces within Iran and developments shaping the regional environment as a whole. Given the close link which exists between the character of a regime and its security perspective, it is possible, acknowledging the February 1979 revolution as a watershed in Iranian foreign policy, to delineate two distinct phases in the pursuit of its irredentist claim *vis-à-vis* Bahrain.

Iran's historical ties to Bahrain — utilized as a rationale by the Shah to justify his regime's claim to the archipelago — date from the early

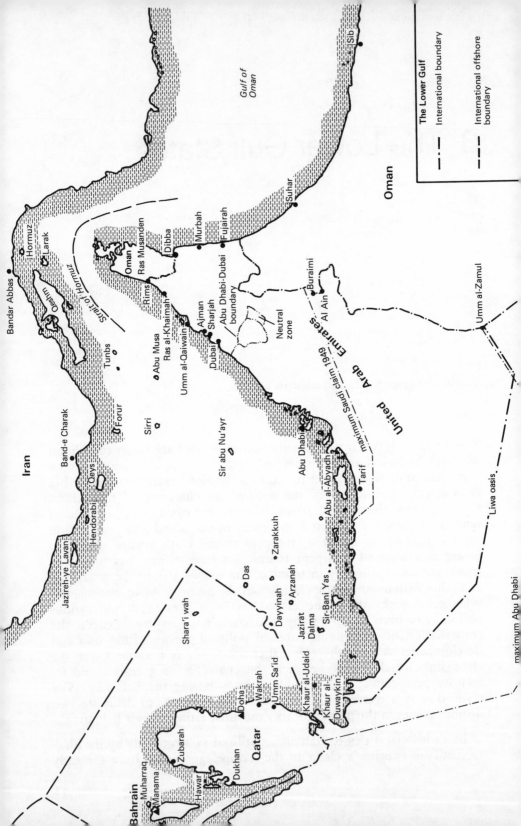

seventeenth century when the Persians successfully expelled the Portuguese occupiers of the islands. After weathering several challenges to its suzerainty from various Arab shaikhdoms of the mainland, Bahrain was finally wrested from Persian control by the powerful 'Utubi rulers of Zubarah on the Qatari coast in 1783.'Utubi sovereignty over Bahrain, as now vested in one of that tribe's leading families, the Al Khalifah, has been continuous since that time.[1]

After 1880, periodic Persian attempts to reassert its authority over the islands were directed towards Britain which, in 1820, had entered into treaty relationships with Bahrain and the other littoral states of the Gulf. Persia's ability to pursue this claim with any vigour, however, was severely circumscribed by its pronounced military weakness. During the oil crisis of 1950, under the reign of Reza Shah, the Anglo-Iranian controversy over Bahrain was revived in the Iranian press as a further manifestation of its hostility toward Britain. By contrast, official reaction remained muted as the Iranian government did not wish to alienate the Americans upon whom it was becoming increasingly dependent for security assistance. As a result, Iranian actions were confined to small-scale gestures to indicate its displeasure over the continuing British relationship with Bahrain. The extent to which the Bahraini dispute was a major factor exacerbating the already fragile set of Iran-Arab relations was manifested in 1957 when renewed Iranian claims triggered strong protests from both Saudi Arabia and, significantly, Egypt.[2]

Remaining relatively dormant after the Iranian government's claims of 1957-58, the Bahraini question next resurfaced in the aftermath of the January 1968 announcement by the British of their decision to withdraw from positions 'East of Suez' by the end of 1971. The announcement, the timing of which clearly caught the Iranians by surprise, was to have considerable ramifications in its policy as it fused the question of Bahrain's status with that of Iran's attitude toward a federation of the Gulf of shaikhdoms.[3] The reassertion of its historical claim to Bahrain necessitated its ongoing opposition to any attempt at federation which might include Bahrain. This wholly negative diplomatic posture had the effect of exacerbating the already delicate state of Iran-Arab relations, raising serious questions in the minds of the smaller littoral states as to Iran's ultimate intentions, and dashing any immediate hopes that there might develop some form of co-operative security

1 For a comprehensive historical account of Iran's historical claim to Bahrain see Hussain M. Al-Baharna, *The Legal Status of the Arabian Gulf States*, chapter 12; J.B. Kelly, 'The Persian Claim to Bahrain', *International Affairs*, 1957, pp 51-70.

2 R.M. Burrell, 'Britain, Iran and the Persian Gulf' in Derek Hopwood (ed.), *The Arabian Peninsula: Society and Politics*, George Allen & Unwin, London, 1972, p 184.

3 See Shahram Chubin and Sepehr Zabih, *The Foreign Relations of Iran*, chapter VI.

system in the wake of the British withdrawal from the region.

Iran's declining material dependency on the United States, as reflected in its shift from grant-aid to credit purchases of American military hardware in 1967, undoubtedly contributed to the Shah's assessment of his increased scope for diplomatic manoeuvre during this crisis. Yet the ability to translate this ostensible potential into influence was hamstrung by the negative, increasingly contradictory nature of Iranian policy. By mid-1969 there was the growing perception in Iran that the credibility of its claim to Bahrain was being eroded by successive political developments in the Gulf and that its continued pursuit would ultimately preclude the possibility, envisaged by the Shah, of Iran's assumption of a predominant regional security role. Having unrealistically revived this dubious historical claim at the time of the British announcement after years of relative neglect, the Shah subsequently found it difficult to shift his stance on this issue as a result of domestic political constraints. Iranian acquiescence in early 1970 to a UN supervised plebiscite in the archipelago, despite the obvious results, was indicative of the Shah's sensitivity to the powerful pan-Iranian political sentiments being voiced internally.[1] The report drafted after the completion of the twenty day UN mission to Bahrain was submitted to the Security Council for consideration on 11 May 1970. It stated that the Bahrainis interviewed by the UN team were 'virtually unanimous in wanting a fully independent sovereign state: the great majority added that this should be an Arab state'.[2] The report's findings were endorsed without dissent by the Security Council on 11 May and approved by the Iranian *Majlis* (186 to 4) three days later. That vote, coupled with the termination of Iranian opposition to the proposed federation of the seven trucial states plus Bahrain and Qatar, made possible a modest *rapprochement* with Saudi Arabia — a development regarded by the Nixon administration as consistent with its evolving 'twin pillars' approach to Gulf security. With the renunciation of its spurious irredentist claim to Bahrain, Iran satisfied the minimum political conditions so as to accord it the legitimacy (in the eyes of other regional actors) to

1 *Ibid.*, pp 219-20. The authors note that the Shah was 'subject to considerable domestic pressures on issues allegedly involving Iran's national heritage. The extreme, often xenophobic, nationalism of both right and left in Iran had manifestly prevented the Shah from acting on this issue at a time when he was politically weak (i.e. prior to the British announcement).' It is significant that once the Shah began to moderate his position on the Bahrain question 'the right wing Pan-Iranist party, which had called for an Iranian invasion of Bahrain in 1961 on the model of India's seizure of Goa, was quickly muzzled'.

2 For the report of the UN mission to Bahrain see Note by the Secretary-General, UN Document, S/9772, 30 April 1970. A senior official at the Iranian Foreign Ministry observed that his nation was 'hurt' by certain 'unnecessary' remarks contained in the report — an apparent reaction to its emphasis on the word 'Arab' in describing the aspirations of the majority of Bahrainis. With respect to the minority of Iranian descent living in Bahrain, the Iranian official said: 'Their safety will be a continuing concern for the Iranian Government'; see *Financial Times*, 4 May 1970.

adopt a more activist security role. At the same time, the altered political atmosphere brought about by this shift in Iranian policy allowed it to press with renewed vigour its claim to the strategically important islands of Abu Musa and the Tunbs in the Strait of Hormuz (see p 56).

Having been ostensibly settled in 1970, the controversy over Bahrain's status curiously re-emerged as an issue of contention in the aftermath of the Iranian Revolution. During that period, those Gulf states with significant Shi'ah populations — specifically, Iraq, Kuwait and Bahrain — became increasingly concerned over statements emanating from various elements of the Tehran ruling circle which called for the 'export' of the Iranian Revolution throughout the region. The dichotomy between the delicately co-existing secular and religious authorities within the country, however, hindered the ability of the surrounding states to ascertain Iranian intentions with any degree of assurance. To be sure, the highly emotive question of transforming the Iranian Revolution into a full-fledged trans-national Shi'ah movement was part of a broader internal power struggle between these contending centres of power.

By far the most inflammatory Iranian statement to emerge after February 1979 came from Ayatollah Sadeq Rouhani, a prominent leader in the Revolution, who baldly reasserted Iran's claim to Bahrain as its 'fourteenth province'.[1] Though considerable concern has been expressed in Bahrain over the domestic implications of the Iranian Revolution, initial reaction, while clearly sympathetic to developments across the Gulf, was confined to small-scale demonstrations in support of Ayatollah Khomeini and calling for the establishment of an Islamic state.[2] In an apparent attempt to distance the Bazargan government from the Rouhani statement, the then Foreign Minister, Ibrahim Yazdi, declared that the Ayatollah's declarations did not represent the 'official' view of Iran and that he 'represents only himself'.[3] This was followed two weeks later by a surprise visit to Bahrain of the Assistant Prime Minister for Public Relations and Transition Affairs, Sadeq

---

1 *MEED*, 22 June 1979, 20 July 1979.

2 *MEED*, 31 August 1979. For a more detailed consideration of the domestic implications of the Iranian revolution in Bahrain see the paper in this series by Avi Plascov.

3 *Le Monde*, 30 September 1979.

Tabatabai, who reportedly sought to reassure the government that Iranian intentions were 'friendly'.[1]

While publicly discounting the seriousness of Iran's renewed irredentist claim, Bahrain did solicit support on the regional level to bolster its political position. The mid-October meeting of Gulf leaders at Taif (Saudi Arabia) to discuss regional security co-ordination was accompanied by the despatch of a number of Saudi naval vessels and a tank brigade to Bahrain. Additional statements of support came from King Hussein and President Sadat, the latter having included an offer of forces.[2] In a move of perhaps even greater long-term political significance, Saudi officials, after years of study, decided to approve the construction of a $1 billion causeway linking Bahrain to the Arab mainland.[3] Renewed political tension between the island state and Iran was apparently the decisive factor in the Saudi decision designed, as one observer put it, to avoid the creation of a 'Cuba' fifteen miles off its shores. While reaffirming the Arab identity of the island, the move is further indicative of the close working relationship existing between these two Gulf states whose ruling families, the Saudis and the Khalifahs, are related.

Questions persist with respect to the factors which reactivated the articulation of Iran's claim to Bahrain in the aftermath of the events of February 1979. Clearly it was a component of the serious debate between contending secular and clerical political authorities over the desirability of promoting the 'export' of Iran's revolutionary expeerience to the surrounding Gulf states. Here, it is interesting to note that although

1 *MEED*, 12 October 1979. It is significant to note that this visit was arranged by President Assad who, given the deterioration in Syria's relations with Iraq, sought to establish a close working relationship with the Bazargan government. The prospects for the creation of a tacit Tehran-Damascus axis based upon a mutual antipathy for Iraq faded, however, when those pro-Syrian elements in a position of authority within Iran were swept from power with the fall of the Bazargan government.

2 Following the Iranian Revolution, President Sadat called for a massive infusion of American arms into Egypt so that it might supersede Iran as the 'stabilizing' power of the region. The ability of Egypt to assume a predominant regional security role of that kind, however, has been severely compromised by its virtual pariah status within the Arab world as a result of the Camp David accords. During the visit of King Khalid to Libya in late September, for example, Colonel Qadhafi took the opportunity to condemn the Egyptian offer to Bahrain as but further evidence of a 'plot' to 'encircle' Saudi Arabia (reported in *Le Monde*, 2 October 1979). Despite his awkward political position in intra-Arab politics, the previous record of Egyptian interventionary actions on behalf of Yemen and Oman reinforced the credibility of the Sadat pledge. The Bahraini Information Minister, Tariq Al-Moayyed, commented that while his country did not face any real external threat 'the statements by the Egyptian Vice President, Hosni Mubarah and Prime Minister Mustafa Khalil about Iranian threats to the Gulf countries show the support Bahrain enjoys at the Arab and regional level'; quoted in *Voice of the Arab World*, November 1979.

3 *New York Times*, 2 December 1979.

Ayatollah Khomeini did issue periodic vague statements calling for a global Islamic upsurgence during that initial post-revolutionary period, he did not specifically associate himself with the Rouhani position on the Bahrain question. The timing and nature of this revival of a previously dormant irredentist claim has prompted some observers to speculate that it may have been motivated by an Iranian desire to counter renewed Arab claims to the three Gulf islands of Abu Musa and Greater and Lesser Tunbs which were occupied by the Shah's forces in 1971.[1] Although it is possible to attribute the impetus underlying Iranian actions to the amalgam of factors suggested above, what is significant is the shift in criteria by which elements within the current theocratic regime sought to publicly justify the revival of its long dormant claim to Bahrain. With a Shi'ah population estimated in excess of fifty per cent, the stability of the island state had the appearance of being particularly vulnerable to the kind of resurgent sectarian politics which the Rouhani statements augured. In sharp contrast to the rationale advanced during the Shah's tenure, the post-revolutionary reassertion of Iran's claim to Bahrain was framed not in terms of the historical Persian connection to the islands but, rather, to the close bond between the Shi'ah populations of the two countries.[2] Following its brief revival in the middle of 1979, the Bahrain question has once again declined in relative salience from the perspective of the Tehran regime. By 1980, more ominous regional developments, in particular the Soviet invasion of Afghanistan and the perception of encirclement which it fostered, and the process of internal fragmentation deriving from revitalized national minority movements were clearly its major preoccupations. Under those circumstances, the stabilization of relations with the Arab states of the lower Gulf, while desirable, was contingent upon a shift in Iranian declaratory policy (i.e. the cessation of calls for the annexation of Bahrain and the 'export' of its revolution). Though moves in that direction temporarily eased the tense state of Iran-Arab relations in the early months of 1980, any discussion of the development of indigenous co-operative security arrangements within the Gulf was precluded by Iranian officials because of the marked differences between the

---

1 *MEED*, 31 August 1979.

2 Previous Iranian references to the sectarian composition of Bahrain were made so as to strengthen its 'historical' claim to the islands by implying that the Shi'ah majority were of Persian origin. In fact, the official 1965 census indicated that a mere four per cent of the population were Iranian.

domestic structures of the states within the region.[1] For the moment, it would appear that with the severe erosion of its position in the Northern Tier owing to the conflict with Iraq, Iran will not needlessly further exacerbate relations with the Arab Gulf states through the pursuit of a wholly specious irredentist claim. Though its reactivation in terms of the priorities of the current Iranian regime is conceivable within the context of a severe deterioration of the Shi'ah position within Bahrain at the hands of the Sunni ruling class — a prospect neither immediate nor likely to become so — the prognosis is that it will remain dormant. That said, an important caveat to this assessment concerns the uncertain future composition of the Tehran regime. Should the more radical theocratic elements, presently in a subordinate position, gain ascendancy as a consequence of the ongoing internal power struggle (i.e. those who would wish to see the Iranian Revolution transformed into a trans-national Shi'ah movement), then the Bahrain question could again become salient as part of a broader effort to destabilize the conservative monarchical Arab states of the lower Gulf.

The dispute between Bahrain and Qatar over Zubarah and the Hawar Islands

Bahrain's claim to Zubarah, a north-western coastal strip on the Qatari Peninsula, is both historical and tribal in nature.[2] As with so many of the territorial disputes in the region, there is a record of attempts on the part of the claimant to have it accorded legal status on the basis of previous occupation. In the case of Zubarah, the claim by the Al Khalifah family is based upon a settlement which they established on that site in 1776 and that was used seventeen years later in their conquest of Bahrain from the Persians. By the last quarter of the nineteenth century nominal Ottoman suzerainty over Qatar, accompanied by increasing British pressure, compelled the Al Khalifah to relinquish control of Zubarah. In 1937 the Al Thani rulers of Qatar, despite the

---

1 In an attempt to improve relations with the UAE, Qatar and Bahrain, the Iranian Ambassador to Kuwait, Ali Shams Ardakani, stated that this government has neither military nor other ambitions in the region. In separate messages conveyed to the rulers of those states the Iranian authorities reportedly affirmed their desire for a different relationship from the alleged 'policy of rivalry' pursued during the Shah's regime; *MEED*, 11 January 1980. This theme was reiterated by Foreign Minister Sadeq Qotbzadeh during his tour of Arab Gulf states in early May 1980; see, for example, his statement in Manama on Iran's relations with Bahrain (*SWB* (ME/6412/A5), 5 May 1980). The improvement of diplomatic relations with adjacent Gulf states clearly remains a divisive issue within Iran's ruling circle. It is significant to note that Tehran broadcast a statement in Arabic by the Islamic Front for the Liberation of Bahrain on the very day of Qotbzadeh's arrival for talks in Manama (*SWB* (ME/6412/A/3), 5 May 1980).

2 See Al-Baharna, *The Legal Status of the Arabian Gulf States*, pp 247-49, 302; J.B. Kelly, 'Sovereignty and Jurisdiction in Eastern Arabia', *International Affairs* 34, no. 1 (January 1958), pp 17-18.

vigorous protest of the Shaikh of Bahrain to Britain, moved to assert their full sovereignty over the Zubarah settlement and its environs along the coast. In addition to the loss of what they considered to be their ancestral home, the Al Khalifah have also sought to substantiate their claim to this territory on the basis of tribal allegiance. Specifically, the Bahrain government has in the past maintained that the Al Nu'aim tribe which settled the area around Zubarah after 1874 have since looked to the Al Khalifah to exercise jurisdiction over them.

A second source of friction between the two countries — again reflecting the historical rivalry and jealousy between the Al Khalifah and the Al Thani — stems from Bahrain's continuing claim to the Hawar Islands situated off the west coast of Qatar. Though Bahrain ownership of Hawar has long been recognised by third parties, its proximity to the peninsula — as well as attempts by Bahrain to attribute continental shelf rights to the reefs and sand islands surrounding it — have precipitated Qatari counter claims.

Despite reports of periodic Kuwaiti and Saudi attempts at mediation in the dispute between Bahrain and Qatar, scant progress has been made in the demarcation of their respective boundaries. The regional political implications of the rift between the two countries was evidenced in 1971 when it greatly contributed to the collapse of the proposed 'Union of Nine'.[1] At the same time, it has precluded the possibility of closer bilateral economic integration, notwithstanding the creation of a Joint Planning Committee in 1972. Of particular political and economic significance, the Qatari proposal to finance the building of a causeway to Bahrain was rejected by that country because of the Hawar Islands dispute.[2] The powerful linkage which exists between specific territorial disputes and the concerns of the broader regional environment was again manifested in the immediate aftermath of the December 1976 OPEC Conference on Doha. During that meeting the Qataris had voted with the majority in favour of an oil price rise substantially above that which the Saudis were advocating. The ensuing deterioration in relations between the two countries was marked by a shift in Saudi declaratory policy in favour of the Bahraini position on the status of the Hawar Islands.[3]

---

1 One observer of Gulf politics observes: 'A great part of the blame for the collapse of the Union of Nine in 1971 should go to Qatar and Bahrain. The historical rift between these two states owing to territorial disputes, with tribal dynastic overtones, naturally spilled over into their attitudes and behaviour toward each other at the negotiating table. The rejection of a proposal by one was in some cases less because of its demerits than the mere fact that the other might have sponsored or supported it'. See Ali Mohammed Khalifa, *The United Arab Emirates*, Croom Helm, London, 1979, p 34.

2 Richard F. Nyrop, et al., *Area Handbook for the Persian Gulf States*, GPO, Washington DC, 1977, p 267.

3 Colin Legum (ed.), *Middle East Contemporary Survey*, vol. I, 1976-77, Holmes & Meier, London, 1978, p 356. Relations between Saudi Arabia and Qatar only began to improve in mid-1977 after a compromise price was reached.

Sporadic reports in 1976 and 1977 of progress towards the resolution of the outstanding territorial issues clouding bilateral relations between Qatar and Bahrain proved unfounded. In April 1978 the Qatari Crown Prince and Defence Minister, Shaikh Hamad Bin-Isa al Khalifa, declared in an interview that the territorial dispute with Qatar was not just over the island of Hawar, but that 'the disagreement in reality is one about the whole border'. While the demarcation of boundaries remained an open question, he affirmed that Bahrain wished to preserve the present ones.[1] The apparent Bahraini negotiating strategy is to maintain a close link between the Zubarah and Hawar questions even though the credibility of its claim to the former has been severely eroded by more than a century of Al Thani predominance on the Qatari Peninsula. In attempting to broaden the scope of any future discussions, it would grant the Bahrain government the opportunity to seemingly make a grand concession on the Zubarah question while concomitantly pushing for an outright recognition by Doha of its sovereignty over the Hawar Islands as a *quid pro quo*. Qatari opposition to such a proposal is premised, needless to say, on the effect which it would have on the demarcation of the continental shelf boundaries between the two countries (see discussion on p 69). It is this feature which militates against a prompt resolution of these contending territorial claims. At the same time, the long-standing process of political polarization between radical and conservative regimes within the region, now complemented by the resurgence of sectarian politics, has created a powerful mutuality of interests amongst the states of the lower Gulf on the basis of their similar domestic structures.[2] Under such conditions of accentuated threat — both religious and ideological — to the legitimacy of these conservative regimes, it is highly unlikely that the Al Khalifah and Al Thani, however acrimonious their historical rivalry, will be prepared to move beyond the bounds of diplomatic posturing in the pursuit of their respective territorial claims.

The dispute between Qatar, Abu Dhabi and Saudi Arabia over the demarcation of their common frontiers

The geographic focal point of this triangular dispute is the Khaur al-'Udaid inlet at the south-east base of the Qatar peninsula and its

---

1 *Arab Report and Record*, 14 April 1978, p 237.

2 The shared perception of an ideological threat emanating from Iraq and the PDRY has increased the degree to which the lower Gulf states seek consciously to concert their actions. In May 1978 the arrest of two Adenis in Abu Dhabi and Ras al-Khaimah after the opening of a PDRY consulate in the UAE prompted the refusal by Bahrain and Qatar to allow South Yemen to establish similar diplomatic missions in their respective capitals. *Arab Report and Record*, 14 May 1978, p 335.

adjacent coastal area. Though ostensibly resolved at the time of the Buraimi Oasis settlement in 1974 (see p 54), it remains a potential source of friction between the three states. Abu Dhabi's claim to sovereignty over Khaur al-'Udaid, supported by British declarations to that effect in 1878 and 1937, was based upon the occupation of that previously uninhabited littoral strip by a certain section of the Bani Yas tribe between 1869 and 1880. While the settlement remained abandoned after that time, the Al Thani rulers of Qatar made periodic attempts to reassert control over the inlet only to be rebuffed by the British. In an attempt to reach a compromise solution, the British government advocated the extension of the Qatar boundary south to the vicinity of Khaur al-'Udaid, but without encompassing it.[1] Saudi Arabia, asserting its own substantial territorial claims against both Qatar and Abu Dhabi, challenged the British right to transfer sovereignty over this particular area. In December 1965 the Saudi and Qatari governments, acting without British consultation, concluded an agreement delimiting their land and offshore boundaries. The British government subsequently notified Riyadh that it did not accept the validity of that agreement in so far as it prejudiced the rights of a third party, namely Abu Dhabi, over the territory demarcated.[2]

The Saudi claim to all territory south of the Liwa oasis in Abu Dhabi was revived in 1970 when Aramco, while exploring one of its new concessions in Saudi Arabia, made a very promising strike at Shuaiba — an oilfield which subsequently proved to be part of the larger Zarrara structure on the other side of the border. It was at this point that King Faisal called for the resumption of negotiations between Saudi Arabia and Abu Dhabi so as to resolve their outstanding differences over territorial demarcation. The complex dialogue which followed during the next four year period culminated in the concluding of an agreement between the two on 29 July 1974. Though the full text has yet to be published, various reports indicate that its terms included two major concessions by Abu Dhabi. In return for the tacit renunciation by Saudi Arabia of its spurious historical claim to the Buraimi Oasis (see discussion on p 54), Abu Dhabi pledged not to exploit that portion of the Zarrara field lying within its own boundaries and granted Saudi Arabia access to the Khaur al-'Udaid inlet via a territorial corridor across its frontier with Qatar.[3]

1 Arabian American Oil Company, *Oman and the Southern Shore of the Persian Gulf*, 1952, p 185; cited in Al-Baharna, *op.cit.*, p 263.

2 Al-Baharna, *loc.cit.*

3 *Arab Report and Record*, 1974, p 307. In a recent move which confirms Saudi annexation of this area, a survey team working for the Saudi Ports Authority is reported to be examining the possibility of building a port at Ras Khumays, *MEED*, 1 August 1980.

In securing these rights with respect to the latter, King Faisal was able to satisfy the long-standing Saudi goal of an outlet on the lower Gulf east of the Qatar peninsula. Though of marginal value in strictly military terms — the inlet being suitable only for small patrol craft — the termination of the Qatar/Abu Dhabi border is of considerable political significance since it reinforces the perception of Qatar as but an adjunct to Saudi Arabia. Some analysts of inter-state relations in the Gulf have observed that the Saudis, having physically isolated Qatar, are now in the position — should the political occasion arise — to outrightly absorb the shaikhdom within their domain.[1] That contingency would appear to rest primarily on the nature of internal political developments on the Qatari Peninsula. Clearly the Saudis would not allow Qatar to be used as a base for subversion against its eastern province should there be a change in the nature of the Doha regime. For the moment, however, the traditional affinity between the Wahhabi regimes of the two countries, operating within the context of volatile political polarization on the regional level, serves to draw Qatar closer to Saudi Arabia. In so doing, the former's capacity for independent political manoeuvrability has been further circumscribed.

The Buraimi dispute

The now famous dispute over sovereignty to the Buraimi Oasis has remained dormant since the bilateral agreement of 1974. According to the terms of the agreement, Saudi Arabia tacitly acknowledged Abu Dhabi/Omani sovereignty over that area in return for the favourable settlement of the Qatar frontier issue described earlier. The disputed territory around Buraimi today consists of six Abu Dhabi and three Omani villages. During the four years of complex negotiations preceding the July 1974 Agreement, Saudi Arabia advanced its claim to sovereignty over Buraimi on the basis of its historical connections to the oasis and its adjacent territory. That tie dates from the turn of the nineteenth century when the oasis was occupied by a Wahhabi expedition despatched from the Nejd.[2] Between 1800 and 1869 Buraimi remained under intermittent Saudi jurisdiction. At the end of that period an Omani force responded to the calls of the Buraimi tribe of Nu'aim and assisted them in the expulsion of the Wahhabi governor from the area.

---

1 See, for example, John B. Kelly, 'Saudi Arabia and the Gulf States' in *Critical Choices for Americans*, vol. X, D.C. Heath, Lexington, Mass., 1976, p 449.

2 For an examination of the historical background to the Buraimi Oasis dispute see Al-Baharna, *op.cit.*, chapter 13; J.B. Kelly, 'The Buraimi Oasis Dispute', *International Affairs*, July 1956.

The shared claim of Oman and Abu Dhabi to sovereignty over Buraimi has been based upon their continuous occupation of the oasis and its environs since 1869. Though there is scattered historical evidence suggesting that the Saudis continued to enjoy considerable allegiance amongst the local tribes even after 1869 (as manifested, for example, in the systematic collection of *zakah*, the religious tithe, from the inhabitants of the disputed areas), no serious effort to re-occupy the Buraimi Oasis was made until 1952. In August of that year the Saudis despatched a small police contingent to the area and were able to reassert their civil authority over the village of Hamasa. This move — condemned as an act of aggression by the British government — led to a series of bilateral negotiations culminating in the so-called Standstill Agreement of 1952. While deferring the final settlement of the dispute to subsequent negotiations, the agreement pledged the parties to maintain their present positions and to desist from any provocative actions. In 1954 Saudi Arabia and Britain, formally acting on behalf of Abu Dhabi and Oman, agreed to refer the Buraimi dispute to a special arbitration tribunal to be convened in Geneva. The breakdown of those proceedings amidst charges of bad faith between the British and Saudi representatives was followed by the announcement from London on 26 October 1955 that the British-officered forces of Trucial Oman had retaken the Buraimi Oasis and ejected the Saudi constabulary force from it.[1] The resumption of diplomatic relations between Britain and Saudi Arabia on 16 January 1963 — relations severed at the time of the Suez crisis — prompted a new initiative to break the diplomatic impasse under the auspices of the UN Secretary-General. These discussions continued throughout the remainder of the 1960s with neither side willing to significantly yield in its position. In 1966 Abu Dhabi and Oman moved to bolster politically their claim to Buraimi by confirming the *de facto* jurisdictional division of the oasis between them.

As the guarantor of Gulf security via the 150 year old network of bilateral treaties linking it with the Trucial states, British policy during the post-war period was motivated primarily by the desire to forestall Saudi hegemony over the whole of the Arabian peninsula. Buraimi became the focal point of that effort. Following the British announcement in January 1968 of their intended withdrawal from the region by the end of 1971, Saudi Arabia supported the concept of a Federation of Gulf shaikhdoms. Yet the continuing pursuit of its claim to Buraimi — as well as territory encompassing one-third of Abu Dhabi — was to preclude the early establishment of diplomatic relations with the newly founded United Arab Emirates just as it fuelled the suspicions long harboured by the surrounding littoral states regarding the ultimate

1 Al-Baharna, *op.cit.*, p 205.

nature of Saudi intentions. The call by King Faisal in 1970 for the resumption of direct negotiations to resolve the issue came at a time when the credibility of the Saudi claim to the oasis was becoming increasingly difficult to sustain, given the legitimacy accorded to the Abu Dhabi/Omani presence at Buraimi by third parties. The ensuing round of bilateral discussions with Abu Dhabi was marked by an important, if tacitly expressed, shift in the Saudi negotiating position. As discussed above, the willingness by Riyadh to acknowledge the *status quo* on the Buraimi question was linked to major concessions by Abu Dhabi on the Qatari frontier issue (i.e. access rights to the Khaur al-'Udaid inlet) and the terms governing the exploitation of the large Zarrarah oilfield straddling their southernmost border.

The 1974 Agreement, accompanied by Saudi Arabia's extension of diplomatic recognition to the United Arab Emirates (UAE), was the prelude to a period of improved relations between the two countries.[1] In 1974 and 1975 it was reported from various quarters that serious technical defects in the supporting maps and documents to the agreement might precipitate a revival of the dispute. Despite the questions arising from the ambiguities of the 1974 understanding, bilateral relations remained close in 1976-77 owing to Abu Dhabi's acquiescence to the Saudi line on oil pricing at the turbulent December 1976 OPEC conference in Doha. In an attempt to move the frontier questions towards a final resolution, the UAE President, Shaikh Zayed of Abu Dhabi, issued a decree in July 1977 creating a committee under the direction of the Federal Foreign Minister to study and delineate the nation's borders with Oman, Saudi Arabia, Qatar and Iran. The impetus behind Zayed's action was clearly the belief that the settlement of these outstanding issues on a definitive basis would further foster a sense of national identity and perhaps, by their precedent, contribute to the resolution of the UAE's internal border disputes.

Concomitant to the establishment of this federal committee within the UAE was the resumption of discussions with Oman concerning the terms of their shared jurisdiction over Buraimi. Though upset at the time of their exclusion from the 1970-74 round of negotiations between Saudi Arabia and Abu Dhabi, this move by the UAE President represented more than an attempt to placate the Omani leadership. At Buraimi there are three Omani villages immediately adjacent to the town of Al Ain, the traditional area associated with Abu Dhabi's ruling Al Nahayyan family. That town and the surrounding mountains which

---

1 Co-operation between Saudi Arabia and the UAE has now expanded into the area of internal security. On 29 October 1976, following a five day visit by the Saudi Interior Minister to the UAE, a security agreement between the two countries was concluded. *Arab Report and Record*, 29 October 1976, p 637.

are contiguous with Oman remain of vital importance to the shaikhdom as they are at present its primary source of fresh water. Despite this potential source of friction over water rights, relations between Abu Dhabi and Oman have continued to be harmonious as a result of the strong support afforded Sultan Qabous by Shaikh Zayed during the Dhofar rebellion.[1]

While the ambiguities clouding the bilateral 1974 Agreement leave the Buraimi frontier technically undefined, there is a clear preference on the part of the parties involved — including Oman — to maintain the territorial status quo at the oasis and its environs. Indeed, the factors which brought about a peaceful resolution of the dispute in 1974 — the mutual desire of conservative monarchical regimes not to destabilize each other needlessly — have, if anything, intensified given the disruptive nature of recent political trends within the region (e.g. the sectarian resurgence accompanying the Iranian Revolution). Under these conditions, it is unlikely that even the discovery of new oil finds in the area would lead to a situation which could not be managed through recourse to diplomatic negotiations.

The short to medium-term prospect for change in the status of the Buraimi question would appear to be contingent primarily upon the internal cohesiveness of the UAE. Though stable at present, the record of recent events — from the domestic impact of disruptive modernization to the process of political/sectarian polarization sweeping the region — underscores the increasing vulnerability of the federal state to pressures generated both within and beyond its borders. Should the cumulative impact of these pressures result in the future fragmentation of the UAE, then it is probable that Saudi Arabia and Oman, faced with the reality of dangerously weak city states on their periphery, would move to adjust favourably their common frontier with Abu Dhabi. Moreover, the advent of any fundamental political transformation within the present UAE state structure — for example, the usurpation of power by left-wing forces as in South Yemen — would most certainly trigger some form of direct Saudi intervention quite apart from any territorial designs Saudi Arabia might continue to harbour.

1 Between 1975 and 1977 Abu Dhabi supplied Oman with approximately $200 million in grant aid.

The current round in the ongoing jurisdictional dispute over Abu Musa, Tunb al-Kubra and Tunb al-Sughra (Greater and Lesser Tunbs) dates to 30 November 1971 when Iranian forces landed on the three strategically located islands near the Strait of Hormuz. The occupation of the islands, then under the titular authority of the shaikhdoms of Sharjah and Ras al-Khaimah respectively, came only two days prior to the inauguration of the UAE. The occupation followed a three year period of discussions conducted at successive stages with both the British government and the individual shaikhdoms directly affected. During those negotiations, the status of the Gulf islands became linked both with Iran's recognition of the UAE and, more tacitly, with the Bahrain question.

In seeking convincingly to justify its claim to and subsequent occupation of the disputed islands, the Iranian government employed two major sets of arguments. First, it maintained its historical rights to the islands on the basis of continuous Iranian occupation until the last quarter of the nineteenth century. At the time of Iran's forced eviction from Abu Musa and the Tunbs by the British, sovereignty — it was argued — was illegally transferred to Sharjah and Ras al-Khaimah. Although it emerged as a serious issue of contention only in the period immediately preceding the British withdrawal from the region, it had been the subject of a number of fruitless exchanges between London and Tehran in the 1920s and 1930s.[1] In the mid-1960s the disputed status of these Gulf islands emerged as a major stumbling block in the complex negotiations between Iran and Britain, the latter acting on behalf of the shaikhdoms, over the demarcation of their continental shelf boundary (see discussion on p 70).[2]

Beyond considerations of historical prerogative, the Iranian leadership also sought to portray its occupation of the islands as an imperative in geo-strategic terms. Given the close proximity of Abu Musa and the Tunbs to the Strait of Hormuz, the Shah argued that freedom of navigation into the Gulf was dependent upon control of the islands by a power committed to the stability of the region. The free flow of oil and goods through these Straits was stressed as a vital interest both to Iran and the West. With the emphasis in American security policy shifting towards the promotion of preponderant regional powers under the Nixon doctrine, Iran regarded its action as being wholly consonant with its assumption of such a role in the Gulf. The actual strategic import-

1 See R.M. Burrell, *op.cit.*, pp 170-79.

2 H.M. Al-Baharna, *op.cit.*, p 306.

ance of the islands immediately adjacent to the Strait of Hormuz remains a point of contention. Contrary to the Shah's contention that the islands were taken to maintain free and secure navigational access through the Strait, one analyst of Gulf security problems has persuasively argued that their control is 'neither essential to block sea traffic in the Gulf, nor sufficient in itself to frustrate a determined naval power from pursuing that objective'.[1]

As noted above, the condition which permitted the reassertion of Iran's long dormant claim to the islands was the announcement by Britain in 1968 of its intention to withdraw from the region by the end of 1971. The two year series of bilateral negotiations which ensued focused both upon the question of jurisdictional rights over the Islands and Iran's assertion of sovereignty over Bahrain. In linking the two issues, the apparent Iranian negotiating strategy was to obtain at least tacit British acquiescence to its intended occupation of Abu Musa and the Tunbs in return for the renunciation of its increasingly untenable claim to Bahrain. Although the negotiations failed to produce an agreement stipulating such an explicit *quid pro quo*, it has been reported that it was the Iranian leadership's understanding that, in the wake of a favourable resolution of the Bahrain question, Britain would not actively oppose Iran's claim to the islands.[2]

During 1970 and 1971 Iranian declaratory policy directed towards the shaikhdoms and other regional states took the form of a subtle admixture of threats and promised benefits designed to move the issue towards a settlement on its terms. For example, in February 1971 the Shah affirmed that, unlike the dispute over Bahrain, Iran would be prepared to resort to force to re-establish its authority over the islands. This was offset by statements throughout the period pledging generous financial assistance to the shaikhdoms should they accede to the Iranian claim.[3] Negotiations between Iran, Britain and the two shaikhdoms continued throughout November 1971 with Iran rejecting 'suggestions' by Arab third parties that Abu Musa and the Tunbs could be leased to it when Britain withdrew from the area.

1 Joseph Churba, *Conflict and Tension among the States of the Persian Gulf, Oman and South Arabia*, Maxwell Air Force Base, Air University Documentary Research Study, Alabama, 1971, p 68; cited in A.M. Khalifa, *op.cit.*, p 152.

2 S. Chubin and S. Zabih, *op.cit.*, p 222. This perception was reinforced by the six day visit to Iran of Sir William Luce, Britain's special envoy in the Persian Gulf, only two weeks prior to the landing of Iranian forces on Abu Musa and the Tunbs islands. Upon leaving Tehran, Sir William stated that Britain and Iran had 'sorted out their differences over the islands'.

3 It should be noted that neither Sharjah nor Ras al-Khaimah is a major oil producer.

On 29 November Iran and Sharjah announced the conclusion of an agreement concerning the status of Abu Musa. While both continued to maintain their respective claim to sovereignty over the island, they were able to agree that:

1 Iranian troops would be stationed in part of the island, and in this area the Iranian flag would be flown and Iran would exercise full jurisdiction.

2 Sharjah would retain jurisdiction over the remainder of the island through the existing police and civil authorities.

3 Both Iran and Sharjah recognized a twelve mile limit of territorial waters around the island and agreed to equally share any revenues accruing from oil exploration.

4 Iran would extend £1.5 million in economic assistance to Sharjah until the latter's revenues from oil deposits reached £3 million per annum.[1]

During the same period, Iran and Ras al-Khaimah were unable to reach a settlement over their contending claims of sovereignty to the Greater and Lesser Tunbs.[2] As a result, the landing of Iranian forces on the morning of 30 November was met by resistance from the Sharjan constabulary force on Greater Tunb with loss of life on both sides.

Predictably, the centre of opposition to Iran's seizure of the islands was Iraq which attempted to depict the question as a major issue in Iran-Arab relations. Amidst charges of collusion between Britain and Iran, the Ba'athist regime in Baghdad severed diplomatic relations with both countries. Kuwait, perhaps fearing the precedent of unilateral military action to resolve territorial disputes given Iraq's irredentist claims against it, also strongly condemned Iran's occupation of Abu Musa and the Tunbs. In terms of criticism within international fora, Iran no doubt benefited from the fact that in the period immediately following the landing of its forces on the Gulf Islands, the great powers were preoccupied by the Indo-Pakistan war and fears of an impending conflict in the Middle East. Though its action clearly precipitated a deterioration in relations with the Arab states of the region, it is apparent that the Iranian leadership was motivated by the not unrealistic belief that such a setback would be a temporary phenomenon given the overriding mutuality of security interests linking the conservative monarchical regimes in the Gulf.

1 *Keesing's Contemporary Archives*, 1971-72, p 25010.

2 The former had approximately 150 Arab inhabitants on it at the time while the latter was and remains uninhabited.

In the aftermath of the Iranian revolution there were reports that the newly-installed theocratic regime in Tehran, having eschewed the Shah's perspective on Gulf security, was considering the relinquishment of the disputed islands. These reports gained further credence following the 'private' visit by a ranking member of the Iranian revolutionary government, Shaikh Sadeq Khalkhali, to the UAE in late May. During a newspaper interview in Abu Dhabi on 31 May he hinted that the three islands seized by the Shah in 1971 might be returned.[1] Despite these signs indicating a possible shift in the Iranian position, the authorities in Tehran have, to date, taken no concrete action with respect to the islands which would constitute a departure from pre-revolutionary policy. In point of fact, it has been suggested by some observers of Gulf politics that one of the factors which prompted the Iranian government initially to emphasize the possible 'export' of its revolutionary experience in its declaratory policy was a desire to counter renewed Arab demands for the return of the islands. In late October 1979, the issue was cited by the Iraqi Ambassador to Lebanon in an interview evidently granted with the express approval of Baghdad. On that occasion, the return of the islands to Arab sovereignty was set as one of the three (largely symbolic) Iraqi preconditions for an improvement in relations with the Tehran regime.[2] Then, as at the outset of the Autumn 1980 war, the heavy-handed manipulation of the islands dispute by Iraq represented the Ba'athist government's attempt to frame the conflagration with Iran in overtly pan-Arab terms.[3] It also served to underscore again the tendency in Gulf politics for differences in one sphere to influence the entire range of relations between the interested parties and their respective supporters.

The Musandam frontier dispute between Oman and the UAE

A long-standing source of tension between Oman and the UAE has been the disputed border separating the Omani enclave of Ras Musandam from the shaikhdoms of Ras al-Khaimah, Fujairah and Sharjah. In the past, Oman has periodically circulated the idea of a 'Greater Oman' which would include large parts of these Emirates so as to establish a direct territorial link with Ras Musandam — the vital enclave on the tip of the peninsula which governs the Straits of Hormuz. In more recent

1   *Arab Report*, 6 June 1979.

2   The other two were a revision of the 1975 agreement on navigation in the Shatt al-Arab waterway and the provision of self-rule for its ethnic minorities, such as the Kurds and the Baluchis. For a summary of the Iraqi Ambassador's interview in the Beirut daily, *An-Nahar*, see *Financial Times*, 1 November 1979.

3   In the initial phase of the Iran-Iraq war there were unsubstantiated reports (e.g. *Financial Times*, 2 October 1980; *Sunday Times*, 5 October 1980) that Baghdad had despatched a small number of men and helicopters to the UAE to attack the three disputed islands near the Strait of Hormuz. According to the *Sunday Times* report, a joint British-American diplomatic initiative halted Iraqi plans to expand the geographical scope of the conflict.

years, the territorial dispute between Oman and Ras al-Khaimah has been compounded by differences over the demarcation of their continental shelf boundary (see discussion on p 71). Though the timing of the Omani claim to the sixteen kilometre stretch of land between the villages of Dawra and Tims in Ras al-Khaimah coincided with the discovery of commercial offshore oil deposits, it was publicly justified by Sultan Qabous in terms of the affinity between Oman and the tribal groupings in that area. In April 1978, no less than three delegations from the UAE visited Oman as part of a sustained drive by the Federal State to resolve this outstanding territorial issue. In those talks, Qabous maintained that the disputed area was populated by the Shihuh and Habus tribes and had been administered by Oman for centuries. Moreover, he accused Shaikh Saqr of Ras al-Khaimah of having initiated the process of territorial encroachment in 1951 when he occupied the village of Rims. Sultan Qabous denied allegations that Oman had reasserted its claim only because of the start of offshore drillings in Ras al-Khaimah and said that bilateral talks on the issue had begun as early as the Lahore Islamic summit meeting in 1974.

The second focal point of the Musandam border dispute has been the village of Dibba in the north-east of the peninsula.[1] Its political division into three component settlements under the respective authority of Oman, Fujairah and Sharjah is indicative of the lower Gulf's fragmented array of territorial units. As with the Oman/Ras al-Khaimah border region, the Dibba area is inhabited primarily by the Shihuh and Habus tribes. In order to bolster their contending territorial claims, both Oman and the UAE have sought to obtain some pledge of allegiance from them. It has been reported that in 1975 some of the Shihuh and Habus accepted an offer of citizenship from Ras al-Khaimah.[2] Given the kinds of goods and services which the UAE as a major petroleum-exporting state is able to provide, it has been difficult for Oman to compete on this basis. The pronounced differential in financial resources between the two is more broadly reflected in the sharp contrast in level of development between the Omani and UAE settlements both at Dibba and at Buraimi.

In an evident attempt to pressure the UAE government on the Musandam border issue (particularly with respect to the potentially oil-rich offshore territory adjacent to Ras al-Khaimah), the Omani government took certain actions in 1978 which indicated that it might seek to

---

1 See J.C. Wilkinson, 'The Oman Question: The Background to the Political Geography of South-East Arabia', *Geographical Journal*, 137, no. 3, September 1971, pp 361-67.

2 *Area Handbook for the Persian Gulf States*, p 354.

revive the Buraimi question. In January of that year, following an unsuccessful round of negotiations and the report that Ras al-Khaimah (with Kuwaiti backing) was to establish an oil refinery in the disputed area, Oman signalled a possible shift in position by putting into circulation a memorial coin bearing a picture of the Sultan's old palace at the Buraimi oasis. Later in the year this was followed by the report that Oman had assembled some 300 mechanized vehicles in the vicinity of Buraimi.[1] As a militarily weak, internally fragmented state seeking to preserve the status quo, the UAE has consistently sought a negotiated settlement of the Musandam border dispute. Towards this end, the UAE has been diplomatically supported by the other littoral states of the Gulf. Efforts at mediation have been made by Saudi Arabia and Kuwait. Significantly, the border dispute between Oman and Ras al-Khaimah is the sole case of the Gulf region in which the Soviet Union has actually taken sides. Its declared support for the latter in 1978[2] was most likely a function of the dispute's relative insignificance[3] and Oman's overtly pro-Western diplomatic posture.

The ability of Oman to pursue its territorial claims against the UAE has been conditioned by the complex interplay between the internal and external political environments in which it must operate. Indeed, it was only after the subsidence of the Dhofar secessionist movement at the end of 1975 that Oman was in a position to direct its attention to the north and reassert its claim to the Musandam border area. In a similar way, the evident threat to the domestic structures of the surrounding states posed by the Iranian revolution militated in favour of a modest *rapprochement* between Oman and the UAE by the close of 1979. During the visit of UAE Vice-President and Prime Minister Shaikh Rashid to Muscat, the Omani Foreign Minister announced the advent of a 'new era' in Oman-UAE relations and that a settlement of the long-standing border disputes between the two countries had been agreed upon.[4]

Given the shared perception of the diverse ideological threats emanating from Baghdad, Tehran and Aden, Oman has been searching for a suitable formula in order to woo the UAE (along with the other

1 *As-Siyassa* (Kuwait), 15 November 1978; cited in *Arab Report and Record*, p 821.

2 For a detailed discussion of the Soviet Union's attitude concerning territorial disputes in the Gulf see Shahram Chubin, 'Soviet Policy Towards the Gulf', *Adelphi Papers*, no. 157, IISS, London, Spring 1980.

3 By way of contrast, it should be noted that the Soviet Union, despite its close ties with Baghdad, has refrained in the past from supporting Iraq in its territorial disputes for fear of alienating Iran and Kuwait.

4 *MEED*, 21 December 1979. Notwithstanding this improvement in bilateral relations, Oman will continue to seek to prevent the consequence of a strong confederation of shaikhdoms. In the past, this interest has been manifested, for example, in diplomatic support for Dubai in its differences with Abu Dhabi.

conservative Arab Gulf states) into a co-operative agreement on both political and security matters. Though the UAE is wary of any proposal which would identify it too closely to Oman, and, by implication, the West, it is reported to be considering two proposals which would indicate the new strategic importance being attached to developments over the past year in Iran: (a) the construction of a military airport in Fujairah just south of the Ras Musandam peninsula, and (b) the construction of a 150 mile pipeline from Abu Dhabi (the state's major oil producer) to Fujairah, thereby allowing it to bypass the Strait of Hormuz in the event of its blockage.[1]

Border disputes within the UAE

The primary impetus which led to the demarcation of the land boundaries of the emirates was the British desire to facilitate the granting of oil concessions in the then Trucial States. A diplomatic mission was despatched to the shaikhdoms in the mid-1950s in an attempt to resolve the various contending tribal territorial claims. Though inter-emirate borders have remained relatively stable since that time, jurisdictional disputes have been a major factor inhibiting the development of a stronger federal identity.[2]

The ongoing problem of political fragmentation within the UAE is evident in the fact that, of the seven emirates, only Abu Dhabi and Umm al-Qaiwain comprise territorially integral units.[3] The mosaic of enclaves and neutral zones which dominates the political geography of the UAE exists today as the result of the lengthy diplomatic process by which the land boundaries of the emirates have been determined. Nonetheless, territorial disputes remain a constant source of tension within the Federation because of internecine familial rivalries. Of the myriad of potential inter-emirate disputes which one might consider, the following are worthy of particular note owing either to their relative importance or to recent history which has witnessed their violent re-activation.

Abu Dhabi-Dubai During the period of the British protectorate, Abu Dhabi laid claim to nearly half of the territory of the adjacent shaikhdom of Dubai. In 1946 fighting erupted between the two parties and continued for over a year. A perennial source of tension, this

---

1 *Financial Times*, 24 October 1979.

2 For a consideration of inter-emirate disputes and their implications see John Duke Anthony, *Arab States of the Lower Gulf: People, Politics, Petroleum*, Middle East Institute, Washington, D.C., 1975, p 22 ff; and Ali Mohammad Khalifa, *op.cit.*, pp 99-109.

3 By way of contrast, the smallest shaikhdom, Ajman, with a total land area of approximately 150 square miles, is sub-divided into three component territorial units.

dispute was provisionally settled in 1968 through the creation of a neutral zone in the contested area. Under the terms of this agreement, it was stipulated that the revenues from any future oil find at that location would be shared equally. As Abu Dhabi is the largest and most wealthy of the then Trucial States, the equitable resolution of this dispute served to further foster the favourable political atmosphere in which the federation of the seven emirates occurred. That having been said, the relationship between Abu Dhabi and Dubai has been a mixed one since the creation of the UAE. At times they have demonstrated a remarkable ability to concert their actions, as in 1972 when a joint decision was taken to despatch the Union Defence Forces to Sharjah to put down an attempted coup. More recently, differences have again come to the fore in a number of spheres of activity.[1] Perhaps most significant are those which have emerged concerning the organization of the federation's military forces. In February 1948, Shaikh Rashid of Dubai is reported to have put his troops on alert following the appointment by Shaikh Zayed of Abu Dhabi of his son to the post of Commander-in-Chief of the Union Defence Forces. Rashid angrily charged that this decision was taken without consultation with other members of the Supreme Council and had the effect of upsetting the delicate balance in the allocation of posts between the emirates. In spite of this ominous deterioration in relations between the two most important members of the federation, Dubai made no move to revive the dormant question of its undefined border with Abu Dhabi. Here, as elsewhere, there is a tendency in Gulf disputes for differences in one area to spill over to encompass the entire range of relations between the states. This frequently takes the form of re-activated territorial claims (whether previously 'resolved' or merely dormant). With respect to the continuing differences between Abu Dhabi and Dubai, however, both states retained a powerful incentive to avoid such an escalation in tension so as not to endanger the federal structure.[2] This interest was further strengthened by the tumultuous events of 1979 on the opposite side of the Gulf — and their implications as perceived by the UAE's conservative monarchical leadership.[3]

---

1 These include the choice of a permanent federal capital (the provisional one being Abu Dhabi city) and commercial policy (i.e. Dubai's complaint that federal travel restrictions hinder its development as a liberal commercial centre by constricting the flow of foreign businessmen and merchants).

2 Although UAE spokesmen discounted Shaikh Rashid's criticism of President Zayed as 'no more than a family argument', there were reports during the crisis of Spring 1978 of foreign diplomats warning their home governments of the federal state's possible dissolution.

3 Even during that period, it is significant to note that arms purchases by the Union Defence Forces were reportedly held in abeyance owing to continuing differences over the allocation of the top army posts; *Financial Times*, 12 January 1979.

Fujairah-Sharjah Fujairah, one of the smallest and poorest of the emirates, was, until 1901, considered a part of Sharjah. Although autonomous from that time, it was not considered an independent shaikhdom until 1952 when it entered into a treaty relationship with Britain.[1] In 1972, less than one year after the founding of the Union, a bizarre episode culminated in the outbreak of border fighting between Fujairah and Sharjah with serious loss of life on both sides. The incident was prompted when the late Shaikh Muhammad al-Shargui of Fujairah announced that he was to present an orchard in his territory to the Federal President, Shaikh Zayed of Abu Dhabi, as a gift. This decision was immediately contested by Sharjah which claimed that, as the orchard was fed by a well that its tribesmen had used for years, Fujairah had no right to make such a presentation unilaterally. In the ensuing period, fighting broke out between the two sides and continued until the despatch of a peacekeeping force composed of Federal and Abu Dhabian troops to the area in contention. The federal government sought to resolve the issue by purchasing title to the orchard and granting Fujairah and Sharjah equal access rights to its well.[2]

Dubai-Sharjah The long-standing dispute over the demarcation of this inter-emirate border again arose in May 1976 when Sharjah began construction of the Charles de Gaulle shopping and business complex on contested territory. Dubai claimed that the site of the planned commercial centre was on its side of the frontier. Hostilities were averted when the issue was referred to a select panel of international lawyers for adjudication.

While inter-tribal feuding and rivalries between ruling elites remain persistent features of UAE political life, recent years have witnessed the emergence of new mechanisms conducive to the amelioration of differences over territorial demarcation. Through them, it is hoped that disputes — whether active or dormant — will be restricted to a level of exchange below that of armed conflict. With the Union about to enter its second decade, only scant progress has been seen regarding the development of a credible mediatory role for the federal government. Of more immediate significance has been the political posture adopted by Abu Dhabi. The pre-eminent economic and military status which that emirate enjoys within the federation confers on it a high degree of potential leverage in its relations with those poorer emirates to the north which remain materially dependent upon it.[3] Shaikh Zayed

1 Al-Baharna, *op.cit.*, p 5.

2 John Duke Anthony, *op.cit.*, pp 214-15.

3 The continuing pursuit by Ras al-Khaimah of a more independent line (e.g. the construction of a hospital outside the federal health service) was met in 1978 by a reduction in the level of development assistance from Abu Dhabi. The effects of this move prompted Shaikh Saqr subsequently to complain that he had been compelled to obtain an international loan at 'commercial rates' so as to finance infrastructure development within his emirate.

appears prepared to exploit this position of pre-eminence as much as possible so as to moderate the behaviour of the other member states within the Union.

Equally important in terms of their potential long-term consequences have been the tentative efforts of Abu Dhabi and Dubai to concert their actions in the area of inter-emirate conflict management. Past episodes have underscored the increasing importance of the Union Defence Forces (UDF) both in terms of the requirements of internal security (e.g. the suppression of the attempted coup in Sharjah in 1972) and the maintenance of order on contested internal frontiers (e.g. the 1972 dispute between Fujairah and Sharjah). The ability of the UDF to play such a role effectively in the future is, to a large extent, contingent on the state of relations between Abu Dhabi and Dubai.[1] Despite the manifestation of periodic differences between the two, recent events of both internal and external origin have, as discussed previously, militated in favour of the strengthening and broadening of their working relationship. Indeed, one could well say the same for the UAE as a whole. For it is clear that under these conditions (i.e. the ideological threats perceived to be emanating from Baghdad, Tehran and Aden coupled with the disruptive impact of the modernization process on the UAE's domestic structure) the emirates' ruling elite retain a powerful incentive to moderate their inter-tribal and dynastic rivalries.

---

1 Another major factor affecting the reliability of the UDF is, of course, its ethnic composition. With an officer corps which remains almost exclusively British, Jordanian and Pakistani, the main force is composed primarily of Omanis, Yemenis and Baluchis. Recent estimates have placed the level of indigenous Arabs as low as ten per cent.

Continental shelf boundaries

Stretching from the mouth of the Shatt al-Arab waterway to the Straits of Hormuz, the Persian Gulf (as noted in the previous discussion), is a body of water whose depth rarely exceeds fifty fathoms (100 metres). Therefore the entire sea bed of the Gulf has been designated as continental shelf in international legal terms.[1] As was the case in the Upper Gulf, the problem of the demarcation of submarine boundaries arose as a result of the discovery of the considerable offshore oil reserves which lie in that area. The settlement of the continental shelf questions became imperative when various oil concessionaires refused to proceed with drilling operations in disputed zones until such time as the disputes had been resolved. The process of delimitation has been seriously hampered in the past, however, as a result of the ongoing sovereignty disputes concerning the status of various Gulf islands. Though none of the Persian Gulf states is a signatory to the 1958 Geneva Convention on the Continental Shelf, large tracts of their shared sea bed have been demarcated in tacit accordance with its principles (as adapted to local geographical and political realities).

Those submarine boundaries which have been resolved on the basis of the conclusion of bilateral agreements are as follows.

Bahrain-Saudi Arabia

Concluded on 22 February 1958, this was the first continental shelf boundary in the Persian Gulf to be defined by treaty.[2] The agreement is noteworthy in two respects. First, the boundary line (extending some 98.5 nautical miles) is not a strict median based on the configuration of the coastline, but rather a series of equidistant points between predetermined landmarks on both Bahraini and Saudi Arabian territory.

Second, while placing the vast Fasht Bu Saafa oilfield under Saudi jurisdiction, the Treaty stipulated that one-half of the net income which accrued as a result of its exploitation should be granted to the Bahrain government.

---

1 In 1945 the United States established international legal precedent through the unilateral declaration of continental shelf rights to the 600 fathoms level. For an extended consideration of continental shelf questions, see Barry Buzan, 'A Sea of Troubles? Sources of Dispute in the New Ocean Regime', *Adelphi Papers*, IISS, London, Spring 1978. Continental shelf disputes of the Lower Gulf are surveyed in Ali A. El-Hakim, *op.cit.*

2 US Department of State, Office of the Geographer, Bureau of Intelligence and Research, 'Continental Shelf Boundary: Bahrain-Saudi Arabia', *International Boundary Study: Limits in the Seas*, series A, no. 18, 29 May 1970.

On 20 March 1969 Abu Dhabi and Qatar concluded an Agreement demarcating their continental shelf boundary for a distance of 115 nautical miles. In so doing, the jurisdictional rights to a number of disputed offshore islands were resolved.[1] The status of Halul, the largest of this group (situated some sixty miles off the Qatar Peninsula), had long been a source of contention between the two emirates. The dispute was intensified following the start of oil exploration in the continental shelf area adjacent to it. Though a panel of British 'experts' determined that Halul should be under Qatari sovereignty in 1962, it was the 1969 Agreement which confirmed that ruling.[2] Other islands similarly affected were those of Dayyinah (granted to Abu Dhabi) and Al-Ashat and Shara'iwah (now considered to be part of the territory of Qatar). In the case of Dayyinah, the settlement of the jurisdictional rights to that island necessitated a deviation in the continental shelf boundary line so as to mark its three mile territorial sea. The precedent for such a deviation had been established in the 1968 Agreement between Iran and Saudi Arabia *vis-à-vis* the islands of Arabi and Farsi.

It is significant to note that the continental shelf boundary line between Qatar and Abu Dhabi was not delimited according to the strict application of the equidistance principle. Although the endpoints were fixed so as to be equidistant from the coasts of both states, its most prominent intermediate point was adjusted to coincide with the location of the al-Bunduq oilfield. The bilateral accord concluded in 1969 stipulated that the development of this field would be undertaken by one concessionaire (Abu Dhabi Marine Areas) and that its total revenues (i.e. royalties, profits and other governmental fees) were to be equally shared between the two governments.

One remaining source of uncertainty with respect to the demarcation of the submarine boundary in this particular area of the Gulf centres around the intentions and prerogatives of Saudi Arabia. It will be recalled that one of the reported terms of the 1974 Agreement between Saudi Arabia and Abu Dhabi (see p 51) was the establishment of a Saudi territorial corridor across Abu Dhabi's frontier with Qatar in

---

1 US Department of State, Office of the Geographer, Bureau of Intelligence and Research, 'Continental Shelf Boundary: Abu Dhabi-Qatar', *International Boundary Study: Limits in the Seas*, series A, no. 12, 10 March 1970.

2 See al-Baharna, *op.cit.*, p 304; El-Hakim, *op.cit.*, pp 95-9.

return for the tacit renunciation by Riyadh of its spurious historical claim to the Buraimi Oasis. Its possession of that corridor to the Khaur al'Udaid Inlet would confer on Saudi Arabia at least the theoretical right to lay some claim to the continental shelf running adjacent to it. To date no move has been made in that direction. Given the Saudi interest in maintaining favourable relations with the Gulf's other conservative monarchical regimes under current politico-economic conditions, it is highly unlikely that the Saudi ruling elite would consider doing so.

Iran-Qatar

The continental shelf boundary agreement between these states was concluded on 20 September 1969 and came into force on 10 May 1970.[1] Extending for a distance of 131 nautical miles and composed of five demarcated points, the Iran-Qatar submarine border was delimited on the basis of the equidistance principle with the exception that the presence of all islands in the Persian Gulf was disregarded. The northwestern terminus of this boundary line remains undetermined owing to uncertainty as to where a potential continental shelf agreement between Bahrain and Qatar (see p 69) would intersect that of the one between Iran and Qatar.

Bahrain-Iran

Concluded on 17 June 1971, the continental shelf agreement between these states came into force on 14 May 1972.[2] The boundary line extends for 28.8 nautical miles with terminal points determined by the adjacent continental shelf agreements (i.e. the western terminus coincides with the endpoint of the Iran-Saudi Arabia boundary line while the eastern one is coterminous with the final demarcated point of the Iran-Qatar continental shelf boundary). The two intermediate points of the Bahrain-Iran boundary line were evidently based on the principle of equidistance although the agreement does not state that the equidistance principle was utilized.

1 US Department of State, Office of the Geographer, Bureau of Intelligence and Research, 'Continental Shelf Boundary: Iran-Qatar', *Limits in the Seas*, no. 25, 9 July 1970.

2 US Department of State, Office of the Geographer, Bureau of Intelligence and Research, 'Continental Shelf Boundary: Bahrain-Iran', *Limits in the Seas*, no. 58, 13 September 1974.

Iran-Oman

The continental shelf boundary between these states extends for a distance of 124.85 nautical miles from the eastern section of the Persian Gulf through the Straits of Hormuz to the Gulf of Oman.[1] Concluded on 25 July 1974, the agreement came into force on 28 May 1975. Most of the boundary line's twenty-two demarcated points are equidistant to both coasts although, in a number of instances, it is evident that various Omani and Iranian islands were utilized as a coastal baseline. The endpoints of the Iran-Oman continental shelf boundary were left undemarcated since the lateral offshore boundaries between Oman and the shaikhdoms of Ras al-Khaimah and Sharjah have yet to be defined.

Those continental shelf boundaries in the Lower Gulf which remain outstanding are as follows.

Bahrain-Qatar

As discussed earlier (see p 49), the sole issue precluding the conclusion of a continental shelf boundary agreement between Bahrain and Qatar is the dispute over jurisdictional rights to the Hawar Islands. Bahrain, which currently exercises control over these islands situated only some 900 metres off the north-western shore of the Qatari Peninsula, has in the past maintained that they are required for its burgeoning population. This rationale defies credibility, however, as the largest island in this chain has an area of roughly five square kilometres. In an attempt to move the issue to a negotiated settlement Qatar is reported to have made two recent proposals: (a) the offer to accept a deviated continental shelf boundary line ceding Bahrain part of its territorial sea in return for Hawar; and (b) the additional offer to share equally any revenue derived from oil exploration in that contested area.[2]

Qatar-Saudi Arabia

Though an agreement delimiting the continental shelf boundary in the Bay of al-Salwa (west of the Qatar peninsula) was reportedly reached in December 1965, it has neither been officially ratified nor published.

---

1 US Department of State, Office of the Geographer, Bureau of Intelligence and Research, 'Continental Shelf Boundary: Iran-Oman', *Limits in the Seas*, no. 67, 1 January 1976.

2 Cited in Ali A. El-Hakim, *op.cit.*, p 121. The Kuwait daily, *Al-Qabas*, has reported that Saudi Arabia is currently mediating between Bahrain and Qatar over the status of the Hawar Islands. The Saudis' first step was to ask both sides to stop making public statements about the dispute; cited in *MEED*, 21 March 1980.

UAE (inter-emirate)

Of the seven emirates making up the Federal State, only Abu Dhabi and Dubai have concluded an agreement defining their lateral offshore boundary. In 1965 British mediation between the two parties led to a settlement which was unilaterally abrogated by Dubai a year later following Continental Oil's discovery of a major new oilfield in the area. On 18 February 1968, Abu Dhabi and Dubai agreed to a modification of the original agreement which confirmed Dubai's sovereignty over the Fateh oilfield and otherwise adjusted the continental shelf boundary to its advantage.[1] The remaining submarine borders between the emirates have yet to be delimited.[2] That their ambiguity has not resulted in a proliferation of inter-emirate disputes may be attributed to the fact that substantial offshore oil discoveries towards the northern emirates have not occurred. A dispute arose in 1970 between Sharjah and Umm al-Qaiwain, and their respective oil concessionaires, over drilling rights following the discovery of a major new field nine miles off the coast of Abu Musa Island. Whereas an agreement concluded between the two emirates under the auspices of the British government had stipulated that the island (then under the sole control of Sharjah) would enjoy the customary three mile territorial sea, this was unilaterally extended to twelve miles by Sharjah in 1969. At this moment the dispute is still the subject of adjudication both between the emirates and their respective oil concessionaires.

Iran-UAE

Since 1971 the major factor precluding the final conclusion of a continental shelf boundary agreement between Iran and the UAE has been the former's invasion and continuing occupation of Abu Musa and the Tunb Islands. As noted earlier (see p 56), jurisdiction over those strategically located islands governing the western mouth of the Straits of Hormuz had been previously in the hands of Sharjah and Ras al-Khaimah respectively.

1 El-Hakim, *op.cit.*, p 99.

2 This notwithstanding the fact that in 1963-64, the British government, acting in its role as the protecting power, determined the continental shelf boundaries of the Trucial States and proposed those lines of demarcation to the shaikhdoms' rulers.

In view of the presence of considerable oil reserves in their offshore territorial waters, Iran and the emirates of Abu Dhabi and Dubai have conducted active negotiations to delimit their continental shelf boundary. In the period prior to the Iranian naval landings on Abu Musa and the Tunb Islands, it was reported that Abu Dhabi had actually initialled an agreement with Iran.[1] On 31 August 1974, Dubai — which had long sought to foster closer ties with Tehran so as to serve as a counterbalance against Abu Dhabi's paramountcy within the Federation — concluded an accord with the Iranian government, though it has yet to be ratified.[2] The boundary line extends for a distance of 39.25 nautical miles with endpoints which coincide with those of the 1968 lateral offshore boundary line between Abu Dhabi-Dubai and the unilateral declaration made by Sharjah in 1964 concerning its continental shelf border with Umm al-Qaiwain.

UAE-Oman

The Omani continental shelf boundaries with both the emirates of Ras al-Khaimah and Sharjah remain undefined. The former, as discussed above (see p 60) re-emerged as a source of contention in 1977-78 following the start of oil exploration in the waters adjacent to a disputed stretch of territory (i.e. between the villages of Dawra and Rims in Ras al-Khaimah). At one point, oilmen from the Zapata Company drilling off Ras al-Khaimah were forced to suspend work when Sultan Qabous despatched a warship to the area to reinforce his claim.[3] This coincided with the movement of elements of the Omani army — ostensibly on manoeuvres — five kilometres into the territory of Ras al-Khaimah.[4] These military moves were accompanied by statements from the Omani Foreign Ministry indicating a desire to move the issue toward a negotiated settlement. This interest was acknowledged by both parties in the aftermath of the Iranian Revolution and the politically charged regional security environment which it engendered.

1   Richard Young, 'The Persian Gulf', in R. Churchill, K.R. Simmonds and Jane Welch (eds.), *New Directions in the Law of the Sea*, vol. III, London, 1973, p 233. One problem in these negotiations apparently centred upon the status of Bani Yas Island (145 miles to the west of Abu Dhabi) and whether it would be considered part of Abu Dhabi's coast for the purpose of determining baselines.

2   US Department of State, Office of the Geographer, Bureau of Intelligence and Research, 'Continental Shelf Boundary: Iran-United Arab Emirates (Dubai), *Limits in the Seas*, no. 63, 30 September 1975.

3   *MEED*, 16 December 1977.

4   *Arabia and the Gulf*, 28 November 1977.

4 Southern Arabia

Relations between Oman and the PDRY

The principal focal point of tension between these ideologically hostile parties has been the intermittent support proffered by the Aden regime to insurgents operating within the bordering Dhofar region of the Sultanate.[1] These links date to the mid-1960s when the Dhofar Liberation Front (DLF), created in 1964 through a union of the Dhofari chapter of the Arab Nationalist Movement (ANM) and the so-called 'Dhofari Benevolence Society', forged ties with revolutionary groups in Aden. In the early years of the movement, additional assistance was lent by the Saudis owing to the traditional rivalry for influence (e.g. the Buraimi Oasis dispute) waged between themselves and the Sultan of Muscat and Oman. Until the establishment of the PDRY in 1967, Dhofari resistance was confined primarily to small-scale military operations from mountain sanctuaries against the British-dominated forces of the Sultan. During this period, the DLF was politically divided between tribesmen, who regarded the rebellion less as a secessionist move-

---

1 A secondary issue (though one not recently referred to by either party) is that concerning sovereignty rights over the Kuria Muria Islands (located off the Dhofar coast). Having been ceded to Queen Victoria in 1854 by the Sultan of Muscat, they were returned by the British government to Oman through means of a bilateral agreement concluded on 30 November 1967. Three days later, the first President of the PDRY disputed the Omani right to sovereignty over this island chain. Since that time, however, scant mention has been made of this wholly unfounded claim in the Aden regime's declaratory policy; see El-Hakim, *The Middle Eastern States and the Law of the Sea*, 1979, p 18.

ment than a drive for autonomy against the repressive rule of Sultan Said bin Taimur, and the ANM faction, which viewed the Dhofar campaign as but one component of a broad ideological struggle in the Arab world.[1]

The accession of the Marxist-oriented National Liberation Front (NLF) to power in South Yemen in December 1967 was to have a profound impact on the course of the Dhofar insurgency. In the ensuing period, this relationship would ensure the DLF a secure training and staging area from which it could carry out military activities across the Omani frontier. An added consequence, however, was the dramatic change which it brought about in the ideological complexion of the DLF.[2] This was evidenced in the adoption of an overtly Marxist-Leninist programme at the 'Second Congress' of the DLF at Himrin in the Dhofar interior in September 1968. The ascendancy of the ANM faction (with external NLF backing) within the Dhofari movement was confirmed when the DLF Congress voted to change the organization's name to the Popular Front for the Liberation of the Occupied Arab Gulf (PFLOAG)[3] in order more accurately to reflect its new trans-national political orientation. At this time, external assistance began to be channelled to the PFLOAG from the People's Republic of China and, subsequently, the Soviet Union via the PDRY.

In the wake of this augmentation in the PFLOAG's military capabilities, the Dhofari rebellion entered a new phase. Indeed, by the early months of 1970, insurgent units (which had previously been responsible for bringing a considerable proportion of the rural population under PFLOAG authority) were, for the first time, able to engage the Sultan's Armed Forces (SAF) in conventional battles and vie for control of the region's few semi-urban areas. Despite this marked deterioration in the government's military situation, the PFLOAG suffered a major political setback in July of that year when Sultan Said bin Taimur was deposed

---

1 For an historical analysis of the Dhofar rebellion see: J.B. Kelly, 'Hadramaut, Oman, Dhofar: the experience of revolution', *Middle Eastern Studies*, 12, no. 2, May 1976, pp 213-29; and Richard F. Nyrop, et al., *Area Handbook for the Persian Gulf States*, pp 385-99.

2 The increasing radicalization of the DLF which prompted the Saudis to cut off their assistance to the Dhofari insurgents even prior to the establishment of the PDRY. In spite of the political polarization within Southern Arabia which that event augured, however, the Saudis refused to assist the combined British-Omani force in their counter-insurgency campaign. This stemmed from the latter's continued resistance to Saudi territorial claims (e.g. the Buraimi Oasis dispute). For a discussion of Saudi policy towards the Dhofar rebellion see Mordechai Abir, *Oil, Power and Politics: Conflict in Arabia, the Red Sea and the Gulf*, Frank Cass, London, 1974, pp 13-15 ff.

3 In December 1971, the word *Oman* would be substituted for *Occupied* so as to form the Popular Front for the Liberation of Oman and the Arab Gulf.

by his son, Qabous, in a bloodless coup initiated with British abetment. The offer of political reform and economic development which the new Sultan brought with him to power did much to bolster the sagging morale of the SAF and enhance the legitimacy of the central government. Within eighteen months, Qabous's skilful diplomacy was responsible for cementing a new relationship between Oman and Saudi Arabia. As a *quid pro quo* for Muscat's support of Riyadh's policy in Eastern Arabia, the Saudi leadership agreed to extend considerable economic assistance to Oman as well as to interdict those PFLOAG supply routes which passed along its frontier with the Dhofar region.[1]

In 1972, fighting along the South Yemen-Oman border intensified as the PFLOAG reached the apex of its power. A major incident occurred on 6 May when the Sultanate's Air Force bombed South Yemeni gun positions near Hauf in response to a thirty-six hour artillery barrage on the Omani border post at Habrut. Two months later, the PFLOAG mounted their largest operation of the war. In a bid to symbolize their new status through the seizure of a major government stronghold, a force totalling some 250 guerrillas attacked the coastal town of Marbat, approximately fifty miles east of Salalah. The SAF, backed by British aircraft and ground personnel, were, however, able to repulse successfully this major PFLOAG military effort.[2] To many observers, the setback sustained by the insurgents in July 1972 (suffered despite the direct commitment of PDRY forces on their behalf) constituted a major turning point in the Dhofari conflict. Thereafter, the PFLOAG were forced to revert to their earlier pattern of low-level guerrilla activities from mountain base camps.

The modernization of the SAF initiated by Qabous upon assuming power continued apace in 1973. Made possible by both foreign assistance (primarily British and Saudi) and revenues generated through domestic oil production, this programme further served to turn the military tide against the PFLOAG. One indicator of this deterioration in the Front's position was a steady flow of defections over to the government side.[3] In that same year, Sultan Qabous used the Iranian *Tudeh* party's declaration of support for the Dhofari insurgents as the occasion for requesting direct assistance (including an Iranian military presence) from the Shah. The latter responded immediately, despatching a battle group of 1,200 men to Dhofar in November 1973. On

---

1 Abir, *op.cit.*, p 26.

2 *Keesing's Contemporary Archives*, 1973, pp 25654-25655; Nyrop, *op.cit.*, pp 391-92.

3 By the end of 1974, the number of defections are reported to have reached over a thousand men. Many of these former guerrillas subsequently served in irregular units of the SAF (referred to as *firqat*) to great effect.

19 December, this force, called the Imperial Iranian Task Force (IITF), assumed the defence of the seventy-five mile road stretch connecting Salalah with the vital trail junction at Thamarit to the north.[1] This was part of the broader 'Operation Thimble' in which the IITF combined with the British led SAF moved to consolidate the government's military gains of that year.[2]

Having seized the military initiative in 1973, the Muscat government's position in Dhofar was further bolstered through the Sultan's domestic and regional foreign policies. Indeed, the combined effect of these was such as to bring about an almost complete reversal of the position in which Oman was enmeshed prior to the accession of Qabous. The military and political reversals suffered by the PFLOAG during 1973 and 1974 prompted a structural reorganization of the party as well as an adjustment of its political manifesto. On 9 August 1974, the PFLOAG announced that the importance accorded its trans-national revolutionary ideology (as translated into a programme of action) was to be downgraded in favour of a renewed emphasis upon the primary goal of 'liberating' Oman. In keeping with this narrowing of geographical scope, the party's name was recast: hence, the Popular Front for the Liberation of Oman and the Arab Gulf (PFLOAG) became merely the Popular Front for the Liberation of Oman (PFLO).

Despite this attempt somehow to revitalize the Dhofari movement, various foreign policy initiatives, occurring concomitantly, contributed to the continued deterioration in the Front's overall position. The process of *rapprochement* between Iraq and Iran (initiated in 1974 and culminating in the Algiers Accord of March 1975) was a principal factor hastening the former to subdue its previously vociferous support for the PFLO in inter-Arab politics.[3] The attempt by Iraq during this period to re-enter the Arab political mainstream through the moderation of its foreign policy posture within the Gulf region prompted it to join Egypt and Kuwait in a diplomatic initiative to effect a like change in PDRY policy. Though clearly a divisive issue within the South Yemeni leader-

---

1 *Ibid.*, p 395. The presence of Iranian forces in Oman quickly became a significant issue in inter-Arab politics due to the suspicions surrounding the Shah's increasingly activist policy in the Gulf. Reported attempts by the Arab League to have Oman substitute Arab forces for the IITF proved unsuccessful. Though the IITF was briefly withdrawn for the above mentioned political reasons in October 1974, they returned at increased strength (totalling some 2,500 men) in early 1975.

2 Chubin and Zabih, *The Foreign Relations of Iran*, 1974, pp 310-12. Complementing its active military role in Dhofar, Iranian diplomacy was successful in securing a pledge of non-interference from Peking (i.e., a cut-off in military assistance to the PFLOAG).

3 In June 1976, the Ba'athist government closed all PFLO offices within Iraq as a final means of indicating the termination of its support for the Dhofar rebellion.

ship (see p 89), the lure of outside economic assistance as a means of ameliorating the country's desperate fiscal plight did encourage tactical steps to reduce the revolutionary content of its foreign policy. On 10 March 1976, the direction of this process was confirmed when the PDRY established diplomatic relations with Saudi Arabia to end the nine year period of their mutual isolation.

This development was followed soon thereafter by reports which indicated that the Aden government had acted (upon Saudi instigation) to curtail PFLO movements into Dhofar and was considering a normalization of relations with the Sultanate.[1] From the PDRY's position, the major provision of the March 1976 agreement was that which called for the withdrawal of all foreign military units. This was taken to mean specifically the evacuation of the IITF from Dhofar. Though the Iranians came under increasing pressure from the Saudis to take this action the Shah maintained that Imperial Forces would remain in Oman until such time as Muscat requested their withdrawal. Despite Omani claims in 1976-77 that the PFLO had been crushed and that military clashes along PDRY border had ceased, Sultan Qabous was reluctant to yield to Arab League pressure concerning the continued presence of the IITF. This was motivated less by the actual military situation in Dhofar (PFLO resistance having been reduced to sporadic, small-scale operations) than the strengthening of PDRY ties with the Soviet bloc (e.g. its support of Soviet policy in the Horn of Africa).[2]

For its part, South Yemen fervently denied that any understanding had been reached with Oman about the curtailment of PFLO activities in Dhofar. It asserted that the stationing of Iranian forces along its frontier remained the main obstacle to the normalization of relations.[3] The diplomatic impasse between Oman and the PDRY was further reinforced when the June 1978 coup in Aden brought to power that faction of the National Front (NF) which reportedly opposed the

1 This was announced by the Sudanese President, Ja'Far al-Numayri, at the Red Sea Conference held in Ta'izz (North Yemen) on 23 March 1977.

2 Following the tenuous victory of the MPLA in Angola, it was reported that a Cuban military contingent had been transferred to the PDRY to replace Soviet and East German advisers.

3 MEED, 8 November 1977. In addition to the withdrawal of the IITF, it was unofficially reported that the PDRY's terms for the establishment of diplomatic relations with Muscat included the demand that Qabous should accept a member of the PFLO into his cabinet. Both conditions, of course, were rejected out of hand by the Sultan. With respect to the Iranian military presence in Dhofar, it was reported at the time of the Shah's four-day visit to Oman in December 1977 that one brigade of the IITF remained in the province (International Herald Tribune, 6 December 1977).

policy of *rapprochement* with the Gulf region's conservative monarch-ical regions (see p 82). At the same time, Oman's position within inter-Arab politics was severely compromised to the indirect benefit of South Yemen as a result of its sole support of Egypt and the Camp David process. Reports in the month of Khomeini's accession to power in Tehran, indicating the presence of a few small Egyptian military units in Dhofar, reflected the developing security relationship between Cairo and Muscat.[1] This assistance (fully in keeping with President Sadat's attempt to supplant Iran as the 'stabilizing' power of the region) was not surprisingly condemned by both the PDRY and the Soviet Union.[2]

As will be discussed further, the April 1980 shake-up in the South Yemen regime has been accompanied by a reversion to the previous pattern of policy (i.e. the fostering — whether for tactical reasons or not — of closer ties with more moderate Arab Gulf states). Though relations between Oman and the PDRY remain, at best, strained, Saudi Arabia and Kuwait — seeking to minimize the dangers of political polarization within the region — have made efforts to mediate their differences.[3] Though the PDRY continues to pose the only major external threat to Oman, the consensus amongst informed observers is that the combination of internal divisions and the ongoing danger of revived conflict with North Yemen precludes the immediate possibility of renewed large-scale PDRY/PFLO military operations against the Muscat government.

1 In one report (*Financial Times*, 15 February 1979) the size of the Egyptian contingent was placed at around 200.

2 See *TASS* statement cited in *MEED*, 4 May 1979.

3 Recent attempts by Kuwait, with Saudi encouragement, to arrange a meeting between the foreign ministers of the two countries reportedly foundered on rumours that Oman had granted the USA air and naval facilities at Masirah.

Relations between the Yemens

The history of strained relations between the Yemens dates to the end of Ottoman rule in Southern Arabia in October 1918. During the ensuing period, North Yemen's temporal and religious leader, Imam Yahya, moved to consolidate control over the areas previously under Turkish suzerainty in a concerted attempt to forge a unified and independent state. Differences with the British government quickly arose when Yahya sought to assert authority over frontier territories that the former considered to be part of its Western Aden Protectorate. Intermittent border incidents led to bilateral negotiations which failed, however, to produce an agreement until 1934. In that year, a forty year Anglo-Yemeni Treaty of Peace and Friendship was concluded in Sanaa which (amongst its other provisions) conferred on North Yemen a boundary slightly more favourable than the one agreed between Britain and Turkey in 1914.[1]

The revival of North Yemeni claims to the Protectorate came shortly after the accession of Yahya's son, Ahmad, to the Imamate in 1948. Skirmishes along the frontier were discussed during a series of meetings in London in 1950 which, in turn, resulted in the creation of a joint committee to study and make a final determination of the disputed boundary. The inability of the commission to reach agreement was accompanied by the resumption of sporadic, small-scale border incursions by North Yemen.[2] Having adopted this course so as to force Britain's hand, Sanaa received the full diplomatic backing of the Arab League. The establishment of relations with the Soviet Union and the conclusion of a military pact with Egypt and Saudi Arabia in 1956 signified the advent of a new, more activist, foreign policy posture on the part of North Yemen. A reflection of this shift (with its attendant accentuation of external influences) was the subsequent influx of arms and technicians from the Eastern bloc (including China). Two years later, the Sanaa government, in an evident bid to bolster its pan-Arab credentials, acceded to membership in the short-lived United Arab Republic (UAR) under President Gamal Abdel Nasser.

Within North Yemen, the revolution of September 1962 quickly devolved into a protracted civil war, pitting the contending Republican and Royalist factions against one another. From the outset, the

---

1 Peter Mansfield, *The Middle East: A Political and Economic Survey*, Oxford University Press, New York, 1973, p 157.

2 *Ibid.*, p 158.

conflict was marked by the significant participation of outside powers on their behalf: whereas the former (based in Ta'izz) benefited from the direct involvement of Egyptian forces, the latter (clustered around the Imam's power base in Sanaa) were actively supported by Saudi Arabia.[1] After five years of inconclusive fighting, the turning point in the conflict came, paradoxically, with the 1967 Arab-Israeli conflict. In the aftermath of the staggering defeat sustained by the Egyptian Army in the Sinai during the Six Day War, Nasser decided to withdraw his forces from Yemen. This was coupled with a successful appeal to Saudi Arabia (conveyed by Sudan during the Khartoum Arab Summit Conference in late August of that same year) to match Egyptian restraint through the curtailment of its own military assistance to Royalist forces. This joint initiative was eventually translated into a pronounced reduction in the overall level of fighting within North Yemen. In 1970 (at the end of a three year period which witnessed the continuation of intermittent fighting between the two sides, as well as significant political power jockeying within each faction), moderate Republicans and Royalists were able to reach agreement on the abolition of the monarchy and the establishment of a reunified state to be known as the Yemen Arab Republic (YAR).

Though propelled by different dynamics, the course of events in North Yemen during the 1960s did have a significant impact on political developments to the south during the same period. Indeed, the arms which permitted the National Liberation Front (NLF) to inaugurate its military campaign for independence in October 1963 were supplied by sympathetic parties in North Yemen. Four years later, the NLF emerged as the dominant politico-military force in South Yemen when it received the open support of the British-trained South Arabian Army. With this decisive backing, the NLF was soon able to eclipse its primary rival for power, the Egyptian influenced Front for the Liberation of South Yemen (FLOSY). In November 1967, as the British evacuated Aden and the remnants of FLOSY fled to political refuge in North Yemen, the NLF formed the government of the unified People's Republic of South Yemen (PRSY).[2]

The Aden government's adoption of a more explicitly Marxist-Leninist political programme coupled with the receipt of large-scale Soviet military aid resulted in the steady deterioration of its relations with neighbouring Arab states. South Yemeni abetment of the

1 A detailed historical consideration of the Yemen civil war would clearly be beyond the scope of this book. For such a study see, for example, Dana Adams Schmidt, *Yemen: The Unknown War*, Bodley Head, London, 1968.

2 In December 1970, the country's name was changed to its present one, the People's Democratic Republic of Yemen (PDRY).

PFLOAG in its conflict with the Oman government in Dhofar was but one move which called into question the PRSY's long-term intentions and regional aspirations. The June 1969 change in regime which brought President Salem Rubai Ali and Party Secretary Abdul Fattah Ismail to power produced a further hardening in the attitude of South Yemen towards the more conservative states adjacent to it. With the assistance of radical political refugees from the north, the NLF began a subversion campaign against the Sanaa government at the precise moment when the latter was adroitly moving to broaden and strengthen its relationship with Riyadh. Indeed, it was the mutual fear of such a development which had initially prompted Saudi Arabia and the YAR to move towards a *rapprochement* of this kind.

Counter-attempts by Sanaa to use political dissidents from the PDRY[1] to destabilize the Aden regime were accompanied by increasingly serious border incidents. In late September 1972, these escalated to the point of full-scale hostilities. Though neither side was able to gain a decisive military advantage along the frontier, North Yemeni forces were able to seize and occupy the long disputed island of Kamaran, a few miles north of the port of Hodeida.[2] The Arab League was instrumental in effecting a ceasefire which left each holding small territorial pockets of the other. Both Libya (with the evident diplomatic backing of the Soviet Union) and Egypt were quick to offer their services in the mediation of the dispute. A preliminary round of talks in Cairo in October was followed by the conclusion in Libya of the so-called Tripoli Agreement on 28 November 1972.[3] The major provision of this accord was to pledge the PDRY and the YAR to work towards the creation of a united Yemeni state within one year of its signing. While failing to address the underlying problems which had precipitated the 1972 crisis, the net effect of the Tripoli Agreement was to defuse temporarily tensions between the two Yemens.[4] In its wake, various joint committees were established to discuss the mechanics of unification. The eventual collapse of these efforts may be attributed to three main factors: first, the ideological chasm separating the PDRY and the

1   In July 1972, negotiations amongst the various anti-NLF political factions within the YAR (e.g. ex-FLOSY members) led to the formation of the 'United National Front of South Yemen'.

2   Another ongoing source of controversy centres around the status of Perim Island (strategically located at the narrowest point of the Straits of Bab el-Mandeb). Though under PDRY occupation since the British withdrawal from Aden in 1967, Sanaa continues to maintain its claim to sovereignty over the island. See El-Hakim, *op.cit.*, pp 17-20.

3   *Keesing's Contemporary Archives*, 1972, p 25654. A major stumbling block to the implementation of the ceasefire was the announcement by the National Democratic Front (or NDF, a PDRY-based amalgam of left wing parties opposed to the Sanaa government) that it would not be party to the Arab League's agreements.

4   For a discussion of the 1972 conflict and its implications see Abir, *op.cit.*, pp 110-13.

YAR; second, the clash of personal rivalries between their leaderships for dominant political influence in any settlement; and third, opposition within each state to the unification process.[1] Although the breakdown of negotiations over unification was in many respects predictable, the pursuit of that goal as a long-term political objective was not abandoned.

In the period following the 1972 crisis, relations between the Yemens were governed largely by internal developments within each state. Under the leadership of President Salem Rubai Ali, South Yemeni foreign policy took a decidedly more pragmatic turn. This new posture was marked by the incremental improvement of Aden's diplomatic ties with the West and moderate Arab governments. The culmination of this process came in 1976 with the establishment of relations with Saudi Arabia and the ensuing reports of a tacit ceasefire in Dhofar between the PDRY/PFLO and Omani forces (see p 78). Rubai's policy of accommodation was not without opposition within the ruling NFL. The Party's Secretary-General, Abdul Fattah Ismail, became chief spokesman of the rival faction which favoured the continuation of a more militant foreign policy orientation. In October 1975, the latter's personal power and prestige had been significantly enhanced when the Vanguard Party (supported by the Iraqi Ba'athists) and the People's Democratic Union (South Yemen's Communist Party) were absorbed within the NLF to form the United National Front Political Organization (UNFPO). With Ismail maintaining his position as Secretary-General of this expanded political party, the power struggle within the PDRY intensified. These differences between the Rubai and Ismail factions emerged over such issues as South Yemeni support for Soviet policy in the Horn of Africa.[2] The ousting and execution of Rubai by Ismail and Prime Minister Ali Nasser Mohammed on 26 June 1978 were accompanied by charges that the former President had been planning a *coup d'état* in the light of his waning influence within the UNFPO. These events followed the assassination two days earlier of the North Yemeni President, Lieutenant-Colonel Ahmed Hussein el Ghashmi, in

---

1 Opposition, primarily tribal, to the proposed union was most intense in the YAR. In the north, the Zeidi tribes (a local Shi'ah sect comprising some fifty-five per cent of the YAR's present population) feared that unification would transform them into a minority owing to the adherence of the remaining northerners and virtually the entire southern populace to the Shafii sect of Sunni Islam. Many residents of the PDRY also opposed the creation of a single Yemeni state for fear that its renewed emphasis upon tribal and sectarian affiliation would compromise their relatively secular life-style.

2 President Rubai is reported to have been opposed to Soviet use of South Yemen as a base for airlifting men and material to Ethiopia for that country's campaign against Somalia and Eritrean secessionists.

which President Rubai was alleged to have been involved.[1] In the aftermath of Rubai's overthrow, Ismail transformed the NLF into the Yemeni Socialist Party, thereby making PDRY the first Arab state to be governed by an explicitly Marxist-Leninist party.

Amidst charges of South Yemeni complicity in the murder of Ghashmi, tensions along the YAR/PDRY frontier quickly began to escalate. On 3 July, Aden announced that North Yemeni forces had penetrated the Beihan border region (some 160 kilometres south-east of Sanaa) and had occupied two villages within the PDRY. Official YAR spokesmen denied the South Yemeni charge and, in turn, blamed the latter for the initiation of hostilities along the frontier. In mid-July, the Arab League (responding to a proposal from North Yemen) moved to avert a further deterioration of relations between the two countries through the establishment of a committee to study their respective grievances. In spite of these efforts at mediation, the latter half of 1978 was marked by the continuation of serious border incidents with both sides exchanging charges of subversion[2] and the massing of troops along the frontier.

On 24 February 1979, North Yemen accused South Yemen of launching a three-pronged ground attack across the border and called for an emergency meeting of the Arab League to consider this renewed act of 'aggression'. The Aden government countered with the claim that it was merely responding to an attack by North Yemen and asserted that its own forces had penetrated some thirty miles into the YAR, capturing the border towns of Al Bayda, Qataba and Harib. Within a week of the outbreak of hostilities came reports that the Carter administration, at the express request of President Saleh, had agreed to expedite delivery of the Saudi-financed arms package previously ordered by the Sanaa government (see p 90). Owing to the mediatory efforts of Iraq, Syria and Jordan, a ceasefire was announced on 2 March to take effect on the following day. At the same time, it was agreed that the Arab League Council of Foreign Ministers would meet in Kuwait (4-6 March) in order to secure the mutual withdrawal of forces and the normalization of relations.

1   The consensus of informed Western opinion is that the assassination in Sanaa was organized by elements within the PDRY who wished to discredit Rubai and thereby cause his downfall. For a detailed chronological review of events during this period see *Keesing's Contemporary Archives*, 1978, pp 29290-29291, and *Arab Report and Record*, 1978, pp 496-98, 609-10, 735-36, 865.

2   The Aden regime was accused of complicity in the October 1978 attempt to overthrow North Yemen's new head of state, Colonel Ali Abdullah Saleh.

Though both sides agreed to the Arab League ceasefire at the conclusion of the Kuwait conference, the disengagement of forces did not begin until a meeting in Sanaa on 16 March between their respective Chiefs of Staff. Twelve days later, Presidents Saleh and Ismail arrived in Kuwait to consider the nine point peace plan developed at the meeting of Arab League Foreign Ministers earlier in the month. In a move which caught most observers by surprise, the two leaders revealed their intention on 30 March of reviving the moribund 1972 Agreement on unification.[1] Subsequent meetings involving senior officials of North and South Yemen have failed, however, to produce any tangible results towards that end. In late October, the Kuwait daily, *Al Anbaa*, reported that an understanding had been reached between Presidents Saleh and Ismail to 'postpone the unification until circumstances are mature for the merger'.[2]

Although both sides continued in the following months to make ritualistic official affirmations of the desirability of unification, it was clear that the implementation of the 1979 Agreement had encountered much the same difficulties as its 1972 predecessor. Relations between the Yemens were slightly buoyed in February 1980 when the main North Yemeni opposition group, the Aden-based National Democratic Front (NDF),[3] concluded an agreement for political co-operation with the Sanaa government.[4] Despite this development, the NDF has been reported to be continuing small-scale guerrilla activities along the YAR border. The relationship between the Aden government and the NDF has since been complicated, however, by Premier Ali Nasser Mohammed's replacement of President Ismail on 21 April. The former has been described as being particularly eager to impose tight political controls on the Front's scope for independent military action.[5]

---

1 *Keesing's Contemporary Archives*, 1980, pp 30197-30198.

2 Cited in *ibid*., p 30199. This report came in the wake of the 4 October meeting in Sanaa between the PDRY's Premier, Ali Nasser Mohammed, and the North Yemeni President, Colonel Ali Abdullah Saleh.

3 See note 3 on p 81).

4 *International Herald Tribune*, 19 February 1980. In the wake of this tenuous agreement, North Yemeni Prime Minister Abdul Aziz Abdul-Ghani was quick to discount reports that several high ranking NDF officials were to be invited to join a re-constituted Cabinet in Sanaa (*Financial Times*, 19 March 1980).

5 *International Herald Tribune*, 7 June 1980.

Under present conditions, the internal preoccupations of both Yemeni regimes, coupled with the reluctance of their respective outside patrons to become directly implicated in renewed fighting in Southern Arabia, would appear to militate in favour of the maintenance of the political *status quo*. While the long term conflict between the Yemens is at heart a structural one (given their contending notions of national order), the immediate threat to stability arises from the persistence of serious, often unreported, border incidents with their attendant danger of unintended escalation.

Relations between Saudi Arabia and the Yemens

The complex and subtle inter-relationship with the Yemens remains one of the most sensitive aspects of Riyadh's regional policy. Relations between these two contending national groupings on the Arabian Peninsula have always been strained. The historical bases of this underlying animosity have been both dynastic rivalry and sectarian differences. Since the September 1962 revolution in Sanaa and the subsequent accession to power of a Marxist-oriented regime in Aden five years later, the nature of the competition between Saudi Arabia and the Yemens has been overtly ideological.

The dispute between Saudi Arabia and North Yemen over the determination of their still largely undemarcated boundary dates from the end of the Ottoman period. Following the withdrawal of Turkish forces, Imam Yahya (as discussed on p 79) quickly moved to assert control over those adjacent border areas which he considered to be part of a 'Greater Yemen'. In Asir, the region lying south of the Hijaz on the Red Sea, this drive brought him into conflict as successive stages with both the British and the Saudis. Though British forces occupied Hodeida in 1919 in order militarily to bolster that branch of the Idrisi family which then ruled Asir, they were withdrawn in the following year. At that time, Ibn Saud, seeking to further extend Wahabbi rule on the Arabian Peninsula, sent his son Faisal to annex the northern highlands of that province.[1] Throughout the late 1920s and early 1930s, Asir remained the focal point of Saudi-Yemeni hostility, with each side lending assistance and political backing to its favoured faction of the Idrisi family. The outbreak of open hostilities between the two sides in 1933 resulted in the speedy rout of Yemeni forces. On 20 May 1934, the Treaty of Muslim Friendship and Arab Fraternity was concluded at Taif confirming Saudi control over the disputed Asir and Najran territories. Though the return of the port city of Hodeida to Imam Yahya has been cited to demonstrate the moderate nature of the Taif settlement, the influence of outside pressure was evidently a major factor in the Saudi decision. Whatever the intentions harboured by each side,[2] the importance of the 1934 agreement was that it served as the basis of stable relations between Saudi Arabia and Yemen (Sanaa) over the next quarter century.

---

1 Peter Mansfield, *op.cit.*, pp 156-57.

2 Manfred Wenner reports, for example, that as late as 1940 Yemeni school textbooks divided the country into three areas: independent Yemen; Asir (under Saudi occupation) and Hadrawmaut and Oman (under British occupation); cited in Richard F. Nyrop, et al., *Area Handbook for the Yemens*, GPO, Washington, DC, 1977, p 27.

As discussed in the preceding section, the establishment of a republic in North Yemen in the wake of the September 1962 revolution was regarded by the Saudi leadership as a direct ideological challenge.[1] In a reflection of the growing political cleavages within the country, King Saud's decision materially to assist Royalist efforts to restore the Imamate was immediately followed by the desertion of several Saudi Air Force officers to Egypt with their aircraft. It also provided President Nasser with the political means to justify the continued build-up of Egyptian forces in Yemen. During the period which followed, the Saudis were repeatedly humiliated by the penetration of regular forces (both Republican and UAR) across their southern frontier which they were militarily unable to check. Upon the accession of King Faisal to the throne in November 1964, there occurred a marked, albeit gradual, shift in the Saudi attitude towards the civil war. Increasingly, the presence of Nasserite forces in Southern Arabia was perceived as posing a more immediate threat to Saudi security than that of ideological contagion from a republican Yemen. Thereafter, the restoration of dynastic rule in Yemen was consistently subordinated by Faisal to the overriding objective of securing an Egyptian military withdrawal.[2]

The Arab League conference of September 1964 in Alexandria provided an opportunity for Faisal and Nasser to discuss the evolving situation in North Yemen. Both publicly committed themselves to the principle of terminating all outside interference so as to facilitate an internal settlement between the contending factions. The Alexandria summit was succeeded in August of the following year by a further round of bilateral discussions in Jeddah which culminated in a formal disengagement agreement. The Haradh peace conference (convened on 24 November as a direct result of this accord) quickly foundered owing to the implacable attitudes of both the rival Yemeni factions and their respective patrons. A reflection of the deadlocked state of the negotiations was the YAR delegation's insistence that the republican regime should solely preside over the country during any transitional period.[3] Relations between Egypt and Saudi Arabia concomitantly deteriorated when King Faisal journeyed to Iran in order to forge what was widely interpreted an an anti-Nasserite alliance of Islamic states.

The resounding Egyptian defeat in the June 1967 war compelled Nasser to shift dramatically his policy in Southern Arabia. At the Khartoum Conference in late August, he reached tacit agreement with

---

1   This perception was reinforced by President Sallal's announced intention of establishing a 'Republic of the Arabian Peninsula'.

2   Stookey, *op.cit.*, p 247.

3   *Ibid.*

King Faisal on the withdrawal of Egyptian forces from North Yemen in return for Saudi post-war economic assistance. And yet, just as the perceived threat posed by the continued presence of a UAR contingent on its southern frontier ended,[1] Riyadh faced an even more disturbing challenge in the form of the newly installed National Liberation Front (NLF) regime in Aden. In the aftermath of this emergence of revolutionary republicanism, Saudi Arabia worked towards the establishment of a pragmatic relationship with the Sanaa government in order to promote a common front against South Yemen.[2] The necessity of such an arrangement was soon confirmed in the eyes of the Saudi leadership by the support proffered by the Aden regime to the Dhofar insurgents in Oman (see p 74).[3] In 1969, two sets of events precipitated a further deterioration in relations between Saudi Arabia and South Yemen: first, the abortive coup attempts of June and September by Arab nationalist elements within the armed forces which the Saudi leadership believed stemmed from the increasing radicalization of politics on the Arabian Peninsula; and second, the occurrence of sporadic attacks by South Yemen forces on Saudi outposts along their common frontier during the autumn.

In response to these developments, Saudi Arabia permitted dissident tribal leaders from Hadrawmaut to resume using its territory as a base for operations against the Aden government. As in 1967, the evident purpose of this move was to create some form of buffer state between Saudi Arabia and South Yemen. During the period between October 1970 and June 1971, these irregular forces launched a series of unsuccessful military raids into South Yemen. This campaign (confined primarily to the Hadrawmaut region) coincided with the resumption of clashes along the YAR-PDRY frontier. By February 1972, these had escalated to the point of open hostilities (see p 81). The agreement concluded in Cairo on 28 October 1972, committing both Yemen leaderships to the amalgamation of their states, clearly caught the Saudis unawares. Fearing the political and military potential of a unified 'Yemeni Republic' (i.e. that the ideological orientation of this nine million strong state would more closely conform to that of the PDRY than the YAR), Riyadh joined other conservative members of the Arab League in counselling Sanaa against such a move.

1 It is evident that the Saudis harboured the unfounded hope that the withdrawal of Egyptian troops would result in the collapse of republican forces within North Yemen.

2 The establishment of diplomatic relations between Saudi Arabia and North Yemen occurred on 23 July 1970.

3 During the period in which the NLF was solidifying its hold over the country, Saudi Arabia made an abortive attempt to establish a protectorate over the Hadrawmaut region of South Yemen. The clear purpose of this effort was to create some form of buffer between the two states.

Immediately following the 1972 conflict between the Yemens, Saudi Arabian policy assumed a markedly more accomodative posture. The mediatory efforts of Kuwait resulted in the onset of informal discussions between Riyadh and Aden at ministerial level. From the position of the South Yemen government (then under the increasingly pragmatic rule of President Salem Rubai Ali), two major factors militated in favour of participation in these preliminary negotiations: first, the waning state of the PDRY-based insurgency movement in Dhofar (see p 75), and second, the desire of the Aden regime to end its political isolation on the Arabian Peninsula. As discussed above, the culmination of this latter process was the establishment of diplomatic relations between Saudi Arabia and the PDRY in March 1976.

Over the same period, Saudi policy towards North Yemen remained centred on efforts both to reduce Sanaa's dependence on Soviet military assistance and to forestall the possibility of its unification with South Yemen. Owing to the magnitude of Riyadh's subventions to the YAR's armed forces, as well as its traditional relationship with the Hashed and Bakil northern tribal confederations,[1] Saudi Arabia retained a number of effective policy instruments in its dealings with the Sanaa regime. The timing of the assassination of President Ibrahim al-Hamdi by local tribesmen in October 1977 (on the eve of his scheduled journey to Aden to discuss possible steps towards unification) led to reports suggesting Saudi complicity.[2] Indeed, Riyadh's sway over al-Hamdi's successor, President Ghashmi, was such that he deemed it necessary to vet his cabinet selections with the Saudi leadership.[3]

Relations between Saudi Arabia and South Yemen further declined in the first quarter of 1978 as a consequence of Aden's vocal and material support for Soviet policy in the Horn of Africa. Though subsequently denied by Saudi officials, a serious clash between Saudi and PDRY forces was said to have occurred on 22-23 January at the village of Wadiah in the Hadrawmaut border region.[4] With additional incidents reported during February and March, Kuwait diplomatically intervened in the dispute so as to prevent any further escalation in fighting. Owing to these mediatory efforts, the South Yemen Interior Minister, Saleh

1 It has been reported that relations between the Saudis and the Hashed and Bakil tribes were such that it was necessary for the Sanaa government to conduct negotiations with them through the good offices of Riyadh. For a more comprehensive discussion of Saudi policy see Adeed Dawisha, 'Saudi Arabia's Search for Security', *Adelphi Papers*, no. 158, IISS, London, Winter 1979-80, p 21.

2 Both the Saudi and South Yemeni ambassadors were withdrawn following the Aden regime's charge overtly linking Riyadh to the assassination of al-Hamdi.

3 Dawisha, *op.cit.*

4 *Al-Manar*, London, 27 January 1978; cited in *Arab Report and Record*, 1978, p 69. This battle took place on the same site as that of the November 1969 round of Saudi-South Yemeni border fighting. For reports of subsequent clashes see *Ibid.*, pp 144, 177.

Musleh Qassem, visited Riyadh in mid-April for a discussion of the border situation. The political backdrop to these negotiations, however, remained their broad dichotomy of interests in the Horn of Africa. This divergence, in turn, served as but a further reflection of the structural ideological nature of the conflict between Saudi Arabia and the PDRY (i.e. one rooted in their contending patterns of national order). Hopes that the April meeting might ameliorate their strained relations were dashed upon the assassination of President Ghashmi in Sanaa on 24 June. The death of this overtly pro-Riyadh North Yemeni leader occurred when a bomb carried in a briefcase by a special envoy from President Rubai Ali of South Yemen exploded in his office. In response to this action, Saudi Arabia took the unprecedented step of sponsoring sanctions against the Aden regime within the Arab League. The recognition, however, that the political and economic isolation of South Yemen would only increase its dependence on the Soviet Union prompted the Saudi leadership to accept Iraqi mediation during the Baghdad summit in November 1978.[1]

The onset of fighting between the YAR and PDRY in February 1979 (see p 83) occurred at a time when Saudi Arabia was seeking to improve its relations with South Yemen. On 24 February, the PDRY's Foreign Minister, Mohammed Saleh Muti, had arrived in Riyadh to discuss arrangements for a visit to Saudi Arabia by President Ismail.[2] Four days later, in response to this outbreak of hostilities on its southern frontier, Saudi Arabia placed the nation's military forces on alert and announced its intention to withdraw its 1,200 man contingent from the Arab Deterrent Force (ADF) in Lebanon.[3] On 28 February, the Carter administration, responding to a direct request from President Saleh, announced that it would expedite delivery of the $100 million arms package previously ordered by North Yemen. At the same time, it was revealed that Saudi Arabia would underwrite an additional $390 million worth of American arms (including 12 F-5E fighter aircraft and 64 M-60 tanks) over a longer period subject to Congressional approval.[4] Though ostensibly motivated by Riyadh's desire to preserve the military balance in Southern Arabia, the speed and magnitude of this

1   Dawisha, op.cit.

2   Keesing's Contemporary Archives, 1980, p 30197.

3   The purpose of this latter move was to prompt Damascus to pressure the PDRY by threatening to take away the pan-Arab legitimacy of the Syrian presence in Lebanon.

4   Ibid. It was reported that this supplementary arms package would bring the overall cost of American arms supplied by Saudi Arabia to the YAR since 1976 to $540 million.

move reflected, at least in part, the profound impact of the Iranian Revolution on the political psychology of the Saudi leadership. However, with the cessation of fighting between the Yemens in March, their position *vis-à-vis* the arms package underwent a marked shift. Once the South Yemeni threat to the Sanaa regime had subsided, Saudi Arabia was clearly hesitant to further augment North Yemen's military capabilities, which later could be turned against their source. This represented a re-assertion of Riyadh's traditionally ambivalent attitude towards its military assistance relationship with the YAR (i.e. the Saudi desire to promote the development of a force structure within North Yemen adequate to deter attack from the PDRY, while at the same time insufficiently large to challenge the primacy of its own position on the Arabian Peninsula).

In June, the Saudis, who were serving as the conduit for the flow of American arms into North Yemen, began to hold up delivery of military equipment (particularly aircraft) earmarked for the YAR. This was a sign not only of lingering doubts over the long-term reliability of its Yemeni client, but of immediate disaffection with the Sanaa government's entry into negotiations with the Aden regime on the question of unification. In retaliation for this cut-off, President Saleh despatched a North Yemeni delegation to the Soviet Union to secure an alternative source of weapons.[1] On 30 August, reports indicated that the first shipment of Soviet arms (10 MiG-21s and 100 T-55 tanks accompanied by some 100 military advisers) had arrived in the port city of Hodeida. This development accelerated the deterioration in relations between Riyadh and Sanaa. The Saudi attempt in December further to punish the North Yemen regime through the unofficial suspension of its economic subventions had the net effect of increasing the YAR's dependence on the Soviet Union. This drift was reflected, for example, in the abstention of North Yemen on the United Nations General Assembly vote of 14 January 1980 which overwhelmingly called for the withdrawal of foreign troops from Afghanistan.[2]

Jarred by the prospect of losing some $700 million in annual economic assistance, President Saleh sent diplomatic envoys to Riyadh as part of a concerted effort to heal the political rift between the two

---

1 The humiliation of having to deal with Washington *via* Riyadh was clearly an additional factor militating in favour of this decision by the Sanaa government.

2 For an insightful discussion of political developments in Southern Arabia during this period see the articles by Patrick Seale in the *Observer*, 21 October 1979 and 17 February 1980.

countries. In March, amidst reports of two serious incidents along the still largely undefined Saudi-North Yemen border,[1] came word of the conclusion of an agreement on the aid question. In return for a resumption of Saudi economic and military assistance, Sanaa is reported to have pledged to loosen its relationship with the Soviet Union.[2] On 13 May, the Saudi Defence Minister, Prince Sultan Bin Abdel Aziz, and Foreign Minister, Prince Saud al-Faisal, paid an unusual visit to Sanaa to review the state of Saudi-Yemeni relations with President Saleh. Though the Saudi leaders expressed disquiet over the continued presence of Soviet military advisers within the country, no renewed threat to suspend or reduce the level of subventions was reportedly issued.

Given the demographic size and political orientation of the Yemens, Saudi Arabia continues to regard the long, largely undemarcated frontier in Southern Arabia as her most strategically vulnerable.[3] Though the territorial disputes between Saudi Arabia and the Yemens remain dormant at present, the recently renewed search for oil by both the PDRY and YAR in areas adjacent to the Kingdom may serve as the occasion for the revival of this set of issues.[4] From Riyadh's security perspective, the long-term challenge to its attempt to maintain a favourable status quo within the sub-region is posed by the possible — albeit improbable — unification of the two Yemen states. It is the prevention of this contingency which, as in the past, provides the motivating force behind Saudi policy in Southern Arabia. That said, the course of events since February 1979 (e.g. the dispute between Saudi Arabia and North Yemen over the supply of American military equipment) again demonstrates the limits of Riyadh's ability to manipulate its relations with the local actors so as to attain its desired political outcomes in this strategic tip of the Arabian Peninsula.

1 The first of these clashes was reported to have occurred on 17-18 February. See Le Monde, 19 March 1980 (quoting Arab diplomatic sources in Beirut). These claims were subsequently denied by high-ranking Saudi officials; see MEED, 14 March 1980.

2 International Herald Tribune, 20 March 1980; MEED, 28 March 1980. One feature of the accord was a Saudi commitment to recruit military instructors from Arab or Moslem countries to replace Soviet advisers.

3 It has been reported, for example, that in explaining the decision in February 1979 to withdraw the Saudi contingent from the Arab Deterrent Force (ADF) in Lebanon, Foreign Minister Prince Saud al-Faisal told the Lebanese Prime Minister: 'Just as you are burdened with your problems in the south, we also have a southern problem at the Saudi-Yemeni border'. Quoted in Al-Hawadith (Beirut), 13 April 1979; cited in Dawisha, op.cit., p 32.

4 For the first time, the Aden regime has invited foreign bids for oil concessions within the PDRY. Two of the five territorial blocks on offer border Saudi Arabia. For a report on this development see MEED, 31 August 1979. In North Yemen, oil exploration is currently under way along the Tihama coast between Hodeida and Saudi Arabia; see MEED, 2 May 1980.

5 Conclusion

In approaching any contemporary regional security study, one is immediately confronted with an analytical problem which is twofold: first, that within a region there is often no common perception of threat and its definition; and second, that what one means by security (i.e. the criteria themselves) may vary significantly from region to region. This necessity — that of critically differentiating amongst conceptions of security both *within* and *between* regions — remains a certain prerequisite for any serious appraisal of the nature and broader policy implications of inter-state conflict in the Gulf.

Recent events have served to highlight the declining utility of many of the traditional distinctions made with respect to Gulf security questions. In the contemporary period, such terms as regional and extra-regional, internal and external, appear to be less dichotomies than part of a broad continuum upon which interactions occur.

An analysis of the sources of inter-state conflict within the Gulf region (in contrast with those which could be made for other discrete geographical areas) is noteworthy in one major respect: no conflict is inherently unimportant. This circumstance may be attributed to at least two sets of factors. First, while it is a truism that domestic/local conflicts have become 'internationalized' owing to the ability of the great powers to project their military capabilities globally,[1] it is import-

1 The case of Iranian participation in the Dhofar war established the fact that this ability does not rest exclusively in the domain of the superpowers.

ant to underscore that their propensity to do so in any particular case (or region) remains subject to a complex calculus of risks and benefits. The magnitude of outside power interests in the Gulf region for at least the next two decades and the absence of a viable regional framework for security co-operation ensure the continuation of a high level of active involvement on their part. In an area of chronic domestic instability — one in which the so-called process of conflict resolution has more often been a function of manipulation than management — the problem of conflict escalation remains acute. The second set of factors exacerbates the implications of the first: namely, the manner in which the persistence of inter-state disputes contributes to the political polarization of the region as a whole. Again, it is this process which establishes at least some of the prerequisites for extra-regional intervention.

Patterns of inter-state conflict in the Gulf

Though there is the tendency of analysts — particularly in the political realm — to focus upon the *sui generis* nature of all phenomena, the findings of this study suggest a number of loose patterns to which the Gulf conflicts would appear to conform. First, in terms of their relative salience, it is evident that the traditional sources of inter-state conflict (e.g. disputes over water and tribal grazing rights) have given way to novel ones reflecting different criteria (e.g. competition for the control of strategic geographical locations, continental shelf disputes, etc.).

Second, with respect to the mechanisms affecting the activation of disputes and the perception of threat, an assessment of the historical record leads to the conclusion that both remain functions largely of the character of the regime in question. When a radical change in the domestic structure of a state occurs, one is confronted not only with a new regime, but, indeed, with a wholly new set of circumstances. The reassertion of Iran's claim to Bahrain by nature of their populations' shared religious affinity (i.e. Shi'ahism) is indicative of the manner in which ostensibly 'resolved' claims may be re-activated in the wake of a regime change through reference to a completely different set of criteria.

The third general proposition suggested by this regional security study stems from the second, and revolves around the relationship between the contending notions of legitimacy and national order evidenced within the Gulf political context. Here, it is necessary to differentiate critically between cases in which neither party accepts the domestic legitimacy of the other and those in which this fundamental question is not at issue. The inter-dynastic quarrels examined in Chapter 3 constitute ready examples of the latter type. In those instances, it was argued that the similarity in the domestic structures of the conservative monarchical states of the Lower Gulf was perhaps the principal factor militating in favour of the limitation of disputes. This characteristic has been reflected in the propensity of inter-dynastic questions to retain their narrow focus and thereby be more susceptible to 'resolution'.

By contrast, it has been witnessed that disputes involving ideologically hostile parties — that is, those stemming from radically different conceptions of domestic legitimacy and national order — are prone to draw in other issues and thus encompass the entire range of their bilateral relations. With respect to the disparate set of disputes between Iraq and Iran examined at length in Chapter 1, the contending nature of their domestic orders supports the conclusion that the problem between them is, at heart, a structural one. Within this context, specific bilateral differences (such as the Shatt al-Arab question) should be regarded not as the *stake*, but, more appropriately, as the *occasion* of conflict. The attendant danger of this kind of ideologically motivated dispute is that through broadening the scope of conflict, it might tend to implicate other states within the region. It is this ongoing possibility, for example, which has prompted the Arab Gulf states to explore ways in which to contain the Iraqi-Iranian dispute within those states' frontiers.[1]

The preceding analysis leads to a fourth, and final, set of considerations, namely the complex and subtle feedback relationship at work between the domestic and foreign policy postures of the local actors. In any study of Third World security questions, it is accepted as almost axiomatic that the factors governing the activation of inter-state conflict are largely reflections of internal weaknesses. Indeed, regimes are prone to utilize external threats as a means of distracting public attention from the more immediate problems of national integration and development. The findings of this paper indicate the degree to which many of the inter-state disputes within the Arabian Peninsula and the Gulf devolve from such domestic sources. Across this region, the clash between the notion of 'nation' and 'state' — that is, the conflict of contending nationalisms both *within* and *between* state structures[2] — remains a persistent source of instability. As evidenced in the case studies discussed above, this pattern of conflict may be manifested either as domestic struggles in which a central government attempts to forestall the process of national fragmentation within that country's borders or as a wider conflict across state frontiers.

Related to the problem of national integration is that of development. Here, the dilemmas of modernization often serve to exacerbate relations at the inter-state level through the accentuation of differences between contending conceptions of domestic order. This 'development problem' more overtly intrudes into the foreign policy realm in those instances when a concerted effort is made to 'export' a particular ideology. It has been observed that Nasser's attempt to have other states in the region emulate the model of Egyptian socialism stemmed from the belief that this was the necessary prerequisite for moderniza-

---

1 Five months prior to the outbreak of hostilities, the Qatar agency cited diplomatic sources for reports that the Gulf states were engaged in intensive contacts 'aimed at co-ordination and consultation on the necessary means to face the consequences of the worsening Iraqi-Iranian dispute'; *SWB* (ME/6391/i), 10 April 1980.

2 I am indebted to Philip Windsor for this point.

tion and Arab resurgence.[1] In the aftermath of the Iranian Revolution, the dominant faction of the Tehran leadership has similarly sought to 'export' that country's revolutionary experience and model of 'Islamic modernization' to adjacent states (particularly Iraq). As during Nasser's period, the net effect of such an exercise has been to translate previously discrete bilateral differences into a matrix of ideological hostility. In so challenging the domestic legitimacy of other Gulf regimes, the scope of conflict has been broadened and the potential for conflict management significantly reduced.

1 This point is made by Udo Steinbach in 'Sources of Third World Conflict' paper delivered at IISS Annual Conference: Stresa, Italy, 11-14 September 1980; to be published in a forthcoming *Adelphi Paper*.

Conditions for conflict management

The attempt to identify mechanisms for the prevention and amelioration of conflict in the Gulf is confounded by the close linkage which exists between the nature and dynamics of individual regimes and the activation of disputes involving them. In assessing the conditions and potential for conflict management, it is necessary to return to the basic dichotomy evidenced within this book between ideological disputes and those in which the fundamental questions of domestic legitimacy and national order are not at issue. As discussed above, it is this divergence which largely determines whether or not the scope of conflict expands to encompass the entire range of relations between the disputants.

The trend towards political polarization within the Gulf region has been accompanied by a proliferation in the number of disputes rooted in ideological hostility. In these instances, the potential for conflict management (let alone conflict resolution) is severely circumscribed owing to what might be characterized as the structural dissonance in the relationship between the parties. It is this underlying nature of the conflict which ensures that territorial questions (as well as other traditional *casus belli*) remain distinct from the primary political objectives of the combatants. As witnessed during the Iran-Iraq war, this characteristic of ideologically motivated disputes precludes the delineation of criteria for settlement and, therefore, severely reduces the effectiveness of institutions with a conflict management potential. The outbreak of hostilities (as distinct from the activation of a dispute within a state's declaratory policy) is not solely linked, however, to regime dynamics. It is also a function both of the prevailing military balance within the region and the relationship between the local actors and outside powers. The *timing* of Baghdad's decision to initiate a war against Iran was thus shaped by a confluence of three trends: first, the Khomeini regime's self-generated diplomatic isolation; second, other events within the international system which served to divert the attention of the superpowers (e.g. the US presidential election campaign, events in Poland and Afghanistan); and third, perhaps most importantly, Iraq's perception of a decisive military tilt in its favour owing to the degeneration of Iran's armed forces. Within this context, the maintenance of a regional power balance — while not addressing the root causes of conflict between ideologically hostile disputants — does emerge as a primary requisite for the prevention of open hostilities.

The experience of the Iran-Iraq war serves to highlight the limited utility of bilateral and multilateral mechanisms for conflict management in those instances where one of the principals involved in the dispute (i.e. Iran) remains non-receptive to such initiatives.[1] That said, however, the efficacy of multilateral efforts has been evidenced in certain cases in which political penalties have been collectively invoked or threatened so as to deter a unilateral move to alter the territorial status quo. The deferral of Iraq's irredentist claim concerning Kuwait, for example, should be attributed not solely to the deterrent posture of outside powers (i.e. the American and British readiness to assist Kuwait in the event of Iraqi aggression). The moderation of Iraqi policy with respect to this question — though clearly of a tactical nature — also stems from Baghdad's desire not to jeopardize its nascent position within inter-Arab politics. The consensus amongst Arab League member states in support of Kuwait's position is thus a factor contributing to stability through its impact on the Iraqi calculation of political costs attendant to this dispute's re-activation. As a general proposition, the effectiveness of this multilateral mechanism for conflict management is clearly contingent upon the maintenance of cohesion within the organization. The likelihood, however, is that such consensus within inter-Arab politics will remain elusive given the prevalence of disputes in which the *casus belli* is more ambiguous and where the combatants are of contending ideologies and foreign policy orientations.[2]

During a period of increasing political turbulence across the region, many observers have come to regard the formation of an indigenous security system — whether tacit or formal — as perhaps the most effective means of containing Gulf conflicts. At the time of the Muscat security conference in November 1976, for example, hope was expressed that this type of informal multilateral forum might eventually serve as the clearing house for the management of crises and conflicts within the region. Then, as during the present period, the problems precluding such a schema for regional order are manifold. Though the viability of regional security as an approach to contain conflicts in a central area of great power competition is at best doubtful, the main factor hindering such a development remains the contending perceptions of security and definitions of threat amongst the local actors. It is the contending patterns of interests reflected in these divergent security perspectives which militate in favour of the Gulf region's continuing volatility.

---

1 During the Gulf war, unsuccessful mediatory attempts have been made by the PLO, Cuba, the United Nations and the Islamic Conference.

2 For a detailed analysis of the Arab League's record and potential for conflict management see Mark W. Zacher, *International Conflicts and Collective Security, 1946-77*, Praeger, New York, 1979, pp 192-201.

Index

PRSY *see* People's Republic of South Yemen
PUK *see* Patriotic Union of Kurdistan

Qabous, Sultan, 55, 60—1, 71, 76, 77
Qaru Island, 40
Qasim, 2—3, 11, 14—5, 25, 27—9
Qasr-e-Shirin, 10
Qatar, 39, 44—45, 48—52, 68—71; continental shelf, 68—71; dispute, 48—52; Al Thani, rulers of, 48—51

Ramadan Revolution, 28
Ras al-Khaimah, 56, 58, 59—61, 72—3
Ras Musandam, 59—62; dispute between Oman and UAE, 59—62
Rashid, Shaikh, 63
Rejection Front, 32, 34
Riyadh, 34, 35, 54, 68, 75, 81, 86, 89—92
Rostamkhani, Abdolhassan, 21
Rouhani, Ayatollah Sadeq, 45, 47

Sadat, President, 31, 46, 78
SAF *see* Sultan's Armed Forces
Safaniya Oilfield, 40
Salalah, 76—7
Saleh, President, 84, 91—2
Sanaa, 82, 88—92
Sanandaj, 19
Saudi Arabia, x, 7, 32—6, 39—40, 43, 44, 49—53, 67, 69, 75, 77, 78, 80—2, 86—92; boundaries, 39—40; continental shelf, 67, 69; dispute, 50—2; Neutral Zone, 40; relations with Yemens, 86—92
Saudi-Iraqi border, 33—5; Neutral Zone, 33—4; Security Alliance, 35

Saudi-Kuwaiti border, 36, 38
Shah, Reza, 13, 44; *see also* Iran
Shara'iwah, 67
al-Shargui, Shaikh Muhammad, 63
Shariat-Madari, Ayatollah, 21, 22
Sharjah, 56, 58, 59, 60, 63—5, 71—2
Shatt al-Arab, 1—16, 28—31, 38, 66, 95
Shi'ah sect, 8, 13, 20, 33, 35, 41, 45, 47, 48, 95
Shihuh tribe, 60
Sistanis, 23
Six Day War, 80
South Yemen, 55, 75, 77—9, 79, 83—4, 86—92; relations with Saudi Arabia, 86—92; *see also* Yemen and North Yemen
Standstill Agreement of 1952, 53
Strait of Hormuz, x, 8, 9, 32, 45, 56—7, 59, 62, 66, 70
Suez Canal, 43, 53; crisis, 53
Sultan's Armed Forces, 74, 76
Sunni Moslem, 17, 22, 48 *see also* Baluchistan
Syria, 5, 16

Tabatabai, Sadeq, 45—6
Tabriz, 22
Taimur, Sultan Said bin, 75
Takriti, Saddam Hussein, 6
Talabani, Jalal, 16
Tehran, 2, 4—6, 8, 11, 13—20, 23, 32, 34—5, 41, 45, 47, 48, 56, 59, 61, 62, 65, 71, 79; Government, 4, 5
Thamarit, 77
Tigris, River, 1
Treaties of Lausanne 1923, 27
Treaties of Sevres 1920, 27
Treaty of Friendship, 16
Treaty of Muhammarah, 33
Treaty of Muslim Friendship, 86
Tripoli Agreement, 81
Trucial States, 62—3

Tunb Islands, 8, 10, 45, 47, 56–9, 70–1; occupation by Iran, 56–9
Turkey, 16, 18, 25, 27

UAE *see* United Arab Emirates
UAR *see* United Arab Republic
UDF *see* Union Defence Forces
Umm al-Maradim Island, 40
Umm al-Qaiwain, 62, 70
Umm Qasr, 28–32
UNFPO *see* United National Front Political Organisation
Union Defence Forces, 63, 65
Union of Nine, 49
United Arab Emirates, 53–5, 59–65, 70–1; continental shelf, 70–1; Musandam dispute, 59–62
United Arab Republic, 79, 87, 88
United National Front Political Organisation, 82

Vanguard Party, 82
Warbah Island, 25, 28–32, 38
Washington, 16, 35

Yemen, x, 36, 79–80, 82–92; Arab Republic, 80, 81–4, 88–92; relations with Saudi Arabia, 86–92; Treaty of Peace, 79; *see also* North and South Yemen
Yahya, Imam, 79, 86
YAR *see* Yemen Arab Republic
Yemeni Socialist Party, 83 *see also* National Liberation Front
Yom Kippur War, 5

Zahidan, 23
Zarrara Oilfield, 51
Zayed, Shaikh, 55, 63–4
Zubarah, 48–50

SECURITY IN THE PERSIAN GULF

1   **Domestic political factors**
     Shahram Chubin (editor)

2   **Sources of inter-state conflict**
     Robert Litwak

3   **Modernisation, political development and stability**
     Avi Plascov

4   **The role of outside powers**
     Shahram Chubin

The International Institute for Strategic Studies was founded in 1958 as a centre for the provision of information on and research into the problems of international security, defence and arms control in the nuclear age. It is international in its Council and staff, and its membership is drawn from over fifty countries. It is independent of governments and is not the advocate of any particular interest.

The Institute is concerned with strategic questions — not just with the military aspects of security but with the social and economic sources and political and moral implications of the use and existence of armed force: in other words, with the basic problems of peace.

The Institute's publications are intended for a much wider audience than its own membership and are available to the general public on special subscription terms or singly.

Security in the Persian Gulf 3:

Modernization, Political Development and Stability

AVI PLASCOV
Research Associate
International Institute for Strategic Studies

Published for
THE INTERNATIONAL INSTITUTE
FOR STRATEGIC STUDIES
by
Gower

© International Institute for Strategic Studies 1982

Published by

Gower Publishing Company Limited,
Gower House, Croft Road,
Aldershot, Hants GU11 3HR, England.

British Library Cataloguing in Publication Data

Plascov, Avi
Modernisation, political development and stability — (Security in the Persian Gulf; v.3)
1. Security, International
2. Persian Gulf — Foreign relations
I. Title   II. Series
327'116'09536   DS49.7

ISBN 0-566-00450-X

Printed and bound in Great Britain by
Biddles Ltd, Guildford and King's Lynn

Contents

Introduction

That there have been many kinds of rapid changes in the states which comprise the Gulf is self-evident. Yet the nature of each change is not always understood nor is the inter-action of the different kinds of change. The aim of this study is to assess the nature and magnitude of potential domestic sources of conflict and the conditions under which they might become salient, contributing to the acceleration of certain political trends which, in turn, may induce instability in the Gulf.

In introducing modernization without an adequate infrastructure and with an extremely limited absorptive capacity, the Gulf states were bound to confront various problems — some of which have yet to surface. Beyond their immediate and long-term economic significance, the very nature of these potential sources of tension could, in many cases, prove counter-productive politically to the region's regimes who are totally dependent on a single, yet diminishing, source of income for sustaining their economic performance and on an immigrant labour force for executing their ambitious projects.

By its nature this unparalleled modernization cannot be confined to the economic sphere — as perhaps at least some of the Gulf regimes would like it to be. The rapid social and political changes that these traditional societies are undergoing involve far-reaching, irreversible effects on the relationship between the regimes and their subjects. Confronted with previously unknown challenges which may question their very legitimacy, these governments may be forced to face some of the consequences of their own economic policies as well as being affected by the onset of other problems. As the Iranian Revolution shows, groups, alienated by a process which pushes them to the sidelines and ignores their grievances, could combine, despite the fact that they remain worlds apart, to undermine the prevailing political order, the consequences of which are incalculable.

A number of 'indicators of change' were identified[1] for the purpose of the study. These fall roughly into three inter-related categories — economic, social and political — which have a bearing on one another and are influenced by the regimes' own policies as well as by the external environment of inter-Arab relations, the continuation of the Arab-Israeli conflict and superpower rivalries. A number of those elements contain stabilizing effects. Others by their very nature are destabilizing. Some are old and the rest are new, though they feed on one another. All, however, are likely to be with the Gulf states for a long while.

Rather than deal individually with each of these states in assessing its potential sources of conflict, the approach followed here is to attempt a comparative perspective of every issue through an overview of the region which highlights certain issues which will affect them differently. Whilst some of these potential sources of conflict are imminent, others are incipient or even latent. Most attention is given to long-term problems though the scarcity of reliable sources makes such judgements difficult.[2]

This study will look first at the religious, social and economic factors of domestic instability. It will then attempt to evaluate which policies could ameliorate or accentuate these states' vulnerabilities. It examines policy choices and the various types of mechanism open to governments in attempting to confront the prospect of internal challenges. The role of the existing political institutions in a number of those states is examined together with their ability to adapt by combining both the perpetuation of the *status quo* and apparent change.

---

1   See also discussion in Michael Nacht *Internal change and political stability in developing countries*, Committee Paper presented in the International Institute for Strategic Studies 23rd Annual Conference, Stresa, Italy, 11-14 September 1980, published in Third World Conflict and International Security, Adelphi Paper 116, IISS, Summer 1981.

2   The author wishes to express his sincere thanks due to all those whose advice had been sought in the course of this project, and he is also indebted to the Shiloah Research Centre for Middle Eastern and African Studies in the Tel Aviv University for allowing him to consult the Press Collection.

PART I

AN ANALYSIS OF THE
FACTORS OF DOMESTIC
INSTABILITY

1 The effects of rapid modernization

Tribalism, Islam and statehood

By virtue of its size and demographic composition, the Gulf displays a mosaic of racial, ethnic and religious diversity which is criss-crossed by political boundaries. The way in which those states were formed is indicative of the degree of strength inherent in their social and political fabrics. The intention here is not to provide a historical background of the region[1] — a much needed dimension for understanding current and future trends — but rather to highlight a few milestones along the road of these states' emergence which are of relevance for any debate on the present regimes' capability to meet the old and new challenges they will be forced to face. It is pointless to discuss the dramatic changes the Gulf is undergoing without alluding, if only briefly, to the foundations upon which such a rapid process is taking place.

The history of the region since the nineteenth century can be described as the product of a complex, fluctuating relationship between three concentric circles of peoples and states: the inner ring embraces the people of the Gulf coasts; the intermediate one is made up of the regional powers based in Baghdad, Riyadh and Tehran; and the outer ring consists of external powers whether Middle Eastern (Egypt and the

---

1 See J.B. Kelly, *Arabia the Gulf and the West. A Critical view of the Arabs and Oil Policy*, Weidenfeld and Nicolson, London, 1980.

Ottoman empire) or international such as Russia (later the Soviet Union), India, Western Europe and later the United States.[1] Accordingly, the political structures of the emerging states changed. As power shifted, spheres of influence were constantly altered. As the strategic and economic value of the Gulf became a matter of international concern, the dependence of the local regimes on, and their interactions with, the external powers changed in essence. Thus internal and external forces have combined to influence the evolution of the political identities and institutions which developed in the region.

Islam — the pillar of legitimacy

In pre-Islamic days, tribes were the dominant form of social and political organization among the Bedouin and even among the city dwellers. Tribes varied in their form of organization and in their lineage and these determined their pride and strength and consequently their elevated or inferior status. Every tribe was led by a *Sheikh* (Arab), *Khan* (Iranian) or *Agha* (Kurd) who was elected by the elders from among the most prominent family in the tribe. Where associations of tribes were established, they were led by the stronger tribe. The need to face common enemies produced federations of such associations (like the Shammar and the Anaiza).

Not all tribes, however, were nomads. The urbanization of certain tribes in the Gulf dates back centuries but sedentarization did not entail abandoning all the traits of nomadism. Some tribes clung to their old mode of life, and became semi-nomadic. In that respect the division into 'desert' and 'town' patterns of life, or rather the nomadic pastoralist versus the settled merchant or sedentary farmer, was slightly blurred, although deep animosity characterized these communities, interdependent co-existence. The garrisoned city was to become the base of the ruling dynasties and from here they tried to control the countryside by manipulating rivalries and shifting alliances.

Islam was certainly the strongest and most revolutionary force to affect the crystallization of nation-states in the Arab Peninsula. Born 1400 years ago in Arabia, Islam (meaning submission to Allah) was always a source of pride to its adherents. Its strength lies in its substance — a code of laws and traditions which is assumed to have the answer to everything rather than merely to serve as a religion. For devout Muslims, all aspects of life and society are regulated by the Qur'aan — held to be the infallible word revealed by Allah to the

1 See Malcolm Yapp 'The Nineteenth and Twentieth Centuries' and 'British Policy in the Persian Gulf' in Alvin J. Cottrell, C. Edmund Boseworth, R. Michael Burrell, Keith McLachlan and Roger M. Savory (ed.) *The Persian Gulf, A General Survey*, The Johns Hopkins University Press, Baltimore and London, 1980, pp 41-100.

4

Prophet Muhammad — and the Shari'ah (Islamic religious law). The tribal inhabitants of the region were thus embraced by the expanding Islamic notion of community of faith (Ummah) which was meant to serve as a powerful force for equality and cohesion, especially when one of its main tenets was governing by consensus (ijma').

But even though the entire region adopted Islam, the diversified interpretation by its adherents regarding the succession to the Prophet and his responsibilities prevented it from becoming a unifying force. Rather the clash between the different doctrines proved to be a constant source of tension in the Gulf which harbours the followers of the three major branches of Islam: the Sunnis, who argue that the successors to Muhammad as the leader of the Ummah must be elected from his own tribe of Quraish by the religious scholars (Ulama'); and the Shi'ia who believe that the Prophet's successors should be exclusively from the descendants of his cousin and son-in-law Ali. Prominent among other sects of Islam are the Kharijis who contend that the leader of the Islamic community should be elected. These sharp divisions reinforced tribal differences and exaggerated the hostility between them.

Saudi Arabia and Qatar

Obviously the most dramatic development came in the eighteenth century with the rise in Arabia of the Wahhabi movement which brought about the emergence of the Saudi state. Wahhabism followed the most strict and least tolerant of the four schools of Sunni ('Orthodox') Islam and the Saudi state was based on the Wahhabi creed, and enforced Islamic law rigidly[1] by installing the Qur'aan as the constitution of the Kingdom.

The Saudi and Wahhabi fortunes and strengths have been inextricably linked since the Wahhabi state was born in 1745.[2] They both originated from the Najd — the strategically crucial highland area of central, tribal Arabia, which remained virtually intact even after the Ottomans, the

1 Women in Saudi Arabia are banned from mixing with men in public places, driving, smoking in public etc. Drinking alcohol is disallowed, adulteresses are stoned to death and thieves lose their right hand. Observation of religious restrictions is closely watched by the government through the Committee for the Prevention of Vice and Promotion of Virtue. There are no cinemas in the Kingdom and the introduction of TV resulted in violent clashes even though the programmes focus on religious teachings. Those who opposed TV, however, were proved right when it became obvious that video tapes of a promiscuous nature were finding their way into many young Saudis' homes. Elsewhere in the Gulf the atmosphere is far more relaxed: Bahrain, being a tourist centre, serves as a haven for many Saudis seeking pleasure. Even in Iran, some of the things outlawed by Khomeini are gradually being resumed.

2 For details see George Rentz 'Wahhabism and Saudi Arabia' in Derek Hopwood (ed.) *The Arabian Peninsula, Society and Politics*, George Allen and Unwin, London, 1972, pp 54-66.

Portuguese and the British established themselves in the coastal areas of Aden, Muscat and in Bahrain. The Najdi spirit of political independence joined hands with the religious ferocity of the Wahhabis. Their politico-religious 'confederacy' sought to assert itself over the entire Peninsula and far beyond by replacing the existing tribal anarchy and sectarian diversity with purified Islam as a unifying force. It was zealously imposed upon all Muslims and 'infidels'. They succeeded in galvanizing their tribal recruits and utilizing their combined force to pursue their territorial ambitions. However, once Wahhabism moved out of the desert and was enforced upon the Peninsula's cities, it lost much of its impetus as a unifying power behind the Bedouin.

It was there that the Saudi/Wahhabi alignment confronted more formidable foreign forces and so the peak of territorial expansion marked the beginning of the decline. The Saudis made forays as far as Damascus in the north and Yemen and Oman in the south only to be stopped in the nineteenth century by an invasion of the Pasha of Egypt into Hijaz (1811). At one point the Saudis even lost their main base of Riyadh. Eventually, however, the Saudi dynasty managed to overcome dissension within the family and succeeded in reviving its fortunes and consolidated its hold over most of Arabia. It put an end to the power of Turkish-backed Al Rashid and, in 1926, ousted from the Hijaz their sworn enemy — the Hashemite dynasty which claimed direct descent from the Prophet and held the post of the Sharif of Mecca. Now, however, the Saudis found it difficult to control their own army — the Ikhwan (Brethren) movement — who constantly raided the areas of Shi'ah Iraq and Trans-Jordan (both the new havens of the British-backed Hashemites) and went as far as questioning the religious commitment of their creators, the Saudis, whom they accused of abandoning the main idea of Wahhabism which to them meant endless expansion. Consequently the latter unleashed their army against them in the late 1920s. The Ikhwan, who had previously carried the Saudi-Wahhabi banner in capturing Jabal Shammar, Asir and Hijaz, were now suppressed by an urban/Bedouin force to pave the way for the establishment of a modern state with recognized borders.

Gradually the Saudi Kingdom (which was proclaimed by name in 1932) became stabilized but it was far from being homogeneous. King Ibn Saud strove to consolidate his hold by strengthening the allegiances of the tribal and urban leaders so as to diminish the Kingdom's regional differences. However, control of the Hijaz by the Saudis after centuries of Ottoman rule could only exacerbate the old deep animosity between the proud, independent conservative Bedouin of Najdi origin and the urbanite cosmopolitan Hijazis known for their mercantilistic, pragmatic approach to life, which they had developed through their constant contact with the outside world with whom they traded or were subdued by, and which made the Najdis always full of contempt and mistrust towards them. This was partly the reason why the Ikhwan were infuriated by Saud's attempts to consolidate his position in Mecca and Medina through incorporating Hijazis into his new administration and through his debasing the Holy Cities by turning them into commercial centres. Traces of this disenchantment are still found today within the less developed Najd.

A worse fate was that of the oppressed Shi'ah in the Kingdom's oil bearing Eastern Province (al-Ansa' — commonly known as Hasa) and even that of the Sunnis living there (some of whom followed the Maliki branch of Islam). The Saudis were also reluctant to trust the Shammar tribes even though they adopted the Wahhabiyah. Whereas the tribes of Northern Saudi Arabia traditionally had close ties with Iraq and Syria, Asir in the south, which had been occupied, was a Shafi'i, Yemeni-inspired region.

Close contact is maintained with the Ulama', the learned divines. Descendants of the al-Wahhab (al-Sheikh) family are regarded as the partners of the dynasty. The Ulama' became, for all practical purposes, a prestigious clerical class with religious and social authority. They were given the role of interpreting the law and teaching religious values along Islamic lines as an integral part of the Kingdom's infrastructure. In return they pledge allegiance to the throne and extend their much needed support for the regime. This alliance is reinforced by marriage. Thus, the uncompromising puritanism of the Wahhabi was the force which has provided the religious basis for the Saudi (and Qatari) societies and has proved instrumental in developing their political systems.

Presenting itself as protector of Islam and cultivating its relations with the tribal heads has enabled the House of Saud to cement its position within the Kingdom. The extended family ties of King ibn Saud (who had some fifteen wives from different tribes and forty-five sons who continued to marry within the constantly growing family, producing thousands of princes and princesses) means that the family reaches practically every corner of the country and includes a large proportion of the indigenous population. Thus Islam and the tribal fabric are inter-woven to provide the regime with its legitimacy.

Oman

In Oman, the second largest state in the Peninsula, a different type of relationship existed between the centre and the periphery and between Islam and the ruling dynasty. The country was the centre of Ibadiyah — another fundamentalist brand of Islam of the Khariji movement which, unlike the conflicting but well preserved hierarchy in Sunni and Shi'ah Islam, displays a measure of egalitarianism, with the ruler deriving his power from general consensus rather than by lineage. The Ibadiyah's early militant nature developed as a result of its exposure to Wahhabi incursions as well as a result of conflicts with the Sunni tribes populating Oman. The movement was based in the interior mountains and in the plateau of Oman, whereas the Sunni tribes (and Shi'i merchants from across the Gulf) populated the coastal northwest area — eventually the seat of the ruling dynasty. The situation was complicated by the fact that Oman has two confederations of tribes: one is predominantly Ibadi with a minority of Sunnis, the other has the opposite. Those living in the province of Dhofar — who were to pose a serious challenge to the regime's survival — belong to the Shafi'i rite of Sunni Islam. Thus Oman's history is one of continuous strife. The country's integrity has been threatened by civil wars and by external forces. The split between the Al Bu Sa'id-led secularly oriented coastal sultanate and the orthodox inhabitants of the interior culminated in the removal in the mid-1950s of the Saudi and Egyptian-backed Imam by the British-backed Omani force. Yet Ibadism became the ideology of Omani particularism and the sultanate's official religion.[1]

The littoral city-states

The development of the sparsely populated littoral sheikhdoms of Eastern Arabia based on the 'cities' stretching from Kuwait down the coast to Sharjah took a different course. In each case, after prolonged wars, a tribal dynasty assumed control over a settled, coastal community of mixed ethnic, sectarian and social background.[2] However the scale of what developed into city-states meant that the contact, and hence mutual influence, between the rulers and the ruled was far more intimate than inside the Peninusla or even in Oman. It also meant that conflict could prove decisive for the existence of certain tribes.

Whereas the relatively insulated interior of the Peninsula preserved much of its old characteristics, the coastal sheikhdoms, engaged in pearling and commerce, were more exposed to external forces and underwent more rapid demographic change. Their cosmopolitan nature was reflected both in their social composition and in their dealings with the forces which dominated them, whether regional or international. Such was the case in Bahrain following the Persian-controlled island's occupation in 1783 by the Al Khalifa dynasty. From the time of its foundation, in the second decade of the eighteenth century, the

1 See James E. Dougherty 'Religion and Law' in A. Cottrell (and others) *The Persian Gulf op. cit.* p 306.

2 For an historical account see John Duke Anthony, *Arab States of the Lower Gulf: People, Politics, Petroleum*, Middle East Institute, Washington DC, 1975.

Al Sabah-led Kuwait was also largely influenced by the surrounding forces. Kuwait, which up to her independence in 1961 was a British protected 6800 square mile principality, was not the only sheikhdom which tied its destiny with such powers. This was a common feature to varying degrees of the other Gulf littoral units. Indeed, the history of the lower Gulf is one of continuous competition between external forces and accompanying tribal feuds, with sheikhdoms trying to assert themselves over their neighbours and, in the nineteenth century, with the Wahhabi-Saudi coalition trying to gain influence there in the face of British attempts to contain the Saudis.

With Britain's decision to withdraw its presence from East of Suez by 1971, Bahrain, Qatar and the Trucial sheikhdoms agreed, in 1968, to establish a federation between themselves. Facing Iran's apprehension that such a regional pact was, in fact, designed to pave the way for an American presence to replace that of Britain, the sheikhdoms, not wishing to antagonize Iran, quickly backed down. Iran's long-standing claim to Bahrain (which it regarded as its province) was enough to deter the other parties of the proposed federation from associating themselves too closely with Bahrain. This fear was coupled with their apprehension of Bahrain's superiority through her economic experience and more educated, advanced community which was larger than that of the other components of the proposed federation combined.

The dynastic animosities and territorial disputes between Bahrain and Qatar — a desert peninsula of 4000 square miles, once governed by the Al Khalifa dynasty — and between Qatar and Abu Dhabi made the proposed federation only a remote possibility. Not even the existence of common enemies and their fears of being engulfed by Saudi Arabia could bridge their own mutual suspicions and antagonisms. These remained at the core of the United Arab Emirates (UAE) — the Federation established on 2 December 1971 between six of the tiny city-states of Abu Dhabi, Dubai, Sharjah, Ajman, Umm al-Qaiwain and Fujairah (the seventh state of Ras al-Khaimah joined only in February 1972).

9

The legacy of tribalism

The process of welding these heterogeneous societies into larger and more cohesive units transcending the old loyalties and enmities was hindered in the larger states (Saudi Arabia, Oman, Iraq and Iran) by the measure of autonomy traditionally enjoyed and fiercely defended by the various groups comprising the domain of the new central authority. Exercising jurisdiction did not automatically win the loyalty and earn the respect of the tribes whose members remained primarily loyal to their tribal frameworks, even if their leaders' control over the tribes was reduced by the upgraded presence of the state and even if the Bedouin do not constitute a separate society. The fact remains that, in the Peninsula, tribalism, regionalism and the notion of a bureaucratic nation state were at first largely incompatible, although the central authority is maintained by dynasties who are themselves of tribal origin. Many people still identify themselves as Hijazis or Najdis rather than Saudis — as indeed the regime would want them to.

Turning a country of tribes into a modern industrial state imposed many strains. The Bedouin themselves found it difficult to adjust. Nevertheless the dynasties continued to push for rapid transformation, being insensitive to the long-cherished life-style of their brothers, and encouraged many of them to resettle and others to move to industrial sites. Hence the tribes began to disintegrate in the face of the changes introduced by the governments, with new roads cutting across, or laws abolishing, their long-preserved grazing rights which regulated the wandering of different tribes through particular seasonal range-lands (*dira* or *hema*). In fact all governments want to control the Bedouin and their movement by breaking down Bedouin individualism and tribal alliances in the hope that it would bring about greater national cohesion. To achieve that, they aim to settle them and transform them into a productive agricultural society. But by doing that they destroy their old way of life, forcing them to adapt to the 'state' and obey 'their' government, concepts which are still foreign to many of them.

Thus a consequence of the expansion of the bureaucracy and the strengthening of the urban element has been the weakening of tribal solidarities — a main component of the power-base of the Saudi regime. The political significance of the tribal framework diminished (as did the numbers of true Badu who in Saudi Arabia number perhaps only just over half a million) as the government introduced new territorial divisions for administrative purposes. Tribal leaders were further alienated by the nomination of government-employed Emirs from a different tribal background and in general by the regime's treatment of the Bedouin as a single category — which is insensitive to the traditional divisions among the tribes, ignoring the fact that not all tribes regard the House of Saud as their patron.

Many Bedouin were as exasperated with the swift change of the environment around them as they are with the new social order governing the Kingdom which has given prominence to young princes and their entourages of rich urban entrepreneurs. It is difficult to see the Bedouin readily acquiescing to a drastic change of his old lifestyle of which he is immensely proud, nor will he be willing to be sucked into the ever expanding, mechanized world. In that respect the 'oil revolution' had the opposite effect on the Bedouin to that of the revolution of the Wahhabiyah: the latter urged them to be mobile so as to spread the message of Islam whilst modernization aims to settle them, forcing them to abandon their traditional way of life. Whether spontaneous, caused by droughts forced or encouraged by governments, by the 1980s about 85 percent of the Bedouin in the Peninsula have been settled.[1] This is certainly the case in the Lower Gulf where the establishment of the city-states marked the decline of the tribe as a political force.[2]

Yet though regarded by the world as 'states' these family-ruled entities are essentially tribal in their composition and way of ruling because they are merely an extension of the traditional tribal order. High-rise blocks and a 'modern' bureaucracy have not yet been able to change the basic nature of these countries: instant modernization does not mean an instant departure from a tribal way of thinking. Beneath the newly-imported Western infrastructure, populated and maintained by immigrants, lie the traditional foundations which, under the present leaderships, still have more to do with tribal, sectarian and ethnic matters than with anything else. Accordingly, political boundaries within the Peninsula have little significance for many Bedouin.

Long-standing blood ties and old feuds could prove to be more important than relations between governments across the borders which divide or embrace the respective clans. To that extent, it may well be the case that, so long as the will of the older, more conservative rulers prevails there is still much to be said for the old ties between the Al Saud dynasty and the Al Khalifa ruling family in Bahrain (or Al Sabah of Kuwait), which are rooted in their common ancestral

---

1 Brian D. Clark 'Tribes in the Persian Gulf' in A. Cottrell (ed.) *The Persian Gulf, op. cit.* p 492.

2 Even in Iraq, where the confrontation between government and tribes was once a problem and where forceful sedentarization aimed at reducing the power of the sheikhs, conscription and taxation, today only 1% of the country's population is nomadic, and its size is constantly dropping. Iran has still some 3 million nomads.

11

origin,[1] than perhaps the affinity of the former may have with the Hijazis within their own country[2] (whose acquiescence they nevertheless seek for the sake of stability). This is so despite the persistence of old unsettled territorial claims and the bitter memories from the past, for the nature of these conflicts differs completely from that between the Saudis and the Hashemites — who had global political and religious aspirations concerning the title of the Calif (Khalifa) ('Commander of the Faithful') and the attached legitimacy of appearing in the name of the Ummah. Moreover, though Saudi Arabia is undoubtedly the most important state in the region, the dynasties in the Gulf (and for that matter in the Middle East as a whole) have a direct interest in strengthening each other out of fear of a chain reaction triggered by the downfall of any one of them. They know that the strength of the 'chain of solidarity' which holds them together is the strength of its weakest link.[3] There is much to be said for the fact that some of these dynasties have ruled their domains uninterrupted for hundreds of years and derive enormous latent strength and resilience from Islamic and tribal legitimacy which they anxiously preserve. To date, their strength lies not only in their ability to wield power but in their action as a powerful group within their respective countries and as one family in the region.

1 These ruling dynasties are part of the Bani Utub group of tribes who descended from the Jamilah of the far flung Anaiza confederation from North Central Arabia, who settled on the shores of the Gulf in the 18th century. After leaving Kuwait and controlling Qatar, Al Khalifa was aided by Al Saud in gaining control over Bahrain. (For further details see Ahmad Mustafa Abu Hakima 'The development of the Gulf States' in Derek Hopwood (ed.) *The Arabian Peninsula, op.cit.* p 32.

2 See also Michael Field 'Warning Signs the West should look for' in *Financial Times*, 29 November 1979. The author envisages that should the lower Gulf regimes begin to disintegrate, their communities of Central Arabia origin would probably turn to the Saudi dynasty which never shelved its ancestral claim to the entire Gulf Coast.

3 Such solidarity prompted Kuwait's authorities to suspend the *al-Tali'ah* leftist weekly for contravening the press and publications law in two articles criticizing Saudi Arabia (KUNA 12.16 GMT 28 August 1980).

Iraq and Iran

Though they differ substantially from each other in their political evolution, it is the changes that Iraq and Iran have experienced which places them, at least for the sake of this study, in a different category than the rest of the Gulf. Both underwent national revolution by overthrowing foreign-imposed monarchies. But whereas Iraq oriented herself after the 1958 Revolution along radical socialist but secular lines, Iran emerged as a republic governed by Islam after deposing the Persian monarchy.

Unlike the rest of the Gulf where 'patriotism' is still tantamount to loyalty to the ruling dynasty, both states gradually developed their own particular identities. But even here these features failed to conceal the deeply-rooted ethnic and sectarian affiliations which hindered the transformation of these states into more cohesive societies. The feeling of nationality which developed in Iraq was fostered by those of the ruling élite and as such it was essentially sectarian and divisive, with Islam providing the focus of opposition to the regime. In Iran, the only non-Arab state in the region, Islam was the force behind which gathered those who opposed the Shah — on religious as well as secular grounds. Following the Iranian revolution, Islam became the *raison d'être* of the new government.

2 Islam's reaction to modernization

The Iranian experience

Serious strains in Persia between secularization and Islam erupted as early as 1891-92 over the monopoly of a tobacco trade grant to a British firm. The divines had championed the Constitutional Revolution as early as 1906, with demands for the restoration of the rule of the Shari'ah embodied in a new Persian Constitution. In both instances the ulama' revealed their popular following and their strength to resist foreign encroachment. At that stage, they refrained, however, from impugning the monarchy as such and confined themselves to portraying it as a foreign-manipulated tool.[1] To them, westernization represented not only moral corruption but centralization which, in turn, meant a reduction of their power, which reflected the widening gap between the religious world of the Mullahs in Qom and the commercial life in Tehran — the seat of temporal power.

The Shah subsequently strove to win the loyalty of his subjects by using the country's oil wealth for very rapid modernization but his policies were bound to alienate most of Iranian society primarily owing to constantly rising inflation which not only robbed the population of any real economic benefits but which was for many the cause of hardship at a time when the Shah's inordinate expenditure on arms procurement imperilled the economy.

---

1   Eli Kedourie, *Islam in the modern world*, Mansell, London, 1980, p 49.

The Shah also tried to diminish the influence of the religious establishment. His 'White Revolution' reforms, which reduced the Mullahs' landholdings and curbed their power in matters relating to education and the administration of justice, once their exclusive traditional sphere of influence, could only exasperate the threatened Mullahs, especially when the growing number of western-educated, secular technocrats who, ranged against the religious traditionalists, went along with these policies.

After all, unlike the Sunnis whose generally quiescent ulama' are expected to perform their solemn duty to confer legitimacy on whoever happened to be the effective ruler, the more vigilant Shi'ah ulama' never recognized the legitimacy of the Khalifa and regarded as usurper anyone but Ali's descendants[1] who claims supreme authority. They tolerated a monarch only as long as he accepted their guidance in defending Islam and upholding the Shari'ah. Unlike their Sunni colleagues, the Shi'ah divines potentially carry great political influence and are financed by their communities. Traditionally they have always resisted central authority for the task of governing inevitably meant accommodation of the imperatives of faith with daily practical compromise. Moreover the Sunnis do not have popular religious leaders because there is no role in their form of Islam for an intermediary between God and man. At the basis of Sunni (orthodox) Islam lies the belief that its followers should co-operate and obey the authorities who in turn appoint and pay the salaries of the religious officials who serve in a sense as their 'representatives'. Hence whereas the Sunni Saudis regard the Head of the House of Saud as their recognized leader (even if they may be aggravated by his behaviour), the Shi'ah divines in Iran have always viewed the Shah as evil even if they sometimes reluctantly co-operated with him.

The fortunes of any ulama' in Iran depended on the strength of the ruler. Accordingly, the Iranian ulama' did not intend to give up the accumulated power which they had gained in the nineteenth century under the weak Qajar rulers who, unlike their predecessors of the Safavid dynasty, failed to check the Mullahs. Thus the traditional contest between the mujahidin and the regime persisted. To broaden their support prior to the Revolution in Iran, the Mullahs began articulating more general public grievances which had little or nothing to do with their basic right authoritatively to interpret Islam, a right which

---

1   Unlike the Sunnis, the Shi'ah (Shi'at Ali i.e. the Party of Ali) believe that the long-awaited Iman — the 12th in line who disappeared in the 9th century, remained in Ali's family and is bound to re-appear and establish a state based on the Qur'aan. (Thus, apart from the Yemeni (Zaidi) Shi'is, other Gulf Shi'is are called the Twelvers.)

was now attacked by the modernizers. Being accused of rejecting progress for reasons of self-interest and, moreover, of perversion of Islamic values, the 'clergy' fought back by charging the Government with dictatorship, with misappropriation of the country's wealth and corruption and inflicting torture — charges which had a wide and constantly growing appeal uniting all alienated elements of Iranian society. The latter's accumulated bitterness, which was championed by the Mullahs, was bound to burst out. What began as a conflict of interests between Islam and secularization developed into an inevitable struggle for survival between two powerful forces who could not co-exist for long in any form. One of them had to give way.

Now that the ulama' are on top, however, they have yet to prove that they can rule the country effectively or that they can grapple successfully with the problems produced by both modernization and their own reaction to it before they themselves lose control.

The Grand Mosque Incident of 1979 in Saudi Arabia

Iran cannot be compared directly with the countries across the Gulf, particularly Saudi Arabia, for they differ totally in the essence of their statehood, the nature of their governments, the role of Islam, the position of the salaried ulama' and the impact of western forces. Nevertheless the attack on the Grand Mosque in Mecca in 1979 (November) was also a protest against the secularization of the ruling dynasty, which is increasingly being perceived by a number of Saudi subjects as abandoning, under the pressure of western-inspired modernization and its associated temptations, their true mission of governing according to the true spirit of Islam.

In the past, the ruler was expected to act, simultaneously, as the upholder of the Shari'ah, the military chief, the guardian of morals and the administrator of justice as well as public benefactor. However the widening gap between changing social reality and the religious ideal of Islam forced the courts to develop more suitable codes which would accommodate the new pressures more adequately and meet the new needs which were no longer amenable to old solutions. Obviously the Saudis were careful, in the process of accommodating to such new elements, to ensure that the spirit of the Shari'ah and traditional ways of doing things would prevail so as to avoid conflict between Islam and modernization. Even so the Kingdom moved gradually away from its exclusive Wahhabi posture. With the death of King Faisal, a religious but pragmatic leader who had proceeded cautiously and slowly along the road to modernization, more technocrats entered into government and economic pressures accelerated the process of change. Some conflict was inevitable even under King Faisal for the influence of the Najdi ulama' influence was being reduced, even though the newly-established al-Medina religious university urged a more orthodox and rigid quiescence. Change was marked by the previously unthinkable introduction of cars, the telephone systems, and, after quelling by force the divines' opposition to innovations, the opening of a girls' school in 1960 and television in 1969. The opening of the television station in Riyadh was, indirectly, to cost King Faisal his life. Nowadays the most rapidly expanding sector is that of the previously non-existent secular curriculum incorporated into the still largely theological educational system.

The contradiction between maintaining high western-style economic growth and preserving the religious and moral values as preached by the Wahhabis soon became apparent. Reconciling spiritual fundamentalism and materialism in the course of changing a predominantly rural society into an urban industrial society was a difficult task and was bound to loosen the delicately interwoven and carefully balanced tribal and religious social fabric in the newly-established industrial theocracy. Ironically, it was the most orthodox and traditional regime in the

17

region which was forced to face opposition on religious grounds.

The attack in Mecca which was carried out by hundreds of Wahhabi fundamentalists[1] who stormed the Masjid al-Haram (The Holy Mosque) was a carefully planned attack. Led by Juhaiman ibn Saif a Utaibi, they demanded that the worshippers recognize Muhammad ibn Abdallah al Qahtani (whose family was said to be related to the Prophet's Quraish lineage in the House of Hashem) as the long-awaited Mahdi ('Messiah'). The intruders who were, ironically, inspired by the same Wahhabi model which created the Saudi state itself, distributed a prepared statement which stridently condemned Al Saud and challenged its legitimacy on the grounds of corruption and of befriending the infidels. They denounced 'impure Islam' and called for the eradication of any signs of Western influence in the Kingdom, including television.

There are, of course, many among the ruling families who eagerly imitate the Western life-style but the strict conformism prevailing in Saudi Arabia forces them to conduct two ways of life: at home they make it a point to appear as if they adhere to Islamic tradition and to criticize all those who do not, despite their own behaviour to the contrary; abroad, where many of them invest their assets (perhaps in anticipation of trouble at home) and where they have houses, some of them live in marked extravagance. News of this other life reaches the Gulf via the Western and Arab media. At home corruption is also widespread and deeply embodied in the blurred distinction between public property and that of the Royal Family. Corruption is even built into the Five Year Plan.[2] The young princes of the Royal Family tend to conclude lucrative deals from which they derive commission and so add to the wealth they derive from oil revenues. Corruption is endemic and becomes part of the entire system and not merely the bureaucracy[3] and it is impossible to regulate. Rumours fuel discontent and envy, a recipe

1 Some estimates run as high as 1,000.

2 An article in *al-Hurriyah* weekly (the organ of Na'if Hawatimah's Popular Democratic Front for the Liberation of Palestine), Lebanon, 6 February 1980, argues that some 300 members of the Royal Family are engaged in private business side by side with their governmental jobs, which they use to enhance their economic interests by acquiring indispensable knowledge concerning future development projects which enables them to make a fortune through wide scale land speculations.

3 See 'Friction over Saudi business corruption seen as a threat to monarchy' in *International Herald Tribune*, 26 April 1980; *al-Dustur* (Lebanon) London, 10 December 1979 and *al-Hawadith*, 4 January 1980.

for potential instability.[1] It is the *extent* of corruption and the consequent growing economic disparities within the Saudi society and *not* the phenomenon of bribery as such (which tends to be an accepted way of doing things in that part of the Arab world), which could trigger indigenous anger.

Much of the criticism levelled against the double standards of the Saudi regime is based on religious grounds and it emanates also from the ranks of the educated, for not all the intelligentsia work in the direction of secularization. What is surprising is that the authorities, who knew of Juhaiman's political work in the previously purged al-Medina University, attributed so little importance to his group of followers prior to the attack on the Mosque. In fact, he and one hundred or so of his followers were jailed the previous year, following the distribution of a number of pamphlets which contained strong criticism of the House of Saud. Juhaiman's pamphlet No. 1 (printed in Kuwait) argues:[2]

> The Royal Family is corrupt. It worships money and spends it on palaces not mosques. If you accept what they say, they will make you rich; otherwise they will persecute and even torture you.

Vigilant Sunnis have for some time been accusing the Najdi religious establishment of becoming bureaucratized and of permitting the erosion of Islamic values and of giving tacit approval to the corruption which has come with modernization. By not protesting strongly and publicly against the new phenomena of secularization, Westernization and permissiveness, they were seen as betraying their sacred duty. In fact the ulama's position has already been eroded: the new administration and the expansion of education meant that the bureaucracy was gradually diminishing the role of the religious dignitaries even in Saudi Arabia — where the dynasty still continues to maintain close contacts with the divines and where, unlike Iran, the latter sided with the regime.

---

1 See Sabri al-Magid's articles in *al-Musawwar* weekly, Egypt, 14 September 1979; 1-8 February 1980. Also Abd al-Aziz Khamis 'Fahd and the Saudi policy' in *Ruz al-Yusuf* daily, Cairo, 28 January 1980, who warned Fahd to learn from the Shah's experience, for whom neither his enormous wealth nor his superior army helped when it came to the crunch.

2 Juhaiman ibn Muhammad ibn Saif Al Utaiba's four pamphlets are: Rules of Allegiance and obedience (Misconduct of tribes) (n.d.); the Unity of God (n.d.); the call of the Ikhwan — how it began and where it is leading (Published 1979); the balance of Man's life (n.d.) (Published by Taliah Press, Kuwait). See James Buchan *Secular and Religious Opposition in Saudi Arabia*, paper prepared for Symposium on 'State, Economy and Power in Saudi Arabia', held at the Centre for Arab Gulf Studies, University of Exeter, 4-6 July 1980, (hereafter Exeter Papers).

The composition of the group which broke into the Mosque was another reason why the authorities failed to anticipate trouble. Many of them were said to have belonged to the al-Mushttarin sect which had broken away from the Wahhabis in the late 1920s, professing a stricter brand of puritanism. In many ways they resembled the Ikhwan Bedouin warriors. A large number were from the Utaibah tribe, old supporters of the ruling family (some of them served in the Royal Guard) who were reported to be exasperated by the expropriation of some of their land (near al-Ta'if) by the Deputy Commander of the National Guard, Amir Badr bin Abd al-Aziz.[1] The insurgents were reported to have been joined by other Bedouin from the Shammar and the Harb as well as by Muslim Brotherhood supporters[2] from the Hijazi element who are striving for full autonomy for their region. Others are known to have been aggrieved by the fact that Jiddah has lost its seniority to Riyadh, so reviving the long-standing Najdi-Hijazi rivalry. Yet others might have been motivated by the old Hashemite-Saudi animosity. What is more, the group included immigrants from South and North Yemens (Zaidis — a Shi'ah sect), Egyptians (affiliated to the Muslim Brotherhood) and even Kuwaitis. This diversity may suggest that it was not merely a fanatical religious group as some observers have argued.[3] Its composition and the skilful way it operated suggests also that they probably came from an urban centre (like Jiddah) — the only place where such a wide range of people could meet. Being heavily armed, they may also have been aided by Saudi military personnel, or have had connections with external forces such as the Soviet-backed People's Democratic Republic of Yemen (PDRY), or both. After all, co-operation between leftists and radical Islamic groups is not unknown — as the Iranian revolution demonstrated. The group managed to hold out for some two weeks before they were flushed out by the Saudi Army, reportedly aided by Jordanian troops and French advisers. The 63 who were publicly executed (one-third of whom were expatriates) were beheaded in accordance with Saudi custom in all eight urban centres.

1 See *al-Yasar al-Arabi* (Egypt), Paris, 6 January 1980.

2 However, in response to an article in *al-Ukaz* newspaper (Saudi Arabia) dated 26 November 1979, in which the writer asks whether the Ikhwan al-Muslimin, which caused havoc in Egypt and Sudan and now in Syria, is connected to the attack on the Mosque, an article appearing in *al-Medina* newspaper dated 13 December 1979 rejected that allegation whilst praising the Association.

3 See Adeed Dawisha *Saudi Arabia's Search for Security*, Adelphi Paper No. 158, International Institute for Strategic Studies, Erratum Page.

Regardless of their dismissive public response to the siege, the challenge to the House of Saud's unrivalled position as the incarnation of purified Islam and as the Guardians of the Holy Places (haramain) — the major source of legitimacy the House of Saud retains — clearly shook the dynasty and increased its nervousness over internal security. After all, unlike other dynasties, the Saudi regime's *raison d'être* is Wahhabi Islam. Previously, small and weak opposition groups had challenged the monarchical nature of the regime, but this assault was directed against the very foundations of the regime and could come to have a wider appeal.[1] The strange coalition which invaded the Mosque gave an expression to religious, tribal and perhaps even expatriate grievances, thus alerting the Royal Court to the fact it was not immune from such a popular opposition and that it had failed to overcome the old divisions and to synthesize tradition with modernization.

The authorities concluded that they must pay more attention to potential sources of internal disaffection — not unconnected to the regime's pro-Americanism — rather than devote all their attention to external dangers. This is true throughout the Peninsula where less orthodox regimes[2] could also prove vulnerable to protests which question their very legitimacy, though to date there are no such signs. Measures were rapidly introduced to emphasize the 'commitment' that the Gulf regimes have to Islam and to reinforce the states' Islamic character. In the case of Saudi Arabia, such measures were accompanied by grants of land and soft loans to poor Saudis and, later, by the doubling of the Imams' salaries[3] and by modest attempts to stamp out corruption.[4] However none of this was likely to impress those whom

1 In response to the Mecca incident the Central Committee of 'the Saudi Communist Party' argued in a document smuggled to the West dated March 1980: 'For the first time, religious groups played an important role in the democratic national struggle..... this fact points to the ever increasing popular opposition to the existing Saudi regime' (see *Israel and Palestine* journal Paris, May 1980). A stronger language was used by the 'Arab Socialist Labour Party' in Saudi Arabia which condemned the government for the execution of 85 people who participated in the attack on the Mosque and called upon all the national forces abroad 'to help bring down the reactionary Saudi regime and the country's liberation'. Published in *al-Hadaf* weekly (George Habash's PFLP organ), Lebanon, 3 May 1980, p 23.

2 It is noteworthy that in the UAE such measures were taken — with Saudi inspiration — as early as the latter part of 1977 when the Shari'ah laws were implemented more strictly in the courts. The government also considered ending the duality of the legal system by blending it into the Shari'ah code (see Haim Shaked and Colin Legum (ed.) *Middle East Contemporary Survey* (MECS), Vol. II, 1977-8, published by the Shiloah Centre for Middle Eastern and African Studies, Tel-Aviv University, Holmes and Meier Publishers, US 1980, p 454.

3 See *al-Riyadh* daily, 29 May 1980.

4 Photographs of people punished by the authorities appeared in the press — *al-Watan* daily, Kuwait, 8 July 1980.

these regimes wanted to appease. If anything, it exposed these dynasties' weaknesses and vulnerabilities despite, if not because of, their entrenched economic position.

Islam and the West — a clash of cultures

The revolution in Iran which culminated in the expulsion of the Shah and the occupation of the American Embassy in Tehran, encouraged Muslims all over the world, regardless of their sectarian differences. Khomeini successfully portrayed the Shah's removal as the outcome of a clash between Islam and the US and as heralding a new freedom from economic, political and cultural domination of foreign powers. In that respect Khomeini succeeded not only in galvanizing the Iranian masses but also in implanting in Muslims the profound hope that they would ultimately have the upper hand against the West and its Muslim allies, i.e. their 'corrupted rulers'. Cutting oil production to the point where it served national interests only, cancelling armaments' contracts with the US and others and making the USSR pay far more for natural gas all indicate the break with the past.

It was oil which gave the Muslims power for it enabled them to reverse the pattern of dependence upon the west. Yet oil not only corrupted a large part of the Gulf's population (including many of those who criticize their governments for abandoning Islamic values and traditions) but it also gave the West a new if different kind of dominance in many spheres of life. At first many Arabs, who felt that the industrial revolution had passed them by, had hoped that industrialization would restore the glory of Islam. They were to discover however that, although they had been able to rid themselves of the West's political patronage, they were now forced to accept Western economic tutelage and influence, which implied their lack of competence, despite their newly discovered wealth, to modernize by themselves. This is an extremely painful thing for religious and secular scholars alike to admit.

To the ulama' modernization, at least in the manner it was introduced, implied intolerable social change, their own lowered status and an admission that Islam does not contain all the answers to the 'world of progress'. They are not against science as such, but modernization in its imported form is seen as the West's victory in that it proves that a continued adherence to true Islam is irreconcilable with industrialization. Modernization which is insensitive to Islamic culture and heritage is regarded as undesirable 'bad development'. It harms the traditional foundations of the state by exposing Islam to previously unknown challenges and reveals the inadequacy of the tools at the disposal of the government. The West — with whom the newly imported secularization and corruption are associated — became the target for those discontented with the process.

This new dependence on the West — and its manifestation in the presence of thousands of businessmen, most of whom are there with the intention of making quick profits — is profoundly irritating. Add to that the close US affiliation with Israel and American policies towards the Palestinian question and you have an explosive mixture. American policy is not only seen as being insensitive to the Arab cause but as valuing an Israeli alliance above the friendship of Saudi Arabia. The latter is taken for granted despite the West's increased dependence on Arab oil.

It was the successful use of the oil embargo following the 1973 War which alerted the Arab world to the potential of oil to secure influence and power. The temptation to resort to the weapon remains. Many of these states can afford to forgo oil revenues for a considerable period if it suits their non-economic interests and accords with their list of political priorities. Such a 'linkage' is urged by Arab states bordering Israel, by the Palestinians and even by many educated middle-class Saudis and Kuwaitis, all of whom argue that the Arabs need to be taken more seriously. They expect their oil producers to manipulate the west's vulnerabilities so as to advance all-Arab interests. Ignoring the limitation and dangers contained in the application of this weapon,[1] they maintain that their states' oil production is far beyond their financial needs and is far more than is desirable for moderate and manageable industrial development. They argue that the only reason why it is necessary to produce so much oil is to satisfy and protect the West's high standards of living. In the case of Saudi Arabia, these so-called 'young Turks' maintain that conservation for future generations is a necessity which will also shield the Kingdom from a high rate of inflation and vast corruption which are the inevitable by-products of excessive oil production.

Contempt for the western way of life yet envy of western industrial success sharpens the dilemma for many proud Muslims who would like to advance themselves by taking advantage of western technology[2] and the spirit of western democracy without having to absorb 'western greed and decadence'. To them the West is the source of all evils and maladies which have afflicted the Arab nation. Readily accepting western assistance or even the trappings of westernization does not make them 'pro-western'. On the contrary, their sense of cultural

---

1 For further reading see Hans Maull *Oil and Influence: the Oil Weapon Examined* , Adelphi Paper No. 117, The International Institute for Strategic Studies, London, 1975.

2 Khomeini is perhaps the best example of a man full of hate towards the West yet using its technology to advance his own interests.

inferiority, especially when some of them are western-educated, makes them search for their lost identity, self-respect and dignity while seeking a way to give expression to their own authenticity.[1] Disillusioned with Arab Nationalism ('Nasserism'), once the most powerful, albeit anti-clerical, manifestation of Arab protest against the West, more Arab intellectuals are turning back toward an Islamic revival. Pan-Islam is therefore both a vehicle for mobilizing public support and an outlet for airing this bitterness and frustration even if many of those protesting remain non-believers. Moreover no ruler professing to govern in the name of Islam can afford to condemn such a form of expression, even if it combines rejection of western imperialism with Marxist rhetoric. These groups' tenacity and firmness when criticizing the subordination of their countries to the West (rather than to pan-Arab and pan-Islamic aims) finds support among more orthodox elements who are exasperated with the moral results of modernization as well as among the still small but steadily emerging middle class. The growing danger for the Gulf regimes is increasingly that of being identified by their own subjects as 'western stooges' who are collaborating willingly with the west in exploiting their countries' gift from God to undermine Islam against the interests of the Arab Nation.

Ironically, the too-explicit link between these dynasties and the US, motivated primarily by hopes for rapid modernization and fear of *external* threats to their very survival, might become the unifying force behind *internal* opposition aiming at their overthrow. The rulers need American assurances but do not wish to be too closely associated with the US and its interests in the region. As a result of America's decline, the cornered dynasties are coming to view their special relations with the US, at least in their present form, as a prime threat to their own survival.[2] Calculating that the US would have to come to their aid *in extremis*, they prefer to be seen to distance themselves from the US and to promote links with Western Europe in the hope that they can use the Western Europeans to put pressure on the US to, in turn, exert pressure on Israel. Lately the Saudis even repeated that they are maintaining an

1 See the three articles by Flora Lewis in the New York Times, 28-29-30 December 1979. Also Muhammed Ayoob ` *The Politics of Resurgent Islam* , published by The Strategic and Defence Studies Centre, Australian National University, Canberra, 5 March 1980, p 12.

2 How far this has gone could be detected from the Saudi embarrassment caused by the Libyan campaign concerning the despatch of the four American AWACS radar surveillance planes to Saudi Arabia, when in reply to the Libyan charge that 'the pilgrims' prayers to God on Mount Arafat (Holy Hill near Mecca) has been disturbed by the sound of American aircraft' the Saudis replied that the prayers 'saw only the helicopters flown by Saudi pilots in order to control traffic between the Holy Cities' (Riyadh Home Service 11.30 GMT, 21 October 1980 — BBC SWB ME/6556/A/2-3, 23 October 1980). The Kuwaiti authorities suspended from publishing for two weeks the leftist weekly *al-Tali'ah* for criticizing Saudi Arabia for obtaining the AWACS following the outbreak of the Iran-Iraq War.

ongoing dialogue with the USSR.[1]

Whether or not Islamic fundamentalism will remain as a lasting form of expression, it certainly should not be dismissed. It will remain a potent force around which a wide coalition of those alienated by modernization can gather. Nevertheless one should not exaggerate Islam or view things exclusively in its terms. There is also a powerful process of secularization at work in the region, especially among the young and educated whose general inclination is to lean towards secular political ideas and to view with derision the conservative way of life of the older generation. Moreover secularization has value for heterogeneous societies for it helps to blur the sectarian and ethnic differences which divide the Gulf states. Yet, however desirable such a development might be, it is at present a remote one. Religious antagonism between the Sunnis and the Shi'is exists and the war between Iraq and Iran has served, at least for the time being, to make this distinction even more pronounced.

1 Interview with the Saudi Foreign Minister, Saud al-Faisal, in Ukaz, Saudi Arabia, 26 May 1981.

3 Sectarian and ethnic strife

Prior to the Iraq-Iran War

The Shi'ah Challenge

Apart from Oman (which has few Shi'is) and excluding Iran, all Gulf states have Sunni regimes governing Shi'is. In Iraq, Bahrain and the Emirate of Dubai Shi'is form the majority; in Kuwait and in Qatar they are just under 20 percent of the inhabitants. For the bigger states (Saudi Arabia and Iraq) their importance lies in their populating — like the Kurds — the sensitive oil-bearing regions.

The rise of Khomeini to power inspired this leaderless, scattered community to voice their protest in a more confident way than ever before. In the first year following the Iranian revolution, a serious challenge to the existing regimes would have been posed should the scattered Shi'is in the Gulf have come to regard the Iranian 'clergy' as their sole moral leaders and political representatives and to respond to Khomeini's trans-national anti-western Islamic revolution as a means of redressing their economically backward and politically inferior status. Many of them eagerly listened to the voices from Iran urging them to rise against their masters. Indeed this was a fear which united all the regimes in the Gulf who were terrified by the possibility of the Islamic revolution being 'imported' to their domain by Shi'is. As one Kuwaiti Minister put it:

The Iranian revolution does not seem to accept the legitimacy of our system of government. It exports Shi'itism in the
guise of pan-Islam, and pan-Iranianism underlies both ... I
suppose he (the Ayatollah) might try to unleash a local fifth
column on the oilfields.[1]

The Shi'is thus came to be regarded as a security threat. Bordering
paranoia, this brought back memories of sectarian conflict in Islamic
history of the ninth and tenth centuries AD.

However, the danger of this challenge was reduced with the outbreak
of the war between Iraq and Iran which tarnished Khomeini's image as
omnipotent. Among his staunch supporters in the Arab states, feelings
of disillusion and despair replaced those of hope and confidence. Fewer
photographs of Khomeini are now on display.

Yet the sectarian problem remains and it could be despair which
could make it surface once again. Discrimination and suppression could
hardly serve as a solution. That the Shi'is of Bahrain or Kuwait might
join other organizations which would oppose the regimes by champion-
ing their grievances remains a possibility much feared by the authorities
who also worry that tension in one state could spill over to its neighbours, even though the Shi'ah community is far from being a homogeneous group because of their disparate origins and subordinate economic
status.

Bahrain

Bahrain's Shi'ah community is comprised of Arab Shi'is (mainly of Iraqi
origin) and non-Arabic speaking Iranians who came there either in the
nineteenth century or following the discovery of oil. Unlike many of
those living in the Saudi Eastern Province, most of Bahrain's Shi'is are
part of the island's indigenous population. They are nevertheless to a
large extent denied access to the country's wealth, despite the fact that
many of them form the backbone of the urban middle class. The
merchants among them are pushed aside by the preferential positions
acquired by a Royal Family increasingly preoccupied with trade. Moreover, the Al Khalifa Sunni dynasty of tribal origin favours their kin
despite the fact that more than 60 percent of this category are illiterate
(they are similar to the rural Shi'ah living in dispersed surburban

---

1 See David Hirst, 'Iran driving the Kuwaitis into the arms of Iraq', *The Guardian*, 13 May
1980.

settlements).[1] Thus, urban Sunnis as well as urban Shi'is (both of Arab and Iranian origin) are excluded from the top of the pyramid regardless of their relatively high economic status.

The Iranian revolution could only encourage Bahrain's Shi'ah. After years of relative calm, demonstrations broke out. Demands in favour of an Islamic state and the prohibition of alcohol and for closing all leisure centres[2] — one of the main sources of Bahrain's economy — were accompanied by protests against the state's security law, the behaviour of the security police, and unemployment. The combination of such Shi'i-championed demands was designed to recruit wider support from other alienated elements in the hope that this would force the government to consider their grievances in a far more serious manner. The Palestinian issue — through the Iranian-initiated 17 August 1979 Jerusalem Day — provided the common denominator for all opponents to join in a protest against both the regime's secular behaviour and its pro-western posture. In response, the government arrested some of the sect's divines who were allegedly co-ordinating their action with Iran's new leaders but the government also tightened up, at least for a while, on public entertainment and restricted the sale of alcohol. The Shi'ah, however, were unimpressed by the government's announced religious, social and economic reforms. Demonstrations, although on a small scale, continued throughout 1979 especially centring around religious celebrations — traditionally the occasions for heightened emotions — but they included nationalist secular elements. In the words of one of the latter:

> The revolution has kindled a new zeal among the people, and it has kindled conflicts. It has made the people hate these regimes. Their sympathy for change in the area existed, but the revolution unveiled it. Thus, we observed the spontaneous movement of the people, which was an expression of their solidarity — not only their solidarity with the revolution in Iran and the Palestinian revolution, but they express local feelings, democratic feelings, feelings hostile to America, the elimination of American principles and the American presence.[3]

1 For further details on Bahrain's society see Fuad I. Khuri 'Oil and socio-economic transformation in Bahrain' in *Man and Society in the Arab Gulf*, Papers of the Third International Symposium of the Centre for Arab Gulf Studies, Basrah, Baghdad, 1979, Vol. III, pp 565-93.

2 See for example a list of demands presented by Shi'ah leaders in *al-Nahar* daily, Beirut, 15 September 1979.

3 Husain Musa of the Popular Front-Bahrain in a discussion with other Gulf organizations in *al-Safir*, Beirut. 18 November 1979 (English version in *Near East/North Africa Report* published by Joint Publications Research Service, 25 January 1980).

The Bahraini government was forced to use tougher measures and demonstrators were dispersed by tear gas with more arrests, whose release was now demanded by the Iranian government. Bahrain obviously could not be seen to give in out of fear that this would only place it in a still more difficult position.

A second wave of demonstrations broke out in Manamah in April 1980. The focus of these protests, however, was directed against the close ties of Al Khalifa with Iraq as 'plotting against the revolution' and for arresting Khomeini's supporters and expelling his representative in Bahrain. Wide publicity was given to statements issued by the Iranian-backed Islamic Front for the Liberation of Bahrain on Radio Tehran International Service broadcast to the Gulf.[1] Demonstrations marking 40 days' mourning for the Iraqi Shi'ah leader, who had been killed by the Ba'athist regime, owing to his tendency to oppose it, heightened tension in Bahrain. The cycle of demonstrations and arrests repeated itself. Shi'ah leaders renewed their demands for the release of those detained since the dissolution of the short-lived National Assembly in 1975. Yet even more arrests were said to have taken place.[2]

The regime was now sensitive not only to the direct impact of the Iranian revolution but that 'over-reporting' and much exaggerated coverage given in the Iranian media on internal unrest would result in undermining the West's financial confidence in Bahrain, further harming the island's already weakened economic capability. This, in turn, would make it difficult for the ruling dynasty to embark on housing schemes and other economic projects mainly directed to that part of the population whose unrest it feared.

The limited support the authorities obtained from the more affluent urban Shi'is (whether Arab or Iranian) reflected the latter's concern at the possibility of the Iranian chain of events repeating itself. Economic chaos could, they fear, ultimately bring to power the strong leftist elements existing in Bahrain which could jeopardize their present economic status.

However, one of the greatest sources of concern of the Bahraini regime remained its fear of Iran reviving its claim to the island as its 'fourteenth province'. Although the Shah renounced Iran's interest in Bahrain following the 1970 Referendum supervised by the UN in which Sunnis, like Shi'is, rejected the Shah's claim, the shadow of this claim and the fear that Iran's 'clergy' want to assume control over all Shi'is,

1 2 May – DR, 13 May 1980; 13 July 1980 – SWB ME/6471/A/1, 15 July 1980. 5 August 1980 (Front's appeal on Jerusalem Day) – SWB ME/6491/A/7, 7 August 1980.

2 al-Kifah al-Arabi, Beirut, 16 March 1981 provided a list of the names of over fifty new detainees.

regardless of existing national boundaries, loom over Bahrain's dynasty. Indeed the declaration of Ayatollah Sadiq Ruhani in mid-June 1979 (that the island is an indivisible part of Iran) strengthened these fears, even if the new Iranian government made it clear that he was not reflecting an official position. However it is the very nature of the Khomeini government which could prompt disaffected Bahrain's Shi'ah to adopt a new posture.

Iraq's readiness to defend the island from an Iranian invasion was no comfort to the regime which rejected — again like all other Gulf states — Iraqi attempts to enhance its own regional position. Moreover, Bahrain never wanted to become a party to the Iraqi-Iranian rivalry. It sees its security in preserving good-neighbourly relations with Iran, for the alternative could only exacerbate sectarian strife within the island.

Kuwait

Kuwait has the same interest as Bahrain, even though its Shi'ah community is fairly small, its history essentially one of quiescence and although the spreading of Kuwait's wealth meant that there was little in common between its Shi'ah minority and the poor Iranian masses. But the rise of Khomeini changed all that and the Shi'ah came to be regarded as a menace which further complicated Kuwait's demographic mosaic. Hence precautions have been taken since the Iranian revolution and the authorities have clamped down on any sign of Shi'ah unease.[1] Not wanting to take any chances of Shi'i demonstrations spreading and engulfing other elements who have political rather than religious grievances, the government swiftly acted against Ahmad Abbas al-Muhri — a nephew of Khomeini and the son of Bahrain's Shi'ah leader[2] — who incited those coming to the Mosque's Friday prayers. He was stripped of his Kuwaiti citizenship and deported with his family to Iran.

Saudi Arabia

If the Kuwaitis were aware of the seeds of dissent contained in the presence of Shi'is, the Shi'i rising in Hasa (the Saudi Eastern Province), which took place whilst the Mecca siege was taking place, alarmed the Saudis. This was primarily, though not exclusively, owing to the strategic

---

1 The government disallowed the taking place of a Shi'i symposium in Hajj Sha'ban mosque, situated in al-Darb region which was closed for the Shi'is (al-Mustaqbal, Lebanon (Paris), 29 September 1979). al-Sharq al-Jadid daily, London, 10 December 1979 described a division in an Islamic group based in Switzerland over the issue of the need to topple the entire Al Sabah dynasty or only its present head. The new group declared its aim of changing all the Arab regimes around Iran and amalgamating them into one state under Khomeini.

2 Middle East Intelligence Survey (MEIS), 1-15 October 1979, p 101.

importance of the Eastern Province where the oilfields are located. The estimated 400,000-strong Shi'i community comprises a large share of the workers in the oil terminals, although they form just over half of the entire population of Hasa, which the Saudis are attempting to dilute primarily with Sunnis from the Najd. Commemorating the death of the Prophet's grandson (the Ashura) in November 1979, the Shi'i community living there paraded in Qatif's streets carrying banners and pictures of Khomeini and chanting anti-western slogans. A few were killed when the military stepped in.

Another demonstration took place on 1 February 1980, the anniversary of Khomeini's return from exile. On both occasions the Shi'is protested bitterly against their inferior economic status, the squalid conditions in which they live and the discrimination they face at being excluded from the bureaucracy and the military. Their antagonism towards the Saudi regime is sharpened by their mutual animosity towards the local Sunnis[1] (like that occurring in the town of Hufuf). Although many of them are of Bahraini, Iranian and Iraqi origin, they claim to be descendants of the old inhabitants of Hasa. Thus these grievances were not aired merely by immigrants but by inhabitants and workers (some of whom with leftist tendencies) who feel discriminated against and that they have a right to a better share in the country's wealth, especially when they are responsible for extracting oil and populating Jubail, the new industrial site situated between Juaymah and Ras Tannura oil terminals. They could hardly be expected to be content with empty government promises to ameliorate their status, especially when their request for the removal of the Province Governor's post from the hands of the ibn Jiluwi family went unheeded. If anything, the failure of the Saudi regime to respond to their pleas could make them only more angry, especially when they are constantly reminded that their present economic condition is far better than in the days of King Abd al-Aziz (when they were accorded the status of a protected minority). Though unprecedented in the form of violent expression of ordinary people, it may not be the last such expression, even if for the last sixteen months the region has been quiet.

Upheaval in the Eastern Province along sectarian lines could bring the Saudi oil industry to a standstill — as the ARAMCO unrest of the 1950s showed. This might affect not only the Kingdom's economy but that of the West also, which imports 9.5 (or more) million barrels of crude oil a

---

1 Without trying to take credit, an Egyptian leftist magazine appearing in Paris argued that those communists who marched in the demonstrations refrained from emphasizing their presence because they knew the religious dignitaries refused to co-operate with them and they did not want to do anything which could harm the chances of a successful anti-government expression (al-Yasar al-Arabi, January 1980).

day from Saudi Arabia. The stakes involved are enormous. Hence the sensitivity of the Shi'i issue in Saudi Arabia, whose regime feared that the new government across the Gulf could exploit this thorn in the Saudi side. There were indications that, on both occasions when the Shi'is were rioting, they were being encouraged by the Iranian media[1] and the new consciousness which surfaced among Saudi Shi'is was evidently inspired by Khomeini. The Iranians tried to tarnish the Saudi image through the so-called Islamic Revolution Organization of the Arabian Peninsula which accused the Saudi regime of forcefully putting down demonstrations in the Eastern Province on the occasion of the International Jerusalem Day and charged that the dynasty only 'pretends to want the return of Jerusalem and (is) making commercial deals at the expense of the Palestinian issue'.[2] They also continuously and sharply criticized Al Saud's failure to adhere to Islam in an attempt to undermine the other pillar of its legitimacy.

Iraq

In Iraq the problem is, of course, of a totally different magnitude. With the rise of Khomeini, Iraq and Iran were on a collision course. The Ba'ath secular Sunni regime feared that its narrow power base might be manipulated by its eastern neighbour's 'clergy' in a way which might foment unrest among the country's Shi'ah, exacerbating the old sectarian rift within Iraq. But Shi'i dissent did not start with Khomeini's revolution. Riots in Najaf and Karbala', the Shi'ah's religious centres and strongholds, were not uncommon in Iraq's history. The Shi'ah community, who form about 60 percent of Iraq's 13 million inhabitants and who populate the wealth-producing southern rural part of the country as a demographic 'buffer' between the rest of the Gulf and the 'Sunni Triangle' (the area ranging from Baghdad to Mosul in the north and down to Rutbah in the west and which does not contain any of Iraq's oilfields[3]), is economically backward. So at the centre of the challenge to the Ba'athist regime lie religious and economic grievances.

---

1 Iranian sources, which reported that a hundred Shi'is were wounded and many arrested, published a statement by a group called the Organization of the Islamic Revolution in the Arabian Peninsula about the incident saying that the Islamic revolution in the peninsula would 'continue to intensify until the tribal Al Sa'ud regime is defeated and the Islamic republic established on the ruins of that oppressive regime'. (Tehran Radio Arabic service citing *Jomhuri-ye Eslami* paper of 6.2.80 — see BBC Monitoring Report ME/6339/I, 7 February 1980.)

2 Tehran Radio 1630 GMT, 10 August 1980 — SWB ME/6496/A/1, 13 August 1980.

3 See map in Abbas Kelidar, *Iraq: the Search for Stability*, published by the Institute for the Study of Conflict, No. 59, July 1975, p 13.

The lack of leadership[1] among the Shi'ah made it easier for the Ba'ath to consolidate their position. However, their hopes of neutralizing the Shi'is by bringing some of their members into the government failed. If anything, many young educated Shi'is rationalized their stand and joined the Iraqi Communist Party (ICP). This alliance became intolerable for the regime and, as early as the early 1960s, Shi'i radicals were being massacred or executed by the Ba'ath. Rebellion of Shi'is grew out of a religious procession in Najaf and Karbala' at the beginning of 1977. The Iraqi Army was called in and the demonstrations were suppressed and some Shi'i leaders were sentenced to death. Personal and ideological issues rather than sectarian conflicts manifested themselves in the brutal purge which followed Saddam Hussein al-Takriti's rise to the presidency (July 1979). The purge was conducted against all those suspected of being his opponents and included the Secretary of the Revolutionary Command Council and other prominent Shi'i ministers known to be connected with the Communists. These executions were nevertheless a reminder to the local Shi'is that the Iraqi regime would not tolerate[2] any internal opposition. Simultaneously, President Saddam embarked upon a wide economic programme designed to improve conditions for the Shi'ah community and oil revenues were put back into the oil-producing region.

But if in the past Iraq feared the Shah's strong army, regarding it as a threat to its security interests and regional position, following the Islamic revolution the Iraqi regime viewed a Shi'i-ruled Iran as a threat to its internal stability. The Iraqi authorities were uneasy about the possibility that many Iraqi Shi'is would regard Khomeini as their spiritual leader knowing him well from the 14 years he had spent in Najaf in exile from Iran. The regime also feared that, while other Shi'i leaders would try to imitate Khomeini's success, he could seek to embarrass the Iraqis for expelling him at the Shah's request.

Indeed, the Iraqi authorities were troubled by the establishment of a clandestine Shi'i body known as the Islamic Call (al-Da'wah al-Islamiyah) Party which both those initiating it and those backing it from across the border (Iran) had hoped would develop into a mass movement and fare more impressively than it did. The Da'wah was

1 The Fatimid Party established in Iraq in 1959 failed to achieve mass support amidst the Shi'ah community. Its leaders were later executed by the Ba'athi regime which nevertheless occasionally coloured its words with Islamic phrases, especially when appearing in carefully orchestrated rallies held in predominantly Shi'i cities (see the words of Iraq's President when speaking in the holy city of Najaf — press release by the Iraqi Embassy in London dated 18 October 1979).

2 Apart from showing its firmness, the secular Ba'ath regime tried to appease the Shi'ah by tightening regulations on the observance of the Ramadan fast and outlawing the gambling through the national lottery and horseracing.

nevertheless responsible for the attempted assassination of Deputy Premier Tariq Aziz in April 1980 as well as other acts of sabotage within Iraq.

Needless to say the Iraqi regime could not tolerate the Da'wah's existence and did its utmost to thwart it. President Saddam Hussein was not going to allow anything to stand in his way when bidding for all-Arab leadership, certainly not within his own domain. Internal stability was essential and he stopped at nothing to ensure it. Harsh measures were always used when he was trying to assert himself and consolidate his position and that included liquidation of any pockets of opposition. The Party was outlawed on 9 April by the Revolution Command Council, with the death sentence imposed for anyone connected with its activities. Those caught were frequently executed. Ayatollah Muhammad Baqir al-Sadr, their leader, was put under house arrest and then executed. The authorities were extremely sensitive to the possibility that the Da'wah was co-ordinating part of its action with the other implacable enemies of the Ba'ath, the Communists and Kurdish groups, and that it maintained contacts not only with Iran but with the Lebanese al-Amal Sh'i group.[1] The Da'wah also extended its operations to the neighbouring littoral states and declared that it was behind the murder of an Iraqi diplomat in Abu Dhabi as revenge for the Iraqi execution of its own members.[2] This pattern continued with reported acts of sabotage and terror and Iraqi suppression in response or pre-emption.

It is difficult to estimate the Shi'is' success. Certainly their achievements in Iraq were inflated by Iranian broadcasts. Nevertheless, the Da'wah had nuisance value and it revealed the extent of the internal discontent within Iraq. It added to the festering problem of Iraq's restless Kurds.

1 Baghdad Radio, 9 April 1980 — SWB/Monitoring Report ME/6392/i, 11 April 1980; also 6471/A/5, 15 July 1980.

2 Tehran (in Arabic) 2200 GMT, 28 April 1980 – *ibid.*, ME/6484/A/3, 30 July 1980.

Secessionist trends

Essentially minorities with distinct identities exist only in the two most powerful states: Iraq and Iran. The perennial question of minorities coming to the fore could nevertheless unsettle the region because, unlike other issues, their claims involve territories. After all, the borders of the relatively new states in the region were generally defined by the colonial powers and some of the minorities have never accepted these lines which they regard as artificial, especially when they separate them from their relatives living on the other side of these borders — as the case of the Kurds demonstrates.

The Kurdish question

With a population (mostly Sunni) ranging between 6.5 and 17 million,[1] populating five different states (predominantly Turkey, Iraq and Iran with smaller numbers in Syria and the USSR), living in hilly regions and retaining their tribal way of life, the Kurds' history is one of a continuous struggle for genuine autonomy. Despite having different enemies and allies, their common goal is perceived by their 'hosts' as aspiring for secession, even if they are careful to demand only autonomy within their respective states. Promised independence by the Treaty of Sèvres of 1920, the unification of independent Kurdistan is probably regarded as their ultimate goal.

Conversely, the regimes of the states where the Kurds live have a common interest: to thwart any notion of Kurdish (and for that matter any other minority) separatism. But whereas each state has regarded Kurdish aspirations as a challenge to its own authority, legitimacy and ability to rule, both Iran and Iraq have sought, while attempting to control their own minority at home, to manipulate each other's ethnic vulnerability so as to increase their own leverage over the other.[2] Hence alliances were sometimes made across the border.

For Iran the Kurdish question had religious facets (most Kurds are Sunnis) and ideological overtones (part of their leadership is communist or is aided by Marxist non-Kurdish elements). For the Ba'ath in Iraq, which was trying to present itself as a socialist popular regime, Kurdish nationalism posed a challenge to the only force which could possibly unite the country under one leadership — Iraqi nationalism. The Kurds' mountainous bases, the arms at their disposal and their ties with other

---

1 Whereas the Kurds tend to inflate their numbers the governments concerned minimize their size.

2 For further reading, see Edgar O'Ballance *The Kurdish Revolt, 1961-1972*, Faber, London, 1973.

discontented Iraqi elements, as well as with some external forces, made them a potent force to be reckoned with.

In their attempts to come to terms with the Kurds, who comprise 20 percent of Iraq's population of 10 million, different Iraqi governments have tried intermittently to crush the Kurdish revolt by force. Failing to achieve this, other means were sought to appease the Kurdish community and weaken the appeal of its militant leaders. 'Divide and rule' tactics were intended to fragment the KDP (Kurdish Democratic Party) led by Mullah Mustafa Barazani, and to recruit members from break-away groups to join the government's lower echelons. When the Ba'ath failed to win massive support from the Kurds and to neutralize Barazani, it tried to reach an arrangement with him. The March 1970 Agreement acknowledged the territorial gains made by the Kurdish militia — the *Pesh Merga* — and offered the Kurds self-rule. The agreement, which granted the Kurds many other concessions, lasted four years (granting the regime the stability it sought) but in fact it was never put into practice. Mutual suspicion and contempt continued to govern the actions of both sides.

The major, though certainly not the only, bone of contention was the oilfields in Kirkuk, an area the Kurds regard as 'theirs' by virtue of it being predominantly Kurdish whereas the Iraqi regime naturally disputed this, arguing that the Turkomans and the Assyrians make it a mixed region. Kurdish leaders accused the government of trying to dilute the Kurdish nature of the area by 'Arabizing' it so as to undermine both the Kurdish influence there and their claim over a share of the oil revenues to be carved out for their own development.

Moreover, the newly-appointed Kurdish Legislative Council and Executive Council neither legislated nor governed. Kurdish institutions, set up in the early 1970s to promote their own culture, were banned and, moreover, even the Arabic language was imposed on the Kurdish education system. The regime also declined to respond to the Kurdish (and Communist) demands for establishing the long-awaited parliament, which might challenge the Ba'ath's monopoly of power. The latter tried to play the Communists and the Kurds against each other and succeeded in further fragmenting the already sharply divided Kurdish leadership[1]

---

1 For further details see A. Kalidar, *Iraq, op.cit.*, p14, and Amanda Cuthbert 'The Kurds' in *Arab Report* (AR), February 1979, p5 (listing the seven different Iraqi-Kurdish political organizations). A 42 page-long document published by the al-Hizb al-Dimuqrati al-Kurdistani, al-Lajnah al-Tahdiriyyah (the Kurdish Democratic Party — Preparatory Committee) founded in 1976 by one of the Barazani's close men, criticized Barazani and called for building the KDP on genuine progressive and democratic foundations (published in 1977).

by nominating Kurdish Ministers and by playing off the various Kurdish groups against each other. Deterioration of relations resulted in the resumption of hostilities.

When war between them finally broke out in March 1974, the Iraqi regime gained the upper hand and the Kurds, considerably weakened after a year of war, were pushed back to the region adjacent to Iran and Turkey. The latter, fearing that conflict would spill over into its own territory, also had an interest in weakening the Iraqi Kurds. Border villages were demolished by the Iraqi Army and the authorities thinned out the Kurdish areas by deporting between 100,000 and 350,000 Kurds to the south of Iraq.[1] Another 200,000 Kurds were reported to have fled to Iran. Unemployment in the Kurdish region meant that many young men migrated to towns, depriving the guerrillas of recruits and weakening the tribal framework, though this also meant that the influence of their tribal chiefs was perpetuated. Few Kurds were absorbed into the oil industry but Kurdistan remained economically backward, with a large share of the budget allocated for its development being spent on roads which would no doubt aid the Iraqi Army if and when the next clash with the Kurds takes place.

The Kurdish cause received a setback once Iran and Iraq mended their fences at Algiers in March 1975, ending a decade in which the Shah had manipulated the Iraqi Kurds to advance Iran's regional stand at the expense of its neighbour. The agreement meant that, in exchange for granting Iran control of the Shatt al-Arab on the basis of the median line, the Shah withdrew his support of Iraq's Kurds' rebellion which as a result collapsed a few days later. In fact, the Kurds' fortunes and the power of their 'host' governments in both states could be depicted as connected vessels. Hence, with the weakening of the central authority in post-revolution Iran and its unwillingness to respond to Kurdish demands, the problem came on the agenda of both states yet again, especially when Iraq, which has never managed to subdue its Kurds for long, was now supporting the revived thrust of Kurdish insurgency directed against Khomeini. So the old pattern repeated itself but with a different motivation. Whereas the Iranian 'clergy' were trying to promote the plight of their Shi'i brothers in Iraq in an attempt to subvert — not merely weaken — the secular, Sunni regime there, the latter was striving to cripple the Iranian regime and seeking to profit from its internal struggles by aiding not only the Iranian Kurds but also the other ethnic groups living adjacent to Iran's border with Iraq.

1   Andrew Whitley, 'The Kurds: pressures and prospects' in *Round Table* quarterly, July 1980, p 251.

However, the Iraqi government failed to weaken Kurdish separatism and, as in the past, Kurds continued in their struggle, making it difficult for the central authority to govern the area. Despite Iraqi-Iranian agreement a new wave of Kurdish activities started in the summer of 1976. The radical Patriotic Union of Kurdistan (PUK), which broke away from the disintegrating tribal-based KDP, also managed to reassert itself in certain villages and was backed by Syria in doing so.[1] The short period of *rapprochement* between Syria and Iraq which followed Camp David deprived the PUK of Syrian help although various groups of Kurds were heartened by the fall of the Shah which encouraged a revival of Kurdish action in Iran, though Kurds were also fighting each other.[2]

Iran harbours more than 4 million Kurds (about one-third of all Kurds) who live astride her border with Iraq and it was not long after the revolution before the well-trained and well-armed Kurds fell out with the Pasdaran (the Revolutionary Guards) in the rugged mountain terrain. Prominent among the rebel forces were the banned Kurdish Democratic Party of Iran (KDPI) and a leftist conglomeration of groups (the Komala Party) known to be aided by the Peykar Party, a communist group hostile to Iran's Tudeh (Communist) Party. The authorities were also aggravated by the Kurds' connection with the Feda'iyun-e Khalq, and the Iranian Army issued a warning to the 'leftist counter-revolutionaries ... fomenting disturbances and bloodshed contrary to the interests of our Kurdish brothers'.[3] Thereafter the guerrillas were driven into the hills after the towns they held were mercilessly bombed. The war continued but negotiations were resumed. The Kurds demanded the evacuation of all Iranian forces occupying parts of Iranian Kurdistan and the implementation of immediate and full autonomy 'within a single united Iran',[4] and a halt to the atrocities

---

1 The PUK was established in 1975 and is led by Mustafa Barazani's former aide, Jalal Talabani. Its publications condemn both Barazani's leadership and the Ba'ath regime which the PUK vowed to overthrow. The PUK's mouthpiece *Sawt al-Ittibad* (No. 3, March 1979) gives an account of nearly two hundred incidents its people were involved in against the Iraqi regime. Talabani's group cooperated with the KDPI across the border.

2 Voice of Iraqi Kurdistan (in Surani Kurdish) 16.00 GMT, 24 July 1980 — SWB ME/6481/A/6, 26 July 1980.

3 Tehran Home Service, 16.30, 23 November 1979 in BBC *Summary of World Broadcasts* (SWB) ME/6281/A/2.

4 National Voice of Iran (in Azarbaijani) 17.45 GMT, 19 April 1980 — SWB ME/6404/A/8, 25 April 1980. The KDP constantly repeated this message and in January 1981 it denied reports of its alleged intention to proclaim a Kurdish state (Voice of Iranian Kurdistan (Surani and Persian)), 2 January 1981 — ME/6615/A/2, 6 January 1981.

and executions of Kurds. The authorities, however, could not be seen to give in to the Kurds' demands from a position of weakness even though they were anxious to end the unrest, fearing its impact on Iran's other minorities.

In a sense, the war with the Kurds was a test case for the central authority. The dilemma was clear. The Iranian army was demoralized and the government wanted to play for time. Losing face would only encourage the other ethnic groups to persist in their own struggle, resulting probably in the fragmentation of the country. Like everything else in Iran, decisions rested with the Ayatollah Khomeini who was reluctant to negotiate with the Kurds in the first place. He was convinced that the Iranian army would shortly put an end to the rebellion and isolate their present leadership, believing history would repeat itself. In 1946 the government had put an end to the short-lived Soviet-backed Kurdish secessionist state set up in Mahabad. However, the escalation of violence along the Iraqi-Iranian border in the months leading up to the war aided the Iraqi-backed Kurds and intensified their struggle, although this was replaced by a short-lived vacillation once the war broke out.

Iran's other minorities

Khuzistan

Far smaller than the Kurds but strategically more important are the Arabs in Khuzistan. These could complicate relations with Iraq and cause a real problem to the Iranian regime. They live — some 2 million of them — near the head of the Gulf in the oil fields of Khuzistan which have provided about 600,000 barrels of refined oil per day, the economic life-blood of Iran.

Strikes among the oil workers played an important role in bringing about the Iranian Revolution. Disenchanted by their economic deficiencies — which the new regime has done nothing to alter — they have demanded autonomy. To emphasize this point, the more militant among them managed to sabotage (with Iraqi aid) the vulnerable oil industry and stated that they would 'not put down their arms and will fight against Persian injustice'.[1] With the new regime asserting its Shi'i nature, the Sunni feelings of some Arabs were also reinforced. Thus national and religious sentiments were intertwined and, to complicate the issue further, many Arabs in Khuzistan are Shi'is.

Some of the fighting between pro-Irani Shi'is and Iraqi Ba'athists took place as far away as Lebanon, nor was the conflict between the Iranian regime and the Arabs of Khuzistan confined to Iranian territory. The seizure of the Iranian embassy in London was evidence that the secessionist Arab guerrillas were encouraged by the escalation of fighting along the borders between Iran and Iraq. Clashes between Iranian forces and armed Khuzistanis followed. The authorities believed nevertheless that the core of the problem was economic rather than political and that agricultural and industrial development would be an adequate answer. However they became increasingly nervous with the intensification of the Iraqi-backed Arab demands for autonomy. Owing to the region's wealth, Iraq had an interest in reviving its old territorial claim to Khuzistan, which it calls 'Arabistan'. Iraq's ability to foment this dormant issue and to create unrest amongst the province's Arab population (through the Khuzistani National Liberation Front) was an integral part of its invasion plan.

Azarbaijan

Bordering the USSR and Turkey and separated from their families there are the Turkish-speaking Azarbaijanis. Like the Kurds, they have rejected

---

1 Radio Baghdad (INA) 2055 GMT 1 May 1980. Throughout the period, Iraq gave wide publicity to political and military activities allegedly carried out by the Arabs of Khuzistan (Baghdad Voice of the Masses 1600 GMT 2 June 1980, SWB ME/6463/A/3, 4 June 1980).

the new Islamic constitution which not only places enormous power in the hands of the country's supreme religious leader but also does not guarantee them any ethnic rights. The influential Ayatollah Shariat Madari, the community's spiritual leader and one of Khomeini's more prominent opponents, also rejected the awarding to Khomeini of seniority in Islamic jurisprudence, though he never disputed the latter's political role in defending Iran and Islam.[1] Being extremely popular country-wide, the aged Madari also has immense influence amongst other minorities and in the Muslim People's Republican Party (MPRP) and he enjoys the support of many other religious leaders. Though refraining from politics as such, he has become a focus for many Iranians. He is therefore perceived by Khomeini's people as a threat. Thus in the first four months following the revolution, the question of autonomy for the Azarbaijanis was further complicated by having a personal dimension added to it, with Khomeini even more reluctant to concede anything that could strengthen Madari.

The revival of the Azarbaijan Democratic Party (ADP) annoyed and worried the regime owing to its known pro-Soviet orientation. The Shah's forces had removed the ADP in 1946, a year after it was installed by the withdrawing Russians to head the short-lived independent Azarbaijan republic. Thus the issue of Azarbaijan could eventually become a bone of contention between Iran and the USSR which the present regime, like its predecessor, fears.

Baluchistan

Similarly, the Iranians are uneasy that the Soviet Union might manipulate the Baluchis — many of whom are known to support and to receive aid and training from the USSR — to advance Soviet influence and to fulfil the age-old dream of gaining access to warm waters near the oil-rich Gulf. Their homelands astride the shortest route from Afghanistan to the approaches of the Straits of Hormuz — through which much of the non-communist industrialized world's oil is carried — makes them of great strategic importance. The Soviet invasion of Afghanistan is a source of great concern to both Pakistan and Iran since, apart from creating a new precedent with all its implications, it could encourage the Baluchis to become more militant.

The Baluchis' demand for the establishment of Baluchistan worries not only Iran but Pakistan and Afghanistan also, both of which harbour a large segment of this ethnic group. It is Pakistan's ability to control 'their' Baluchis which could affect Baluchis in Iran — known to be connected with the Pakistan-based Baluchistan's People's Liberation Front, a Marxist guerrilla movement. Another new Baluchi group, called

1 See interview with him published in *The Middle East*, January 1980, p 33.

the Islamic Unity Party, is also striving for autonomy with the intention of establishing Baluchistan.[1] Already there are signs to that effect, with news percolating from Iran of small-scale clashes between Iranian government forces and Baluchi rebels.

It was more than fifty years ago that Reza Shah succeeded in bringing to a halt a Baluchi secessionist attempt. The rough terrain of Baluchistan and Seistan, however, made it difficult to subdue this group permanently to the central authority. Therefore, the government resorted to the methods it employed elsewhere of 'divide and rule' coupled with modest economic aid but the backward nature of the region did not change.

Moreover, the Islamic revolution opened up a new era for the Baluchis who are Sunnis.[2] Their fear of a Shi'i rule aggravated even the feelings of those who traditionally tended to co-operate with the government. That their demands for autonomy coincided with those of the other Iranian minorities did not help their cause. To what extent they can succeed will depend on their own cohesiveness, military capability, alliances with other domestic forces, aid from external forces such as the USSR or Iraq[3] as well as the central authority's weakness. The fact that they inhabit a remote but strategic region which could prove instrumental for outside forces may prompt the authorities to deal firmly with future Baluchi unrest but the mountainous terrain and Baluchi soldiers serving in Oman and the UAE (where they form a large part of the country's army in special units)[4] could serve to alter the military equation. The mercenaries are known to be staunch supporters of an independent Baluchistan.

Needless to say Iraq has sought to manipulate the separatist aspirations of the various Iranian minorities, at first as a way to off-set the Iranian leverage over Baghdad, and later as an instrument which would force Iran to divert attention and split its military forces. In that respect, the Soviet invasion of Afghanistan indirectly helped the Iraqi invasion of Iran for it forced Iran to focus its political and military attention also to the east and the north.

1 For further details see Eric Pace 'Iran's minorities: a history of conflict' in the *New York Times*, 23 December 1979, p 14.

2 In April 1980 the government closed down the University of Seistan and Baluchistan after Sunni students demonstrated in support for changing the education system (Tehran home service 0930 GMT 23 April 1980 — SWB ME/6403/A/9, 24 April 1980).

3 Iraq may renew its support for the Baluchis so as to offset the prospects of Soviet domination of the Straits of Hormuz — a situation which would hinder Iraq's regional supremacy and make it more dependent on the USSR.

4 Two Baluchi regiments are based in Salalah and the third in the adjacent Dhofari Coast (see Leigh Johnson 'Oman, a rock in the sands' in *Defence and Foreign Affairs Digest*, June 1979, p 9).

The Iran-Iraq war and its internal implications

The intention here is to examine briefly some of the internal implications of the war between Iran and Iraq. In the context discussed here,
these are related primarily, though not exclusively, to sectarian and
ethnic problems.

In launching the war against Iran, Saddam Hussein appears to have
had two related objects. First, to relieve his regime from Khomeini's
challenge by humiliating him and setting in motion a process for his
collapse. Second, to project himself as the new unrivalled regional
power in the Gulf if not in the Arab world. He believed he could achieve
his long-standing aspirations. There was a regional vacuum to be filled.
He faced only a weakened faction-ridden and polarized enemy which
had previously dominated the region. He anticipated the acquiescence
of his other neighbours, particularly when the war was to be presented
in the name of pan-Arabism facing up to a destabilizing brand of pan-
Islam, and his Syrian foes were entangled at home and in Lebanon. He
saw the preoccupation of both superpowers with their own affairs and
expected them to fear the consequences of getting physically involved.
The strengthening of his ties with western European states at the
expense of his patron — the USSR — was to provide him with a more
palatable, and hence more acceptable, ideological posture among his
southern neighbours as well as to allow him to limit further Soviet
leverage by diversifying his sources of arms. Saddam's quest for world-
wide influence was to be enhanced by oil bartered for a newly acquired
French-supplied nuclear potential.

Finally his stand in the Third World was to be promoted by adopting
a non-aligned position. These external policies were to further bolster
his position at home, where his charisma and the new-elected parliament were to cloak his totalitarian rule with a more relaxed and positive
image and overpower any internal opposition he might continue to
have. President Hussein believed that Iraq's resources and military
might would grant him a decisive victory and that the Arabs of
Khuzistan would act as a fifth column and help him to turn that
province into 'Arabistan'. Saddam clearly seems to have calculated he
would immediately be in a position to turn his territorial gains to
political advantage.

From his point of view, everything went wrong. 'Qadisiyat Saddam'
— as he termed his war with Iran — was nothing like the battle carrying
that name in 636 AD in which the victorious Arabs precipitated the
downfall of the Persian empire. If anything it was a blunder. Iraq set
itself an unattainable target. Short-term miscalculations and an over-
optimistic appraisal of the situation backfired and turned the war into a
long-term problem for Iraq despite of, if not because of, its continuing

presence on Iranian soil.

At first the sheikhdoms were pleased with Iraq's invasion which revealed Iran's military weakness. Like Iraq the dynasties had hoped that the war would result in the collapse of Khomeini and his replacement by a more 'responsible' and predictable moderate regime. However, with Iraq's exposed frailty, these dynasties became more concerned that what amounted to a prolonged war of attrition could prompt external intervention or at least force them to provide Iraq with certain air and naval facilities. Beyond paying lip service to the Arab cause, they were unwilling to do anything, fearing both Iranian retaliation and their own Shi'is reaction. Given both the uninhibited approach of both Iran and Iraq with regard to destroying each other's oil installations and with the stakes already so high, the sheikhdoms were anxious to remain aloof. They soon took comfort from the military stalemate which meant that the two most powerful states continued to weaken each other. So long as the sheikhs could persist in their non-involvement and so long as the war produced no winners and the conflict remained unresolved (thus constraining the main actors), neither could dominate the region and their ability to manipulate the internal vulnerabilities of their other neighbours would be hindered, though not lost.

Kuwait was less relaxed. It is strategically wedged between Iraq and Iran. The Al Sabah dynasty feared the consequences of being sucked into the war and of being identified by Iran as siding with Iraq — which ironically, has never relinquished its claim to Kuwait's territory. With its mercantilistic instinct, Kuwait adopted 'neutrality' as a means of allaying Iranian fears. The weakening of the Iraqi thrust enabled Kuwait to refrain from overtly supporting Iraq.[1] Iranian air-raids on Kuwait's border posts in mid-November 1980 (and again in June 1981) served as a reminder to that effect and strengthened Kuwait's (and, for that matter, all the other dynasties') resolve to avoid being perceived as supporting Iraq against Iran.[2] Unlike the other states, Kuwait feared also the possibility of the extension of the Gulf war to its soil through a flare-up between the Iranian Shi'i community and the Iraqi refugees who had arrived there.

Yet the war set the Shi'ah problem in a narrower context than before. Unlike previous occasions, when in Tehran a wave of Iranian nationalism had embraced the population, very few expressions of solidarity

---

1 The possibility of its territory serving as the haven for anti-Iraqi activities was feared by Kuwait. In July 1980 its government and that of the UAE were threatened by the Iranian-sponsored 'The Islamic Movement in Iraq' of helping Iraqi intelligence track down its opponents on their soil (see Tehran Radio (Arabic) 17.30 GMT 28 July 1980 — SWB ME/6484/A/2, 30 July 1980).

2 Iran warned Saudi Arabia not to supply Iraq with oil as the former alleged it did (Tehran Radio 20.30 GMT 30 December 1980 — SWB ME/6612/A/3, 1 January 1981).

with Iran took place among the Shi'is in other parts of the Gulf. Even in Bahrain such demonstrations did not last. This could be primarily attributed to the unimpressive way in which Iran fared in the war which revealed its new military weakness. Of course the war shattered the hopes of the Shi'is living in the Gulf, but Khomeini's appeal had appeared to decline even before the war. Calls to overthrow their government were directed at Iraqi soldiers — most of whom were themselves Shi'is — but these went unheeded.

Indeed an important feature in the first stages of the Iraqi invasion was Saddam Hussein's unwillingness to put to the test the loyalty of Shi'i soldiers fighting against their co-religionist Iranians. He also feared the reaction of Shi'is at home should the army incur heavy losses. Hence the Iraqi regime 'encouraged' Shi'i leaders to side openly with the invasion and to support the nation's attempt to 'recover the Iraqi rights and territory usurped by Iran'[1] and to send cables of solidarity to the President and to the soldiers. Members of the Shi'i ulama' were escorted to Iraq-occupied villages across the Shatt al-Arab where, however reluctantly, they were expected to give their public blessing to Iraq's army,[2] so as to grant a wider appeal to Iraqi unity as well as demonstrate to Iran that sectarian affinities prove invalid when subordinated by the far more powerful feelings of Iraqi patriotism.[3]

Iran was unimpressed. Its broadcasts continued to tell of unrest in the Iraqi Shi'i as well as Kurdish areas. Reports on the continued terror activity of the Da'wah were given prominence in the propaganda warfare which accompanied the skirmishes at the front. Each side was magnifying and fabricating news as to the clandestine activities happening on the other side of the border whereas in reality, at least in the first stages of the war, neither the Iraqi Shi'is nor the Kurds on either side were very active. If anything the war limited the scope of their activity. Their fears of being perceived as collaborating with the implacable enemy and their understanding that they would be deprived of much needed legitimacy forced them to remain aloof. In due course, however, this was to change.[4] The Kurds soon began taking advantage of the

---

1 Embassy of the Republic of Iraq Press Release dated 24 September 1980.

2 See *Qadisiyat Saddam* (published by the Iraqi Embassy in London) 30 December 1980.

3 The Iraqis were at pains to convince also their diaspora in the west of this newly crystallized spirit of Iraqi solidarity through their publication in Arabic *Qadisiyat Saddam* mentioned above.

4 In early December Pasdaran guards clashed with the disbanded KDPI 20 km. from Mahabad. Both sides declared they dealt painful blows to the other (SWB ME/6597/A/3-4, 10 December 1980). The Iraqis were quick to report such incidents much earlier.

situation to further their cause with the usual patterns of each faction being aided from across the border repeating itself. From their sanctuaries, the Kurds on both sides of the border sought to advance their interests in the face of the poor military performance demonstrated by their 'hosts'. To that end, Iraqi Kurdish groups co-operated with communist compatriots.[1] The Kurds in them felt increasingly confident and spurned Tehran's offer of pardon. By April 1981 the Iranian Kurds were in full control and had established a 'free zone' within Iran's theocracy.

With no end to the war in sight and with more arms reaching the Kurds, both states would have an intensified guerrilla war on their hands. It is difficult to see which side stands to gain from this competition which would parallel a war of attrition between the two states. Obviously any concessions one government makes will have a bearing on the Kurds on the other side. As to Iran's other minorities, the longer the war goes on, the more they are also likely to press their claims. The fact that a considerable part of Iran's forces will be tied down in the border area with Iraq and in areas close to the Kurdish region could mean that Iran's other minorities will enjoy more breathing space. A less affluent and weaker central authority might be forced to make more concessions. In that respect much may come to depend on the struggle for power within Iran following Khomeini's demise.

A similar situation could occur in Iraq. With war dragging on and more casualties incurred, more doubts will be raised in Iraq as to the wisdom of the whole exercise in the first place. Saddam's miscalculations may have provided his rivals within the party and the military with much needed political ammunition. The Israeli air raid on 7 June 1981 which destroyed Iraq's newly constructed nuclear reactor, dealt a blow to his already waning prestige. One thing is obvious: the economic cost of the stagnant war could deny the regime the support it was gathering among the poorer segment of the population, the bulk of which are Shi'is.

One of the most important lessons that minorities carry out of this war is that, when put to the test, the loyalty of sectarian and ethnic 'minorities' does not reflect itself in siding with the all-embracing transnational notions of pan-Islam (for the Iraqi Shi'ah) or pan-Arabism (for the Arabs of Khuzistan[2]), not even in adopting a particularistic line

---

1 Voice of Iraqi Kurdistan (in Surani Kurdish) 15.30 GMT 29 November 1980 announced the establishment of the Democratic Iraqi Front comprised of the Democratic Party of Kurdistan, the Unified Socialist Party of Kurdistan and the Iraqi Communist Party (SWB ME/6590/A/10 2 December 1980). For their Charter — see 6592/A/4, 4 December 1980.

2 See the Iraqi-published appeal from 'the Arab Masses Movement in Arabistan' to the 11th Arab Summit in Amman (INA 13.10 GMT 26 November 1980).

associated exclusively with their distinctive narrow affinities. Rather they feel more comfortable in clinging to the nationalism of 'their' state – not out of loyalty but simply for no other viable alternative which would prove safer and contain less uncertainties. Thus to the disappointment of Iraq and regardless of all publicity given to the contrary,[1] rather than help the Iraqi army many Khuzistanis fled eastwards where they were not trapped with split loyalties between the adversaries and where it was less dangerous. What follows is that, despite the sectarian and ethnic divisions, the idea of a state is predominant in both Iraq and Iran, even among those who have grievances. Both 'separatism' and 'trans-nationalism' do not seem to serve as a unifying force for the community nor do they serve as a viable alternative. This, however, should not be taken to imply identification with the state or the regime and certainly not as a sign of loyalty. Rather it is an expression of helplessness and fear of the unknown and, among the younger more educated generation, a yearning for an equal chance and a desire for trust and recognition.

This, however, is not the case among the Kurds who, despite their heterogeneity, do regard themselves as a distinct national group with their own culture and history which makes them entitled, in their eyes, to possess something different. Kurdish consciousness is strong among the educated, more militant, young who feel alienated by the fact that their people are excluded from the benefits of modernization. This is especially true in Iraq where some of them are inclined to believe that they would best serve their cause by carrying out their struggle along class rather than along ethnic lines and that, in order to convince their government of their serious intentions they should resort to the sabotage of oil installations. The question is how persistent will the bulk of the Kurdish population prove in supporting Kurdish nationalism. One way or another, Kurdish fragmentation would probably deny them their long-term achievements.

---

1 Throughout the war, the Iraqis were at pains to show that the Arabs of 'liberated' Khuzistan are contributing their share by 'bravely' fighting the 'Iranian forces' (see *Qadisiyat Saddam*, 25 November, 15 December 1980, 19 January 1981 and *Baghdad Observer*, 9 February 1981). In fact, a large part of this population deserted their villages in the first few days of the war. Only a few of this previously vocal segment of population aided the advancing Iraqis. The Iranians in Khuzistan reported the arrest of four groups of spies which helped the Iraqis since the outbreak of the war. Among them there were elements from the Mojahedin-e Khalq and its off-spring the Marxist-Leninist 'Peykar' (all together they were reported to have numbered just over 100). (Pars in English 08.00 GMT 6 January 1981 – SWB ME/6616/A/4, 7 January 1981.) It may be the case that the publicity given to these arrests was designed both to despair the Iraqis and deter others from co-operating with them as well as an attempt to further de-legitimize the leftist opposition in Iran and depict it as Iraqi stooges. The regime also arranged for votes of support of the Khuzistanis themselves in the Islamic Republic and Khomeini (ME/6447/A/5, 12 February 1981).

The main weakness of the Kurds on both sides of the border remains their lack of leadership. No one could easily step into the late Mustafa Barazani's shoes and even he could not unite the Kurds behind him. The Kurds' traditional divisions, whether geographical, tribal, linguistic, religious (Shi'i-Sunni) or personal, cannot be easily overcome, and certainly not by transferring allegiance from tribal leaders to nationalist groupings of leftist ideology. The generation gap only exacerbates these rivalries and will further hamper the Kurds' cause.

Thus much will depend on future Irani-Iraqi relations. An agreement between Iran and Iraq, for whatever reason, would certainly limit the Kurds' room for manoeuvre, both militarily and politically. Kurdish strength also depends largely on the weakness of each of these states' central authority. They have always been quick to take advantage of regime vulnerabilities to promote their interests and enlarge their bargaining position, aligning themselves not only with other internal leftist forces who have their own aspirations and different motivations and who look toward the disintegration of central rule, but also with outside powers and interests.

Manipulation cuts both ways. The Kurds might be willing to put themselves as 'clients' at the disposal of external forces. But they may also desire to manipulate their 'patrons' against their respective governments and drag them into conflict with their neighbours whether Iran, Iraq, Syria, Turkey, or the USSR. For the Soviet Union supporting the Kurds (or for that matter any minority) could prove counter-productive at home. But it may just be the case that, if Soviet relations with Iraq or Iran deteriorate, the USSR would covertly aid not only the communist parties there but other ethnic groups if only to remind these two states of Soviet leverage. This would not be something new.

It is quite obvious that it is not in the interest of Iraq to trigger off a process which could split Iran into several ethnic regions for such a break-up could result in the rise to power of a communist government or supply the USSR with a pretext for intervention — neither possibility would be to Iraq's liking. Of course these things may happen anyway, but the point here is the relationship between internal festering problems, external manipulation, superpower competition and the possible spill-over effects of internal developments. This was demonstrated by the Omani war in Dhofar.

Dhofar

After a 31-year guerrilla war on Omani soil, Sultan Qabus bin Sa'id managed, in 1975, with Iranian and British help, to effectively crush the Soviet-backed Dhofari rebels who were striving to take over the province adjacent to the PDRY from where they operated. Today the 60,000 Dhofaris, who are concentrated around Salalah (which has grown into a town), are more or less economically integrated into the rest of the sparsely populated Sultanate. The Sultan has consolidated his hold on the territory in question and has a far better equipped army at his disposal which could hardly be matched by the remaining rebels across the border. However the challenge remains not only in the mouthpieces of the latter: Dhofar is Oman's Achilles heel.

The transformation of many Dhofaris was caused by the process of emigration to the Gulf and to other parts of the Arab world where they not only acquired skills and education but also became increasingly exposed to new political ideas. On their return in 1960, a branch of the radical Arab Nationalist Movement (ANM) was established in Dhofar. Following a split in their ranks, the highly politicized Dhofar Charitable Association (DCA) was set up with the purpose of undermining the Omani regime.[1] In 1964 the Dhofar Liberation Front (DLF) was established to include various small groups. Some of them were soldiers who served in Oman's and the UAE's armed forces. The DLF received limited military and financial support from Egypt, Iraq and Kuwait. They also maintained contact with the exiled Omani Imam, Ghalib bin Ali, who lived in Saudi Arabia.[2] The latter also extended some help to the Dhofaris owing to the Kingdom's conflict with Oman.[3]

However it was not only the limited external support it received which crippled the DLF. The movement failed to establish itself in the Dhofari urban centres primarily owing to the efficiency of the authorities, who arrested many DLF supporters. The movement's greatest failure, which was inherent in its composition, was its internal divisions. Whereas there were those separatists who confined themselves only to the liberation of Dhofar, others regarded the sole aim of the DLF as the bringing about of a social-political revolution which would extend throughout the Gulf. This polarization between the DCA and ANM,

---

1   For further reading see Walid W. Kazziha, *Revolutionary transformation in the Arab World — Habash and his comrades from nationalism to Marxism*, London, 1975.

2   See Joseph Churba, *Conflict and tension among the states of the Persian Gulf, Oman and South Arabia*, Air University Documentary Research Study, 1971, p 58.

3   See M. Burrell and A. Cottrell, *The Indian Ocean — a Conference Report*, CSIS, Washington, 1971, p 105.

which had accompanied the movement since its inception, only further weakened its cohesion.

They were nevertheless united in their struggle against the Omani regime. Their successful 'hit and run' operations and sabotage activities made the DLF a threat to Sultan Sa'id bin Taimur's rule. The rebels gained the support of those alienated by his policies which specifically aimed at perpetuating their economic backwardness and isolation and asserting the puritan Islamic way of life of the Ibadiyah on the country in a way which rejected any economic, social and certainly education changes. In that respect his reaction only played into the Front's hands. More recruits joined the movement which was greatly aided by South Yemen's independence in 1967. Being ideologically motivated, the DLF turned, now that it occupied areas beyond the Jabal (mountains), to focus on social, agricultural and educational reforms. They tried the indoctrination of Marxist ideals aimed at unifying their ranks and doing away with old tribal framework and clannish loyalties. They also strove to reorganize their guerrilla forces. By now they were being aided by communist states (including China),[1] radical Arab states and the more militant Palestinian groups of George Habash (originally one of the founders of the ANM) and Na'if Hawatimah of the PLO.[2]

In 1971 the DLF amalgamated with another umbrella organization comprising small groups which operated in northern Oman to form the Popular Front for the Liberation of Oman and the Arab Gulf (PFLOAG).[3] By the time Sultan Qabus deposed his father in 1970 in a British-engineered bloodless coup, the PFLOAG was at the peak of its success and the war entered its fifth year.[4]

Unlike his father, the Sandhurst-educated Sultan Qabus strove to modernize the country, introducing economic reforms even into Dhofar. In so doing he hoped to weaken the appeal the rebels had to the then 35,000 strong tribal population of the Dhofari province. He soon discovered, however, that the ideological and political motivation of the movement was secession and that the confrontation between them was over his own legitimacy and political position. Thus the answer could

1 See Stephen Page, *The USSR and Arabia*, Central Asian Research Centre and the Canadian Institute of International Affairs, London, 1971. pp 84-5, 115-16.

2 Seren David 'The Dhofari rebel movement 1965-1975' in *Maarachot*, monthly Hebrew, December 1976, p 44.

3 For further reading see 9 June studies, *Documents of the National Struggle in Oman and the Arabian Gulf*, translated and published by the Gulf Committee, London 1974, p 106.

4 For details see Fred Halliday, *Arabia Without Sultans*, Harmondsworth, Penguin Books, 1971, pp 318-60.

not be merely economic. Determined to crush the rebels, the British-backed Sultan recruited the support of the UAE and Saudi Arabia who by then realized that the Dhofaris had never really abandoned their old dream of changing the political nature of the entire Gulf.[1] The fear of another Soviet-backed regime in south Arabia was sufficient to prompt them to bury their differences (as over the Buraimi Oasis). The Shah, who wanted to bolster his own regional position, sent his troops to Oman.

By now the aid the PFLOAG received from all those who had supported it in the first place had dwindled. Not only did the Dhofaris suffer from internal splits, which made them change their name to the PFLO, but they were further crippled by a wave of desertions. Militarily they could hardly prove a match for the Omani-Irani-British 'front',[2] especially once they had failed to transfer part of their struggle to northern Oman so as to alleviate some of the pressure they faced in Dhofar itself, from which they were finally ejected in 1975.

With the mentality of an islander — Oman being isolated by water and by a vast desert — the ruler of Oman is still extremely uneasy about his south-western flank. Now that he has lost his Iranian ally, who assisted him greatly in putting down the Dhofari rebels and whose strength had deterred the PDRY from pushing for an all-out confrontation, Sultan Qabus is growing increasingly worried at the constantly expanding military strength of his Yemeni neighbour as well as at the presence of many Soviet, East German and Cuban advisers stationed in the PDRY.

What might constrain the USSR is the knowledge that the Reagan Administration's threshold of tolerance to Soviet-inspired subversive activity is almost certain to be lower than that of his predecessor. This is especially true in Oman which, following the Iranian revolution, is regarded as being indispensable strategically for the US as a bridgehead for American operations in the region. That could mean that an overtly Soviet-backed assault across the border in Dhofar might touch-off a direct superpower confrontation, or at least would supply Sultan Qabus with the pretext for granting the Americans not merely facilities but bases. The US might be only too eager to restore its lost credibility and to prove that American vacillation is a thing of the past. Another unpalatable possibility for the Soviet Union would be the arrival in Oman of a large Egyptian expeditionary force (in addition to the Egyptian troops already stationed on Omani soil) to do what the Iranian army did in the 1970s.

1 PFLOAG cells were exposed in Abu Dhabi and Ras al-Khaimah. The Bahraini regime also clamped down on their supporters.

2 Jordan, which trained Omani forces, sent troops to aid Qabus.

Indeed these contingencies are much feared by the remnants of the PFLO themselves who would like to keep Oman free of foreign presence.[1] Accordingly, part of their much exaggerated[2] limited action was directed against foreigners and, in an attempt to discredit Sultan Qabus, most of their Aden-broadcasted propaganda is levelled against his ties with the US, Britain and Egypt.[3] Propaganda warfare is in fact the main avenue of the PFLO to try to offset the Sultan's political and economic projects which have made him far more popular in his state and diminished the economic grievances of those the PFLO would like to recruit. The Omani regime has used the time since the war ended to raise the standard of living of the Dhofaris and integrate them into the state. New roads have been built to ease such integration as well as to enable the army to be far more mobile in its pursuit of rebels. It is also a reminder of the presence of the central authority — which is being felt increasingly in Salalah.

Conversely, time has been wasted by the rebels. With their numerical weakness[4] and limited appeal when confronting a far superior Omani army (which is now nothing like the force they fought a decade ago) it is no wonder that there are those who out of desperation, disillusioned with both the PFLO's limitations and its divided leadership as well as with the message of Marxism which failed to provide the answer for the PDRY's dire economic problems, have seized the opportunity of an amnesty to defect to Oman[5] where they are co-opted into the system.

However this is not the end of the movement. Sultan Qabus' current popularity may serve to weaken the appeal of the PFLO, but it is certainly not a guarantee that his rule is secure. The fall of the Shah boosted the PFLO and we could well witness attempts to revitalize their actions from their haven in the PDRY. Learning from bitter experience, they may find it more useful to concentrate, at least initially, on

1 Leader of the PFLO in an interview in Libya suggesting that the closure of the Straits of Hormuz or bombing the Omani oil fields would prove counter-productive, for that would result in the US taking over the Gulf, arguing its interests were damaged and that this would hurt PFLO interests (al-Kifah al-Arabi Lebanon, 17 September 1979).

2 See for example Aden Home Service 12.30 GMT 12 April 1980 on heavy losses incurred by Oman etc., SWB ME/6395/A/7, 15 April 1980.

3 See declaration on the occasion of the PFLO Anniversary — Aden Home Service 16.30 GMT 9 June 1980 — SWB ME/6442/A/1, 11 June 1980 and ibid. ME/6569/A/1, 7 November 1980. See also al-Jumhuriyah daily, Cairo, 7 June 1981.

4 A PFLO spokesman admitted that their numbers are far less than the level of 1975. Interview with Salim Gharib in charge of propaganda of the PFLO in Bratislava Pravda in Slovak, 1 July 1980, p 6 in DR 9 July 1980.

5 See interview with Salim Ahmad al-Ghassini, former member of the PFLO who surrendered to the Omani Government, Salalah Home Service 13.00 GMT 31 July 1980 — SWB/ME/6487/A/1, 2 August 1980.

underground urban operations rather than on rural guerrilla action culminating in direct military confrontation. Their small, though capable, Soviet-trained force could prove quite dangerous. With oil recently discovered in Dhofar, their leaway may grow considerably. Side by side with reported desertion of rebels, there are sporadic attempts to revitalize the movement's activity.

Conclusions

The history of hatred and bloodshed in the region may repeat itself, with minority or sectarian unease resulting in an intensification of political unrest. Given that such ferment could be aided by domestic leftist groups and be encouraged or mitigated by external forces — whose help is always required owing to the military weakness of the indigenous elements — the potential dangers posed by the secessionist movements are real. The chain reaction such struggles could trigger off might, in the long run, culminate in the disintegration of existing states, spill over to neighbouring territories and further complicate superpower relations.

4 The strains of modernization

With the discovery of oil in the Gulf came dramatic change, though again the Peninsula's interior retained its close inward-looking character and it was some time before oil revenues were to leave their mark on the small and scattered population there. Those who first benefited from oil — Kuwait and Bahrain — were the first ones to experience abrupt change, being unwittingly propelled into a new era. Their compact nature and their close contact with the external world meant that — unlike Iraq, Iran, Saudi Arabia and Oman — their pace of social, demographic and cultural transformation was alarming. It took some time before the rest of the region was affected by the soaring oil revenues when the first attempts to integrate the countryside into the state's economy came about. This did not take place until the great oil boom of the mid-1970s and especially the period inaugurated by the 1973-74 quadrupling of oil prices.

Oil revenues have determined the frantic pace of economic development. Wild spending, huge imports and sheer waste have all marked the new phase of attempting to create the much needed infrastructure. A large share of the Arab oil-producing states' returns was spent on creating and expanding a local administration and in developing modern education and health systems. The foundations of a welfare state have, in most cases, been built, with new services being provided for the indigenous population as well as for the numerous expatriates — without whom the process of modernization could not have taken place. A large proportion of the expenditure included housing, water supplies, electricity and new roads, which connected the urban centres with isolated regions.

Initially, rather than devoting attention to traditional economic activities and developing the agriculture and the fishing industry so as to improve the conditions for that part of the population who form the backbone of their countries and whose cohesion the regimes need to maintain whatever the financial costs, the Gulf governments opted for rapid industrialization regardless of the obvious social and economic implications. In the Peninsula this trend was encouraged by the Western educated princes who, upon their return from their studies abroad, tried to superimpose the western capitalist system on a primitive economy, confident that, with wealth at their disposal, they could attain in a short while at least what the inflation-stricken, less affluent western economies had managed to achieve. Given this eagerness, it is precisely the rapid *pace* and deformed *quality* of development which may make modernization contribute to internal instability.

Urbanization

The oil industry has made the Gulf one of the most urbanized areas in the developing world. Again Iran and Iraq are different from the rest of the Gulf owing to the sheer size of their population. Moreover urbanization in the city states has a totally different meaning from that in the vast and scarcely populated states of Saudi Arabia and Oman. The growth of urban population of the littoral states is caused almost solely by the influx of foreigners. The concentration of the bulk of heavy and light industry and other sources of livelihood in and around the urban centres has meant that demographic structures are constantly changing, turning the indigenous urban population into a minority through the numerous expatriates of different origin being joined by a young, local, rural element.

In contrast to Iraq and Iran, the original policy in the predominantly rural areas of Oman and Saudi Arabia was to encourage deliberately the migration of the countryside's population (amongst whom the regimes enjoy immense support) into the cities — the seat of the central government — so as to try and balance the increasing numbers and weight of immigrants there and, in the Eastern Province, to dilute the political weight of the Shi'i population. The alternative contains many political dangers. Owing to his pro-Egyptian and pro-Western orientations, which have isolated Oman to a certain extent, Sultan Qabus is not supported by the middle class which populates Muscat, Mattra and Salalah, composed primarily of non-Omanis, mainly Zanzibaris (some of whom hold Omani citizenship), Lebanese, Cypriots and Syrians, all of whose numbers have increased in the last decade. But the migration on a daily basis of rural Omanis from neighbouring areas (who are working in the towns or are marketing their products there) could hardly change the demographic composition of these towns which have in any case absorbed Omanis who migrated from the interior as well as Omanis who returned from other parts of the Gulf where they had gone in search of employment.

In Saudi Arabia on the other hand, being a very large country with poor communications, the trek towards the ever-expanding cities — which harbour most of the population — is still on a modest scale. Moreover, unlike Iran, where urbanization gathered momentum in the 1970s with many peasants streaming into the cities in the hope of being incorporated into the labour market, the widely dispersed and isolated Saudi rural and semi-nomadic populations received large sums of money through various governmental and other patriarchal channels *without* being integrated into the economic development taking place elsewhere in their country. Therefore the economic incentive for these farmers and Bedouins to substitute their old way of life for a 'modern' way of life, is lower than elsewhere in the Middle East. In other words, though the industrial development centred around the existing seven urban centres has meant that the Saudi periphery was excluded from the main orbit of the economic boom, many of these inhabitants nevertheless (unlike the rural Omanis) have enjoyed the fruits of an industrial revolution of which they are not part.

This, however, does not mean that the Saudi rural sector was not affected by the process of modernization. The small scale of urbanization as well as the participation of some Saudis (on a seasonal basis) in industrial projects, the spread of such schemes to some of the more distant but mineral-rich areas, as well as the new highways joining these sites with the cities, have all meant that the Saudi countryside is being increasingly exposed to the consequences of industrialization. Although the growth of the sprawling Saudi cities should be largely attributed to immigrants, the employment opportunities in the Eastern Province and other centres have attracted many Bedouins to the cities, further decreasing the already falling numbers of nomads.

Urbanization resulted in the establishment of shanty towns on the outskirts of the cities where land is available and the Bedouin could retain their life-style and not mix with the urban population. In response to such a common phenomenon, the governments of Saudi Arabia, Kuwait, Qatar and Bahrain embarked on construction programmes in an attempt to settle the Bedouins by providing them with housing despite the fact that the latter prefer living in a shanty area. As far as the Saudis are concerned, such a process has advantages for it helps to dilute the territorial and tribal divisions which have hitherto characterized the Kingdom. Thus the government encouraged, for example, the move of the Qahtan tribe of the south to other areas where economic development is taking place. The movement of tribes from central Arabia to the Gulf's coast in search of work began in fact in the pre-oil days. Thus descendants of different tribes are found among the leading business families in the Eastern Province where settlements of Bedouins arose through employment with ARAMCO as early as the 1930s. Soon the Damman-Dharan-al-Khubar and Qatif complex became a magnet to many Bedouins. Riyadh also attracted many rural inhabitants and Jiddah has increased from 60,000 twenty years ago to over 1,000,000 today.

The Saudi intention of incorporating the local backward rural economy with the foreign-manned, urban, modern industrial sector was envisaged through the newly-established complexes of Yanbu and Jubail. Bringing industrial development into the countryside will, it is hoped, attract many young villagers and Bedouins without causing a harmful effect on their traditional social fabric. Moreover, the government is confident that the new adjacent cities built with all ultra-modern amenities, schooling and hospitalization will encourage young members of the nomadic sectors to come and live there, despite the fact that such a way of life is totally alien to them.

Nevertheless the traumatic effect of this change and its tempo has left its mark on some of these bewildered, unskilled workers. The high cost of living, limited space and the overcrowded, noisy way of life could not be conducive to mass departures into the city, but nevertheless it has its temptations with its secularized way of life which is free of the restrictive milieu of the conservative family.

In Saudi Arabia, the desertion of the rural and tribal structures by some of their younger members, albeit on a small scale, has harmed the economy of the families remaining behind, which have become increasingly dependent on the women and the children, further crippling the already weakened economic viability of the countryside's traditional social order. The *cabilah* (the federation of Bedouin tribes), once a unit of immense prestige, has lost much of its unifying force. Similarly, the *hamulah* (clan) is weakened considerably by the government-encouraged departure of its young members. Even the unit of the family, once built on firm foundations, is becoming fragmented, especially in places remote from areas of economic development.

Urbanization has also other political implications because this growing drift to the towns could eventually result in the emergence of new, inter-related sets of conflict — within the local population and between the population and the governments concerned — all of which could prove costly to the Gulf's regimes.

By virtue of bringing together different sections of the population, urbanization could lead to further confrontation between religious sects and ethnic minorities on the one hand and the governments on the other. These sections of the population tend to stick together, preserve and even reinforce their social and religious affinities, especially if they are confronted by alienation. A prime example is that of the Shi'ah migration from the rural areas to the capitals of Bahrain and Iraq, although in the latter it is on a very much larger scale. But in both states the Shi'ah population is generally economically backward and feels to some degree alienated.

Over half of Iraq's 13,000,000 population is concentrated in the cities. Baghdad, which has 35 percent of the country's industry, contains over 3,000,000 people. The rapid growth of Mosul and Basra has meant that the capital's rate of expansion slightly declined. Nevertheless the Iraqi government is alarmed by the rapid growth of the cities' population and the corresponding rural depopulation for this trend not only jeopardizes the development of Iraqi agriculture but also brings into the urban centres many frustrated inhabitants — Kurds into the northern cities and Shi'is into the southern cities and the capital, most of the latter coming from the Amara province where land tenure conditions are intolerable. Not even the ill-executed land reforms which followed the 1958 revolution could stop this trend.[1] If anything it was the disparity in wealth distribution which induced the flight from the backward, impoverished countryside to the cities where most economic development was taking place. Becoming daily wage earners in building or service industries appealed to these migrants more than the miserable life of a tenant farmer. But in the cities, construction could not keep pace with the residential explosion. With the shortage of housing and the absence of adequate sanitation, the squatter settlements constructed by the migrants created enormous social and political problems for the authorities. Government attempts to reverse the movement to the town failed. It was its fear of a coup by the Communists in 1963 which probably prompted the Ba'athist government to tear down tens of thousands of the squatter dwellings in Baghdad, many of which were populated by Communist Shi'is.[2] New overcrowded quarters were built for their inhabitants on the east and later on the west banks of the Tigris but Iraq's shortage of skilled manpower and her determination to rely upon her own labour meant that the problem was not solved.[3]

1 Compare Rony Gabbay, *Communism and Agrarian Reform in Iraq*, Croom Helm, London, 1978, p 179 and Edith and E.F. Penrose, *Iraq, International Relations and National Development*, Ernest Benn, London, 1978.

2 Fuad Bali 'Social factors in Iraqi rural-urban migration' in *American Journal of Economics and Sociology*, 1966, p 362.

3 Michael E. Bonine 'The Urbanization of the Persian Gulf nation' in A. Cottrell (ed.) *The Persian Gulf States, op.cit.* p 244.

The decline of agriculture

Urbanization and the continued concentration on industrialization in Iraq caused the further stagnation of agriculture with governments failing to carry out the much needed and often promised agrarian reforms. The method of collectivization the Iraqi government introduced did not succeed in solving the problem of this sector which still employs over half the labour force and is still engaged in primitive cultivation which utilizes only a half of the available arable land. About 45 percent of Iraq's population live in villages without electricity. The slow rate of progress on land reclamation and irrigation accelerated the process of urbanization. This in turn forced the government to attend more seriously to developing agriculture with oil revenues.

The extent of real damage caused by the war with Iran is still far from clear. However, the longer the war goes on, the more serious its economic implications will become and the government will find it increasingly difficult to shield its citizens from the harsh realities. Whatever the outcome of the conflict, Iraq will have to continue to focus on her eastern front and attention will continue to be paid to the military. Consequently many of the planned economic and social projects aimed at developing the countryside will have to be shelved, at least for the time being. In turn, this will mean a continuous urbanization of angry peasants of primarily Shi'i origin.

The decline of agriculture was not unique to predominantly agricultural Iraq. Throughout the Gulf, the oil industry has dramatically reduced the already meagre contribution of agriculture and fisheries to the gross domestic product (GDP). With such a list of immediate priorities the urgent need to modernize agriculture was pushed aside. But although some of the richer states do not have to rely on agriculture — being endowed not only with large oil reserves but also with other non-oil resources — the stagnation experienced by Omani agriculture could destroy its only real non-oil source of potential income. This is why Qatar is devoting more attention to its meagre agricultural sector.

To a lesser extent that has been the case in Saudi Arabia. Saudi statistics suggest a decline in the workforce engaged in farming from 40 percent in 1970 to 28 percent in 1975. With agriculture preserved in its relatively unproductive form, its share of the Kingdom's non-oil GDP has dropped from 12.1 percent in 1970 to 2.4 percent in 1978. The total cultivated area[1] has also declined (a third of 2m hectares the

---

1 *al-Jazirah* newspaper, 30 December 1979.

government believes are arable).[1] Indeed, in some of the states the growth of the cities was at the expense of agricultural land. In Bahrain, palm cultivation declined with the expansion of the capital Manama and previously cultivated land became extremely valuable real estate, particularly the area between Manama and Budayya where new government-sponsored housing projects were instituted.

Iran is of course a totally different example owing to the magnitude of the problem. With her 35,000,000 inhabitants, Iran's population is larger than that of the rest of the Gulf combined. Half of the country's population lives in the four largest cities. The concentration of industrial development in and around Tehran has meant that one in seven Iranians lives in the overcrowded capital, which simply cannot cater for such a massive population. The government's attempts to induce industrial development in nine other centres away from the capital did not bring the hoped for results, despite the fact that the development of the oil industry increasingly attracted many Iranians to the south-west of the country.

With the Shah's concentration on the over-expansion of the industrial sector, agriculture lost much of its attraction. Thus urbanization in Iran resulted in a country once self-sufficient in agriculture having to import food. The low prices their products fetched could only push more peasants towards the city. There they confronted another aspect of maldistribution of income. In Tehran the waves of poor local landless migrants pouring into the city found an affluent Irani community which had acquired much of its status under the Shah's regime. Daunting inflation and high rents prevented the migrants from any chance of bettering their lot. Popular disaffection with the Shah's economic policies and priorities ran deep in the cities and culminated in the alliance of the bazaar and the Mosque which caused the downfall of the Shah.

The rise of Khomeini raised expectations to an unrealistic level. Being confident of finding employment — the very reason for their migration in the first place — these frustrated migrants were not able to digest the fact that there would be no panacea for their economic predicament. In response the new regime tried to reverse the trend back to the countryside. Indeed 1979-80 witnessed an agricultural boom but even the upsurge in agricultural output could not alter Iran's dependence on food imports. Nevertheless, the governmental emphasis on agriculture and the high urban unemployment encouraged some Iranians to return to their villages and others to remain in the countryside.

1 For further details see Tim Sisley 'Workforce depleted by move to towns' in *Financial Times* Supplement on Saudi Arabia, 24 April 1980.

However Iran's economic problems remain insurmountable and the new government did not succeed where the Shah has failed. The problem of unemployment in the countryside was compounded by the desertion of many land owners who left their farms unmanaged. Industry and construction suffered even more owing to the yawning gap created by the departure of some 80,000 foreign technicians and moreover there is an acute shortage of working capital caused by reduced oil production and the mass exodus of more than 100,000 rich and middle-class Iranians who smuggled out with them a large part of their liquid assets. The remaining private investors are discouraged by the economic chaos and by the persistent calls of the fundamentalists of the Islamic Republic Party, the Mojahedin and the leftist Fedayeen all of whom demand the limiting of private ownership, industrial nationalization and land reforms.

The war with Iraq introduced a new dimension. Oil production came virtually to a standstill. The government was forced to devote attention to the military sector and consequently priorities changed. The problem is further complicated by the numerous refugees, many of whom refuse to be confined to the newly established refugee camps and instead flock into the cities, adding to the reservoir of unemployed Iranians, whose numbers were reported to have reached 4 million by the summer of 1981.This situation can only get worse and patience will run out. It is difficult to see these peasants going along with policies whose implications might slide the country back to mediaeval conditions.

There are already signs of dissatisfaction with the government's economic policies. The new regime has not addressed itself to the daily needs of a large part of the population.[1] Unemployment is rising. The frustration is greater because, while the Shah attended to their problems, however symbolically and inadequately, the new regime which they believed would change everything for them, has done nothing to reduce their miseries. Many who marched in protest against the US are expressing their deep sense of frustration and disillusion with present day policies as well as a yearning for an immediate and drastic change. Government declarations and religious fervour can hardly substitute for facing up to the mounting economic problems. The system itself could become the focus of complaint.

---

1   Over two-thirds of Iran's sixty thousand villages are reported to have no piped water. Tehran still has no adequate sewerage system.

Conclusion

In conclusion, the process of urbanization contains serious economic, social and political implications which are related. Though in countries like Saudi Arabia, Oman and Qatar migration to the cities helps to balance the sizable immigrant community already present in the cities, it affects the delicate social fabric of these traditional societies which form the power base of the regimes. Urbanization in Iraq and Bahrain means the presence of many alienated Shi'is in the capitals. In Iran, which is the only country in the region to have a proletariat, urbanization was bound to be politically explosive. The masses which brought down one regime could prove crucial in any ensuing future struggle for power.

Urbanization contains the seeds of political upheaval. Urban slums are natural breeding grounds for agitation. The pace of the influx of the rural population into the cities puts enormous pressures on housing and infrastructure. Yet it would seem that the Gulf governments, the Iranians included, are either unimpressed by this danger or else they are helpless to confront it.

5 Regional demographic patterns

Unlike Iran and Iraq, the rapid economic growth of the underpopulated Arabian Peninsula could not have materialized without foreigners, attracted to the region by the opportunities of earning high wages. Whether the expatriates outnumber the indigenous population, as in the case of the UAE, Qatar or Kuwait, or whether they form a smaller group as in the other states, this constantly expanding foreign workforce has proved indispensable for any state embarking on economic development. These expatriates are found in all sectors of the economy and at all levels of skill, at times dominating both owing to their ability or to the lack of inclination on the part of the locals to engage in hard labour. Indeed the foreigners are relied upon to do the work in place of nationals as did the slaves of the past. This symbiotic arrangement which enables the Gulf to industrialize and develop as well as providing the foreign workers with the opportunity to better their lot and support their families who remain behind means that they both need and depend on one another.

Accurate information as to the size of the expatriate community in each state is difficult to find, being a politically sensitive issue and a source of embarrassment to some of the Gulf regimes. Government statistics aim to diminish the size of the immigrant population and to inflate their own. Nevertheless, the data provided by some demographers[1] has shed sufficient light, enabling us to appreciate the magnitude of this phenomenon so as to study some of its wider economic and political implications.

Prior to examining the constantly changing demographic composition in the Gulf, the economic and political motivations of the manpower-exporting states — mainly Jordan, Egypt and the Yemens — should be looked at so as to evaluate long-term considerations which would have a direct bearing on future inter-Arab relations.

---

1 A most valuable source on the Peninsula are the studies written by J.S. Birks and C.A. Sinclair for the International Labour Office in Geneva entitled *The International Migration Project*. Also A.G. Hill, 'Population Migration and Development in the Gulf States,' in *Domestic Political Factors* (ed) Shahram Chubin, Gower, 1981. For details on the patterns emerging in the early 1970s — see Gerard Fischer and Abdul-Muhsin Muzaffar, *Some Basic Characteristics of the Labour Force in Bahrain, Qatar, the UAE and Oman* (monograph), February 1975).

Jordan and the Palestinians

Jordan, which, following the 1948 war, annexed most of Palestine and was consequently forced to harbour most of the Palestinians, was the only Arab state which in 1950 — against the opposition of all other Arab governments — granted citizenship to its refugee and non-refugee Palestinian subjects. The United Nations Relief and Work Agency for the Palestine Refugees (UNRWA) which was established with the purpose of caring for the needy amongst the refugee population, soon found its task an impossible one, especially in view of Jordan's economic handicaps. The failure of UNRWA's work projects, the gloomy prospects for employment in Jordan, and the meagre salaries paid, only encouraged Palestinians to take advantage of their newly acquired citizenship. To the envy of the Gaza Strip inhabitants — the second largest Palestinian concentration who were under Egyptian control and were prohibited from emigrating elsewhere — the Jordanian passport proved an indispensable asset[1] to the needy Palestinians living in the West Bank and East Bank of the Hashemite Kingdom of Jordan.

With the refugees realizing that there was no chance for an immediate settlement of their plight, many young Palestinians were inclined to travel abroad. UNRWA, taking advantage of this trend, hastened to expand its education system and established specially designed Vocational Training Centres which in fact catered for the growing needs of Kuwait, Saudi Arabia (and to a lesser extent Iraq) through 'exporting' their newly graduated Palestinian professionals who could not be absorbed into the limited Jordanian market. This was an arrangement satisfactory to all the parties concerned: the oil producing states could easily 'import' the workforce that their expanding economies needed; the refugees were pleased that their sons could be gainfully employed and sent back sums of money to their families remaining behind in Jordan with which they could purchase land, build houses, open shops and raise their standard of living; and the Jordanian government was happy, not only with this substantial input into the country's economy but that it managed to rid itself of many potential trouble-makers.

Yet emigration was not characteristic solely of the refugee community. Many non-refugee nomadic, rural and urban Palestinians travelled to the Gulf as did a constantly growing number of Trans-Jordanians. Thus the majority of the Palestinian immigrants present in Kuwait and

1 The Syrian and Lebanese *laissez-passer* and for that matter the mid-1950 Arab League Travel Document, institutionalized especially for the Palestinians, were not respected by the Gulf governments who feared that none of these states would readmit the Palestinians once they terminated their contract and decided to return.

Saudi Arabia are holders of Jordanian citizenship.[1] Iraq also absorbed a small share of skilled Palestinians in addition to those who fled there as a result of the 1948 war.

Owing to the fact that the other Gulf states embarked on this rapid economic development slightly later, and because of the Palestinians' inclination to join their relatives and friends, the lower Gulf states, which already had Iranian, Asian and even African workers, acquired a relatively small, though important number of Palestinians in their workforces.

However, the second big wave of Palestinians poured into the region after the 1967 war — again mainly to Kuwait, but this time also to Qatar, UAE and Bahrain. Now not only skilled refugees entered the Arab Gulf but also poor labourers from the occupied West Bank and, for the first time since 1948, from the Gaza Strip. The right to travel abroad, which was denied to the Strip's population under Egyptian control, was granted by the Israeli authorities with Jordan providing special 'passports' (without which no Arab state would admit Palestinians) so as to acquire political influence among the Gaza Strip's population for whom Jordan became the gateway to the rest of the Arab world. This movement slowed down for a while owing to the economic boom in the areas under Israel's occupation, but, with the rise of inflation in Israel, even prior to the 1973 war, and with the lucrative opportunities in the Gulf, especially for the white collar workers for whom there was no work in Israel, the more skilled Palestinians left for the Arabian Peninsula.

Egypt

It is difficult to assess the size of the Egyptian population in the Gulf. Some suggest that there are over one million Egyptian workers there (most of whom are found in Iraq). Even if this number is highly exaggerated,[2] their role is of great importance. If in the 1960s a large proportion of Egyptian emigrants to the Gulf were unskilled, professional people are found in larger numbers in the 1970s group. Many of them assumed an indispensable brokerage role in terms of technology

---

1 The failure of most demographers to distinguish between Jordanians proper (i.e. Trans-Jordanians) and Palestinians holding Jordanian citizenship accounts for the existence of an amorphous category of 'Jordanians' or 'Jordanians and Palestinians' — the latter being in many cases the relatively few Palestinian refugees who come from Syria or Lebanon, or later, the Gaza Strip.

2 See J.S. Birks and C.A. Sinclair 'Egypt: a frustrated labor exporter' in *The Middle East Journal*, Summer 1979, p 303.

transferred from the West to the Arab world.[1] In Kuwait the Egyptians numbered in 1965 some 10,000; by 1970 they had tripled in number, comprising 4.1 percent of the population. At present their number is put at 150,000. A need for their skills became more acute with the dwindling numbers of Iraqis and Iranians working there. Their numbers are increasing in Abu Dhabi, North Yemen and Qatar (with whom Egypt signed an agreement in 1974 for sending Egyptian workers). In Saudi Arabia there are as many as 250,000 Egyptians.

Egypt's considerations here are somewhat similar to those of Jordan but economically the situation in Egypt is far more serious. With its population of 40 million increasing annually by another million and with larger numbers of unemployed villagers and jobless university and high-school graduates saturating Cairo, the need to provide an economic outlet is much greater. Sadat's liberal economic policies enabled many Egyptians to return with luxury goods impossible to come by at home with the low salaries and relatively high taxes. Egypt now encourages even skilled workers to emigrate to the Gulf. Shortening the compulsory military service accelerated this movement. The rapidly rising standard of living of those who sent their remittances back home or returned after a short while prompted others to join this group. While remittances provide Egypt with much needed hard currency, they also harm its economy (as in Jordan, Sudan and North Yemen) by contributing to inflation.

There were also domestic and inter-Arab political considerations which coincided with the government's economic policies. As with Jordan, the emigration of some of the constantly swelling ranks of the intelligentsia enabled the Egyptian regime to get rid of part of a discontented, politicized element as well as large numbers of disillusioned and ill-educated poor who could be mobilized for political purposes.

The Yemens

If the Palestinians and even the Egyptians are difficult to replace because of the key role they play and because of the inter-Arab implications of such a policy, the Yemenis, who heavily populate Saudi Arabia (between 1 and 2 million) and primarily take unskilled jobs, although very numerous, are quite dispensable and the Saudis are encouraging their departure. Already many North (and even South) Yemenis are returning with their earnings from Saudi Arabia to North Yemen which is itself experiencing a period of rapid economic growth. The Saudis, who are

---

1 For further reading see Nazli Chourci 'The new migration to the Middle East' in *International Migration Review*, Volume II, Winter 1977, pp 421-43.

aiding North Yemen's economy in other ways, are encouraging this trend. To the disappointment of some Yemenis, their jobs are quickly manned by waves of Asian workers now saturating the Gulf as a whole.

Asia and the Far East

If the phenomenon of Orientals arriving in the region is a recent one, the presence of Pakistanis and Indians in the lower Gulf is not. Prior to the discovery of oil, Oman, Qatar and Bahrain had trade connections with East Africa and Asia respectively. In fact the lower Gulf was in a sense isolated geographically from the rest of the Arab Middle East hence, once oil began to be exported, it was quite natural for these states to rely on immigrants from those places. In Qatar in 1970, the Asians, primarily Pakistanis, roughly equalled the Iranian contingent and together they amounted to 60 percent of the immigrants. In Oman by 1978, Indians accounted for more than half and Pakistanis for 36 percent of the non-Omani population. The Asian contingent in Bahrain nearly trebled in the 1970s to become two-thirds of the labour force, and in the UAE the proportion was roughly the same. This trend manifested itself elsewhere in the Gulf, albeit on a smaller scale, with the Asians taking not only the unskilled places but, in places like Qatar, controlling the entire private sector. Projected figures of the mid-1980s suggest that, with this trend continuing, the Arab component of the migrant workforce would decline in the Peninsula from 75 percent in 1975 to 40 percent.[1]

With the entry into the Gulf's market of South Korean, Japanese and other Far Eastern industrial concerns, a new type of arrangement was reached whereby these firms bring with them the necessary number of skilled and unskilled workers. They come without families, live in special work camps and leave with their earnings once the project is completed. These Far Easterners are found in growing numbers in the region's industrial sites. In 1978 the South Koreans totalled 52,000. Two years later their number had nearly trebled. Recently there is even talk of China supplying workers under special contract to Kuwait.[2]

1 See Birks and Sinclair's article in the *Financial Times* Supplement on the UAE, 22 January 1980, p viii.

2 See *Middle East Economic Digest*, 10 October 1980, p 43.

The ratio of expatriates to locals

The fact that the indigenous population dominates only the traditional and backward economic sectors (agriculture and fishing) while the modern sector almost totally depends on foreigners, has long-term economic implications. The patterns in the UAE, Qatar, Kuwait and to a certain extent Saudi Arabia are roughly similar. In the latter, about half of the employed nationals participate in and dominate the 'old' economy which accounts only for about 1 percent of the national income. Birks and Sinclair argue that from a total Saudi population of six million or so, some 1,026,400 accounted in 1975 for about 57 percent of the total workforce and that the immigrant population amounted to a quarter of the states' population.[1] But the 1980 numbers suggest that the expatriates formed, by then, some 75 percent of the 2 million strong workforce.[2] In Kuwait today (1981) the expatriate community amounts to about 60 percent of the total 1.3 million population. A higher proportion still exists in Qatar: of 230,000 inhabitants, 170,000 are immigrants and they are an even larger proportion of the total workforce. The UAE's population in 1968 was said to be 180,000 of which the nationals comprised 90 percent. Ten years later, with a population of 840,000, they made up only a quarter. Today their relative share has shrunk further in a total population of nearly one million. But these figures are somewhat misleading if they are not qualified by stating first, that 96 percent of all workers are immigrants[3] and, second, that about 90 percent of all employment is concentrated in the three main partners of the seven-member federation; Abu Dhabi, Dubai and Sharjah. Third, as in Qatar, not all UAE nationals are indigenous. However, the data published by the government inflates the size of local population to over 30 percent.[4]

Oman is an example where the dependence on expatriates extends across the whole spectrum[5] and, unlike the UAE, to the higher echelons of government. If anything, this dependence will increase.

---

1 See Birks and Sinclair *Saudi Arabia, op.cit.*, p 33.

2 See *al Shakq al-Awsat* (Saudi Arabia), London, 14 May 1981.

3 Quoted from a study carried out by Abu Dhabi University — BBC, 24 June 1980.

4 See *Middle East Economic Digest*, 8 January 1981, p 38.

5 By 1975 two-thirds of the trade was in immigrant hands, who found it quite easy to compete with the locals, whilst in 1973 they stood roughly equal — see the Omani National Statistical Office, *Survey of employment in the private sector 1976* (table 24) in Birks and Sinclair, International Migration Project: *The Sultanate of Oman* (1977), pp 45-9.

On the other hand, Bahrain's population growth was far slower than in Kuwait and Qatar owing to migration to the Peninsula[1] and, in contrast to those two states, the size of the expatriate community did not grow rapidly in relative terms even though it did grow substantially in absolute terms. Whereas in 1941 Bahrain's population was assessed at 90,000 of whom 16 percent were immigrants (owing to its traditional trading position), in 1976 non-Bahrainis numbered some 70,000 out of the total population of 300,000 (23 percent). A recent census published by the government suggests that 32 percent of Bahrain's 358,857 population are foreigners.[2] The composition of the expatriate community changed, with the Asian community becoming the dominant factor. Once Bahrain's oil production dwindled and it became less attractive owing to its economic limitations, fewer Arabs have come and more Arabs have left. Between 1971 and 1977 the Arab share of employment dropped from 54 percent to 16 percent, whereas the Asian share rose from 27 percent to 65 percent. The numbers of Asians have increased since then.[3]

There is no clear demographic pattern and every state has a blend of nationalities. Some of the states in the region, like Oman, are exporters as well as importers of manpower. Though thousands of Omanis are reported to have returned home from elsewhere in the lower Gulf with the liberalization marking Sultan Qabus's accession, numerous Omani labourers are known to have left their state in the hope of earning higher salaries elsewhere. This propensity only drains the local manpower further, forcing Oman to rely on expatriates even in the unskilled sector. In the other states the outflow of their own citizens is hardly noticeable when compared with their immigrant populations.

Only Iran and Iraq are in a sense self-sufficient in terms of labour and importation of manpower is on a limited scale, although Iran had many American specialists who were crucial for her economic and military development and Iraq began absorbing immigrants in the mid-1970s. Prior to the war with Iran, Iraq had 20,000 Indians, 2,500 Chinese and many Moroccans in addition to Egyptians, Palestinians and Western and Eastern European and Soviet advisers. However, both states, and particularly Iran, have exported labour. In Qatar there are 40,000 Iranians. They are also present in Bahrain and Dubai. Iraqis can be traced in small numbers throughout the Gulf and there are a few Kuwaitis and Saudis in the UAE and Qatar.

1 Tribes such as the Jau, Askar and Dur left the island. Others lost many of their members. See Fuad I. Khury 'Oil and socioeconomic transformation in Bahrain' in *Man and Society in the Arab Gulf* (Papers of the third symposium of the Centre for Arab Gulf Studies) (Basra, Baghdad, 1979), Vol. III, p 569.

2 *al-Qabas* daily, Kuwait, 14 June 1981.

3 See Birks and Sinclair, *Bahrain*, pp 2, 34-5, 41.

The immigrant labour pyramid

The Gulf's dependency on immigrants is not evenly spread, even though the pattern at the top of the expatriate pyramid is fairly similar. Many western consultants are found in the private sector and they advise the rulers of these semi-feudal societies, at times serving as government employees. This is particularly true of Oman where there are many British advisers at all levels. In Qatar there are about 15,000 western expatriates. In Saudi Arabia their share in the total workforce is lower (30,000 Americans and 25,000 Britons) but they are also indispensable.

The second group of expatriates which hold highly ranked positions within the government and form the backbone of expanding ministries are of Arab origin. Many sensitive key positions are filled by Palestinians, Egyptians and Jordanians. This is true mainly in Qatar, UAE and Kuwait. Oman is an exception with a large part of its civil service being manned by Zanzibaris. Sudanese are prominent in the UAE's municipal services. Baluchis are found in large numbers in the non-commissioned levels of Oman's army and many Omanis serve in the UAE's military forces. Bahrain and Qatar's police have many North Yemenis. The Palestinians are found in the media and practically control the education system in the Gulf. Many Egyptians too are teachers, being traditionally very poor in their performance in trade — a sector which contains many Palestinians, Syrians, Lebanese and Adenis and, in the lower Gulf, many Pakistanis and Indians.

The other categories of expatriates down the ladder of semi-skilled and unskilled labourers in the public and private sectors are less definable in terms of nationality but, as noted earlier, the numbers of Asian and Far Eastern workers are increasing.

Immigrants and politics

The process which aims to preserve the locals' complete control of their governments by replacing expatriates with skilled nationals is far from being successful. The economic temptations outside government and the shortage of skilled and experienced local administrators (attributed mainly to the relatively late establishment of the education system) cripples the rulers, attempts to ease out foreigners manning sensitive governmental positions.[1] Moreover, the Gulf regimes have failed in their attempts to limit the number of immigrants so as to try to reverse, or at least preserve, the ratio of locals to foreigners. Granting citizenship, or more commonly naturalization, to a fraction of their early immigrants, as in the case of the UAE, Bahrain, Qatar and even Kuwait, could hardly affect the demographic balance which, with the ever-expanding economic schemes demanding an even larger workforce, is only further changing the balance in the immigrants' favour.

The fact that some governmental jobs carry prohibitions (non-Saudis for example cannot serve as policemen or even taxi drivers) only further sharpens the existing differences and mistrust between the Arab expatriates and the locals. Wage discrimination, which gives the locals a higher salary than any immigrant filling a similar post as well as the right to replace any foreigner manning a senior administrative position, has already left its mark on many expatriates who feel bitter and insecure.

Bitterness is developing too amongst the Asian and Far Eastern labourers many of whom are living in appalling conditions in an attempt to avoid high rents and evade the police searching for illegal immigrants. But it is not so much the conditions under which they live which aggravate them. Rather is it the accumulated feeling of being regarded as modern slaves. Non-Arab expatriates have, in consequence, played a prominent role in the few demonstrations which have taken place in Bahrain, Saudi Arabia,[2] Dubai and Oman.

Another group in this category are the Iranian immigrants to whom, following the Islamic revolution, the authorities are devoting far more attention. Many of them are poor, attracted by economic incentives and have left their families in Iran. They are a reservoir of dissent and in Bahrain and Kuwait they have proved fairly active in response to Shi'i sentiments.

So, beneath the industrious atmosphere, lies a great deal of simmering strain. Tension could arise from political as well as economic grievances.

1 On Saudi intentions see *al-Jazirah* daily, Saudi Arabia, 16 February 1980.

2 In 1978 the Saudi security forces clashed with immigrants and killed a number of demonstrators.

In the UAE restrictions on the immigrants are perceived to border on 'subtle social apartheid'.[1] Arrogance and harshness are bound to breed hostility. Signs to that effect were seen in a recent strike by oil workers in Kuwait in late April 1981.

In some places a political tinge is attached to what many immigrants regard as social discrimination. While the Palestinians and Egyptians are reminded of their inferior status as aliens who should be grateful for being supplied with work, they, in turn, secretly accuse their 'hosts' of making their fortunes at the expense and on the back of those who carried the burden of the war with Israel. They also argue that the Gulf's modernization should be attributed to their own hard labour rather than to the local dynasties − from whom they might demand a larger share of the cake. This argument would probably be supported by the governments of some of the manpower-exporting states which are becoming increasingly resentful of the way their citizens are being treated in the Gulf.[2]

Many immigrants are also angry at their paymasters for not aiding their own countries of origin and easing the sufferings of the masses there. To date none of those groups has dared to express such feelings in public for fear of losing their jobs but the potential is there for more politically-orientated underground elements to attempt to take advantage of such sentiments. Theoretically, they might respond to any political movement which would take up their plight and champion their cause. Then their grievances would be focused against the system rather than be open to amelioration by it and their economic interests, which until now are mutually exclusive and complementary, would cease to be so.

So politically, sharp distinctions need to be made between Arab and non-Arab workers, between educated and uneducated Arab immigrants, and between immigration within the Gulf and from outside the region. Whereas the Iranian, Asian and Far Eastern workers are merely interested in bettering their lot,[3] intending to return to their places of origin with their savings, the educated Arab immigrants are perceived by the local

1 See Kathleen Bishtaivi's articles 'Between Islam and Travolta' and 'Population shift threatens stability' in *Financial Times* Supplement on the UAE, 23 June 1980, p xiii.

2 This is the main theme of an article in *al-Jumhuriyah* daily (Cairo), 2 May 1981, entitled 'The Egyptians who are suffering in Kuwait'.

3 Pakistani sources estimated that remittances sent home by Pakistanis working in the UAE totalled just above 88 million dollars last year compared with 106 million dollars in 1978 − *Middle East Economic Digest*, 27 June 1980, p 43. Another Pakistani source suggested that in 1980 the Pakistanis in the Gulf are expected to send home 1,600 dollars (*Ibid*), 16 May 1980, pp 6-7.

governments as being interested, in addition to raising their standard of living, in participating politically and contributing their share to inter-Arab politics. After all, many young Arabs regard the existing international borders as artificial lines imposed by Western imperialism and consequently might have greater political expectations beyond the economic reasons which prompted their immigration. Moreover, should conflict erupt between their state of origin and their host country they might have divided loyalties, being regarded as a 'fifth column' by both states and it could be assumed that, whatever their origin, some of these expatriates maintain contact with their respective governments. It would seem that this is the reason behind the Gulf regimes' fears that the presence of Egyptian immigrants could be used by Egypt[1] as a lever over them, especially when many Egyptians are employed in the administration and in the educational system — politically sensitive posts which might give Egypt a potential weapon should the oil producing countries attempt to carry out economic sanctions against Egypt. Gulf rulers are not necessarily impressed by the tendency of Egyptian immigrants to shy away from politics and concentrate on earning money, fearing that there are Egyptians who are antagonized by the present economic policies of the host countries.

However perhaps the most important group is that of the Palestinians, nearly 300,000 of whom live in Kuwait. Their potential in the other Gulf states is not reflected in their relatively small numbers: they are usually found in the urban centres and, apart from Saudi Arabia (80,000) and Iraq (50,000), have high ranking jobs within the local government. This accounts for their political importance. The Palestinians' importance lies well beyond their numbers and the economic role they play. Given their declared desire to return to Palestine and their hopes for Arab unity, regarding it as providing the only combined military force which could regain their lost country, the gap between the declarations of Arab governments and the reality of their lack of positive action to support the Palestinian cause could destabilize the region. The Palestinians have no state to return to and their sojourn in the Gulf is heavily dependent on the resolution of the Arab-Israeli conflict. Thus their mere presence in the Gulf is regarded by the local regimes as a menace by virtue of their persistent political expectations regarding their yet unresolved plight and the duties of their 'hosts' which stem from that.

---

1 *al-Wahdah*, UAE 27 April 1980 argued that the Egyptian Intelligence (together with the American CIA) have established a number of secret military organizations from among the Egyptian immigrants for the purpose of destabilizing the Gulf so as to pave the way for external intervention (as well as follow closely political tendencies among their brothers who opposed President Sadat).

The main problem is in Kuwait, not only because of its sizable Palestinian community (300,000) but because of the role that Palestinians play, the positions they have acquired and the influence they carry with the rest of the Kuwaiti population. Kuwait is thus constrained by the Palestinian question in a way different to that of other states in the region and must, therefore, present itself, on certain occasions, as taking the lead on this issue, not merely toeing the line. In agreeing to allow the PLO to open offices on its soil, Kuwait was motivated by the need to indicate her commitment to the Palestinian cause for fear of Palestinian reaction should Kuwait deny the PLO this minimal status at a time when other western states had licensed such offices. The Kuwaitis were also guided by their preference for controlling open rather than underground political activities. Nevertheless, the authorities are carefully watching the Palestinians' movements: for it is obvious that, beyond running its own independent education the PLO there is indulging in other ventures, and that, as elsewhere in the Gulf, there are secret Palestinian cells in constant contact with their affiliated counterparts outside the state — whether Communists, Ba'athists and, more commonly, Arab Nationalist Movements or the Muslim Brotherhood — all of whom run their operations independent of, and at times in conflict with, the PLO's network.

What terrifies the Gulf regimes is the possibility of the PLO engaging in terrorism on their soil. The lessons of the civil wars in Jordan and particularly Lebanon, where the PLO through co-operation with Muslim elements managed to undermine the state's central authority and to bring about a *de facto* partition of Lebanon and the creation of an independent Palestinian base in the form of a 'state within a state', are still fresh in their memories as is that of the mid-1970s upheaval in Kuwait.

The reluctance of the Peninsula states to license open PLO political activity — beyond opening offices — stems also from fears of the uncontrollable consequences of the Palestinians being able to function and strengthen their position and influence whilst other groups of expatriates and indigenous minorities, let alone the local intelligentsia, are prohibited from freely organizing themselves.

6 Changing political priorities

By its very nature, modernization is not confined to the introduction of industrialization. Many social and organizational changes accompany this process or are a by-product of it. Growing political awareness could not be divorced from the import of technology and expectations of greater participation in political life have followed modernization. A failure of the regimes to pay due regard to such demands could breed tension.

Generally, ideological demands are slow to emerge, allowing the rulers to be relatively free from political challenge in the first decades of the flow of oil revenues. This, however, is almost bound to change. Enormous disparities caused by an uneven distribution of the newly-acquired wealth feed political radicalization. It was hoped that, with the local populations' dependence on the newly created sources of livelihood, it would prove relatively easy to insulate the states from socialist ideas and other undesirable and unwarranted side-effects of modernization. This was enforced by the adoption of strict measures designed to withstand pressures from within the system. But the rulers' task became more difficult with the fragmentation of the traditional tribal order and new strains appeared, caused by changing expectations. There is a direct relationship between economic conditions and political stability.

The rapid expansion of the education system

Side by side with economic growth and as part of the establishment of basic infrastructure, the Peninsula governments strove to build an adequate education system so as to leap decades technologically. Lagging behind Iran and Iraq, where modern education was introduced in the previous century,[1] these states embarked on schemes which sought to replace the old traditional educational system, which had bequeathed them a high rate of illiteracy,[2] with a modern one. Bahrain and Kuwait started earlier than the other states but all the rest are following. With half of the Gulf's indigenous population being under 15, education received top priority, with the vision of creating a capable young generation. Given this commitment to education, large sums were allocated to build schools and enrolments were expanding accordingly. The UAE in 1979 allocated 23.9 percent of its budget to education. Vocational training centres were built in the Gulf states (at times by the oil companies — as in Oman) to reduce their dependence on foreign labour. The most rapid growth took place in Saudi Arabia. In 1979 there was a total of 4,645 schools,[3] 41,565 teachers and some 40,000 students in the Kingdom's seven universities, though the quality and standards of education were affected by the desire of the government to increase the number of graduates.[4]

Yet the rapid transformation of the education system created a number of problems. In places like Oman, where the bulk of the population resides in the countryside and is generally excluded from the process of modernization, there has been little readiness to adopt any

1 In Iran by 1978 there were roughly some 8 million students of all kinds in some 50,000 schools with nearly a quarter of a million teachers. Higher education included 21 universities and 80 institutes of higher teaching. Iraq's education system had in 1977 twice as many students than it had a decade before: 555,184 pupils in the secondary schools. But the real jump is in her vocational training system [7,626 (1965-76) to 28,363]; technical 4,389 to 21,186 respectively; and in her eight relatively newly established universities and academic institutions; 2,222 to 81,498, (details found in Cottrell *The Persian Gulf, op.cit.* Appendix 1). These universities absorb many students from elsewhere in the Arab world and this is also used to dilute the impact of the Kurdish students in the northern Sulimaniya University.

2 Even Iraq is still struggling to no avail to eradicate its high rate of illiteracy which is reported to reach 72% of females and 30% of males in the 15-45 age group — see Susannah Tarbush 'Early success for Iraqi literacy drive' in *Middle East Economic Digest,* 21 September 1979, p 8. The UAE is reported to have 91,000 illiterate inhabitants out of her 862,000 population (Qatar News Agency, 7 September 1979).

3 Excluding the military institutions with faculty numbering 4,159 (*Financial Times,* 28 April 1980).

4 By 1985 the Saudi government expects to have a total of 1,027,396 in the entire education system including 73,490 students (*al-Riyadh* daily, 11 May 1980).

new system which did not correspond to their strong Islamic values.[1] In Saudi Arabia with the process of expanding education came the erosion of the old traditional rural framework because it encouraged migration and it included the young women as well. Furthermore the aspirations of the younger generation far from coincide with their parents' more traditional outlook. This manifested itself also in the relatively slow growth of higher Islamic studies. Moreover education further deprives the market of indigenous labour in the short term.

The fact that the schools had to absorb not only the locals' but the immigrants' children also left its mark on the construction and size of the education system. With the need to cater for the second generation of the constantly rising numbers of expatriates, the relative expenditure on education has become very high.

Moreover, the ambitious education programmes meant that the teaching posts had to be staffed largely by expatriate Arab teachers. In Oman this was mainly due to the high level of illiteracy and the shortage of local trained teachers and in the UAE and Kuwait it was due more to the tendency of the few indigenous teachers to abandon the education sector for the more lucrative jobs of trade, business or even other government areas and it is difficult to see a large proportion of those acquiring higher education opting for teaching posts.[2]

The political implications of such a state of affairs is proving to be a source of unease to the regimes which recall that the Middle East has a long history of political demonstrations starting with students moving from the classroom into the streets, incited by their teachers. Nevertheless, these rulers are intent on expanding their education systems as a sign of progress, prestige and above all concern for their people.

A more complicated situation is bound to develop in the Gulf universities. Universities could produce either a brand of Islamic fundamentalists or a breed of Marxists — both of whom are totally unacceptable to the Gulf regimes — or ideas steeped in western capitalism.

In Kuwait, political life on campus is already a source of concern for

1 In 1969 there were only three modern schools side by side with the traditional education system. By 1977 there were 261 schools with a total of 64,975 pupils. (A corresponding growth in the education system marked the development which took place in Dhofar since the end of the war there in 1975.) Today there are some 100,000 pupils (out of an estimated population of 1.5 million) in 357 schools, and a university is planned to be established in Nizwa.

2 In 1976-7 there were 769 foreign teachers which represented 27% of the total. (Birks and Sinclair, *Bahrain*, *op.cit.*, p 13.) The employment of women as elementary school teachers (followed later by Qatar and Kuwait) helped in maintaining the balance. But there is evidence to suggest that many local teachers later deserted this branch for more tempting jobs in the private and even public sectors.

the authorities. Established in 1966, the student population is 9,000 and is taught by 650 lecturers (mostly expatriates). Some of the students also come from other parts of the Arab world and this has led to conflict between pro- and anti-government groups of the country of origin. In 1978, the Kuwaiti authorities had to arrest a number of students following a fight between left wing and right wing Bahraini factions. Such activity could not leave the Kuwaiti students themselves untouched and clashes between the 'democratic group' and the more influential 'Islamic group' marked the election campaign for the students union.[1] Obviously, the Kuwaiti government is fearful that such conflicts would be manipulated by opposition forces.[2]

Islamic sentiments appeared also in the small Al Ain University in the UAE where students are seeking to organize themselves politically. UAE officials have grown worried and recently the President of the UAE ordered a purge of the faculty of its 'liberal' thinkers.[3] The Saudis, who had hoped that education would develop a feeling of patriotism,[4] are similarly troubled by attacks on Islam by foreigners in contact with local students.[5]

Iran has different problems to contend with. If under the Shah the university campuses were bastions of struggle against the regime, in post-revolutionary Iran this did not change. Conflict between the new regime and its opponents has extended to the campus. The rapid growth of the Iranian secondary education system means that many of those wanting to continue with higher education have to travel abroad. The universities can absorb only 8 percent of the 300,000 or so applicants but the new government is trying to discourage students from going abroad to complete their education. In the words of Iran's Under Secretary of the Ministry of Culture and Higher Education, Dr. Jahanshahlu:

> If the aim of study abroad was a graduation certificate, that could be obtained in this country, and if the objective was an advance in knowledge in accordance with Islamic principles, study abroad was not useful.

1   *al-Siyasah* daily, Kuwait, 30 April 1979.

2   *al-Jumhuriyah* daily, Cairo, 18 May 1980.

3   Doyle McManus 'Radical ideas taking root in the oil emirates' in *International Herald Tribune* (IHT), 7 January 1981. The university has 1,800 students and is expected to take 5,000 in the next few years.

4   Interior Minister Prince Na'if in a symposium in the University of Riyadh, *al-Jazirah*, 9 January 1980.

5   Prince Na'if warned Saudi students in a seminar in Riyadh that contacts with western society put their Islamic faith in danger, see *Gulf Mirror* weekly, Bahrain, 10 May 1980.

82

He justified the government's position also on ecomic grounds arguing that the amount of money spent on aiding students abroad was two-and-a-half times more than the total annual expense of all Iran's universities.

Whereas the sheikhdoms and Saudi Arabia are sending their sons to study abroad at government expense, with the aim of equipping them with the necessary knowledge to form the higher echelons of the ever-expanding bureaucracy and thereby to diminish these states' dependence on immigrants to fill such jobs, in pre-revolution Iran and Iraq this process has enabled the regimes to rid themselves of potential dissidents but many of the students who travelled to the West to complete their higher education are reluctant to return to their places of origin. Unlike other students from the Gulf who return to well-paid, prestigious positions in their countries' administrations, the employment opportunities and the attendant salaries present no economic incentive to many Iranians and Iraqis. The latter in many cases seek employment in other Gulf states. Moreover the political atmosphere in both states tends to deter many graduates from returning home. The Iraqi regime now restricts travel for study to members of the Ba'ath, a policy which also helps the government to confront the acute problem of the 'brain drain'.

Prior to the revolution, many Iranian students indulged in anti-Shah activities in western universities whither they were followed by the Iranian secret police. Now a large part of the intelligentsia has left the country to live abroad. Thus, unlike other Gulf states, a large proportion of the Iranian political opposition lives in the West.

The anti-Ba'ath Iraqi opposition in the West is far more modest in size and less organized. Only Kurds[1] and Iraqi communists seem to be occasionally active, mainly through verbal clashes with Ba'athi students who are carefully watching their rivals' steps. Needless to say, all dissidents are constrained by fear for the safety of their relatives remaining behind who, in many cases, are prevented from leaving the country. The limited weight of the intelligentsia in Iraq and its ineffectiveness abroad makes it easier for the regime to neutralize such opposition, especially as the Ba'athi have adopted a policy of incorporating intellectuals into the establishment to defuse political opposition.

The intelligentsia in the rest of the Gulf surfaced only recently but the rapid expansion of the education system, the establishment of universities and the rising numbers of students encouraged by their governments to study abroad have all manifested themselves in the emergence of a new group with distinct political aspirations. The students having experienced a new way of life in Egypt, Iraq, Syria and

---

1 The Kurdish underground organizes part of its European propaganda activities from Finland and London and Paris.

particularly in the West and having absorbed new ideas, now confront the old reality at home with its enveloping traditional and restricted atmosphere and become discontented and unwilling to abide by the existing limitations[1] which prevent them from debating what they freely debated abroad.

If anything, the political orientation of many of these educated youngsters would be to support pan-Arabism or radical pan-Islam in an attempt to turn the Arab world into an international political force which would suit its newly acquired economic power. Such perceptions would encourage political initiative rather than passivity. Being educated in the west will not ensure a pro-Western orientation. Many Third World revolutionary regimes are led by those who received their education in the West. Nor will those from Iraq, the PDRY or even Kuwait[2] who have acquired their education in the USSR necessarily become communists by conviction. Some of them have come to dislike the Russians during their sojourn in the Soviet Union where they are looked down upon and patronized. Others see the failure of the Soviet economic and social system. Nevertheless, the new experience of all students going abroad must be expected to shape their political thinking and so present a challenge to existing regimes.

1 Bahrain's government was reported to have deprived some 400 students of their passports 'until they gave a pledge not to indulge in political activities abroad' — see 'The story of Bahrain's unrest' in *Middle East Economic Digest*, October 1979. Oman on the other hand is fearful to allow many of her students to return, especially when some of them are known to be associated with the Rejectionists of the PLO, the Syrian Ba'ath and of course the PFLO — see SWB ME/6451/A/1, 7 August 1980 on Oman's students meeting in Syria.

2 Kuwait is reported to have sent in 1980 some 21 students to the USSR.

The emergence of a new middle class

One of the most significant and far-reaching effects caused by modernization of the Gulf has been the emergence of a new and rapidly growing middle-class comprised of merchants, businessmen, civil servants, journalists, teachers and the military. In Iran and Iraq it is exclusively indigenous. In Bahrain it is also predominantly local, but in the city states it was, at least initially, foreign immigrants who made up both the new 'industrial class' and the expanding bureaucracy. In Saudi Arabia the pattern is less clear owing to the Kingdom's size and diversity. In certain parts of the state there is a predominance of an aristocratic merchant class whereas in the Hijaz, side by side with this mixed group and the noble families, there has developed — as in Kuwait — a cadre of local non-royal professionals.

Yet unlike the other states in the region, which were once either under Ottoman rule or British influence, the penetration of external bureaucracies never really left its mark on Saudi Arabia. Thus the new administration developed alongside the existing traditional tribal structures and did not initially replace them. Indeed the traditional modes of government were maintained for they gave the ruler contact with tribal leaders. Yet the old channels of communication between the ruler and the ruled became a bone of contention when the new centralized administration began to fill its ranks. Favouritism led to unqualified people joining the administration.

The rapid expansion of the petroleum industry and government bureaucracy during the 1950s meant that, side by side with the foreigners recruited to fill these jobs, came the first secular-educated Saudis. With the expansion of secular education, the middle class too expanded. The Royal Family has been careful to leave the Ministry of Education in the hands of the religious authorities (members of the Al Shaikh) but other ministries are increasingly staffed by more secular-oriented academics. Antagonism has developed between these two groups[1] as it has between the technocrats and the business class (which includes both royalty and commoners).[2] Though still numerically small, this rapidly growing and increasingly influential middle class, which has already gained economic privileges and social status, is bound to leave its mark on the nature of the political system in the Gulf and hence pose a dilemma for the regimes: they need the indigenous middle-class but its growing strength, weight and influence is worrying. Furthermore the middle-class, although it has hitherto subordinated itself to the system,

---

1 See William Rugh 'Emergence of new middle class in Saudi Arabia' in *Middle East Journal*, 1973, pp 7-20.

2 See Martin Woollacott 'A share in everything except power', *The Guardian*, 18 April 1981.

could hardly fail to worry the dynasties who are aware of their political aspirations. In the UAE there are already signs of western-educated technocrats chafing under absolutist sheikhs.

Apart from Iraq and Iran, the new and rather thin layer of the emerging urban intelligentsia has influence only on the younger generation. It generally lacks cohesion and conflicting ideologies tend to polarize its members but their importance lies in their ability to become a focus for a consensus against the regimes.

Open political activity

Clubs and unions

Open political activity is limited in the Peninsula. Apart from post-revolutionary Iran, only Bahrain and Kuwait display any such activity. One unique feature of Bahrain's community is the existence of over 90 social clubs and a number of professional societies. In the absence of political parties and trade unions, these officially apolitical bodies serve as a platform for open if cautious debates. The clubs' membership includes a cross-section of the community, ranging from civil servants to university graduates, Arabs and non-Arabs, immigrants and locals.[1] Their concern with political matters, such as labour unions, freedom of speech etc. troubled the Bahraini regime which has kept an eye on their activities. With the establishment of the Bahraini Constitutional Assembly they lost part of their influence but, following its demise, they have served as a 'substitute' for public debate, albeit restricted.

The only other place which resembles Bahrain is neighbouring Kuwait which has a far more politically-aware intelligentsia. Discussion takes place mainly in informal social gatherings (diwaniya[2]) but, as elsewhere in the region, the debate is inhibited out of fear of the presence of government agents.

A far less-relaxed atmosphere than the social clubs manifests itself through the action of manual workers in the region. Trade unions have always been regarded by governments as a possible Soviet-inspired instrument for political agitation and hence they have sought to prevent their existence unless they came under strict governmental control (as in Iraq and, to a certain extent, in Kuwait)[3] or unless the political consequences of outlawing them were likely to be severe (as in Iran which has over 900 labour syndicates).

Bahrain stands out as an important exception for, although no unions exist there, the struggle for a licensed labour movement had a serious impact on the government's relationship not only with the newly emerging working class but with the Bahraini society as a whole. Much of the continuous protest which has come from the newly emerging working-class has been over the issue of the right to unionize labour.

---

1 For further details see Emil Nakhleh, *Bahrain: Political development in a modernizing society*, Lexington Books, Mass. 1976.

2 See Tawfic E. Farah, 'Incubating supportive attitudes in an emerging state: the case of Kuwait' in *Journal of South Asian and Middle Eastern Studies*, Volume II, No. 4, Summer 1979, p 61.

3 Kuwait limited such unions by preventing expatriates from becoming officers. Qatar on the other hand licensed some workers' committees whose mandate was severely restricted.

For the government (and perhaps for at least some of those behind the popular movement) this is seen as the way to bring about its own collapse — through the development of political polarization in which extreme nationalists would take the lead. The incompatibility of ideas as to the nature of Bahraini society manifested itself in the major labour strikes which developed into uprisings in 1954, 1956, 1965, 1970 and 1972 and in the harsh measures introduced by the government when quelling these protests. At the core of the confrontation was the tension between traditional family rule and popular participation. In fact most political crises in Bahrain have centred on the Bahraini workers' determination to unionize.[1] But, unlike labour strikes in the Eastern Province of Saudi Arabia in 1953 and 1956 which concentrated more on protesting against working conditions, the presence of many students in the Bahraini demonstrations indicated that these expressions of bitterness were not confined to the right to establish trade unions, nor even to a growing exasperation and impatience with what they perceive to be an archaic feudal superstructure — though they refrained from openly advocating its overthrow. Rather the growing impact of Arab solidarity was inspired by pan-Arabism which expressed itself through waves of hostility against western imperialism. The presence on Bahraini soil of the British, against whom much of this anger was directed, especially following the British/French invasion of the Suez Canal, sufficed to unify the ranks of the angry demonstrators who, like their brothers in Kuwait, were protesting against the strong link between their government and Britain. Many of them came to regard their dynasties as an extension of western colonialism. Calls for higher wages and improved working conditions were carefully blended into pleas for democratization and greater liberalization. Events elsewhere in the Arab world continued to influence attitudes of the 'opposition'. The collapse of the Hashemite monarchy in Iraq in 1958 encouraged the radicals.

The Arab defeat at the hands of Israel in 1967 shook the region. Through the pain and shame of immigrants from the Arab states bordering Israel, the educated local population came to sense the magnitude of the frustration. A reason explaining the defeat had to be found. Both superpowers were now accused and demonstrators in Saudi Arabia's eastern province marched against the American installations, expressing the new mood.

The debate within the Arab world reached the Gulf through the Arab radio stations and by following the imported Arab press.

The media

If prior to the 1970s the Arab desert sheikhdoms were backward and

---

1 Nakhleh, *Bahrain, op.cit.*, p 75.

largely tribal societies hardly affected by international and even inter-Arab affairs, modernization put an end to their isolation and they became increasingly exposed to political developments around them. With the exception of Kuwait, which has a relatively liberal press not to the liking of the regime, most of the sheikhdoms' press is state controlled. Unlike Kuwait, where Palestinians influence the press and consequently strong pan-Arab, non-aligned sentiments dominate its content, in Saudi Arabia and elsewhere journalists have tended to be local. However this is changing. A more critical note is appearing in the press but once it exceeds certain limits it will probably not be tolerated by governments.

Censorship and the banning of the appearance of newspapers serves to moderate criticism levelled against the regimes by the non-state controlled press as well as to deter the printing of 'rumours' and 'fabrications' which could trigger off unease. This has not stopped the arrival of underground publications printed at home or smuggled in by local dissident groups or other illegal bodies. Regulating the entry of Arabic press from abroad, especially at times of inter-Arab conflict, ensures that the bulk of the population is exposed primarily to the government's propaganda. This is enforced by the state controlled radio and television which now reach the most remote regions, providing a direct contact between ruler and ruled — giving the former more power. The media is also an important tool at the disposal of the religious establishment in maintaining and enriching their listeners' exposure to religion and Islamic cultural revival. In Iraq, the Ba'ath-controlled organs are an integral part of the Party's indoctrination machinery.

Yet, so long as the governments do not jam radio transmissions from abroad, many people also tune in to other Arabic stations which enables them to acquire a wider view of events and to maintain contact with those they look to for guidance. Inflammatory radio propaganda has always been a common feature in Middle East politics. Recently, the Iranian Shi'ah clergy constantly encouraged the Shi'ah community in Iraq, Bahrain and Saudi Arabia to rise against their governments. In the past Egypt used this technique to incite the masses in the region against their leaders. The memory of President Nasser's speeches which resulted in upheaval in the Middle East, fierce demonstrations in Bahrain and an all-out strike in Saudi Arabia's oil fields is still fresh in the minds of the rulers. Egypt, with the Voice of Cairo remaining a popular station in the Gulf even after her peace with Israel, is widely heard but, as far as the Arabs are concerned, Sadat (or for that matter any other leader in the region) does not have Nasser's charisma and certainly not his popularity (even before his historic visit to Jerusalem).

Those educated in the West listen eagerly also to the Voice of America and the BBC World Service Arabic, Persian and English programmes and

Radio Monte Carlo which provide a more objective and reliable source of information and commentary than Arab sources. The role of the BBC was referred to by the Shah who was aggravated by what he regarded as 'the hostile tone of the radio's transmissions'. However, a similar complaint was registered by his successors. International dialling also makes it easier for any dissident group to receive instruction from abroad. Technology can, therefore, prove two-edged. Whilst it enables the regime to maintain contact with its subjects in trying to create a cohesive and loyal society, it also makes this task far more difficult when adversaries use the same techniques to manipulate existing sectarian or minority conflicts or to challenge the policies and credibility of the regimes.

Clandestine political activity

Middle East political life is carried on at two inter-related levels: open government or a sanctioned 'democratic' process and a rich underground political activity. In the Gulf sheikhdoms it is generally the latter which predominates although its magnitude is still limited. At the outset it should be stressed that, perhaps with the qualified exception of Iran, practically all political movements in the area have been inspired by forces outside the region, whether pan-Arabism or socialism.

But in observing Middle Eastern politics and trying to ascertain what forces are at work behind certain political groupings, terms such as 'left' and 'right' can prove misleading, if not meaningless. As events in the region have revealed, Marxism and Islam are not necessarily incompatible. Despite their total rejection of each other's ideology and, although the existence of one structure precludes by definition the spread of the other's doctrine, their common denominators could provide a base for convenient *ad hoc* marriage. With both groups' shared and widely appealing animosity towards western imperialism and capitalism (which they take as the reason for their exploitation by corrupted rulers co-operating with the west) and with their shared view of the need to re-establish society on a classless basis (which would mean a fairer distribution of wealth, embodied in the term Islamic socialism or Arab socialism), the rest becomes of secondary importance if they are to unseat governments which pursue their own self-serving policies. Each group, of course, is confident that once the main obstacle is out of the way, it would throw aside its erstwhile partner.

Indeed, the Iranian revolution has demonstrated not only how the 'left' and the 'right' can, however temporarily, put aside their deep enmity and unite behind a common aim[1] — the overthrow of the Shah and the neutralizing of the army — but that a Marxist wing and a progressive-Muslim wing could even be synthesized to provide the foundation of one of the most important opposition guerrilla groups — the Sazman-e Mojahedin-e Khalq-e Iran (Organization of Freedom Fighters of the Iranian People). Evidently it is clear that co-operation between the latter and the other two forces — the Tudeh (Masses) Communist party and its offshoot the Marxist Feda'iyin-e Khalq (People's Fighters)[2] — is becoming more complicated with their clashing aspirations and hence conflicting definitions of their respective roles.

1 See David Menashri 'Strange bedfellows: the Khomeini coalition' in *The Jerusalem Quarterly*, No. 12, Summer 1979, pp 34-48.

2 For an analysis of the Left — see Shahram Chubin 'Leftist forces in Iran' in *Problems of Communism*, July-August 1980, pp 1-25.

This situation is not unique to Iran. A tense co-existence between Iraqi radical leftist forces has marked the history of the country since the 1958 revolution, and especially following the rise of the Ba'athists to power in 1963. Given the Ba'ath and communist mistrust and mutual suspicions of each other's ultimate intentions, let alone their conflicting ideology and the stigma the communists carry of being a tool for Soviet conspiracy, co-existence between the two has always been extremely delicate.

In addition to being perceived by many Arabs as being antithetical, it is the communists' association with, and subordination to, the USSR which has always made it difficult for Communist parties and their off-shoots to make headway, despite the fact that the Soviet Union generally preferred, whenever possible, to maintain close relations with the region's governments even at the expense of the communists. But once government-to-government relations soured, the Communists again assumed the role of agents in Soviet strategy, enjoying clandestine support in money, arms and other forms of aid — whether extended from across the border (as in the case of Iran) or infiltrated from the USSR's strongholds in the region (Syria, PDRY and Ethiopia). This form of oscillating relationship has characterized the co-operation between the Iranian Tudeh party and the Iraqi Communist Party (ICP) on the one hand and the USSR on the other, a relationship which was also influenced by the desire of both parties to relieve themselves of their handicap and act independently on issues like the Arab-Israeli conflict where the ICP's stance is far more radical than that of its sponsor.

But in both Iran and Iraq the communist parties have found it diffi-cult to stay intact. Fragmentation occurred on ideological lines before and after the 1965 Soviet-Chinese rift. In Iraq, sectarian, ethnic and regional tensions proved also decisive in these divisions, with the young, more militant, Shi'i radicals in the south gravitating away from the Sunni communist leadership. The latter opted to co-operate with the regime in forming in August 1973 the short-lived Ba'athi dominated coalition as a way of advancing communist interests. Thereafter many pro-Soviet Iraqi communists fled the country; others were arrested, the rest joined the underground movement. In Iran, the Tudeh was further weakened prior to the revolution by a number of groups pulling out of the party in an attempt to gain where the Tudeh's image was blackened. Following the revolution, the 'legitimized' Tudeh entrenched its position and gained lost ground among Iran's minorities. Its members joined other subversive groups and tried to infiltrate the military. The Tudeh even went as far as to cloak its rhetoric in language steeped in Islam, but the memory of its role in undermining the short-lived Mossadegh-led nationalist government will not be quickly forgotten.

Despite occasional schisms, the communist parties and associated splinter groups are perhaps the most tightly-knit organizations in the region. Their strength lies in their efficiency, experience, careful recruitment (which partly accounts for their small size), ideological cohesiveness and Soviet backing. They have survived waves of persecution and arrests. Nevertheless, their failure in Iraq to recruit among the Iraqi peasantry and in Iran from the urban proletariat has proved their weakness.

In small numbers communists are found throughout the region. Iraqi exiles seek refuge in the PDRY, Lebanon and Syria — which aids any Iraqi group striving to overthrow the present regime (such as the so-called Democratic National and Patriotic Front).[1] Elsewhere the situation is less clear. The Gulf governments are united in their fear of communist penetration of the immigrants. Even if they are inactive, it could be assumed that some communists are to be found in Kuwait[2] despite the fact that the authorities there have from time to time purged the country of scores of expatriate political activists.

The National Front for the Liberation of Bahrain (known as the NLF-Bahrain) has communist inclinations, though those were not necessarily reflected in this group's manifestos which are designed to emphasize the more general Bahraini grievances in the hope of having a wider appeal.[3] It sought to take the lead in Bahrain by forming both some kind of grouping based on a minimum programme around which the various small groups would gather[4] and by co-ordinating action with other democratic and nationalist groupings in the region. Members of the NLFB were nervous that the fall of the Shah and the loss of this US ally in the region would put the onus on Bahrain to refrain from carrying out its promise of dismantling the Dhzu Fajr naval base which

---

1 SWB ME/6575/A/1 and 6586/A/1, 27 November 1980.

2 Secret Jordanian documents suggest that in the late 1950s there were a number of Palestinian communists active in Kuwait and Iraq. (Data found in the Jordanian files confiscated by Israel in the 1967 war: Israel State Archives, Jerusalem, Section 65 reports: MN/20/1/57 dated 20 February 1958; MKH20/1/1551 dated 23 September 1958; MQ/20/15/5992 dated 6 May 1959 and others.)

3 See article explaining the National Front for the Liberation of Bahrain's programme in al-Hadaf weekly, Beirut 15 September 1979, p 30.

4 Interview with Abdallah Khalid, member of the Front in Bratislava Pravda (in Slovak), 5 July 1980, p 6 in Foreign Broadcast Information Service Daily Report, 9 July 1980, chapter 1.

is an American military installation — 'a promise forced from it by progressive forces'.[1] The NFLB was not alone. Another group called the Popular Front of Bahrain, an Arab Nationalist offspring of PFLOAG, strove to achieve the same things but under its own leadership.

But if the Communists are among the strongest opposition forces in Iraq and Iran, Kuwait, as noted earlier, is the centre for political activity carried out by Palestinians. In fact, the Fatah was established there by Yassir Arafat, who moved to Kuwait from Cairo and the various factions comprising the PLO have always regarded the opportunities offered by Kuwait, which harboured a large segment of the Palestinian diaspora, as granting the Palestinian movement ample scope for political action. Another group which regards Kuwait as its stronghold is the leftist Arab Nationalist Movement (ANM). In a sense it is an 'expatriate movement' which has gradually become mixed in its composition though the driving force behind it remains Palestinian. The rapidly expanding University of Kuwait has become a centre for their political agitation but the ANM's weakness lies in its failure to catch the imagination of those outside the intelligentsia. The immigrants depended on capitalism and on the high salaries paid by those dynasties the ANM wanted to subvert. Its Kuwaiti branch declined to engage in terror, reasoning that the conditions were not ripe, either socially or politically. Nevertheless the Gulf governments have become immensely troubled by the stated priorities and intentions of the ANM and were thus only too happy to witness its fragmentation and to assist it in its new form — the Popular Front for the Liberation of Palestine (PFLP) — which meant that they would carry on their armed struggle on Israel's borders rather than in the Gulf. However in 1973 Kuwait expelled a number of South Yemeni and Hadrami expatriates for belonging to the ANM. A similar reaction followed the anti-government activities in Kuwait in 1975/76. On that occasion Iraqis, Syrians and Lebanese all expressed their disenchantment with the Kuwaiti government's passive policies over the war in Lebanon. This culminated in the government expelling some 10,000 Arab immigrants, most of whom were Palestinians. In fact the security forces in Kuwait and Bahrain (where the ANM also tried to function[2]) were well

1 *Ibid.* Indeed these fears were shared by representatives of other 'fronts' in a round table discussion held in Beirut in which members of the following groups participated: Popular Front for the Liberation of Oman (PFLO); Kuwaiti Democratic Grouping; YAR Democratic National Front; Yemeni Socialist Party; Popular Front-Bahrain and NLF-Bahrain (*al-Safir*, Beirut 18 November 1979), *Journal of Political Research and Sociology*, 25 January 1980, p 3.

2 *al-Jumhwiyah* daily, Cairo, reported on 12 December 1979 that ANM cells were recently discovered in the Gulf responsible for an explosion in Manamah and the distribution of leaflets in Kuwait which call for social justice and fair distribution of wealth.

placed to watch its clandestine operations and it remained fairly inactive although it was obvious that it had arms at its disposal.

On the surface it would seem that in the UAE there are no traces of such anxieties. Despite its enormous expatriate population, the situation is different to that in Kuwait. There are no indications of any kind of political activity there. However, there are those who suggest that beneath the surface, the Iraqi Ba'athist ideas appeal to some members of the sheikhdoms' younger intelligentsia and that they maintain contact with the Iraqi diplomatic mission there.[1] At the moment, the only signs of mild discontent are those expressed by educated nationals who are disenchanted with the presence of numerous immigrants who would tend to weaken any demand for change emerging from the local but narrowly-based intelligentsia.

Saudi Arabia is again different for, beyond the short-lived outburst of anger in the oil fields in 1953 and 1956 — in which both locals and expatriates participated — it is the only country whose recent history has revealed conflict within the ruling dynasty on ideological rather than personal grounds. The protest was over the absolutist nature of the regime and a few members of the Royal Family were willing to put themselves at the disposal of Saudi Arabia's adversary, Egypt. In 1962 the Saudi Liberation Front, a Cairo-based group better known as the 'Free Princes', led by the former Finance Minister Prince Talal ibn Abd al-Aziz and several other brothers and half brothers, amalgamated itself with the Front for National Reform (established in 1954, later known as the Front for National Liberation of Saudi Arabia — a bourgeois group established in 1958 which was in contact with the communists) and called for the overthrow of the Saudi monarchy and its replacement by a constitutional democracy. The incident ended with the dissident princes being granted clemency upon their return to the Kingdom in early 1964. But the whole affair, which was manipulated by Abd al-Nasser, who never hid his aim to overthrow the Saudi monarchy, left its mark on the Royal Court. Thereafter the Saudis have occasionally faced other ineffective opposition groups[2] all of whom denounced the

1 See *The Security of the Middle East Oil,* Institute for the Study of Conflict (ISC) Special Report, May 1979, p 22.

2 *Middle East Intelligence Survey* listed other groups of an obscure nature. These included: the Revolutionary Najd Party; the Popular Democratic Front in Saudi Arabia and the Committee for the Defence of the Rights of the Saudi People which was said to be operating from Iraq and Western Europe — see Volume 7, No. 16, 16-30 November 1979, p 124. Another group called the Popular Democratic Party is said to have been formed in 1970 by Ba'athists and Nasserites (see Michael M.J. Fisher 'Competing ideologies and social structures in the Persian Gulf' in A. Cottrell (ed.) *The Persian Gulf, op.cit.* p 523. For further details on the various oppositionary groups — see Helen Lackner *A House Built on Sand, a Political Economy of Saudi Arabia,* Ithaca Press, London, 1980, pp 103-9.

family's extravagance and its connections with the US and have called for the removal of the ruling dynasty and the establishment of a republic in its place.

In 1969 the Front for National Liberation of Saudi Arabia participated in an unsuccessful coup and some 300 Air Force officers were arrested. Up to then and thereafter it was hardly active. On 31 August 1975 it changed its name to the Saudi Communist Party and was reported to have co-operated with the Iraqi Communist Party (ICP) and the pro-Communist National Front for the Liberation of Bahrain. Its meagre activities were confined to printing a handful of clandestine leaflets. It is doubtful whether such a party really exists. However, in a document smuggled abroad, the 'party' criticizes the Saudi regime as a police state 'which suppresses all freedom of thought and exploits religion to further its reactionary interests'. The paper went on to attack the Saudi foreign policy as being 'at the service of imperialism'.[1] In an interview published in Paris by the leftist organ *al-Yasar al-Arabi*, two Saudi communists claimed that the party is attempting to establish a front which will unite all the other opposition forces functioning underground in the Kingdom which are united in their aim to overthrow the Saudi Monarchy.[2] However, it would seem that any leftist force would concentrate its activities among the immigrants and, in view of their alleged success in instigating the popular protests of the mid-1950s and following the 1967 war, they would probably focus on the Eastern province, trying to take advantage of the existing grievances of the local and expatriate workers whom they believe to be by now a conscientious working-class.[3]

1   Extracts from the document were published in *Israel and Palestine* bi-monthly, Paris, May 1980, p 11.

2   The interviewees list the following parties: al-Ba'th; the Arab Socialist Labour Party; the Revolutionary Labour Party (a Marxist-Leninist offspring of the ANM); the Peninsula's People's Union (Nasserites). On the other side of the political spectrum are: al-Da'wah (a Sunni Party which stretches to Pakistan) [to be distinguished from the Iraqi Shi'i Da'wah — AP], the Muslim Brotherhood and the Fatimi Party (Shi'i). Reprinted in *al-Ittihad* (daily of the Communist Party in Israel), 5/9 October 1979.

3   A view shared by other revolutionary forces — see interview with Saudi oppositionary elements in *Nidal al-Sha'b* weekly, Beirut, 12 January 1980 and *al-Hadaf* weekly, Beirut, 9 May 1981.

Left and right

In summary, it should be said that the combined impact of the various leftist groups in the Peninsula — unlike Iran and Iraq — has been extremely limited. They have acquired a small following, primarily from the expatriates and a handful from the middle-class, and as such they have not yet posed a serious challenge. Starting with the ARAMCO struggle in 1953, it is evident that the organizers of the strikes in Saudi Arabia underestimated the entrenched position of the Royal Family on the one hand and overestimated their own power and appeal. They were also to realize that many of the immigrants in fact underwent a process of 'de-politicization' owing to the economic penalties involved in participating in any political movement. Their purpose for being in the Gulf is to make money and not to indulge in any form of political activity that could endanger that. As to the local workers, they were either immature politically or simply not interested. However, this was not the case either in Bahrain or in Kuwait although in both states the governments were in control and their fierce reaction to any hostile political expression was to deter others from joining in.

Dependent on external aid, the vitality of all these 'parties' would hinge on their ability to function and recruit in the face of a tighter regional co-ordination in internal security and intelligence designed to monitor their movements and activities.[1] Disappearance and re-emergence under different names, with the intention of deceiving the authorities and attracting more attention, is no substitute for action. The formation of the Gulf Co-operation Council is, at least in part, intended to facilitate the sharing of political intelligence.

Regimes are not notably tolerant of opposition. Nasir al-Sa'id, for example, was kidnapped from Beirut when he published articles in al-Safir newspapers against the Saudi dynasty.[2] But the weakness of these groups should not be taken for granted and their potential success among Arab immigrants should not be dismissed. The relevance of these leftist groups lies in their links to other local groups, whether dis-enchanted younger members of the intelligentsia, clerks or young officers. If aided by individuals from the armed forces, they clearly

1 In Saudi Arabia the annual *hajj*, which means the saturation of the Kingdom by roughly 2,000,000 pilgrims, is probably used by subversive political bodies and other governments for planting new recruits from abroad. Some of them are found among the thousands of pilgrims who, contrary to the authorities' wish, remain illegally in the Kingdom after the *hajj* is over.

2 The kidnap was probably launched by Palestinians of the Fatah who wanted to demonstrate their value to the Saudis and were accordingly rewarded. Rejectionist Palestinians were annoyed by the act and sharply criticized the Saudi regime — see *Nidal al-Sha'b* weekly of the PFLP, Beirut, 12 January 1980.

could come to possess the potential to cause instability. They may even seek a tactical alliance with Islamic groups which usually operate through the mosques and enjoy an edge in terms of mass support.

Hence attention should also be paid to forces found on the 'right' such as the Muslim Brotherhood Association and its offshoots which recently have revealed their vitality in Syria and in Egypt. As a funda-mentalist Sunni movement, it advocates running the Islamic state according to the Qur'aan, which must provide the social and political guidelines for state order. The Brotherhood are implacably opposed both to western imperialism and any form of Marxist doctrine and they blame the Arab leadership for the failure of the Islamic world to assert itself.

The Brotherhood have gathered an impressive following from the masses as well as from students and officials. Persecuted by the Egyptian authorities, they functioned underground and directed their limited but tenacious struggle against the various secular regimes in the Middle East through their regional cells. Some fled to Saudi Arabia where they found an atmosphere conducive to Islamic teaching and they were instrumental in the establishment of the al-Medina Islamic university, from where they proved very influential in shaping the thinking of the ulama, and in educating a new generation of orthodox Saudis as well as many foreign students attracted by the Holy Cities. Their Friday sermons (Khutbahs) in the mosques were always carefully watched by the authorities. Members of a more militant Egyptian Islamic group, al-Takfir wa-al-Hijrah, also took refuge in the Kingdom whose govern-ment in 1977 declined to extradite them to Egypt where they had previously carried out terrorist operations, the most prominent of these being the assassination of the former Egyptian Minister for Awqaf Affairs.[1]

Though watchful of their host governments' policies (particularly in respect of relations with the US, ties with Iraq as well as Islamic purity), the Muslim Brotherhood appears to tolerate monarchies, regarding them as a buffer against the 'spread of communism'. Therefore they are perceived as a useful instrument in balancing left-wing influence. Never-theless all governments are wary of these militant groups for they are known to receive money and arms from external sources (such as Libya's Muemar al-Qadhafi) and are strongly based in Jordan yet no regime presenting itself as the guardian of Islam can outlaw their activities. Hence the dilemma of the Saudis who fear that the Brother-hood could become a channel for disaffection and, at least in the Saudi context, it is perhaps the opposition from the right which is of greatest

1 Cairo Middle East New Agency (MENA) 16.20 GMT 10 January 1980 in *Daily Report*, 11 January 1980.

98

concern because of their appeal to the lower strata of population (whether local or expatriate). Moreover they are opposed to rapid and 'bad' development, to the liberalization of society and to the relaxing of religious restrictions. In contrast to other faiths, there is no real separation in Islam between the 'state' and 'religion'. In that respect Islamic thinking has not changed.

In summary, Islam itself could become a destabilizing force, not only through rifts within sects or between sects but also as a violent anti-dynastic expression. The 'western link', as already mentioned, could form the base for co-operation — however tentative — between various groups found on opposite sides of the political spectrum which nevertheless share the same aim of overthrowing the ruling dynasties.[1]

---

1 This is the main message of a spokesman for the Islamic Revolution Organization which claimed credit both for the seizure of the Grand Mosque and the Shi'ah protest in the Eastern Province (see al-Mawaqif al-Arabi, Lebanon, 20 April 1981).

7 Politico-military relations in the Gulf

Faced with all these potential threats, the regimes in the Gulf have always believed that their own loyal armed forces would be able to handle the situation should ethnic or other internal political forces attempt to change the *status quo*. This too was shattered by the Iranian revolution, having witnessed there the performance of the army from the first stages of the confrontation to its final collapse. Although their populations (except for Iraq) are far smaller and less homogeneous than that of Iran and the danger of mass demonstrations in the Iranian style could be dismissed, the fact that the military to all intents and purposes deserted the ruler alarmed them.

It was, however, fears of *external* aggression associated with the void created by Britain's withdrawal which prompted these regimes to enhance their armies' military capability. Apart from Iran and Iraq, whose armed forces were always relatively large owing to their mutual fears and to their regional political ambitions (Iran in the Gulf and Iraq initially in the Arab-Israeli arena), the other states had relatively small, poorly armed forces which were essentially regarded as an internal arm of the central authority. These forces were nevertheless the corner stones of the regimes. They were mainly comprised of carefully selected Bedouins. The rulers made it a point to be accessible to their soldiers whose personal loyalty was a prerequisite for continued stability.

With the financial revolution came a change of emphasis. The excessive wealth and the associated sense of both power and vulnerability pushed the regimes to modernize and to expand their armed forces. Air forces and navies were established. Security needs were re-defined as to protect the states not only from external threats but also from unadmitted potential internal challenges. Enormous quantities of advanced western-produced weapons found their way into the Gulf. Western arms dealers and western European governments tried to tempt the rulers not only to purchase their products but to invest in their arms industries. Again, prestige played an important role with the sheikhdoms competing with each other. They were united in their attempts not only to upgrade the quality of their military but they were anxious that they would be perceived by their internal as well as external foes as strong. For Saudi Arabia this was an essential ingredient in her overall strategy of trying to gain a leading position in the Arab world and distancing itself from American patronage. Rhetoric was, of course, interwoven into these attempts with states competing vocally over the need 'to liberate Jerusalem' and their indispensable military contribution to that cause.

Absorbing the new and sophisticated weapons called for fundamental changes: more soldiers were recruited; new training systems were introduced; officers were sent for instruction abroad; the ranks of the non-commissioned officers and especially those of the technicians swelled; and the structure of the army was altered accordingly. This meant that the new armies ceased to be the 'bodyguards' of the dynasties and virtually lost their previous characteristics. In the smaller states and Oman, the main change was that the new forces were comprised mainly of foreigners. Consequently, the modernized army ceased to be a personal army having personal contact with its tribal leader. The new chain of command put a distance between the soldier and the ruler, with many of the officer posts in these states being manned by expatriates.

The lucrative economic opportunities outside meant, however, that many locals left and few joined the forces. Governments found it more difficult to recruit and thus they had to compromise on the standard of their new soldiers as well as having to pay enormous salaries to those serving. These payments were both to provide the economic incentive and to create a stake for the army in the well-being of the regime.

But this did not prove sufficient in the UAE whose 25,000 man army is comprised mainly of Omanis (85 percent) and Baluchis and even the officer corps is dominated by expatriates. Outstanding among them are

Jordanians[1] but contract officers from Pakistan (some of whom form the backbone of Abu Dhabi's air force), Britain and many other nationalities also serve. Non-nationals dominate all technical positions. The implications of such a composition could be far-reaching, especially when one of the UAE's main concerns is a threat coming from their southern neighbour, Oman, which has never shelved its aspiration for a Greater Oman. The wealth of the vulnerable UAE could tempt any Omani regime. But Oman itself suffers from the same problem. With a tiny army of roughly 1,000 soldiers in the mid-1960s, prior to the Dhofari rebellion, the Sultanate has now absorbed many Yemenis and especially Baluchis into its 15,000-strong armed forces.[2] The fact that they form separately manned units[3] could prove difficult for the Omani regime if trouble were to erupt in Baluchistan.[4] It would then be up to the British-piloted air force to deter any attack from, say, the PDRY. On a more modest scale, Qatar's 5,000 strong armed forces include many Omanis, Dhofaris, Yemenis, British, Pakistanis and Iranians seconded or under contract to the government. But Qataris now comprise the backbone of the officer corps. Kuwait has many poorly-educated Iraqis and Saudi Bedouins as well as Iranians and Asians in her 12,700 strong armed forces.

Failure to recruit more locals to the army means that the ratio of expatriates to locals can only grow. Lavish inducements, however, cannot buy from foreigners that sense of commitment and reliability for which the reigning dynasties yearn. Lack of loyalty, homogeneity and cohesiveness calls into question not only the army's readiness to

---

1 The proportion of Jordanians in the officer corps is higher than reported because many of them were naturalized. In fact even the first UAE Chief of Staff, Awwad al-Khalidi, was of Jordanian origin; he was selected as a compromise so as to avoid the thorny question of control over the UAE armed forces – a complicated and emotionally charged source of conflict between Abu Dhabi and Dubai. In June 1980 he was replaced and nominated as a military adviser to the President of the UAE (al-Fajr, Abu Dhabi, 3 June 1980). UAE officers train in Jordan (al-Shurtah, UAE August 1979).

2 The Omani armed forces also include Dhofaris who defected from the PFLOAG guerrilla group, whom it uses as paramilitary forces against their brothers (for further details see Leigh Johnson, 'Oman', op.cit., p 9).

3 Unlike the northern Oman recruits who have their own command, the Baluchis are under British officers.

4 Should the Baluchi soldiers, out of solidarity with their brothers across the water in Iran and in an attempt to extend them help, take control of the strategically located Musanadam Peninsula (a non-contiguous part of Oman which is separated from it by an 80-km-wide strip of desert which belongs to Fujairah and Sharjah) things could be seriously complicated for the Omani regime. Another perhaps more serious complication could occur should the Baluchi soldiers desert Oman en masse; that would expose the country to the danger of the PDRY-backed Dhofari rebels taking over 'their' province. Indeed the latter argue that the Baluchis comprise 60% of Oman's army (Aden Voice of the PFLO, 15 March 1980).

defend its paymasters but also its capability to do so. What is more there is little to stop ideologically-motivated expatriate officers trying to stage, or help others to stage, a coup. They could well be targets for subversion. But the opposite is also arguable: an expatriate-dominated army would constitute less of a security risk as being less politicized.[1] Of the smaller states only Bahrain is spared this dilemma as it can find enough local youths to join its small army.[2]

In view of local manpower shortages, there are regimes which are examining the possibility of introducing conscription in the hope that it would not only expand the army but it would also help to reduce the social differences in their heterogeneous societies by instilling a sense of pride and identity and developing feelings of patriotism. In Iraq conscription has proved, to some extent, instrumental in winning a measure of identification of the young with the regime. Officially, Kuwait has already introduced conscription (mainly in an attempt to offset the numerical weight of its Bedouin soldiers of Shi'i/Iraqi origin) and the UAE is considering doing the same which will exclude the non-indigenous segment of the population whose loyalty is doubted. Saudi Arabia is also looking into the implications of a flexible, though compulsory, draft with the view of enlisting as many school-leavers and university graduates as possible in a way which nevertheless would take into account civilian manpower needs. However, embarking on such a policy could tend to dilute the more reliable part of the dynasty's military forces and eliminate the existing economic incentives[3] which serve to encourage the army's loyalty,[4] thus running the risk of facing the consequences of a self-defeating policy. Moreover, conscription there would be rejected by the educated, as reports suggest has already happened in Kuwait.[5]

---

1 Though they were not required to use real force, the Palestinian officers and Yemenis who served in the Qatari forces at the time of the 'strike' in 1963 proved loyal to the Qatari regime.

2 Interview with Bahrain Chief of Staff in al-Qabas daily, Kuwait, 5 June 1979.

3 In urging people to join the army the government emphasized the high salaries paid to soldiers (see al-Jazirah, 18 August 1979). Oman's schemes also speak of handsome loans and lodging – Oman, Oman, 17 July 1979.

4 The Saudi regime was reported to have paid each officer who participated in freeing the Mecca mosque the sum of 50,000 dollars and each soldier a bonus of two month's pay. See Muhammad Hasanin Hykal, 'Mini-Shahs trust evolution to avert revolution in the Gulf' – Sunday Times, 30 December 1979.

5 al-Nahar Arab Report and Memo, 13 August 1979. Kuwait was the first state to introduce conscription.

Saudi Arabia

Saudi Arabia already faces potential tensions regarding control over the military. It maintains three separate armed forces which complement yet counterbalance one another. Internal security is assigned to the police, to the small Royal Guard (RG) and, primarily, to the National Guard (NG) — 'the White Army' — a capable and loyal Bedouin force whose task is to defend the monarch and guard the oilfields. The regular army handles the country's external defence. The air defence forces have a role to play both internally and externally. This classification is reflected in the internal divisions of the Royal Court: the National Guard, which played an important role in the smooth accession to the throne of King Khalid, is under the command of conservative Amir Abdallah; the army is the responsibility of the more progressive Amir Sultan, the Minister of Defence and Aviation. The power struggle over the control of the forces is part and parcel of the issue of succession to the throne among the contenders for power.

The various forces also differ in their composition. Entrusted with the responsibility for the safety of the Royal Family, the 30,000 strong National Guard and the 1,200 strong Royal Guard are composed of carefully selected regular and semi-regular dedicated Bedouins mainly of Najdi origin. They are armed mainly with light and medium weapons. The regular army, air force and navy are together about twice the size of the National Guard. It is planned to increase the size of the forces to 300,000 by 1985 whereas the National Guard will be only 75,000. Many of the recruits to the three regular armed services are of urban origin and are generally thought to be less reliable and less attached to the House of Saud. Their record of attempted coups testifies to that.

Rivalries within the Saudi military came to a head following the Mecca Grand Mosque affair which exposed its poor performance and raised doubts about its ability to defend the present regime. Discontented tribal elements within the army, especially from Hijaz, could be expected to express some sort of dissatisfaction and Saudi officers may also react against their diminishing role and status *vis-à-vis* the bureaucracy.

The Emirates

Problems of amalgamation of a different sort exist in the Emirates. Though seemingly small in size, the UAE has the highest ratio of defence forces to civilian population in the world, having to defend only a quarter of a million UAE indigenous citizens (and three times as many immigrants). Primarily this is because each of the stronger Emirates insists on maintaining its own separate military force and even purchases its own weapons, regardless of the formal military merger which took place in May 1976. The troops are stationed under distinct commands which correspond to the sheikhdoms of the UAE, although Abu Dhabi supplies 75 percent of its own troops to the UAE's forces. This fragile situation could spell disaster if conflict were to erupt within the UAE or between Ras al-Khaimah and Oman.

Iraq

Power struggles within the military could prove to be just as unsettling as rivalries between the regular armies and the militias. In Iraq, the Sunni-dominated Iraqi military élite, primarily of Takrit origin, has always been suspicious of anyone outside their clique. To ensure that their control continues they promote their fellow-Ba'athists over others whose loyalty they question. But the military cannot be isolated and depoliticized as the regimes would like it to be. Consequently the regime has strengthened its own militia, the People's Army.[1] Iraq's Ba'athist Revolutionary Command Council is no longer dominated by army officers, and it tries to keep track of undesirable trends developing in the military through thousands of Ba'athist commissars who, apart from spreading the Party's message, inspect the officers and report back on their conduct and political views. It follows that the militia's present head, Deputy Prime Minister Taha Yasin Ramadan, has great political power. Such mechanisms, which are being increasingly resented by the military and could not, in any case, create genuine loyalty, are nevertheless essential for the regime's rule in a country which has known many attempts by the military to seize power since 1936. Occasional purges of the army's higher ranks enabled the Party to assert itself over the military, though this did not eliminate the continuous rift between the civilian and military wings within the Ba'ath which are still jockeying for power.

But whereas the former President, Ahmad Hasan al-Bakr, himself a professional soldier, earned the respect of the military who regarded him as their own representative, the likelihood of Saddam Hussein winning their support seems highly questionable, especially following the war with Iran which has tarnished the military's image. If anything, the putting on of a general's uniform without ever having served in the army only antagonized the officer corps. This could not be altered by the generous pay increase he gave the army. The military have always resented Hussein, regarding him as a threat to their supremacy. This manifested itself in the attempted coups of 1970 and 1973 when he maintained control over the Party's militia and strove to eliminate anyone who stood in his way. The most recent purge which accompanied Hussein's final promotion was designed to enable him to consolidate his position as President and also to warn the army against any disloyalty. However conflict at the top may well resurface and might again destabilize the country.

---

1 By 1978, it had a strength of 75,000. In 1981 it is 300,000 strong and many of these are with Iraqi forces in Iran, probably to forestall any dangers of an uprising there.

Iran

In Iran confrontation between the 'clergy' on the one hand and the military and their supporters on the other seems imminent, especially because of the way the war with Iraq has been going. Since it came to power the new Iranian regime has been suspicious of the military which was, in fact, seriously disorganized. Lacking spare parts for the sophisticated equipment which had escaped rust, and suffering from mass desertion and low morale, the Iranian army was further weakened by the new regime's policy. Apart from purging the army, the new government set up an independent 30,000 strong para-military force, the Pasdaran (the Revolutionary Guards) who are unquestionably loyal to the 'clergy'. Nevertheless the militia's training was entrusted to the army (which resented this task) while the Revolutionary Guards continued in their attempts to discipline and subdue the military to their control through thousands of Mullahs who were assigned to all units, serving as political and spiritual commissars. It was soon obvious, however, that the newly established urban Pasdaran could not fulfil even the duties of maintaining law and order: and their image was further tarnished in their confrontation with the Kurds and the Azerbaijanis. Specially formed army units were called in and carried out their task somewhat reluctantly. They remembered that Khomeini was still executing soldiers.

Of graver consequence was the failure of the Iranian army, once the most powerful force in the region, to defend Iran from the Iraqi invasion. However the army soon became a focal point for expressing Persian nationalism. Under whatever Iranian regime, the cry for revanchism will be salient and will shape future relations not only with Iraq but with the other Arab states in the region. And that will mean a prominent role for Iran's military which would not only prove a potent threat to long-term regional stability but also a focus for alternative internal power.

In fact, such a competition surfaced between the acting head of the army, (then President Bani Sadr) and the Mullahs. The latter, fearing his growing influence, were ready to go as far as to create obstacles for him. Soldiers even charged the divines with not allocating money needed for the war and criticized them for interfering with the conduct of the war. Neither the tenacity nor courage shown by the Pasdaran in Khuzistan allowed them to regain their position. It is obvious, however, that they would not easily give in and the Mullahs, by unseating Bani Sadr, finally managed to assume control over the military. Despite its reduced military capabilities and the fact that it lacks a large part of its chain of command, the Iranian army might still pose a threat to Khomeini and certainly to any less popular successor. When the confrontation between the Pasdaran and the army takes place, the former could hardly prove a match for the latter, assuming that the military leadership acts in harmony. However, as events are showing, the real challenge to the Mullahs comes from the armed left or from a radical Muslim-Leftist alliance which may be assisted by a number of high-ranking officers. Such a coalition might be able to take control of the country. On the other hand, the military, fearing a leftist takeover might, in anticipation of the latter's reaction, instigate a coup to forestall such a danger. Either way the military could enter as an 'accepted' arbiter, and might prove themselves the only force under the circumstances able to enforce the resumption of full oil production needed for the domestic economy and for restoring the military machine.

Military modernization

In the Peninsula, cash is found more easily than local manpower. The sums used to augment these states' military capability are staggering, commanding a large share of the total budget. Following the unrest in Mecca and in the Eastern Province, Saudi Arabia increased defence spending by 18 percent for the year 1980/81 to 19.8 billion dollars. The UAE has, as noted earlier, the highest per capita defence expenditure in the world. In 1980 it reached 1.26 billion dollars or 40 percent of the total budget.[1] In other states it was about 20 percent.[2] Spending vast amounts of money on defence does not seem to have negative effects for it does not come necessarily at the expense of the needs of local (and immigrant) population. But in Oman, Iraq and even Saudi Arabia, alienated segments of the population (Dhofaris in Oman and Shi'is in Iraq and Saudi Arabia) realize that the cost of military modernization not only deprives them of economic reforms but is, in fact, directed largely against them, especially when, as in some of these states, they are excluded from the military. Such priorities could come to trigger unrest — as indeed was the case in Iran. Under such conditions military modernization reinforces rather than defuses internal contradictions.

Military modernization is accompanied by Western (and Soviet)[3] experts and instructors, often with their dependents. In places like Saudi Arabia and Iran, this irritates the religious establishment because of all the effects of such a visible foreign presence and the ensuing process of westernization. There are already nearly 2,000 American military personnel on Saudi soil and over 300 British officers and NCOs in Oman whose number will shortly grow if Chieftain tanks reach the Sultanate.

The diversification of arms-suppliers, which aims at diminishing a country's dependence on its sole supplier, with all the attached military and political implications of limiting a patron's leverage over the client, creates additional problems. Not only is that state's military capability seriously affected by the need to grapple with problems flowing from the existence of a number of different kinds of weapons, their absorption and maintenance, but such a process means the influx of even more

---

1 *Strategy Week*, 11-17 August 1980, p 5.

2 For further details see IISS, *Military Balance 1980-81*.

3 Indeed this was a problem for Kuwait which was reluctant to allow the presence of Soviet instructors and technicians on its soil, and confronted the opposition of its main arms-supplier, the US, which was uneasy about the possibility of its sophisticated weapons reaching the hands of the USSR. (See also A. Cottrell, *The Persian Gulf, op.cit.*, p 166.) Nevertheless Egyptian instructors trained Kuwaitis in previously purchased Soviet weapons.

foreign military experts. The latter serves to underline the chronic inability of these states to run their own armies without foreigners. An ultra-modern arsenal can only be operated with external assistance and this could create destabilizing anti-foreign sentiments among the local officers. It follows that leaning toward western European arms producers may not necessarily pay the hoped-for political dividends. This is especially true of Iraq, unless it gradually replaces all its Soviet equipment with say, French weapons, taking advantage of Iran's present military weakness.

The concentration of large quantities of arms in the hands of the military grants the army a capability to seize power. Middle Eastern history is full of examples of coups, counter-coups and aborted coups. Iraq's regime, having already experienced 20 such coups, is prone to such a danger: and Kuwait is not immune, despite the 'clean' political record of its army until now. The stronger Saudi Arabia's army gets, the more difficult it will be for the National Guard to defend the monarch against a coup instigated by or backed by the other armed services. The National Guard is already reported to have prevented a number of coup attempts by the regular army.

The Gulf armed forces now include highly politicized, ambitious officers who will doubtless demand accelerated modernization of the armed forces. Older commissioned ranks are being gradually replaced by eager, young academy-trained officers, many of whom were exposed in the course of their instruction to new ideas. These might come to present a real threat to the present regimes.[1] Arab officers returning from military training in the West[2] or the USSR, could cast their lot with educated revolutionaries of one type or another. Enlarging the officer corps increases the chances of a military coup and isolating the army from the main centres of population in a number of large, self-contained military cities (like those in Tabuk near Jordan, Khamis Mushait near the Yemens or the planned King Khalid City near the Iraqi-Kuwait border) may not necessarily enable a dynasty to stifle disaffection, though it might provide it with much-needed time.

Modern weapons, supersonic fighters and different types of missiles do not serve to protect the regime internally. The Iranian military forces may have had the capacity to contain the Iraqis, to put an end to the Dhofari war and enable the Shah to assert himself regionally, but it proved a weak instrument at home once the soldiers were forced to confront their unarmed but adamant fellow-citizens.

1   It is estimated that some 5,000 Saudi officers underwent such intensive courses. (See also *Ruz al-Yusuf* daily, Cairo, 28 January 1980.)

2   Qatar News Agency quoted Kuwait's Minister of State for Cabinet Affairs as saying that matters were settled with the Kuwaiti cadets in the Infantry College and that there was no trouble there. Doha, 27 November 1979.

Whether the regimes can depend on their armies as pillars of their own regimes and prevent them, in spite of constantly swelling ranks, from becoming a threat to their own existences remains to be seen. The policy of military modernization — like some other facets of rapid transformation — is a two-edged sword.

PART II

POLICY CHOICES:
MANAGING CHANGE IN AN
UNCERTAIN ENVIRONMENT

The various 'agents of change' and potential locally-generated sources of conflict raise questions about the adequacy of governmental mechanisms for attaining stability. The next section examines selective governmental policies and the role and capacity of existing political institutions in an attempt to evaluate the regimes' policy choices when facing the challenges and trying to contain them.

8 Industrialization

If I were to use economic justification for every project I try to build in Saudi Arabia, then we would not build many of these projects..... Our primary goal here is to change a human being from illiterate to literate — to educate our people. How can you put a price tag on that?[1]

Encouraged by their enormous financial surpluses and motivated primarily by non-economic considerations, Gulf governments have competed with one another in rushing to modernize along western lines. Prestige played a dominant role in decision making. Determined to achieve the unthinkable and seeking to demonstrate their power and economic 'capability', all rulers have aimed at bolstering their internal, inter-Arab and international political position through industrialization. One result has been little, if any, regional economic co-ordination. This will prove costly, especially for those whose oil expectancy is shorter.

This trend has been reflected in development plans: government expenditure (apart from Iraq) was in many cases planned in excess of their rapidly rising revenues. Adopting stricter measures could have perhaps enabled the richer states at least to come to terms with some of the economic and social problems prompted by rapid industrial development. This is not to say that they ignored the social and political implications of rapid modernization and diversification, which in turn means

1 Mr. Faisal al-Bashir, the Saudi Government's Deputy Planning Minister in an interview — see Youssef M. Ibrahim 'Saudi Arabia determined to modernize despite monetary, social price' in *New York Times*, 7 March 1980.

ever growing dependence on an imported workforce, but that they placed themselves, willingly, in a delicate position despite their understanding of those built-in implications. The alternative courses of action open to them is a subject for debate.

'Diversification' means waste?

Endowed with a cheap and available source of energy, all Gulf governments attempted to diversify their economy so as to create alternative sources of income to this non-replenishable asset. 'Exchanging hydrocarbon resources for modernization', as one oil minister put it, 'is geared to assuring the oil producers' economic future.' With this in mind, a handsome slice of the budget was allocated to building non-oil as well as oil-related heavy industries which included processing plants for steel and aluminium, fertilizers, petrochemicals and refining. Unlike Third World states, the overriding drive towards industrialization as such was not merely to provide employment but for the sake of creating non-oil income alternatives.[1] In fact between 1974 and 1979, over 250 billion dollars were spent by the Gulf regimes (excluding Iran and Iraq) to modernize their primitive economies. However, excessive spending on ambitious industrial schemes, inadequate planning, the absence of an economic rationale justifying the projects, rising inflation, budgetary and balance of payment deficits were all part of the 'modernization fever' which swept the region. The Saudi First Five Year Plan's actual expenditure totalled 23.4 billion dollars. The Second Plan (1975-80) went far beyond its planned 142 billion dollars and the Third Plan, while officially set at 235 billion dollars, is expected to pump another 300 billion dollars into the Kingdom's economy to accelerate the already frantic pace of development. Not even the Grand Mosque incident has prompted the Saudis to slow down modernization though it did encourage them to change certain policies and to shift their focus.

Earlier IMF experts warned the Saudis against any abrupt change in their fiscal policy which could have a negative effect on the local private sector they wanted to encourage.[2] The Saudis were also advised to restrain their growth, to pursue a sober, gradual rise of oil prices and to

---

1 See 'Economic Problems of Arabian Peninsula Oil States' in S. Chubin (ed.), *op.cit.*, pp 38-57.

2 Quotations from an allegedly IMF unpublished report appeared in *Middle East Economic Digest*, 19 October 1979, pp 6-9.

refrain from sharp increases which could backfire[1] owing to their world-wide implication. They were also recommended to spend less on heavy industry so as not to squander resources or create 'white elephants', to invest more in developing human resources and traditional economic activities rather than in infrastructure, and to control the rocketing prices of projects by budgeting for the medium term rather than on an annual basis. Other Gulf states were urged to establish a similar list of priorities. But this was to no avail, especially when this advice confronted urgings to the contrary on the part of private western consultants who had vested interests in accelerating economic development and who — like the regimes themselves — were interested in short-term results.

By 1978 the non-oil sector's contribution to the gross domestic product (GDP) was reported to be quite impressive — despite the parallel process of cooling down the economy and cutting back on schemes in mid-1977, which was reflected in the decline of imports, budget expenditure cuts and the consequent drop in inflation (estimated at 18 percent in 1978). In 1979 the oil price rise gave the Saudi government a surplus of 20 percent.[2] The magnitude of the new industrial schemes in Yanbu (on the Red Sea) and Jubail (on the Gulf), where the Saudis are building hydrocarbon, petrochemical and metal industries as well as other projects, leaves no doubt as to the direction the Saudis are taking.

Yet even in the long run it is difficult to see these big industrial projects as income-generating assets which would justify their economic investment. Harsh climatic conditions, leading to vast sums spent on annual maintenance and low production rates, and the relatively high cost of foreign labour, coupled with difficult conditions in the world

1 The issue of oil pricing is outside the scope of this study. It should be pointed out, however, that unlike other Gulf states, large new oil fields are discovered every year in Saudi Arabia which, at the present rate of production, would have oil for at least the next 50 years. Sharp oil price increases could prove counter-productive to the vast desert empire (which would need an enormous annual income just to sustain what has been already created) simply because such price rises would force the industrialized world to nuclearize and devote more attention to substitutional sources of energy faster than would otherwise be the case. As for the more immediate future, Saudi Arabia's planned industrial projects are mainly gas-associated or spin-off industries. Moreover, damaging the western economic system (which is interdependent with the economy of the desert kingdom) is feared also for political reasons. The Saudi regime is worried that under such conditions it will deprive itself of the indispensable American support, if not bring about the seizure of the oil fields. Saudi Arabia stepped up its oil production (10.3 mbd.) once the Iraqi-Iranian war broke out, to compensate for what was lost, and went as far as to create a world glut to keep prices down. It is through such measures that the Saudi regime is trying to deepen the west's commitment to Gulf security.

2 James Buxton 'Kingdom's fortunes are soaring' in *Financial Times* Supplement on Saudi Arabia, 28 April 1980.

markets and international competition could all work against them being profitable.

Even in the Sultanate of Oman, the poorest amongst the oil producers, there is little indication to suggest that Sultan Qabus is motivated solely by economic considerations. He is confident that the mere presence of oil and the recent discovery of new oil deposits, along with Oman's strategic importance, will eventually grant him the unconditional Arab and western economic and military aid he seeks. This has been reflected in Oman's growing deficit which, in 1979, was estimated at 312 million dollars. In that respect Sultan Qabus behaved as if his country can afford expenditures as high as the surplus economies of his neighbours. Yet, unlike other Gulf rulers, he has not so far invested in 'white elephants'. Industrialization on a small scale was introduced only on his accession in 1970.

Unlike Bahrain, which is a tiny island where oil was discovered early in the 1930s and whose reserves will dry up in a few years[1], Oman is a late-comer to the oil producers and started exporting only in 1967 yet its proven oil reserves are currently only ten times annual production. Oil production peaked in 1976 (134 million barrels) dropping the following year to 123 million. In 1979 it exported only 107 million barrels, 7 percent less than in the previous year. The recent discovery of oil in the northern part of the Dhofar province could account for an increase in oil production, estimated to reach about 120 million barrels in 1981.

On the other hand Bahrain was aided by Britain in establishing the foundations for economic development and in embarking on an early and logical diversification, whereas Oman remained a backward country up to the 1970s. Nevertheless, Oman was quick to take advantage of her relatively meagre oil reserves. Her light crude fetches high prices. This has enabled Sultan Qabus to channel large sums into the country's backward economy which also relies increasingly on foreign financial aid (mainly from Kuwait). But the high cost of the war in Dhofar and the considerable sums being spent on the expansion of Oman's armed forces (40 percent of the budget) have slowed down Oman's economic progress. Now, however, more money is being allocated to economic growth. The 1980 budget was estimated at 2.87 billion dollars of which oil revenues were expected to come to 2.72 billion dollars. The ambitious Five Year Plan beginning in 1981 is expected to cost more than 20 billion dollars, which seems to show that the mistakes made by other Gulf states have not been heeded.

1 Bahrain's oil production in 1980 was 47,500 barrels a day, decreasing at a rate of 4% a year. Its 1980-81 budget of 1,803 dollars (though up 20% on the previous two year period) reflected this factor.

Whereas the richer states (including Qatar) emphasized industrialization, Bahrain has concentrated more on the non-energy consuming industries such as dry docks, banking, communications, insurance and tourism. In doing so Bahrain appreciated its limitations as well as some of the consequences of an accelerated growth, opting for strengthening those components of its economy which could prove 'indispensable' to the economies of the oil-endowed states like Saudi Arabia, Kuwait and the UAE. In fact, Bahrain was already in 1978 drawing roughly 40 percent of its 0.4 billion dollars income from non-oil sources. Taking advantage of its geographical position, its relatively well established infrastructure and the business acumen of its inhabitants, Bahrain emerged as a regional centre through entrepôt activities, tax-free short-funding offshore banking units (OBUs) system, its sophisticated international communication centre and its recreation facilities. The income derived from these and other industrial projects helped to balance the budget despite an oil income which has been declining since 1970. Bahrain received a boost to its economy by the demise of Beirut as a result of the war in Lebanon and is aided by Saudi Arabia — with whom Bahrain shares an offshore field and for whom it serves as an extension of its banking system. Nevertheless, it has encountered severe competition from Dubai's entrepôt trade and dry docks as well as from the UAE's offshore banking system. It has also suffered lately from Kuwait's newly-imposed restrictions on liquid assets and reserve requirements which was intended to reduce the flow of funds to the island.

Kuwait, with its large concentration of banking firms and financial companies and with its determination to slow down the growth of non-profitable industries (which would turn its citizens into a minority in their own country), is now concentrating on banking and equities (held both at home and, especially, abroad) rather than on heavy industrialization. But, unlike Qatar, Kuwait did not cut government spending on infrastructure and services, even though in the mid-1970s the government cancelled a number of projects[1] and it decided in April 1980 to further cut oil production from 2 million barrels a day to 1.5 million barrels a day. Oil revenues rose with higher prices, still leaving it in surplus. Given Kuwait's proven oil reserves (estimated at 71.2 billion barrels), oil would comfortably serve as an 'insurance policy' for the next fifty years, guaranteeing the expansion of Kuwait as a financial rather than an industrial centre. But such a course of action, which implies duplication within the region, is likely to cripple the poorer countries like Bahrain, Qatar, and even Dubai, because bolstering Kuwait's financial position in this way can only be at the expense of

1 See *Middle East Economic Digest*, 18 July 1975. But thereafter others were licensed in the hope they would serve as an economic incentive to the local entrepreneurs.

others, especially once their own oil dries up. This in turn might create a new situation of 'haves' and 'have-nots' within the Gulf,[1] adding yet another element to the region's instability.

The second set of questions relates to some of the social and political costs of industrialization rather than the choices of economic policies *per se*. The main dilemma confronting the Gulf regimes is how to continue the process of modernization and simultaneously cushion themselves against the threats engendered by this rapid transformation.[2] Economic policies have far-reaching social and demographic effects which in turn raise other problems, challenging the power structure of each of the regimes. They may be forced to redraw their list of priorities.

---

1   With oil becoming for the less endowed states an indispensable source of revenue the Peninsula might witness the surfacing of old conflicts which centre around boundaries, continental shelves and oil fields. (See R. Litwak's book on inter-state conflicts in this series.) Discovery of new oil could in itself prove destabilizing, therefore.

2   The above mentioned article by Y. Ibrahim, *New York Times*, 7 March 1980 also quotes a senior member of the Royal Family who holds a key government post as saying: 'Saudi Arabia 'is determined to develop and to pay the price that comes with that in terms of social change. Change will come to this country even if it means that, with education and industrialization, we will have to put up with alien ideologies and cultures such as leftist tendencies'.

The 'enrichment policy': indigenous manifestations

Concentration of wealth in few hands is a feature common to all Gulf states. To mitigate this, governments, social welfare disbursement, patronage, gifts, pay-offs, interest-free loans, 'development funds' and subsidies — all of which constitute the non-wage income enjoyed by the unskilled which is easily spent rather than used as an investment — have tried to redistribute wealth but this has proved to be economically counter-productive for it does not involve the nomadic and rural sections of the population in the actual development of 'their' state. These unconditional payments are not only militating against the local population's change of life style, but are in fact crippling even the traditional subsistence-oriented rural economy which is in the hands of the relatively non-productive older generation. In that respect modernization has failed to accommodate the bulk of the Gulf's pastoral, nomadic and rural population which cannot easily be converted to an industrial society.

A more constructive alternative with regard to the Bedouin in Saudi Arabia would be to try to integrate them into modern society by harnessing their traditional way of life to serve the economy. This could be achieved through range-land projects which would restore nomadic pastoralism with the purpose of encouraging them to raise animals for the meat market rather than to maintain large herds as a mark of wealth. This would provide for gradual 'absorption' of the Bedouin and allow those who want to retain their lifestyle to do so. A pre-requisite for such a policy, however, is the gradual phasing-out of the different types of donations the Bedouin receive as part of the 'enrichment policy' for, without an economic incentive, there is little chance of the Bedouin selling their flocks in the markets. Of course, to stop abruptly such unconditional payments after they have been given for years while other sectors of the population continue to enjoy wealth would prove extremely difficult and politically undesirable.

The urban population is also seeking to take advantage of the new situation. This does not mean that they are becoming participants in the productive workforce, rather that they are attempting to exploit the situation to their own benefit. Kuwait and the UAE could serve as examples where the proliferating, speculative real-estate, financing and overbanking have left their negative mark on the economy, with most private businesses being directed at short-term gains at the expense of a government interested in developing long-term diversification. Local businessmen pride themselves on being able to manipulate the system through their personal contacts in the administration which enable them to receive special loans etc. This in turn has given a boost to the notion of *umulah* — to be interpreted loosely as a 'commission' paid

122

to those who handle the mediation as the go-betweens — without whom Western firms would find it impossible to operate. Enormous sums of these corrupting payments are thus spread within a thin layer of society, adding another element to the constantly changing social pyramid.

Speaking about the imminent dangers emanating from greed and corruption practised by his neighbours, President Saddam Hussein said in summer 1980:

> Some Arab rulers have followed their personal interests, being concerned with gratifying their own desires and increasing their riches, while neglecting their responsibilities and the affairs of the people. Some of these rulers have become so covetous in heaping millions of dollars into millions, that these millions and tens of millions have not been enough for them, but their wealth has expanded into billions of dollars. These riches are being plundered from the wealth of the people.[1]

Indeed, increasingly this is how many people in the Peninsula are coming to view things. They are told they are the richest citizens on earth and yet they feel that whatever they get is insufficient. They want a far greater share of the oil revenues without having to work for it. The present mechanism by which wealth is dispensed means that the big cities, where the merchants and the Royal Families live, get the lion's share. Those excluded or not 'compensated', as they believe they ought to be, are disenchanted with their portion. More people believe they have the right to know how 'their' money is being spent for not all of them are impressed with industrialization and its associated facilities, which, in practice, have little meaning for them. From the external media and talks with people they come to appreciate many of these projects as a waste. They also learn about the behaviour of the royal courts abroad and many of them do not share their rulers' view that they should be grateful for what they are given.

So, once practised, the 'enrichment policy' becomes a problem in itself. On the one hand the wealth that is distributed becomes eventually insufficient. On the other hand, rather than strengthening the cohesiveness of society, the unevenly distributed wealth further fragments the indigenous population, creating envy and potential antagonism between the rich and the less affluent and between the rulers and the ruled. This is true even in oil-less Bahrain where, as elsewhere in the Gulf, people are coming to question secretly their rulers' economic policies. The question is whether the ruling dynasties are mindful of the warning contained in the message of the greatest Arab historian, Ibn Khaldun,

---

1 Speech on the anniversary of the 17th July Revolution — Press Release by Embassy of the Republic of Iraq, London.

who cautioned:

> The things that go with luxury and submergence in life of ease break the vigour of group feeling, which alone produces superiority. When group feeling is destroyed, the tribe is no longer able to defend or protect itself, let alone press any claims. It will be swallowed up by other nations.[1]

Nevertheless, most regimes are convinced that, on balance, the economic benefits to the individual would outweigh all the other disruptive costs involved and that a firm commitment to such progress would earn them the wide popular support they yearn for rather than undermine their own power base. However more members of the royal courts are having second thoughts. There are already signs that some of the regimes are feeling uneasy that things are getting out of control, with their economies developing too far too fast. A more cautious note is discernible in recent economic decision making. Qatar was one of the first states to control expansion, reduce inflation and cut oil production. The UAE ordered a reduction in pumping oil by 80,000 barrels a day by 1981-82. Its industrialization scheme is coming under scrutiny with a great deal of rethinking as to the benefits of such plans. If it is impossible to admit failure in public, it is still likely that the regime will cut duplication within the UAE itself and attend to more immediate problems. Indeed there are those who suggest that, as the sheikhdoms (with the exception of Bahrain) are low absorbers by virtue of their relative high oil production and small population, a more sensible path would be to increase investments abroad and become 'rentiers'.

But a drastic cut in the pace of industrialization, with which the regimes may eventually be contented, could mean not only severe western and inter-Arab pressures but also the surfacing of serious internal upheaval with neither the lower strata of the local community nor the immigrant population willingly accepting a course of action which forces a revision of their expectations and aspirations.

---

1 Ibn Khaldun *The Muqaddimah, an introduction to history* translated and edited by Franz Rosenthal, Princeton, 1967, Volume I, p 287. Ibn Khaldun (d. 1406).

The demographic dimension

> The truth is that every additional job provided by a project will have to go to a non-national, and this will in turn entail considerable added investment in services and infrastructure..... I'd hate to see a series of White Elephants draining the economies of the oil exporting countries under the guise of industrialization.[1]

Diversification inevitably means the presence of more foreigners in the Gulf which in turn disturbs the social fabric. Without the immigrants, industrialization could not take place. Even with the projects currently under way and the present level of spending the numbers of immigrants will increase.[2] By the mid-1980s, an additional two million expatriates are expected to join the more than two million foreigners already working in the Gulf. The indigenous population, particularly in the UAE, are increasingly feeling that they are being swamped and their identity diluted. Calls are heard for drastic reductions of the concentrations of non-nationals. 'The safety of the homeland and the protection of society against the internal dangers is a national duty that is no less important than defending the country against foreign dangers' said the editorial of the *al-Ittihad* daily in Abu Dhabi (17 September 1979). It went on:

> The state which spares neither funds nor man in the defence of the homeland's borders, airspace, waters and territory is at the same time seeking to safeguard its internal structure so that there will be no imbalance and so that its citizens do not become a small minority in a sea of foreign communities......... we do not want to bequeath our sons a homeland whose identity has been defaced.

The plea reflects the growing fear of nations throughout the Gulf who are disenchanted by this rising tide of immigration which could jeopardize the social, cultural, and ultimately, the political identity of the city states and seriously affect that of the larger states. The protest against this 'open door' policy is indirectly against the pace of development which determines the need for additional manpower. It is dawning upon many people that both control of the pace of change and the reins of government are gradually slipping out of their hands and that their leaders are simply ignoring the threat or are powerless to do anything about it.

---

1   Ali Khalifah Al Sabah, Kuwait's Under Secretary Ministry of Finance's words in November 1976 — see *Middle East Economic Survey*, Volume 20, No. 4, November 1976, pp 1-2.

2   'Saudi Arabia's foreign labour force growth exceeded by 75%.' See David Sherriff 'Consensus back Saudi political stability', *Middle East Economic Digest*, 30 November 1979.

In an attempt to regulate immigration, to limit the expatriates' presence and to prevent them from acquiring the means which would enable them to translate their *de facto* presence to a *de jure* one, the governments have made visas and work permits more difficult to obtain. They have also enacted a number of complementary nationality, labour, property and business laws[1] aimed at preventing the long-established immigrants from having citizens' rights or being naturalized, unless the governments deem this necessary.[2]

Those caught violating these laws were deported. The Saudis expelled in 1979 some 80,000 immigrants who tried to enter the Kingdom, remain there illegally after the *hajj*, or whose contracts terminated,[3] as well as a few Arab expatriates suspected of political activity. A few of the latter category were also found among the 18,000 foreigners Kuwait has recently deported.[4] Qatar also followed with a crackdown on employment irregularities but the Gulf states have found it extremely difficult to confront the labour-supplying companies which sprang up in the Arab world, India, Pakistan and the Far East[5] to exploit the situation. Moreover, the authorities have not been able to prevent the old phenomenon of clandestine immigration[6] from the Yemens, Iraq, Jordan and Egypt. Many of those who opted for illegal entry were unskilled workers who took advantage of the Peninsula's long, unpatrolled

---

1 For further reading see Enid Hill 'The modernization of labour in the Arab Gulf states: an interpretation of political economy with special reference to labour laws' in *Man and Society, op.cit.* pp 257-373 and A. Hill, *Population Migration, op.cit.* pp 67-8.

2 A few Omanis and Yemenis (some of whom were political exiles) managed in the 1960s to become naturalized in Saudi Arabia. In the UAE and Qatar this was more common in the early 1970s. Kuwait also naturalized many Bedouin (she has a two-stage nationality procedure). The prime motivation of these regimes was to balance the number of expatriates by granting a civil status to those believed to be loyal to the dynasties.

3 Interior Minister Prince Na'if Ibn al-Aziz said on Saudi television that the Kingdom is determined to fight such malpractice and that the authorities were examining ways of narrowing down the huge number of immigrants which since November 1978 amounted to 1 million who were joined by another half a million dependants (*Middle East Economic Digest*, 26 October 1979). In the first part of 1980, 11,000 people were expelled from Jiddah alone (*al-Jazirah*, 16 April 1980).

4 *al-Hadaf*, weekly, Kuwait 17 January 1980.

5 The government of Thailand opened a labour department office in Saudi Arabia to investigate malpractices by Thai export companies which take money from immigrants without finding them jobs, send agricultural workers presenting them as skilled labourers, and smuggle workers into Saudi Arabia. The Thais were reported to be considering opening a similar office in Iraq. (*MEED*, 25 January 1980, pp 40-41 and February 1980, Special Report p 11).

6 *Monday Morning* weekly (Beirut, 26 May 1980) quoted *al-Ittihad* the semi-official UAE newspaper which wrote that 35% of the immigrants are illegally resident in the country.

borders.[1] For others, forged papers and bribes for middlemen have ensured the provision of visas, with local sponsors granting asylum in exchange for low paid employment.[2] Thus the governments' attempts to 'balance' the inflow of skilled workers with the departure of similar groups has proved impossible to operate owing to the economic boom which has, if anything, demanded an even larger workforce and made the Gulf a magnet.

In the meantime, governments are troubled by the steady rise in the urban population and are trying to reduce the numbers of immigrants flocking to the cities. Housing projects were planned for the sizable pop-opulations working in the industrial sites (such as Yanbu and Jubail in Saudi Arabia, Shuaiba in Kuwait, Umm Sa'id in Qatar, Jabal Ali in Dubai and Ruwais in Abu Dhabi) which were in many cases planned to be some distance away from the towns. Decentralization of both industry and population in selected parts of the Gulf is seen also as a security precaution as it would be easier to isolate a remote place should unrest surface among the immigrants. It would also limit contact with the local population. The authorities believe that with modern recreat-ional facilities provided at those working centres but not available in the towns, there would be little leisure incentive for the immigrants to flock to the cities after working hours. However, should the governments modernize the areas adjacent to the industrial complexes where the expatriates are temporarily housed, then these would soon become towns. Though admittedly they would be foreign communities,[3] the cultural and political risks they pose to the regimes could be severe, requiring the security forces to cope with large and potentially disloyal groups. Such towns, of course, would demand schools, clinics, hospitals, social services and mosques. Should the governments not provide the immigrants with anything beyond their basic needs, this too could be a source of discontent.

Kuwait's segregation policies, which prohibit immigrants from own-ing property, were designed to protect Kuwait's own citizens[4] but this

1 Even Bahrain, an island, found it difficult to track down such a movement conducted by professional 'go-betweens'. But because most immigrants preferred the richer oil-producing states the burden on Bahrain's authorities was relatively small.

2 *al-Bilad* Saudi Arabia, 20 December 1979 quotes a police commander who complains about this phenomenon. *Ukaz* reported on 27 April 1981 that 9,400 illegal immigrants were caught in Jiddah alone. Kuwait announced she would severely punish anyone co-operating in aiding illegal immigrants (*al-Ra'i al-Am* daily, Kuwait 15 March 1980). The press reported the arrests of many Egyptians who infiltrated Kuwait (*Mar'at al-Ummah* 13 May 1981).

3 Bahrain is an exception in that the new Isa town (35,000) houses both locals and immi-grants. The same applies to the other planned towns.

4 Businesses require 51% Kuwaiti ownership.

could also create among the immigrants the unrest which Kuwait hopes to avoid by granting them certain social and health services.[1] Up to now the economic interests of both the host states and the Arab expatriates have complemented one another yet, once the immigrants start taking social benefits for granted they could cease to be a force of stability and start to protest against discrimination.

The lessons of countries such as Malaysia and Singapore have not gone unlearnt. The Gulf regimes' predicament is clear: so long as the immigrants are effectively excluded from political life, they become resentful, especially if their living conditions are poor; but granting them a degree of participation and a more adequate share of financial rewards may encourage them to stay, thus further diluting the local population. Thus the Gulf regimes tend to compromise, providing the immigrants with better facilities so as to reduce their economic grievances while not granting them any political rights. The argument is used that if the expatriates do not like it they can always leave.

Levying tax on migrant earnings or remittances as a means of diminishing the economic incentive is practically impossible and politically undesirable, though the larger states may consider adopting the Libyan model which stipulates that the expatriates' transfer of earnings outside Libya is restricted to 60 percent of their salaries if they work in urban centres but 90 percent if they work and live on a desert site — an economic measure geared to moving expatriates to the countryside which might prove more desirable politically.

The Gulf regimes have calculated that their leverage over *non-Arab* workers would be greater than over Arabs and they therefore opted for gradually replacing the potentially-politicized Arab labour force with the more obedient and politically docile Asian and Oriental workers, hoping that this in itself would make the Arab expatriates more amenable. Experts have forecast that, by 1985, more than a million Asian and Far Eastern workers are expected in the Gulf[2] forming about 60 percent of the expatriate workforce. Ten years earlier, in 1975, there were only 15,000 Asian immigrants. Thus with construction outpacing manufacturing and with the expansion of the service sector, a new type of expatriate could flood the labour market.

As far as the local governments are concerned, the Far Eastern immigrants who have no roots in the region and have a vested interest in

---

1 Bahrain, which is far from being affluent, might consider a change of policy for, in the words of the Director of Labour 'expatriates are costing Bahrain too much money (265 million dollars a year)' *Gulf Mirror* weekly, Bahrain 3 January 1981.

2 Finding presented by S. Birks and C. Sinclair in Arab Gulf Studies Conference held in Exeter University, June 1979.

the stability of the political system, are more 'convenient':[1] they are brought in by an Eastern contractor and are expected to leave once the project is completed. They live apart in self-contained cantonments, are accustomed to a modest way of life and low salary, and carry little influence over the local population — even if the authorities may suspect that some of them may have a communist 'label', an 'affiliation' with the West[2] or previous military training.[3] There are, however, those who warn that history in the Gulf could repeat itself with expatriates rising and taking over the cities — as happened in the ninth century at the height of Islamic power when the imported East African blacks revolted.[4]

But the inter-Arab implications of the so-called 'oriental and asian connection' could be far-reaching for North Yemen, Jordan and Egypt — all of whom depend heavily on the Gulf absorbing their surplus manpower, even if this deprives them of much of their best trained personnel which, in turn, hampers their own economic growth.[5] A reduction in opportunities abroad would create unemployment in these states which could in turn create unrest. No economic aid could substitute for the enormous indirect 'subsidy' paid by the Gulf States to the citizens of Yemen, Jordan and Egypt through transferred earnings. Moreover, should the Arab immigrants feel threatened by the waves of Asian and Oriental workers, who would lessen the Gulf's dependence on them, they themselves may react politically in the host countries.

Ironically, those whom the Gulf regimes would most like to replace

1 Also see Birks and Sinclair, *UAE op. cit.* p 26 and *Qatar op. cit.* p 30.

2 Iraq condemned the UAE for taking in South Koreans, 'the American imperialistic agents' who will facilitiate the US.'endeavouring to use a new form of indirect intervention through its world's agents and tools' in order to maintain oil supplies (*Baghdad Observer*, 12 September 1978).

3 Arguing that it is not the Palestinian immigrants who need to be feared, especially when they have proved their loyalty, *al-Kifah al-Arabi* (Lebanon, 29 September 1979) argued in its article that it is rather the Koreans and the Pakistanis who are connected to the West and when given the sign they would use their military expertise. But Amir Na'if, the Minister of Interior, announced that he is not troubled by the fact that the South Koreans have undergone compulsory military training in their country as part of their conscription (*al-Jumhur*, Lebanon 5 June 1980).

4 Mohammad Shaaban's words in the Exeter University Conference *op.cit.* — in *Arab Oil and Economic Review*.

5 Already in December 1978 the Jordanian government ordered a stop to the emigration of skilled workers from both the West Bank and the East Bank. Recent statistics show that 77,000 workers left for Saudi Arabia, Kuwait and the UAE (*al-Quds* daily, East Jerusalem, 18 December 1978). In January 1980 Jordan cancelled such travel restrictions (Jordan News Agency 14.45 GMT, 30 January 1980, SWB ME/6334/A/4, 1 February 1980). To compensate for the outflow of workers, Jordan is forced to import many Egyptians, Pakistanis and even Orientals.

are the educated Palestinians and Egyptians who will continue to be indispensable by virtue of the posts they fill in the ever expanding education system which requires knowledge of Arabic. The Saudis, to avoid permanency, want to devise a system which would 'loan' such teachers for four years after which they would be replaced by other expatriates.[1]

The expatriates who could most easily be replaced are the unskilled and semi-skilled workers — many of whom are Yemenis. However a strike of Yemeni workers in the Saudi installations could have far-reaching effects and if a revolution were to take place in North Yemen or the two Yemens somehow overcome their differences and unite, the Yemeni workers would then be even less welcome.[2] Another group which is already regarded with disfavour are the Iranians, many of whom own small businesses in Bahrain and Qatar. Although they do not comprise a large part of the manpower needed for diversification, their departure could nevertheless harm the private sector. In the UAE, however, an attempt to replace them, besides aggravating relations with Iran, could result in severe economic damage, as the strike in the port of Dubai has already shown.

Policies designed to replace as many Arab workers as possible with Asian and Far Eastern labour could therefore prove counter-productive both externally and internally. Moreover, it will not prove possible to promote economic development without further upsetting the existing demographic balance. 'Gulfanization' (which means replacing foreign workers with locals) is a mirage. The scale of development envisaged entails increased reliance on immigrants with all the problems that will entail.

---

1 (MENA 8 April 1980.) In July a number of Palestinian teachers whose contracts were terminated reached the West Bank (ha-Aretz daily, Tel-Aviv, 23 July 1980).

2 Both Bahrain and Qatar expelled many North Yemenis who served in their respective police forces once the war in Yemen took place, regarding them as a potential 'fifth column'.

Ethnic and sectarian policies

Unrelated directly to economic development, yet being increasingly influenced by it, are the various religious sects and minorities living in some of the states. Although their problem is not merely an economic one, the fact that they have been denied a share in their countries' new wealth as part of the policy of thwarting separatism has further alienated them. Such discrimination could only strengthen the appeal of secession. Repression aimed at ensuring their obedience has had the opposite effect. The Iraqi policy of diluting heavily populated regions by transfer to other areas (Kurds) or expelling thousands of Shi'is (mainly of Iranian extraction) across the border has not brought about the stability the Ba'ath seeks. The dilemma is clear: granting such groups a measure of local autonomy as a sign of goodwill can only be perceived by them as a sign of weakness on the part of the central authority.

What is needed is to make these communities feel more wanted rather than alienated. A mixture of far more generous economic incentives and some political measures should be used, directed particularly at the younger generation. The divisions would not disappear but the very attempt to erase them, if carried out sincerely and consistently, could have some positive effects. What has been done until now is only a fraction of what is required bearing in mind the pace of developments in other parts of Iraq.

Iraq is devoting some attention to the integration and assimilation of minorities in an attempt to promote a new brand of Iraqi nationalism. On 20 September 1980, elections took place to the newly established Legislative Council Law of the Autonomous Region of Kurdistan. The council elections, in which everyone living in the region — not only Kurds — had a right to vote, was in charge of 'drawing up and ratifying laws concerning the region's affairs and discussing its general budget'. The government gave much publicity to the elections (which took place two days before the invasion into Iran) which were intended: 'to complete the construction of the democratic institutions and to develop and deepen the exercise of democracy in Iraq'.[1]

Co-opting Kurds by giving them governmental posts or even having a Vice President of Kurdish origin would not amount to very much for those the government seeks to appease, but it could help to isolate them. The less sophisticated part of the Kurdish population might be easier to impress with economic reforms.

Indeed an integral part of this policy is a widespread economic development of the more backward parts of the country — the enclaves

---

1 Iraq News Agency — SWB ME/6530/A/1 23 September 1980 and 6578/A/1 18 November 1980.

adjacent to the oil-bearing regions in the south (Shi'i) and the north (Kurds)[1] as well as in the cities where there are large concentrations of migrants from the countryside. With the war likely to prove a burden for the foreseeable future, any setback to what has already been achieved (and partly damaged by the war) could prove costly for the state's fragile social fabric.

However, the chances for real autonomy as a way of handling such intractable issues appear slim in both Iran and Iraq for regional devolution goes to the heart of the problem of both states' identity: consolidation of power at the centre will not suffice so long as the regimes' hold over the periphery remains fragmented. Nevertheless serious efforts to include the countryside in the process of modernization would help to lessen grievances and dilute the distinctive character of minority areas.

As in Iraq, so also in Iran much will hinge on who is in power and how strongly the various minorities press their claims for a far more generous distribution of wealth and the right to run their own affairs — at least in the traditional sphere. One thing is clear. Without resuming full production of oil there is no chance of those expectations being met.

As far as Saudi Arabia is concerned, what is needed is not only a continued effort to dilute the ethnic composition of the oil-bearing Shi'i-dominated Eastern Province and a Shi'i-oriented comprehensive economic development plan on a far larger scale than that already initiated but also a concerted effort to make the Shi'is feel that they are an integral part of the Kingdom. This could be done by putting an end to the discrimination and exploitation of this traditionally down-trodden and exploited segment of the population and through the integration of the younger Shi'is into the armed forces and especially the upper echelons of the government's bureaucracy — not only in the Eastern Province but throughout the Kingdom as a whole. A Najdi-dominated centralized administration which spends vast sums of money on prestige projects yet consistently ignores those who make the oil revenues possible is bound to trigger dissent. Moreover a strong army cannot compel obedience or loyalty, as Iran has demonstrated.

In Bahrain it remains to be seen whether or not the Al Khalifa will attend to the plight of the Shi'is who, though disunited nevertheless comprise the majority of the population. Whereas the poor amongst them will demand far-reaching economic reforms and housing, the more affluent Shi'is will have to be appeased economically and politically co-opted if trouble is to be avoided. Kuwait, which has in any case far

---

1 The 1980 budget allocated 31,256 million dollars for Kurdistan — see Christine Osborne 'Kurds enjoy autonomy in Iraq', *Middle East Economic Digest*, 28 March 1980, p 31.

fewer Shi'is than Bahrain can probably contain the problem for, unlike Bahrain, the poor Shi'is hardly exist in Kuwait but Bahrain is not in any case endowed with Kuwait's wealth. This will make it more difficult for the Bahraini dynasty to carry out any large economic projects and housing schemes designed to placate Shi'is. This is a case where a co-ordinated economic policy in the Gulf could ease a problem which ultimately affects them all.

Bahrain faces another problem that Kuwait is spared: economic demands from Bahraini Shi'is accompany demands for the right to unionize as well as for other far reaching social and political reforms which challenge the entire political system. Even so it might prove more desirable for Bahrain to allow a restricted labour union than prevent it. The risks involved could prove more manageable than those posed by continued denial.

9 Mechanisms for maintaining control and managing change

Can these regimes manage the new challenges with the old tools? What options are open to the governments, given the external and internal contradictions? If there are no 'remedies', are there any devices for gaining time? These questions are discussed in the following pages.

The rapid population growth and the extensive process of urbanization have altered the very foundations upon which central authority rests. The new situation has fragmented the old social order. Not only have the concentrated expatriate communities diluted local populations but they have forced at least some governments to contend with problems emanating from the exposure of the local populations to the 'agents of change'.

Using new democratic trappings when implanting modern systems on top of traditional ones have until now proved sufficient to maintain internal control while indicating both apparent change and a readiness to adapt to the new needs. Thus the authoritarian regimes in the Gulf have managed so far to avoid changing their basic characteristics by employing simultaneously the old and tried methods of distributing largesse, buying-off opponents, neutralizing rival interest groups, and repression. Politics has so far been restricted to the top of the pyramid and has excluded the bulk of the population who continue passively to accept this or are still powerless to change it if they so desire.

But the rapid changes which are taking place as a result of modernization manifest themselves in the rising expectations of the lower strata of population, in the surfacing of new social groupings with distinctive political aspirations, and in demands for greater participation by the newly-emerging middle class which, in contrast to their economic participation, are denied *any* political power and are deprived of even those limited rights accorded elsewhere in the Arab world. These challenges and others have alerted the regimes to the possibility that things could get out of control if they do not introduce new measures (despite the fact that these would be risky) so as to gain time in the hope that somehow they will succeed in maintaining stability and cementing their position while avoiding having to introduce sweeping changes that might threaten their very existence. Rather than accommodating at least part of these new pressure groups, the governments have opted for limited social reforms so as to try and gain the loyalty of the population by creating vested interests for them in the well-being of the regime. The process of decision making in all those states remains exclusively in the hands of small groups — whether senior technocrats in Iraq, the ruling families in the sheikhdoms or the 'clergy' in Iran — all of whom to some degree take account of public opinion in the hope this will bolster their own position while granting a sense of participation to those excluded from power. This limited action is unlikely to prevent opposition from the rapidly growing intelligentsia but the fact that the educated classes remain disorganized, divided and have demonstrated little readiness for sacrifice has made it easier for the regimes. This is true throughout the Gulf, where some problems were left purposely unattended to and a gradual, controlled evolution was sought as a means of avoiding revolution. Yet the main question remains: how to reconcile the process of rapid modernization with traditional values while perpetuating the existing monopoly of power and social patterns?

The dynasties' reluctance to make real changes stems from their fears that nothing that they can grant could satisfy the expectations of those outside the present system. The latter will insist on far-reaching changes and will view any minor modifications as simply a step on the way to full participation. The regimes are nevertheless aware that they had better institutionalize such reforms from a position of strength before changes are imposed on them by events. After all, the|*way* things are handled could prove far more important than the changes themselves. A similar distinction needs to be made between policy and structure for, despite the rapid changes the sheikhdoms have undergone in the process of modernization, the centralized political system under which those states are governed remains virtually untouched.

The revolution in Iran and the recent incidents in Saudi Arabia have forced the regimes to examine their respective forms of government. This chapter assesses the adequacy of some of the mechanisms and the old and new institutions used by the different regimes in their attempts to perpetuate the political *status quo*. Basically these could be classified into:

1 Mechanisms which relate to the royal families and which lend themselves to strengthening relations *within* the pyramid and ensuring smooth succession;

2 Mechanisms which relate to the way that the regimes handle those *outside* the immediate circle of decision makers. These institutions aim at granting the subjects the feeling of political participation through nominated bodies for consultations or through elected bodies which, theoretically, function as 'legislatures' albeit restricted.

Strengthening dynastic cohesion

For their part, the dynasties believe that a prerequisite for maintaining the *status quo* is that the ruling families must be able to face external and internal challenges to their authority. This means that, apart from being flexible, they must demonstrate a high degree of real cohesion and solidarity within the royal families themselves and put aside their differences.

On the face of it, it would seem that Saudi Arabia is far less vulnerable in that its sheer size and its countrywide network of intertwined family interests allows it to extend its control to all spheres of life without having to accommodate other internal forces. Moreover, the common fear of the ruling class of losing their favourable position, in which all members of the huge family have vested interests, ensures their crucial loyalty to the throne and promises a united front against any opposition emanating from outside the royal court, regardless of all quarrels inside the ruling family. Yet it is these internal conflicts and rivalries of individuals and groups jockeying for positions of power and influence within the royal court which could upset the delicate balance within the Saudi regime.

In maintaining a tight grip over their domains, the rulers of the sheikhdoms and Saudi Arabia are assisted by the other members of the royal families. Most of the important political decisions take place in this forum in accordance with tribal tradition. The Family Councils also allocate much of the states' income to the families' private treasuries. In fact, these bodies are authentic institutions which predate the establishment of the state. They give expression to the existing centres of power, reflecting the prevailing attitudes and even conflicting positions. Underlying this framework is a bond of solidarity which has allowed these councils to weather many storms. The state's affairs remain primarily a family issue.

Saudi Arabia: cohesion and succession

Although the Saudis have generally succeeded in preserving the secrecy of internal debates, disputes between princes over the question of succession, over control of the armed forces, over the extent of Saudi support for Arab 'hardliners' opposed to the Egyptian-Israeli peace treaty, or the ongoing debate on the pace of modernization and the associated perils of excessive dependence on the US, have all polarized the apparently unified ranks of the Al Saud. In many cases these divisions coincide with the traditional competition between the three main branches of the Saudi dynasty: the Jilwa, who include the late King Saud and the present King Khalid; the Shamar tribe to whom Prince Abdallah (Second Deputy Prime Minister and Commander of the

National Guard) and Prince Muhammad are affiliated; and the Sudairi tribe to whom the powerful Crown Prince Fahd belongs as well as his other influential full brothers — Sultan (Minister of Defence), Na'if (Minister of Interior), Turki (former Deputy Minister of Defence), Salman (Governor of Riyadh), Ahmad (Deputy Minister of the Interior) and Abd al-Rahman (Counsellor of the Royal Family Affairs). In practice neither group is all that homogeneous, especially when the generation gap parallels the education gap between the orthodox conservative tribal chiefs and the 'progressive', urban, young and ambitious princes. But such polarization is not confined to the Jilwa and Sudairi branches. There are other branches, including families (like the Al Sheikh[1]) and cliques of brothers and half-brothers, sons and grandsons which cut across the traditional divisions who all expect to play a decisive role with regard to the government's policies. Unlike the past, these groupings of princes are struggling from *within* the system against policies practised by the monarchy. Such is the *ad hoc* pressure group known as the 'Young Turks' who urge an immediate and drastic cut in oil production to conserve the state's asset for generations to come and to allow the ensuing rise in oil prices to compensate for the cut, if the Kingdom's real financial needs are not met by the reduced production.

Until now the question of the smooth removal of 'inadequate' rulers regarded by the family as acting against the regime's interests has been resolved in Saudi Arabia — as in Abu Dhabi and Qatar — by unanimous decision of the Family Council. This was the case in 1964, when King Saud ibn Abd al Aziz was replaced by his second brother, Faisal, who had headed the internal opposition. When the latter was murdered in 1975 by a discontented relative, King Khalid took over but, in mid-1977, the Family decided that his poor health required that he should go into semi-retirement and, while retaining the royal title, would cede power to Crown Prince Fahd. Prince Abdallah will probably be selected as Crown Prince once Fahd becomes King. Considered as a conservative Muslim who is not enthusiastic about modernization, Abdallah has strong support among the ulama' tribes within the Western Gulf and the National Guard — a power-base he would not easily give up. Indeed he was partly eclipsed following the mishandling of the uprising in Mecca for which Prince Sultan was praised even though many Saudi soldiers were killed. He will nevertheless probably step into Abdallah's shoes once succession takes place. Thus Abdallah may be outflanked by two Sundairis who hold similar 'progressive' views, to the disenchantment of

1 This was mainly because King Faisal, who originated from the Al Sheikh, elevated this Wahhabi-related branch and installed three of his sons in key positions.

the ulama'. No final decision has yet been made and the question is still open.[1]

The royal court is torn between two unpalatable choices when trying to avoid the perennial question which has plagued many monarchies: the absence of an obvious succession line, just as its existence might have unsettling effects. Fearing the consequences of rift over the ranking positions, the Saudis have striven to establish a system of balances along the line of succession whereby seniority passes horizontally from the eldest brother to the next brother in age — thus from one branch of the family to another — rather than from father to son. It is believed that once this issue is settled, devotion of the princes to the survival of the system would transcend any competition between them.

But the system of succession, which passes through the sons of the first King rather than from father to son, means that, before the second generation of grandsons can mount the throne, the last of the 29 sons of King Abd al-Aziz ibn Abd al-Rahman ibn Faisal al Saud has to be considered first. Age and sickness could allow for minor changes but essentially the system points to gloomy prospects for the grandsons.

The sheikhdoms

Elsewhere such issues are of a lesser magnitude and either have no urgency or are postponed to the days when the question becomes acute. This is done so as to prevent unnecessary internal rifts from surfacing early. In Kuwait the problem of the succession line troubled the Royal Family for a short while following the death of Sabah Salim al Sabah (the 12th ruler of the dynasty founded in 1756) in December 1977. Uncertainty prevailed as to the way the dynasty would settle the issue of selecting the Crown Prince. In the past this was based on rotation between the two branches of Al Sabah — al-Salim and al-Kafir. This model has recently been broken[2] but the issue was settled swiftly according to the old principle. Abu Dhabi already has a designated Crown Prince but he may have to overcome the rising power of Prince Muhammad.

Qatar is an example where persistent feuds in 1977 within its ruling family over the issue of succession — though on a totally different scale to the feuds of their relatives in Saudi Arabia — remained in practice unresolved. The struggle is between the younger brother of the present

1 For an analysis of the Royal Family politics — see Jacob Goldberg 'The Saudi Arabian Kingdom' in Colin Legum, Haim Shaked, and Daniel Dishon (eds.) *Middle East Contemporary Survey* (MECS), Volume III, 1978-79, The Siloah Centre for Middle Eastern and African Studies, Tel Aviv University, Holmes and Meier, New York and London 1980, pp 737-40.

2 For full details see Aryeh Shmuelevitz 'Kuwait' in *Ibid*. Volume II, 1977-78, pp 424-7.

ruler, Sheikh Suhaim, the Minister for Foreign Affairs, and the ruler's younger son Sheikh Abd al-Aziz, the Minister of Finance and Oil, over the position of Prime Minister[1] — a rivalry which might engulf other members of the Al Thani Family, the armed forces and probably also the Saudis who have tried to help reconcile these differences. In the absence of an heir to the throne, Oman might also witness bitter feuding between claimants.

1 *Middle East Contemporary Survey, Ibid.*, Volume I, 1976-77, pp 354-5.

Broadening the top

Apart from attempting to keep its house in order and to attend promptly to any grievances, each dynasty has sought to widen its base of power by broadening the foundations of government. This has coincided with other needs including building a welfare state which has demanded the establishment of an administration which would handle new types of problems. To that end, and in order to adjust to the rapidly changing circumstances in the process of building an infrastructure, the regimes have incorporated the previously excluded but rapidly increasing number of educated middle class technocrats in the process of decision making — though without granting them real political participation. Thus the autocratic top of the pyramid remained practically untouched and tribal whereas the rest of the pyramid was changing fundamentally. Control over the armed forces and the higher echelons of the administration have remained in the hands of the Head of State, whether King, Amir, Sheikh, or Sultan. Prominent members of the dynastic families head the newly established, centralized ministries. Gradually, however, some less sensitive governmental posts are being manned by ministers who do not belong to the ruling families. In Kuwait this had also much to do with the challenges the regime was facing from within the country. In an attempt to broaden its support, to appease other influential merchant families and to give them a sense of participation in the running of the country's affairs — while continuing to exclude the 'lower' strata of local population from the political process, giving them instead a share in the country's wealth — a number of 'outsiders' were brought into the Kuwaiti government. They serve side by side with members of the Sabah Royal Family,[1] who have nevertheless retained control over the key positions of foreign affairs, interior, defence and oil.

Broadening the top in Bahrain has also served a different purpose. The Al Khalifa ruling family, which began to face opposition as early as the mid-1950s, has followed the Iraqi pattern, in an attempt to defuse sectarian strife from tearing Bahrain apart. In 1975 five Shi'i ministers were brought in to head the less important offices in the Sunni-dominated seventeen-member cabinet. Today over half of the Ministers and most Heads of Government Departments are non-Royal. In the course of transition from a country of villages and tribes into a semi-modern state, the Sultan of Oman has also shown some readiness to

---

1 Since 1962 when the constitutional assembly was established there were ten successive cabinets with a total of 14-16 members. Whereas the first cabinet included eleven members of the Royal Family the 1971-5 cabinet had only three such members. For further details see Abdo Baaklini 'Patterns of participation in development in Arab Gulf experience' in *Man and Society in the Arab Gulf, op.cit.* Volume 3, 1979, pp 50-51.

make his government 'more representative' so as to weaken the urban opposition and to avoid domestic rivalries and tribalization. As Prime Minister, Qabus changed the structure of government at the end of 1980, nominating two Deputy Prime Ministers.

Elsewhere 'commoners' have been incorporated into government primarily on professional grounds, though they always remain inferior in their political status. Qatar nominated 'technocrats' to head the Ministries of Public Works, Labour and Social Affairs, Transport and Communications, Public Health and Information. Although the UAE's government is different from the other Gulf cabinets (it has to balance representation of the ruling families of the federation's components), a few technocrats have been admitted to serve as ministers. In Saudi Arabia the need became more acute with the expansion of the oil industry which required technical knowledge and expertise within the government. Prominent among such nominations was that of Sheikh Ahmad Zaki al-Yamani to head the Oil Ministry.

But, unlike elsewhere in the Gulf, the Saudi regime has had to accommodate not only skilled commoners but also numerous educated (and uneducated) senior members of the Royal Family itself. For that purpose many posts were created and new ministries established for absorbing the generation of sons into the system. This has not contributed to the administration's efficiency but this is obviously of secondary importance for a dynasty intent on defusing family rivalries and broadening its base. Will this satisfy the large number of Western-educated grandsons? Or will the knowledge that the present system has little substantial to offer them militate towards growing discontent within the Royal Family? These are questions which remain unanswered.

The UAE: problems of regional integration

A different type of dynastic cohesion has been sought in the UAE where the federal framework has been used to protect the seven diversified but fairly homogeneous principalities.[1] Common fears of external forces such as the USSR, Oman, Saudi Arabia and Iran as well as internal subversive movements, and the constantly expanding, politicized, expatriate community, all make the city states instinctively combine into a union. Indeed, external events such as the fall of the Shah, the invasion of Afghanistan and the siege of Mecca have all combined to convince the rulers of the Federation of the need to cement their ties. For the smaller Emirates, there were also economic incentives.

1 For a discussion of the disintegrative forces and integrative factors in the UAE see John Duke Anthony, *Transformation amidst tradition: the UAE in transition*, in S. Chubin (ed.) *op.cit.* pp 19-37.

142

To that end, new institutions were set up alongside existing ones. Special Consultative Assemblies, which have grown out of the tribal system, have been established within the federal system to provide the channels of communications essential for such a fragile union. Though each principality has continued to maintain its own institutions independent of the wider framework (whether the private *majlis* or the advisory councils), the union's institutions were strengthened by a 40-man Federal National Council, by a cabinet consisting of over twenty members and a seven-member Supreme Council of Rulers, all of which give wider representation, albeit not equal,[1] to all components. Pragmatic considerations have led to compromise in favour of a gradual change in the UAE's composition so as to avoid friction, maintain unity and lessen the contradictions inherent in the federal arrangement.

But many questions were purposely left unresolved or were not attended to despite resolutions to the contrary and these might have unsettling effects in the near future. Troublesome tribal conflicts continue over border issues, and over economic and demographic imbalances. Furthermore the Amirs' suspicion of each other's intentions as to the binding nature of the Federation make it difficult to maintain a measure of real unity essential for the Federation's existence.

The rivalry between the rulers of introverted Abu Dhabi and cosmopolitan Dubai over hegemony and their conflicting attitudes regarding the eventual substance of the federal framework makes it difficult for the parties concerned to subordinate their own interests and prestige to the political unity to which they pay lip service. Although they have managed to put aside many of their differences they still lack the ability to overcome parochial interests. Much will continue to depend on the individualistic and highly contrasted personalities of Sheikh Zayid ibn Sultan Al Nuhayan (aged 63), the ruler of economically-stronger Abu Dhabi who currently serves as the UAE's President, and Sheikh Rashid ibn Sa'id Al Maktum (aged 70), the Ruler of Dubai who is the UAE's Prime Minister. Whereas the former is the proponent of a strong federal framework which would ultimately lead to full unification, the latter represents the majority view in advocating a loose federation which would leave the principalities in full control of their own affairs. Sheikh Rashid's nomination for premiership of the fourth government since the UAE was founded in December 1971 (previously headed by one of his sons), paved the way for overcoming the traditional enmity between Abu Dhabi and Dubai.

An official superstructure, however, does not make the principalities feel that the federal union is anything but artificial. Loyalty to the

1 The two bigger Emirates have eight members each, Sharjah and Ras al-Khaimah six members and the other Emirates send four members each.

federal concept — a notion utterly foreign to many of the Bedouin who understand loyalty and allegiance only in personal terms — has yet to strike roots beyond the palaces of the rulers. The fact that the UAE functions as an economic entity means little politically to many of its inhabitants who still identify themselves with their places of origin. Jealousy and envy, especially on the part of the rulers of the five poorer and smaller Emirates, who resent the political constraints emanating from their inferior economic and demographic status, can only complicate mutual relations. They nevertheless welcome the enormous financial contributions coming from Abu Dhabi which provide 98 percent of the UAE's budget. In fact the continuing tension between Abu Dhabi and Dubai produces both economic and psychological benefits for the smaller Emirates whose leaders not only gain from the carefully engineered compromises but see this conflict as a guarantee of their own independence.

This view is not necessarily shared by the second generation. Political impetus for keeping the federal momentum is provided from all parts of the Federation by the educated younger generation which is exasperated by the petty quarrels of the older leaders. Unlike Qatar, the UAE is spared at least some of the tensions arising from the generation gap. Representatives of this younger generation, to whom the idea of Arab unity appeals ideologically, politically and economically, are now manning high-ranking posts in both local and federal governments. However it remains to be seen whether the fear of the Federal Union falling apart and the need to stand together to withstand challenges will help to smooth the process of succession in the principalities. In the past, dynastic intrigue has been the norm when resolving the question of who should succeed to the throne. Only in Dubai have the rulers for the last 150 years died natural deaths. Since the establishment of the UAE, Sharjah's ruler was murdered by the cousin he had himself deposed in 1965.[1]

The issue of succession is also likely to loom large in the UAE should Sharjah's demands for an equal footing[2] to that of Abu Dhabi and Dubai not be met. The emnity between Sharjah and Dubai dates back to the days of the British with the Al Qasimi families of Sharjah and Ras al-Khaimah resenting the right of veto on federal matters granted to both Abu Dhabi and Dubai. The Al Qasimi look down on the rulers of

1 Rosemarie said Zahlan: 'Britain played vital role in formation of the emirates' in *Financial Times* Supplement on UAE, 23 June 1980, p xvi.

2 Sharjah is demanding a better share in the UAE institutions also owing to its exit to the Gulf of Oman which might make both Fujairah and Sharjah (Khor Fakkan port) strategically important once arteries of communication are paved and pipelines laid to bypass the Straits of Hormuz.

Abu Dhabi and Dubai whose money they badly need. Led by a young university graduate, Sharjah has developed politically far more than the other Emirates. Selecting Sharjah's Abdallah Omran Taryam (aged 34) (a former Education Minister) as the Speaker of the Federal National Council could only alleviate part of the pressure. Members of Sharjah's dynasty still entertain hopes — like certain elements in Ras al-Khaimah[1] — for full independence. The situation is further complicated by the fact that, except for Abu Dhabi and Umm al-Qaiwain, all the other Emirates have territorial claims on non-contiguous areas.

But perhaps the most crucial issue which demonstrates, more than any other, the brittle nature of this political hybrid is its separate military forces. The problem of blending together half a dozen private armies to form the UAE's military armed forces remains. Some rulers are reluctant to hand over the control of their armies to unified federal command. Relinquishing personal power to an amorphous body makes little sense for Dubai, Ras al-Khaimah and even Sharjah. On the other hand, for the poor Emirates of Ajman, Fujairah and Umm al-Qaiwain amalgamation is seen as contributing to their own security. Full integration is remote. The way in which Abu Dhabi's ruler decided in 1978 to assume full control over the army through the nomination of his son to be its Commander — without consulting Dubai's ruler or the Minister of Defence (Dubai's ruler's son) — speaks for itself. The ruler of Dubai would not easily forget what was behind this unilateral move, even if it was in fact implementing a decision arrived at two years earlier. Political rivalry and fierce economic competition within the UAE could indeed blow the federation apart.

---

1 Unlike Sharjah, Ras al-Khaimah along with Dubai and Umm al-Qaiwain did not abolish their flags in favour of the UAE's flag.

Tribal channels of communication

Formal and informal institutions exist in the sheikhdoms as a means of communication between the ruler and his subjects. They serve to keep the subjects in contact with the dynasty through open audience ('Majlis') with the ruler. Providing subjects with direct access to the palace — where they can air their grievances, present their petitions and be rewarded if the 'giver of gifts' deems it necessary — is a long-held tribal tradition which enables the ruling dynasty to exert influence. Oil revenues now give immense power to the rulers at the expense of both the merchants and ulama'. Modern communication systems serve to cut down time and distance (especially in Saudi Arabia and Oman) between the ruler and ruled and, to a certain extent, tend to diminish the intermediary power of heads of tribes. But, despite the rapid growth of a Western-style local bureaucracy, which has created a kind of a buffer between the ruler and his people, the latter still seek redress through the Majlis before they approach the ministry concerned.

On a wider and more formal level, consultation with tribal chieftains, religious dignitaries and family leaders still precedes the formulation of policies. This is to avoid friction and establish a consensus. To strengthen their relations with the Bedouin chiefs, the rulers tend to visit them from time to time to seek their advice and to listen to their appeals. What is regarded in the West as a long drawn-out process of decision making is viewed by the more conservative regimes as normal. Consultations are required for internal stability, and are for the bulk of the orthodox population an accepted form of 'democracy' enshrined in the true spirit of Islamic values rooted in tribal notions of government. In fact, practically every powerful sheikh runs his own periodic Majlis sessions both as a form for debate and for resolving disputes in accordance with ancient tribal customs as well as a means of elevating his position and prestige. These institutions have withstood the test of time and crisis and have enabled Bedouin leaders to maintain control and to extend their influence over the members of their tribes.

Recognizing the need for an informal consultative assembly, and hoping to win over tribal chieftains in a country where tribalism is far more influential than the religious ulama', Sultan Qabus felt strong enough in mid-1978 to establish a national tribal advisory body in Dhofar. The Sultan makes a point of being accessible and his tours are a way of maintaining contact with his subjects. Sultan Qabus is not yet under real pressure to change this system of government. Nor is President Saddam Hussein, who uses such tours to raise his popularity.

A different situation exists in Saudi Arabia where such informal institutions are proving insufficient to bridge the growing gap between the regime and its people. To broaden support for the government and

146

to widen the base from which decisions are made, the Saudis have reiterated their promise that they will appoint provincial councils and reform the consultative assembly (Majlis al-Shura). These would include previously unrepresented elements loyal to the throne such as younger princes, scholars, religious leaders, military officers and tribal sheikhs. The manner in which they will be selected remains unspecified. Nothing has yet been done.

The Majlis al-Shura is currently an ungainly body. It was formed in the Hijaz in 1926 by King Abd al-Aziz in recognition of the Hijazis political sophistication and in an attempt to accommodate any opposition. His successors have made many promises, beginning with an attempt to defuse the oilfield troubles of the early 1950s, that the Majlis al-Shura would become some sort of 'legislature'. Since the Mecca Mosque incident, promises to set up the Majlis have been reiterated as a preventive act and an attempt to placate the fundamentalist Islamic opposition and to weaken its appeal. Promises were made that regional administration would be decentralized but the Saudi rulers continue to play for time. The regime has disclosed vague details of its plans. The Consultative Council, which is said to be complementary to the cabinet and to act as its advisory body, is expected to include some 70 to 100 nominated members. The Saudi justification for avoiding elections is that elections would bring in only affluent urban representatives, as has happened in the case of the Municipal Councils.[1] Moreover it is not clear how such a new body would impinge on the traditional consultative role of the ulama'.

More than a year has passed and the Majlis' deadline has still not been met. Endless promises and declarations on its imminent establishments continue to be made. Once the regime regained its confidence, it proved unwilling to honour its promises. This has been perceived by educated Saudis as a sign of a lack of leadership[2] with the usual dragging of feet.[3] In characteristically Saudi fashion, a combination of money

1 See interview with Crown Prince Fahd in *al-Safir* daily, Beirut, 9 January 1980. This view should be seen more as an expression of suspicion towards the rich merchants, whose political power declined once oil revenues were earned and the rulers' dependence on the merchants diminished.

2 See Tim Sisely 'Saudi Arabia: the political future' *Middle East International*, 20 June 1980.

3 It is noteworthy that a long statement prepared by the 'Saudi Council for Solidarity and Peace' (a leftist clandestine opposition group which co-operated with radical Palestinians) charged Fahd for failing to keep his promises, made after King Faisal's assassination in 1975 to set up a Consultative Council. The group saw proof in such policies of the 'ruling clique's intention to defend its interests indefinitely. The statement was published in the Iraqi Communist paper *Tariq al-Sha'b*, 26 September 1977 — see Haim Shaked and Tamar Yegnes; 'The Saudi Arabian Kingdom' in Colin Legum and Haim Shaked (ed.), *Middle East Contemporary Survey*, Volume II, 1977-78. The Shiloah Centre for Middle Eastern and African Studies, Tel-Aviv University, Holmes and Meier Publishers, New York and London, 1979, p 679.

and promises was seen as a way of removing grievances and gaining time.

The Saudi regime is well aware of the mood of discontent yet it is fearful that the establishment of a new body will be perceived as a sign of weakness and lack of leadership. Another serious possibility is that such a body would become a place for debate. In its proposed form such a body would satisfy neither the conservatives nor the more progressive and impatient third generation princes.[1] So in its revived form — which is nevertheless derived from the Shari'ah[2] — this body can hardly close the gap between ruler and ruled — nor would the rulers want it to. It is difficult to see the Royal Family surrendering any portion of its power unless forced to do so for fear of worse to come. Should the Saudis nevertheless eventually establish the Council, it will probably be large so as to give maximum representation but this will make it politically unwieldy. Moreover such a body will not have fiscal control.

Given that none of those in line to inherit the Saudi throne appear to have the leadership that has characterized their predecessors, the Saudi regime may be forced to reconsider once again its old promise to establish a body of which two-thirds of its members would be elected. The question remains: can the Saudis ensure their hold on power by balancing traditional and religious values or will they be forced to formalize a political system to satisfy the aspirations of the increasing numbers of Western-educated, secularized and ambitious younger men?

Only in Qatar, whose relatively small and less politically developed population has always been less exposed to the external world, has the ruling dynasty managed to avoid implementing its Provisional Constitution, let alone having to go beyond a nominated Advisory Council. Elections were rejected by a regime which feels confident of being able to continue governing uninterruptedly along the principles of the Islamic *Shura*. Qatar's dynasty has provided an effective and acceptable leadership whose rule has not so far been questioned. Qataris have shared in the state's wealth and the concentration of the non-ruling elite on business has sufficed to remove most grievances and to limit the interest in politics *per se*.

---

1 The debate in the Saudi press on the *Majlis al-Shura* is instructive, for from the various articles the gap between conservative and more progressive elements could be discerned. While the former strictly limit the proposed council's function to a consultative body (*Ukaz*, 22 March 1980, *al-Jazirah*, 11 May 1980), there are those who hint that it should be able to question the government's action (*al-Medina*, 19 April 1980, p 11).

2 *Saudi Economic Survey* weekly reporting on the Crown Prince's explanation of the work of the special committee established to draw up a constitution for the new Consultative Council (Volume XIII, no. 648, 16 January 1980).

In the UAE however there are already signs of discontent among the educated younger members of the ruling dynasties who openly call for free democratic elections to the Federal National Council (FNC) — the consultative body which must approve any legislation presented by the government — rather than the present custom of nominating its members according to tribal and family ties. Failing to get their way, a few young and talented ministers have already resigned senior posts in protest against the centralized manner with which the old leaders run the UAE's affairs and they have supporters among the influential Bani Khalifa branch of Abu Dhabi's Royal Family as well as among other young members of Royal Families throughout the UAE (especially in Sharjah). At Al Ain University there have been debates on the nature of the federal system as well as on the way its representatives are selected. Demonstrations occurred in Abu Dhabi in March 1979.[1] Sharjah's newspapers (*al-Khalij* and *al-Azmina al-Arabia*) continue to reflect this feeling of frustration.[2] With the extended Provisional Constitution expiring in 31 December 1981, it might be assumed that the present low profile of these 'Young Turks' will not last,[3] especially when they will be watching the progress of the reinstituted Parliament in Kuwait.

In justifying their total rejection of democratic institutions, the dynasties claim that importing alien Western forms of democracy would undermine Islamic tradition. They also argue that they have yet to see one Arab state in the Middle East where such a system really works in a 'democratic' fashion but, sooner or later, the UAE rulers will have to come to terms, publicly, with the limitations of their own political system. In their attempts to stave off democracy, the rulers might devise a system whereby some members are elected while others are nominated.

1 The protesting students demanded democratization and strengthening the federation as a guarantee for each state's own development. (See M. Vassilyev 'What would the rain of gold bring' in *Novoy Vhemia*, 7 December 1979.)

2 *al-Khalij* and *al-Khalij Times* newspapers were reported to have been shut down in mid-1981 by the UAE's government following their reporting on strikes carried out by local government officials and teachers in protest over not receiving a salary rise (to compensate for the rising inflation and high cost of rent) at a time when their rulers were living lavishly.

3 See also Ann Fyfe 'Democracy in the Gulf: the UAE' *The Middle East*, June 1980, p 33. Crown Prince Sheikh Khalid of Ras al-Khaimah called for a permanent constitution which would grant equal rights to all UAE citizens. (*Middle East Economic Digest*, 9 January 1981.)

The parliamentary experiments: Kuwait and Bahrain

Unlike Saudi Arabia and the UAE, in both Kuwait and Bahrain the demands for democratization emanate from outside the royal families. In these cases, the traditional tribal institutions of government could not possibly defuse pressures from a far more politically sophisticated and advanced urban society. In wanting to continue to reign as a sole, unaccountable arbiter, the rulers had to devise new institutions which would not eliminate the tribal base of legitimacy but would permit the population to provide advice through a system granted by the ruler on his own terms as a gesture to his loyal subjects. The restricted type of responsible popular participation should not be taken as participatory democracy yet the various family-ruled states fear that, though the rulers of Kuwait and Bahrain do not intend to drop the tightly-held reins of government, even the precedent is dangerous. The experiment may acquire its own momentum and its impact could carry deep into the Peninsula.

Following Kuwait's independance in 1961, the Al Sabah dynasty established a quasi-constitutional monarchy. Elections for the Constitutional Assembly were held in December of that year. Ten months later a Constitution, which remained in force until 1976, was signed. The first elections to the Legislative Assembly took place in January 1963. They were followed by further elections in 1967, 1971 and 1975. Although the Cabinet was constitutionally responsible to the National Assembly, the Amir, as Head of State, was not. He was empowered to dissolve parliament and his title remained hereditary. The National Assembly had 50 members who were elected by ten districts, providing roughly every 10,000 citizens with a representative. The authorities intended that elections in such small constituencies would preclude the need for political parties. Indeed political parties were outlawed in Kuwait as elsewhere in the Gulf, making politics personal rather than institutional. In fact the Ruling Family originally wanted the Assembly to be limited in its functions to a kind of consultative body not authorized to legislate (similar to the 14-member Kuwaiti Council selected in 1938) but which would nevertheless give its elected members a feeling that their views were being taken into account.

Both Kuwait (and, later, Bahrain) preferred to license limited open political activity rather than to drive the opposition underground. They also calculated that they stood to gain politically should they be regarded as liberal when compared to others in the Gulf. However, terms such as 'democracy' and 'freedom of the press' in their Western interpretations remain unthinkable. The rulers of Kuwait and Bahrain sought parliaments which would rubber stamp their decisions but which would nevertheless prove useful in venting pressure. Yet both unleashed the very forces they had hoped to contain. Conflict erupted between the Parliament and Cabinet and the legitimacy of the regimes was increasingly being questioned. In Kuwait, the regime reluctantly allowed candidates who were affiliated to the Arab Nationalist Movement to stand for election. Control over leftist political groupings was further complicated by the fact that their activists were in most cases Palestinian and Egyptian immigrants who were careful not to exceed the bounds of legitimate political activity, fearing their own expulsion.

By 1975 the leftists had strengthened their appeal. The elections of that year brought in a relatively large number of anti-government groups which co-operated in delaying government bills. They urged the government to cut oil production, to involve itself in the Palestinian question and to abandon its traditional neutral position on inter-Arab affairs. It was not long before, for the first time, sharp criticism was levelled against the Royal Family itself. The indigenous opposition co-ordinated its activities with subversive action carried out by immigrants (primarily of Palestinian origin) who distributed anti-government leaflets, and even engaged in terrorist activity once it became clear that Kuwait would refrain from condemning Syria's brutal action against the Palestinians in the war in Lebanon. Acting swiftly in response, the government expelled thousands of Northern Arab immigrants, banned all political parties, trade unions and youth clubs and curtailed the freedom of the press and speech. Parliament was dissolved for four years in the summer of 1976.

Bahrain had dissolved its parliament a year earlier, only twenty months after its inception. The Bahraini National Assembly, which was established in mid-December 1973, replaced the Constitutional Assembly established a year earlier. The latter was composed of 42 members of whom 22 were elected, 8 appointed by the Amir and 12 Ministers. It presented a Draft Constitution which called for the creation of a National Assembly whose members would be directly elected by the public. The Ministers would be *ex officio* members in that Assembly which would function, under the Amir, as the sole legislative body of the country. He had the right to dissolve the Assembly, but a new one had either to replace it within two months or else the dissolved Assembly would regain its constitutional authority.[1]

Under such terms it was soon clear that the highly politicized left and the Shi'is[2] would challenge the dynasty's internal and pro-American

1 Emile A. Nakhleh 'Political participation and the Constitutional experiments in the Arab Gulf: Bahrain and Qatar' (Paper presented in Inaugural Conference of the Centre for Arab Gulf Studies, University of Exeter, England, July 9-13, 1979), p 16.

2 *al-Nahar al-Arabi wa al-Duwali*, Lebanon (Paris) 7 September 1979, suggested that the Shi'is, who did quite well in the elections (65%), had demanded the premiership and hence the parliament was dissolved.

policies. If the Bahraini dynasty had hoped to acquire greater legitimacy far beyond its narrowly-based autocratic tribal system, it soon realized that forming the Assembly could only accentuate the contradictions within Bahrain. Like Kuwait, Bahrain had set in motion a political process which could only be controlled by force. Once the opposition groupings were allowed to function, it would prove extremely difficult to restrain them. Political competition within the opposition tended towards extremes, with each party trying to outbid the other and to prove itself the only one able to champion the grievances of the underdog. In Bahrain the opposition has been more sophisticated than elsewhere in the Gulf, forcing the extremely efficient security services (headed by British expatriates) to clamp down on all those suspected of maintaining contact with the PFLOAG, which had aligned itself with other 'progressive' forces committed to destroying the political systems in the Gulf. With the intention of deterring the public, a number of executions took place yet these harsh measures were followed by economic and social reforms with the intention of appeasing the population.

In Kuwait, however, the issue was far more complicated. The challenges of 1976 left their mark on the Kuwaiti regime which continued to search for some accommodation with its opponents. Putting emphasis on the welfare of the local inhabitants and making itself more accessible to its citizens has helped the government to cement its position but it has not been enough. The fundamental problem remains. Since the government reiterated its promises that parliament would be reactivated (after the 1962 Constitution had been 'adequately' amended), it had to decide what type of formal institution would be re-established. In view of the public's expectations, would the Kuwaitis approve of something which would take them back many years and give them less than they had before? Would a restricted form of Western-type democracy prove manageable and beneficial in the long run? Can free parliamentary debate take place while political parties remain outlawed? And would such an institution add a measure of stability to the other states in the Gulf? Again these are questions which cannot be answered with confidence.

The changes produced by rapid modernization cannot make the pressures any less. The dynasty is itself deeply involved in business and is taking advantage of its position at the expense of the other local merchants and, more generally, at the expense of the state (if one does not accept the definition that the Royal Family is coincident with the state). There are those who are increasingly disenchanted with favouritism and corruption. So great is the disaffection that the authorities have proscribed discussion of public issues by the press and in the informal gatherings of the *diwaniyah*, limited it to twenty people.[1]

Aware of the current mood and the voices of educated Kuwaitis suggesting that the Al Sabah should become a figurehead in a constitutional democracy like that prevailing in Britain and under pressure from events in Iran and in neighbouring Saudi Arabia, the Kuwaiti regime decided once more to move towards a parliamentary form of government as a way of relieving pressure. Determined to keep things under full control from the start, the authorities appointed a special commission to revise the Constitution. Some Kuwaitis were suspicious from the start of the recommendations the Commission would present. As put by Abdal-Latif al-Dueij in an article published in mid-1980 in *Arab Oil and Economic Review*:

> The choice of the 35 members of the Committee merely seems based on a fair distribution of Kuwaiti families, parties and tribes — a system we thought had been abandoned. One of the negative aspects of the former parliamentary life was the division of the constituencies according to group and parties, which meant that rather than representing the people, a Deputy symbolised the authority of a single family.

Like others, the writer demanded that, before revising the Constitution a report should be published as to the reasons for the dissolution of the National Assembly.

The proposed 1980 amendments suggested only that the Constitution should read 'Islam is the religion of the state and Islamic laws are the main source of legislation' and that the number of deputies should be 60 not 50 and be elected for a five-year rather than a four-year term. The authorities warned against 'reviving the bickering and factionalism which led the former Amir to suspend the assembly'.[2] A bomb exploded outside the offices of the Kuwait Oil Company in London, which some observers suggested was related to Kuwaiti Shi'ah demands for appropriate representation in the future parliament.

The results of the February 1981 elections reflected the success of the regime in uniting its Bedouin supporters (23) and encouraging the fragmentation of the radicals' vote. Some 500 candidates competed for 50 places with only 43,000 male Kuwaitis (3 percent of the population)

---

1 *al-Hadaf* weekly, Kuwait, 11 October 1979; David Hirst 'Iran driving the Kuwaitis into the arms of Iraq' *The Guardian*, 13 May 1980.

2 Sheikh Saad al-Abdallah al-Salim, Kuwait's Prime Minister — *Middle East Economic Digest*, 29 August 1980, p 23.

voting.[1] The large number of candidates harmed the chances of the divided leftists whose popularity had in any case dwindled because some of them had sided with Iran against Iraq. The redrawn voting districts fragmented the vote of the Shi'ah's constituency.

So far the opposition's reaction to its defeat has been mild. 'We accept the election results because we asked for democracy and we did not make conditions as to the results' said Dr. Ahmad al-Khatib (who, together with four other radicals, failed to be re-elected). He went on to say: 'The democracy does not manifest itself (only) in the activity of the Members of the People's Council. In all authorities and public institutions should the spirit of democracy beat'. If this would prevail, he promised, 'those rejecting democracy would not have the opportunity to attack it from within and without...... The elections are just the starting point'.[2] Such sentiments clearly demonstrate the gap of expectations between the Kuwaiti regime which will insist on having a compliant Parliament, and the local intelligensia, which is mainly excluded from this body.

Needless to say, these elections in Kuwait contain serious implications also for its neighbours, especially Bahrain. But unlike Kuwait — to the satisfaction of the Saudi regime — Bahrain has never declared its intention to revive its National Assembly. As Bahrain's Prime Minister Sheikh Khalifa bin Salman declared, when he warned those bent on 'destabilizing the island':

Our past democratic experiment gave us experience which would enable us to base our future processes on foundations suitable to our society's values and heritage.

Our democracy is derived from our values, culture and society. We should not import foreign democracies.

He added: Our democratic experience failed and this should make it necessary to contemplate about and revise the style of democratic processes for the future.[3]

---

1 Excluded from the vote were naturalized Kuwaitis, women, soldiers (army officers who stood as candidates resigned from the army). Immigrants were also excluded. Calls to grant franchise to those among them living many years in Kuwait were aired earlier by radicals (al-Nahar Arab Report and Memo, 13 August 1979, pp 6-8), who also demanded that women should be allowed to vote.

2 al-Tali'ah weekly, Kuwait, 4 March 1981.

3 Interview in al-Bahrain weekly in Gulf Mirror, 20 December 1980.

Bahrain's firmness could be deduced from the resignation (six months earlier) of the Minister of Labour who was known to support greater labour representation at plant level in preparation for recognized trade unions. However, in its attempts to indicate some change, the Bahraini government is considering the introduction of elections at local level for municipality councils.[1] Obviously this cannot solve Al Khalifa's predicament. And there are members of the Ruling Family who argue that more than a superficial move will be needed.

For the UAE and Saudi Arabia the consequences of the 'Kuwaiti gamble' could also be quite severe. Disenchanted with the nature and the content of the political debate and liberalization of the political systems in both Kuwait and Bahrain and assuming that this has some impact on its own intelligentsia, Saudi Arabia has always exerted pressure on both states to do away with their parliamentary systems which, in the opinion of the Saudi rulers, must ultimately result in dislocation and the collapse of the existing central authority. The Saudis fear that the re-introduction of the Kuwaiti Parliament (even if it remains limited in power and co-opted in its membership) would present the Saudi dynasty in an unfavourable light and might result in increased demands within the Kingdom to follow the same path — something the Saudi regime has never intended to do. The countries in the region are no longer as isolated as they were in the past and their populations are bound to be influenced by events elsewhere in the region. Though they differ in some respects, all dynasties face unpalatable choices. They fear that introducing any kind of participatory democracy would hasten their demise and that any change would ultimately mean polarization and the use of more repression which could result in political decay and collapse. Yet, although the pressures for something more than cosmetic measures are likely to grow, they remain reluctant to put to the test the resilience and flexibility of their own political systems.

1 *Ibid.*, 3 January 1981.

Dictatorship in the name of ideology: the case of Iraq

In Iraq a new and inverted type of regime has replaced the monarchy. Once the Ba'ath took over (ten years later in 1958) it declared its intention to implement its ideology of Arab Unity, freedom from western imperialism and statism (meaning socialism). 'Democracy' was said to be the way to bring about the Ba'ath's ideology. Yet the Iraqi regime has been employing basically the same kind of safety measures used by its southern neighbours, sharing with them the perennial dilemmas associated with neutralizing the opposition. Assured succession, systematic purges, repression, nepotism and co-option have all been employed by Saddam Hussein. Similar methods were used by his predecessors in response to challenges from the opposition which have demanded a broadening of the top of the pyramid in exchange for a provisional armistice. This was done through the establishment in August 1973 of the Progressive Patriotic and National Front (PPNF), a Communist initiated yet Ba'athist-controlled body which included, in addition to its two main rival components, a number of ephemeral Kurdish groups (the pro-Ba'ath Kurdistan Democratic Party) and 'progressive' Nasserite organizations led by the Lawyers Federation. Shi'is were also included but only as members of other parties. Some members of the Front were then invited to join the 'Cabinet' or Council of Ministers which, once augmented, was then made irrelevant. It was not its size which prevented the Council of Ministers from leaving its mark on Iraq's political life. Power remained exclusively with the Ba'ath's 20-member Revolutionary Command Council (RCC). The Iraqi regime never intended to allow the PPNF to be a platform for power-sharing. Rather the Ba'ath hoped that the opposition's limited participation would be sufficient to neutralize, if not win over, some of its opponents.

The parties differed in their views of the nature and purpose of the PPNF. The Communists regarded it as a transitional phase leading to free parliamentary elections; the Ba'ath viewing it as an instrument which would enable it to weaken and control the opposition while playing for time and attempting to consolidate its hold on power. The inevitable clashes between both sides of the PPNF have occurred since its inception yet neither party wanted to do away with it. The Ba'ath had no wish to tarnish its image and preferred to pursue a dialogue with its rivals. The Communists hoped to take advantage of the PPNF to advance their own interests.

With the rise of Saddam Hussein al-Takriti to the Presidency, a new era opened. Hussein, fearful of his opponents both within the Ba'ath and outside it, strove to narrow still further the top of the technocratic-military pyramid which his predessor Ahmad Hasan al-Bakr had wanted to widen. He assumed the posts of Chairman of the RCC, Secretary-General of the Regional Leadership of the Ba'ath and

156

Commander-in-Chief of the armed forces and the Premiership. Saddam had learnt from the Ba'ath's failure in 1963. Total control over the state and party apparatus enabled him to carry out, following his accession, a ruthless purge against his opponents within the Ba'ath and the military, some of whom were executed following a short show-trial on the 8th August 1979. The latter were replaced by people loyal to him, primarily from his own city of Takrit — the cradle of the Ba'ath.[1] Saddam Hussein nominated his cousin and brother-in-law (now Major-General) Adnan Khairallah to be Defence Minister and Deputy Commander-in-Chief and his step-brother Barazan Takriti to head the internal security apparatus while its previous director Sa'adun Shakir was made Minister of Interior and Party Security.

At the same time he turned against the communists (at home and abroad), executing some and arresting many. He also dealt a blow to Shi'i and Kurdish radicals. Saddam Hussein's version of 'democracy' aimed at downgrading the importance of the RCC while upgrading that of the government[2] and elevating his own stand beyond any kind of accountability. That did not mean that he ignored the RCC, rather that he handled it through a series of nominations of unknown or less ambitious personalities and by counter-balancing potential rivals. Having secured his position, he released many prisoners and allowed some political activists to return from exile. Moreover, he invited the Iraqi Communist Party (ICP) to resume the dialogue in the PPNF. He then proceeded to establish new democratic trappings by a carefully engineered election to a newly-established Parliament. The latter's purpose is to encourage patriotism through popular participation and to accommodate popular pressures and demands.

On 20 June 1980, a few months before the Iraqi invasion of Iran, Saddam ordered the holding of elections for the National Assembly — Iraq's new legislature. 840 candidates ('whether they are organized Ba'athists, non-organized Ba'athists, members of a fraternal party or members of the Front'[3]) competed for 250 seats in 56 constituencies.

1 For further details see A. Kelidar, *Iraq, op.cit.*

2 This was done through the nomination of five senior members of the RCC to the posts of Deputy Prime Minister (which coincided with Hussein's policy of balancing the members of the Ba'ath's elite against one another) and widely publicizing the Council of Ministers' meetings so as to create the impression that the Cabinet became indispensable in the process of decision making. A detailed account of the mechanism used by him to consolidate his position is described in Ofra Bengio *Centres of Power and Centres of Opposition in Saddam Hussein's Regime*. Published by the Shiloah Centre for Middle Eastern and African Studies, Tel Aviv University, Data and Analysis Serial, March 1981.

3 INA 15.50 GMT, 30 June 1980 — SWB ME/6460/A/7, 25 July 1980.

Every man and woman over 18 could vote.[1] But, beyond the widely publicized speeches, it is still unclear what are the practical implications of the President's warning:

We want the National Assembly to be the genuine representative of the people in their struggle to achieve economic prosperity through socialism, and not to protect the interests of the bourgeois or to promote the revival of the interests of the minority.
The President continued:
We want it to be a sharp sword (word indistinct) and not a spade for destruction or a treacherous knife to slaughter masses in the dark for the sake of securing the interests of an evil minority at the expense of the masses' interest.

Doubtless, the setting up of the largely decorative parliament was a significant move in the process of building democratic institutions under a one-party system but much will depend on how strong (or how weak) Iraq's leader feels. The war has already cost Saddam his pre-eminence in the Arab world and this could weaken his image internally. Yet, though shaken by the way the war has developed, he is still firmly in charge. Perhaps the greatest danger to the survival of the regime lies in growing discontent within the military whose officers might conclude that, given the failure in Iran, it would be prudent to distance themselves from Saddam Hussein and stage a coup before they are themselves blamed for Saddam's Iranian miscalculations. Paradoxically, the destruction of the Iraqi nuclear reactor may have served, among other things, to set back such sentiments.

1 In Kuwait the age was limited to men over 21. Women were not granted franchise.

Iran — the absence of order

Like Iraq, Iran has replaced its monarchy with a different type of regime but it provides an extreme example of what happens when a political system breaks down and chaos reigns. If all other states in the region have a recognized and ruling regime and established procedures for handling government affairs (even if the dividing line between those supporting and those opposing the government is sometimes blurred), in post-revolution Iran such elements do not exist. Its political system is characterized by a struggle for succession which began even before Khomeini's rise to power. A ferocious jostling for power and influence parallels the internal ethnic conflict, paralysing an already unstable political system.

According to the Islamic Constitution, Ayatollah Khomeini became the official *Velayat Faghih*, the country's supreme religious father-figure. He assumed full control over the state with the sole right to veto anything of which he disapproves. Real power, therefore, rests exclusively with Khomeini. A new theocratic form of dictatorship has replaced the old one. Khomeini dominates practically all spheres of Iranian life through the clerical machinery at his disposal and the 15-man Revolutionary Council which he heads controls thousands of local revolutionary Komitehs (Committees) headed by Mullahs which have come to overshadow the government, which is reigning but not ruling.

Far from trying to accommodate their opponents, the clergy are attempting to neutralize, if not crush, anyone outside their clique. The Mullah-dominated Islamic Republic Party (IRP) imposed a constitution on Iran which aimed to thwart any separation of church from state and vested absolute power in the divines. With 80,000 Mullahs operating from more than 20,000 mosques, its network of dedicated zealots Hezbollahi (Partisans of Allah) and its armed Pasdaran, the clerical regime embodied in the IRP is striving to consolidate its power by manning all levels of government, parliament,[1] and judiciary, security organs and the mass media. They replace the educated secular class whom the Mullahs resent and mistrust.

But Khomeini is an old and sick man. Many of the other religious leaders are also elderly and none have his stature. Moreover, the clergy is far from united and a power struggle is taking place within its ranks. Some religious elements are disenchanted either because they have been excluded from power or because the clergy is playing a role in spheres beyond the traditional boundaries of religion. The fact that five of the

---

1 See Amir Taheri 'Top hat gives way to Turban in Iran majlis' in *International Herald Tribune*, 22 March 1980.

Grand Ayatollahs[1] were not included in the Revolutionary Council aggravated their followers. Prominent amongst these is Shariat Madari from Azarbaijan.

Many technocrats have left the country, exasperated at being dictated to by Mullahs who clearly lack competence. They are also alienated by the religious and regressive nature of the regime and this sense of frustration and powerlessness is reinforced by the actions of the revolutionary courts which are still carrying out executions, regardless of protest from the government. The newly established SAVAMA resembles too closely the SAVAK security service it replaced. Finally the rapid deterioration of the economy is laid at the door of the IRP.

In the political sphere, the *modus vivendi* between the IRP and the Tudeh Party is extremely tentative, though the communists are careful not to give the clerics any excuse to end it. Being 'inside' the system rather than 'outside' it, gives the Tudeh some advantage over the other groups jockeying for power. The Tudeh is ideally placed to fill any future vacuum, probably in alliance with the Mojahedin. Meanwhile they are keeping a low profile and hoping to profit from the contradictions in the government.

Bani Sadr was the only one (apart from Khomeini) to have a public mandate with his landslide presidential victory in January 1980. He had hoped to consolidate his own power and advance Iran into a new modern era while the clerics wanted him to be a figurehead only, dealing with ceremonial affairs. President Bani Sadr had soon to acquiesce in the nomination for the post of Prime Minister of a man that he had earlier rejected, and regarded as incompetent.

Nominated Premier on 11 August 1980, Muhammad Ali Rajai (the former Minister of Education) had the flawless credentials of a freedom fighter. He represented a new generation of young, anti-western Muslims who had never travelled abroad nor tasted power.[2] It was not long before conflict between the President and his Prime Minister came into the open. In early August, a National Consultative Council was elected, whose duty was to finalize the draft of the Constitution due to be submitted to yet another referendum. It was this multiplicity of power centres and the existence of different decision-making organs which prevented Iran from proceeding to the next phase of building new, properly functioning governing structures. The country was bedevilled

---

1 Ayatollah (*Ayatallah*) meaning 'Sign of God' is an elevated religious appellation — a recognition which has no formal way of being bestowed. There are some 60 Ayatollahs in Iran and a larger number of those carry the more junior title of *Hojatoleslam*.

2 Vahe Petrossian 'Iran's premier Rajai: a new generation Muslim', *Middle East Economic Digest*, 15 August 1980, p 21.

not only by acute economic problems but by deepening political divisions between modernist and traditional factions. This happened in the Revolutionary Council — a body which was established prior to the ousting of the Shah and continued to function as a shadow government even after Mehdi Bazargan became Prime Minister. This manifested itself also in the new parliament and, in short, in every corner of the country and in any sphere of life. In that respect the issue of the American hostages became increasingly a pawn in the game of power inside Iran and was instrumental in constraining the secular group around Bani Sadr. The Mullahs tried to tarnish Bani Sadr's image and any attempt by him to compromise was depicted as counter-revolutionary and anti-Islamic. His resignation was demanded by the leaders of the IRP who were always suspicious of him and feared he would advance himself at their expense in anticipation of a showdown between the various contenders for power. Bani Sadr's tolerance of the strong Mojahedin was anathema to the clergy which continue to be obsessed with the possibility of a plot or a coup undermining their present relatively entrenched position. After all, in the first 30 months of the revolution some seven attempted coups took place but also two attempts on the life of Bani Sadr. The violence and assassinations continue.

The war with Iraq introduced a new dimension into the struggle for power. It gave a boost to the position of Bani Sadr, who, having failed to establish a political power base, now projected himself as a wartime leader and outraged the IRP which was prepared to undercut him at whatever cost, even when the war was going on. The ill-equipped Pasdaran and the newly-established Mustazafin (the forsaken) army of volunteers were rushed to the border region to fight the Iraqis single-handed. This situation hampered any attempts to co-ordinate military action. Army officers were not unnaturally angered by the clergy's intervention in military decisions, even if they feared that when the war ended the army would be purged once again. Ironically, the IRP has been in favour of the war continuing. At first, it hoped that the 'pro-American' Bani Sadr could thus be blamed for his failure to defeat the Iraqis. After the IRP had managed to oust him, it wished to keep the army busy and far away from Tehran — where the first signs of a civil war surfaced with the bomb blast at IRP Headquarters in July 1981.

The bombing killed 72 people — including four government ministers, six deputy ministers, twenty members of Parliament and Ayatollah Muhammad Beheshti, the IRP General Secretary who was expected to succeed Khomeini. This created a new vacuum, for it followed the removal of two other confidants of Khomeini: Mustafa Chamran, Commander of the Pasdaran on the Iraqi front, who was killed in an ambush, and Hojatoleslam Sayyid Ali Khameni, who was seriously injured in an attempt on his life. Among the contenders seeking to fill this vacuum are not only the Executive Affairs Minister Behzad Nabavi, the House Speaker Hojatoleslam Akbar Hashemi Rafsanjani, the new leader of the IRP Hojatoleslam Muhammad Javad Bahonar as well as other Mullahs, but also members of the now more daring Opposition.

The IRP retaliated for the bombing by executing scores and arresting hundreds of the Mujahedin, who were blamed for the attack. It was concerned lest the loose alliance between Bani Sadr — now in Paris — and the Mujahedin prove to be a bond linking together all those striving to topple the Mullahs. These include General Gholam Ali Ovaisi (the former Commander of the Army), General Palizban, the aged General Bahram Aryana, the former Premier Shahpur Bakhtiar, the son of the late Shah, Reza Pahlavi, and his mother, ex-Empress Farah Dibah — all of whom are operating separately from outside Iran. So far, however, they have failed to unite their ranks, let alone succeed in gathering a popular following within Iran, which is crucial for any movement. The struggle for power continues within Iran as the Mullahs strive to consolidate their position against non violent change.

It seems clear that, in the Iranian case, as perhaps in some other States, there is little expectation that succession will be orderly or free of violence. Moreover, the Iranian Revolution has made it abundantly clear that the transfer of power from one absolute ruler to another, albeit of a different kind, does little to propitiate all sectors of society. It only brings new tensions and schisms to the fore.

Conclusions

The vicious circles

'There is one certain fact — we are the losers in the end.'[1]

It was the collapse of the Shah which alerted the West to the dangers contained in and exacerbated by wild spending and extravagance which create, rather than bridge, social gaps.

Though it is pointless to compare the Arab states in the Persian Gulf with Iran, it is nevertheless of some interest to look at the similar patterns which are emerging in the region, if only to study the relationship between rapid economic growth and political instability. For the non-homogeneous, essentially tribal sheikhdoms could also prove vulnerable to such pressures. Excessive wealth created the illusion of the ability to import modernization and make all the requisite changes without complications. However, modernization taking place so rapidly with practically no preparation sets in motion new, previously unknown processes by virtue of the changes it introduces as well as sharpening old potential sources of conflict which have a bearing on one another. The seeds for the kinds of change which the various regimes proceeding with industrialization wish to avert are there, with the potential political instability growing out of economic development. The 1980s will probably prove far less tranquil for at least some of the local govern-

---

1 OPEC president and UAE Oil Minister, Dr. Mana Sa'id al-Utaiba's words on the purchasing power of oil (made at an OPEC seminar, Vienna) — see *The Middle East*, December 1979, p 85.

ments. Their own policies of pushing ahead with rapid modernization could well serve to precipitate the breakdown of their own political foundations.

In addition to their fears of external threats, each of the Gulf regimes is troubled by persisting challenges from within. Given that politics cannot be divorced from economics and that political problems feed on social tensions, two intertwined vicious circles which grow out of the process of swift modernization can be discerned. The first circle relates to the local scene: economic development has led to the crumbling of existing social frameworks and Islamic values which in the past managed to weather changes and proved the cornerstone of the tribal order; urbanization further weakens tribalism; old loyalties are consequently dissolved; the general expansion of education resulted, as indeed the regimes initially hoped, in the emergence of a new white-collar strata; however, the political expectations of this ambitious, politicized, westernized and secularized younger generation are incompatible with those of the regime which has enriched them; this potential unrest could breed conflict between a given regime and both the military and civilian establishments on whom it depends.

The second vicious circle relates to the implications of newly created demographic patterns in the Peninsula: economic development and industrialization cannot take place, at any level, without a foreign workforce. This mutual dependence, which could be depicted as a symbiosis, is not confined to the economic sphere. The immigrants bring with them foreign cultures and political influences which leave their mark on the traditional fabric; the presence of these expatriates creates new types of constraints for the regimes owing to the former's expectations and inter-Arab pressures which may manipulate immigrants' grievances and exacerbate old and new potential sources of uneasiness among the indigenous population.

Associated with both circles are more general issues such as the Palestinian question which has ceased to be a problem only between Israel and its neighbours. In the absence of a 'satisfactory' political solution to the Palestinian question, refraining from real participation in the struggle against Israel (through the deployment of the oil weapon) could only be perceived by the Palestinians as a betrayal of their cause. For those bent on attracting world public opinion to their plight, oil is an obvious target. Needless to say the Gulf rulers are terrified by such a possibility. Western European governments accept the linkage between oil and the Palestinian issue,[1] which is the main reason for their exerting pressure on the American Administration to change its posture over the Palestinian question.

1 See also Valerie Yorke, *The Gulf in the 1980s*, Chatham House Papers No. 6, The Royal Institute of International Affairs (London, 1980), p 64.

But any political subversive movement, minority, or sect struggling for recognition, autonomy, secession or social revolution could be tempted to strike at the oil in Iran, Iraq, Saudi Arabia and Oman and disaffected groups populate the oil fields and the industrial regions dependent on oil. The Gulf's source of power is also its Achilles heel. Indeed sectarian and ethnic problems – to which the collapse of the Shah acted as a catalytic agent – might challenge the regimes' very legitimacy. While criticisms coming from Sunni quarters toward Sunni regimes attest to the cracks in the pillar of Islam – the cornerstone of the Saudi regime – grievances expressed by downtrodden Shi'i minorities scattered around the Gulf contain the danger of their looking elsewhere rather than to their respective governments for redress.

The Shah's downfall also exposed the inadequacy of existing political institutions and the weakness of safety mechanisms designed to manage change and withstand pressure of the discontented. Yet the dynasties are confident that they can succeed where the Shah failed, for they do not intend to bring about their own destruction. Unlike the Shah, they are distributing their wealth and creating stakes in the well-being of the system for the entire population – be it local or foreign – believing that raising standards of living would grant them public approbation. At any rate this is their intention.

What puzzles many observers is the extent and pace of modernization maintained by the sheikhdoms. The philosophy behind this rush to develop is instructive. When asked about the means and conditions used for achieving stability, Bahrain's Prime Minister Khalifa bin Salman al-Khalifa answered:[1]

By development plans. By economic projects. By joining with the people in the development process and making them partners in the economic cycle...... By providing for the Bahraini individual, who is our true resource, in the areas of education, housing and economic needs. By giving him opportunities for work and growth. By distributing the wealth of this small country as a recognition of the effort of the citizen who helped produce this wealth, rather than as a gift of the government. By the security which protects property and possessions as well as liberties. It is the wise government which achieves true stability.

But when further asked to identify what threatens the Gulf's stability he said:

1 'Before the glass of stability is broken' in *al-Mustaqbal*, Paris, 12 January 1980.

The entire world is plotting against our stability. The western and world information media are not interested in our accomplishments...... World information media cover our news if a group of boys throw a small firecracker at a building and break the windows. Within a few hours you get a reaction from Washington, and immediately a 'liberation front' is formed and claims responsibility for the incident. The concern of the world has become to wait for the smallest incident to occur among us, as if it were a sign of instability so that all the resentments it contains can be reported by the vast world information media in order to shake confidence in us.

Such expression reflects the general mood among practically all dynastic rulers who argue that the danger to their survival is external, primarily from super-power competition.[1] But what clearly flows from the interview is first, the conspiratorial approach concerning myths in the Gulf and second, the real fear of indeed being perceived by all parties concerned as unstable. The possibility that rapid industrial expansion in itself contains detrimental factors which militate against stability seems to be totally discounted. The question is whether, beyond publicly denying that their own policies might prove counter-productive, these regimes really do understand the contradictions inherent in economic expansion, which is not necessarily conducive to the kind of development they are seeking. Are they carried away and deceived by numerous western consultants, businessmen and western governments who — like those rulers themselves — are motivated by hopes for short-term gains and the desire to make the most of things as long as it is possible? Or are they, as is more probably the case, sober enough, after the first years of intoxication, to realize the long-term threats they are bound to face because of their deliberate policies? Rather than opt for steady but limited evolutionary change as practised by Iraq,[2] prestige and other political considerations prompted the dynasties to revolutionize their countries. Soon these rulers will have to come to terms with the consequences of their own development policies which threaten to tear the

1   In the words of the Saudi Crown Prince Fahd to *al-Riyadh* newspaper: 'The countries of the Gulf have never sensed any menace from within, because the real dangers have been converging on the region from remote areas' (in *International Herald Tribune*, 19 January 1981).

2   Unlike the other Arab oil producing states in the Gulf, Iraq enjoys a relatively high absorbtive capacity, and has a reservoir of local manpower, and, theoretically, has greater potential for modernization than its southern neighbours. But the gradual pace of Iraq's economic development had more to do with the political instability which bedevilled the country, than with a more cautious economic strategy adopted by its government. Nevertheless, Iraq has learned from some of the mistakes committed by the other Gulf regimes in their ambitious schemes.

166

seams of the social fabric of their states. The first phase of implanting or establishing the previously non-existent infrastructure is a relatively easy task compared with the tasks lying ahead, especially when, for example, Saudi Arabia, under the present ruler, is deprived of the calibre of leadership displayed by those leading the Kingdom in the early days.

The threats are real but their unpredictable and varied nature renders the problems of countering them more difficult. They need to be dealt with in a comprehensive manner for the alternative could sooner or later backfire. There are no easy solutions: short-term gains do not necessarily confer long-term advantages, even if what these governments are after is essentially buying time. Still the governments are adamant; money commands all. What the dynasties seem to suggest is that economic growth can take place while conditions for social change are managed, slowed down or, preferably, eliminated. In other words, no political modernization need accompany economic modernization.

Development and 'enrichment policies' were intended to acquire power for the regimes, internal support and a measure of legitimacy. In due course, it was hoped, this combination would buy time they needed. The dilemma was that instituting a more 'liberal' system, apart from its being counter to the regimes' instincts, was bound to trigger off an uncontrollable chain reaction which would weaken if not fragment the traditional formal and informal institutions which provide the regimes with legitimacy. Setting such a process in motion, moreover, creates continuous strife between the regimes and their subjects rather than defusing it. Cosmetic change could not last. Drawing the line between what was desirable and what was feasible proved in practice impossible.

Transformation cannot be stopped for it carries its own momentum. Slowing down modernization, after it has laid the foundation for change, could prove difficult. At this juncture the Rulers would have very few means at their disposal which would enable them to control all other spheres but the economic and even there their leverage is limited. In any event, it is the next generation which will have to face most of the problems currently being created. Perhaps its members will be better equipped in having a higher degree of flexibility.

But there is much to be said for the integrative forces and pragmatism which mark the way in which the present regimes handle problems. So far, the traditional social and political systems have proved remarkably stable by virtue of their inherent ability to adapt, and a growing awareness of the need to meet and accommodate challenges in a flexible manner. Technological innovation has increased their capacity not only to promote change but also to cope with some of its undesirable manifestations. The real questions are: can the regimes synthesise the various challenges, or will they, instead, produce a highly unstable patrimonial, corrupt and repressive bureaucracy? Can free economic enterprise be indefinitely divorced from other notions of western political order yet avoid being pushed to 'revolutionary' Marxism or 'reactionary' Islam? As the example of Iran shows, the birth of a new order and the pains of transformation may not only introduce a new measure of domestic instability but even shake the entire region to its foundations.

The future

It is extremely difficult and it may even be pointless to try to devise a scale which will quantify how potent are the various sources of conflict in each of the states of the Gulf region. With the different issues interwoven and mutually reinforcing, not recognizing territorial boundaries and subject to external influence, any attempts to point to the saliency of certain factors, to attempt to create a hierarchy of threats could be misleading: to say that the Kurdish question in Iraq is more acute than in Iran or that the Shi'i problem in Bahrain is more persistent than the question of the immigrants in the UAE, would be pointless. Perhaps the possibility of a coup in Saudi Arabia may indeed be more likely than elsewhere owing to the army's past record but that does not mean that, because the Kuwaiti army has proved passive until now, Kuwait is immune from a military takeover. This, and other potential sources of unrest, could erupt any time and anywhere in the Gulf regardless of what has happened in the past.

So listing these inherently unstable states according to their potential strengths or weaknesses so as to forecast the likelihood of survival of the regimes could prove a futile exercise. Although comparing the Kingdom of Saudi Arabia with the tiny island of Bahrain could be regarded as inappropriate because the collapse of the Bahraini dynasty would not have the same catalytic affect on the entire region as a collapse of the Saudi regime, it is nevertheless worth looking at the existing patterns and trends in all states of the region because they are intimately linked. A chain reaction in the region might be triggered off not only by a change in Saudi Arabia. Moreover, the fact that there are many in Saudi Arabia who would like to see change does not make change imminent. Similarly the fact that people in Kuwait might conclude that they would be worse off under a different regime does not preclude the possibility of an internal flare-up.

By looking at Iran, Iraq and Saudi Arabia, three different patterns of instability seem to emerge. The war in Iran appears to have deprived the state of what was left of the momentum created by the revolution. For the foreseeable future, Iran seems set to remain a country at odds with itself. Islamic fervour, Iranian nationalism, separatist tendencies and democratic aspirations (of one type or another) will collide and produce havoc between opposing contenders for power, once driven by their common exasperation with the Shah and rapid westernization. It was this process which caused immense dislocation in this largely feudal society in the past and it is the problems associated with rapid modernization which will continue to bedevil a country troubled by different dichotomies. Much, of course, will depend on the outcome of the war with Iraq. Its prolongation is, ironically, in the interest of many of those striving to seize power or keen to take advantage of the weakness at the centre.

The economic chaos plaguing Iran could ultimately destroy the present regime. It was the frustrated masses which brought Khomeini to power and it could be they who turn eventually against the clergy. The only group which stands to gain from such disillusionment are the leftist groups which would strive to fill the vacuum and champion the economic grievances of the unorganized masses. Thus the very forces that the Islamic revolution unleashed could ultimately turn against it. Balkanization could follow.

The stability of the present Iraqi regime will depend largely on events in Iran. While Iraqi leaders managed in the past to defuse some of their domestic problems, President Hussein's policies seem set to aggravate them while simultaneously polarizing the Ba'ath party and alienating the military — something his predecessor managed to avoid. The aggressive manner in which he is trying to maintain exclusive control over the whole state apparatus, together with the lack of sensitivity to sectarian issues, seems likely to prove counter productive. This may enable his enemies to put aside their longstanding differences and to co-operate politically. With no real consensus even within his own party, it would seem that the present regime in Iraq has seriously undermined its power base by going to war with Iran.

Far wider is the base of the Saudi regime. The Royal Family is not just a tribe: in a sense it is the state itself. Its members occupy almost all the important jobs in all strata of the bureaucracy and in the economy. This is true also in security services, in the army and air force and in the intelligence bureaux: the State is the Family. Ironically the Kingdom's size, with its scattered and sparsely populated urban centres, makes the co-ordination of opposition far more difficult. Even if taking over one of the Provinces may prove possible, anyone trying to instigate a palace coup (perhaps the most plausible possibility) would confront many difficulties. There are numerous claimants to the throne, each with his own network of followers. Jealousies between Princes are not uncommon, and the sheer size of the family could diminish its unity. Power struggles and conspiracies and even belated blood feuds could repeat the history of Arabia with the prospects of elements from within the political system aligning themselves with alienated groups from outside or external forces. Being an oil superpower does not make Saudi Arabia immune to such challenges. On the contrary, the existing vulnerabilities inherent in the Kingdom's composition, all point to the yawning gap between Saudi Arabia's image as a politically powerful State and its actual strength. The resilience of the political system will be increasingly tested by the gathering forces which challenge Al Saud's legitimacy.

In the long run it would seem that at least some of the other dynasties in the Gulf would be ill-equipped to handle such potential threats, being further crippled by their own lack of cohesion. The absence of capable leadership means that arguments over foreign policies and conflicting concepts of how to defuse internal opposition may increasingly be enmeshed with jockeying for power within the ruling dynasties, with quarrels over succession threatening to result in fragmentation and, in some places, even secession.

Whatever their orientation, what unites these authoritarian regimes is the way in which they handle questions of their own legitimacy by avoiding major changes, by playing for time and by postponing the day when they will have to accommodate the demands of those opposing them. But failure to establish new mechanisms and institutions for coping with perennial problems does not mean that these governments will necessarily succumb to pressure. Throughout the world there are regimes which have managed to survive despite the fact that observers have numbered their days. The Hashemite monarchy in Jordan, for example, has managed to survive, initially because the opposition was too weak but also because it has managed to retain flexibility in meeting challenges and in making adjustments and concessions in the course of confrontation. It continues to exist and even to assert itself. This does not mean that the King could not be toppled tomorrow. The example of Jordan is cited not so much because it is the closest in nature to the Gulf sheikhdoms but rather to illustrate the importance of flexibility for any regime and to demonstrate that stability, or the lack of it, does not automatically translate itself into immediate collapse. Regimes continue to exist for all their enduring vulnerabilities.

But the present calm in some of these states should not be seen as stability nor as a reflection of their governments' capability to withstand internal challenges. Until now, only Kuwait and Bahrain have been put to the test and their regimes have survived. The Mecca Mosque incident revealed how little the world knows of existing pockets of opposition and it also exposed the limits of Saudi ability to handle such challenges. It would be undesirable to fall into the temptation of extrapolating capacity and stamina from a given regime's past performance and present situation.

So long as there is no serious opposition, the most ramshackle government could prove stable. On the other hand, a regime's opponents could gather momentum in spite of or because of its policy. Yet, whereas in the past internal opposition was mainly local and personal and could be contained, today that opposition is strengthened by a number of domestic factors and by regional and external forces which might widen the appeal of opposing groups.

Regardless of their social reforms, the very identification of certain regimes in the West could create the widest coalition of forces against them. Rival political groups could subsume their differences under common aims. To that end, highly emotional crowds could be inflamed and rapidly mobilized especially where religious sentiments can be manipulated. Much would thus depend on when and if such forces could put aside their differences and manage to articulate other more widely supported public grievances. But as one member of the PFLO put it:

> One of the ironies and anomalies in this region which is seething with events and developments is that the spontaneous political movement among the masses is evincing an obvious and growing state of restiveness and impatience, while the organized political forces or the organizing instruments of struggle have still not risen to the level of events, largely incapacitated by their maladies and side squabbles.[1]

Nevertheless, the conditions for dissident forces who might wish to change the *status quo* have been unintentionally improved. Such forces may include not only those who rejected modernization in the first place but also those who have been aided and elevated by it. The gap between the rising expectations of the lower echelons and the intentions of those at the tops of the pyramids cannot be easily reconciled. More and more people after establishing themselves economically, question the prerogatives of the ruling families. Their demands for real political power are echoed by many who are in any case increasingly exposed to new political ideas through the media and the constantly expanding higher education systems and studies abroad. This is true throughout the Gulf. The revolution in education is a source of pride to the regimes but it could ultimately serve to unsettle those who have introduced it.

Whatever may be the eventual outcome of the revolution in Iran, it has already had a profound impact on the entire region in prompting and accelerating change. Although these changes have proved destabilizing, they might nevertheless engender some kind of regional co-operation — however fragile and provisional. This may go beyond exchanging information on subversive elements in order to confront the common menace of domestic 'agents of destabilization' which do not recognize territorial boundaries. Yet with some of those governments attempting to manipulate each other's internal problems to acquire leverage over their neighbours, and to promote their own regional interests, permanent co-operation is simply unlikely. We must suspend judgment on the effectiveness of the Gulf Co-operation Council. The participating states may be able to subsume their differences in a common endeavour, but equally they may not. The absence of co-operation would make it more

---

1 In *al-Dustur* weekly, London, 11-17 February 1980 (JPRS, 2 April 1980).

difficult to confront internal dangers. However effective, co-operation by itself is unlikely to substitute for regime competence should these regimes need to face domestic challenges.

'Remedies' are likely to be unrealistic or counter productive. The dilemma for the regimes remains: how to keep hold on unshared power while accommodating or defusing internal and external pressures for some devolution of power. How long can they buy off the opposition? For how long can modernization proceed without creating precisely those kinds of challenges which they are ill-equipped to withstand? Can they control the pace and direction of change once set in motion? The future of the industrialized West depends in large measure on the answers to these questions.

Index

Abbas al-Muhri, Ahmad, 31
Abd al-Aziz, King, of Saudi Arabia, 32, 139, 147
Abd al-Aziz, Sheikh, of Qatar, 140
Abd al-Rahman, Prince, of Saudi Arabia, 138
Abdallah, Prince, of Saudi Arabia, 104, 137, 138
Abu Dhabi, 9, 35, 72, 105, 138, 139, 145: Bani Khalifa branch of Royal Family, 149; controls UAE army, 145; Egyptian workers in 70; finances UAE 144; Pakistan officers in Air Force, 102; problem of excessive immigration 125—6; rivalry with Dubai, 143, 144
Aden, 6
Afghanistan: Soviet invasion, 42, 43
Ahmad, Prince, of Saudi Arabia, 138
Ajman, 9, 145

Anaiza tribes 4, 12n
Arab Nationalist Movement, 50, 51, 78: Kuwaiti branch, 94, 151
Arab Oil and Economic Review, 153
Arafat, Yassir, 94
Aryana, Gen. Bahram, 162
Azarbaijan, 41—2, 160: Democratic Party, 42; Muslim People's Republican Party, 42
Aziz, Tariq, 35

Badr bin Abd al-Aziz, Amir, 20
Baghdad, 60, 61
Bahonar, Hojatoleslam Muhammad Javad, 162
Bahrain, 6, 9, 27, 28, 46, 56, 75, 94, 97, 124, 150, 171: Al Khalifa dynasty, 8, 11, 28, 30, 132, 141, 155; Asian workers in, 71; broadening government, 141; decline of agriculture, 63; economic development, 119,

120; education in, 80; emergence of new middle-class, 85; government measure against demonstrators, 30; housing programmes, 59; Iranian workers in, 73, 75, 130; labour unrest from 1954, 87–8; NLF-Bahrain, 93–4, 96; North Yemenis in police force, 74; Palestinian workers in, 69; Parliament, 151–2, 154; Parliament dissolved, 151; Popular Front of Bahrain, 94; question of elections, 155; ratio of expatriates to natives, 73; Shi'ah community, 28, 132, 133, 141, 151, 169; Shi'ah unrest after Iranian revolution, 29–30; social clubs and societies, 87; urbanization, 60, 64–5

Bakhtiar, Shahpur, 162

Baluchistan, 42–3: demands for independence, 42–3; Islamic Unity Party, 43; soldiers' service in Oman and UAE, 43, 74, 102; Soviet influence, 42

Bani Sadr, Pres., of Iran, 107, 160, 161, 162: attempts to assassinate, 161

Barazani, Mullah Mustafa, 37

Basra, 60

Bazargan, Mehdi, 161

BBC World Service, 89, 90

Bedouin: as soldiers, 100, 103, 104; conflict with authority, 10–11; in UAE, 144; Majlis sessions, 146; policy of absorption of, 122; settlement of 11, 59–60

Beheshti, Ayatollah Muhammad, 161

Birks, J.S. and Sinclair, C.A., 72

Britain: backing for Omani

forces, 8, 50, 52; consequences of withdrawal from the Gulf, 9, 100

Chamran, Mustafa, 161

Dhofar, Oman, 50, 109: Dhofar Charitable Association, 50; Dhofar Liberation Front, 50, 51; national tribal advisory body, 146; oil discoveries, 54, 119; outside support for rebellion in, 50, 51; rebellion in, 50–4, 102, 110; Salalah, 50, 53; Soviet backing, 50; wish to secede, 51–2

Dubai, 9, 27, 72, 75, 145: entrepot trade, 120; Iranian workers in, 73, 130; rivalry with Abu Dhabi, 144, 145

Dueij, Abdul-Latif al-, 153

Egypt, 98: Egyptian workers in Gulf states, 69–70, 74, 77, 130; forces in Oman, 52; Gaza Strip, 68, 69; invades Saudi Arabia (1811), 6; reasons for encouraging emigration, 70, 129–30; surplus manpower, 129–30; Voice of Cairo broadcasts, 89

Ethiopia, 92

Fahd, Crown Prince, of Saudi Arabia, 19n, 138

Faisal, King, of Saudi Arabia: death of, 17, 138

Farah Dibah, Ex-Empress of Iran, 162

Fatah, 94

Fujairah, 9, 145

Ghalib bin Ali, Imam, 50

Habash, George, 51
Hasan al-Bakr, Pres. Ahmad, of Iraq, 106, 156
Hashemite dynasty, 6, 12, 88, 171
Hawatimah, Na'if, 51
Hussein al-Takriti, Pres. Saddam, of Iraq, 34, 47, 106: establishes democratic trappings, 157; governing technique, 156, 157, 170; loss of face through Iran-Iraq war, 158; meet the people tours, 146; nepotism, 157; on enrichment of Arab rulers, 123; on the National Assembly, 158; outlaws Da'wah Party, 35; reasons for attacking Iran, 44; woos Shi'is, 46

Ibn Khaldun, 123: warns about luxury, 124
Ibn Saud, King, of Saudi Arabia, 6, 7
India: workers in Gulf states, 71; workers in Iraq, 73
International Monetary Fund: advice to Saudi Arabia, 117–18
Iran, 56, 168: armed forces, 100, 107; bombing of IRP HQ 1981, 161–2; claim to Bahrain, 9, 30–1; decline of agriculture, 63–4; education in, 80n; effect of revolution on Gulf states, 28; emergence of new middle-class, 85; Fedayeen, 64; fragmentation of Communist Party, 92–3; Hezbollahi (Partisans of Allah), 159; intelligentsia now living abroad, 83; Islamic Republic Party, 64, 159, 161, 162; Kurdish Democratic Party of Iran, 39; Kurdish question, 36, 38, 39–40, 169; loss of oil production

through Iran-Iraq war, 64; minorities, 36–43, 132; Mojahedin, 64, 160, 161, 162; *Mustazafin*, 161; nomads in, 11n; opposed to study abroad, 82–3; Organization of Freedom Fighters of the Iranian People, 91; Pasdaran (Revolutionary Guards), 39, 107, 159, 161; People's Fighters, 91; Peykar Party, 39; political unity behind revolution, 91; post-revolutionary divisions, 91, 159–62, 169–70; post-revolutionary fight for control of armed forces, 107–8; refugees, 64; religious revolution against Shah, 13, 16, 172; Revolutionary Council, 160, 161; SAVAMA security service 160; Shi'ah opposition to Shah; strains between secularization and Islam, 14–16; theocratic dictatorship, 159; trade unions, 87; Tudeh (Communist) Party, 39, 91, 92, 160; unemployment, 64; urbanization, 65
Iran-Iraq war, 28: failure of Iranian army, 107; failure of Iraqi plans, 44–5, 47; internal implications for combatants, 44–9, 161, 169–70; war of words, 46
Iran, Shah of, 19n, 23, 30, 42, 65, 93, 163, 165: attempts to curb Mullahs' powers, 15; criticizes BBC, 90; helps Oman during Dhofari rebellion, 50, 52, 110; industrialization policy, 63; relations with Kurds, 38; use of oil wealth for modernization, 14
Iraq, 27, 56, 84, 166: armed forces, 100; Ba'ath/Communist

177

mistrust, 92; Ba'ath regime, 33, 34, 36, 37, 61, 83, 106, 156, 170; Communist Party (ICP), 34, 92, 96, 157; decline of agriculture, 62; dictatorship post-1958, 156—8; elections of 1980, 157—8; emergence of new middle-class, 85, 86; fragmentation of Communist Party, 92—3; illiteracy, 80n; immigrants and advisers, 73; Islamic Call (Da'wah) Party, 34—5, 46; Israeli attack on nuclear reactor, 47, 158; Kurdish question, 36—8, 39, 131—2, 169; Kurdistan Democratic Party, 156; Lawyers Federation, 156; media control, 89; opposed to study abroad, 83; Palestinian workers in, 69, 73, 77; People's Army, 106; Progressive Patriotic and National Front (PPNF), 156; prone to coups, 110; Revolutionary Command Council (RCC), 156, 157; sedentarization of nomads 11n; Shi'ah unrest, 33—5, 131, 156, 157; socialist revolution of 1958, 13, 88; Sunni-dominated military, 106; trade unions, 87; urbanization and rural depopulation, 60—1, 65; weakness of intelligentsia, 83

Islam, 4, 99: cultural clash with West, 23—6; divisions in, 5; reaction to modernization, 14—26; Shari'ah (religious law) 5, 14, 15, 17, 148; Ummah (community of faith), 5, 12

Islamic Front for the Liberation of Bahrain, 30

Islamic Revolution Organization of the Arabian Peninsula, 33

Israel, 24, 69, 164; victory in 1967 war, 88

Jahanshahlu, Dr., 82

Jiddah, 20

Jordan: acquires most of Palestine 1948, 68; emigrants to Gulf states from, 68—9, 74; grants passports to Palestinians, 68; officers in UAE forces, 102; strengths of monarchy, 171; surplus manpower, 129—30

Juhaiman ibn Saif al Utaibi: criticizes House of Saud, 19; leads attack on Mecca 1979, 18; pamphlets, 19n

Khairallah, Major-Gen. Adnan, 157

Khalid, King, of Saudi Arabia, 104, 137, 138

Khalifa bin Salman, Sheikh: on democratic experiment in Bahrain, 154; on economic development, 165; on threats to Gulf stability, 165—6

Khameni, Hojatoleslam Sayyid Ali, 161—2

Kharijis, 5, 7

Khatib, Dr. Ahmad al-, 154

Khomeini, Ayatollah, 23, 28, 30—3 passim, 38, 42, 44, 45, 47, 63, 107, 161, 170: as leader of Shi'is, 27; exile in Iraq, 34; power in Iran, 159

Khuzistan, Iran: little help for Iraqi invaders, 48; militant Arabs of, 41, 44; National Liberation Front, 41; oil fields, 41

Kirkuk oilfields, Iraq, 37

Korea, South: workers in Gulf states, 71, 129n

Kurds, 36—40: aspirations, 36; countries containing, 36; Kurdish Democratic Party, 37, 39; Patriotic Union of Kurdistan, 39; population, 36; relations

178

with Iran, 36, 38, 39—40; relations with Iraq, 36—8, 39, 48, 131—2; take advantage of Iran-Iraq war, 46—7; war with Iraq 1974, 38; weakness of, 48—9

Kuwait, 8, 19, 27, 28, 56, 71, 73, 75, 84, 88, 93, 97, 169, 171: Al Sabah dynasty, 9, 11, 45, 139, 141, 150, 153; attitude to Iran-Iraq war, 45; British presence, 9; broadening government, 141; conscription, 103; Constitution, 150, 153; dealing with Shi'ah unrest, 31, 132—3; development as financial centre 120—1, 122; education in, 80; Egyptian workers in, 70; elections, 150, 151; emergence of new middle-class, 85; expatriates in armed forces, 102; expels illegal immigrants, 126—7, 151; housing programmes, 59; Iranian workers in, 75; oil reserves, 120; oil strike 1981, 76; Palestinian political activity in, 94—5; Palestinian workers in, 68, 69, 74, 77, 78; Parliament, 150—1, 152—3, 154, 155; Parliament dissolved, 151; PLO in, 76, 94; politics on the campus, 81—2; possibility of army coup, 110; press, 89; ratio of expatriates to natives, 72; social gatherings, 87; succession in, 139; trade unions, 87; use of expatriate teachers, 81

Kuwait Oil Company: bomb outside London offices, 153

Lebanon, 93
Libya: rules for immigrants' transfer of earnings, 128;

Madari, Ayatollah Shariat, 42, 160
Majlis (open audience), 146—7
Mecca, 7, 109: Grand Mosque Incident of 1979, 17—22, 104, 138, 147, 171; Masjid al-Haram (Holy Mosque), 18; Mosque's attackers, 20
Medina, 7: al-Medina religious university, 17, 19, 98
Mosul, 60
Muhammad, Prince, of Abu Dhabi, 139
Muhammad, Prince, of Saudi Arabia, 138
Muhammed, the Prophet, 5
Muscat, 6
Muslim Brotherhood, 20, 78, 98

Nabavi, Behzad, 162
Na'if, Prince, of Saudi Arabia, 138
Nasir al-Sa'id, 97
Nasser, Pres. Abd al-, 89; conspiracy against Saudi Arabia, 95

Oil: Arab embargo of 1973, 24; modernization consequent upon, 56—7; power conferred by, 23; quadrupling of prices 1973—4, 56
Oman, 7—8, 27, 43, 56, 75, 105; as US bridgehead, 52; British advisers, 74, 109; British-piloted air force, 102; broadening government, 141—2; decline of agriculture, 62; dependence on expatriates, 72; Dhofari rebellion, 50—4, 102, 119; education in, 80—1; Egyptian forces in, 52; expatriates in army, 102; Ibadiyah movement, 7—8, 51; Indian workers in, 71; industrializa-

tion, 119; oil production, 119; Pakistani workers in, 71; urbanization, 58, 65; use of expatriate teachers, 81; Zanzibari workers in, 74

Ovaisi, Gen. Gholam Ali, 162

Pakistan: Baluchistan People's Liberation Front in, 42; officers in Abu Dhabi air force, 102; remittances from workers in UAE to, 76n; workers in Gulf states, 71

Palestine Liberation Organization (PLO), 51, 76, 94; Gulf states' fears of, 78

Palizban, Gen., 162

Persian Gulf and adjacent states, 3: armed forces, 101; arms sales to, 101; Asian workers in, 71, 74, 129; broadening governments, 141—5; clandestine political activity, 91—6; 'commission' payments, 122—3; Communist parties in 92—4; decline of agriculture, 62; discrimination against immigrants 75—6; educational expansion, 80—4, 130, 164; effect of left- and right-wing groups, 97—9; emergence of new middle-class, 85—6; 'enrichment policy', 122—4, 167; ethnic and sectarian policies, 131—3; expatriates in, 66—7, 74; expatriates in armed forces, 101—2; expatriates in education, 74; Family Councils, 137; foreign broadcasts to, 89—90; immigrants and politics, 75—8, 164; industrialization, 115—16, 117; inner ring of states, 3; Islamic divisions in, 4—5; legacy of tribalism, 10—12; manpower 'exporters' to, 68—71; media,

88—90; media censorship, 89; military modernization, 109—11; open political activity, 87—90; outer rings of states, 3—4; plans to replace immigrant Arab with Asian workers, 129—30; political aspirations of graduates, 83—4; politico-military relations, 100-11; pre-Islamic tribal state, 4; problem of excessive immigration, 125—7, 128; proneness to coups, 110; question of government and people's expectations, 134—6, 164; ratio of expatriates to locals, 72—3, 75; reactions to Iraqi invasion of Iran, 45, 46; segregation of immigrants, 127—8; strains of modernization, 56—7, 163—4, 165, 173; Straits of Hormuz, 42; strengthening dynastic cohesion, 137—40; threats to stability, 165—7, 171—2; trade unions, 87; tribal channels of communication, 146—9; tribal dynasties, 12n; urbanization, 58—61, 65

Popular Front for the Liberation of Oman (PFLO), 52, 172; propaganda, 53

Popular Front for the Liberation of Oman and the Arab Gulf (PFLOAG), 51, 52, 152

Popular Front for the Liberation of Palestine, 94

Qabus bin Sa id, Sultan, of Oman, 52, 53, 58, 73, 119, 142, 146: deposes father 1970, 51; puts down Dhofari rebellion, 50; reforms in Oman, 51, 53

Qadhafi, Pres. Muemar al-, of Libya, 98

Qatar, 5, 7, 19, 27, 62, 65, 75,

110, 138; nineteenth-century forays, 6; oil reserves, 118n; opposition groups, 95n; organizing the Bedouin, 10-11, 59—60; Palestinian workers in, 69, 70; politics on the campus, 82; position of women in, 5n; possibility of army coup, 110; problem of secularization, 17, 21; Qahtan tribe, 59; question of conscription, 103; ratio of immigrant workers to indigenous, 72; reasons for attack on Mecca 1979, 18; Royal Guard, 104; Saudi Communist Party, 96; Saudi Liberation Front ('Free Princes'), 95; Shammar tribes, 4, 7, 20, 155; Shi'ah dissent 1979-80, 31—3, 132; stabilization of kingdom, 6; strength of Shi'ah in oilfields, 32; Sudairi tribe, 138; Sunni support for dynasty, 15; support for Oman against Dhofaris, 52; use of technocrats in government, 142; Utaibah tribe 20; Wahhabi movement, 5—6, 7, 8, 17, 18, 21; Western expatriates in, 74, 109; Western oil imports from, 32—3; Yemeni workers in, 70—1

Shakir, Sa'adun, 157

Sharjah, 8, 9, 72, 145, 149: Al Qasimi family, 144; murder of ruler 1965, 144; resentment at Dubai and Abu Dhabi's UAE veto, 144—5

Shatt al-Arab, 38, 46

Shi'ah, 5, 7, 8, 165: challenge to Gulf regimes, 27—8, 89, 109; dissent in Arab states, 28—35; distribution of Shi'is in Arab states, 27—8; political influence of ulama', 15; reactions to Iran-Iraq war, 45—6

Suhaim, Sheikh, of Qatar, 140

Sultan, Prince, of Saudi Arabia, 104, 138

Sunnis, 5, 7, 8, 165: quiescent ulama', 15, 19; ruling regimes, 27

Syria, 36, 39, 92, 93

Takfir wa-al-Hijrah, al- (group), 98

Takriti, Barazan, 157

Talil ibn Abd al-Aziz, Prince, of Saudi Arabia, 95

Taryam, Abdallah Omran, 145

Tehran, 14: occupation of US embassy, 23

Turkey, 36, 38

Turki, Prince, of Saudi Arabia, 138

Ulama' (religious scholars), 5, 7, 146: problem of modernization for, 23—4, 138—9

Umm al-Qaiwain, 9, 145

Union of Soviet Socialist Republics: Arabs educated in, 84; invasion of Afghanistan, 42, 43; possible help for Kurds, 49; question of interference in Oman, 52; relations with Middle East Communist parties 92

United Arab Emirates (UAE), 9, 43, 73, 75, 95, 103, 155: Al Ain University, 82, 149; armed forces, 105, 145; Asian workers in, 71; Baluchis in military forces, 101; Consultative Assemblies, 143; cut oil production, 124; defence budget 1980, 105, 109; education expenditure 1979, 80; expatriate officers in forces, 101—2; Federal National Council, 143, 149; Iranian workers in, 130;

middle-class unrest, 86; off-shore banking system, 120, 122; Omanis in military forces, 74, 101; Palestinian workers in, 69, 74; politics on the campus, 82, 149; problem of excessive immigration, 125, 169; problems of regional integration, 142–5; Provisional Constitution, 149; question of democracy in, 149; question of industrialization scheme, 124; ratio of expatriates to natives, 72; restrictions on immigrants, 76; Sudanese workers in, 74; support for Oman against Dhofaris, 52; Supreme Council of Rulers, 143; use of expatriate teachers, 81; use of technocrats in government, 142

United Nations Relief and Work Agency for Palestine Refugees, 68

United States of America: clash with Iran, 23; relations with Arab states, 24, 25; Voice of America broadcasts, 89

Yamani, Sheikh Ahmad Zaki al-, 142

Yasar al-Arabi, al-, 96

Yemen Arab Republic (North): Egyptian workers in, 70; surplus manpower, 129–30; workers in Saudi Arabia, 70–1, 130; Yemenis in Oman forces, 102; Yemenis in police forces of Bahrain and Qatar, 74

Yemen, People's Democratic Republic of (South), 20, 50, 53, 84, 92, 93, 102: help for Dhofari rebels, 52; workers in Saudi Arabia, 70

Zaidi sect, 20

Zayid ibn Sultan Al Nuhayan, Sheikh, of Abu Dhabi, 143

SECURITY IN THE PERSIAN GULF 4

SECURITY IN THE PERSIAN GULF

The International Institute for Strategic Studies was founded in 1958 as a centre
for the provision of information on and research into the problems of international security, defence and arms control in the nuclear age. It is international
in its Council and staff, and its membership is drawn from over fifty countries. It
is independent of governments and is not the advocate of any particular interest.

The Institute is concerned with strategic questions — not just with the military
aspects of security but with the social and economic sources and political and
moral implications of the use and existence of armed force: in other words, with
the basic problems of peace.

The Institute's publications are intended for a much wider audience than its
own membership and are available to the general public on special subscription
terms or singly.

Security in the Persian Gulf 4:

The Role of Outside Powers

SHAHRAM CHUBIN
Project Director, Regional Security Studies Programme
International Institute for Strategic Studies

Published for
THE INTERNATIONAL INSTITUTE
FOR STRATEGIC STUDIES
by
GOWER

© International Institute for Strategic Studies 1982

Published by

Gower Publishing Company Limited,
Gower House, Croft Road,
Aldershot, Hants GU11 3HR, England

British Library Cataloguing in Publication Data

Chubin, Shahram
    The role of outside powers — (Security in
    the Persian Gulf; 4)
    1. Security, International 2. Persian Gulf —
    Foreign relations
    I. Title   II. Series
    327'.116'09536   DS49.7
    ISBN 0-566-00449-6

Printed and bound in Great Britain by
Biddles Ltd, Guildford and King's Lynn

Contents

Introduction

For the decade of the 1980s, even with the greatest success for oil conservation, diversification of supplies and the substitution of other products, Western dependency on Middle Eastern oil will continue. The Persian Gulf, and particularly Saudi Arabia, will be the critical states yet their future political orientations and oil policies are uncertain.

Inhabiting a region undergoing rapid and fundamental changes, their political future cannot be guaranteed even with (perhaps especially because of) their financial assets. The types of challenges to these states' security are neither clearly identifiable nor easily met by traditional diplomatic instruments. Yet outside powers will be importantly affected by the consequences of change and instability in these states.

Not only are the challenges and threats to Western interests more inchoate and less soluble by traditional means, but those erstwhile instruments themselves, (such as raw military power) are progressively less valuable or indeed relevant to a broad range of foreign policy problems. The narrow utility of force has raised questions as to the effectiveness of the residual instruments in the armoury of Western diplomacy in their relations with their local allies. What, in short, does the West have to offer these states in a partnership? What is the currency to be offered in exchange for those governments' willingness to accommodate Western interests — the pursuit of moderate price increases, raising oil production or recycling petro-dollars?

The West is not without instruments for influencing these states. These range from implicit security relationships to mutually beneficial trading ties constituting a web of incipient interdependence. The manipulation of these instruments, and the mutual perception of common interests, however, are subject to limitation and even complete reversal, dependent as they are on political conditions within the region.

Political forces within the Persian Gulf (inter-Arab, and Iran-Arab) condition the political environment of the states in the region and hence the choices of their elites on how best to respond to assure their security. Although inherently marginal, the role of outside powers in responding to these forces and in addressing these priorities of the regional states, need not be insignificant, and indeed, may be decisive.

In addition external powers may, through their policies, aggravate indigenous instabilities — by inconsistent policies, by precipitate withdrawals of political support, or military over-reactions to local incidents. Policies designed to enhance immediate interests, such as encouraging higher oil production, may undermine longer term interests of stability and assured supplies. The manipulation of instruments of influence such as arms sales designed to aid military modernization, must be used with discrimination if they are not to endanger the regime they are intended to protect. In the long term, military modernization may itself prove a threat.

Apart from short versus longer term trade-offs, choices between regional and wider interests must be made. Both these elements are present for example in US policy choices on the Palestine question. Failure to tackle this problem will affect Saudi security and Saudi relations with the West, while energetic pursuit of a particular settlement may increase short-term problems with the Saudis. Similarly, responses to events in the Persian Gulf that see it as an autonomous region would have quite different implications for superpower relations to responses that link it with their rivalry elsewhere.

Primarily but not exclusively due to the region's oil wealth, both the West and the East have become progressively more interested in the Persian Gulf in the 1980s. This interest will endure. Each superpower will seek access to the region's resources on privileged terms, denial of the area to the other's predominant influence, and the use of strategic facilities in one form or another. This interest coupled with political and even military involvement will raise the stakes of the competition in the region and affect the capacity of the superpowers to manage indigenous conflict in the region. This intensified competition will in turn underscore the differing priorities and perspectives existing between local and outside powers. Seen from the standpoint of the superpowers, the Persian Gulf region will be a test-case for their relationship in which the extent of competition and its forms will unfold in the 1980s. Seen from the viewpoint of the international system, the volatility of politics in the Persian Gulf, together with the dependence of outside powers on the region (coupled with a narrow range of instruments of influence), will in combination be reflective of the international environment in the 1980s. Regional security will be an issue involving both local and outside powers, but the balance of responsibilities have yet to be worked out.

It is, however, with the responsibilities of the external power with which we are concerned. How can it meet these without exacerbating local tensions? What types of relationships are most conducive to regional order? Will its role be a primary or supplementary one? What formal structures, or informal patterns of co-operation hold the most promise for success in conflict management?

The nature of 'influence'

Outside power 'influence' is limited both by the nature of the challenges confronting the regional states (such as modernization, which is open-ended and intangible), and by differing perspectives and priorities. Regional co-operation, or indigenous moderate forces, cannot be created by outside powers. They can only be stimulated and reinforced by them.

'Influence' as a concept is ambiguous. It may refer to a product (outcome) or a process (a relationship). It may be narrowly issue-specific or refer to a quality in an overall relationship. As a result it may be either declining or durable. It is usually difficult to identify with precision.

It is also difficult to operationalize. Often it reflects joint or parallel interests, sometimes it involves a tacit reciprocal bargain. The desired outcome may be achieved prior to the use of 'influence' due to an anticipated reaction. What are the indicators of influence? An extensive presence? A large aid commitment? A major aid commitment? Military dependency? An institutionalized channel for influence?

Our aim is not a discussion of the general theory of influence but rather a focus on the instruments of influence available to the super-powers in their relations with specific regional states. While not oblivious to the phenomenon of reverse influence which constrains the mighty, the focus is on the use of influence as a means of managing or ameliorating or promoting instability. In the Persian Gulf this leads inevitably though not exclusively to an examination of arms sales — as

3

a means of influence and as a source of security. Arms sales constitute a visible, tangible and central tool in the relations between regional and external power. The salience of arms transfers as an instrument of influence requires examination. Here the relevant distinctions are among supplies as an inducement, or as a coercive instrument; as a specific need, or as a *symbol* of a wider relationship. Under what conditions are they an effective means of influence? What is the salience of other, general, factors in a relationship, such as economic strength (technology transfers), or a reputation as an ally? Our emphasis is on influence as an 'ordering' mechanism, as a means for affecting the policies of states and their interactions, in the service of a larger goal.

Arms transfers and policy

With the UK's withdrawal from the Persian Gulf, Western policymakers looked to local states with compatible interests to assume responsibility for security. This was generalized in the Nixon doctrine enunciated in June 1969 in Guam. In the Persian Gulf it meant reliance on Iran and Saudi Arabia as 'twin-pillars' of local strength. It implied a US willingness to build up these states for the execution of these responsibilities, by arms sales and military training.

With the dawning of the energy crisis and growing dependency on Gulf oil which was fully visible by mid-1973, the issue of Gulf security gained further prominence. Additional reasons for arms sales to the region sprang up, first the 'demand-pull' of the Shah, eager for new arms and wider responsibilities, and second, the 'supply-push' of the West, eager to 'recycle' the large revenue surpluses accruing to the oil producing states.

There remained nevertheless within the US foreign policy elite (if not in actual policy) a deep ambivalence about policy toward the region. Henry Kissinger emphasized the geo-political importance of the region, the necessity of buttressing friendly states and the imperative of maintaining a reputation for dependability and firmness; others were not so sure. Growing dependence on Gulf oil was a fact. That the answer to this fact was the buttressing of local states through arms sales which, it was argued, implied or necessitated an indirect US security commitment, was however seriously questioned by some. This school of thought did not see the choices as between a direct and indirect US security role in the region. It argued, rather, that Western interests (access to oil, moderate oil prices, and regional stability) could be achieved by different policies and policy instruments. It saw a natural conjunction of interests between the Gulf states and the West requiring little cultivation, and saw threats to security as primarily local, requiring little in the way of modern arms to meet them, and as essentially 'political', necessitating reforms rather than repression.

This broad (and over-simplified) dichotomy in approach which persists is noted for it serves as a useful benchmark in assessing the record of US policy in the region in the 1970s.

In the Persian Gulf, arms sales became a central part of the US relationship with the major littoral states. Iran and Saudi Arabia ordered arms worth $30 billion between 1973 and 1980 and were the largest importers of arms. Arms became the central component of this relationship due to the interaction of each state's requirements and needs rather than to any clear or autonomous decision by any one state.

The incentives for arms sales to the Gulf states were clear: for strategic (or defence) purposes to bolster their capacity to resist aggression; for 'influence' as a channel for creating a dependency; and for economic reasons – such as the improvement of balance of payments, to reduce the unit costs of one's own weapons, to provide employment, etc. A variety of benefits were assumed from arms sales. Joseph Sisco referred to their 'moderating influence' (1973), and Eugene Rostow to the maintenance of 'regional balances'. David Packard argued that the US would gain more influence as a supplier than as a bystander,[1] while James Schlesinger noted, astutely, that while the US sold arms for its own reasons, the views of the recipients were not necessarily identical to those of the US. If the incentives for selling arms were theoretically clear, which arms or weapons systems should be sold was not. This was the product of the buying state's own appreciation of its needs and its persuasiveness within and importance to the US.

The use of arms sales as the central instrument of foreign policy was neither totally purposive nor unilateral at this time. The general interests of the US argued for it and regional friends demanded it. Arms became the central component in the relationships because they were at once tangible, symbolic and available. Their importance transcended their practical utility or the ambiguity behind the suppliers' motives and particularly the recipients' assumptions about Western commitment, implicit in arms sales. They became the currency in relations between the US and Saudi Arabia and Iran.

From this certain consequences followed. Starting as an instrument intended to facilitate the achievement of certain goals (regional stability and advancing bilateral relations), they tended to take on a life of their

1 Also that the US by pre-emptive selling could actually reduce purchases by them from other sources.

own. As the symbol of the relationship, arms transfers became hard to deny or even to regulate.[1] It is even more difficult to manipulate arms transfers for other ends or interests. The arms relationship in short has its own dynamic: it is difficult to deny *Phoenix* air-to-air missiles if F-14s aircraft are sold, or *Sidewinder* missiles, if F-15 fighters are approved. Furthermore the large-scale provision of arms to a regime (whether the Shah or the Saudi Royal Family) restricts the ability of the supplier either to 'influence' that regime or to cultivate options with respect to it. Politically identified with the recipient regime, the supplier is locked further into it and finds it difficult to avoid acquiescence in that state's definition of its needs. Accentuating this is the arms sales constituency (the US armed services, MAAG, and the manufacturers among others), which comes to see military assistance as an end in itself rather than a means. Advocacy thus often replaces responsible criticism. Furthermore, as arms become a substitute for alliance, they take on almost mystical qualities. Impervious to arguments about their intrinsic worth, they acquire great political and symbolic value. If restricted or denied they can weaken or destabilize the recipient politically, domestically and regionally. For the supplier state too they acquire greater importance as they come to be seen as a product or service that it is relatively much easier to supply to fortify the bilateral relationship than alternatives such as a formal defence treaty or a solution to the Palestine question.

The nature of a relationship in which arms sales occupy a key role is thus inherently complex and muddied. The important question is whether the record of its use as an instrument in diplomacy in the Persian Gulf is clear as to its effectiveness. Has it contributed to the achievement of US goals, and with what consequences?

In the section that follows I examine US relations with Iran and Saudi Arabia and Soviet relations with Iraq. In the case of Iran and Saudi Arabia, I make a distinction between the phases 1973-76 and 1977-80. In Iran's case a further division is made in the second phase to distinguish between the pre-revolutionary and post-revolutionary periods. This enables us to assess arms transfers as an instrument for durable influence in quite different political settings. In the case of Iraq—Soviet relations, the arms relationship is especially important in that arms sales are one of the few instruments of Soviet influence in the Third World, while Iraq is one of their older clients, dating back two decades.

---

1 Many observers have noted that when a particular arms request is under consideration the wisdom of the specific item is not at issue. Rather the entire relationship and the dependability of the supplier become the stake.

6

The three states contrast in their relations with the superpowers. Unlike Saudi Arabia, Iran has had a military assistance relationship with the US dating back over three decades. This was originally a government-to-government relationship with US advisers (MAAG) and it was strengthened by a bilateral Executive Agreement on Defence (1959) and participation in CENTO, in which the US was an associate member. In addition, Iran has diplomatic ties with the USSR. By contrast a Saudi defence relationship with the US is recent — starting in the 1970s — and only in the late 1970s did it become government-to-government, and more intensive. It is still informal with no express security commitment. Moreover Saudi Arabia does not have ties with the USSR.

Iraq, like Saudi Arabia, has ties with only one superpower, the USSR. The 1972 Treaty of Friendship contains a defence clause roughly comparable to Iran's rather weak assurance under the Executive Agreement. The Soviet Union is Iraq's major though not exclusive arms supplier. As with the US, arms transfers have been the major instrument in Soviet diplomacy with her ally in the Gulf, perhaps even more so. What is its record of achievement?

The second part of the book examines the potential contribution of the outside powers to conflict management in the region against the backdrop of trends in regional politics. The role of regional powers and regional structures is the related concern of this section which also evaluates the regional potential for conflict management.

1 The Record of Outside Power Influence

US—Iran 1973-80

The background: 1973-76

The US involvement in Iran's military programmes dates to the late 1940s. From the immediate post-war period onward, strains developed between the Shah's view of Iran's defence needs and those of the US. American assistance in the restoration of the Shah in 1953 increased the psychological dependency of Iranian leaders on Washington. To this was added a real material dependency on US grant and budgetary assistance until 1967. By the mid-1960s, as Iran's oil income increased, Iran moved from grant-aid to credit-purchases from the US. This in turn gave way to outright purchases in the late 1960s and Iran's choices and bargaining power increased. US views of the optimum size for Iran's armed forces, or the appropriate weapons-systems for them were still heard, but increasingly ignored. By the early 1970s these American views, which had counselled restraint on an arms build-up for over two decades, were no longer offered. In part this was because Iran's oil wealth enabled it to reject views which it earlier had no choice but to accept. But equally important was the changed international context within which the Shah's perennial appetite for arms appeared intelligible and even welcome.

Foremost among these was the need for a strong and friendly state to protect US (and Western) interests in the Gulf.[1] The Shah was not only eager for Iran to do this and at her own expense but was prepared to do so on a wider canvas including the Middle East and the Indian subcontinent. US interests thus coincided with those of the Shah and a relationship was fashioned that not only avoided the need for a direct US military role but also promised support for its growing interests at a very low cost. The (only) identifiable costs were the sale of arms to the Shah's regime, a dependable but not formal ally. The strategic benefits from the point of view of a Republican administration contending with a public intent on retrenchment and selective commitment, were obvious. Equally clearly, a role as principal arms supplier implied concomitant influence which could be manipulated as the recipient's dependence (on spare parts and training) grew. Hence Kissinger's cryptic reference in 1974 that he was fashioning with these states 'reasons for restraint'.

Apart from the longstanding arms relationship with Tehran and a willingness to strengthen a 'moderate' state able to assume wider responsibilities, the US had concrete political–military objectives in the Gulf. The establishment of a regional security system was one priority. Another was the strengthening of Iran itself *vis-à-vis* the Soviet Union, which was increasing its military potential. An Iran assured of its defence needs would be less prone to buckle under Soviet pressure. Often forgotten today, the May 1972 Nixon–Kissinger decision to allow the Shah to buy any conventional arms he wished came a month after the Soviet–Iraqi defence agreement and several months after the dismemberment of Pakistan. It also came before the quintupling of oil prices at the end of 1973. It was thus something less than the *carte blanche* it has been made out to be. Nevertheless the 1972 understanding was an order of magnitude change in US policy which formalized the US' transition from restraining patron to acquiescent partner. It could be argued that this reflected a new interdependent partnership rather than created it. Internationally this may have been the case. Domestically, it sealed the future of the US interests with the Shah's fate. Yet in 1972 this appeared neither avoidable nor unwelcome. The Shah's was apparently the most stable and certainly the longest lived regime in the Middle East.

How successful was US policy in obtaining its objectives within Iran in 1969-76? As far as security interests were concerned the record is clear. The Shah's role enhanced Gulf stability by containing Iraq, pacifying the Dhofari rebellion which had been abetted by South

---

1 This is not to suggest that many of these interests did not coincide with what the Shah considered in Iran's interests.

Yemen and the USSR and establishing working relations with Saudi Arabia. Further afield, Iran's diplomatic initiatives in Egypt and in the Indian subcontinent also worked in favour of diminishing conflict and strengthening peace.[1]

Militarily Iran's arms build-up and their assimilation was not tested. Yet it was already clear that rather than diminish US involvement, in at least its initial stages, the military component of the Nixon Doctrine (arms sales) actually increased the US physical presence. By 1976 there were some 25,000 military-related personnel (and their dependents) in Iran.

On the other hand the build-up of Iran militarily held the potential for a regional equilibrium less susceptible to disturbance by outside powers. The fact that Iran's arms were US supplied and largely compatible with those of US forces, together with the availability of Iran's military facilities, enhanced US and allied capabilities for rapid reaction in grave contingencies. Furthermore use of Iranian territory for intelligence and Soviet missile test monitoring were useful by-products of the arms relationship.

In the area of oil pricing, Iran and US interests diverged. While Tehran saw its interest in increasing its revenues (and even thereby discouraging consumption), Washington saw oil price rises as politically unpalatable and economically inflationary. The Shah's pursuit of Iran's interests to increase its revenues were historically justifiable and economically defensible. The difference between the two states' economic interests here was not allowed to wreck the compatability of interests on other security questions. Suggestions from various sources to invade the oilfields (Robert Tucker), encourage the break-up of OPEC (Professor Adelman), stimulate divisions between Iran and Saudi Arabia (Treasury Secretary Simon and Senator Frank Church) or favour Saudi Arabia over Iran (Ambassador J. Akins) were rejected by Nixon and Kissinger. Whether real or not,[2] linkage between the security dimension of US—Iranian relationship and oil-price questions (and Iran's role as advocate of price increases) was never formally invoked. However, careful consideration was given to a policy of such a linkage in the closing months of the Ford Administration.[3]

---

1 To these could be added the supply in 1974 of F-5s to South Vietnam at US request; the provision of oil to the US Navy in late 1973, and the supply of oil to Israel.

2 Adherents to the view that the oil-price increases were the result of expensive arms sales which necessitated greater revenues, (cf. Dale Tahtinen, 'Arms in the Persian Gulf') and Senator Frank Church (among others of the American Enterprise Institute for Public Policy Research, 1974) are unpersuasive.

3 Leslie Gelb, *New York Times*, 12 November 1976.

The Nixon-Ford presidencies were the highpoint of US—Iranian co-operation in which a tacit partnership evolved covering defence and security affairs in the Gulf and Middle East. Iran's policies were largely congruent with those of Washington and furthered their joint interests; differences on oil prices were submerged; and bureaucratic procedures were circumvented to facilitate this close relationship. Something approaching a 'special relationship' had indeed evolved largely due to the personal relationships between Nixon, Kissinger and the Shah.

The stability and durability of this personal (rather than institutionalized-bureaucratic) relationship was, however, suspect — largely for this very reason. There was no real consensus within the US, either in the bureaucracy or in the public at large, as to the wisdom of this close relationship. Some argued that oil prices were more important than military—security issues; others that the 'over-arming' of Iran threatened either regional or domestic stability, or that Iran's arms expenditures diverted resources from her economic development.[1] There was also a general hesitancy to embrace any further a regime with an 'unattractive' record on human rights. No matter that there were few suggestions as to how the US might extricate itself from dependency on the region without greater, and more direct, military involvement, there was a clear trend toward questioning the wisdom of the Republican administration's policies. By 1976 the consensus was unravelling and the tone of comments in that election year affected US—Iran relations.

The relationship underwent a marked shift in that year, losing its special status and reverting to straight bargaining. Sensing the new mood in Washington, the Shah resorted to earlier and successful tactics. In 1976-77 he hinted obliquely in interviews that if arms sales to Iran were curtailed he would:

1 Retaliate by limiting trade with the US.
2 Reconsider Iran's regional role promoting stability.
3 Buy arms from the USSR.
4 Be 'difficult' on issues relating to non-proliferation. (The latter was in fact used as an 'inducement' — that is, to show

---

1 Senator Church (1977); Lincoln Bloomfield (1976); Edward Kennedy (1974); Theodore Moran (1978); Leslie M. Pryor (1978). None of these authors suggested how the US could expect Iran to support Western interests if the US did not in turn meet some of the Shah's concerns.

his good faith, he supported US policies noting that he had the option not to do so.)[1]

A much clearer example of Iranian bargaining was in November 1977 on the Shah's visit to the US. In Washington he announced his support for an oil-price freeze in that December's OPEC meeting (in his hosts' idiom) by 'giving the US a break'.

The mood in Washington reflected a marked change in US priorities. Less geo-political than the Republicans, the Democrats were also less comfortable with the Iranian Shah who appeared arrogant, demanding and aloof. Defining security in other than purely military terms, the Carter administration sought to promote universal values such as human rights, particularly among its Third World allies. This implied greater popular political participation and more debate within those countries as to their policy choices and direction. In this view, stability in a region began with political stability at home. As regards Iran, the close — even cordial — relationship was gradually changed to a correct, working relationship. Standard comments of respect and public reassurance were still forthcoming from Washington but they carried less conviction. In fact, the Carter administration subtly shifted to a twin-pillar policy in which Saudi Arabia rather than Iran was given pre-eminent weight.[2]

In arms sales this shift was most apparent. Iran's requests were now routed through bureaucratic channels rather than allowed to short-cut them. US arms sales guidelines announced in May 1977 shifted the 'burden of proof' on to those requesting a particular purchase (rather than those rejecting it). This less permissive approach had an immediate impact. In July 1977 Iran's request for 250 F-18L aircraft was refused.[3] In July 1978 a request for advanced electronics on the F-4G was also refused. In addition the Carter administration sought where possible either to defer, or to scale down requests. Iran's request for a second tranche of 150 F-16s was accordingly postponed in 1977-78.

The Carter administration, though insensitive to the domestic political impact of such refusals within Iran, still sought to maintain its

---

1 *Business Week.* Note also that in 1976 when questions were raised about the activities of Iranian security personnel in the US, the Shah hinted that any restriction of their activities would be followed by Iran imposing restrictions on CIA activities within Iran. This implied a *quid pro quo* with the intelligence facilities used by the CIA–USA in Northern Iran for monitoring missile tests and signals and radio communications in the USSR. *Washington Post*, 1979.

2 Jim Hoagland and J.P. Smith, 'Saudi Arabia and the United States'. *Survival*, vol. XX, no. 2, March-April 1978, pp. 80-7.

3 The reason given was that the aircraft was not operationally deployed with US forces, a qualitative control outlined in the May 1977 guidelines.

ties with Iran despite Iran's human rights record. It thus supported the arms commitments it had inherited from the preceding administration. It expended considerable political (and presidential capital) in the latter part of 1977 in convincing a sceptical Congress of Iran's need for six AWACs early-warning aircraft. It also supported the request for the first tranche of 150 F-16s for delivery to Iran early in the 1980s. The AWACs affair, exacerbated by the administration's own 'open' approach to government which revealed differences within its own ranks (notably the CIA's opposition) and its own innocence of relations with Congress, also demonstrated the difficulties of shifting policies in such a sensitive area. Commitments were hard to stop, not merely because they were inherited, but because they were part of a process symbolizing the overall relationship.[1]

The more sceptical view of arms transfers as a tool of influence for promoting either bilateral relations or regional stability was paralleled in Carter's more low-key approach to political crises in the Third World. In neither Afghanistan (1978) nor Somalia—Ethiopia (1977-1978) did the United States respond militarily to these events, despite indications of Soviet complicity in the disturbances. The divergence between Iran's (and Saudi Arabia's) perceptions of the threat and that of the US were quite clear. Washington used its closer relationship with Iran to prevent the transfer of US-supplied arms to Somalia.[2] This affected both states' perceptions of their ally's dependability and willingness to meet their security needs.

The revolutionary upheaval

With the emergence of widespread unrest within Iran in 1978, US policy shifted and with it the utility of its policy instruments. From pursuing a close but measured relationship with an Iran considered a 'force for stability in the area' and a dependable ally, pursuing policies supportive of US interests, it became necessary to seek to contain that country's turbulence before it disrupted those wider interests. In the fluid politics that characterized the disintegration of the Shah's regime, the arms relationship was of limited value. The US sought

---

1   'Our willingness to sell arms is seen by many, indeed most, friendly governments, as a litmus test of our bilateral relationships. . . . a refusal to sell invariably touches an extremely sensitive nerve, and tends to raise doubts in the minds of the affected country about the assumed strength of the bilateral relationship in security affairs and about the future reliability of the United States as an arms supplier'. Lucy Wilson Benson, 'Turning the Supertanker: Arms Transfer Restraint', *International Security*, Spring 1979, p. 17.

2   Under the traditional 'end-use' agreement governing arms transfers giving the supplier the right to veto third party transfers by the original recipient. This veto was not exercised by the US in Iran's involvement in Oman because the arms remained in Iran's hands.

'damage limitation' and counselled political rather than military 'solutions'. There was no identifiable or discrete military threat that could be met by new, better or more arms. The close military relationship with the Shah's regime, a crucial asset in the event of aggression from external sources, was too blunt an instrument for this contingency.[1] Nor could less equivocal US expressions of support for the Shah or even the deployment of US troops to Iranian territory have materially affected the outcome of the revolution unless perhaps they had been forthcoming early in the upheavals. This was not possible because the initial unrest was not seen as the beginning of a momentous revolution but rather as sporadic and isolated disturbances. In the event, the US arms relationship with Iran, symbolizing its close ties with the Shah,[2] was transferred from an asset for influence in a peaceful era into a liability in a revolutionary situation. Even as a deterrent against external intervention in Iran's crisis, the demonstrative use of force by the US could have been counter-productive. Hence Washington's reluctance to allow the sailing to the Gulf of a carrier task force from the Philippines, which it had initially considered. The danger that such a move might be construed domestically in Iran as opposition to the revolution and set off still wider disturbances[3] overrode the initial impulse either to signal support for the Shah or deter Soviet involvement.

As the Shah's fate was sealed in the streets of Tehran, Washington re-examined its options. It found that the military relationship still conferred on it certain advantages. The fact that Iranian officers had been largely trained in the US (over 12,000 since 1947), could speak English and were well acquainted with their American counterparts, gave the US a natural channel for communication to the still intact armed forces. It was evident to all that this could still be a considerable advantage in the bargaining that would shape the future course of politics in Iran. The dispatch of General Huyser (Deputy to the US Commander in Europe) in December 1978 was intended by the US to establish an independent line of communication to these military

---

1 Ironically the Shah's regime had planned its security forces to meet isolated low-level guerrilla violence through SAVAK, and high-level military threats through its armed forces. The interface of these two categories of threat, widespread civil disorder which might have been met by mobile, tactical police forces armed with shields, rubber bullets and incapacitating gases, was not anticipated probably due to bureaucratic jealousies and a refusal to admit, even privately, its possibility. This question is important for its potential relevance to other states in the Gulf.

2 In addition to the co-operation between intelligence services spanning the decades, with which we are not here concerned.

3 The British Ambassador Antony Parsons who was in close touch with US Ambassador William Sullivan has argued that this move would have enraged the crowds still further rather than cowed them. (Personal interview, London, 1979).

commanders. Despite the controversy surrounding the mission,[1] this much is clear – the existence of an independent channel to the armed forces derived from the close military relationship with the US. Second, this channel was an important and potentially crucial one for influencing politics in Iran after the departure of the Shah.[2] The maintenance of an intact military as an institution could confer considerable bargaining advantages in managing both the post-revolutionary politics of Iran and the transition. How this channel of communication was used and what other forces bore on it is however more contentious. For our purposes it is sufficient to note the US dilemma in using this channel. The impulse to use the military to support the Bakhtiar government to extract assurances and concessions from the Bazargan–Khomeini forces competed with the conclusion of many US officials that the victory of the latter's forces was inevitable. The argument for recognizing the 'inevitable' and urging the military to withdraw support from Bakhtiar by announcing 'political neutrality' (with specific assurances from Khomeini about the military's welfare) was especially tempting for a United States that wanted above all to maintain its position within the country. Whether it was this that precipitated the Iranian generals' decision to opt for 'neutrality' in mid-February is still not clear. Evidently the generals were divided. Some saw the Shah's exile as temporary, others sensed the end of an era and a shift in American policy toward accommodating Khomeini. Whatever the relevance of the various factors, the channel available to the US was not used productively. The neutrality of the military was followed by its destruction and its senior officers were executed. The US' ambiguous role was condemned by royalist and republican alike.

Post-revolution

The immediate consequence of the revolution was the virtual disintegration of the armed forces (desertion ran at 60 per cent), the purging of senior officers, and the withdrawal of US technicians and advisers. (The MAAG for example was reduced to six from approximately 400). In addition six intelligence gathering bases run by the CIA and NSA were lost. Advanced military equipment like the 77 F-14 aircraft and their *Phoenix* missiles were also at risk in the anarchy that followed

---

1   The Shah believed the Huyser mission was intended to undermine him and expedite his exile.   General Haig and others are sceptical about the US role as well. See also Michael Ledeen & William Lewis, 'Carter and the Fall of the Shah', *The Washington Quarterly*, vol. 3, no. 2, Spring 1980.

2   Ambassador William Sullivan appears to have recognized the importance of the military as a channel to post-revolutionary Iran. See 'The Road Not Taken', *Foreign Policy*, no. 40, Fall 1980, pp. 175-86.

February 1979. In this new era it was the task of US diplomacy to prevent a total break in relations that would jeopardize its economic and political-military interests in the country. To do so it had to show a less conspicuous presence in the country but to conserve what contacts it had initiated with the new regime, and patiently to await the emergence of order in the country. In time, it was expected, a hierarchy would be established, priorities would be identified, and pragmatic considerations, both strategic and economic, would impel Iranian—US co-operations — albeit on a lower key.

American caution after February 1979 was understandable. Totally identified with the Shah over three decades, it had a burdensome past to live down with the new authorities and in the new anti-Western ethos in Iran. At the same time important interests were at stake: the prevention of a communist or leftist takeover in Iran which would further unsettle the Gulf region; the continuation of the export of oil to the US and, more important, to her European and Japanese allies.[1] The US therefore attempted to 'normalize' relations and to avoid giving offence or fostering the notion that she was intent on containing or isolating the new regime. Care was exercised to prevent provocation, criticism of massive human rights violation were perfunctory, and the best possible construction put on statements of intent emanating from Tehran. Where possible the 'moderate' forces' comments were singled out, and stressed, implicitly distinguishing between PM Bazargan and Ayatollah Khomeini. In short Washington sought to show that it was prepared 'to do business' with the new authorities in Tehran.

Events in Iran in mid-1979 seemed to support this approach. Despite statements to the contrary, the armed forces were not completely disbanded. In May, relations with Iraq and in August, relations with the Kurds deteriorated sharply and the Iranian authorities rediscovered the need for a military system that functioned. Despite the cancellation of $11 billion worth of US arms ordered by the Shah, the country had taken possession of $8 billion worth which were still largely unassimilated. If these were not to become scrap, spare parts and maintenance assistance would be required from the United States. Furthermore continued technical training of Iranian personnel was necessary for much of this material.[2] In addition, the Iranian logistical system had been computerized by the US. Without adequate skilled personnel the

---

1   The US normally imported 9 per cent of her energy imports (4 per cent total consumption) from Iran. In Europe the proportions were higher. In Japan Iran accounted for 20 per cent of her imports which were 90 per cent of her needs.

2   This in fact still continued. Despite revolutionary rhetoric some 250 Iranian military were being trained in the US in November 1979 (contrasted with 2,500 in 1976).

location of spare parts already in the country's inventory would be impossible. In short the umbilical cord leading from Iran to the US was still very real. The US, aware of this objective dependency, was anxious to use it discreetly as a basis for preliminary co-operation. To do so, it needed to avoid any public reference to it or to appear to be driving a hard bargain. Washington was extremely sensitive lest an attempt to exploit it should backfire and terminate the only existing channel for contact and co-operation. Thus it was hoped that the military relationship would prevent too complete or too rapid a break-down in an overall relationship that was politically strained. Any unwillingness to respond sensitively to any Iranian requests was thus seen in Washington as potentially damaging to US interests, for this would drive the new regime elsewhere. Moreover the option of outright rejection was discarded because it might force the regime's hand and drive it into a corner, and possibly toward the USSR.

Washington thus found that Iran's military dependency, far from strengthening America's hand, inhibited it from the exercise of influence lest it jeopardize that channel. No matter that Iran's dependence was real, that Iran had tangible security problems that needed to be met, that Iran still required a counterpoise to the USSR, and that shifting arms supplies is a lengthy and costly business in which the transition period could be particularly dangerous – and that all of these considerations could be expected to militate in favour of US not Iranian leverage – supplier leverage simply did not materialize.

In practice the reverse happened. In mid-1979 the US, while continuing the technical training of Iranians, agreed to provide non-lethal spare parts, which (it was argued) had already been paid for. In addition there were reports of supplies of diesel fuel for military vehicles used in Kurdistan. US refined heating oil was also made available to the Iranian government. Negotiations for the resale of F-14s to the US were also announced but not initiated in 1979.

The semblance of 'normalization' was as illusory as was Washington's expectation that 'moderates' would emerge in Iran's revolutionary condition. The cultivation of the moderates in this situation was the kiss of death. The fear of Iran's disintegration, of a replacement by a leftist regime or even of further chaos, were powerful incentives arguing for 'doing business' with Khomeini's regime. Yet it was difficult to establish direct contact with the Ayatollah, who had in any case a totally different frame of reference. For Khomeini 'security' was to be achieved through revolutionary unity and purity not through arms. This meant that practical considerations held less importance than the manipulation of symbols. The occupation of the US Embassy in October 1979, supported by Khomeini, brought down the Bazargan government. In this episode the limits of American influence were further exposed. Khomeini's willingness to invite an American military response, to claim martyrdom or to expose US weakness while objectively foolhardy, was nonetheless tactically irreproachable for mobilizing revolutionary zeal and unity.

The US' responses were limited by a variety of factors. The well-being of the hostages ruled out any precipitate military rescue while regional and global considerations deterred a major punitive military operation. Furthermore the use of force might consolidate Iranians behind Khomeini and frighten US allies in the region. However, the failure to respond would also be costly. It could strengthen Khomeini's image among the Iranian masses, advertise US impotence and frighten US allies. The use of non-military instruments, such as trade embargoes, would hurt the Iranian people rather than the government and might, in any case, have proved ineffective, at least in the short run. Multilateral actions with Western allies confronted the problem of the greater dependence of these states on Iran's oil.[1] Furthermore the American freezing of Iranian funds inside the US (applying also to foreign banks) created strong resentments among US allies about a unilateral measure which affected multilateral interests.

The military relationship and the hostage episode

The seizure of some sixty US citizens, mostly diplomats, in the US Embassy in Tehran by militant students on 4th November, supported by the Iranian authorities, ushered in a new phase in Washington's relationship with the revolutionary regime. No longer so anxious to reassure Tehran about its 'acceptance' of the revolution and its willingness to work with it, Washington now sought to convey to the Iranian leaders the costs involved in supporting such hostile activities. In attempting to communicate this over the next fourteen months, Washington was constrained both by its continuing interest in Iran's political cohesion and by the refusal of the authorities in Tehran to acknowledge their continuing dependence on the US for arms. This failure to recognize or act upon an 'objective interest' made the Iranian leadership impervious to the types of sanctions and incentives that could be manipulated in the arms supply relationship. Normal assumptions about dependency fostering a business-like attitude or inhibiting extreme measures did not therefore hold in a situation where the dependent partner was prepared to sacrifice his material interests for a 'higher' goal.

---

1 Especially Japan's reluctance to forego Iran's oil or jeopardize her reasonably good economic relations with the new regime.

The Bazargan government had quickly recognized the reality of this military dependency and the necessity for the maintenance of a defence establishment. With considerable pragmatism they had embarked in the summer of 1979 upon re-establishing links with the United States — which had proved to be equally business-like. Foreign Minister Yazdi had put the matter very simply: 'We have bought billions of dollars worth of military equipment from the United States, and for the maintenance of this equipment we need parts. So obviously there will be, and there are, some contracts — you may say a purchasing contract — for the parts'.[1] Yazdi was aware that the issue of any type of military relationship with the US was a potentially contentious one. This was not merely a matter of emotions or revolutionary rhetoric. In the continuing power struggle in Iran it was clear that the future role of the armed forces could be decisive. Who supplied, advised and influenced these forces could play an important role in Iran's future. Nevertheless he and Bazargan still underestimated the power of the militants within Iran. By showing a willingness to acknowledge the necessity of a continuing Iran—US relationship, they inadvertently provided a pretext for those seeking a total rupture of relations.

The subsequent details of the saga of the US hostages concerns us only to the extent that the military component of the relationship was utilized. On 9 November the United States halted and impounded a $300 million shipment of aircraft spare parts; the announcement for the resumption of deliveries having been made on 5 October. On 23 November, the US announced that flight training for the 273 or so Iranian military personnel[2] still in the United States would be terminated, although other instruction courses would continue. The effect of these measures was to inhibit any commercial relationship in the military field by independent businesses and contractors. US companies complied with a government request to reduce their number of representatives in Iran.[3]

A second set of pressures were set in motion in the Spring. On 17 April President Carter declared that the $300 million in spare parts which had been paid for would now 'be made available for use by United States' military forces or for sale to other countries'. The bulk of this equipment comprised aircraft and helicopter parts. The practical effect of this move was that, if future US—Iranian relations should

---

1 *International Herald Tribune*, 5 July 1979.

2 The figures vary but appear to have consisted of 249 undergoing training with the USAF of which 200 were pilots, and 24 with the Navy of which 19 were pilots. See *Air Force Times*, 19 November 1979.

3 *Boston Globe*, 15 November 1979.

improve to the point of a renewal of the arms relationship, 'it will be longer and harder for them (Iran) to recover' because now there would be no parts in the pipeline.[1] Ten days earlier the severance of diplomatic relations had ended the remaining military training relationship and all Iranian military personnel had been returned to Iran.[2] A consequence of the measures undertaken by Washington after November was the severance for all practical purposes of any form of co-operation — official or commercial — in areas related to technology likely to have potential military application. This was due as much to the anger of US companies at the seizure of the hostages as to specific or express government prohibition. Nevertheless the implication of Washington's actions was clear: no company could expect government support in any claim against Iran if no diplomatic relations existed. Washington's measures therefore had the wider effect of inhibiting the continuation of normal commercial contacts such as the provision of 'customer service' by aircraft companies such as Boeing.[3]

Frustrated by the failure of these and other economic sanctions to make an impression on the Iranian government, the United States launched a rescue mission to free the hostages on 24 April 1980. Two aspects of this aborted mission concern us: the decision to launch the incursion by air from eastern Iran; and the expectation of some co-operation by Iranian military units within the country. Both of these components relate directly to the military and arms relationship. The choice of approach site was almost certainly due to the United States' knowledge about the likely blindspots in Iran's radar coverage — information that was due to its own contribution in their construction. Second, the military assistance expected from within the Iranian armed forces was due to the longstanding and extensive contacts between the two countries' military services.[4] In the context of the April mission, James Schlesinger's remarks six years earlier are apposite. Asked whether the United States had considered the effects of the sale of arms to countries that it might in future have to fight, the Defence Secretary said: 'In the extreme and highly unlikely circumstances (suggested) . . . it is not clear that American forces would prefer to come face-to-face

---

1 For the text of Carter's statement see *The New York Times*, 18 April 1980. See also *Wall Street Journal*, 18 April 1980.

2 See *Aviation Week and Space Technology*, 14 April 1980, p. 23.

3 See *ibid*., p. 15.

4 This expectation of assistance appears to have been justified. The Iranian Air Force's destruction of the helicopters left behind at Tabas before they could be examined for information was much remarked upon in Iran and appears to have been due only partly to caution relating to their physical security. The former Chief of the Iranian Air Force, General Bagheri was subsequently arrested on charges of collusion with the US. See *International Herald Tribune*, 26 February 1981.

with equipment supplied by some other power as opposed to the US'.[1]

It was soon clear that the severance of spare parts from the United States and the prohibition of all arms transfers to Iran from any country possessing US-made equipment[2] was exacting a price on Iran, particularly in aviation. Iranian agents attempted unsuccessfully to circumvent the embargo by purchases in Europe.[3] In November 1979 Western observers reported that the radar systems were unserviceable and that the F-14s (of which Iran had 77) were barely operational. The 380 F-4s and F-5s were said to be 50 per cent operational. The helicopter force of nearly 1,000 was reported to be largely grounded.[4] The computerized logistics system was now in total disarray. As a result it was impossible to locate the existence of spare parts or supplies which might exist in inventory. Whether this was due simply to the lack of adequately trained manpower and inadequate assimilation of the technology, or due to actual sabotage — as implied by President Bani Sadr — is unknown. He observed that the operational readiness of the three armed services in January 1980 varied between 5 and 25 per cent.[5] A more obvious case of US sabotage related to the *Phoenix* air-to-air missile. Sensitive components of this missile were disassembled and removed by American technicians before their departure from Iran — a clear case of supplier leverage.[6]

Iran's efforts to procure military supplies through West Germany and Italy proved unsuccessful.[7] By January 1980, Iran's helicopter force of 1,000 was down to an operational readiness of some 15 per cent, due in large part to the lack of support personnel and spare parts from the US. The Italian government refused to supply the fifty CH-47C *Chinook* (Agusta-Bell) helicopters ordered by Iran pending the release of the hostages.[8] The effect of this was felt not only in the

1 Department of Defense News Release, 14 January 1974 (Pentagon Press Conference), as cited in James Noyes, *The Clouded Lens*, Hoover Institution, 1977, p. 197.

2 Or with a licence to manufacture it.

3 *Baltimore Sun*, 19 November 1979.

4 The articles by Robert Fisk in *The Times*, 27, 28 November 1979 and US Defense Department evaluations in *International Herald Tribune*, 19 November 1979.

5 Bani Sadr, interview *Le Monde*, 8 October 1980. The logistical system cost, according to the President, $250 million.

6 See *Aviation Week and Space Technology*, 20 October 1980.

7 *Newsweek*, 31 December 1979, p. 17.

8 See *Aviation Week and Space Technology*, 28 January 1980, p. 11; 18 February 1980, p. 15; 14 April 1980, p. 20. Agusta had 100 technicians in Iran and had provided 60 helicopters before the revolution.

military field where Iran's new defence officials with extraordinary naiveté had recently discovered the usefulness of the helicopter force inherited from the Shah's regime.[1] In fields of civil application (such as in flood relief operations) the spare parts for helicopters were missed and this was readily and publicly admitted.[2]

By mid-1980 it was clear that Western sanctions, especially in the military field, were exacting their toll. In addition to the political purges, desertions and the decline in discipline and morale in the armed forces and the low esteem in which they continued to be publicly held, the loss of technical assistance together with the severance of spare parts had reduced the Iranian military's capabilities even further. In the context of its international isolation, Iranian officials used their one remaining bargaining card *vis-à-vis* the West — the 'threat' to become dependent on the USSR. This had already been implied by economic agreements with the Eastern bloc announced the day after EEC sanctions were agreed on 22 April. In May this threat was revived in the context of potential arms supplies from the USSR to reduce Iran's dependence on the United States.[3]

The threat was significant for it reflected Iran's awareness of the limits to Western pressures. US measures after 4 November had been intended to impress upon Iran's leaders the costs of supporting such illegal actions as hostage-taking while continuing to offer the prospect of a normal relationship once the issue was resolved. Washington's responses had been gradual and calibrated, sensitive to both political pressures building up within the United States and the need to avoid precipitate action by offering Tehran the possibility of a peaceful solution. After the Soviet invasion of Afghanistan, President Carter and, after the rescue mission, Secretary Brown, each offered to normalize relations if the hostage issue were resolved. Indeed Carter in January had even offered to resume the sale of arms to Iran.[4] The United States' strategic interest in Iran had now been heightened by the presence of Soviet troops close to the Gulf. As a result, Defense Secretary Brown observed: 'We are quite eager to restore good relations . . . We do want to be friends with the revolutionary government . . . A strong, stable Iran, neutral and Islamic would be good for the area and

1 See Defence Minister Mustafa Chamran's comments, *International Herald Tribune*, 22-23 March 1980.

2 See *Daily Telegraph*, 23 February 1980.

3 It was raised but not acted upon by Foreign Minister Sadeq Ghotbzadeh. See *Daily Telegraph*, 9 May 1980.

4 *International Herald Tribune*, 24 January 1980.

for the United States. Moreover it would help to block Soviet expansionism'.[1]

As long as US strategic interests required a strong Iran that remained independent of the USSR and these interests dominated the US approach to the hostage issue, there were bound to be limits to the effectiveness of its measures aimed at Iran. Particularly in the psychological dimension affecting bargaining, the US need for Iran was clearly more evident and more publicized than the Iranians' need for a connection with the United States. It was only with the arrival — and perception — of a new and greater threat that the Iranians were persuaded to negotiate the issue realistically.

The Iran—Iraq war

The escalation from border clashes to more significant conflict — without a formal declaration of war — was a direct result of Iran's military weakness. Differences between the two neighbours had periodically surfaced in the past two decades, ostensibly on the issue of their riverine frontier on the Shatt al' Arab.[2] But, despite occasional clashes, skirmishes, and exchanges of fire in the border region, there had never been a serious risk of war due to Iran's acknowledged military preponderance and its interest in the maintenance of the *status quo*. Iran's international isolation and particularly her military weakness — in part as the result of the US' embargo — changed the military balance of power in the Gulf. Iraq perceived an opportunity to score a rapid and decisive military victory and took it. The onset of the first Gulf war in modern times may largely be attributed to Iran's military weakness, in part caused by the severance of its military relationship with the US.

The war from Washington's view was a mixed blessing. While it might convince the Iranians of the futility of retaining the hostages, it might also weaken that country either leading to its disintegration or driving it into reliance on the USSR. Constrained by domestic political requirements and regional and international interests, Washington sought to dangle the possibility of a military relationship before the Iranians while seeking to limit the adverse consequences of the war.

The constraints operating on the US government domestically were clear: a passionate distaste for the Iranian regime combined with a fervent desire both to see it punished and have the hostages released. Electoral considerations impelled President Carter to seek the release

1 *International Herald Tribune*, 28 April 1980.

2 For background see the companion paper in this series by Robert Litwak. 'Sources of Inter-State Conflict', *Security in the Persian Gulf*, Gower, Aldershot, for IISS, no. 2, 1981.

of the hostages without sacrificing US honour through making concessions to blackmail. Yet the Iranians would need to be enticed by
subtle incentives for the threat of increasing punishment had not
worked and, if applied, could prove counterproductive from the standpoint of US strategic interests. US regional and global interests also
required a delicate touch to ensure that neither Iran nor Iraq won a
decisive victory; to ensure that the USSR did not benefit from the war;
to limit the escalation of the conflict through prevention of competitive
arms supply policies; and to retain its credibility as a partner of the
Arab oil-producing states, particularly Saudi Arabia. The difficulties
of balancing these considerations were made more difficult both by
Washington's lack of diplomatic ties with either contestant and by the
growing daily need of returning the hostages before election day.

   To reduce the possibility of misunderstanding, the US and USSR met
on 25 September and co-ordinated their positions by agreeing to
neutrality. A week later the US dispatched early-warning aircraft to
Saudi Arabia to allay its regional partner's anxieties. At the outset of
the war President Carter announced that the US was 'not taking a
position' on it, going on to explain that the conflict might convince the
Iranians of their need for friends 'and therefore induce them to release
the hostages'.[1] This was followed by hints of US concern.   Warren
Christopher, Deputy Secretary of State, noted that while the US
remained neutral it would certainly oppose 'the dismemberment of
Iran'.[2] By the first week in October, Washington had publicly warned
Jordan against the transfer of US supplied arms to Iraq.[3] On 19
October President Carter alluded to the US interest in a strong Iran and
Secretary of State Muskie made public reference to Iraq's 'invasion'.[4]
By the end of the month, Washington had returned to its by now
traditional ploy, that of holding out the possibility of restoring a
military supply relationship once the hostage issue was resolved.[5] A
mouth-watering list of equipment paid for and ready for delivery was
made public. It included parts for F-4s, F-5s, F-14s, C-130s, *Dragon*
anti-tank missiles, land-mines, 155 mm howitzer and tank ammunition
and air-defence missiles.[6] Explanations for the American readiness to
supply arms were various. Secretary Muskie, for example, argued that

1   See *International Herald Tribune*, 26 September 1980.

2   See *International Herald Tribune*, 29 September 1980.

3   See *International Herald Tribune*, 8 October 1980.

4   See *International Herald Tribune*, 20 October 1980.

5   See *International Herald Tribune*, 25-26 October 1980.

6   See *International Herald Tribune*, 31 October 1980. See also *Aviation Week*, 3 November
    1980, p. 15.

retention of the embargo on parts favoured Iraq. The President made a distinction between supplying equipment already paid for and selling additional equipment.[1] Within a week these signals to Iran had been further refined. It was now observed that much of the material formerly ordered by Iran might not now be required while other orders, such as ammunition, might present the US with diplomatic problems if supplied during a conflict. It was suggested that, if Iran requested supplies, perhaps the provision of non-lethal equipment such as aircraft parts (rather than ammunition) might be appropriate.[2]

In the event the Iranians failed to rise to this bait and neglected to ask for spare parts. Indeed, despite setbacks on the battlefield, the Iranians apparently concluded the final agreement on the release of the hostages without any specific reference to the military supply relationship, or even the material already bought and embargoed. After this agreement there were no immediate signs of Iran's interest in the resumption of supplies. It became clear in January 1981 that Iran owned $1 billion-worth in arms, equipment and cash held by the US Department of Defense. Of this, approximately half derived from a cash trust fund customarily maintained by large-scale customers of US arms, the remainder was in equipment, some of which had been ordered before the advent of the revolutionary government in Tehran.[3] The new Republican administration expressly rejected its predecessor's policy of using the arms as an inducement for Iranian good behaviour. It immediately ruled out any military supply relationship with Tehran, cancelling the standing order (with reimbursement) and rejecting consideration of any future requests that Iran might be inclined to make.[4]

Why was the United States unable to use its past (and potential) role as an arms supplier to improve relations with Iran? After all, with Iran now at war and militarily disadvantaged, the opportunity for the re-establishment of US influence seemed obvious. The manipulation of arms supplies might be expected to provide the US with increased leverage on the contestants and in the Gulf as a whole. The reasons why this opportunity had not materialized by the spring of 1981 are attributable to two sets of discrete factors rather than to the inherent limitations of leverage in an arms-supply relationship. The first set of constraints revolves around the nature of the war itself, the impact of

1 President Carter's Campaign Debate in Cleveland, 28 October in *Selected Statements*, 1 November 1980, p. 26; *International Herald Tribune*, 31 October 1980.

2 See *Washington Post*, 4 November 1980; *Washington Star*, 4 November 1980.

3 *Baltimore Sun*, 22 January 1981; *Washington Star*, 22 January 1981.

4 *The Times*, 28 January 1981.

the embargo on Iran's preparedness and Iran's immediate military needs. The second lies outside strictly military considerations and originated in the nature of Iran's (domestic) politics, the power struggle within and the pressures that this created on the prosecution of the war.

Preparedness. The war demonstrated at its outset the failure of the early warning system to detect intruding Iraqi aircraft that were able to strike more than 300 miles deep into Iran. Although this was attributed to US—Iraqi collusion,[1] a more plausible explanation, given the same phenomenon on the Iraqi side, was the lack of expertise in maintenance.[2] In its initial phases the air war was quite intense. By the end of the second week of the war, Iranian aircraft losses were believed to be up to 100, twice those of Iraq.[3] It was evident that Iran was relying on the F-4s and F-5s (rather than the F-14s which were more difficult to service) and that these remained operational partly because the large inventory (totalling 343) enabled technicians to cannibalize many for needed parts. By the end of the third week of the war, Iran had begun a limited use of its *Cobra* helicopters, *Tow* and *Dragon* anti-tank missiles and the *Maverick* air-to-surface missile. Their limited use in the war, despite large Iranian stocks, suggested that lack of ammunition was less a problem than the inadequacy of maintenance and a dearth of spare parts.[4] The infrequent use of the large helicopter fleet certainly sustained this reasoning. Despite its clear superiority in airpower, in training and in aircraft performance and the flying of up to 100 sorties a day, Iran made no systematic use of airpower for close support, for interdiction, or to gain air superiority. This suggested weakness in logistics and in command and control. In addition a shortage of pilots and navigators as a result of frequent political purges seriously impaired the Iranian war effort. The brunt of the air war was sustained by the F-4s and F-5s while the F-14 was only used infrequently, primarily as a radar platform. Iran's primary reliance on these two aircraft and on C-130s and Boeing 707s for transport and supply (together with its need for helicopter parts) had indeed been apparent before the war. As a result of the systematic use of these aircraft against Iranian Kurds in 1979, they had needed repair and maintenance and it had been parts and ammunition for these aircraft that Iran had sought before the events of November 1979.

---

1 By Iranian officials, see *The Times*, 25 September 1980.

2 See *Aviation Week and Space Technology*, 29 September 1980, p. 27.

3 *Ibid.*, 6 October 1980, pp. 20-21.

4 See *ibid.*, 13 October 1980, pp. 24-25.

After the first weeks of the war, the level of air activity declined appreciably, leading in the winter months to a static land war punctuated by the sporadic exchange of shelling and occasional tank battles. In this kind of warfare, military equipment of US origin was less important. With the exception of its tank force (which included US-supplied M-60s and M-48s though it consisted predominantly of British-built *Chieftains*)[1] most of Iran's artillery needs were obtainable elsewhere. For example 105 mm, 130 mm and 155 mm artillery shells could be bought in the arms markets of Europe. Furthermore the sheer number of weapons systems and bulk of ammunition bought and stored in the Shah's day provided the Iranian armed forces with a considerable buffer against any immediate needs. Stocks could be extended by cannibalization particularly since the diminishing tempo of the land war necessitated the commitment of only limited numbers of vehicles, tanks and artillery to battle.

Substitution. The move from an air to a land war and the diminution of the intensity of the conflict thus reduced Iran's needs for spare parts from abroad, and specifically removed any immediate necessity of compromising its revolution (as Iran saw it) by re-establishing direct or indirect links with the United States to obtain spare parts for its aircraft. While reducing Iran's immediate needs it did not eliminate the necessity of acquiring replenishment for an arsenal which was bound to need ammunition and parts as the war continued. There was considerable evidence of Iran's search for new sources of equipment. For the exclusively US-supplied Air Force (which included Army and Navy aviation) there was the most difficulty. Even six months before the war Iranian agents had reportedly been trying, with little success, to obtain parts for F-4s and F-5s.[2] Iran continued without success to press Italy for the release of *Chinook* helicopters it had paid for earlier.[3] Iranian representatives — again without success — sought assistance from Greece for spare parts and the servicing of F-4 aircraft.[4] The Iraqi government claimed that Iran had received US-made supplies particularly for its Air Force with US approval from Japan and Taiwan.[5] Another source alleged that Israel was providing Iran with US equipment, particularly spares for the F-4, but neglected to state

---

1 875 *Chieftain* and 250 (light) *Scorpion* tanks of UK origin, and 400 M47/48, and 460 M-60A1 US tanks.

2 NATO intelligence sources are quoted in *International Herald Tribune*, 6 October 1980.

3 *Aviation Week*, 24 November 1980, p. 26.

4 *The Times*, 2 October 1980; *International Herald Tribune*, 10 October 1980.

5 *The Times*, 2 October 1980.

whether this was with or without US assent.[1] Still another source reported that Iran had obtained 'American-made spares' manufactured under licence in Italy.[2] Despite these allegations, which were cloudy and confused, two points were clear. First it was highly unlikely that the US would supply Iran either directly or indirectly with spare parts for aircraft without some sort of political understanding or *quid pro quo*. This meant that, with the possible exception of captured US-built equipment (as in Vietnam),[3] no major recipient of arms would risk its arms relationship with the US by contravening US law and policy. Second, it was always possible for Iran to obtain certain categories of material such as some artillery pieces and ammunition for them on the open market.[4] Clearly however Iran could not easily find radar equipment, avionics packages or the spare parts for aircraft that would be needed routinely for maintenance. The more extensive usage made of equipment during warfare (such as aircraft tyres) and battle damage would require considerable quantities of such items.

Iran achieved some success in obtaining arms and parts from countries outside of the West. Syria, Libya and North Korea are reported to have provided Soviet-bloc material. This consisted chiefly of ammunition, explosives and medical supplies. They were ferried by Iranian transport aircraft who were permitted access to Soviet airspace.[5] Direct Soviet assistance was more limited. The report of an offer to supply arms to Iran was denied by Moscow.[6] However, it appeared consistent with the Soviet interest in increasing the USSR's role in Iran for the Soviets to depict the US as poised to invade that country — the implication being that the USSR would then 'protect the revolution'.[7] Soviet supply of jet fuel directly to Iran was

---

1   *The Observer*, 2 November 1980. This charge was denied by Israel, see *ibid.*, 9 November 1980. It was confirmed subsequently by various sources, see *International Herald Tribune*, 24 August 1981.

2   *The Observer*, 25 January 1980.

3   These arms may have reached North Korea, a limited supplier of arms to Iran. See *Aviation Week*, 13 October 1980, p. 24 and *International Herald Tribune*, 10 October 1980.

4   This would account for claims by Iranian officials including Bani Sadr that obtaining US equipment in the arms market had posed no problem. See *Le Monde*, 8 October 1980. Another official specifically exempted certain categories of aircraft from this. See *The Times*, 31 October 1980.

5   See *International Herald Tribune*, 10 October, 5 November 1980; *Financial Times*, 1 November 1980.

6   See especially *International Herald Tribune*, 9 October 1980; *Le Monde*, 22 October 1980.

7   See *Pravda*, 17 January 1981.

reported.[1] Soviet bloc equipment could be of assistance to Iran in several areas. In air defence, ammunition for the ZSU-23-4 anti-aircraft guns would be useful. Ammunition and spares for armoured vehicles, SA-7 man-portable air defence missiles, all of which could supplement Soviet supplied equipment already existing in the Iranian inventory, would be helpful to Iran's war effort. Yet none of these would provide Iran with anything other than a limited capability to remain in the war — they could not furnish the basis for victory.

In sum the impact of the US-led sanctions on Iran's military preparedness was considerable. Iran's isolation and apparent military weakness had invited an Iraqi attack. *Inter alia* lack of spare parts and poor maintenance impeded Iran's capacity to use its air superiority to great effect and was reflected also in poor air defence due to the incapacitated *Hawk* defence system. Exclusive reliance on the US for supplies of aircraft and helicopter parts hampered Iran's search for alternative sources of supply. Such equipment as could be bought on the open market was at premium prices[2] and consisted of ammunition or small artillery pieces. Eastern bloc material, though available, was of marginal rather than decisive importance for Iran's military capability. As the war shifted to ground engagements, Iran's war effort was hampered not only by an embargo on US equipment but also by Britain's refusal to supply arms or spare parts during the conflict. As a result Iran's tank force, split almost equally between US and UK tanks, was in potential jeopardy. Extensive use of *Chieftain* tanks would require the replacement of their power packs (engines) and in due course[3] this might result in Iran's armour grinding to a halt without even encountering its adversary.

Although the costs of the embargo for Iran's preparedness and military capabilities, for her hard currency reserves in seeking substitute sources, and for her pride in failing to expel the Iraqi invader, were considerable, they were still in fact mitigated. The winding-down of the war after two months necessitated the commitment of fewer resources to it. Equipment could be husbanded and reconstituted through improvisation. The air-war particularly became less important. This enabled the Iranian regime to avoid (or put off) facing the reality of its military needs — which were now less pressing. It also allowed the politicians in Tehran to continue their power struggle without

1 *International Herald Tribune*, 5 November 1980 (The report cites *Aviation Week* as its source.)

2 This was an additional cost, and admitted by Iranian officials. See Bani Sadr's comments quoted in *International Herald Tribune*, 10 October 1980.

3 After 700 miles. See *Financial Times*, 21 January 1981.

30

identifying their priorities. It meant that there was no need to choose between confronting Iraq or the United States; both would continue to be the implacable enemies of the revolution. For the United States, this slow-motion war meant that the leverage that would logically accrue to it as the main supplier of arms to Iran in a situation of conflict remained potential rather than actual. Influence unacknowledged is not real.

Quite apart from the slow pace of the war which provided Iran with a breathing spell to ponder the hard choices of the future, there were domestic political constraints in Iran impeding any acceptance of a renewed military relationship with the United States. This was evident in the curious fact that, throughout the negotiations on the release of the hostages, the issue of the resumption of supply of spare parts came up only once, and that was in an exploratory meeting in September. It was never raised again. Nor, evidently, was there an implicit expectation that once the issue was resolved, the acquisition of arms would be easier,[1] for Iran's leadership interpreted the war with Iraq as a conflict launched by a US proxy.[2] At the outset of hostilities Iran's Foreign Ministry had put this clearly:

> . . . we consider all our domestic and external problems, including the aggressions launched by the Iraqi regime and the provocations they are mounting in the borders, to be a product of the provocations launched by the US superpower against us and our Muslim nation before the triumph of the revolution.[3]

With the perception that 'the hand of the US had appeared from the sleeve of Iraq'[4] in the war, it would be difficult to justify negotiations for arms with the United States. Indeed political in-fighting combined with revolutionary self-image made it hazardous to support the idea of any negotiations with the US. For by acceding to negotiations, it could be argued, Iran would be conceding defeat and indicating its willingness to sue for peace on terms dictated by the United States. Others within Iran argued in less doctrinaire terms and sought to define Iran's

1 For an authoritative discussion of the course of negotiations see *New York Times*, 28 January 1981. The issue was brought up by Sadeq Tabatabai, a relative of Khomeini, in discussions with Warren Christopher in Bonn.

2 See the comments of Iran's Minister of State for Executive Affairs, Behzad Nabavi in *Le Monde*, 29 January 1981.

3 Text of Foreign Ministry statement, Tehran, 18 September 1980 in Sound World Broadcasts (SWB) ME/6528/A/3 20 September 1980.

4 This was Khomeini's comment in mid-September; he had prefaced it with the statement 'We are at war with America'. See *International Herald Tribune*, 15 September 1980.

priorities accordingly.[1] One exchange in the Majlis (Parliament) captured this nicely: 'The Imam (reported one cleric) has said we are fighting against America. How can we have discussions and talks with our enemy?' To which a leading secular moderate replied: 'This is the first time I have heard that we are fighting against America . . . it is very dangerous for us not to contact America'.[2] Prime Minister Rajai in October asserted that: 'Negotiations will not be considered even though they (the US) might for example offer to provide us with spare parts'.[3]

The political competition within Iran resulted in a cacophony of voices arguing for quite different responses to the war. In this context it was clear that no person, Ayatollah Khomeini included, felt strong enough to pursue negotiations with the United States to their logical conclusion. Such consensus as was to emerge would have to be the product of time, of battlefield losses, and of economic privation rather than of artful persuasion or logic. Even then domestic politics precluded any serious quest for the resupply of arms from the United States. Revolutionary rhetoric and self-image had created hostages of the Iranian leadership which now found itself imprisoned by the web they themselves had spun. A decision to seek to reactivate the military supply relationship with the US would be an admission of defeat on several levels. It would imply that Iraq's attack was not inspired by the US and that such an interpretation had been erroneous. It would also be an admission that such a relationship would not tarnish the purity or integrity of the revolution and that such ties did not necessarily entail either dependency on or subservience to the supplier. The domestic political implications of such a relationship would also have to be considered. Would the build-up of the army and the resurrection of an *ésprit de corps* and military morale, together with contacts with a foreign government, be neutral in its consequences for Iranian politics? An admission that that foreign government, the United States, was neutral and not an active foe of the revolution would erode one of the pillars of the revolutionary edifice so ardently constructed among the masses. For these reasons the costs of even tacit co-operation − let alone a military supply relationship − would be too costly for the Iranian government. Domestic ferment and revolutionary propaganda constrained the range of responses available to Iran during its conflict with Iraq.

1 For example, the notorious Ayatollah Khalkali strove to make the war with Iraq the priority item even if it meant a settlement with the United States. He apparently did not accept Khomeini's view that these were an inseparable menace.

2 See *The Times*, 30 September 1980.

3 *International Herald Tribune*, 22 October 1980.

The limits and conditions of influence in wartime. If the United States failed in the first six months of the war to gain influence commensurate with what might have been expected, given Iran's continued dependence on her for replacements, the reasons for this are many and relate only partly to the actual supply relationship. On the purely practical level, it was not yet clear that Iran had exhausted its existing stocks. Nor was it certain that Iran's major problems of resupply had yet crystallized. In the early phases of the war morale and leadership may have been the major shortages. The declining use of air power after October reduced attrition (and so temporarily Iran's need for parts) in the one area of undoubted US monopoly. The embargo on parts had exacted some costs through increasing the price of purchases on the open market, and in virtually grounding the helicopter fleet but it had not yet convinced the Iranian leadership of the need to seek a reconciliation with the US.

The political inhibitions against such a *rapprochement* were various but may be reduced essentially to one factor in the continuing power struggle any person or faction advocating ties with the United States was open to criticism as a counter-revolutionary and subject to removal. The very idea of a renewed arms connection — with all its perceived implications for the importance of the armed forces in politics, the reassertion of American 'control' (i.e. leverage), and the consequences of this 'dependence' for Iran's revolutionary gains — was clearly too high a price to pay to expel Iraq from Western Iran. According to this mind-set, the risks of prolonged war *vis-à-vis* Iraq paled into insignificance when compared with the risks of renewed dependence on the US.[1] The Iranian government was thus not tempted by the inducements and signals emanating from the increasingly desperate Democratic administration in Washington in the Autumn of 1980 and, as noted earlier, it made no effort to include the issue of military supplies in the final negotiations over the hostages.

That Iran has been impervious to past US blandishments does not necessarily mean that it will remain frozen in its decision not to reactivate the military relationship. Two factors could decisively reverse the current decision, one political, the second an outgrowth of developments on the battlefield. A change in the leadership in Iran, or the emergence of a strong pragmatic figure from within the current leadership could enable Iran to reverse its policies, including its phobia about relations with the United States — an issue which has acquired the status of legend in the revolutionary mythology. Such a prospect does not seem to be too distant for neither sloganeering nor the

---

1 Indeed many of Iran's more militant revolutionaries saw in a long war with Iraq an opportunity to consolidate the revolution and suppress differences emerging within Iran.

preservation of the revolution's rectitude is sufficient to meet the needs of the Iranian people over time.

The second factor which would increase the attractiveness — indeed the necessity — for US arms and enhance US supplier leverage would be a reintensification of the conflict. Whether the war heats up to include large-scale engagements or drags on into a long war of attrition across the front, Iran's lack of spare parts will prove a major and growing weakness. The continuing lack of support for its aircraft will cripple its chances of success in the event that Iran seeks to launch a decisive counter-offensive to expel the Iraqis completely from Khuzestan.

Unable to win the war without spare parts and unable during a conflict to shift weapons-systems and sources of supply, Iran will find itself ineluctably drawn toward the US. Unless the war winds down with the tacit consensus of the belligerents, or Iraq withdraws unilaterally, Iran will be forced to expel the Iraqis and to do this without adequate air cover will be hazardous indeed. As a result, it may well be that the point of leverage accruing to the supplier of arms has yet to be reached.[1]

Conclusion

What was the arms relationship with Iran designed to achieve?
With what degree of success and with what limitations?
How does the Iranian experience translate elsewhere?
What are the conditions for influence?

The intensification of the arms relationship with Iran coincided with the increased importance of the region and the growing willingness of Iran to assume responsibilities which the UK was shedding and the US was unwilling to assume. The emergence of parallel interests and the Shah's requests for arms made this intensification inevitable. It reinforced relations between Tehran and Washington. It brought nearly ten years of relative political stability to the Gulf region at a time when no other littoral state could assure the region's security. In the event, the arms and the relationship with Iran were tools ill-designed for the test that confronted them in late 1978 — a widespread Revolution. Whether Iran's arms purchases decisively contributed to the economic

---

1 This is not to deny that Iran still retains residual leverage. The threat in extremity to 'go to the USSR' or the possibility of disintegration may prove so damaging to US interests that Washington would allow a discreet, indirect resupply operation without requiring any political conditions from the regime.

problems and hence the Revolution is not at all clear.[1] What is clear is that the refusal of the Shah's request for arms would have weakened the US—Iran relationship.[2] In some respects this had already happened after 1976.

The military supply lever of the US was thus in practice of limited utility in the revolutionary period in Iran. In theory access to the senior military officers should have been a considerable asset; in practice it proved irrelevant at best. As a base on which to build with a new government in Iran, it proved, despite the tangible dependency it entailed, disappointing. It locked-in the supplier to an accommodating posture lest that channel be jeopardized. Despite palpable security problems, the new Tehran regime preferred political posturing to pragmatic policies. The upshot was a dependency that remained real but politically irrelevant in the short run. As long as no overwhelming security threat was perceived by Khomeini, the suppliers' leverage remained notional. The liability of intimacy with the Shah's regime still overshadowed everything else. In this setting the only consolation for the supplier was itself bitter-sweet; the deterioration of Iran's military machine, while constraining any effective aggression by Tehran in the region, also limited its capacity to deter aggression. A weakened, unstable Iran might threaten US interests as much as it did its own leadership. Iran, militarily weak, had proved a far more destabilizing regional force than ever was the case when the Shah's legions were intact. If this proved anything it was that a fixation on arms transfers as regionally disruptive had obscured the less tangible but more real threats to the region. The US' continued interest in a strong Iran also laid to rest the hoary notion that US entanglement derived from the arms transfers, rather than an antecedent interest which these arms transfers only reflected.

1 Despite T. Moran, *International Security*. But it is a relevant question for the rest of the Gulf. Contrast S. Neuman, 'Iranian Defense Expenditures and the Social Crisis', *International Security*, vol. 3, no. 3, Winter 1978-79, pp. 178-92. Stephanie Neuman, 'Arms Transfers, Defense Production and Dependency: The Case of Iran' in H. Amirsadeghi (ed.), *The Security of the Persian Gulf*, Croom Helm, 1981.

2 As Barry Blechman has argued: 'The sale of sophisticated weapons is a significant political act. It associates the seller with specific personalities and policies of the purchasing government, thus involving the seller in the foreign government's domestic politics. A decision to sell arms is viewed as a sign of approval and encouragement; a decision in favour of restraint is taken as a signal of disapproval'. *New York Times*, 2 April 1980.

US—Saudi Arabia 1973-80

The nature of the relationship

The US relationship with Saudi Arabia is at once more complex and simpler than that with Iran — more complex in that it embraces much more than arms in its mutual dependence, simpler because it is not one of near equals in a partnership.

From the US perspective, Saudi Arabia's importance is obvious. Saudi Arabia produces 30 per cent of OPEC's oil output and it supplies 10 per cent of total US consumption (20 per cent of imports). Only Saudi Arabia has the spare productive capacity to unilaterally determine the scale of price rises agreed in OPEC. As the most important single country in OPEC, Saudi Arabia is thus important as a dependable supplier of oil, able to moderate price increases to minimize their damage on the international economy, and in a position to increase its own production capacity to ameliorate world shortages, and largely to regulate prices.

In addition to this, Saudi Arabia as a monarchy is instinctively hostile to communism and radicalism. It is interested in stemming these forces in the Middle East and in supporting 'moderate' governments that seek evolutionary change. Oil revenues have enabled Saudi Arabia to exercise influence in its diplomacy in the Middle East in a direction generally favourable to Western interests.

Though delicate, the relationship with Saudi Arabia is less brittle than that with Iran. Saudi ambitions and capabilities are limited and there are fewer misgivings regarding her military build-up. With a population of at most six million and with a land-mass as large as the US east of the Mississippi, her vulnerability and insecurity in a region full of threats is easily acknowledged. In addition, Saudi policy, the outgrowth of consensus in the royal family, is more subtle, given less to posturing than to allusion and indirection and to postponing issues rather than risking confrontations. There is no question in American minds of Saudi Arabia playing a security role in the Persian Gulf comparable to that entertained in the past for Iran. Her military build-up is clearly 'defensive' and her foreign policy goals are circumscribed. She is often exasperatingly reticent rather than overly activist.

The Saudi military build-up has also given critics in the US less cause for concern. Although Saudi Arabia has been the largest importer of US arms in recent years and spends vast amounts *per capita* on military expenditures (and more than 10 per cent of GNP on the military), the results have not been spectacular or divisive of US public opinion until the AWACs deal. This is principally due to two reasons: Saudi

Arabia's evident importance and military weakness; and the large amount of money allotted to services, training and the improvement of physical infrastructure (calculated to be as much as 60 per cent of 'arms' imports). (These services were exempt from the Carter May 1977 guidelines limiting arms exports.) Also the scale of Saudi Arabia's military modernization and expansion has involved fewer US government personnel. It has created fewer problems for US governments because the Saudi style of diplomacy acknowledges its limitations. Fewer requests are made of the US for weapons that are 'inappropriate' and the Saudi style builds fewer resentments within the US bureaucracy than did the Shah's, with its pretension to equality and partnership. Again this may be tending to change if arms sales to Saudi Arabia are seen to be at the expense of Israel's security.

As with Iran, the security dimension is central to the relationship but it has given rise to fewer problems than with Iran. Unlike the relationship with Iran, which was orientated at times almost exclusively on the military dimension of the partnership, involving mutual expectations which could, and frequently were disappointed, with Saudi Arabia this is but one component of a more complex package. The military ties with Saudi Arabia are, in any case, relatively new (dating back a decade) and have been, until recently, less intensive and formal. In part this is due to the constraints on Saudi foreign policy arising from inter-Arab politics which militate against any formal or conspicuous alignments ('the Baghdad Pact syndrome').

The genuine interdependence existing between the US and Saudi Arabia is not more stable or impervious to disruption because it is very real. Indeed its very stability depends on political assumptions and expectations which may be reversed overnight by a change either in the orientation of the Saudi elite, or its physical replacement. It is nonetheless based on a partnership which has tangible benefits — for both parties.

What Saudi Arabia brings to this partnership is an ability to moderate oil prices, to increase its own production, to assure supplies, and to play a constructive role in preserving stability on the Arabian Peninsula. The willingness to pursue these policies depends very much on what is to be gained from doing so. For example, the willingness to expose itself to political attacks in OPEC or within the Gulf, by policies limiting its own potential oil revenues, or decisions to increase its maximum sustainable daily production capability (which involves technical and investment judgements), all involve important political calculations and decisions which converge on one question: is her security thereby enhanced? Another way of putting this is that Saudi oil and foreign policy decisions will depend on her leaders' assessments of the forces at work in the region and the instruments available to deal with them.

It is here that Saudi expectations of the US role enter the Saudis' part of the package deal. The principal point to be made is that Saudi expectations of the US have been excessive. This is due both to an exaggerated view of superpower omnipotence and to a 'psychological dependency' that reflects both a genuine acknowledgement of indigenous technical deficiencies and an acute sense of insecurity and military weakness. Excessive expectations derive from immense needs. A primary requirement is for 'reassurance'. This pertains most concretely to security-related matters such as guarantees for the Kingdom (and regime) and to a more general measure of assurance in a volatile *milieu* and against an uncertain future. By its very nature, this type of 'requirement' is difficult to meet — yet it underscores the importance of 'atmosphere' and 'symbolism' in an unequal relationship. The development of a modern armed force positioned in the border regions is one response to insecurity. The Air Force with F-5s, F-15s, and *Maverick* air-to-surface missiles is also being developed for defensive operations on the periphery of Saudi territory. Where specific weapon systems (such as the F-15 in 1978 and 1980-81, and AWACs) become an issue in Saudi-US relations, they become symbolic of the entire relationship and critical to its continued well-being.

Other regional threats, particularly if they involve any form of Soviet activity as an arms supplier, or arms transporter, or through surrogate forces (such as the Cubans), are expected to be met by Saudi Arabia with the assistance of the US in a similar capacity — as arms supplier, transporter, or even as ultimate guarantor. The US' willingness to use force demonstratively for political purposes to assure Saudi security is not new. In 1963 a US squadron of aircraft was despatched to Saudi Arabia both to reassure King Saud and to deter Abdul Nasir from any involvement in Saudi Arabia. In February 1979 and October 1980 both aircraft and ships were despatched to warn the PDRY (and Iran) and to give substance to the US (implicit) commitment to Saudi Arabia's security.

Against major threats to its security emanating from beyond the region, for example from the USSR, the Saudis rely on US assistance and involvement. This is primarily a deterrent function but also includes a requirement for rapid and major interventionary forces (by sea and air). This in turn requires both the strategic infrastructure for rapid deployment and political relations facilitating it. In addition what Saudi Arabia tangibly requires of the US can swiftly be enumerated but it is important to stress the significance of 'atmosphere' and perceptions to the lesser partner. For the US arms are far easier to provide for their very concreteness as a visible symbol of the bond can satisfy the recipient, reassure it and serve to advertise its importance to other states in the region. Arms act as symbolic substitutes for alliances.

Saudi 'concerns' or demands for 'reassurance' are nonetheless real for being intangible, inchoate and difficult to assuage. For example, Saudi fears of Soviet 'encirclement' through the PDRY, Iraq and Ethiopia, and the emphasis on the geo-political,[1] on the importance of American 'will' and the credibility of her commitments should not be understood in concrete or literal terms. Their importance derives rather from the shift they may give to the balance of indigenous political forces, and hence to Saudi political calculations made to meet them. A circle of adversaries would increase pressure on the Saudi government to accommodate them and inhibit the Saudis from adapting the best means of securing their defence. Increased indirect pressure, in short, will mean a loss of autonomy and choice for Saudi leaders directing foreign policy.

Saudi security concerns start with regime survival and stability. For internal and lesser contingencies, Saudi Arabia expects arms and training in modernizing its National Guard and improving its intelligence agencies. To deter regional threats emanating from other states, such as Iran or Iraq, a floating 'over the horizon' presence is likely to be useful in most military contingencies.

In this as in other aspects of relations with Saudi Arabia there are paradoxes:

1 Only the US can provide a balance (often psychological) to the Soviet threat but the physical presence of the US could exacerbate regional problems of instability and US over-reactions could stimulate Soviet responses.

2 Against regional threats, specific or ideological, the US potential role is also important especially its reputation for reliability and commitment. A strong arms relationship is central for advertising Saudi Arabia's importance but an overt alliance is still impossible politically.

3 Against factors strengthening radicalism, the US connection also has a role to play. For example, only the US is in a position to defuse the political pressures that bear on Saudi Arabia from a 'no-war, no-peace' situation, by pushing a Middle Eastern settlement. Yet the path chosen to achieve that goal (Camp David) may itself exacerbate those pressures on Saudi Arabia in the short run.

4 In a period of sustained instability, the US connection becomes a liability yet the option of cutting loose from the

---

1 Saudi geo-political concerns can sometimes be met more easily by marginal actions than their other worries. The US supply of arms to King Hussan of Morocco in late 1979 was undertaken partly to reassure Saudi Arabia, for example.

US is limited by the lack of a realistic alternative for security. Thus 'distancing' occurs to reduce the Kingdom's exposure.

The relationship between Saudi Arabia and the US is by no means exclusively related to security, even on the Saudi side. Interdependence constrains and channels choices. Saudi Arabia's leaders have looked to the West for technology and training to develop their country, diversify their economy, build their infrastructure and train their people. This requires the provision of services, large-scale imports and access to technology. The accumulation of revenues, which cannot be absorbed domestically, has been met by making large investments in the West, thereby increasing its interest in Western stability.

Saudi Arabia has the largest foreign exchange reserves of any country ($60 billion), and most of it is invested in the United States. This and her diversified investments provide her with several assets and (potential) economic levers in her relations with the US, including:

1 A reduction in US dollar holdings.
2 Withdrawal of deposits from US banks.
3 The sudden sale of large quantities of US government scrip.
4 Discontinuance of purchases of additional US government securities.
5 Closure of US portfolio accounts on fixed income and equity securities.

Saudi funds are a potential source of international financial instability and provide potential leverage *vis-à-vis* the US. Yet this can be overstated. Saudi Arabia would itself be affected by these actions. Saudi development (as well as defence) is dependent primarily on access to Western technology as well as to investment markets. As a large foreign investor it has a vested interest in international stability.

Saudi oil and investment policies are particularly sensitive to Western economic policies and subject to change. For example weakness in the dollar could eventually encourage an oil pricing policy on a basket of currencies or Special Drawing Rights (SDRs)[1] (though the effects of this would be complex). More important, the Saudi oil production rate is strongly dependent on two factors. In the short run, willingness to increase production temporarily to assist the West in its difficulties (or in the long run to increase its production capacity)

---

1 The Saudis' strong economic involvement with the US in particular results in a shared commitment to a strong dollar and to Saudi concern in the absence of a strong US energy policy. Saudi officials are said to refer to 'our dollar' in private talks with their US counterparts (Interview, Washington, October 1979.)

turns on the willingness of the US in particular to implement a strong energy policy. Second, a production rate which is geared less to investment needs than to alliance considerations requires at least assurances that its surplus investment will be safeguarded against inflation (or confiscation)and that such policies are 'appreciated' politically, by the consumers.

This requires amplification. In the oil market up until 1979, Saudi Arabia's oil production-rate has been in excess of its own economic needs. In an inflationary world economy, the return on investments overseas could scarcely be economically justified (given their vulnerability to confiscation) against the conservationists' argument in the oil producing countries that the best possible oil investment was to leave it in the ground where it would appreciate in value without being a hostage to the West. Saudi willingness to produce more oil than was justified by its revenue requirements has been in essence political, though admittedly the economic argument for preventing a world recession or contributing to inflation which would increase the price of its own imports is also important.

As in its foreign security policy, its oil policy is also subject to reversal depending on the balance of multiple considerations. Some of these it is in the power of the US to effect:

1   A strong US energy policy, conservation and realistic prices.
2   Protection of Saudi investments, and perhaps privileged status for them (guarantee of real value for surplus revenues) to encourage a stake in moderation.
3   Assurances of access to advanced technology.
4   Revision of tax laws making the employment of US personnel in the Kingdom less costly.

Perhaps most important in the short run is the first. The continuous pressure on Saudi Arabia to increase its maximum sustainable daily production-rate to meet other shortfalls (especially in 1979-81 when the Saudis' official ceiling of 8.5 million b/d was surpassed by 1 and on occasion by 2 million b/d for a year) may be short-sighted.[1] It increases Saudi Arabia's political isolation and her identification with the West at a time of strong conservationist and nationalist trends in the region. It therefore threatens the long-term security of supplies by

---

1   Saudi capacities are a source of dispute. In mid-1979 estimates were revised downward from 16 to 10.5 million b/d. At the end of 1979 Saudi officials declared that it had now risen to 11 million b/d and would increase to 12 million b/d within a few years. Clearly production capacity is not the same as actual production-rate, which will be dependent only partially on technical questions.

41

exposing the Saudi regime to the charge of collusion with the West and to parting with the national patrimony at a discount.

Related to Saudi production-rates is the general question of Saudi development. There exists a basic quandary for Saudi developmental planners in a tight oil market. Cuts in production do not automatically adversely affect revenues, indeed they rather stimulate increases in prices with the resultant effect of equal (or possibly) increased revenues for a diminished quantity of oil exported. This situation may vanish as worldwide production picks up or demand dries up and the scarcity vanishes. It is important nevertheless that Saudi planners are not encouraged by the West to pursue indiscriminate industrialization programmes in order to foster a false appetite for revenues designed to increase their incentives for maximum oil production to alleviate Western problems. This too will undermine the regime politically with long-term implications for the security of oil supplies.[1]

The interdependence between the US and Saudi Arabia is real. Each brings something to the relationship that the other requires. In economic terms the US is acutely dependent on Saudi Arabia but the dependency is by no means one-way. For its ultimate security Saudi Arabia is almost totally dependent on the US. Each has assets and instruments in the relationship but these cannot be converted into 'leverage' except with political will in a specific context. The components of the package comprising the relationship are linked implicitly. In a web of interactions both sides exert general influence. Saudi dependence on the US goes beyond the material. The US is the only congenial superpower and it is a preferred and trusted economic partner. The US is the only state that can reduce pressures on Saudi Arabia by a settlement of the Palestine issue and is the only market large enough for investment on the scale of the Saudis. Saudi sensitivity to US policies and its reputation are intelligible by reference to this broad enmeshment of ties. This interdependence militates against any sudden swings in the political relationship, barring any fundamental political reassessments by either party. The military component of the relationship is designed to deal with the exogenous threats to the Kingdom and it is with its dynamics that we are concerned.

The record of the military relationship

Saudi Arabia's importance in US security policies was marginal in the 1950s and 1960s. Government-to-government relations scarcely existed.

---

1 See the companion paper by Avi Plascov, '*Modernization, Political Development and Stability*', Security in the Persian Gulf, no. 3, Gower, Aldershot, for IISS, 1981.

ARAMCO represented the major US institution doing business with Saudi Arabia. The UK remained paramount in the Gulf and the major arms supplier to Saudi Arabia in the 1960s. Saudi interest in developing relations with the US government was nonetheless clear. Partly this was due to its experience with ARAMCO and to the trust and respect that had been engendered in that relationship. It also arose partly from a degree of scepticism regarding the UK (for example over London's support for Abu Dhabi on the Buraimi dispute). The importance of the US connection had already been demonstrated in 1963 by the rapid deployment, as noted above, of US aircraft to Saudi Arabia for reassurance at the time of the Yemen civil war, when President Nasir's ambitions in the Arabian peninsula were suspect.

The importance of the US for assuring the security of the Gulf after the British withdrawal made relations even more important on the eve of the 1970s. Though militarily weak, the Kingdom was relied upon by US policy-makers and encouraged to become one of the 'twin-pillars' designed to assure the security of the region. Interest in Saudi Arabia picked up slowly as the recognition of an imminent and growing 'energy crisis' seeped through the Washington bureaucracy. By April 1973, when Saudi Arabia made its first allusion to the 'oil weapon', the central importance of that country's resources to the health of Western economies was, at last, painfully clear. The 1973 war also brought Saudi Arabia directly into the issue of Israel and the occupied territories.

The Saudi government began to look to the United States as a partner in security affairs at the turn of the 1970s. Initially this meant an interest in the United States for arms and advice, while Washington was keen to assist in strengthening Saudi Arabia and to promote close political and economic ties. A study of a possible Saudi naval expansion programme was initiated in 1968 and agreed in 1972. In the spring of 1971, a request for assistance in modernizing the Saudi National Guard led to an initial survey by mid-1972 which was completed by the autumn of 1973. An overall defence study requested in December 1973 was completed by September 1974. Despite the spectacular growth in Saudi military-related purchases in the 1970s there is thus considerable evidence of planning rather than *ad hoc* purposes unrelated to any programme. By the end of 1973 it had become a deliberate part of US policy to 'entangle' Saudi Arabia into a nexus of relations which would give it a tangible stake in moderation and would constrain any sudden, disruptive, policy reversals. Saudi Arabia, for its part, welcomed this new attention. Its experience with the US Army Corps of Engineers in various projects in the Kingdom had been an agreeable one. The expansion of contracts covering ports and general infrastructure grew apace.

As part of the new emphasis on Saudi Arabia, two government-to-government Joint Commissions were set up in 1974. One covered economic affairs, the other security affairs. Meeting twice a year, the Commissions increased the number and breadth of official consultations between the two states.

The sale of arms to Saudi Arabia came to symbolize the deepening relationship with that state. Unlike Iran, however, Saudi Arabia's value came primarily from her oil, not from her potential as an ally with regional influence.[1] Thus, although for Saudi Arabia the prime importance of the US was as a guarantor of her security, arms as such were less important as a currency of that relationship. This was evident in the nature of the Kingdom's arms build-up. Limited in particular by deficiencies in technically trained manpower and in physical plant facilities, the great bulk of her 'arms' purchases (60–65 per cent) were in fact spent on training, spare parts, and on the construction of infrastructure — roads, airports, barracks, and ports. The scope of the military build-up is exemplified by the comment of a US official in 1976 that, while other states in the Gulf dealt with divisions in their armed forces, Saudi Arabia counted only brigades. The military co-operation programme was also less 'intensive'[2] involving fewer US government personnel and more contract personnel.

Between 1973 and 1976 Saudi Arabia ranked second only to Iran in arms purchases and signed $8 billion-worth of foreign military sales agreements with the US. Military expenditure leapt from $1 billion to over $9 billion in the same period. Military expenditures per capita were the highest in the world after 1975 (averaging $1,250). The principal component of the military training mission was the US Army Corps of Engineers.

Necessarily the American presence in Saudi Arabia increased in proportion to the expansion of the military modernization programme. In 1976, US defence-related personnel in uniform numbered 300, with another 900 civilians working on defence-related contracts. Including dependents military-related US personnel totalled 3,450 comprising some 21 per cent of the 16,000 Americans in the Kingdom. By 1978 the number of Americans had doubled to 30,000 but military-related personnel still numbered only 3,200, accounting for less than 11 per cent of the American community.[3] These figures show that the size of

1 That is there was no question of Saudi Arabia playing a regional military role.

2 The number of Saudi military officers trained by the US, even allowing for differences in armed forces size, was considerably fewer than Iran. See *Security Assistance*, (1979). By 1981 the US had 400 military personnel in Saudi Arabia with an additional 750 Defense Department civilians (excluding AWACs personnel) loaned to the Kingdom. See *International Herald Tribune*, 28-29 March 1981.

3 Uniformed military in 1978 had been reduced by one-third, to 200. These figures are taken from James Noyes, *The Clouded Lens*, Hoover Institution, 1977, p. 65.

the US military contingent remained small in relation to other activities by Americans.

The United States' involvement in Saudi development covers a wide range of fields:[1] planning (Stanford Research Institute); construction (Bechtel); oil (Aramco); and military modernization. The use of private enterprise in this last area is especially notable. The Saudi government contracted with the Vinnell Corporation of California to assist in the modernization of the National Guard. This force is comprised of the most loyal Bedouin elements, known as the White Army, and is structured primarily for an internal security mission. While Vinnell is responsible for training this force (with 1,500 US personnel on contract), the US government is involved in sales of armoured cars and tanks. In 1979 the US approved the sale of $1.23 billion-worth of equipment as part of this modernization programme. There is little doubt that the Saudi government values the involvement of the United States in its defence build-up. Although it is keen to keep the US military presence in the Kingdom limited, the presence of a sizeable US military training mission is a form of reassurance that a security commitment would be activated in a crisis. As such it is a substitute for a formal defence arrangement which the Saudis are unable to accept.

The Saudi military expansion programme encompasses five principal areas: the modernization of the air force; the creation of a coastal navy from scratch; the modernization of the National Guard; the construction of an air defence capability; and the establishment of the basic infrastructure required for defence and civilian projects. The modernization and construction of a very modest but technically advanced armed force has created problems for a state lacking trained manpower or a well-developed system of communications. The physical size and climatic inhospitability of the country makes the assurance of the territorial integrity of the country difficult. The defence of long borders against hostile incursions requires air mobility for troops and supplies necessitating multiple airfields, depots and long-range capabilities for aircraft.

It would be surprising if such an ambitious development programme progressed without complications and serious problems abound. While Western critics often emphasize the dollar value of 'military sales' they neglect to note the percentage of expenditure that relates to civilian-sector infrastructure. Reports of large contracts, such as the recent $2 billion in construction, services and spares for the Saudi navy

---

1 As a result in most years US–Saudi trade was in the US favour despite the heavy importation of oil.

and air force,[1] should not therefore routinely be equated with military capability. Similarly the shortage of skilled manpower has acted as a serious constraint on the programmes. Foreign personnel have to be contracted, often at high price and with potentially disruptive consequences for society. Over 950 specialists were sought in the US for two years' service in Saudi Arabia to train the Saudi Air Force on the F-15s purchased in 1978.[2] Manpower from Pakistan has also reportedly been sought.

A third issue is the general impact of the military build-up on Saudi stability. In its extreme form, Western critics argue that the arms build-up destabilized the Shah and contributed to the revolution in Iran. Sometimes this argument is made (as by US Representative Rosenthal) as a means of denying Saudi Arabia arms: 'We're seeing the exact same scenario that we saw in Iran — dumping a vast amount of highly sophisticated American equipment into an area where the stability of the government is highly unpredictable'.[3] Others, like George Ball, appear to have changed their minds. Ball had argued against the military build-up in Iran — a country with six times the population, a greater manpower base, and a more prominent security problem in the shape of the neighbouring USSR. However, Ball now writes:

> We sold military hardware to the Shah on the assumption that he would be the protector of the Gulf and we would stay out of it. If today the Gulf is to be protected we ourselves must pull the laboring oar, yet, to be fully effective, we shall need the co-operation of the Saudis.[4]

The distinction is unconvincing as it begs the question how much the Saudis need if the US back-up is there as the 'laboring oar'.

It is evident that the United States' prominent role as arms supplier to the Saudi government entails a measure of support for and identification with the current Saudi regime. Intrinsically involved in the supply of arms, in the advice offered on the structure of military forces, and in the choice of weapons systems are assumptions about domestic stability and the impact of military modernization on the society. Rapid expansion of the military may, as in Iran, dilute the base of

1 See *International Herald Tribune*, 21 January 1981.

2 See *Aviation Week and Space Technology*, 2 June 1980.

3 See *International Herald Tribune*, 28 February—1 March 1981.

4 George Ball, 'Reflections of a heavy year, America and the World 1980', *Foreign Affairs*, vol.59, no.3, 1981, p.484 *et seq*.

loyalty in the ranks. In Saudi Arabia tribal loyalty of the White Army may survive military modernization but the experience elsewhere in the Middle East is mixed on this issue. In the military relationship it will be important, as Bill Quandt has reminded us, that the United States does not promote its own ideas of military organization and seek to ensure their rationalization at the expense of traditional procedures which exist. The Saudi leadership may prefer reliability to efficiency in their military.[1]

We should not be surprised at the difficulties of building effective modern armed forces rapidly in a society lacking infrastructure and trained manpower, and constrained both by domestic political considerations and dependence on a supplier that is sometimes uncertain of its goals. It was bound to lead to high expectations that could not be met and to consequent frustration. Despite the commitment of over $35 billion in orders for military equipment largely over the past decade, by the 1980s the Saudis were still not in a position to meet their primary security threats by themselves.[2] As we shall see, both this inescapable dependence and the difficulties encountered in obtaining some of their arms requests from the United States have led to disenchantment in Saudi Arabia about the arms relationship with the United States.

The F-15 aircraft: a case study in supplier-recipient relationship

The first round: 1978. In its programme of air force modernization, the Saudi government in the 1970s sought to replace its aging *Lightning* aircraft (sold by the UK in the mid-1960s) with an aircraft that was capable, long-range and most important, advanced. The Ford administration promised a sympathetic hearing but it fell to the Carter presidency to reply to the Saudi request for 60 F-15s. A military case for the F-15s could be made: their range was a necessity given the Kingdom's area, and their greater capabilities did not entail correspondingly greater difficulties in maintenance or a significantly larger manpower requirement. But from the Saudi perspective the importance attached to the request was political. The supply of arms is above

---

1 William Quandt, 'Saudi Arabia's Foreign and Defense Policies in the 1980s', unpublished paper prepared for the *European—American Institute Workshop*, June 1980, p. 18.

2 For a parallel view see the Report of the Delegation to the Indian Ocean Area Committee on Armed Services, House of Representatives, 96th Cong., 2nd Session, Washington DC: USGPO 1980, pp. 26-27. For an excellent if overstated analysis see Abdul Kasim Mansur (pseud.), 'The Military Balance in the Persian Gulf: Who will Guard the Guardians?', *Armed Forces Journal International*, November 1980, excerpted as, 'The American Threat to Saudi Arabia' in *Survival*, January-February 1981.

all a political act representing for both parties a concrete indicator of the relationship. For the Saudis it was supremely important that its intimate and evolving ties with the United States be given tangible and public expression and that the worth and importance of the Kingdom's importance be publicly acknowledged in this way.

The Saudis saw in the request a test case for the overall relationship and a symbol of Saudi—US ties. An American decision to sell the planes would be an affirmation of Saudi Arabia's importance. A denial, deferral or reduction of the request would be a concrete indicator that the Kingdom was taken less seriously than either Israel or Iran, both states which were receiving state-of-the-art military equipment. Such a rebuff would have adverse consequences domestically and regionally. Within the Kingdom it would undermine those factions arguing for close ties with the United States and provide them with little to show for an accommodating oil policy. Regionally it would have been damaging to Saudi prestige, raising questions about US perceptions of Saudi reliability and stability and of its importance in relation to Israel or Iran. By undermining the Saudis, a refusal would have weakened the prospects for political co-operation on the southern littoral of the Gulf.[1]

The Saudi request for the F-15s thus represented far more than a preference for a particular weapons system. It was a demand for a political response, for reassurance, and for 'hand-holding' that could not be understood in technical terms or in relation to strictly or solely military criterion. The United States' response was indicative of the difficulties in the relationship.

The actual passage of the request with the administration's support through Congress in the spring of 1978, need not detain us here. The sale was agreed in the Senate by a vote of 54—44. It comprised part of a 'package' deal in which sales to Saudi Arabia and Egypt (50 F-5Es of the 120 requested) were 'balanced' by selling to Israel an *additional* 20 F-15s over the original Israeli submission of 15 F-15s and 75 F-16s. The end result was however less important than the process through which the Saudi request passed. To gain assent, the Saudi government was subjected to questioning of its motives and final agreement was made conditional on restrictive conditions that constituted a political embarrassment to the Kingdom.

---

1 These arguments apply equally to a US refusal of the subsequent Saudi request in 1980 for additional equipment. For the 'political' importance of arms sales and the relationship between the Saudi defence build-up and its credibility in the Arab world, see Andrew Pierre, 'Beyond the Plane Package: Arms and Politics in the Middle East', *International Security*, vol. 3, no. 1, Summer 1978, pp. 150-51, and Abdul Kasim Mansur, 'The American Threat to Saudi Arabia', *passim*.

It was no surprise that pro-Israeli forces within the US Congress exaggerated the potential of the F-15s for strikes against Israeli positions or for possible transfer to some other Arab state for it was clear that the most galling aspect of the Saudi request, and the subsequent package for the Israelis was the political symbolism of 'relative evenhandedness for US arms transfers'[1] to the region. But the requirement of an assurance from the Kingdom on the stationing of the aircraft away from its western frontier and their configuration to preclude their use against Israel was needlessly humiliating to the Saudis. Prince Fahd publicly declared: 'We only purchase the weapons necessary for defending our borders and our vast territory'. King Khaled in a letter to President Carter acknowledged a 'linkage': 'I would like to emphasize that the planes are being acquired for defence and Saudi Arabia is continuing to make every effort in pursuit of a just, comprehensive and lasting settlement in the Middle East'. The specific restrictions governing the sale included:

1   No transfer of F-15s or the training on them of third country nationals.
2   No equipment or special auxiliary tanks would be permitted to increase range.
3   Saudi Arabia would not request multiple ejection bomb racks or seek them elsewhere.
4   Saudi Arabia would not acquire other combat aircraft pending delivery of the F-15s.

Secretary of Defense Brown assured Congress that the planes would not be based at Tabuk, 125 miles from Eilat.

It was clear that these conditions and US hypersensitivity to Israel's security needs embarrassed the Saudis who publicly chafed at the restrictions. Prince Saud, the Foreign Minister, observed: 'As far as I am concerned, why should Saudi Arabia be the sole country to have a condition imposed on it? We are as much threatened as anyone'.[2] Politically these restrictions shed doubt on Saudi Arabia's Arab commitment, implying the acceptance of conditions separating the Palestinian issue from its own defence.

Saudi Arabia made the sale of the F-15s a test case of the overall relationship. It used the willingness of France to sell the F-I *Mirage* aircraft, with a quicker delivery schedule and no restrictions governing their deployment or re-transfer to third countries, as a lever to pressure

---

1   See Andrew Pierre, 'Beyond the Plane Package', *ibid.*, p. 155.

2   US TV interview. In fact similar, and equally embarrassing conditions had been demanded of Iran the previous year during the hearings on the sale of AWACs. Saudi Arabia has so far consistently rejected conditions on the AWACs sought by them.

Washington. Both Cyrus Vance and Harold Brown warned Congress that if the F-15 sale was not approved, Saudi Arabia would obtain its needs from France without controls guaranteeing Israel's safety.[1] In the event, the agreement to sell the aircraft was a pyrrhic victory for the Saudis who had been subjected to Congressional criticism and to what amounted to a pro-Zionist veto. Treated as a second class client rather than a regional partner it had been somewhat less than successful as an exercise in reassurance.

The second round: 1980-81. The bitter after-taste of the experience in 1978 however was not a deterrent to a new contentious Saudi request made in 1980. As in 1978, it is best understood for its political connotations — as a demand for reassurance and as a reaffirmation of a US commitment. But in the wake of Iran's revolution and the Soviet invasion of Afghanistan, it is equally intelligible in terms of a changed security environment in the region. Although annoyed by the 1978 experience, the Saudis had reason to suspect that a more acute security problem in the Gulf would now make the US more amenable to a request for arms, and that the conditions imposed in 1978 were in any case subject to bargaining.

The issue was first raised in February 1980 when Saudi officials discussed Gulf security with Zbigniew Brzezinski and Warren Christopher in Riyadh. Rather than offer the US military facilities in the region, Saudi officials sought to improve their own defence capabilities. The Saudis sought extra fuel tanks for the F-15, together with an aerial refueling capability in the shape of 4 KC-135 tankers, plus an unspecified number of AWACs early warning and command and control aircraft for directing the F-15s. In addition, Saudi Arabia asked to purchase the improved *Sidewinder* air-to-air missile (the AIM-9L). The additional refueling capability would have stretched the range of the F-15 from 450 to at least 1,000 miles.

The initial response by the US Executive Branch was encouraging. Brzezinski is reported to have told Crown Prince Fahd: 'For the defence of Saudi Arabia we will do anything'. General Jones and the Joint Chiefs of Staff were also keen to see the Saudis purchase the AWACs originally ordered by Iran.[2] The Saudis were then (a) asked to 'justify' the request; (b) told to be aware of possible political problems

---

1 Also it would deny the US influence over their use in conflict in the manipulation of spares, ammunition etc. An identical argument is being used over British Nimrod as an alternative to AWACs.

2 *Washington Star*, 18 July 1980.

in Congress in an election year and (c) appraised of the US doubts' about its absorptive capacity for new equipment.[1]

When the Saudi request for 'enhanced' F-15s became public, the responses were similar to 1978. Some, like Senator Jackson, saw 'blackmail' in the Saudi request. This phrase, most commonly used by pro-Israelis, was not confined to that group. Many in the United States saw its own influence as 'leverage' while other states' power was seen as 'blackmail'. *The New York Times* saw no difference between Saudi Arabia and the other states, and showed no recognition of a partnership and asked: 'If every Saudi desire is America's command', it asked 'then what of Iraq's desires and Libya's . . . ?[2] A more sophisticated response came from the *Washington Post* which saw the issue as balancing reassurance and credibility with Israel with consistency and reliability with the Saudis. It accurately diagnosed Saudi motives as being at least part psychological 'to remove the stigma of being a second class arms recipient' and it identified Israel's anxiety as political as well: ' . . . it is a reminder that Saudi Arabia is cutting into Israel's political edge in Washington'.[3] With the 'attentive public' as split as the US government (between NSC and Defense for, and Congress against) the possibility of a bruising public debate again looked imminent in mid-1980.

A major problem for those legalistically inclined was the express denial in May 1978 by the administration that the Saudi government would seek to add to the capabilities of the F-15. Secretary Brown had sent a letter to the Chairman of the Senate Foreign Relations Committee: 'Saudi Arabia has not requested nor do we intend to sell any other systems or armaments that would increase the range or enhance the ground attack capability of the F-15'.[4] Congress could now argue that this request was in violation of the administration's promises. Sixty-eight Senators (more than two-thirds of the Senate) duly did so in a letter to the President in the summer.[5] Senator Byrd, Majority leader, referred to the equipment requested as 'offensive' implying some imaginary criteria for distinguishing between arms

---

1 *Washington Star*, 20 April 1960.

2 *New York Times* (Editorial), 18 June 1980. The Editorial sought to balance between those who would confront the Saudis and those who would appease them.

3 See the Editorial, *Washington Post*, 20 June 1980.

4 John Sparkman, Alabama.

5 *The Times*, 9 July 1980; *International Herald Tribune*, 9 July 1980.

legitimately needed for 'defence' and other purposes.[1] By mid-1980 it was clear that the Saudis had decided not to press for a decision before the elections which were now looming large. In deferring the request, however, they made it clear that they would expect a rapid answer on the morrow of the election results.[2]

The administration was relieved at the Saudis' willingness to await the elections. It anticipated problems in Congress and did not expect President Carter to court electoral problems by raising the issue. It denied however that this 'breathing spell' constituted a 'back-door rejection'.[3] In October, as a prelude to a subsequent decision, the Defense Department undertook a study of the Saudi request to be completed by 30 November. By this time the eruption of the Iran-Iraq war and the request for the stationing of 4 US AWACs on Saudi soil had further changed the political environment in the Gulf. As a result many Defense Department officials were hopeful for more intensive military relations in the future between the two states.[4]

At this point one of those events which are explicable only in terms of US domestic politics intervened. President Carter, anxious about the softness of his support in New York State, appealed to the Jewish vote by observing on 24 October that the US would not reverse its May 1978 assurances; it would not provide 'offensive' equipment to Saudi Arabia. Subsequently it transpired that the President was attempting to distinguish between 'bomb racks' and refueling capability.[5] Besides undermining the Pentagon study, the President annoyed the Saudis. He lost the state anyway.

The Saudi perspective. From the outset the Saudis made it clear to their American counterparts that the request would be an 'important test case' which could damage relations.[6] In part the Saudis were motivated by competitiveness with Egypt and the need to be reassured that Cairo had not replaced Saudi Arabia as the centre of US attention. Egypt, which had felt able to ignore the Arab consensus and had allowed US F-4s and AWACs to be stationed on its soil, had also under-

---

1 *International Herald Tribune*, 23 June 1980.

2 The report in *Aviation Week and Space Technology*, 14 July 1980, p. 17, that the Saudis sought 'an immediate answer' which Defense Secretary Brown answered would not be forthcoming, is not corroborated elsewhere.

3 *International Herald Tribune*, 23 June 1980.

4 *International Herald Tribune*, 22 October 1980.

5 See *International Herald Tribune*, 27 October 1980.

6 See *International Herald Tribune*, 18, 23 June 1980.

taken joint military exercises with the US. The US had provided and subsidized Egypt's purchase of the AIM-9L *Sidewinder* missile which the Saudis now sought.[1] It was important in terms of regional politics and the Saudis' reputation that the Kingdom be allowed to buy for cash what another Arab state was obtaining at a discount.

More important, the Saudi government believed that a change in its security environment necessitated an acceleration of its military build-up which had been shown to be inadequate to meet even minor threats.[2] The Saudi government expressly rejected two types of linkage (or *quid pro quo*) in exchange for US arms: firstly, the provision of military facilities to the West on Saudi soil and secondly, support for the Camp David peace process.[3] Either of these concessions in the Saudi view would compromise rather than strengthen Saudi security. In combination they would entail a departure from the Arab consensus which has been the mainstay of Saudi foreign policy, resulting in an isolation which would increase the Kingdom's vulnerability to terrorism and subversion. Western expectations along these lines were, in the Saudi view, evidence of ignorance rather than malice, an ignorance that neglected to note that Saudi security was underwritten in large part by the sanction of the Arab–Islamic world which constituted a defence and psychological umbrella for Saudi Arabia that it could ill afford to destroy. Attempts by US Congressmen to link the sale of arms with explicit changes in Saudi policy toward Egypt and Israel were, in the Saudi view, unacceptable.[4]

The area of linkage or reciprocity in the Saudi view was in the Kingdom's oil policies. Saudi officials hinted that 'civilian authorities' were beginning to ask what the Kingdom was getting in return for stepped-up crude oil production and the establishment of oil prices several dollars per barrel lower than that being charged by other

1 See *Washington Star*, 15 June 1980.

2 The border war between the Yemens, the Mecca incident in November 1979 and now the Iran–Iraq war contributed to the feeling of weakness. In addition there was a regional perception of Saudi military weakness, that Saudi Arabia was a 'cheque book' state that had to be reversed. On the latter see Abdul Kasim Mansur, 'The American Threat to Saudi Arabia', *passim*.

3 The most authoritative report is in the *Washington Star*, 18 July 1980.

4 Eighteen of thirty-five members of the House, Foreign Affairs Committee (including three Republicans) opposed the sale arguing that if the sale was a 'test of friendship' that friendship was reciprocal and demanded in effect Saudi support of the Camp David Agreement before approving the sale, *International Herald Tribune*, 27 February 1981. This was supported by a *New York Times* editorial, see *International Herald Tribune*, 8 April 1981. The tendency of US legislators to link everything indiscriminately must baffle the Saudis. During the 1980-81 AWACs debate some argued that the Saudis' failure to restrain Syria in Lebanon constituted an argument against the sale.

producing states.[1] Oil Minister Zaki Yamani put this clearly: 'We've gotten no sign of appreciation for everything we've done'. Saudi development needs would require oil production of only half the current rate of 10.3 million barrels per day. 'Why should we accumulate a surplus of funds'?[2]

As in 1978, it was particularly galling to the Saudis to have their arms requests subject to what they saw as an Israeli veto. The Saudi Ambassador in Washington argued that the US was putting Israel's interests before its own and hinted (as in 1978) that there existed other sources for arms 'without restrictions and conditions'.[3] This was put more strongly after Carter's electoral gambit. A Saudi press statement noted that: 'Nobody has the monopoly on the Kingdom's friendship'. The Saudi press agency pointed out that 'if the Kingdom does not get a response it may knock on all doors to obtain necessary requirements to realize the defence of the homeland'.[4] In the Saudi view its ability to buy arms should be subject only to the limits imposed on it by the United States nuclear non-proliferation policy.[5]

The Saudi arguments[6] to the US government illustrate their perception of the nature of the relationship. In considering their request for the arms as a test of the relationship, they see the relationship as one 'carefully balanced' between the two parties and subject to adverse consequences if refused. While not threatening specific retaliatory action, they imply that a rejection would make future co-operation politically difficult. Furthermore although much of the equipment is available elsewhere, the Saudis insist that ' . . . as a matter of principle we want to purchase it from the US'. Conceding that the election posed problems for the administration, the Saudis did not push for an early decision but they did not conceal their belief that with more courage the United States government could always stand up to 'Zionist pressures'.

1 *Washington Star*, 18 July 1980.

2 *New York Times*, 19 October 1980. In 1978 Yamani had related Saudi oil production level and support for the dollar to US arms sales. *Washington Post*, 2 May 1978.

3 Sheikh Faysal al-Hejelan, *The Times*, 10 July 1980.

4 See SWB BBC/ME/6563/i 31 October 1980; *Financial Times*, 30 October 1980; *New York Times*, 31 October 1980; *The Times*, 31 October 1980.

5 See the comment by Mohammed Abdu Yamani, Information Minister, *New York Times*, 19 December 1980.

6 These are well compiled in a report in the *Washington Star*, 18 July 1980. Other useful sources on the Saudi perspective include George Ball, 'Reflections on a Heavy Year', *Foreign Affairs*, America and the World 1980, pp. 488-494 and Abdul Kasim Mansur, 'The American Threat'. I have drawn on all three in the next two paragraphs.

The Saudis' arguments in support of their specific request is enlightening. Reference has been made to a refusal to accept a *quid pro quo* between arms and either bases or support for Camp David. In the Saudi view the key linkage that exists is between its oil policies and western security. The arguments in favour of the Saudi request are subtle and relate to the impact of a rejection on Saudi security. Allusions are made to domestic pressures and public dissatisfaction over the Saudis' return on the relationship. This is not argued as a future possibility: 'That point has already come. The questions are being asked today'. The Royal Family implies that it is under considerable pressure from the military for equipment, and that the greatest threat to stability is internal and possibly from a discontented military. 'We are talking about helping the stability of our government'. A refusal may entail instability. Finally the argument is made that the USSR provides arms to its allies in the region, why then should the US remain unresponsive to its allies' needs?

The denouement. The election of a Republican President to the White House reduced the US domestic political calculations surrounding the Saudi request. Seeing the world largely in East—West terms, the new government could view both Saudi and Israeli needs as complementary. In February 1981 the pro-Israeli elements in Congress moved towards dropping their opposition to the Saudi request, provided the United States' offer to Israel was 'sweetened'. It became clear that, as in 1978, opposition to Saudi requests had become a means of increasing Israel's leverage for better terms from Washington. By the end of February the elements of a new package were discernible. In addition to the earlier 40 F-15s Washington would provide Israel with ten more on preferential financing terms. In addition Israel would have the restrictions on the sales of her *Kfir* aircraft (with a US engine) to the Third World removed, and would receive an enhanced early warning capability — probably a ground radar station and access to US intelligence. Thus in FY 1982, $2.18 billion in aid is to be allocated to Israel, of which $1.4 billion will be military aid and the remainder economic. In addition $600 million is to be provided for the building of new bases to substitute for those given up in the Sinai.[1] The Saudi request therefore seemed set for eventual approval by Congress in 1981 but it then ran into further difficulties. The agreement when it comes will not be a resounding affirmation either of Saudi importance or of the weight attached to the relationship with the Kingdom by Washington.

1   See *International Herald Tribune*, 21-22, and 27 February 1980.

After massive expenditure on the modernization and expansion of defence capabilities, Saudi Arabia still remains severely limited in its ability to meet threats to its territorial integrity, and is likely to remain so for the next decade. Despite exasperation in certain quarters with this state of affairs, the Saudi leadership is aware of the inevitably lengthy process that military modernization entails especially for a country starting from 'scratch' with little in the way of infrastructure and skilled manpower. This recognition does not however diminish the Saudis' quandary: how to maintain a defence link with the United States to meet the major threats to its security while diminishing its own political exposure to criticism within the Arab world of collusion and collaboration with Israel's foremost ally. The acute tension arising from the attempt to balance these two requirements has not been eased either by recent US foreign policy or by the intensification of threats to Saudi security within the region. Reliance on the United States remains a principal feature of Saudi defence planning but the political costs of identification with Washington have risen. Saudi attempts to reduce the conspicuousness of this link and to distance itself from the US have taken various forms including the diversification of arms suppliers (see below), and the refusal to support US policies in the region, but this has not severed that nation's continued *ultimate* dependence on the US for security. As its credibility as an ally declined and its liability as a partner increased, the US' ability to influence or persuade the Saudis on various issues has accordingly shrunk. The leverage of the arms supplier diminished as that supplier itself became at once less credible as a supplier of security and a magnet attracting regional hostility likely to undermine the recipient's security.

Doubts about the United States as a security partner can be traced to developments in 1978-79. It was not the fact that the United States could not prevent regional instabilities that impaired the US' reputation, but rather the nature of its lackadaisical and equivocal responses to them. It was not US military capabilities but rather its political judgement that was thrown into doubt, confusing and unnerving its regional partners.

The revolution in Iran was a traumatic event for the Saudi leadership. It took the (for it) unusual step of condemning the disturbances against the Shah in August 1978. The replacement of a pro-Western monarchy, which was moderate, with a militantly anti-Western republic was bad enough. But the uncertainty of the region in the face of the unpredictability of the new regime generated further insecurities. The very nature of the revolution, the alliance between secularists and fundamentalists, and between the middle and lower classes could not fail to find an echo elsewhere in the Gulf. Furthermore the prospect, in the Saudi view, was for the emergence of the Left as victors as the revolution became increasingly radicalized. The incapacity of the United States either to save the Shah[1] or to diminish the repercussions of his removal were closely studied in Riyadh. The parallels for themselves of US acquiescence in the change of leadership was obvious: 'better to lose a Shah than a nation' implied a priority commitment to the flow of oil, not to regime security. The inability of the US to influence the new Iranian authorities after the revolution was a continuing source of concern in Riyadh. For, whatever worries may have existed about Iran under the Shah, the Saudis had counted on the US' influence in Tehran as a potentially restraining factor. Now this had gone, to be replaced by tension between Washington and Tehran which caught Saudi Arabia in the centre of contradictory pressures. Above all though, the revolution in Iran raised questions about the relevance of the security relationship with the US. If threats materialized internally or in murky conditions, it was now clear that the US could not be counted upon for support.

The second regional event that unsettled the area was the unveiling of the Camp David agreements with simultaneous deterioration of stability in Iran later in 1978. The failure of the United States to consult with the Saudi leadership in advance and its assumption that Saudi Arabia's support (or at least its neutrality) would be automatic, demonstrated an egregious insensitivity to Saudi political concerns. From the Saudi perspective, any departure from the security reassurance provided by the umbrella of the 'Arab consensus' risked the intensification of pressures and threats to the Kingdom not only by radical Palestinian elements but by militant governments including Libya, South Yemen and possibly Iraq. The need to reinsure by maintaining its credentials as a good Arab nation was all the more pressing in the light of the wave of anti-Western sentiment emanating from Iran and finding responses in the region and beyond. To much of the Arab world, the Camp David agreements looked like an American sponsored plan to eliminate the Arab military option and hence to reduce any Israeli incentive to compromise. To expect Saudi Arabia's support for this in the light of its military weakness, the pressures of inter-Arab politics and the revolution in Iran, was to expect rather more influence than the arms relationship alone could muster.

In response to these developments (together with the brief Yemen war) the US in early 1979 sought to lay a new basis for its relationship

---

1 Or to grant him and his family a haven after thirty-seven years of 'friendship', something which is understood in personal terms in the Kingdom.

with Saudi Arabia. On a tour which also embraced Egypt, Israel and Jordan, Defense Secretary Brown in February 1979 offered the Saudi leadership a more explicit defence arrangement. This was apparently tied to Saudi support both for Camp David and a greater US military presence in the region. The Saudi response, while acknowledging the 'Communist threat', was to emphasize as a priority the necessity of revising the Camp David accords. The Defense Minister, Prince Sultan, argued that 'the situation in the region will become more critical unless Israel withdraws completely from the occupied territories, including Jerusalem, and grants the Palestinian people the right to self-determination in their homeland'.[1]

Nevertheless the US–Saudi military co-operation increased. Commercial sales, the hiring of civilian personnel, the building of infrastructure ('pouring concrete') continued. But to these activities was added in 1979 a new dimension: the US now assumed a direct training and advisory function with the Saudi armed forces including field and combat manoeuvres and the identification of contingencies and missions — in short a role more direct than that of mere salesman. This reflected a recognition in the aftermath of events in Iran that Saudi Arabia, with vast land space and limited military potential, could not soon expect to become self-reliant for defence against local threats.[2]

More generally it meant the effective end to the Nixon doctrine, for with local states unable to assume primary responsibility for the region's security, the US would have to play a more active forward role. In pursuit of this, talk of 'pacts' with states in the region and 'bases' for access to it increased. The prospect of an increased naval presence either within the region or 'over the horizon' was discussed publicly. In this connection, while consideration was given to the permanent deployment of a larger naval presence (perhaps by the creation of a Fifth Fleet), the MIDEASTFOR naval operations in Bahrain were reinforced in mid-1979 by the addition of two destroyers. Implicitly acknowledging the relationship between security in the Gulf, access to the region and the Palestinian issue, the US sought without success throughout the year to obtain the support of 'moderate' Arab regimes for the Camp David approach to a settlement.

1 *Okaz* (Riyadh) 12 February 1979; quoted in Adeed Dawisha, 'Internal Values and External Threats: The Making of Saudi Foreign Policy', *Orbis*, vol. 23, no. 1, Spring 1979, p. 143 f.n. Particularly annoying to the Saudis was the attempt by some quarters in Washington, e.g. Frank Church, Chairman of the Senate Foreign Relations Committee on February 1 1979 to link the sale of US aircraft with Saudi support for Camp David.

2 The acquisition of a purely defensive capability requiring air-mobile units and the construction of an air defence network would require time during which the US role as guarantor would be indispensable.

The utility of the US connection — 'liabilities and all'

The case of the Yemens. Lacking military power, Saudi Arabia has sought to use its vast financial assets to strengthen its security. Dispensation of subsidies to friendly governments has been a feature of this 'chequebook diplomacy' while financial incentives have been held out tantalizingly to poor and hostile neighbours. The limits of this as a substitute for military power are nowhere better illustrated than in Saudi Arabia's relations with the People's Democratic Republic of Yemen (PDRY). Saudi offers of up to $125 million in aid in 1977 were unable to persuade the Aden government to stop backing radical movements in the Arabian Peninsula. The PDRY's disruptiveness in the region increased, culminating in June 1978 in the assassination of the relatively pro-Saudi President Ghashmi. The Saudis were successful in obtaining sanctions, including the severance of economic and technical assistance against the PDRY, the first such decision by the Arab League against a member state.

Despite this success, relations between North (the Yemen Arab Republic) and South Yemen (PDRY) deteriorated and led to border clashes in February 1979. The pro-Saudi regime of the North Yemen formally requested an Arab League meeting on the PDRY's 'military attack' on 25 February. Saudi Arabia responded by cancelling all military leave and placing its forces on alert. Three days later the United States agreed to speed up arms deliveries previously promised to the YAR. By the beginning of March, South Yemeni forces were reported to be deep inside North Yemen and close to cutting the Taez-Sana road. Despite a ceasefire arranged by Syria and Iraq in the Arab League, South Yemeni planes attacked North Yemen. While Arab League meetings continued to seek agreement on a ceasefire proposal and on a mediation committee to visit both countries, the United States assumed a more direct role. On 6 March a naval task force was despatched to the Arabian Sea to strengthen a warning given the previous day by Secretary Vance to the USSR against any USSR–Cuban involvement in the conflict. On 9 March, under emergency provisions of the 1976 Arms Export Control Act (circumventing the need for Congressional approval), President Carter approved the delivery to the YAR of $300 million-worth of arms including twelve F-5E aircraft within two weeks. A squadron of US F-15s together with ninety military advisers were also rushed to Saudi Arabia and, in addition, the US made an offer to provide early-warning (AWACs) aircraft if the Saudis required them. By the end of the month the crisis had subsided and the YAR and PDRY were engaged in discussions about eventual 'unification'. The incident underscored Saudi Arabia's military impotence in the face of even a limited regional threat.

59

Saudi Arabia's relationship with North Yemen — always ambivalent because of the persistent Saudi desire to control its more populous neighbour[1] — was at least partly responsible for that government's military weakness. The United States' reaction, in part a response to Saudi Arabia's panic, was designed primarily to reassure the Kingdom of its reliability as an ally. Whether the PDRY attack was a Soviet-sponsored probe was unclear, but it was manifestly Soviet-assisted as relatively large infusions of Soviet arms in the preceding months had made it possible. The Saudis' perception of the incident was that it represented a carefully calculated PDRY—Cuban—USSR probe designed to unseat the YAR government and to test Saudi and Western reactions. Though grateful for the prompt US response, the Saudi government was also embarrassed by the revelation of its military weakness and by the publicity surrounding the provision of assistance. It continued to remain opposed to any public support for either Camp David or an American military presence in the Gulf. This reluctance was if anything reinforced by the diplomatic assistance furnished by Iraq in the dispute — for Iraq remained adamantly opposed to both elements of American policy.

The Iran—Iraq conflict. Towards the end of 1979, two distinct but inter-related developments in the Gulf region punctuated the evolution of the US—Saudi security relationship: the crisis between Iran and the US over the seizure of American hostages; and the invasion by the Soviet Union of neighbouring Afghanistan. Both underlined the continuing instability and tension in the area and both focussed attention on the growing need for the West to develop military facilities in the region for rapid access and to the necessity for Western countervailing power to offset nearby Soviet forces. Yet neither was able to shake the Saudis from their resolve not to increase their identification with the West.

This determination if anything increased throughout 1980 as the Carter administration reversed its earlier policies and loudly proclaimed a rhetorical doctrine which it admitted it was incapable of supporting. Pleased by the willingness of Carter to at last question Soviet policies, and at being courted by National Security Adviser Brzezinski in early February 1980, the Saudis still remained adamant, seeing this as only the latest and not necessarily the last American 'flip-flop'. Accordingly they rejected a further US request for the use of military facilities on 8 April, 1980.

1 For a useful discussion see the Congressional testimony of US officials, in *Aviation Week*, 26 May 1980, pp. 79-83.

In the course of the year this judgement hardened. Washington's alternation between threat and whimper on the hostage issue was unimpressive. Threats to use force, to mine the Gulf's waters or to exact reprisals by military attacks did little to encourage Saudi Arabia (or the other Gulf states) to formalize any military relationship with Washington. The April rescue mission in Tabas was seen as a further indication of the erosion of American power.[1] Nor was Washington's response to the invasion of Afghanistan impressive enough to encourage the solidification of ties. Having failed to fully mobilize its allies on the issue, Washington failed also to convince Pakistan that it was seriously concerned and could be counted upon.[2] Subsequently it found, in the weakness of the Pakistan regime, in the sensitivity of India and in the disunity of the Afghan opposition, reasons for not supporting resistance to the Soviet occupiers. The US failure to 'draw the line' in Afghanistan[3] but to respond by flexing military muscles elsewhere did little to reassure the Saudis about the astuteness of American political judgements. The sheer volubility of US statements, punctuated by political rhetoric and contradictory leaks, gave the impression neither of consistency nor of purpose. Yet it was precisely at this time, with Washington in the throes of a premature election campaign, that the Carter administration sought from its regional partners open identification, oblivious to their political needs and domestic constraints.

The conflict between Iran and Iraq which had festered since the spring of 1979 escalated into large-scale hostilities in the second half of September 1980. Initially the Saudi response was low-key, advocating restraint and cautioning against an 'over-reaction' by the West. Saudi Foreign Minister Faisal specifically referred to the dangers of a superpower action-reaction syndrome and to the dynamic of a logic which, in seeking to meet 'every eventuality', actually 'tends to increase the threat'. In his view the dangers of Saudi involvement or the closure of the Straits was exaggerated. Outside forces, he believed, would 'only complicate the situation'.[4]

---

1 The fact that it was launched via Oman embarrassed that country and cast even more doubt on the predictability of US actions and on US judgement. For the general Arab perception of the pressures building up on them see *The Sunday Times* (Mohammed Heikal), 28 April 1980, and *International Herald Tribune*, 18 April 1980.

2 Reportedly the Saudis offered to participate in a 'joint consortium' with the US — 'Saudi Arabia would organize Arab funds, the United States would rally the West'. — Washington ignored this and failed to inspire Pakistan by itself. See *International Herald Tribune*, 19 February 1981.

3 On this issue see 'The Comments of a Saudi Leader', *The Times*, 10 February 1981.

4 See the reports based on interviews with him in *The Washington Post*, 28 September 1980; *Wall Street Journal*, 30 September 1980.

As a result of developments in the war (specifically the use of other Gulf states' territories by Iraq for the dispersal of its aircraft, and for access through them to the islands in the Lower Gulf), this initial Saudi evaluation was hastily discarded.[1] Fearing Iranian air attacks because of assistance to Iraq, the Saudis looked to the US for aid. On 29 September, US and Saudi officials conferred on the text of an announcement regarding US assistance. In Washington consideration was given to the provision of air defence aircraft (F-14s or F-15s). The subsequent decision to send four AWACs was considered a minimal response by Washington. In its deliberations Washington was guided by several considerations:

1 A need to reassure the Saudis about the US commitment.
2 A desire to meet the Saudi request to encourage Saudi Arabia later on to replace whatever oil short-falls occurred as a result of the war.
3 To stop the 'mindless gravitation' of Saudi Arabia toward Iraq.

Consideration was given in Washington to the opportunity presented by the Saudi request for military assistance to press for a longer-term arrangement but this was discarded. It remained nonetheless part of the US motive for its swift response that its actions might make the Saudis more prepared to envisage military co-operation to meet future contingencies.[2]

The upshot of these considerations was a formal Saudi request for defence assistance from the United States. Four AWACs early-warning aircraft, to be flown, maintained and protected by American personnel (numbering 300), were sent to the Gulf on 30 September. The cost of the operation was to be largely borne by the US with some contributions from Saudi Arabia. The aircraft were based in Dhahran. Two tanker aircraft (KC-135s) with support personnel (40) were also sent. The AWACs were considered an appropriate response, symbolizing US commitment (with its advanced early warning capability against air attack), yet remaining unprovocative. The US position was made clear; neutrality in the war did not mean that the US was '. . . neutral in meeting the legitimate defense needs of our friends'.[3] The US commit-

---

1 Indeed the differences between Prince Faisal's comments in the US and the activity of the Saudi government *at the same time* suggests differences in their evaluation of the problem that is greater than a simple matter of information. The subsequent Saudi request for assistance may well have been controversial within the Saudi leadership.

2 See the reconstruction of US decision-making by Richard Burt and Bernard Gwertzman, *International Herald Tribune*, 13 October 1980.

3 See the *Wall Street Journal*, 1 October 1980; *The Times*, 1 October 1980.

ment was augmented the same week by a mobile ground radar station and by additional communications equipment and 96 support personnel. The following week the US offered to share the information derived from the AWACs with the other non-belligerent Gulf states provided they eschewed any involvement in the conflict.

The US' aims during the conflict were straightforward: to keep open the Straits of Hormuz and to maintain access to the non-belligerents in the region. In showing its concern for its vital interests in the region it sought to protect the oilfields from any expansion of the war which might arise from Iranian reprisals for the involvement of the other Gulf states. At the same time as it asserted its own interest in the course of the war, and responded to its ally's needs, the US was constrained by two other necessities: the avoidance of any military action inconsistent with neutrality which might provoke a commensurate Soviet response; and the continuing need to demonstrate to its regional friends that its military activities were geared to the protection of the oilfields rather than from any design to seize them.

Within these constraints the US role in the war was successful.[1] The Iranian government on 1 October, 'fully aware of its international obligations', pledged not to attempt to block the Straits. The Saudi leadership's willingness publicly to request US military assistance demonstrated that *in extremis* their reticence could be overcome. It was a clear sign of the Kingdom's dependence on the US in an emergency. Even Iraq temporarily dropped its loud objections to a US presence after the Saudi request. The American action was a clear extension of US involvement in the region and an assumption of a direct military responsibility for the defence of Saudi Arabia's oilfields. It went beyond even the Carter doctrine which had claimed a right to involvement against an 'outside' threat to the region, for this was a local issue.

The war clearly showed that sources of threat to the region's security lay principally in the Gulf region itself and not, as had become a hardened cliché, from the Palestine question. It also demonstrated that the 'exclusion of the superpowers' from the Gulf could not be a realistic formula if one of the principal Gulf states had rapid recourse to one of those superpowers in the face of threats emanating from a regional conflict. Yet, despite the inadequacy of this formula for meeting even contingencies within the region, the political inhibitions on accepting alignment with the US persisted for the Saudis. To be sure Riyadh increased its oil production to full capacity (10.5 million

---

1 The best initial discussions of the war and its political repercussions are *Wall Street Journal*, 15 October 1980; *International Herald Tribune*, 15 October 1980.

b/d — 20 per cent more than its official ceiling) to compensate for any shortfall due to the war. But it still remained reluctant to cement its military relationship more formally. While it may have become more receptive to a discreet American presence in the region, it is doubtful, given the nature of US government, that this is feasible. To justify a US military presence on its territory, the Saudi government would need something tangible to show for it, not merely to its own populace but to the Arab world at large which would be in a position to undermine its security.[1]

So, despite the continuing need for a security guarantee from the US, Riyadh finds itself unable to provide the means to make this credible. It reverts to the traditional formula — 'We can't accommodate your security interests without substantial progress on our political problem, the Palestinians'[2] — and it indulges in flights of fancy with no relationship to reality but of great political appeal within the Arab world. Even as the conflict continued, Prince Fahd was quoted as saying that there were no threats to the region from within but rather from dangers 'converging in the region from remote areas'. He asserted that the Gulf nations do not need foreign help in maintaining their security because 'Gulf security is exclusively the affair of the Gulf nations'.[3]

How this Gordian knot will be cut continues to mystify observers. In his 'farewell comments', Secretary Brown noted the dilemma without suggesting any solution by observing on the one hand the Saudis' increased need for a US security commitment in the light of the War and of events in Afghanistan and, on the other hand, the damage any formal Saudi alliance with the US or the granting of permission for US troops to be stationed on its soil would do for both internal and regional security. However, this did not deter the Defense Secretary from calling for a more 'explicit military arrangement'.[4]

The continuing Saudi ambivalence toward the US is very clear. The US is often a source of embarrassment. Lacking discretion it tends to overwhelm its partners rather than the threats to them. Its embrace is still considered almost as dangerous as its withdrawal. The linkage between the security of the Gulf and the issue of Palestine has been

1 Libya's severance of ties with Riyadh because of the Kingdom's acceptance of the AWACs is illustrative of the types of pressures that could be concerted in the event of a permanent presence.

2 In the words of one Saudi official, quoted in the *Wall Street Journal*, 25 November 1980.

3 *International Herald Tribune*, 19 January 1981.

4 See *New York Times*, 7 December 1980.

weakened by the war but that linkage persists. The importance of the US connection for Gulf security has not weakened the pressures on the US to produce a settlement on Palestine. The risks that Saudi Arabia is prepared to run depends on both issues:

1   The relevance of the US to its needs in the Gulf and further afield.
2   One of those needs is the pressure the issue of Palestine continues to exert on its policies.

The risks of departure from the Arab consensus, of isolation and vulnerability to terrorism inhibit any change in Saudi policy on this issue. While greater Saudi activism in shaping that consensus is possible, withdrawal from it, as Egypt has done, is unthinkable for the security of the Kingdom is partly sanctioned by it and, dependent as it is on inter-Arab politics, it cannot afford the risks of its alienation.

Arms diversification

Despite the preponderant role of the US in its defence programme, Saudi Arabia has not sought to obtain all its defence needs from one source. Diversification of sources of supply has been a feature of its arms purchases in recent years. France, in particular, has become a major supplier responsible especially for much of the Kingdom's armour and air defence. Total purchases from this source had reached by the Autumn of 1980 some 12 billion francs, a quarter of which is attributable to training and technical services. Included in the equipment transferred have been some 450 *Panhard* APCs, 250 AMX-30 tanks, 150 AMX-10P Infantry Combat Vehicles, *Gazelle* anti-tank helicopters, *Crotale* (Shahine) air-defence missiles and 155 mm howitzers. In addition an electronics industry is being set up with aid from Thomson-CSF for the manufacture of radar and radio equipment.

In October 1980 Saudi Arabia signed a major new defence purchase agreement with France. Totalling 14.4 billion francs ($3.5 billion), a third of which comprised services and training systems, this agreement extended the French role to the expansion and modernization of the Saudi Navy. The package included the supply of six ships (four frigates of 2,000 tons plus two tankers) together with *Otomat* anti-ship missiles and 24 *Dauphin* helicopters together with the AS-15-TT anti-ship missile. In addition France is to provide logistic and support services and extensive training for the Saudi Navy. France is to send 45 officers and 125 petty officers for temporary service in the Royal Saudi Navy. This training, which is to be extended to hundreds of Saudis, will be done in Saudi Arabia. Reportedly a major consideration for the Saudis in favouring France (over Italy which also competed for the order) was the training component offered.[1] The agreement was understandably seen in France as a sign that Saudi Arabia wanted to intensify its military relationship.

Another indication of the Saudis' new interest in European arms suppliers was their indirect approach to the Federal Republic of Germany in late 1980 for *Leopard II* tanks and *Tornado* aircraft. The numbers discussed were respectively 300 and between 75 and 100. The implications of the approach were more profound than the numbers. There were suggestions that requests for other systems would follow — up to 10 billion marks in value — and there were hints of a possible 'special relationship' developing. As the principal supplier of oil to the Federal Republic (25 per cent of its needs), the reported Saudi offer of linking the arms purchases with the guaranteed supply of oil for ten years to cover the costs may have been especially attractive. The Federal Republic had strong economic incentives to examine the request seriously, including a large trade deficit with Saudi Arabia (together with a $2–3 billion loan from the Kingdom) and cost overruns on its weapons systems which could be reduced by exports extending their production run and so lowering their unit costs. Against this the Republic had political constraints both in the form of an established policy against the export of arms to 'areas of tension' and in the shape of a vocal faction of the SPD opposed to such sales.[2] Prime Minister Begin was not slow to play on memories of the 'holocaust' and Germany's moral obligations to Israel.

The Saudi overture may well have been timed for political reasons to pressure Washington to lift the restrictions on the F-15s but there were practical considerations as well. The *Tornado* aircraft, in which Italy and the United Kingdom are partners with the FRG, could be absorbed more easily than French aircraft given the continuing training programme provided by the UK in Saudi Arabia. A maintenance and logistics base was therefore already in place and diversification would thus create fewer practical problems.[3] The German answer to the Saudi request had not been given by April 1981 and may be postponed for some time but, in the context of a Western policy toward assuring Gulf security and given the Federal Republic's reluctance to commit

1 For sources on this transaction see, *Aviation Week and Space Technology*, 3 November 1980, p. 33; *Le Monde*, 14 May 1980, 15 October 1980; *Middle East Economic Digest*, 24 October 1980, pp. 3–5, 23 January 1981, p. 31.

2 See *inter alia Le Monde*, 10 January 1981; *Financial Times*, 13 January 1981; *The Times*, 13 February 1981; *International Herald Tribune*, 23 February 1981.

3 See *Aviation Week and Space Technology*, 9 February 1981, p. 30.

armed forces or ships to the area, the provision of arms has a certain logic. It would entail the supply of some advisers and technicians as well. Bonn's interest in the political dimension of security with an emphasis on economic assistance to the region may well continue but it may be supplemented in the future by a discriminating policy of arms supply to important states.

Dependence and leverage

The Saudi relationship with the United States has undergone a marked change in recent years. Difficulties in obtaining advanced armaments like the F-15 and AWACs have been embarrassing for the Saudi leadership, while America's continuing alignment with Israel has made a close relationship a growing political liability for them. Furthermore the trend toward non-alignment, so prevalent in the rhetoric of the Gulf, has created its own pressures against a tight exclusive relationship with either superpower. Nor has the extensive military relationship with the US been totally satisfactory for some in the Saudi leadership who attribute the Kingdom's still weak military capability, after massive expenditures, less to the inherent problems of modernization than to a purposeful US policy of stretching out this dependency. An intention to reduce both this dependence and the political exposure attendant on such a close relationship has served as a strong incentive for diversifying arms suppliers. The European states are natural candidates as additional suppliers. They are usually more forthcoming in supplying sophisticated equipment, motivated largely by commercial incentives, and they are less inhibited by hostile domestic interest groups. Above all they are less politically controversial as suppliers within the Arab world.

The diversification of sources of supply does not, and is not intended, to reduce the dependence of Saudi Arabia on the US as an ultimate guarantor, or to substitute for US equipment and training in, for example, its air force, but it does act as a means of spreading the risks of dependence on one source. It is also a way of asserting independence and of achieving political distance from the US. To be sure there are problems and risks. Diversification complicates logistics, maintenance and training[1] and may, in introducing a strong element of commercialism, dilute the essentially political feature of commitment that the supply of arms has meant to the recipient state. Against this has to be balanced the advantages which enable the recipient to

---

1 Furthermore the after-sales service of countries such as France have in the past been criticised.

threaten to go elsewhere for equipment denied by its principal supplier, as Saudi Arabia has done in the case of the F-15 and AWACs. The strengthening of links with other Western suppliers, while it may mean a reduced dependence on the US, does not entail a reduction in aggregate Western influence in Saudi Arabia. Moreover this sharing of influence, if it is not *politically* competitive, need not be unwelcome to Washington. Indeed to the extent that it 'spreads the load' and implies a multilateral Western approach to the question of Gulf security, it may well serve Washington's interest to have its own potential influence somewhat reduced. The conclusion of an agreement between Saudi Arabia and France on the training of police and in internal security affairs[1] is an example. The Saudis, doubtless encouraged by France's prompt and discreet assistance during the disturbances at Mecca in November 1979, decided to extend this relationship. From the US' viewpoint such agreements could only be beneficial, for equivalent American assistance would be controversial domestically and more disruptive politically within the region. In the context of the Gulf, the Saudis' diversification of sources of arms supply need not be unduly worrying to the United States. The basis for the relationship is far broader than that of arms supply alone, and the basis for influence will survive its diminution.

Perspective and style

It would be surprising, given their cultural differences and the dissimilarity of their political systems, if US–Saudi relations were without problems of communication. There is foremost on the US side the problem of stereotyping which arises largely from ignorance.[2] This colours the US perception of the Arabs — especially of the oil-rich states. Oil is seen as 'unearned income' or a 'windfall' and sheikhs are associated with 'blackmail', with 'extortion' and with camels. There has been a recurrent political temptation — as in the Eisenstadt memorandum of mid-1978 — to place the blame of the energy crisis on OPEC and specifically on the Arabs. Inadequate knowledge and a low level of US attention combined with the fantastic wealth of the otherwise backward Kingdom with its archaic institutions makes Saudi Arabia an ideal subject for simplistic commentary. Public opinion in the United States is ill-informed, and the 'partnership' with Saudi Arabia is often seen with a mixture of derision and envy. How durable

---

1 Concluded on a visit by the French Interior Minister in November 1980. See *Le Monde*, 2–3, 4 November 1980.

2 On the persistence of this see Malcolm Peck, 'The Saudi–American Relationship and King Faisal', in Willard A. Beling (ed.), *King Faisal and the Modernization of Saudi Arabia*, Croom Helm, London, 1980, pp. 230–45.

such a partnership can be under these conditions is a question for the longer term. In the short term it contributes to misunderstandings. These are compounded by differences in style and emphasis. The United States sees Saudi Arabia as too reticent and as demanding security assurances from the West while refusing to help make these possible or credible. It tends to attribute the Saudis' unwillingness to accept an explicit defence arrangement as motivated more by cowardice than by sensitive intra-Arab considerations, and Americans tend to interpret the Saudis' security problems largely in terms of external dangers and in the East—West framework. Saudi reticence, and a style of indirection and allusion which refuses to confront problems head-on, is often seen as being motivated by maddening pusillanimity rather than by political constraints. Saudi caution is rarely viewed with reference to the Kingdom's military weakness and its need to remain within the Arab consensus. Consequently the Saudis are sometimes seen as insufficiently active in substantively pursuing a Middle East peace and given to flights of empty rhetoric.[1] Eager to see its friends stand up and be counted, American public opinion tends to ignore the undercurrent of anti-Westernism and xenophobia latent in the Arab world, including Saudi Arabia, which can be mobilized against its regional friends unless they are careful.

The Saudis have similar problems with the Americans. The trust and dependency that have characterized the relationship in the past have already been noted. Disappointment may provide the basis for more realistic expectations and consequently for a more stable relationship in the future. It is as much the image and the style as the policies of the United States that have complicated relations in recent years. Washington has consistently leaked embarrassing information to the press[2] which has undermined the Kingdom's security. By holding up arms transfers, by placing restrictive conditions on them or by allowing them to be subject to pro-Israeli pressure groups, successive United States' governments have undermined the Saudi position in the Arab world. The inability in Washington to co-ordinate the activity of various agencies often leads to contradictory emphases and pressures on the Kingdom. These are usually questions of style rather than policy. For example the Kingdom cannot afford politically to be seen to be increasing its own oil production beyond its official ceiling while the US uses this to fill up its strategic stockpile, the better to undermine

---

1 The continuing role of rhetoric as an inexpensive functional substitute for action in Arab politics is underestimated.

2 Examples abound the most prominent being reports of feuds in the royal family, corruption, and the instability of the regime.

any future use of the 'Arab oil weapon'. Public pressure on the Kingdom to fall in line with preferred US policy positions is usually counterproductive as it exposes the Saudi leadership to the criticism from factions within the royal family and from enemies abroad of being a 'puppet regime'.

Apart from poor co-ordination of its government agencies and a tendency to indulge in excessive leaking and publicity in its policies, the policies themselves are, from the Saudi view, often ill-conceived. The problem of inconsistency and fluctuation in US policies in recent years is well-known and requires little amplification here. It has created the impression of bad judgement, insensitivity and over-reaction which will take time to efface. This is not a new problem. King Faisal in the 1960s told a US Ambassador: 'You Americans do not make things easier for your friends. You disregard their concerns and thereby weaken their (political) influence in the area'.[1] What is new is the promotion of policies which the Saudis view as positively harmful to them, for example the Camp David agreement. The impatience of the United States with the Saudis' passivity is often understandable but any inclination to believe that 'they have nowhere else to go' and that therefore they can be taken for granted, is dangerously misconceived. At any other time the Camp David process might have stood some chance of Saudi support but, with the slow-motion collapse of pro-Western Iran and with all the pressures that unleashed in the region, it was folly to expect Riyadh to take the risk of identification with the West in 1978-80.

From the Saudi perspective American policy tends to be too one dimensional. Riyadh sees threats emanating from every quarter; internal, on its borders, within the politics of the Arab world, from the USSR and its proxies, and even from the ill-considered policies of its putative protector, the United States. The Saudis want reassurance against these threats but are unwilling to choose any one instrument to meet all of them. Hence they seek security guarantees but are loathe to admit it publicly and want a military relationship but are unwilling to pay the political costs such a relationship would entail. Much of Saudi security policy is therefore one of damage limitation, of alleviating pressures that may create problems rather than meeting them head-on. In this context an issue such as Palestine is directly important — partly because it is a litmus test of the Kingdom's Arab and (because of Jerusalem) Islamic, credentials, and partly because, as it festers, it

1 Herman Eilts, 'Security Considerations in the Persian Gulf', *International Security*, vol. 5, no. 2, Fall 1980, p. 96.

creates pressures within the Arab world which *inter alia* inhibit the development of the Kingdom's relationship with the United States — a relationship which is essential if Saudi Arabia is to meet the other threats to its security.

Leverage or interdependence?

Each party brings certain expectations and requirements to the relationship. Although each has important assets which the other requires, it is essential to differentiate the possession of these assets from their conversion into leverage or influence. To do this one should distinguish between (a) the leverage to achieve specific goals, and (b) the general influence that permeates the relationship. The latter leads to such general notions as 'sensitivity' or responsiveness to an ally's concerns or to an 'anticipated reaction' by one party before the other even articulates its preference. The value attached to a relationship may increase for both parties at the same time hence presumably increasing their assets (and potential leverage) simultaneously. For example, as Saudi Arabia's importance as an oil producer has increased for the US, so also has the saliency of the US security relationship to the Kingdom.

The quality and style of the relationship determines the manner in which influence is, or is not, exerted. Acknowledged differences in priorities, 'reasonable' expectations and the constraints operating on respective policies can avoid clashes and futile exercises in leverage. The time-frame of mutual expectations governs the quality of the relationship. Are trade-offs issue-specific and immediate or do they reflect part of a much more complex stable, institutionalized, relationship?[1] The emphasis placed here on the arms relationship reflects the pronounced concentration on this visible component of relations. As a functional substitute for formal treaty relations, they have also become a palliative for problem areas. It is easier, though still not easy, to grind out arms agreements than to achieve a Middle East settlement or to devise a strict energy policy.

We have already noted that within the relationship there have sometimes emerged differences as to precisely what is linked with what. On occasion the United States has sought to imply a link between supplying arms and support for the Camp David peace process and to hint that a defence commitment is dependent on access to bases on Saudi soil. At the same time the US has expected Saudi Arabia to moderate

---

1 As noted in Iran's case, the Shah tended to widen differences on a single issue to threaten the entire relationship. This conferred short-term advantages to Iran on issues but also made the entire relationship precarious. It also created resentment in the US bureaucracy. This accumulated resentment was evident in Iran's crisis.

oil price rises and maintain the level of production necessary to do this, while ignoring the (admittedly rather slow) build-up of the US strategic petroleum reserve. Moderating the price of oil has been a prime Saudi responsibility — both for the West and its own longer-term interests — and has been acknowledged as such by Saudi leaders. Occasionally Western leaders have made the connection explicit by arguing that oil price increases by the Gulf states 'undermine our very ability to defend them'.[1] Sometimes the linkage is more indirectly evoked as in the case of a notification to Congress of an arms package in mid-1979. The administration had held this up arguing that the circumstances were inappropriate. After Saudi Arabia made a decision to sell its crude oil at $18 a barrel (against the prevailing OPEC price of $23.50) in June 1979 and later increased its production by 1 million b/d, relations were reported to have 'eased'. The arms request followed.[2] Sometimes the American press has baulked at the very ambiguity of the linkages involved in the US—Saudi relationship and has sought, pre-emptively, to sever them. One newspaper editorial argued that any Saudi offer

> ' . . . to trade off dropping resistance to partial filling of the [strategic] reserves for the sale of the offensive [i.e. en-hanced F-15s] military equipment should be rejected. . . . It would be dangerous to concede to Saudi Arabia . . . the right to determine the rate at which the US will fill its reserves and it would be wrong to go back on a written commitment [i.e. that of May 1978]'.[3]

In practice issues are rarely so directly or crudely linked. The relation-ship is not analagous to the bazaar. It embraces a range of mutual interests and cannot be a single issue arrangement.

It is mistaken to see the 'manipulation of levers' or instruments in the service of a specified goal. The overall relationship is important and this consists of clearly identifiable short-term mutual interests together with less tangible long-term mutual interests. The relationship resembles therefore a sophisticated dialogue rather than a simple trading relation-ship.[4]

---

1   Defense Secretary Harold Brown, *International Herald Tribune*, 21 June 1980.

2   A US official referred to this as 'negative linkage' that is a case of 'not penalizing' them for what OPEC does because the Saudis had not 'put the squeeze on us' like the others. In fact this distinction is artificial. The Saudis used their resources against policies harmful to the West, and the US acknowledged this by maintaining a close military supply relationship. See the *Washington Star*, 13 July 1979.

3   *International Herald Tribune*, 18 June 1980.

4   I am indebted to Joe Twineam of the State Department for his observations on the relation-ship.

This is not to deny that either state entertains certain expectations of the other in the relationship. But it does suggest a resistance to the identification of specific levers exercised for carefully defined short-term results which are explicitly set out. More commonly decisions are made in the knowledge that the other party will recognize their meaning. For example, after December 1976, in the OPEC meeting at Qatar, Saudi Arabian leaders indirectly referred to their stand against oil price increases as a 'present' to the new United States President. The implication of this was that it ought to be 'appreciated'. Similarly in 1978-81 Saudi Arabia continued to extend the deadline for the production of oil at 1-2 million b/d in excess of its own formal ceiling on production. The implication of this was that Riyadh, in assisting the US, also expected the United States to implement a rigorous domestic energy policy without any further delay. Since the totality of the relationship is more than merely one of *quid pro quo* and is based on trust, atmosphere matters. This means that declaratory policy, protocol considerations and the symbolic dimension of relations are extremely important, requiring a sensitivity and co-ordination within the US bureaucracy that may be difficult to achieve.[1] Reference has already been made to the 'psychological dependency' that exists (balancing in part the real dependency of the West on Saudi oil). The West is trusted because it is not intent on imposing its system of government on others and can provide security against those who do. A broad co-operative multi-levelled relationship covering a wide range of issues has thus been fashioned — including oil, arms, investment, trade, technology, training, and education. Such a broad-based relationship gives the West multiple sources of entrée into the government and increases the prospects for general influence.

Due to criticisms of the connection with the United States, the Saudis have in recent years been on the defensive, with a drift toward disassociation and an emphasis on the Arab dimension of security policy, best seen in Saudi support for Gulf security arrangements. Within the Kingdom some have pointed to the problems associated with the American link and by no means all of the Saudi leadership are equally in favour of its maintenance, leave alone its intensification. It is not always clear that the mutually advantageous partnership is always equally advantageous. Therefore, in the words of a veteran observer of Saudi affairs 'it may be necessary once in a while to demonstrate its

1 This requires careful tuning of policy statements for the effect it can have on various audiences, including a general Arab audience.

value'.[1] Due partly to Congressional criticism and delay, the Saudi leadership has moved to diversify the sources of its military equipment. This need not mean a corresponding dilution of US influence. The supply of military equipment and services has not been a tool for fine-tuning the relationship. United States' influence in the Kingdom antedates the establishment of a large-scale military tie. It will therefore survive it. But whether the relationship matures to become a durable one depends largely on greater sensitivity on the part of the United States to the priorities and constraints of its vulnerable partner.

USSR—Iraq 1968-80

The Soviet Union as arms supplier

As a supplier of arms to states in the Third World, the Soviet Union has not been exempt from the generic problems associated with the conversion of arms assistance into continuing political influence. The same problems exist for Moscow as for Washington — arms are a blunt instrument for leverage which cannot be fine-tuned through supply and denial. Too generous a supply for reassurance of the recipient risks reducing its dependency; too much denial will alienate the recipient, driving it toward diversification. Once supplied little influence can be brought to bear on how the arms are used and the pressures for maintaining the supply relationship limit the possibilities of frequent denials. While the nature of the supply relationship is dependent on overall political ties that will fluctuate, erratic supply will accelerate the pressures for diversification. Thus, even in periods of strain and tension, the supplier will have a continuing incentive to provide arms for the decline of supplies will tend to go hand in hand with that of the supplier's influence. Even if arms are used for purposes different from those originally contemplated, to retain future influence the supplier will tend to seek to demonstrate its reliability and responsiveness by maintaining supplies.[2]

There is abundant evidence that the Soviet Union regards military assistance as an integral part of its foreign policy and as one component of its strategic posture in the Third World. Its concentration on its border on South-West Asia and on the Middle East is especially notable.

---

1 Eilts, 'Security Considerations in the Persian Gulf', pp. 79-113.

2 The umbilical cord is therefore two-way. The examples of the US and revolutionary Iran in 1979, and the USSR and the Iraq—Iran war are illustrative.

Equally remarkable is the growth of Soviet military aid which in recent years has overtaken that of the US. Military assistance has been used to achieve a number of ends:

1. Preclusively, to deny the dominance of the West or to erode its position by siding with an anti-Western regime.
2. Intrusively, as an opening wedge for subsequent agreements.
3. As an entrée into society through the armed forces.
4. As a deterrent, to balance against and warn hostile states.
5. As a market, for oil or hard currency.
6. As a hedge or buffer against possible setbacks elsewhere in the region or as a bargaining card *vis-à-vis* pro-Western regimes and the West.

Soviet aims are often more concrete than this, seeking to use arms assistance as a *quid pro quo* for strategic access[1] (staging facilities, overflight rights, prepositioning of equipment, etc.). Arms transfers have often been an opening wedge leading to grants of strategic access. The example of Berbera in Somalia is illustrative. Concessions on overflight rights (even for civilian aircraft), servicing agreements (including personnel and technicians) rarely have primarily commercial connotations, being part of an overall programme of political penetration and area familiarization less typical of the United States.

Generally Soviet policy has shown a willingness to offer attractive discounts in the opening phases of a relationship or to grant aid exclusively to needy countries (such as the PDRY and Somalia) and at the same time to restrict high technology and an abundant supply of parts. The Soviets have shown a high degree of continuity of supply, flexibility regarding the ideology of the recipient and an unwillingness to use their supply relationship to enforce an outcome when their interests have not been clear-cut.[2] When forced, however, they have been prepared to take or to change sides (as with Ethiopia and Somalia). Like the US, the Soviet Union has little control over how its arms are ultimately used and even less in ordering local antagonisms to suit Soviet strategic needs.

In addition, Soviet military aid to the Third World contrasts with that of the West in a different way. The USSR does not compete in the provision of economic assistance, high technology or the produc-

---

1 See the discussion by Robert Harkavy, 'Strategic Access, Bases and Arms Transfers' in *Great Power Competition in the Middle East*, Milton Leitenberg and Gabriel Sheffer (eds.), Pergamon, New York, 1979, pp. 173-75.

2 Contrast the US which has been prepared to alienate one or both allies in the India—Pakistan, Turkey—Greece conflicts.

tion of sophisticated consumer goods. Its military industry is by far its most efficient and it enjoys a comparative advantage in arms production.[1] Marginal costs are often low and, in many cases, arms withdrawn from Soviet front-line service are sold from stockpiles. There are thus stronger Soviet incentives to use arms sales for strictly commercial reasons. This is especially true where the recipient has a large hard-currency income and where it is potentially possible to turn soft currency goods like arms into hard currency. Thus economic considerations strengthen incentives to supply arms to oil-producing states.[2] It is thus not surprising that Iraq and Libya have been two of the major recipients of Soviet arms since 1973.

Soviet economic motives in Iraq are clear. Iraq constitutes a lucrative market and Iraq's repayment record has been excellent. Its oil revenues have doubled in the past five years (1976-81) to over $30 billion. Between 1970 and 1976, Iraq's share of Soviet trade with the Third World grew from 2.2 to 10.9 per cent. In 1978 Iraq was still the USSR's most important trading partner in the Arab world. Contracts in 1977 were double those of 1973 (two-way trade equalling $3 billion) but a declining percentage of Iraq's overall trade.[3] This was due to Iraq's increased trade with the West. Even with the US trade was doubling every year after 1977. Nevertheless, even despite the USSR's reduced importance as a trading partner by 1980, it is significant that the number of Soviet and Eastern bloc economic technicians in Iraq doubled in the period 1977-79.[4]

The Soviet Union has earned hard currency from the sale of arms and of machinery and equipment. Originally these were paid for by Iraq in oil. Iraq's crude oil exports to the USSR in 1972-73, for example, grew from 4 to 11 million metric tons. After that year barter arrangements were revised and payments were made in hard currency, leading in 1974 to a drop to less than 4 million tons in oil exports to the USSR in that year.

1 See Gur Ofer, 'Soviet Military Aid to the Middle East — an Economic Balance Sheet' in II. 'Soviet Economy in New Perspective' (A Compendium of Papers), Joint Economic Committee, Congress, October 1976, pp. 216-39.

2 'As the economic function of arms sales becomes more vital to Soviet interests, the Soviets are likely to become proportionately more avid in seeking customers possessing hard currency or its oil equivalent'. CIA, *USSR: Soviet Economic Problems and Prospects*, CIA, July 1977, p. 28.

3 The Communist share of Iraq's trade was halved between 1973 and 1977 to 11.5 per cent. The USSR fell from first to fourth place as a trading partner.

4 To 12,900 if 1,350 Cuban, and 275 Chinese are included. *Contrast*, CIA, 1977 (November 1978), p. 9; and (October 1980), p. 21.

The development of Iraqi–USSR trade is illustrative of the (increasing) role of commerce as a factor in Soviet military sales to the Third World. A major component of Soviet trade with the less-developed countries (LDCs) is arms sales which are accounted for only as 'residuals' in Soviet statistics. The Middle East is a unique market place where Soviet arms have been turned into either oil or directly into hard currency: 'Almost all of Iraq's oil shipments to the USSR either as barter or repayment for past debts are resold for hard currency'.[1] The fact that an otherwise strategically important target state is solvent and able to pay for its arms in convertible currency reinforces the attractiveness of Iraq as a market for Soviet arms and diminishes any tendency toward denial.

Iraq, of course, has not always been wealthy. In the aftermath of the revolution of 1958, it found its choice of arms suppliers severely constrained by financial as well as by political considerations. It was in this period (1958-74) that Iraq–Soviet relations were potentially at their most rewarding for Soviet influence. The grant component in Soviet aid was high, and alternative suppliers limited for both financial and political reasons. Soviet leverage should have been at its zenith at this juncture, particularly since a tacit anti-Westernism brought the two countries into a marriage of convenience. Overlapping interests and the lack of Iraqi options were certainly responsible for the development of relations. The USSR was able to dispose of a large surplus inventory and to deliver arms more quickly and secretly than other potential suppliers. Soviet arms aid, in addition, consisted largely of weapons and ammunition rather than infrastructure. Moreover the simplicity and ease of operation of Soviet weapons facilitated their assimilation and maintenance. In this area, lack of sophistication is not necessarily a handicap.

But even in this period of maximum convergence, Soviet influence was by no means decisive — for reasons we shall discuss. The subsequent period was initially one of growing intimacy (1972-74) to be followed by a loosening of bonds (1975-81) when, although Iraq's strategic importance to the USSR increased, Soviet influence declined. This was due in large part to the nature of the Iraqi government, and to shifts in the regional environment affecting its perceptions and priorities, as well as to the widening options provided it both by oil wealth and a less doctrinaire and more pragmatic approach to its

1 *Communist Aid Activities in Non-Communist Less Developed Countries 1978* (CIA, 1979), p. 34. The Soviets' sale of Iraqi oil at higher prices on the world market was a contentious issue in the relationship in the early 1970s. This was reminiscent of a similar problem with Egyptian cotton and world cotton prices in the 1960s.

interests. In this second period therefore, divergences between Moscow and Baghdad increased despite the existence of a strong military relationship.

The scope of this relationship merits an abbreviated discussion here. Iraq was the Soviet Union's largest arms customer in the Third World from 1974 to 1978. Some $3.6 billion-worth of arms were delivered by 1978 (as against $2.7 billion for Syria, and $3.4 billion for Libya) and, in contrast to Syria and Egypt, it should be noted the equipment provided was not resupply for arms lost in combat. In the opinion of a US government agency: 'Deliveries since the 1977 war have brought in the most modern military equipment ever supplied to an LDC'. The value of Soviet military aid to Iraq outran the economic by 15 to 1. The magnitude of this aid is indicated by noting that in the past nine years Iraq has tripled the size of its armed forces while simultaneously modernizing them. The Soviet Union has assisted this growth, providing, in 1974-78, over 70 per cent of the $5.3 billion spent on imported arms (compared to less than 10 per cent from France).[1] Until the mid-1970s, Soviet arms constituted 75 per cent of the Iraqi inventory.

In addition to the commercial motivation noted earlier, Iraq was becoming increasingly important for strategic reasons — as an ally in the Arab world, as an access point into the Gulf and as a counterweight to Iran. By maintaining a militantly anti-Western tone in its foreign relations, the Iraqi regime could increase the inhibitions of the smaller Gulf Arab states from co-operating with the West. Iraq's rejection of Western formulae for peace in the Middle East — though occasionally embarrassing — could still serve Soviet interests. Iraq's growing power in the 1970s was thus a factor that held promise from the Soviet viewpoint. Yet the course of relations in the past few years has highlighted some of the problems of maintaining influence even in states where the military links are strong.

A number of basic differences have interacted with existing irritants to reduce the margin of Soviet influence appreciably. A basic change (besides Iraq's reordering of priorities and growing options) is the perception within Iraq that Soviet intentions are malign and suspect. This has accelerated a move toward a diversification of suppliers and to an 'even-handedness' toward the two superpowers. This in turn has reduced Iraq's utility to the USSR as an anti-Western ally in the region. Baghdad appears from this perspective to be a political rather than military rejectionist, creating problems for Moscow's regional allies (Syria and

1 The opinion and figures quoted in the above paragraph are taken from *Communist Aid Activities in Non-Communist LDCs in 1979 and 1954-1979*, CIA, Washington, 1980, pp. 156, 160-61.

the PDRY) and complicating the extension of Soviet influence in other states (for example Iran). The fact of arms dependency which remains real (though declining) has not noticeably inhibited Iraq in its policies in the region even where these conflict with the USSR. The Soviet Union for its part has been reluctant to terminate the relationship — not least (one suspects) because it is too entangled in it after over twenty years and would prefer not to jeopardize the relationship until it became absolutely hopeless. It also needs the hard currency. As in the US case with Iran, the supplier's influence is dependent on the overall political relationship which, even if overturned, provides an additional and independent argument for maintaining the arms supply relationship, this time as a possible means of restoring the political tie. Whether the Soviet Union (or the US) can tolerate arms relationships with states whose regional policies regularly clash with their interests appears doubtful. But the arguments against terminating those ties are likely to remain strong as long as the relationships are not confined solely to *quid pro quos*.

The evolution and scope of the military relationship

The background: 1958-72. After the July 1958 Revolution, republican Iraq looked to the USSR for military assistance. In part this was due to the absence of any other major supplier prepared to subsidize sales or able to deliver equipment quickly.[1] Anxious to encourage Iraq's move towards non-alignment, Moscow responded with military assistance — a squadron of MiG-15s plus a military mission. By the early 1960s, Iraq was the first Gulf state to receive supersonic aircraft — the MiG-21. Despite some hesitation about Iraq's repression of communists, and its uncertain political orientation, Moscow maintained the arms link. Henceforth anti-Westernism would be the touchstone for relations and not ideological purity. By mid-1965 any Soviet reluctance to arm a regime engaged in full-scale operations against its Kurdish population had evaporated. An encouraging sign for Moscow was Iraq's growing militance and its severance of diplomatic relations with the United States in 1967.

---

1 France was unwilling to depart from commercial terms. Only the USSR could provide adequate supplies quickly. For a recent affirmation of this see Major-General Fursdon's report in *Daily Telegraph*, 17 November 1980. This capacity distinguishes the superpower from other suppliers. In this connection see Mohammed Haikal's observations on Soviet versus French capabilities. Irritated at Soviet policy, Egypt arranged a 10-year agreement for the supply of *Mirages* from France. Once relations with Moscow improved, supplies were resumed. ' . . . in one month more *MiGs* arrived from the Soviet Union than *Mirages* were due to arrive from France in three years'. Haikal, *Sphinx and Commissar*, Collins, 1978, p. 285.

Baghdad's losses in the 1967 war were quickly more than made up. Between 1967 and 1971 the USSR provided some 110 MiG-21s and SU-7s, 20 helicopters and trainers, 150 tanks, 300 APCs, and 500 field guns and artillery. Soviet economic credits and grants between 1969 and 1971 were nearly double the total in the preceding decade.[1] East European credits and grants from 1969 to 1972 totalled $415 million as against $14 million for the entire decade after the Revolution.

The intensified but still low-level military relationship reflected a convergence of political interests. With the return of the Ba'ath party to power in 1969 and in its hard-line approach to the question of Palestine, Iraq became more strongly anti-Western. The USSR came to be seen as an important power essential for the achievement of Arab interests and as a source of support to balance the conservative states being built up by the West in the Gulf. Iraq's political weakness (the Kurdish issue remained unresolved) and its revolutionary rhetoric, which isolated it regionally, led it toward a dependence on the USSR which the latter welcomed.[2] For the USSR, Iraq would always be important in the Arab world as a hedge against reverses in relations with other Arab states (such as occurred in Egypt in 1971 and in Syria in 1976). Iraq's importance as a Gulf state was daily growing for the USSR which lacked any other friendly littoral state. Furthermore throughout the 1970s, Iraq's good repayment record and growing oil income consolidated the relationship. There was thus a solid commercial incentive lacking in the case of Syria or Egypt.

These ties were further cemented as the Iraqi Ba'ath sought to consolidate their power domestically, to reduce Western influence and to compete with Iran in the Gulf. In February 1972 Saddam Hussein visited the USSR and called for a 'solid strategic alliance'. Responding to this Iraqi initiative, despite some reservations about providing open-ended support, the USSR agreed and concluded a Treaty of Friendship and Cooperation on 7 April 1972. This agreement contained two Articles (7 and 8) relating to consultations in the event of a threat and to defence co-operation. For Iraq it was a way out of regional isolation and domestic disorder. For the USSR it compensated for setbacks in Egypt without providing unconditional support or entanglement. Indeed Moscow was quick to reassure Iran on this point. The Treaty was signed at a time when oil production in the North Rumaila oilfields (developed with Soviet assistance) was inaugurated. It coincided too

1 $365 million versus $184 million (1954-68). See *Communist States and Developing Countries: Aid and Trade in 1972*. Washington DC: State Department, Bureau of Intelligence and Research, June 1973, Tables 2, 10.

2 In 1968 Iraq sought French *Mirages-III* aircraft but an agreement was not reached due to Iraq's inability to pay.

with the visit of a Russian naval flotilla to the Gulf. Finally it formalized the military relationship by providing the basis for a growing pattern of sales, consultations and visits between the two states.

An immediate result of the agreement was the construction of SAM-3 sites in Iraq. In the summer of 1973 a dozen TU-22 (*Blinder*) supersonic medium-bombers were delivered to Iraq, the first such delivery outside the Warsaw Pact.[1] By October 1974 Iraq had received 12 MiG-23s (*Flogger*). Since there were no Iraqis trained to fly these aircraft, Soviet pilots and maintenance personnel accompanied them. As relations between the Ba'athists and the Kurds and neighbouring Iran deteriorated throughout 1974, sporadic clashes grew fiercer in the border areas. There were reports of the use of TU-22s (flown by Soviet pilots) and Soviet ground advisers against the Kurds.[2] Though hardly decisive, this limited involvement, the first use of Soviet personnel since the 1970 Canal War, signified the degree to which USSR—Iraq relations had developed.

Iraq however was dissatisfied both with the level of material and diplomatic support provided by Moscow. After 1974 it sought to order its priorities in such a way as to avoid excessive dependency on any one country. Accordingly 1974 saw its first move to diversify its sources of arms. It concluded a $70 million agreement with France for thirty-one *Alouette* helicopters, (with SS-11 anti-tank missiles) plus mortars and ammunition.

The move toward a balance: 1974-81. With hindsight it is clear that 1974 was the high-point of the Soviet—Iraqi military relationship, although both a growing demand for arms and the assimilation of arms previously ordered would require a continuing flow of spare parts, training and technical assistance. Military dependence would persist for the foreseeable future but the nature of dependency would change. The order for French arms in 1974 was one indication. In April 1975 Saddam Hussein pointedly observed that Iraq would diversify its sources of arms if the national interest so dictated.[3] The settlement of the border conflict with Iran and the pacification of the Kurds

---

1 In speed and range the *Blinder* was superior to aircraft provided to any other Arab state at that time. See Roger F. Pajak, 'Soviet Arms Aid to the Middle East since the October War' in *The Political Economy of the Middle East 1973-1978. A Compendium of Papers*, Joint Economic Committee, Congress of the US, 96th Cong; 2nd Sess, 21 April 1980, pp. 445-85.

2 Officially Soviet pilots were seconded to Iraq for training its pilots. In practice operational activities seem to have been included in a team of 'advisers' under a Colonel Vasilev. See *The Times*, 19 June 1974; *Daily Telegraph*, 11 September 1974; *Le Monde*, 12 September 1974; *New York Times*, 29 September 1974 and *International Herald Tribune*, 7 October 1974.

3 *Washington Post*, 25 April 1975.

reduced the immediate security threats to Iraq.

After 1975 a declining proportion of Iraqi military purchases came from the Eastern bloc. Although Eastern bloc arms accounted for $1,443 millions of a total of $1,721 millions transferred to Iraq between 1966 and 1976, this share was reduced thereafter. By 1976 Eastern arms accounted for only $2,710 million of $3,740 million and by 1978 for $3.6 billion of the $5.3 billion of arms cumulatively transferred to Iraq.[1] The value of Soviet bloc arms thus accounted for two-thirds of Iraq's inventory rather than the three-quarters earlier in the decade. Even these figures understate the degree of diversification as they refer to weapons actually delivered rather than to orders yet to be filled. If orders are included the virtual Soviet monopoly has been truly lost. The value has been reduced to perhaps 60 per cent of Iraq's inventory and is declining. The trend in this direction has benefited France, starting with an order for 36 *Mirage* F-1 aircraft in 1977 (with twenty-four more added in 1979). In addition to medium tanks and missiles from France there have followed large orders for APCs from Brazil, for eleven naval vessels from Italy (1981) and for forty-eight trainer aircraft from Switzerland.[2] While actual *deliveries* from non-Communist bloc countries between 1974 and 1978 totalled only $1,524 million, if *orders* were counted the figure would be greater than $3 billion since 1974 — a more impressive testimony to diversification.

The trend however should not be exaggerated. Iraq's military relationship with the USSR is solidly based. Diversification is costly, lengthy and often a risky enterprise for states with imminent security problems. The incentives for a cautious partnership — perhaps shorn of illusions on either side — remain intact. Despite a coolness in relations arising from Iraq's rapid (and unheralded) border settlement with Iran in 1975, which affected Soviet–Iraqi military relations in 1975 and 1976, Soviet problems with Syria in the Lebanon swung Moscow back toward Iraq. The Soviet Union made a conscious effort to restore and consolidate these ties.[3] An agreement was concluded in mid-1976 on a record $1,000 million arms package involving aircraft, ships, tanks and artillery, placing Iraq first among recipients of Soviet

1 See *World Military Expenditures and Arms Transfers*, ACDA, Washington: 1977, 1978, 1979, pp. 78, 156 and 160-61 respectively.

2 Consult *The Military Balance* 1978-79, 1979-80, 1980-81. See also *Le Monde*, 21 December 1979; 8 February 1980 and the section in the text below on diversification.

3 On Alexei Kosygin's visit to Iraq see *Le Monde*, 2 June 1976.

arms.[1] In 1977 Iraq purchased long-range jet transport aircraft (Il -76s) never before exported by the USSR. At the same time Iraq received nearly $600 million of arms previously ordered, accounting for 20 per cent of the Soviet Union's shipments to the Third World. In 1978 the delivery of aircraft to Iraq accounted for 60 per cent of Soviet aircraft deliveries to the Third World.[2] A visit to Moscow by Saddam Hussein in later 1978 appeared to reflect continued dissatisfaction with the manner in which Soviet deliveries were being implemented. Equally important however were the political differences that had emerged between the two states and which had begun to be reflected in the overall relationship. In Iraq this could be seen by more pointed comments about the need for diversification and relationships which lack 'strings', followed by new orders from European states,[3] and in the USSR by a continued willingness to deliver arms but to try to regulate the flow to extract concessions or to register disapproval. In 1979 the USSR concluded a major new arms agreement with Iraq for additional T-72 tanks and MiG-25 fighter aircraft. Even so Moscow appears to have found it easier to continue to deliver arms in the wake of its invasion of Afghanistan in the hope of neutralizing Iraq's opposition to it, rather than to deny her arms until her response was clearly non-critical.[4]

With the vast scale of deliveries of equipment Iraq's dependence on the Soviet Union for training and spares grew apace. Soviet military advisers in Iraq doubled between 1972 and 1979.[5] One hundred Iraqi military personnel were in the USSR for training in 1978 bringing a total of 3,710 military officers trained there in the past twenty-five years.[6] Iraq's aircraft and tanks will, for the foreseeable future, be dependent on the Soviet Union for spare parts and equipment. While the Soviet Union is no longer the sole supplier, it remains the principal supplier of arms and equipment and reports that it will lose that position are, as of early 1981, at the least premature.

1 *Communist Aid Activities*, CIA, 1977.

2 See *Communist Aid Activities 1978*, pp. 2, 34.

3 On the occasion of the French Defence Minister's visit, senior Iraqi officials made pointed references along these lines. See *Military Aviation News*, June 1978, p. 16.

4 Large-scale deliveries of Soviet arms to Iraq were reported in early 1980. See *Baltimore Sun*, 7 February 1980.

5 From 500 to 1,100 in 1978, 1,069 in 1979. Compare *Communist Aid and Trade 1973* and *Communist Aid Activities 1979*.

6 *Communist Aid Activities 1979*.

With the Revolution, Iraq moved to replace the UK with the Soviet Union as its principal supplier of arms. It might have been expected that the new and vulnerable Iraqi regime would be susceptible to the wishes and priorities of its new foreign patron and that the dependency generated by its needs and regional isolation would result in tangible influence for the Soviet Union. The record of relations is however somewhat more complex. Although there have been discernible attempts by Moscow to use its arms supplies as leverage, the evidence for success in this is scanty indeed. This section looks at a few examples while sketching the political divergences between the two states that continue to exist.

In the 1960s Iraq became the USSR's third largest arms customer, and a valuable ally in the volatile politics of the Arab world. But involvement with regimes like that of Iraq (and Syria) in the 1960s was demanding. It potentially strained Moscow's relations with Egypt and raised issues such as Moscow's appropriate policy in applying doctrinal dictates to the under-developed world. In Iraq's case for example, should the USSR acquiesce in the suppression of Iraq's Communist Party? Or should it try to use its role as arms supplier to pressure Baghdad on its policies in this respect? In February 1963 the Ba'ath party ousted Abd'l Karim Qasim's regime and followed this with an extensive purge of the Iraqi Communist Party and subsequently with a military campaign against Iraq's Kurdish population (traditionally a source of support for the Iraqi Communist Party). After initial warnings about reprisals, the Soviet Union in mid-1963 cut off its military assistance and training programmes. Only after the repression eased and the extreme Ba'ath members were dismissed did the USSR make new military aid credit available. This was the Soviet Union's first use of arms transfers as leverage against a recipient,[1] and appears to have had some success. Soviet sensitivity about Iraq's treatment of its communists is illustrated by Khruschev's refusal to shake the hand of Iraq's President Abd al-Salam Aref in Cairo in 1964: 'I'm not going to shake hands with people whose hands are stained with the blood of Communists'.[2] However when the Iraqi regime resumed its offensive against the Kurds in 1965, Moscow did not again resort to the manipulation of the arms relationship to induce restraint. Indeed Soviet

---

1 For a discussion and citations see Wynfred Joshua and Stephen P. Gibert, *Arms for the Third World: Soviet Military and Diplomacy*, Johns Hopkins Press, London, 1969, p. 17; and *The Economist*, 29 June 1963, p. 1,344.

2 Haykal, *The Sphinx and the Commissar*, p. 21.

appeals to Baghdad for tolerance toward the Communist Party were becoming muffled. By 1967 the USSR had accepted that as a matter of pragmatism state-to-state relations must take precedence over ideological preferences. Illustrative both of the Soviet view of the political uses of military assistance and of the benefits it could provide its clients were two episodes relating to Iran. The Shah of Iran negotiated with Moscow for the purchase of arms at a time when Iranian–Egyptian relations were poor. President Nasir objected to this. The Soviet response was to stress the pragmatic benefits to the Arabs of Soviet influence in Iran: 'We must have a presence in Iran . . . we must have our plan to neutralize the Shah . . . Tell me . . . should we leave Iran alone or try to take care of it? Which is better for you — Soviet arms in Iran or American arms?'[1] In fact it was Soviet influence on Iran (in part a result of improved relations) that elicited reassurances from the Shah that Iran would not take advantage of any redeployment of Iraqi troops away from their joint frontier during the 1973 war.[2]

The return of the Ba'ath to power in 1969, with their uncompromising stand on Palestine and their resultant hostility toward the West, inaugurated a new closer phase in Soviet–Iraqi relations. The new Iraqi leadership, harsh with its domestic opponents and militant vis-à-vis all its neighbours, swiftly became politically isolated within the Arab world and excluded from Persian Gulf affairs. Ba'athist ambitions outpaced its capabilities which were largely consumed by the need to consolidate itself domestically. The revival of border conflict with Iran in 1969 accounted for the balance of its energies. The combination of domestic problems, regional isolation, military entanglement with a neighbour, and a strident revolutionary rhetoric, necessitated greater means than were available to Baghdad. The USSR for its part found the combination tempting but dangerous. Baghdad served as an alternative to reliance on an Egypt whose course appeared uncertain with the death of Nasir. Iraq could at least pay for Soviet assistance and did not constitute a bottomless charity case. Moreover Iraq's militant anti-Western posture was attractive.

But there were some debits. The unscrupulousness and unpredictability of the Ba'ath and the prospect of entanglement with them in an open-ended commitment, either domestically or vis-à-vis other

1 The conversation between Sadat — representing Nasir — and Kosygin is reported by Haykal in *Sphinx and Commissar*, p. 174.

2 *Ibid.*, p. 267.

states, served to impart a measure of caution. Involvement would increase the opportunities for influence while caution would limit them. Soviet policy toward Iraq after 1969 was an attempt to balance the two.

The April 1972 Treaty with Iraq was illustrative of this dilemma. It increased Soviet involvement in Iraq especially under Article 9 in the defence area and yielded concrete benefits. As a result of the Treaty, the USSR was reportedly granted access to Iraqi naval facilities and the use of her military airfields.[1] A more conspicuous result of the Treaty was in domestic politics. In June the Iraq Petroleum Company (IPC) was nationalized, ending Western dominance in the oil industry. Eager to stabilize their client's hold on the country, Moscow promoted a coalition arrangement among the Kurdish leadership (the Kurdish Democratic Party (KDP)), the Communists and the Ba'ath. The Communists agreed to this proposal in July 1973, were legalized, and joined the Progressive National Front with two cabinet posts. The KDP however refused. The Communist decision split the party. The group refusing to co-operate with the Ba'athists became known as the Iraq Communist Party Central Command, comprised mainly of Shi'a from southern Iraq who threw in their lot with the Kurds.[2]

The Soviet promotion of a largely fictitious power-sharing formula in which the Communist Party accepted the Ba'ath's primacy, reflected an important shift in the Soviet commitment. By promoting co-operation between these groups, the Soviets sought to strengthen the Baghdad regime, even at the expense of the Communist Party. The Soviets thus withdrew support from the Kurds when the KDP refused to join this arrangement. The Soviets hoped that the consolidation of Ba'ath rule in Iraq might make it a more reliable and less impulsive ally in foreign affairs.

The Soviet Union nevertheless trod a fine line between reassurance of an unstable regime and encouragement of its wilder impulses. Soviet arms sold to Baghdad could impair relations with the US or antagonize Iran if they were used impetuously by the Iraqi leadership. The supplier

1 Periodically exaggerated reports about a Soviet naval 'base' at Umm Qasr have surfaced. There is no evidence of any base as such. Iraqi naval facilities are poor. The coastline is only *forty-seven kilometres* in length and access to it is further limited by the commanding position of two islands, Warba and Bubiyan disputed with Kuwait. In addition the Shatt al-Arab Estuary leading to Iraqi ports at Basrah and Umm Qasr is marshy and shallow and needs dredging. Work has been going on in improving facilities at Fao, a port near Basrah.

2 For discussion see Abbas Kelidar, 'Iraq: The Search for Stability', *Institute for the Study of Conflict*, no. 59, July 1975.

has always certain residual responsibilities for the ultimate use of the product supplied. The revival of Iraq's claim to Kuwait buttressed by a border incident in March 1973 was illustrative. A Soviet naval visit that coincided with this episode may have been intended as Soviet support for the claim,[1] although the case can equally be made that its timing with the reassertion of the claim was fortuitous and even counter-productive politically in that it further isolated Iraq.

Soviet involvement in Iraq necessitated commitments. The Soviet transfer of twelve TU-22s in mid-1973 was doubtless a form of political reassurance to the Baghdad government that the USSR remained a reliable supplier of advanced weapon systems to match those of the US. The same can be said for the twelve MiG-23s sent in the following year. If these aircraft were in fact used in the offensive against the Kurds in 1974-75, they had no decisive effect. Nevertheless they sent a political signal to Iran while giving the USSR limited operational experience. It did not mean that the USSR fully supported Iraq in its war.

The Soviet Union urged a political settlement with the refractory Kurds on a more liberal basis than that offered by the Ba'athists in their 'Draft Law of the Progressive National Front for the autonomy of the Kurdish Region'.[2] Only after a full-scale military offensive was launched did Moscow side with the Baghdad government. Even then Moscow continued to manipulate the arms supply relationship. Saddam Hussein was reported to have told President Sadat in Rabat in October 1974 that arms deliveries were slow: 'We are suffering from our Soviet friends the same things which you are suffering'.[3] As the war intensi-fied, Iraq's requests for long-range artillery, to match those in Iran's inventory, became more pressing. It was partly this that precipitated the sudden decision by Iraq in March 1975 to settle her border conflict with Iran which came as a surprise to the USSR. The terms of the agree-ment represented concessions by Iraq. Most significant was the accept-ance of the principle not to export subversion throughout the region. This was followed by an approach more favourable to regional co-operation in the Gulf to exclude the superpowers.

---

1 See Anne Kelly CNA paper and Cottrell-Burrell article. Anne M. Kelly, 'The Soviet Naval Presence during the Iran–Kuwaiti Border Disputes' *March-April 1973*, Centre for Naval Analysis, Professional Paper 122, June 1974 .

2 This document, unlike its 1970 predecessor, did not recognize two separate nationalities.

3 Al-Nahar (*Arab Report*) 21 April 1975, pp. 3-4. See also *Washington Post*, 9 February 1975.

The turn in Baghdad's policy reflected a shift in priorities.[1] Domestic instability and regional hostility had necessitated dependence on the USSR which was now considered onerous and potentially dangerous. The Ba'athists now therefore energetically sought to isolate and suppress the Kurds and to defuse this problem even at the price of a settlement in Iran. Such a settlement was in turn made possible by Iraq's decision to reduce its militantly revolutionary policies in the Gulf. Iraq's dependence on the USSR for security had greatly increased with the growth of hostilities with the Kurds and Iran, and the Ba'athists had stepped back from its implications. To reverse this loss of autonomy the Ba'athists now sought first to defuse some of the threats and then to diversify their sources of arms and to establish their uncontested predominance in national politics without being beholden to an outside power. The pragmatic Iraqi leadership had made a decision to keep its options open. If dependency was a matter of degree and unavoidable, loss of control was not. Iraq stepped up trade relations with the West and sought assistance in marketing its oil. To escape domination by an underground Communist Party, Iraq instituted strong measures to ensure that they were kept under control. With the border settlement with Iran in 1975 dependence did not end but it was reduced materially.

After 1976 antipathy to the West because of its relationship with Israel and with the conservative Arab states did not mean an indiscriminate reliance on the USSR. The settlement of issues with Iran and the consequent weakening of the Kurdish cause gave Iraq greater freedom from domestic pressures. A less militant regional diplomacy made Iraq more acceptable in Persian Gulf politics. Rising oil revenues also increased Baghdad's options for acquiring arms, technology and training. This did not lead to a rapid integration of Iraq into Persian Gulf politics after 1975 but it did start a slow process toward rebuilding trust with the other littoral states. Iraq's decision in 1975 to drop support for Liberation Fronts in the Gulf was followed by a settlement of her border disputes with Saudi Arabia in July 1975. Iraq also played down her claim to Kuwait and to the islands of Warba and Bubiyan and joined discussions about regional approaches to security in the Gulf.

Iraq's attitude toward the Palestine question also underwent a significant change. From a militant ultra-rejectionist position at the

---

1 The Soviet connection had not brought the Ba'athist regime adequate tangible results in their rivalry with Syria, conflict with Iran or hostility toward Israel. Soviet refusal to provide full support on these issues limited its attractiveness to Iraq. Caution and a reluctance to take sides had weakened the potential for Soviet influence.

beginning of the decade, the Ba'ath had moved by November 1978 to a tacit acceptance of General Assembly Resolution 242 combined with a political interpretation of 'Rejectionism'. This movement was not necessarily against Soviet interests. Indeed Moscow had long been more moderate than the Iraqi regime on this Middle East question [1] but it symbolized Baghdad's reintegration into Arab politics particularly as the meeting in November 1978 reflected a new (albeit short) reconciliation with Syria which lasted until mid-1979.

Baghdad's regional option was not necessarily in tension with reliance on the USSR, but there were indications that in practice it was seen more as a substitute than a complement to the latter. The conclusion of agreements on internal security with Iran and Saudi Arabia in 1978 and 1979 symbolized this. Certainly Iraq's involvement in regional security discussions was not well received by the USSR who resists any tendency by its partners to be even-handed *vis-à-vis* the superpowers.[2] There were plausible reports that the USSR held up arms deliveries to Iraq in 1975 to signal its displeasure with its involvement in these discussions. The Iraqi Communist Party also criticized these talks.

Dependency has continued and the scope for truly independent positions is limited. Illustrative of this was the continued Soviet use of Iraq for strategic purposes. Even when the Soviet Union supported the opposing side in the Ethiopian–Eritrean conflict 1977-78, Iraq did not refuse it permission to use its facilities. The most it could extract was an agreement from Moscow not to ferry supplies *directly* from Iraqi soil to Ethiopia.[3] Nevertheless Iraq publicly opposed Soviet[4] support for Ethiopia against the (Muslim) Eritrean separatists. This opposition extended to providing military assistance to the Eritreans and later to supplying oil to Somalia. The conjunction of the pro-Soviet coup in Afghanistan in April 1978 and in the PDRY in July 1978 also evoked an Iraqi reaction that was less than receptive to the change in the political environment.[5]

---

1 Differences between the two states on this issue had been a source of aggravation, e.g. the 1970 Rogers Plan.

2 In fact however 'exclusion' of the superpowers from the Gulf would have consequences more serious for the West than for the USSR given the latter's geographical propinquity.

3 Soviet transports therefore touched down in the PDRY en route to Ethiopia. See S. Hussein interview, *International Herald Tribune*, 10 July 1978.

4 *Ath -Thawra* criticism see issue of 16 August 1978 and report in *Arab Report and Record* 16-31 August 1978, p. 675.

5 Saddam Hussein noted that the USSR will not be satisfied until the entire world is Communist. *International Herald Tribune*, 10 July 1978.

The Communist Party

In Iraq the Ba'aths' relations with the Iraqi Communist Party has been a barometer of its relations with the Soviet Union. Iraq's opposition to Soviet advances in the region after 1978 therefore had domestic political ramifications. In April 1978 the Iraqi Communist Party, at that time still in a (nominal) coalition with the ruling Ba'ath, criticized the government's domestic and foreign policies.[1] The Ba'ath responded by asking how, as members, the Communists could be critical of the government, and accused them of being Soviet satellites.[2] Subsequently extensive purges of Iraqi communists were carried out and two dozen were executed for organizing illegally within the armed forces. The Ba'athists were acutely sensitive to such dangers in the light of a similar development in Afghanistan before the coup. A senior official referred to the strain this had caused with the USSR and observed: 'Our differences are with the Soviet Union. Why does the Communist Party take an unfriendly attitude toward us?'[3] Another official observed, 'As far as we are concerned our strategic alliance with the USSR will not change . . . as long as there is no interference in our internal affairs'.[4]

Certainly the strategic relationship with the USSR persisted, but its nature had changed. As the Soviet Union has made inroads into the region – in Ethiopia, in the PDRY and in Afghanistan – so the Ba'athist regime has seen a power originally enlisted to balance the West creeping closer to the 'Arab homeland'. The geopolitical implications of this Soviet presence and its potential political utility within Iraqi politics itself were not lost on the Ba'ath leadership. Furthermore they now found the Soviet Union somewhat reluctant to tolerate these divergences with good grace. Syria – Iraq's Ba'athist rival – appeared to be favoured by Moscow. Soviet arms supplies were manipulated to chasten the Iraqi leadership. Saddam Hussein's visit to Moscow in December 1978 reportedly involved complaints over delays in shipments of spare parts, and over Soviet attempts to co-ordinate and standardize arms supplies to both Iraq and Syria to avoid duplication.[5]

---

1 *Tarikh al-Shab*, April 1978.

2 *Al-Rasid* (29 April–12 May, 1978).

3 *The Times*, 1 June 1978.

4 Naim Haddad (Member of the Revolutionary Command Council and Secretary General of the Ruling Progressive Front.) *The Middle East*, July 1978, p.30.

5 See *Military Aviation News*, December 1978, pp. 14-15 as cited in *Pajak loc.cit.*, 1980.

Ba'athist suspicions about covert Soviet contacts with the opposition within Iraq sharpened. In 1979 two Communist Ministers were dismissed and another purge of the Iraq Communist Party was ordered. The alienation of the communists from the Ba'ath regime became total, the senior leadership fled into exile, and from there maintained a constant stream of criticism directed at the Ba'ath. Iraq was clearly concerned that the Communist Party, working as a fifth column for the USSR, could provide the conduit for Soviet intervention in the country and, possibly through its strength in the Shi'a and Kurdish areas, provide a link with both of Iraq's hostile neighbours, Iran and Syria. The Ba'ath therefore continued their campaign to depict the Communists as agents under the control of a foreign non-Arab power.[1] They were quick to observe that the existence of a Friendship Treaty with Iraq does '. . . not give the Soviet Union any right to interfere in our internal affairs in any way'.[2] Their interpretation of Soviet policy was straightforward: 'The Soviet Union is now seriously working through its communist parties to penetrate and take over Pakistan and other countries'.[3] To prevent any such possibility, the purge of the Communists was intensified. On 25 April 1980, the offices of Georges Habbash's Marxist Popular Front for the Liberation of Palestine were closed. By November 1980 seven opposition groups within Iraq, consisting *inter alia* of Iraqi communists and a Kurdish faction, joined forces against the Ba'ath with the aim of forging closer ties with both the USSR and Iran.[4] Lastly the Iraqi Communist Party, using the platform of the 26th Party Congress in Moscow in March 1981, denounced the Ba'ath regime both for the continued suppression of the Communists and for its war with Iran.[5] Soviet policy during the war suggested parallel reservations about Baghdad's behaviour.

The Ba'ath have always regarded the Communist Party both as an alien threat to Arab culture and a tool of a foreign power. The agreement to form a coalition in 1972 had been demonstrably tactical, necessitated by multiple simultaneous pressures on the regime. This 'Progressive National Front' had come under severe strain as the Com-

1 See especially two *Ath-Thawra* editorials in 1980–81. As broadcast by Baghdad Home Service, 10 February 1980 in ME/6344/A/2, 13 February 1980; and *INA*, 8 February 1981 in ME/6645/A/4, 10 February 1981.

2 Saddoun Hammadi interview with *Newsweek*, 25 February 1980, p.56.

3 Naim Haddad, quoted by *As-Siyasah*, broadcast by KUNA, 7 May 1980 in ME/6414/A/4, 8 May 1980.

4 *The Guardian*, 14 November 1980. See also *The Observer*, 5 April 1981.

5 *International Herald Tribune*, 3 March 1981. (No mention was made at Party Congress of Iraq or of the Iraq–Soviet Treaty.)

munists sought to expand their influence within it, and as the Soviet shadow in the region began to grow, sensitizing the Ba'ath to the implications for their own political survival. The Iraqi leadership, however, sought to separate the issue of its treatment of the communists and its relations with the USSR: 'We will not allow our relations with you to pass through the channel of the ICP'.[1] Moscow was repeatedly advised, 'Our relationship with Moscow is constantly improving . . . while our differences with the ICP are related to security'.[2] The Soviet press was highly critical of Ba'athist attempts to depict the Communist Party as 'anti-Arab' in their efforts to discredit it.[3]

In the aftermath of the Iranian revolution and the Soviet invasion of Afghanistan, Iraq's divergences from the USSR grew wider. Iraq was far from enthusiastic about Iran's revolution, fearing its potential turn to the left more than it was impressed by its 'progressive' credentials. Unsurprizingly the Iraqi Communist Party (and indirectly the USSR) criticized this attitude.[4] Sensitivity about the potential role of the ICP within Iraq was undoubtedly increased as much by events in the region as by its members' (alleged) intervention and recruitment in the armed forces. Nevertheless the fact that the arbiters of change in both Afghanistan and the PDRY had been the military, which had been Soviet-trained and advised, suggested parallels to the Ba'athist leaders of their own potential condition. The military relationship could become the vehicle for Soviet influence and for regime transformation. The subsequent purges in 1978–79 were doubtless to cleanse the armed forces of non-Ba'athists and to serve notice on Moscow as to the limits of the Ba'athists' tolerance for this type of activity. Yet it is doubtful that the principal threat from the ICP came from its potential for organizing coups so much as from its capacity to organize and make common cause with other opposition elements. ICP co-operation with foreign opponents was another possibility, perhaps with the Iranian *Tudeh* (Communist Party) or perhaps with the Syrian regime increasingly aligned to Moscow.

The Ba'ath's understandable sensitivity about their political survival and the threat they saw in the combination of Soviet proximity and its

1 Naim Haddad interview in *Al-Dostour* (London), no.425, 2-8 April 1979, pp.6-7.

2 Saddoun Hammadi (Foreign Minister), *The Middle East Economic Digest*, 18 May 1979, p.3.

3 See for example the *Tass* commentary of 19 December 1979 in SWB SU/6303/A4/1-2, 21 December 1979.

4 See *Financial Times*, 11 April 1980; *Washington Star*, 17 April 1980.

proclivity for domestic interference was sufficient to make any other issue secondary. Sporadic and unconvincing attempts to separate domestic policies from relations with Moscow were made only ritualistically. It was clear that the Iraqi regime was prepared to risk its military relationship with the USSR if its political control was at stake. For its part the USSR found Iraq an increasingly troublesome partner following divergent policies and progressively less susceptible to influence through the medium of arms supply manipulation. Rather than risk rupture Moscow continued the flow of supplies erratically, and one suspects with little expectation that leverage would accrue thereby.

Regional divergences

Increasingly after 1978, Iraqi and Soviet policies in the Gulf region diverged. The PDRY—YAR border conflict in February 1979 saw not Iraqi support for the former but rather intensive efforts (which proved successful) to limit and terminate the clashes. The Iraqi government forthrightly condemned the Soviet invasion of Afghanistan[1] and voted against the Soviet Union in the UN and in Islamic *fora* in 1980. Yet the limits to these divergences were still evident. In their criticism of the Soviet invasion, Iraq's leadership appeared equally worried by the prospect of other states moving toward the US for protection or allowing the West a military presence. Furthermore, Iraq's leaders explicitly confirmed that Iraq would not change its relations with the USSR as a result of the invasion. This was despite the acknowledgement that: 'We think the Soviet Union is trying to expand its sphere of influence via the old game of power politics'.[2] Iraq's expectations were thus realistic in that they accepted that differences with Moscow might arise: '. . . while the Soviet Union is Iraq's friend still we may differ with it politically . . . because our policy derives from National and Pan-Arab interests'.[3]

Iraq's political response was twofold: first an attempt to limit both superpowers' presence in the region, and second to provide a regional alternative to that presence. In February 1980 Saddam Hussein announced an eight point Pan-Arab declaration proposing the rejection of foreign forces or bases anywhere in the Arab world, but linking this with agreement on the renunciation of force in disputes among Arab

---

1 See Saddam Hussein's comments, Press Release, Iraq, 11 February 1980.

2 Saddoun Hammadi, *Newsweek*, 25 February 1980, p.56. See S. Hussein interview, *Al-Watan al-Arabi*, Paris, Weekly, 4 February 1980.

3 Naim Haddad, Iraqi News Agency, 13 July 1980.

states and with their neighbours. Iraq and Saudi Arabia had indeed gradually since 1978 shifted their positions *vis-a-vis* their respective superpower partners and moved toward a non-aligned centre between the two blocs. The Pan-Arab declaration was intended to reinforce the regional option of the Gulf states.

The other component of Iraq's response was related: to limit Soviet influence in the region and to weaken that of its allies. In one sense the competition had become an internecine one among contending radical forces. The Iraqi Ba'ath, highly sensitive to the question of national independence, increasingly saw some leftist groupings, such as the government of the PDRY, as Soviet puppets. In addition the PDRY had granted sanctuary to members of the ICP and had repressed the Ba'ath. On 26 March 1980, Baghdad announced its support for the opposition groups seeking to overthrow the regime in Aden. It did so as an affirmation of its support for the independence of the region. The Iraqi Foreign Minister was quite clear as to the reasons for Iraq's position: 'Every Arab country is free to do anything provided it remains independent, but to bring the physical presence of a superpower to the region is something that causes us concern'.[1] Three months later he referred to the PDRY as being 'under the influence of a foreign power'.[2]

Iraq's sensitivity to competitive intervention by the superpowers in the region did not extend only against the USSR. It was genuinely even-handed to the extent of putting pressure on Oman, but the very fact of even-handedness demonstrates the shift in Iraq's priorities over the past decade. The divergences noted above reflect a shift away from pronounced alignment with the USSR. This can be accounted for in part by increased capabilities and in part by reduced commitments. Increased domestic stability, greater regional acceptance and higher oil revenues freed Baghdad from a dependence on the USSR which had been the consequence of multiple problems, frozen regional relations and a militant foreign orientation. In the process a re-ordering of priorities had also taken place. While this reflected the preference for self-reliance of a regime more sure of itself, more capable of choosing its priorities and less keen on spending itself in diffuse evangelical crusades overseas, it also reflected a changed perception of the USSR and the threat that the USSR poses to Iraq's independence.

1 See *Le Monde*, 28 March 1980; *Financial Times*, 28 March 1980; and Saddoun Hammadi's comments in *Al Jambour*, quoted in *Arab Oil* (Kuwait), March 1980.

2 See his *Press Conference* INA, 15 June 1980 in ME/6447/A/7, 18 June 1980.

The Iran—Iraq war 1980—81: supplier influence?

The war between Iraq and Iran which erupted in the autumn of 1980 had longstanding causes but its immediate antecedents lay in the threat posed to secular Iraq by the militant Shi'ism of revolutionary Iran. Sporadic border hostilities throughout 1979—80 finally escalated into large-scale clashes that consumed quite large amounts of military equipment and ammunition and caused serious human and financial losses. As the war progressed it might have been expected that the war-weary contestants with their equipment spent would be daily becoming more dependent on their major arms suppliers for fresh equipment, ammunition and spares and that this would accordingly increase the leverage of their chief supplier — the more so since the combatants in wartime had few of the options open to a recipient able to move at a more leisurely or measured pace. Therefore it would be reasonable to have expected that, with the outbreak of war, the role and influence of the supplying powers would increase.

This logic was complicated in the real world. First, what may at first glance have looked like a case of a regional conflict reflecting an East—West polarization, with the superpowers as the major suppliers of the two contestants, was deceptive. Iran, since the revolution and especially after autumn 1979, could scarcely be considered a pro-Western power, while Iraq in the same period had drifted away from the USSR toward a truer non-alignment. The result was that the outbreak of the war occurred at a time when the regional states had moved substantially to what amounted to a *de facto* reversal of alignments; Iraq to the West, Iran to the East. The arms-supply relationship to be sure still reflected an East—West division but this was mainly due to the lead-times necessary for supply (and the inertia this was bound to give to acquisition policies) and to the impracticality of rapid or frequent shifts in sources of supply. The superpowers, and in particular the USSR, thus found its interests in the war to be complex and cross-cutting and by no means susceptible to a clear-cut decision for or against either combatant. Soviet attempts to reconcile these interests militated against an unequivocal alignment which in turn reduced its capacity to influence the war — an issue to which we return after we examine Soviet Policy and Iraq's reactions.

As noted above, the strain in Iraq's relations with the USSR had been discernible before the war. Differences in approach to issues in the region's politics had been compounded by mutual distrust. The coldness in the Soviet attitude had been reflected in the virtual silence on the eighth anniversary of the Friendship Treaty and the scanty references to Iraq in the Soviet press. An indicator of the Soviet position was the Iraqi Communist Party's condemnation of Iraq in the April preceding the war. Nevertheless the Soviet Union had to balance a number of considerations in formulating a policy toward the conflict and the continuing rivalry:

1 The exclusion of US influence from the region.
2 The preservation of the possibility of extending influence in Iran.
3 The non-repudiation of an 'ally' which could damage Soviet reputation both as a 'friend' and as a supplier of military equipment.

The outbreak of the war was itself an embarrassment for it demonstrated the suppliers' inability to prevent the recipients' initiation of hostilities. More importantly it increased the pressure on the USSR to choose among the three principal considerations in its overall policy. Under pressure from both belligerents to take sides, the USSR was undoubtedly annoyed by the situation which it saw as a diversion from the principal struggle against the West, and as a pretext which the West would use to increase its military presence in the region. Moscow wanted to balance between keeping its relations with Iraq while not losing its opportunities in Iran for as long as it could. The USSR preferred not to make a choice. Yet the war posed the possibility that a refusal to take sides might risk the alienation of both. Consequently Soviet policy sought to balance these considerations. By declaring its 'neutrality' it sought to avoid antagonizing either State (which in the circumstances implied a tilt toward Iran). But the fear of losing influence over both led the Soviet Union to sanction supplies on a low level and sometimes indirectly to both sides. At worst genuine Soviet neutrality could result in the loss of Soviet influence in both countries and bring about a consolidated Western presence and expanded Western opportunities in the region. It was therefore important for the Soviet Union to retain ties with both states. Assistance had therefore to be provided at a level sufficient to keep the USSR 'in the game'. This assessment reflected a shift in Soviet interests towards Iraq which was no longer the most intimate Soviet ally. As a consequence Soviet policy was not to maximize its influence on Baghdad during the war but to salvage a residual influence there, while pursuing its broader interests in the region.

Before the war Moscow had already found its attempt to cultivate the two neighbouring states under strain. In April and again in August 1980 Iran had asked the USSR to cut off arms supplies to Iraq, depicting it as an unfriendly act toward 'The Revolution'.[1] The Soviets were not willing to comply with this but reportedly offered in August and

---

1 See *Le Monde*, 13-14 April 1980.

again in October to provide Iran with arms if it so requested.[1] Shortly after the hostilities intensified, Moscow rejected Iran's demand that it condemn 'Iraq's aggression' but it tilted toward Iran by declaring its 'neutrality',[2] even so this elicited it no thanks from the Iranians. Moscow however persisted in wooing Iran — judging that Iraq in the short term had fewer options. A public reference to Soviet enthusiasm for Iran's 'historic' revolution and to its support 'for Iran's right to decide her own future without foreign interference' was contained in a joint communiqué with Syria — Iraq's rival and Iran's ally.[3]

The Soviet tilt toward Iran was not merely verbal. It provided Tehran with jet fuel by air-tanker[4] and agreed to a transit arrangement for Iranian commerce. It granted permission to Syria, Libya and North Korea to use Soviet airspace in providing supplies and ammunition to Iran[5] and may indeed have encouraged this flow of arms as an indirect way of gaining favour with Iran without courting confrontation with Iraq. There were no reports of the direct supply of arms by the USSR to Iran but, if Moscow were interested in doing so, it could provide some useful equipment duplicating that already contained in the Iranian inventory such as SAM-7s and -9s, ZSU-23-4s and ZSU-57-2s, and the 85 mm. anti-tank gun.

Initially Moscow was fearful that the war might lead to a reversal of the revolutionary regime and its replacement by a conservative, more Western oriented government. The enhancement of the armed forces' prestige in Iran was therefore viewed with disquiet. But, as the war continued, this threat receded and so did the prospect of a rapprochement with the United States, its principal potential source of arms. The Soviet press was however emphatic in its denials of support for Iraq.[6] Reports of the transport of Soviet tanks for example were quickly and repeatedly denied.[7] When challenged by Iran's Prime Minister to show

---

1 See *The Baltimore Sun*, 23 August 1980; *Washington Post*, 24 September 1980; *The Times*, 6 October 1980; *Le Monde*, 9, 14, October 1980.

2 *Le Monde*, 25 September 1980, and *New York Times*, 24 September 1980.

3 *Le Monde*, 12-13 October 1980.

4 *Aviation Week and Space Technology*, 3 November 1980, p.27.

5 There were numerous reports of this originating mainly in Washington. For example, see *International Herald Tribune*, 11-12 October 1980, and 6 November 1980.

6 See for example *Pravda*, 11 January 1981; *Izvestia*, 10 January 1981 and *Krasnaya Zvezda*, 15 January 1981.

7 See *Tass*, 14 January 1981 in SU/6624/A4/1, 16 January 1981, and Leonid Ponomayov in *Soviet News* (London), 10 February 1981, p.44.

its true colours — imperialist or revolutionary — with reference to its position *vis-à-vis* Iraq (and Israel) 'the regional aggressors', the Soviet official press was quick to respond: 'The reality is that from the beginning of the fratricidal Iran–Iraq war, the Soviet Union has not delivered, and will not deliver, arms to either side in the conflict'.[1]

Soviet reiteration of its neutrality amounted to reassurance of Iran which was unlikely to gain the Soviet Union many thanks in Baghdad. But what was Soviet policy toward its erstwhile client and how did Iraq react? In July 1980 Saddam Hussein, the Iraqi President, observed that Iraq had not been subservient to Moscow nor had it entertained excessive expectations of the Soviet Union: 'We have been and are still friends. But when the Soviet Union fails to give us certain kinds of arms, we will go to any other country in the world to obtain those weapons . . . In fact we have done this . . . But our arms are still basically Soviet'.[2] It was precisely this fact that necessitated two visits to Moscow by Tariq Aziz, the Iraqi Deputy Prime Minister, in September and November after the outbreak of the war. Neither trip was successful in obtaining new arms and the Soviet reaction to the visits was pointedly low-key.[3] The Iraqi attitude was also guarded. Tariq Aziz observed that Iraq had not requested more arms: 'Besides we have the arms to support a long war'[4] while Saddam Hussein argued that the USSR had fulfilled its obligations under the 1972 Treaty and Iraq considered it a friend.[5] Occasionally, however, an undertone of concern was also detectable. In October Saddam Hussein referred to Iran's Western armaments and training in glowing terms when contrasting them with those of Iraq.[6] Criticism of Soviet arms not performing well was made more directly by Iraq's Defence Minister.[7] By the end of the year Iraq admitted that the USSR had interrupted its

---

1   For Rajai's challenge see *Le Monde*, 17 February 1981 and for Moscow's reply see Radio Moscow, 16 February 1981 in SU/6653/A4/3-4, 19 February 1981.

2   Saddam Hussein Press Conference, Baghdad TV, 22 July 1980, in ME/6479/A/13, 24 July 1980. For press reports see *The Times*, and *Le Monde*, 22 July 1980.

3   For a discussion of Soviet policy toward Iraq at this time see Karen Dawisha's two articles: 'Moscow and the Gulf War', *The World Today*, January 1981, pp. 8-14, and 'Soviet Decision-Making in the Middle East', *International Affairs*, London, vol.57, no.1, Winter 1980-81, pp. 43-59.

4   *Le Monde*, 22 October 1980.

5   Saddam Hussein Press Conference, 10 November 1980. Complete text from Embassy of Republic of Iraq, Press Office, London. (See also *Le Monde*, 12 November 1980.)

6   See *International Herald Tribune*, 19 October 1980.

7   Adnan Khairallah, *The New York Times*, 12 November 1980.

supply of arms from the start of the war — arguing nevertheless that this would have no effect on either Iraq's capabilities or its relations with Moscow.[1] By February 1981 the Soviet cut-off appeared to be biting. In welcoming the continuing supply of French weapons, Iraqi officials contrasted the willingness of France to honour agreements with those who sought pretexts to avoid them.[2] The Iraqi First Deputy Premier reported that Moscow had 'stopped implementing pre-war [arms] contracts signed with Iran' adding that Iraq would not forget this.[3] Saddam Hussein claimed that Iraq had concluded arms agreements since the start of the war amounting to several billion dollars, which would allow her arms 'superior to that which it possessed before the start of the war' including aircraft, tanks and artillery.[4] A month later both the Defence and Foreign Ministers acknowledged the Soviet cut-off and pointedly emphasized that Iraq would buy arms from any other source 'with the sole exception of Israel[5]' . . .'including the United States'.[6]

There were indeed signs that Iraq was obtaining supplies from other sources. France delivered four *Mirage* fighters (ordered in 1979) in January 1981 and promised to continue deliveries until the order for twenty-four was completed. In addition France, Italy and Germany were reported to be the source of spare parts and some missile reloads for Iraq. France in particular could play an important role for the supply of the HOT anti-tank missiles, helicopter (*Puma, Gazelle* and *Alouette*) replacements and spares, light tanks (AMX) and artillery shells already in Iraq's inventory (Spain and Brazil were also potential suppliers). The delivery of the *Mirage* though was unlikely to have any practical effect on Iraq's capabilities (*inter alia* because pilot training had not been completed) although it provided a psychological boost to the Iraqi armed forces and served as a contrast to the Soviets' denial.

To what extent the Soviet Union in fact cut off Iraq from supplies is not demonstrable with any precision. It is clear that Moscow could not acquiesce in a major defeat of its arms client but this was not yet a real risk. At the other extreme it was equally clear that the USSR did not

1 Tariq Aziz, *Le Monde*, 24 December 1980.

2 *Le Monde* 4 February 1981.

3 Taha Yazzin Ramadin, *International Herald Tribune*, 5 February 1981.

4 *Le Monde*, 17 February 1981.

5 Saddoun Hammadi, *The Times*, 12 March 1981.

6 Adnan Khairallah interview *Al-Hawedess*, in *Le Monde*, 15-16 March 1980, *International Herald Tribune*, 14-15 March 1980.

wish to identify with or encourage Iraq's prosecution of a war which held risks for Soviet interests in the region. Within these parameters Soviet interests were to retain some influence in Iraq while currying favour with Iran. This might place it in a position to act as peacemaker — or in any case in a position superior to the US which lacked diplomatic relations with either combatant.[1] This still gave Moscow considerable latitude in its supply policy. The definition of 'resupply' was itself subject to considerable debate. It could perhaps be argued that the provision of ammunition and spare parts did not meet the definition of 'resupply' and was merely a 'normal' flow.[2] Semantic distinctions apart, the issue was subject to elastic interpretation. The replacement of arms and equipment lost in the conflict on a one-for-one basis (with no quantitative or qualitative increase) might well be argued to constitute a policy of restraint falling between the extremes of a dramatic air-bridge ferrying in more and better equipment, and its opposite, a complete denial of any equipment whatsoever. There were reports that Moscow had indeed settled for this one-for-one replacement.[3]

The impact of Moscow's policy on Iraq's war effort is equally difficult to pinpoint with precision. What had been Iraqi expectations with respect to the length of the war, the attrition of equipment and Soviet resupply policy? How much stockpiling of ammunition and spare parts had it been allowed to complete by a USSR notorious for the short leash it holds over its recipients? What other sources of supply existed that could make a material difference to Iraq's war effort?

Iraq had entered into its 'strategic' partnership with the USSR under the pragmatic Ba'ath with few illusions. Its movement toward the diversification of arms supplies had accelerated after 1978 as it found its interests less congruent with that of the USSR. The result had been the placement of large-scale orders with France especially, but also with Italy and Brazil. Its determination to diversify its sources of supplies had been constantly reiterated before the war, most recently in the summer of 1980.[4] As a consequence its dependence on the USSR was

1 High-level American acknowledgement of 'no irreconcilable differences' with Iraq in January 1980 which hinted at renewed relations were rebuffed by Iraq. See *Wall Street Journal*, 15 January 1980 and 8 February 1980. Some new movement was evident in April 1981, see *International Herald Tribune*, 8 April 1981.

2 *Daily Telegraph*, 9 October 1980, and *Financial Times*, 3 October 1980.

3 *The Times*, 20 March 1981.

4 See the Iraq Information Minister's comment in June 1980, *Al-Nahar* (Beirut), 21 June 1980.

in the process of being appreciably reduced when the war started.[1] However it was inevitable that Iraq should rely on material already in its inventory and this meant Soviet material. Iraq has thus remained dependent on the USSR — potentially vitally so — for spare parts, ammunition and re-equipment during the war. This dependence could be modified by the course and nature of the conflict and by the availability of alternative suppliers.

It was evident from Iraq's official comments that there was disappointment at the Soviets' resupply policy although there was little sign of panic in Baghdad. As long as the war remained spasmodic and prolonged, alternative sources of supply could be found — from an unnamed East European country[2] (doubtless with full Soviet acquiescence), from the international arms market, and from former recipients of Soviet arms.[3] Iraq had wealthy allies in the Gulf and healthy foreign exchange reserves and could afford premium prices. Furthermore Iran's difficulties in locating sources of supply suggested that the pattern of low-level and desultory exchanges of fire might continue, thus reducing the pressure on Iraq to pay the political price that Moscow might wish to extract from a renewed commitment.

Moscow's price for the opening up of the arms tap would (in all probability) be an Iraqi withdrawal from Iranian territory. Depending on its terms, this might be considered as a considerable defeat for Saddam Hussein in his *Qadissiyah* against the Persians, which would jeopardize his political standing in Iraq and in the Arab world in general. Furthermore acquiescence in such terms as a result of Soviet pressure would be a humiliation for Iraq's aspirations for independence and non-alignment. It therefore appeared unlikely that Soviet influence, deriving from its role as principal arms supplier, could be converted into the kind of leverage that would impel Iraq toward a settlement. If the war revived in its intensity, Iraq could be expected to seek and find other sources of supply while, if it continued to sputter sporadically, both belligerents might tacitly allow it to die down without a formal agreement. In either case it is clear that, even in the case of (some) inter-state wars, the supplier of arms is by no means assured of influence.

1 Many orders had yet to be delivered let alone absorbed into the armed forces. Consequently Iraq's reliance on the USSR remained a major consideration during the war.

2 Probably Poland.

3 Egypt's Agreement to provide 4,000 tons of ammunition and spares in March 1981 was illustrative.

Influence and the 1980—81 war

The onset of a war which consumed military equipment but which yielded no decisive result and promised further rounds of fighting might well have been expected to maximize the influence of the arms-supplying power with regard to its more desperate dependent partner. In some respects the war was in fact a test case of such assumptions. It could for example be argued that the outside powers as arms suppliers were unable to prevent the initiation of the war, to limit its consequences, or to influence its termination or outcome. This was largely though not completely accurate. Limits on 'influence' came in part because of the shift in the political relationships between supplier and recipient, which had not yet been reflected in the military side, and in part because the suppliers' own relationship was under strain and could not have survived a clash in the Persian Gulf.

Furthermore the nature of the war itself limited the influence of the supplier. Neither intense nor short, the recipient was accordingly under less direct pressure to seek resupply rapidly. The actual hostilities did not concentrate on the sustained use of air power — an area where the supplier would have a virtual monopoly and hence maximal leverage. Alternate sources existed for most other material. Iraq was thus less beholden to the USSR than might have been anticipated. This was even more the case because Iraq's adversary — Iran — was in even worse condition in respect to organization, morale and the acquisition of spare parts and replacements. The decline in the tempo of the fighting after the first few weeks testified to this and reduced any likelihood that Iraq would be irreversibly locked into dependence on the USSR as a result of the war.

Soviet influence as a result of the war might have been increased if it had been used to achieve something more compatible with Iraq's war aims — but Moscow's preferred outcome — a reversion to the *status quo ante bellum* — was for the Iraqi leadership a recipe for regional humiliation and possibly domestic political instability. The price of Soviet military assistance — a compromise peace — would leave Iraq 'with nothing to show for its efforts'. Iraq's willingness to accept the USSR's conditions would increase only if the alternatives to it — outright military defeat or an imminent overriding need for resupply due to an expanded war — were the immediate prospect. So long as its leaders felt that it could salvage something better than the unpalatable terms the Soviet Union was offering for assistance, Iraq's leaders would persist in the war and remain oblivious to the incipient dependency on the USSR that only a full-scale war would make manifest. The likelihood in the future, however, was for a winding-down of the war by tacit consent without agreement on a formal settlement. After the hostilities, Iraq's policy of arms diversification can be expected to accelerate further the erosion of Moscow's potential influence in that country.

The conditions for, and scope of, influence

Soviet interests in Iraq are best served by a responsive government sensitive to its wishes, while optimally this 'sensitivity' would extend to tight co-ordination in the diplomatic realm. Specific goals include access to Iraqi territory (especially to airspace, and to air and naval facilities) and preferential terms of trade, particularly for Iraqi oil. The achievement of these interests is dependent on the acquisition of influence in Baghdad, and Soviet policy in the past two decades has concentrated on this. It has encountered setbacks and achieved some successes as the relationship has evolved. Soviet influence too, though it has ebbed and flowed, still persists in Baghdad. This reflects a continued convergence of interest in opposition to 'Western imperialism'. The USSR has sought to reduce Western influence in the region for its own purposes. Iraq has sought and used Soviet power to achieve its own 'independence' and to assist the Arab cause on the issue of Palestine. Overlapping interests have facilitated the extension of Soviet influence but the durability of the relationship is now more in doubt than before while its scope has been reduced in the past decade. Because of the increasing importance of the Persian Gulf, it is unlikely that the USSR will accept such a reduction in influence passively. Iraq's importance in the region has increased, perhaps particularly so in the aftermath of Iran's instability. In addition, Iraq's oil wealth,[1] relative political stability and reintegration into the mainstream of Arab politics increase her influence and hence her value as a regional ally. Yet it may well be that the qualities making a state a valuable regional ally (stability, cohesion and wealth) also make it less likely to need the USSR. The search for influence when its target has choices and exhibits flexibility may prove to be expensive.

The record of Soviet—Iraqi relations to date sheds light on the conditions tending to increase or decrease the scope of external power influence. In a nutshell Soviet influence has depended essentially on its value to Iraq (in terms of the latter state's priorities and alternatives) and on Iraq's strength or weakness. When the Iraqi leadership was domestically challenged, regionally isolated and financially weak in 1969—74 (and in earlier periods) dependence on the Soviet Union increased. Ideological militance at this time further precluded a search for

---

1 Her oil reserves may be as high as 90 billion barrels, second only to those of Saudi Arabia.

alternative sources of arms supply or diplomatic support. A common hostility to the West then cemented a relationship which was already bound by arms supply and commercial links.

All of these elements changed in the late 1970s as Iraq's leaders consolidated their control domestically. They mended their fences regionally, diversified their arms purchases and entered into pragmatic commercial relations with the West.[1] The shift in international orientation which was symbolized by a de-emphasis on spreading revolution and by less intransigence on the Palestine issue, though marked, was by no means a reversal. It permitted a corresponding shift in emphasis from almost exclusive dependence on the USSR to a wider arena where Iraqi interests might be served.

Soviet influence in Iraq in the late 1970s was thus diluted and Western technology, French arms, regional co-operation and more diplomatic activity gave Iraq more options. France appeared keen to further this co-operation by offering arms and technology, including in the nuclear field.[2] Furthermore France shrewdly played on the Ba'athists' attraction to Gaullism; they appeared to share assertive nationalism which judged the two blocs solely in terms of their contributions to national interests. Yet whatever these other sources could offer, they were not yet in a position to replace the USSR as a source of diplomatic support on Palestine. As long as Iraq had Palestine as a priority in its foreign policy and judged other states by their positions on this issue, the Soviet position remained a privileged one. This remains true despite the growing realization in Iraq that the Soviet Union's growing presence on the periphery of the Gulf constitutes a threat to Arab interests. With a priority on Gulf issues, Iraq now judges the USSR by different criteria. Saddam Hussein put this well:

> Our relationship with the USSR . . . is not linked to any special time, but to an understanding of the extent and nature of the Arab struggle, as well as to what the Soviet Union can do to help the Arab nation through agreement on strategies, mutual interests or both.[3]

That the Soviet—Iraqi 'strategic' partnership is solidly based has not meant that it is static or immutable. Its durability could be affected by Western policies. The West could soften Iraqi hostility by modifying its

1 Contrast direction of trade in late 1970s with that in late 1960s. Note especially that from 1972 when USSR was leading supplier of non-military products; by 1980 USSR was fourteenth. (*International Herald Tribune*, 5 February 1980.)

2 Iraq is France's largest supplier of Middle East oil.

3 Quoted in Claudia Wright, 'Iraq: New Power in the Middle East', *Foreign Affairs*, vol.58, no.2, Winter 1979-80, pp. 257-77.

policy toward Israel. A European initiative on this issue may well increase Iraq's disposition to strengthen its ties with states such as France, Italy, Germany and Spain. Similarly, a change in Soviet policy could also affect the partnership. Greater Soviet militance and an increased supply of arms and support for the Palestinians and the Rejectionist Front could see a revival of intimacy in the relationship. Alternatively, continued stalemate and the inability of the USSR to influence events or produce results could accentuate the trend toward a diminished Iraqi reliance on the USSR.

In its relations with Iraq, the USSR has suffered from considerable constraints. Allied with a militant state to which it has supplied arms, it has inevitably been identified with the policies of the recipient. Yet the supply of arms has not given the Soviet Union any control over their use. Failure to support fully and unconditionally the recipient in its regional quarrels (with Syria and Iran) has brought only resentment, weakening any influence the supply of arms might have been expected to bring. At the same time support for the Ba'ath regime has entailed the sacrifice of domestic allies (the Iraq Communist Party) and a switch of support away from erstwhile friends (the Kurds). Finally, as the recipient has become stabilized and more confident, it has sought to loosen the 'unnatural' closeness of the earlier relationship, to diversify relations, and even to be critical of Soviet policies in other areas.

To a considerable extent the consolidation of the Ba'ath's power has meant the diminution of Soviet influence in Iraq. In terms of regional politics the relationship with the USSR has been a liability for Iraq, raising the suspicion of the other littoral states and slowing Baghdad's quest for influence. It may be accurate to suggest that Soviet leverage at present is less positive than negative, conferring the power to cause a nuisance rather than the power to distribute rewards. In a sense it has 'relevant' power through the capacity to meet the Iraqis' principal concern, their maintenance of political control within Iraq. Soviet influence within the Communist Party and the potential use of Kurdish dissidence provide important reminders of the leverage that can be exerted against a recalcitrant Ba'athist leadership. It is not necessary to accept fully the reports of a communist plot for a coup against the regime in 1978—79 (or of Soviet sponsorship of this on the PDRY—Afghanistan models) to remark that the Soviet Union's retention of these levers provides a powerful incentive for Iraq's leadership to remain minimally pliable to Soviet concerns, or risk domestic troubles. If the Soviets can offer the Iraqi leadership a means of staying in power (by not causing them any trouble) their leverage is likely to remain considerable. This is an asset that the West does not possess.

The arms relationship

The supplier's influence is clearly increased if it is the sole (or even primary) source of arms to a state that has both a pressing security problem and few alternative means of meeting it. In the 1960s and early 1970s Iraq faced security problems inside the country and on its borders while dependent on the USSR for military aid. Iraq had neither the luxury of time nor the economic means to diversify her sources of supply. The Soviet position as primary and practically sole supplier carried with it undoubted influence. It enabled the USSR to pressure the Ba'ath into a National Front coalition with the Communist party in 1972–73. It had earlier, in the mid-1960s, used the manipulation of arms to prevent attacks on the Kurds. This was less effective in 1974 when denial of arms contributed to the Ba'ath decision to settle their differences with Iran and no more effective in 1975 or in 1976 when the USSR had agreed to a major new sales agreement. This experience suggests that while supplier-influence varies largely with the imminence of the security threat perceived by the recipient and the feasible alternative sources of arms, it is also dependent on the political context. The overall relationship of the recipient to the regional environment is a conditioner of its dependence. When isolated, Iraq's dependence on the USSR increased; when in tune with the region, the Soviet connection assumed less salience. At times the USSR has provided the means for the fulfilment of the Iraqi leadership's priorities *vis-à-vis* Israel and the Arab world; at other times, these have been best pursued by other means. Relations with the supplier state need not be brittle: Iraq's 'strategic alliance' has allowed for divergences and strains without a total disruption in relations. This is due largely to the make-up of the recipient state which, in the case of Iraq since 1969, has been characterized by both flexibility and idealism.[1] A lack of illusions both about the nature of the supplying state[2] and the recipient–supplier relationship has made for fewer disappointments and shocks than might otherwise have been the case. The Iraqi leadership has started from the premise that 'no country with serious problems which relies on importing its weapons can claim to be absolutely independent with regard to

---

1 Saddam Hussein clearly considers these virtues: 'We are pragmatists. If confrontation doesn't work we change. We haven't closed any doors'. *Los Angeles Times*, 12 November 1978.

2 Saddam Hussein refers to the immobility of Soviet bureaucracy as the 'Siberian mentality', see Haykal, *Sphinx and Commissar*, p.279.

many calculations of politics . . . '.[1] It has seen its relationship with the Soviet Union as essentially one of *quid pro quos* wherein the latter expects returns on its investments:

> . . . we consequently must not expect the Soviets to support us without assuring them of our friendship in the form which they consider would serve the objectives of their international strategy through joint action.[2]

The corollary to these assumptions is that a strategic relationship is also a partnership, the terms of which can be revised by either partner.

There is considerable evidence that the USSR views military aid as an instrument of influence and not merely a commercial commodity. In the 1970s it used this aid both as a punishment and as a reward for its clients.[3] The manipulation of arms supplies is clearly a risky business for both recipient and supplier but the balance of risk varies with the imminence of the threat to the supplier, its choices, and the supplier's own degree of interest in the state. A sustained interruption of the process of supplying arms (rather than a temporary curtailment to signal displeasure) may unnerve the recipient. This would tend to reinforce the permanent incentive that exists for maximizing sources of supply and reducing dependence on a sole supplier. Iraq's move in this direction in the mid-1970s was doubtless accelerated by the Soviet reluctance to provide the arms Baghdad wanted, and to Soviet manipulation of supplies. Nevertheless, to a considerable extent the incentives for diversifying already existed. Once the economic means became available this became possible. The result was to reduce dependency on any one power and hence to forestall or dilute pressure if it were applied. In addition the move toward diversification after a period of near total reliance on one supplier acted as a lever with which to exert pressure on that supplier for more or better arms. If it was to retain influence, the supplier would have to deliver.

For the Soviet Union the military component has undoubtedly been the core of the relationship with Iraq. Arms have been a currency that

---

1 Saddam Hussein Statement to Iraqi Ambassadors in West Europe and Japan, 12 June 1975, reprinted in *Saddam Hussein on Social and Foreign Affairs*, Croom Helm, London, 1979, p.72.

2 Interview given to Egyptian journalist, 19 January 1977 in *Saddam Hussein on Social and Foreign Affairs*, p.101.

3 It increased its supplies to Syria when that state refused to co-operate with the US in 1975, and withheld supplies when Syria refused to end its involvement in the Lebanese civil war in 1976. The Soviet Union used the curtailment of arms supplies as a weapon in its debt negotiations with Egypt after 1974. This contributed to the deterioration of relations, the Egyptian abrogation of the Friendship Treaty and the loss of the largest customer for Soviet arms.

the USSR could provide relatively easily. They provided a tangible bond, an indication of Soviet constancy and goodwill. In the 1970s, as the relationship evolved, the trade and aid pattern of exchanging commodities for arms gave way to payments in hard currency. No longer a favour, the arms were subjected to more critical assessment by the recipient. They became more 'commercial' in nature, particularly as the USSR was known to be less competitive with the West in areas of non-military technology.[1] If the supplier had strong incentives for sales, its capacity to manipulate them for other purposes correspondingly decreased. If they were the one area in which the Soviet Union met Iraq's needs, jeopardizing it would end the only channel of Soviet influence. For, unlike the US in Iran and in Saudi Arabia, the military link was likely to be the only significant link as Iraq's foreign trade expanded in the 1980s. The Soviet ability to use arms as a means of influence is therefore likely to be further circumscribed in the decade ahead. 'Influence' would be derived less from extreme and tangible Iraqi dependence than from a parallelism of view and a convergence of interest. The belief in the importance of the relationship and the indispensability of ties would ensure continuity but the pattern of interactions would be businesslike involving the exchange of favours, *quid pro quos* and bargaining with the reciprocal use of levers. Soviet influence from the military supply relationship would persist but only if it was uninterrupted. Entanglement and loss of 'control' were inevitably the price of supplying arms, an essential by-product of the Soviet quest for influence.

This analysis holds only if the Iraqi leadership remains the same, pursues its pragmatic policy of contacts with its neighbours and is presented with no major and urgent security problem. In a crisis, the importance and the influence of the military supplier tends to increase. The transition from virtually total dependence on one supplier to a more balanced mix of suppliers, consistent with political demands and logistic efficiency, takes time and is costly. Whether it is also risky depends upon the threat environment. The length of the transition, particularly in terms of training, language skills and the like to assure full assimilation of the new arms, may be more than the military as an interest group will tolerate. Whether the USSR or their supporters in Iraq's armed forces are in a position to arrest the move toward diversification seems doubtful. Nevertheless, as a potential interest group they are a powerful reminder of the umbilical cord that binds nations in

---

1 Note Saddam Hussein's comment that the Soviet Union 'believe(s) that their most effective means for changing the world to their advantage is with arms. . . . The Soviets cannot compete with US technology'. *International Herald Tribune*, 10 July 1978.

major military relationships. This cord can only be rapidly severed (as in Iran) if the consequences for the nation's military preparedness are deemed to be tolerable, or if (again as in Iran) the supply link itself is seen as the greatest security threat. There are no reasons to expect Iraq to end its military relationship with the USSR but a reduction in its scope will give Iraq's leaders greater latitude in their approach to their interests. For the USSR the transformed relationship will mean fewer risks of involvement but the cost in influence may well be sorely missed and encourage the promotion of other, more pliable groups in Iraqi politics.[1]

1 The best work on the USSR and Iraq is Francis Fukuyama, *The Soviet Union and Iraq Since 1968*, Rand (N-1524-AF), July 1980. This monograph appeared after the initial draft of this chapter was completed in May 1980. Many of the interpretations of issues are parallel and I have found it instructive and stimulating.

2 The Superpower Contribution to Conflict Management

The record of outside powers

The modern history of the Gulf as it relates to the management of conflict may be divided into three distinct phases. The first was the era of British paramountcy and protection which saw an outside power playing the role of manager, guardian and arbiter of the region. Intervention by other outside powers was deterred, piracy and smuggling were suppressed, interstate conflicts were frozen, and coups were either vetoed or encouraged pre-emptively. As a result of the UK's presence, disruptive forces were contained and their manipulation by outside forces prevented. Saudi Arabia was prevented from acquiring the Buraimi oasis: and Iran was denied Bahrain. Iraq's claim to Kuwait (1961) was balked first by a British military response and subsequently by use of the Arab League machinery. Territorial claims between Iran and Arab states were likewise shelved. Not only in inter-state rivalry, but also in the thwarting of unfavourable internal developments, the British exercised a veto. Sheikh Shakhbut in 1966 and Sultan Taimur in 1970 were ousted to forestall internal discontent.[1] The British role as protector thus guaranteed internal and external security in a region largely insulated from other inter-Arab pressures. But as these pressures grew in the 1960s and the region became politicized, the UK's presence

---

1 However, the revolution in Iraq in 1958 showed the limits of British power in the non-protected states.

111

became more difficult to justify in narrow political-economic terms.

Paradoxically the British withdrawal from the Gulf came at a time when growing Western dependence on the region was becoming evident, with projections that it would become acute in the next decade. The financial cost of the UK's presence was negligible (£12 million) and, although the smaller littoral states offered to pay that cost, the UK's imperial era was terminated with a minimum of attention to future policy interests.

The second phase was characterized by an indirect superpower role in conflict management, confined to the supply of arms and the provision of training and occasional joint exercises (mainly in CENTO and with the US naval detachment MIDEASTFOR stationed in Bahrain). These exercises involved the use by *P-3 Orion* maritime reconnaissance planes of Bandar Abbas in Iran and Masirah in Oman. Besides showing an interest in maintaining some access to friendly states, little was done to maintain an efficient base structure near the Gulf region. Within the region the US ruled out any new or direct physical presence. It was recognized that formal pacts would be targets for criticism and that bases would be vulnerable to subversion and might increase political instability. From this it was concluded that the assumption of primary responsibility for conflict management in the region lay with the local states. The major friendly states, Iran and Saudi Arabia, were encouraged to improve their relations and to assume greater defence tasks for the security of the region. For its part, the USSR also lacked a direct presence while cultivating its ties with Iraq and securing a Treaty of Friendship with Baghdad in April 1972. Relations between the two superpowers throughout most of this period (1969–78) improved and their rivalry in the Gulf remained muted and indirect.

It was domestic not regional tensions which undid the principal pillar of Gulf security – Iran. The Iranian revolution not only undermined the notion that local states could play important roles in the maintenance of regional security, it also unleashed new and very destabilizing pressures which themselves required containment.

The third (and current) phase of conflict management in the Gulf is visible only in outline. With growing interests in the region and a more hostile and competitive relationship, the superpowers' role will be more direct. This is especially clear from the Western perpective where acute dependence and Soviet proximity to the region are even more stark in the aftermath of Iran's upheaval. Past structures have broken down and, without regional states as buffers, the prospect for direct East–West confrontation arising from local instabilities has increased. Unlike the preceding era, the pressures on the superpowers in assuming a greater role in conflict management have intensified. Their interests are greater and no obvious substitute exists. The issue in this phase is not whether but how the superpowers can usefully play this role and what role exists for regional structures.

In the Persian Gulf (more than elsewhere in the Third World), outside powers are confronted by a strong dependence on a region whose stability is precarious. The sources of this instability are multiple and interactive. Limitations on the capacity of outside powers to maintain order exist both because of the nature of the instabilities (modernization and rapid change) which are impervious to traditional instruments of influence and because of political competition within the region itself and between outside powers. The margin for influence, though narrow, is real and requires clear definition if it is not to be further eroded.

The nature of some of the threats to stability are resistant to easy manipulation but they are not immune to some influence. Modernization may be inherently unpredictable and open-ended but it is not thereby inevitably disruptive. Other factors acting as constraints on outside power influence are not immutable either. The regional context which conditions the exercise of influence (unanimity, fragmentation, polarization) can alter as can the cultural historical-legacy (real or fancied slights), the political popularity of a given elite, or even the nature of the interests of outside powers (which may tend to define stability statically or alternatively to promote change indiscriminately to undermine the other bloc's interests). Moreover, all of these can be affected by outside powers' policies. This is most obvious in the military arena where the power balance can sharply affect the range of choice open to either bloc. A pre-condition for any influence is military power. It can balance or deter the other bloc and reassure local allies. By deterring threats to allies, it can prevent the exploitation of local disputes and, by providing reassurance, it can discourage the accommodation or appeasement of threatening forces by local friends. It can therefore affect policy choices as well as constrain military threats. If a necessary instrument, military power is not sufficient by itself. Much depends on its availability, its relevance, its flexibility, how it is used, and how it is perceived.

The region is still recovering from two recent shocks, the revolution in Iran and the Soviet invasion of Afghanistan. After the first, many analysts argued that 'internal' instabilities were the greatest threat to security in the Gulf. The 'lesson' of Iran was therefore to reduce arms sales and to loosen ties with 'unstable' regimes and to play down the military instrument. Within a year the invasion of a nearby state by the Soviet Union served as a reminder that 'lessons' ought not to be digested too quickly or mechanically. Just as there are multiple threats to regional stability (internal, regional and external), a variety of instruments are necessary for managing and containing them. The interesting questions are the priorities and their mix. Threats to regional stability are varied and reinforcing. Although some originate in domestic tensions (for example sectarian or ethnic differences, disagreements on the pace or goal of state policy, income or status inequalities, low levels of institutionalization and highly politicized populaces) these are not purely domestic issues. Moreover they are often harnessed by states (regional or external) for their own parallel or quite different purposes such as support for a secessionist movement to weaken an adversary (Iran/Iraq, Kurds, Arabistan or the USSR/PDRY in Oman). It is then that they become dangerous. 'Simple' interstate or boundary disputes rarely remain self-contained. The search for the 'clear' case of external aggression calling forth a direct military response is chimerical. The military balance (which embraces notions of both reliability and relevant power) overhangs the politics of the region[1] and has an effect on perceptions of the range of choice. It can constrain or widen the margins of choice for both outside and local powers. It can psychologically inhibit and so affect the opportunities and the costs of local aggression. Military power cannot (and is not designed to) prevent social dislocations but it can influence their direction and specifically the degree to which outside forces use it for their own purposes. It may not guarantee political settlements but it can provide the context to make them possible. Military power is one of several complementary instruments in conflict management. That it does not by itself suffice is not an argument for its renunciation. The alleged inadequacy of any one remedy to settle all the region's problems is hardly an argument against that remedy. The choice is not between doing nothing and doing something risky, but between the costs and consequences of two different types of risk.

With the fall of the Shah the Nixon doctrine was buried. With it was interred the attempt to decouple local instability from direct superpower competition. In its place has arisen a highly unstable system to which the linkage between local and global stability is stronger and more direct than anywhere in the Third World. The end of the twin-pillar security era in which local powers insulated local tremors from global rivalry[2] has thus meant a greater potential for direct confron-

---

1 See Albert Wohlstetter, 'Half wars and half policies in the Persian Gulf' in Scott Thompson (ed.), *National Security in the 1980s: From Weakness to Strength*, Institute for Contemporary Studies, San Francisco, 1980.

2 See next section.

114

tation between the blocs in a region where there are no rules defined by experience as there are in other conflict-prone regions (such as the Arab–Israel zone). It has also entailed a correspondingly greater pressure on regional states. With Iran in turmoil, the margin of tolerance for further instability is diminished. Saudi Arabia has come under intense scrutiny as interests and pressures have focused on her. The Western states' dependence in the region means a vulnerability not just to cataclysmic revolutions but also to minor tremors, such as the balance of power within factions in the Saudi leadership which might result in policy reversals.

Yet it would be erroneous to conclude that this vulnerability too is not susceptible to influence. The 'assurance of oil supplies' also requires balancing the USSR, although that is not sufficient in itself as a policy for oil. If the issue were merely one of indigenous instabilities and the social strains generated by rapid growth, the West's task of assuring oil supplies would be radically different. It is the prospect of these instabilities being exploited by hostile powers in ways harmful to Western interests that makes the military instrument relevant. The distinction between deterring the USSR and assuring the flow of oil is not always as clear as it may appear to some.[1]

Western interests are by their nature more difficult to pursue. It is harder to stabilize a region undergoing multiple crises with many regional antagonisms than it is to accentuate and to seek to benefit from them. It is harder to support orderly change without risking either open-ended support of existing regimes than it is to flirt with opposition elements (as a hedge) and hence hasten the shift. It is inherently risky to attempt to assist in fine-tuning social change so as to conserve interests but to accommodate 'reasonable' demands. Mass democracies are rarely equipped with the means to calibrate and subtly sustain that involvement over time whilst eschewing dependence on simple panaceas, be they military–technical fixes or isolationist impulses.[2]

Nevertheless there remains, as asserted earlier, scope for influence. The maintenance of a military balance in the region is a precondition for other forms of influence – it must be credible, relevant and disposable in a timely fashion. The US is unique as the only outside power able at once to deter the Soviet Union and to bring about a Middle East settlement. Nevertheless it is generally recognized that the military instrument can be sufficiently obtrusive to weaken the regime it is

---

1   See Leonard Binder, 'Iran', *Current History*, January 1980.

2   Another set of opposites to be avoided is the alternation between the beliefs that either telescoped, compressed democracy, or the reinforcement of traditional structures, will bring stability to the region.

designed to protect. Yet the reassurance which it provides should not become a license whereby the local powers' concerns come to drive the suppliers' policies. It is also true that a Western policy that concentrates only on 'access to oil' or 'denial of the USSR', invites failure with the populace of the region. An equitable bargain across a much broader agenda needs to be struck for the establishment of more durable relations.

The range of security problems in the Gulf: actual and potential

Although the priorities and vulnerabilities of the local and outside powers to specific threats may differ, the gap between their perceptions of these threats has narrowed. Whereas in the past decade 'local' threats would have been considered a responsibility of the regional powers, this may no longer be the case in the 1980s. The revolution in Iran has at once weakened the basis for a regional response and intensified the threats to Gulf stability. As a result Saudi Arabia (in particular) has become most important for Western interests yet has been weakened at the same time. The critical importance of Saudi stability and the narrower tolerance for (further) disruption has concentrated attention on Saudi security. Although many of the threats to Saudi security could properly be considered local and internal, because of that country's military weakness there is now a clear recognition that outside power assistance may be needed even in meeting some of these low-level threats. The question is how can this be done without weakening the state that is being protected? Because of the extreme dependency of Western states on Gulf oil and hence their interest in stability and access to the region, in an era of uncertainty even the smallest tremors have the potential for escalation into confrontation between the two blocs. This much closer coupling between regional conflicts and global competition is inevitable in an arena where the interests of the two blocs increasingly overlap and where no indigenous 'buffers' yet exist capable of substantially decoupling local from global disturbance.

There is nevertheless no automaticity about this connection; dependence may argue for it but policy decisions still have to be taken. The contrast between Iran's revolution and the probable Western reaction to a coup in Saudi Arabia demonstrates a 'learning process' at work. It also highlights the fact that there is no exact 'fit' between Western notions of 'threats' and those of the indigenous states.

For the latter, threats to regime stability are at least as important as threats to national security. In a state such as Saudi Arabia the two would be considered identical — as indeed the name of the country implies. In all the states the counter-elite or opposition are considered a primary potential threat. Where in this context the maintenance of regime power is the objective, for the *outside* power the assurance of stability which allows the uninterrupted supply of oil is the primary consideration. At least theoretically the outside power may prefer to accept a regime change as a means of preserving its major interest. In the Iranian revolution the West's acquiescence in the change of regime did little to reassure the other monarchical oil producers about their indispensability under similar circumstances.

From these differences in priority and emphasis — on the maintenance of power for the one, and on the continued flow of oil for the other — stem different approaches to conflict management.

1   Starting from the domestic sources of threat, security as defined by the littoral states starts with regime security. Factionalism and divisions within the ruling elite (whether Royal family or Revolutionary Command Council) are urgent matters. For outside powers a principal concern is that a change in leadership will result in differing policies (for example, over oil production) or shifts in orientation.

2   A second threat to security arises in the possibility of political strife such as military coups and revolutions. In the Middle East, coups not revolutions have been the norm. This has meant a continuity in institutions and administrative structures with replacement occurring at the top — usually without much disruption. Revolutions on the Iranian model — or prolonged unrest — threaten not just the loss of an ally but the prolonged loss of oil.

3   In most states the ruling elite do not represent the entire population, and national integration is not far advanced. Ethnic or linguistic minorities, sectarian schisms, and large numbers of foreign immigrants give these states the appearance of a mosaic. Overlapping populations also constitute potential problems as cores for secessionist movements, or as objects of political *irredenta* by neighbouring states, or as sources of domestic opposition.

4   Given the inadequate assimilation of most minorities and the prevalence of existing sources of tension between neighbours, the next category of security threats is external aggression. These are rarely clear-cut and often interact with domestic vulnerabilities. For example assistance by a neighbouring state to armed dissidents within a country (Iraq in Iran; Iran in Iraq; the PDRY in Dhofar) may constitute an unfriendly act, but is it the source or instigator of these dissidents?

The line between internal dissidence and external support (aggression) will be difficult to pinpoint with precision. The provision of arms, sanctuary and diplomatic support still falls short of actual armed aggression. *Irredenta* if periodically revived but not physically pursued (as in Iraq's past claims to Kuwait) are illustrative of a source of tension and threat falling short of actual armed aggression.

A clearer distinction exists between two types of aggression, (a) regional — by a state within the area (such as Iraq or the PDRY), or (b) extra-regional by a state from outside (perhaps Cuba or Libya). These are more clearly identifiable when the aggression is overt. When limited to training and advisory functions, it becomes equally difficult to weigh.

Overlapping the concretely identifiable sources of threat to the security of the region (such as coups, fragmentation and external aggression) are more diffuse sources of instability — rapid, disruptive and unequal growth, radicalism, crises of legitimacy and identity.

Few of the sources of instability and of threat to Gulf security will be susceptible to easy categorization. Internal vulnerabilities and external alignments and opportunities will interact and mutually reinforce each other. Threats will not come clearly and conveniently labelled. The important consideration will have to be what contribution the outside power can make to meeting it. The list below is an attempt to match threats to *appropriate* response from external actors.

Categories of contingency and the range of superpower instruments

Coups, revolutions, domestic unrest:	prior warning; intelligence; political adaptation; accommodation; pre-emption; arms; coup reversal.
Civil Wars; secessionist movements:	Conciliation; recognition or non-; agreement on non-intervention; arms; sanctuary; transport; intervention.
Inter-state conflicts (neighbours):	arms supply/cut-off; tactical intelligence; deterrence of outside intervention; conciliation; good offices; provision of peacekeeping forces.
Extra-regional power involvement:	Military-naval presence; provision of transport; advisers; arms; rapid deployment force; nuclear deterrence.

The outside powers and regional instability

It is by no means clear that the outside powers have similar interests in the Gulf region. On the contrary, differences exist in their degree of dependence on the region (and hence in their interest in its stability) and the range of instruments for influence at their disposal. The following discussion will first emphasize the issues from the Western perspective, that is with the assumption that orderly change is a goal sought by the outside power, followed by that of the USSR.

First it is necessary to identify again a range of contingencies, political and military which the outside power may be called upon to influence:

1   Coups, internal unrest, revolution, secessionist movements, civil war, subversion.
2   Inter-state conflict, local or regional.
3   Superpower intervention.

As already noted none of these are likely to be clearcut. In the first two categories there may be varying degrees of foreign involvement, instigation, and exploitation. The upshot of such crises could be a reversal in policy in a (friendly) oil producing country leading to a shift in its alignment and interruption in the flow of its oil. Specific military threats could involve its oil installations or access to the Gulf itself in the Straits of Hormuz. In terms of East—West competition the threats identified could take various forms:

1   Accession to power of an anti-Western regime (either supportive of, or supported by the USSR), with an alliance of convenience with the USSR.
2   Subversive support for internal dissidents, secessionists or revolutionary groups.
3   Aggression by a pro-Soviet regime (or client) such as the PDRY.
4   Outright intimidation, aggression or invasion by the USSR.

The instruments for meeting these contingencies though limited are by no means negligible. The constraints on them are pronounced and require identification to point to the need for a variegated and multi-faceted policy to address them. The constraints would appear to be:

1   The fluidity of politics in the region. The US cannot guarantee the *status quo*. It cannot stop shifts in alignment. As a resolute, powerful and dependable ally it can increase its attractiveness as a partner. It can defuse the pressures that may encourage defections from its camp (for example, over Palestine).
2   The intractability of many contingencies to clear-cut labelling or to the neat application of influence. US military power is no

119

panacea against threats of subversion. In some cases it may invite them.

In both these cases the value of the Western commitment must be seen to outweigh its costs. This means it must be credible and it must address the needs and priorities of the regional state. This need has two components: *relevance* to the military threats they face, and *appropriateness* to the political environment in which they exist. In brief, Western military power (and policy) must be capable of defending these states without at the same time undermining them. This requires, for example, a Western policy with respect to Palestine in tune with the aspirations of the moderate Arab states. This would insulate them from the pressures of inter-Arab politics that otherwise make a pro-Western connection a political liability.

There are three further constraints:

3   The fluidity of regional politics and the intractability of many regional problems to clear-cut solutions has tended in the past to encourage approaches to regional security which are formal. In part this is due to the technical necessities of military supply, access and rapid deployment. In practice such pressure tends to exacerbate regional political differences, and increase polarization by inviting states to make the USSR (rather than Israel) the priority issue.[1]

4   A further constraint is the very ambiguity of the military instrument in the Persian Gulf. Is it intended to reassure the oil-producing states and to deter attacks on them or to warn them against certain policies ('blackmail', etc.)? The US has specifically declined to rule the latter possibility out. As a two-edged sword ambiguity is useful to the West but it does tend to add to the disquiet of the local states.[2]

5   Finally, practical political-military necessities are an obstacle to the exercise of influence. To be effective the military instrument has to be either in place or able to respond rapidly to sudden threats. Without an extremely rapid response[3] the outside power may be met by a *fait accompli*. The current ability of the US to match the USSR in air and sea lift into the Gulf region in a timely fashion to influence events on the ground early is in

1   See the discussion of regional security below.

2   The possibility that facilities granted to the US might be used for purposes other than defending the Gulf or oil is highlighted by Washington's use of Oman (to that state's embarrassment) to mount the abortive Tabas mission to free US hostages in April 1980.

3   The premium on rapid response, for deployment on warning, also raises the risks of false alarms. Interventions triggered by false claims may politically undermine the protected state, exposing it as a 'puppet'.

some doubt. Yet attempts to improve this capability by a presence within the region runs into the reluctance of the Gulf states to accept the political risks entailed.

The constraints on the exercise of influence in the region should not obscure the fact that these constraints are only partly immutable and that they exist for both superpowers (though not necessarily equally). As stated at the outset, a necessary (but not sufficient) condition for influence is military power, and without it an outside power is likely to be a spectator. Military power affects the perceptions and the policies of regional and external powers. It affects their calculations of the balance of risks to be run in supporting or opposing that power. And it affects the incentives and choices of regional state. It is therefore a precondition for other measures that will stabilize the region. The military power must be real rather than theoretical. It must be relevant to the most plausible threats faced by the regional states, it must be flexible and it must be dependable. If it is all of these, the costs of association with it will rarely be higher than its gains.

Defining conflict management in the broadest terms it may be useful to divide it into three categories: (a) prevention, (b) containment, and (c) settlement.

Prevention

1   This includes the *deterrence* of aggression, whether by a regional state or a superpower, and the maintenance of a *regional balance of power* (through arms, training, advisers). It also includes *reassurance* of regional allies, through a policy of steadfastness, a military presence through occasional naval deployments, joint exercises, and diplomatic support.
2   In addition, outside powers can help by *forestalling* political strains by the provision of advice or political intelligence to preempt pressures likely to weaken friendly regimes, by the encouragement of adaptable political institutions and safety valves, and by assistance in anticipating assassinations or terrorism.
3   Third, outside powers can undertake the amelioration (or nonexacerbation) of political pressures on the regimes. This would include, for example, efforts to settle the Palestinian issue as a means of *defusing* it as a contributory tension and as an instrument used against the pro-Western regimes. It would also include paying careful attention to the longer-run implications of indiscriminate commercialism for Saudi Arabia's security and willingness to forego pressure on Saudi Arabia to increase oil production in recognition of the political exposure it entails for

the Kingdom. Being sensitive to measures which increase Oman's isolation from her neighbours is another example. In the same category would come the avoidance of sudden withdrawal of support or fluctuations in policy that leave the regional partner politically exposed and unprepared.

Containment

This includes a willingness to defend and, if need be, to reverse unwelcome developments and to limit their consequences. It could include, for example, a guarantee of territorial integrity, protection of specific areas (such as oil installations), the provision of air defence or minesweepers, the reversal of a coup, and assistance in counter-insurgency.

Settlement

This may include the freezing of conflicts as opposed to their settlement, through the maintenance of a stable regional balance. The specific contributions of outside powers tend to be limited but they can, for example, seek reciprocal restraints, provide compromise solutions, offer good offices or a channel of communications and assist in setting up an international peacekeeping force. The most important contribution of the outside power is in providing the setting where peaceful settlement is possible. This involves the entire range of activities discussed under these three headings.

The Rapid Deployment Force (RDF)

A dawning recognition of the importance of military power in influencing Gulf politics saw Washington quicken its plans for a quick-reaction force in 1979. If the revolution in Iran suggested that instabilities were primarily internal in origin, the invasion of Afghanistan underscored the interaction between domestic instabilities and external power exploitation. In combination the two events undermined the US military position in the region. The former removed a potentially strong buffer with the USSR and replaced it with a state veering between disintegration and the active export of revolution to the Gulf. In either form Iran became an active force for destabilization of the Gulf. The invasion of Afghanistan, in turn, as it becomes permanent, opens up a variety of means for the extension of Soviet influence and perhaps power into the region. Finally the revival of a border conflict between the YAR and PDRY which threatened Saudi Arabia in March 1979 had the unmistakable appearance of Soviet probing of Western responses. It has already become clear that the US might indeed be called upon to defend one local state against another. The means available to do this effectively are being fashioned as the RDF is accelerated. The reasoning behind it was that contingencies in the Persian Gulf (and elsewhere) might require the rapid deployment of US military power. Related to the need for military means to react to crises was an awareness of the political importance of military power — for reassurance, for deterrence, as a symbol of commitment and as a means of defence (whether of US interests or of friendly states). This reflected the necessity after Iran's upheaval (and the end of reliance on regional states for regional order) of a more direct US role in the region to shore up the regional balance of power, which could now be upset by even the smallest infusion of force. Disagreement nonetheless persists as to the best method by which the US could at once shore up its friends and influence events in the region without further destabilizing it. On the need for greater military capability and for a better and quicker air and sealift capability there is no real dispute. Similarly on the need for more over-the-horizon presence there is little disagreement.

Accordingly in mid-1979 the US MIDEASTFOR stationed in Bahrain was augmented by the addition of two destroyers (from three ships to five) and naval deployments into the Indian Ocean were increased (from occasional to permanent). A decision was made to increase port visits and to 'show the flag' in friendly states more regularly. Consideration was given to the creation of a new Middle Eastern Command integrating the land-sea-air components of US military power in the region. A consensus also existed on the need for continued arms supplies — both as a means of strengthening local states and as a demonstration of the importance attached to them by the US. The possibility of joint exercises and contingency planning with local states was also mooted although it was clear that publicity could jeopardize this type of co-operation. There was also substantial agreement on the need to preposition equipment close to the zone (in floating stockpiles or on the territory of friendly states) and to build up the necessary means for transporting material in bulk over long distances with minimum dependence on permission from other states *en route* for refuelling (the CX cargo plane is seen as the answer to this problem). Access agreements for the use of facilities in four states close to the Persian Gulf had been completed by early 1981.

Generally speaking there was no basic divergence on the need for a quick-reaction force, on what that force should comprise, on the urgency for it, and even on the necessity for some agreement with states *en route* to the Gulf for air-staging and access rights in emergencies. Differences emerged, however, on whether this type of capability, which would not be ready until the mid- to late-1980s, would be enough. Those sceptical about alternatives argued strongly against any attempt to negotiate agreements with local states that would permit the stationing of a skeletal staff of US personnel on their territory. Three arguments were used, two of them serious. Firstly, that such agreements would be regionally disruptive, would undermine the host government politically and expose it to criticism while depicting the US as aggressive. Secondly, that these facilities would be useless against Soviet political penetration and internal unrest, which were primarily political problems. Finally, that the creation of such capabilities would generate incentives for their use and make for unnecessary interventions. The proponents of an RDF plus a military presence in the region started from an assumption that military power could demonstrate US interest, reassure allies and deter disruptors of regional order. They accepted the political sensitivity of the question of a US presence in the region but argued that the military balance of power affected the policies of local states and that, by maintaining a credible and resolute commitment, the US could 'redistribute the risks' affecting the calculations of the local states.[1] They saw a need for an obtrusive or local presence and argued that a tacit, informal but visibly capable ground force was essential for sustaining Western (and local) interests. In this view a naval over-the-horizon presence was doubly inadequate in the same way as the RDF was inadequate. Not only could it not affect events early enough to be meaningful but its very merit as a flexible tool in crises made it a less effective instrument than ground forces as a symbol of commitment.[2] A basic assumption of this school was that crises were likely to erupt quickly, giving outside powers little warning or reaction time. Unless it had the means to respond quickly — before the other power — it would face a *fait accompli* and risk a choice between escalation and acquiescence. Given the geopolitics of the region and Soviet access to the airspace of the countries to its south, the USSR's reaction time would be far less than that of the US if the latter started from the continental US or Western Europe. Over short distances (below 1,000 miles) Soviet airlift was superior to that of the US. To match the Soviet ability to project power quickly into the region it was therefore imperative to set up the local infrastructure. This was essential not only technically but to serve notice on US friends that Washington was serious about their defence.

---

1 See especially Albert Wohlstetter, 'Half wars and half policies in the Persian Gulf' in Scott Thompson (ed.), *National Security in the 1980s: From Weakness to Strength*, Institute for Contemporary Studies, San Francisco, 1980.

2 See Barry Blechman and Stephen Kaplan (eds), *Force Without War: US Armed Forces as a Political Instrument* (Washington, DC: Brookings Institution), 1978, had noted this in their studies of the post-war use of force.

A distinction should be made between policies before, during and subsequent to crises. The first would encompass a range of actions intended to prevent the exacerbation of (imminent) local problems, or to anticipate, warn and forestall them. The second would be intended to contain, limit and freeze actual crises by addressing their causes subsequently.

The types of crises have already been identified. It is evident that, in the range of factors tending toward the destabilization of societies undergoing rapid change, the military instrument is limited but not useless. The greater the obtrusive presence of the superpower in the domestic affairs of a state, the greater its identification with the prevailing regime and, if Iran is an indicator, the greater the difficulties caused for the regime thereby. But this is not immutable. Superpowers' reputations are not static. A breakthrough on the Arab—Israel question or clear signs of commitment could change American reputation in the Arab world. The superpowers' role in conflict management may nonetheless be ambiguous. The extension of a security assurance may deter external aggression but it may also embolden the protected party to resist settlement on any but its own terms. The superpower connection, by transforming the stakes of local disputes, may make them more resistant to solution by quiet diplomacy. An overt superpower presence or connection — whether in military bases or through formal alliance ('pacts') — may exacerbate regional tensions (for Saudi Arabia for example) rather than contribute to their reduction. However it may also deter aggression. It is evident, given the range of security problems, that the superpowers' role is one that is complementary to other structures for assuring security.

Some domestic threats in the region cannot be met efficiently by outside powers[1] unless an external element is identified (or manufactured, as in the case of USSR/Afghanistan) but they can be forestalled by intelligence co-operation.

Clear or even cloudy regional threats are different. Aggression by the PDRY in February—March 1979 was met by a strong US response, including arms deliveries and naval deployments. This prompt response served notice as to the limits of US tolerance and warned the USSR of the probable consequences of its continuation. In this setting, the USSR exercised corresponding pressure for restraint on the PDRY. However, the diplomatic defusion of the conflict came through a regional security structure (the Arab League) and through the efforts of

---

1 Partly because a rapid coup in Kuwait would be difficult to prevent. If it were to be reversed it would have to be by a regional not an outside power. A coup in Saudi Arabia though would require an outside power if it were to be reversed.

Syria, Iraq and Kuwait.

In cases of a major inter-state conflict or large-scale aggression, the infrastructure for a military response by superpowers needs to be in place. For example, an Iraqi attack on Saudi Arabia would require a prompt US response. Hence the Rapid Deployment Force with its attendant problems. But this is not an appropriate instrument for lesser contingencies.

The military assistance instrument has already been noted. Here it is only necessary to repeat that the provision of arms for the attainment of influence and to enable the recipient to achieve a measure of self-reliance is a lengthy process with indeterminate results, which is nonetheless essential for the bilateral relationship.

In the case of arms supply, perhaps one can identify an area of potential compromise and harmonization of policies between the super-powers but, in a period of distrust and uncertainty, this is a chimera as regards practical politics. The arms supplier relationship is central to the diplomacy of both superpowers and especially the USSR. Agreement on restraint in this area will come only when the risks of direct confrontation become stark to the suppliers. However, if the Arab—Israeli case is any indicator, even here restraint and caution will compete unfavourably with the impulse for political advantage.

Soviet interests and policy

As Soviet interests in the Persian Gulf have increased, so have its political and military means of influence in the region. A growing and expansive definition of its security interests (given substance by Eastern Europe's probable incipient dependence on the region's oil), has been strengthened by a military capacity for rapid intervention and the consolidation of a Soviet political presence on the periphery of the Gulf — in Ethiopia, in South Yemen and now in Afghanistan. A permanent presence in the latter country broadens its strategic options and means for exerting pressure on the Gulf states and reinforces the perception of cumulative setbacks for the West in the eyes of the regional states.

Though by no means the primary source of day-to-day influence, the Soviet military relationship with the states on the Gulf periphery has grown. Treaties of Friendship (and Defence Co-operation) now exist with Ethiopia, the PDRY, Afghanistan and Iraq. In the first three states, Soviet power is strongly ensconced and the host state is more dependent and less able to expel Soviet advisers, unlike Egypt and Somalia. At the same time the USSR has since 1979 wooed the YAR back into a military aid relationship and arrested its movement toward the West. Capitalizing on Saudi Arabia's anxiety since the revolution in Iran, the USSR has concluded an agreement allowing it the use of Saudi airspace for its 'Aeroflot' civil aircraft — in practice for its transport and surveillance aircraft. A mixture of threat (military presence and hostile radio propaganda) and reassurance (an alternation between criticism and flattery) is designed to gain changes in the foreign policy alignment of these states. At the same time the USSR has exerted pressure on the Gulf states to oppose Oman's proposal for co-operation on regional security matters, and has been critical of the RDF, underscoring its potential use as an instrument for pressuring them on their oil and Middle East policies. By intensifying regional pressures against the West and by playing on their anxieties regarding the credibility of the West as an ally, the USSR has increased its own relevance as a factor to be reckoned with.

A good example of Soviet capacity for exploiting regional politics is that of the American hostages held in Iran. At the outset Moscow supported the Iranian action but was sensitive to the possibility that, if too overt, this support might jeopardize détente with the US. After December 1979 this inhibition was shed. Iran's position became 'understandable', and the Embassy 'a nest of spies'. The US was accused of using the episode as a pretext for using force and intervention. The US military build-up, it was argued, jeopardized European interests and threatened the entire Gulf. Moscow pointed out that the implication for the Gulf states was clear — the US would not condone their 'independence', and US military forces were designed to intimidate them and to prevent, through intervention, 'unfavourable social changes'.[1] Moscow contrasted US threats against the revolution with its own support for it. A specific feature of Soviet policy in this crisis was the support extended to the most radical elements within Iran and the discrediting of those in favour of ending the impasse through compromise. By radicalizing Iranian politics, the USSR sought to widen the rift with the US and, after the application of economic sanctions, to pose as the saviour of the revolution. Soviet policies in this episode precisely reflected a mixture of insecurity and expansionism so prevalent in its attitude toward events in the region. At once fearful that the hostage issue could serve as a pretext for US intervention in Iran, and that its resolution could serve to normalize ties between Tehran and Washington, Moscow sought to prevent any settlement while blaming the US for its hostility toward the revolution.

1 *Pravda*, February 1980.

Soviet assets and vulnerabilities

In contrast to the West, the USSR is less dependent on the region's resources for its economic well-being, or on the stability which this requires. It is also better equipped with the instruments for covert political—military operations in this region than is the West. These asymmetries are by no means decisive but they reinforce the prospects for Soviet influence. The primary Soviet interest is to attain sufficient influence in the region to ensure sensitivity to its own security needs. Ideally this would involve denial of the region to the West but, at least in the first instance, it requires a diminution of Western influence (and presence). A secondary interest which is growing daily is in access to the region's petroleum supplies for itself and for its East European allies. A third interest might be to use petroleum politics to split the alliance and put pressure on OECD states. Theoretically the second interest could entail a stake in an orderly region for normal commercial relations. More likely, however, given the high cost of OPEC oil, the Soviet bloc's limited hard currency reserves, and the alternative markets available to the producer states, it will entail an attempt to use political—military influence to gain oil on preferential terms — whether for barter agreements or discounted prices. In this essentially 'colonial' approach to the region's resources, the USSR will dispose of numerous assets.

1   It has relevant power and the means to ensure that regimes stay in power, and to threaten them with mischief-making and instability if they are 'unhelpful'. Vulnerabilities in the Kurdish areas or in Saudi Arabia's Eastern province serve as reminders of this.
2   It has a major means of influence through the provision of arms (a sector of her economy which is relatively efficient).
3   It can apply pressure in many ways — through communist parties, secessionist groups and through covert operations.
4   It has political and military staying power, a willingness to invest, hedge, and to persist in the quest for influence, despite setbacks.
5   It has shown a (new) marked preference for satellites over more independent clients and hence a willingness to consolidate control over states.

The USSR is a beneficiary of anti-Western sentiments. Cultural backlashes or reactions to an obtrusive presence, to the extent that they weaken the West, assist the USSR. Political alienation of regional states by the West's policies in, for example, Israel, serve the same function, creating the basis for an alliance as in Iraq. Finally in a region in which the *status quo* regimes are identified with the West, those elements opposed to it look to the USSR. In a region witnessing rapid change this is a not inconsiderable asset.

Against these are arrayed a number of liabilities:

1 The USSR is an atheistic regime in a region where religion is not solely personal or spiritual in connotation.
2 Soviet power and proximity cause unease among even its tactical supporters.
3 The Soviet Union is not an attractive partner as a supplier of technology, in a region where states can afford to choose what they purchase.
4 The Soviet tendency to hedge its bets by supporting several states – often in competition with one another (Iraq–Syria; Iran–Iraq) – and its refusal to choose between them, has limited its appeal as a dependable ally.
5 The USSR has shown itself to be of only marginal relevance to the Palestine issue.

On balance Soviet interests have been pursued relentlessly but with reference to the risks involved. In the Iran–Iraq hostilities of the 1969–75, and in the Dhofar insurgency between 1973 and 1975, Soviet investments were limited and its policy was averse to risk. With the growth of its military power, its incipient oil dependency and the disarray in the West after the upheaval in Iran, Soviet probing increased. With the revolution in Iran and the invasion of Afghanistan, the prospects for the extension of Soviet influence have improved but so too has the prospect of military confrontation with the West which has reacted with sudden alarm. The resultant deterioration in East–West relations in 1980 (which was aggravated by the US diplomats-held-as-hostages issue) has raised the spectre of inadvertent conflict through uncontrolled escalation or miscalculation. In this setting, with the growth of Soviet influence and the volatility of the West's reaction, the risks have grown. The incentives for superpower management of conflicts in this arena – in which both have stakes – have risen proportionately. The Iran–Iraq war thus demonstrated a willingness on the part of the superpowers to forego opportunities for gaining influence through greater involvement. Admittedly the political context in this case was mixed and not conducive to a clear polarization between the superpowers, yet their restraint was due in part at least to the risks of competitive involvement and escalation.

Superpower relations and conflict management

The superpowers are more directly involved in regional politics because of their growing interests, yet this involvement has not been matched by any sustained experience of interaction in this area. No tacit agreements on the scope and legitimacy of their respective positions has been reached. Without any such tacit agreement, or experience of crisis management (as in the Arab—Israeli zone), the attendant risks of confrontation and miscalculation are high — particularly given the nature of the stakes and the volatility of the political environment. The state of the superpowers' overall relationship clearly conditions the scope and nature of their policies in particular regions. When the co-operative dimension is dominant, it affects the incentives for risk-taking in specific areas. When the competitive element prevails, the potential gains in particular regions may look more attractive than the overall relationship. The superpower relationship also affects the regional political context. Extreme superpower competition tends to focus pressures on the local states to stand up and be counted and accentuates pressures toward regional polarization. This may have the effect of either freezing regional disputes or imbuing them with much greater importance, thereby transforming them from a local to a global stake and into a test of power and resolve.

When superpower relations are characterized by muted competition, regional priorities emerge with cross-currents that militate against polarization. Issues are damped down and become significant in terms that can be contained with fewer risks.

The current situation

Politics in the Persian Gulf today are especially volatile and fluid with the local states looking afresh at their alignments. The Iranian revolution and the invasion of Afghanistan have changed the balance of power in the region against the West. The new Iranian regime now acts as an additional and major source of disruption and insecurity in the region. This has had the effect of modifying past orientations and in bringing together the secular Ba'athist Iraqi Republic and the Kingdom of Saudi Arabia. With intensified and growing superpower competition throughout South-West Asia (and continued arms supplies reflecting this interest), the prospect of an unregulated superpower competition subject to fewer constraints and seen in zero-sum terms, has encouraged most of the littoral states to seek security by loosening links with either bloc and by emphasizing their independence. Thus, as the risks of superpower confrontation have risen, so have the incentives for the littoral states to lie low and call down a plague on either side. Differences still exist among the Arab littoral states but they have been reduced. Iraq is now more conscious of the Soviet threat which has moved nearer and which may increase if Iran disintegrates or its clerics stumble. At the same time US credibility has shrunk to a new low in the Gulf as a result of the cumulative impact of the upheaval in Iran, the 'loss' of Afghanistan and the debacle in Tabas over the hostages. If the Soviet threat has increased, the attractiveness of the US as a countervailing power has not correspondingly increased.

Even if developments in the region have so far been adverse to the West, from the point of view of the superpowers the risks in this new era are apparent. Intensified competition in an uncharted area where interests intersect and no learning process has been undergone, threatens inadvertent war or conflict through miscalculation as much as offering the prospect of unilateral advantage. It is still too soon to see what course superpower relations will take but a summary of the choices is merited.

Unregulated competition. This characterizes the current situation in the region and its periphery where the stakes are high, tensions in the overall relationship feed into assessments of policies within the region, and the politics of the region are volatile and sufficiently murky to provide few indicators as to the origin of specific events. In this context each has a stake in the region itself, one (or both) see a means of weakening the other (by denial or by exploiting and redirecting events), and the region is not only the stake but the symbol of a wider value. There is no agreement on 'legitimate interests' and each sees the other as aggressive. No regional buffers exist to insulate or moderate this competition. After several crises the seriousness of the situation may dispose the superpowers to work out some ground-rules. Alternatively the region may continue as the focus of competition with consequent militarization and pressures for alignment.

Regulated competition. A prerequisite to the identification of rules governing competition will be the need to agree on a definition of stability. Current Soviet policy does not see support for revolutions or national liberation wars as incompatible with détente. It argues that repression breeds revolution, that people must be free to choose, and that détente was never intended to consecrate the *status quo*. Whether this attitude toward change and its exploitation can be reconciled with Western views of the necessity of restraint by outside powers in regional affairs seems doubtful. A common interest in a specific access area such as in the 'Free Transit'[1] of ships through the International Straits of Hormuz has resulted in co-operation between the two blocs at the Law

---

1   or 'Straits Passage'.

of the Sea Conferences. But asymmetrical interests, dependencies, and hence opportunities for extending influence, block other avenues of co-operation. For example the fundamentally misconceived notion of Naval Arms Limitation Talks (NALT) in the Indian Ocean overlooked both these asymmetries and the proximity of the region to Soviet land-based airpower which would be unchecked if US carrier-based aircraft were limited.[1] Superpower agreement on limiting arms supplies to the region, potentially a common interest, is unlikely to be effective even if agreed as the oil-rich states can choose their supplier. Nevertheless a situation could arise when even the prospect of unilateral gain *vis-à-vis* the other superpower comes to appear less attractive. This could come about not only if there is a heightened risk of conflict but also if one or both come to see that there is nothing to gain by unregulated competition and that they may lose ground to third parties (Europe, China, or the regional states themselves).

Towards co-management?

The incentives for an accommodation between the superpowers over the Persian Gulf involving tacit recognition of their mutual interests could gradually develop. In theory their interests overlap as each shares an interest in avoiding war through loss of control, and in maintaining its influence in, and preserving access to, the region. OPEC could to some extent be seen as a common adversary. To eliminate the risk of manipulation by local states and to minimize uncertainty about each other's reactions in crises, the prospect of a tacit superpower agreement may in future look more appealing. If détente were to be revived and given substance, the Persian Gulf, where interests overlap, could serve as an important test-case for restraint and for negotiations. Co-management is not of course the only possibility. One can imagine in abstract varying degrees of superpower co-operation and involvement varying from a 'hands-off' agreement to a partition arrangement embodied in a formal division of spheres of influence and working as a condominium. An agreement on reciprocal abstention from the region appears at present less likely than its opposite, but the movement toward an intermediate formula such as co-management appears more likely than either.

The arguments in favour of co-management and especially of Western acceptance of the USSR's 'legitimate interests' in the Gulf region, are

---

1 See Richard Haass, 'Naval Arms Limitation in the Indian Ocean', *Survival* XX, no.2, March–April 1978, pp. 50-8. For background see Joel Larus, 'The End of Naval Détente in the Indian Ocean', *The World Today*, April 1980, pp. 126-32.

seductive. Essentially they revolve around several propositions:

1 That the Soviet Union (and Eastern bloc) have equal interests in the Gulf that must be accepted by the West.
2 That formal acknowledgement of these interests by the West in its security policies in the Gulf will elicit a 'responsible' Soviet policy, whereas attempts at its 'exclusion' through unilateralism will encourage Moscow to play the 'spoiler'.
3 That the current Western policy in respect to the Gulf is doomed to failure. This is so both because of Soviet geographical advantages in power projection and the intrinsic limitations of military force as an instrument of influence in a region of political instability.

Many in the West who make these arguments are not persuaded that Soviet partnership in the region has been truly sought. They believe that the region's problems do not emanate solely or even principally from Soviet activities. Furthermore they do not believe that the 'militarization' of Western policy is a useful or necessary response to issues relating to Gulf security.[1] Others, who are convinced both of the nature of the Soviet threat and the utility of military force, argue for co-management from the allegedly 'realistic' grounds that some parts of the Gulf are militarily indefensible[2] and need to be conceded, the better to defend more vital areas. An underlying assumption of these varied views is that the current Western military build-up is costly and either counterproductive or useless, and that there exists an independent path to Gulf security (seemingly divorced from the military balance) namely a 'diplomatic' solution. The most prominent exponent of this is Selig Harrison who has argued that anxiety about its security was the primary motive for the Soviet invasion of Afghanistan. To allay these anxieties and to facilitate the withdrawal of Soviet troops, he argues for the permanent neutralization of Iran, Pakistan and Afghanistan.[3] He appears to recognize that in this context 'neutralization' would be tantamount to conceding predominant Soviet influence in all three countries, but finds this acceptable.

Still another stream of thought in favour of co-management originates in Europe and prefers this route to the assurance of

---

1 For a discussion of this and citations see my 'US Security Interests in the Persian Gulf in the 1980s', *Daedalus*, (Fall 1980).

2 For example, Northern Iran.

3 Selig Harrison, *Foreign Policy*, no.41, 'Exit through Finland'. Harrison earlier argued that it was Iran's attempts to reduce Afghan dependence on the USSR that prompted the Soviet invasion, see 'After the Afghan Coup: Nightmare in Baluchistan', *Foreign Policy*, no.32, 1978, and *New York Times*, 22 December 1980.

unimpeded oil supplies, primarily because it foresees no security conceivably resulting from an open-ended competition. In this view European powers have as much to fear from a reckless and precipitate military response by the United States as from Soviet expansionism. Here co-management is interpreted not as a superpower arrangement — which is sometimes labelled as a 'Yalta'[1] — but by a more general formula involving European consumers and possibly producers.

The various arguments adduced in favour of 'co-management' (specifically those regulating superpower competition) often tend to be propounded as an alternative to a policy that seeks to restore the military balance in the region. As an inexpensive short-cut to meeting the security needs of the region, co-management is rarely seen in perspective. It is not, for example, asked how a meaningful arrangement between the blocs is to be enforced in the absence of a military balance, or how 'restraint' is to be interpreted when the Soviet Union insists on the right to assist revolutionary forces. Furthermore the notion that the US and USSR have overlapping interests is very far removed from accepting that they have identical interests. The West's dependency on the region is much more acute than that of the Eastern bloc and its involvement in the region has the weight of historical experience. The USSR is a newcomer to Gulf politics, its interests in the region are of recent standing and remain general and diffuse. Acquiescence in the Soviet claim to having 'legitimate interests' in the region would be in itself a considerable concession. Creeping expansionism and extension of claims, though rarely spectacular, require a consistent and predictable Western response if they are to be deterred. The inexorable Soviet push for political predominance in this region, a historic fact accelerated of late, will not be contained when co-management is mooted in the West as a serious solution to the problem of the West's vulnerability. Co-management formulae are only likely to be realistic options where superpower relations are more co-operative and where their overall interests can be defined more compatibly.

To be sure it is in periods of strain that such arrangements are at their most appealing. Spheres of influence would reduce the prospect for confrontation in states that are currently contested and (it is argued) clearly draw the lines of political predominance for both blocs. This would reduce the chance of inadvertent hostilities through the

---

1 M. Jacques Chirac in September 1980 specifically alluded to the need to ensure that there was not 'another Yalta' while proposing that the USSR be excluded from any arrangement to guarantee navigation through the Straits of Hormuz. For the Soviet response see the article in *Sovetskaya Rossiya* as broadcast by Tass, 3 October, in SWB SU/6540/C/2, 4 October 1980, and *The Financial Times*, 4 October 1980.

escalation of local conflicts, and lend to relations an element of predictability. An informal arrangement could not determine oil prices or production policies or prevent shifts in domestic politics leading to a shift in orientations (though these too could be met by a formal condominium or partition of the region), but even so it could reduce even if it could not eliminate regional tensions.

Whether the attractions of predictability weigh equally heavily with the two superpowers is not clear. The extremity of Western vulnerability and the instability of the region combine to make a Western interest in predictability understandable. The Soviet Union, however, may count these as opportunities for exploitation. The risks of unlimited competition which may provide the USSR with an incentive for seeking predictability have not hitherto been self-evident. To be influential on Soviet policy, these risks must be tangible, credible and communicated unmistakably. This requires not only an enhanced presence and improved military capabilities, but also a consistency of practice which will arrest both the erosion in the credibility of American resolve and the decline of its military instrument so evident in recent years.

The search for a regulation of competition between the superpowers must continue but without illusions that the military balance can be divorced from it. Similarly the very process of seeking regulation must be handled with sensitivity by the United States if it is not to create problems with its partners. Conflict-management and co-management may be manipulated by the USSR as a means for weakening the Western alliance. Any hint of a US–USSR condominium in the Gulf would send the West's local partners scurrying to Moscow for protection, and would reinforce tendencies in Europe to seek to mediate between the two superpowers. The risks of 'co-management' need to be assessed as clearly as the risks of less regulated competition.

Soviet proposals for a 'collective solution'

More likely than a formal arrangement is the continuation of the pattern of probing and response which over time may make clear to both sides the limit of its competitor's tolerance. The loss of control over even regional conflicts by the superpowers was made strikingly clear by the Iran–Iraq war which erupted in September 1980. Due to its special circumstances (notably the virtual reversal in alignments by the two regional states which still depended on their original patrons for military supplies), the superpowers had no clear incentive to support either side. The first Gulf war thus elicited a tacitly restrained response from the two superpowers who, aware of the risks involved in these uncharted waters, consulted and agreed to refrain from supplying arms. It was notable, however, how each superpower saw the other as better placed to benefit from the war. The United States feared (a) an Iraqi victory which could fragment Iran and drive it into Soviet arms, (b) an Iranian victory with Soviet support that destabilized the Gulf, and (c) lacking diplomatic relations with either combatant, a negotiated settlement on the lines of Tashkent in 1966 managed by the USSR. Soviet worst case perceptions were a mirror image. They feared (a) an Iranian victory which owed nothing to the USSR but depended on US-supplied arms, (b) an Iraqi victory which consolidated Baghdad's anti-Soviet position without affecting Iran's orientation, and (c) a stalemate or settlement in which the USSR was exposed as conservative, risk-averse and unreliable as an ally.

Despite these mutual fears, the agreement held. There was no evidence of significant or direct supply of arms by the superpowers to the belligerents. The USSR, however, saw in the continued deployments of Western naval vessels in the region, and in the dispatch of four US AWACs early warning aircraft to Saudi Arabia, an example of the United States' search for pretexts to justify its 'militarization' of the region.

Since the invasion of Afghanistan the USSR has sought to underline its own interest in a political settlement of the contentious issues centred in South-West Asia. In so doing it has not departed from the basic principles it first enunciated in its Asian Security formula of 1969 which was elaborated upon in the course of the subsequent decade. Nevertheless, in the light of newly enunciated 'Carter Doctrine' of January 1980 which reserved for the US the right to respond with force if necessary to threats in the Persian Gulf which it claimed as a 'vital interest', there was clearly a need for a reiteration of the Soviet position. This was prominently put forward twice in 1980 — in the Portugalov proposal of February and the Brezhnev proposal of December. In between came various commentaries which elaborated upon the Soviet approach.

The Portugalov proposal was essentially an elaboration of a speech made a week earlier (22 February) by Brezhnev in Moscow. It made four points:[1]

1   It emphasized the risks of instability in the Gulf region which made it a 'powder keg' liable to explode as a result of intervention and miscalculation.

1   The full text of Nikolay Portugalov's commentary was carried by Tass, 29 February, in SU/6360/C/1, 3 March 1980. For comments see Le Monde, 3 March 1980; The Sunday Times, 2 March 1980; The Christian Science Monitor, 15 April 1980.

2   It noted that the European states were more dependent on Gulf oil than the US.
3   It affirmed the Soviet Union's own interest 'in the security of oil supply routes in the Persian Gulf area'.
4   It proposed an 'All-European conference on Energy' [comprising the membership of the Helsinki agreements] to discuss guarantees of:
    (a)   The security of the oil supply routes;
    (b)   Equal commercial access for all countries;
    (c)   The territorial integrity of and independence of the producer states.

In time the European context would be expanded into a United Nations framework.

The proposal was evidently framed as a response to the Carter Doctrine. It contrasted its own peaceful approach to 'American militarism'. It also sought to appeal to European anxieties about superpower relations after Afghanistan. It acknowledged the Europeans' interest in Gulf oil (while affirming its own) and offered a 'diplomatic track' to guarantee it. Lest there should be any misunderstandings, the USSR repeatedly asserted that the concentration of US forces in the Gulf area was 'a direct threat to the southern parts of the Soviet Union'.[1] In May 1980, the Warsaw Pact returned to the theme of guaranteeing the sea-routes in the context of their demilitarization making reference *inter alia* to the Persian Gulf. Brezhnev repeated this theme when acting as host to the Ethiopian president in October.[2]

In December, while visiting New Delhi, Brezhnev elaborated upon the Soviet approach in a five-point proposal aimed at guaranteeing military non-intervention in the Gulf area. Both the timing and the formulation of the proposal were shrewd, coming just before a scheduled non-aligned meeting in India whose members formally supported the idea of a 'peace zone' in the Indian Ocean. Its principal components were an agreement by the great powers to neutralize the region, to:

1   Foreswear military 'bases' in the Gulf area or adjacent islands.
2   Renounce the deployment of nuclear weapons in the region.
3   Abstain from the threat or use of force against states in the area or from interference in their internal affairs.

---

1   For example, the Soviet Ambassador in Paris, Stephan Chervonenko repeated this theme while seeking to accentuate the differences within NATO. See *International Herald Tribune*, 17 April 1980.

2   Declaration of the Warsaw Pact Members' Consultative Committee, 15 May. See *Le Monde*, 29 October 1980.

4   Forego any attempt to draw the Gulf states into 'military group-
     ings'.
5   Pledge non-interference within states or in the use of the sealanes
     linking the states of the area with other countries.[1]

In practical terms the 'peace proposal' sought to inhibit Western
means of naval deployment and regional security arrangements while
leaving unconstrained Soviet land-based power nearby. Soviet commentaries made it plain that the proposal was essentially propagandistic by
contrasting the United States military approach with its own more
reasonable one. The Soviet proposal was portrayed as a 'barrier against
US aggression' while Washington's policy was dedicated to grabbing oil,
shoring up reactionary regimes, dictating economic subservience and
fighting national liberation forces.[2] Precisely how demilitarization and
neutralization of the 'area' could guarantee Western interests while the
Soviet Union remained in the immediate vicinity remained pointedly
unclear. Equally important the Soviet proposal sought to widen the gap
between European and American responses to the task of securing
access to oil by playing on doubts in some quarters of the wisdom of
Washington's leadership. Representative of such tactics is a report by
Anatoliy Gromyko on Brezhnev's proposal which argues that 'the
[United States'] policy of militarization of the Indian Ocean and
Persian Gulf area creates for the Western European powers and Japan
real difficulties on the path of developing broad economic links with
the countries of the region'.[3]

The Soviet appeal for a 'collective solution' found a welcome echo
among those who remained sceptical about the utility of military power
in securing access to the Gulf and those analysts anxious to allay Soviet

1   For references to the proposal made on 10 December, *International Herald Tribune*,
    11 December, 12 December. For reactions, press and governmental, see *The Times*,
    12 December 1980; *The Guardian*, 12 December 1980; *Le Monde*, 13 December 1980; *The
    Economist*, 13 December 1980. Contrast the press reactions of *The Observer*, 14 December
    1980 with *The Daily Telegraph*, 12 December 1980. No Gulf state welcomed the proposal
    and a number like Oman, Iran and Saudi Arabia were in varying degrees critical of it.

2   For a representative sample containing these themes consult *Radio Moscow*, 12 December,
    in SU/6601/A4/1, 15 December; Dmitry Volsky, 'Time will not Wait', *New Times*, 51. (80).
    Pavel Demchenko, 'The Persian Gulf can become a zone of Peace', *Pravda*, 2 January 1981,
    Tass 2, 3 January 1981 in SWB SU/6614/A4/1, 5 January 1981; Vikentcy Matreyev,
    Izvestiya (commentary), 18 January in Moscow, 18 January SWB SU/6628/A4/1,
    21 January 1981. Vladimir Kudryavtsev, *Izvestiya* (commentary), 22 January in Moscow,
    22 January in SWB SU/6632/C2/3, 26 January 1981 and Dmitry Volsky, 'Harder to Build
    than to Destroy', *New Times* 2.(81), pp. 5-7.

3   Report of an article by Anatoliy Gromyko, Director of the African Institute of the USSR
    Academy of Sciences in *Izvestiya* excerpted by Tass, 12 January in SWB SU/6624/A4/3,
    16 January 1981.

security anxieties in their bordering regions. This appeal is likely to grow because, with future instabilities in the region inevitable, Moscow will be keen both to point out its capacity for disruptive behaviour and the price of its restraint. Implicitly (the USSR may argue) with so much indigenous instability would it not make sense to come to an arrangement? Indeed it may condition its good behaviour on joint management — a possibility evidently feared in Washington during the Gulf War.[1] The risks of entering into such an arrangement (rather than agreeing to consult and concert informally during crises) may well be higher for the West given the existing balance of military power.

The role of other outside powers

Extra-regional power

The political problems associated with a superpower presence in the form of 'bases', military advisers, and the like have already been elaborated upon. For Saudi Arabia, for example, an American presence to guarantee its security may be counterproductive, attracting nationalist agitation and focusing attention on Riyadh's ties with a government supportive of Israel. It may well be of little practical use in dealing with many security threats. Less disruptive and liable to provoke a counter-reaction by the other bloc, a contribution by European states to regional security is also less politically troublesome because of the European position on the Palestine question. Furthermore, unlike the United States, some European states are able to react militarily to murky situations without loud and anguished debates and selective leaking of information. France's assistance in meeting the Mecca disturbances of November 1979 and her past activities in Africa bear testimony to this. In addition, her proximity in Djibouti with some 6,000 troops provides her with a flexible instrument for meeting lesser contingencies quickly. The development of co-operation between Saudi Arabia and France in the internal security field over the past two years is ample testimony to Saudi recognition of this important role.[2]

Parallel to this has been a Saudi keenness to diversify the source of its armaments. France has agreed to supply a large part of the Saudi Navy. Germany in 1981 has been sounded out about a possible sale of

---

1 See James Reston's report, *International Herald Tribune*, 25 September 1980.

2 The potential role of Taiwan and South Korea in assisting Saudi Arabia in the maintenance of internal security should also be mentioned. Well-organized and motivated, both states maintain good ties with Riyadh and could provide discreet assistance when necessary.

Leopard II tanks. Although reluctant to embark on large-scale arms exports, the Federal Republic has played a distinctive role in regional security in the economic area. It has disbursed large-scale grants and loans to Turkey and Pakistan with the aim of contributing to the social–economic underpinnings of security.

Britain's contribution to Gulf security has also continued to be low-key. It retains particularly close ties with the smaller Arab states of the Gulf where its relationship has historical sanction. It has on secondment or on contract some 800 military personnel in Oman assisting in the maintenance of security in that state. It has discreetly encouraged co-operation among the sheikhdoms under the umbrella of Saudi Arabia and furthered the cause of a regional security arrangement.

From the point of view of the Western Alliance, too, this division of labour in which the allies, according to their respective strengths, assist in the maintenance of security, makes eminent sense. The European contribution provides a 'third-choice', an intermediate connection which is less polarizing than that of either superpower. The informal co-ordination of policies toward the region thus protects both the regional state and the outside powers' interests. A naval presence in the Gulf of Oman exclusively made up of US ships during the Iran–Iraq war would have been less effective as a symbol of Western concern about the security of the flow of oil than was the inter-allied contribution including elements from France, the UK and Australia. The dangers of *loose* co-ordination reside in the temptation among individual allies to improve their bargaining position *vis-à-vis* the regional state by departing from alliance positions and offering greater concessions in exchange for preferential agreements (for example by 'recognizing the PLO' in return for guaranteed oil supplies). This danger can be exaggerated but it is worth emphasizing that allied policies can contribute to Gulf security in a healthy decentralized way only if they are parallel and not competitive.

Regional power

Less obtrusive than even the Europeans are other Muslim or Arab states which could contribute to Gulf security. Jordan is the pre-eminent example of a state which has long assisted the Gulf sheikhdoms in military training and with the dispatch of military advisers. Economically less well-off than its oil-rich neighbours, there is reason to expect a growing role in this area for Jordan's security forces. Although not quite as well placed, Pakistan has the Muslim connection to recommend it in addition to considerable experience in providing military assistance to the Gulf sheikhdoms. It too could find the economic incentives of such assistance tempting. In the past year there have been repeated rumours of an agreement between Pakistan and Saudi Arabia whereby the former would provide a military contingent (numbers vary from 600 to 10,000) to act as a form of 'Swiss-Guard' for the Saudi Royal Family.[1] In addition they could, as mercenaries, check disloyal elements within the National Guard and provide oil installation security. Although repeatedly denied, there is no gainsaying the logic of such an arrangement which would provide Pakistan in turn with much needed cash.

There may also be roles for other regional states outside the Gulf. Egypt has offered to assist the Arab states in the event of Iranian aggression and to provide the West with facilities for access to the region for its defence.   If relations between the Gulf states and Egypt improve this may become an additional form of security assurance.

The scope and limits of conflict management

The superpowers

The Iranian revolution ended any prospect of exclusive or primary reliance on regional states for assuring the security of the area. The indirect role of the outside powers was jettisoned and followed by more intensified involvement. But this had the potential of polarizing the region, exacerbating internal and intra-Arab problems and triggering counter-reactions by the other superpower. Much of the recent tension in the Gulf is due to the over-hasty US response to a situation which — in a broad sense — was susceptible to anticipation. Under the Carter administration, false assumptions and erroneous distinctions bred transitory comfort, followed by ingenuous alarm.

The role of the superpowers in conflict management is primarily to deter one another. This deterrence must cover a broad spectrum from direct aggression through to covert and indirect exploitation of regional vulnerabilities. The West's difficulties in achieving this have already been noted by reference to the debate concerning the merits of presence-on-the-ground versus over-the-horizon, the trip-wire versus the rapid early projection of power. Just as important is the recognition by the West that distinctions between 'outside' and domestic threats may obfuscate problems. The Carter doctrine referred to 'outside' threats

---

1   See *New York Times*, 20 August 1980; *The Economist*, 13 September 1980; *Washington Star*, 10 December 1980; *International Herald Tribune*, 9 February 1981.

while the dispatch of AWACs in October 1980 was designed to contain a local war.

An acknowledgement by the superpowers of each other's interests may in time be forthcoming in concrete terms but it will not in itself constitute a short-cut to conflict management. Co-management with all its attractions cannot be erected out of phase with a balance of power. Even then its effect on allies and partners will need to be gauged before it is embarked upon. More important in the short run is the need for a shared definition of what constitutes permissible behaviour by outside powers in the region. What degree of involvement under what conditions, is mutually acceptable? Is covert activity acceptable? Is the supply of arms the same as the dispatch of advisers, or the latter equatable with military formations? Because the superpowers share an interest in avoiding conflict that arises inadvertently through miscalculation and in reducing their manipulation by local governments, procedures and guidelines for reaction to crises may well evolve. Consultations on the 'hot-line' during regional conflicts are a logical starting point. Agreement, as in the Iran—Iraq war, to supply no arms during hostilities may be a principle that can be extended to future conflicts. Tacit agreement on non-interventions during civil wars or revolutions could also be agreed, provided it was clear that neither side was directly or indirectly involved in instigating these.

Agreement on such principles will be difficult however as long as Moscow believes in its right to 'protect change' that favours it, extending to them a doctrine of irreversibility and equates adverse changes with 'counter-revolution'. Without a convergence between the two superpowers on the question of change and the *status quo*, and on an appropriate code of conduct, superpower competition will evolve *ad hoc* and unregulated.

The conditions for successful conflict management by outside powers are as simple to identify as they are difficult to achieve. They require:

1 A military balance and a perception of commitment that brooks no doubt and reduces the possibility of miscalculation.
2 A recognition that the risks run through opportunistic unilateralism are greater than the rewards and that the risks include the loss of control, an open-ended commitment and the possibility of escalation, and an understanding that restraint may be mutually advantageous.
3 An agreement or understanding on a definition of respective interests.

Superpower agreement on restraint — a tacit form of conflict management — will not be a panacea. It will not reduce locally driven instabilities or end superpower competition. It will however, provide the possibility of decoupling some local conflicts (such as that between Iran and Iraq) and seek to regulate that rivalry. Nor will it be static. Local opportunities will constantly beckon. The temptation to break the Western alliance if it develops cracks may be irresistible. The price of restraint with regional allies which are anti-*status quo* may prove high (as in Egypt and Somalia). The incentives for restraint may revolve around perceptions relating to whose assets are more effective in peacetime and who time favours. Soviet restraint cannot be obtained solely by manipulating the military risks. Positive incentives will also be needed. But equally Soviet restraint and non-disruptive behaviour cannot be encouraged solely by conceding it a 'stake' in the region nor can it be divorced from an effective military balance in the region.

Regional security

There are six principal scenarios in which the flow of oil may be jeopardized:

1 The political use of the 'oil weapon', as in the producer's embargo in 1973.
2 Prolonged internal instability affecting oil production in a major producer (as with Iran in 1978).
3 Protracted inter-state conflict reducing exports in one or more states (such as happened in the Iran—Iraq war of 1980—81).
4 The control of the choke-points through which most oil exports pass.
5 Attacks on the sea lines of communication outside the Persian Gulf.
6 Invasion by a hostile outside power of one or more oil producing states.

Of the six contingencies, the first three have already occurred and are liable to recur. In these the role of the superpowers has not been primary. However it must be conceded that their future role in regional conflicts is likely to be important as in the most recent case, if only to communicate their interest in its geographical containment to areas away from other producers and the Straits of Hormuz. In the three other scenarios, which have not yet occurred, the role of the outside powers is critical. In providing for the security of navigation in the Straits and beyond, and in deterring major aggression they are essentially irreplaceable.

It is in the lesser threats to the region that hope is often placed in a regional security arrangement. This approach to conflict management should be seen not as an alternative to security arrangements with outside powers but as a complement. In the past, progress toward regional co-operation was bedevilled by a legacy of distrust and tension attributable less to any Arab—Persian differences than to differences in orientation and disparities in power. These impediments have not disappeared with the Shah, and they remain in the Iraq—Saudi relationship. Nevertheless the twin shocks of the Iranian revolution and the Soviet invasion of Afghanistan have galvanized the Arab states into greater co-operation. In meeting common threats — from Iran, from sectarian disputes, from sabotage to oil installations — the co-operation has been effective.

In addition the shared fear of intensified superpower rivalry has contributed to a growing (rhetorical) emphasis on the exclusive rights of the regional states to manage the security of the region. Apart from erecting norms to complicate the superpowers' quest for facilities in the region, this co-operation has had a substantive value. It contributed, in the case of the YAR—PDRY border war of March 1979, to a search for a regional solution. In the event of future conflicts among the smaller states this type of regional approach can be helpful in decoupling local from outside power competition. Yet it is evident, as in the Iran—Iraq war, that such co-operation will not be effective in the event of a major regional war. And, even in the events of March 1979 just cited, it was necessary (as in October 1980) to call in an outside power patron to signal its concern about the conflict.

There is no reason to expect that the maintenance of Gulf security will be a matter exclusively for outside powers or conversely solely the task of regional states. A variety of elements will be needed, comprising military and economic measures, political and institutional responses, local arrangements (formal and informal), co-operation with states situated nearby, and measures designed to buttress security through relations with European states as well as ultimate reliance upon the United States.

3 Regional Co-operation and Conflict Management

The superpowers' most obvious contribution to regional security is in deterring one another while reassuring local allies. But here the problem of asymmetrical interests and assets arises. While Western interests are served by change that is not disruptive of regional order, it is by no means clear that regional forces left to themselves will work in this direction. The West must seek to support the forces of order unobtrusively without suppressing evolutionary change. To do this, as we have seen, it is necessary both to deter outside powers and to reassure and buttress friendly regional states to enable them to meet and to adjust to the varied pressures working on them. This requires the extension of a defence commitment to the region (and especially to Saudi Arabia) that is at once credible and relevant to their needs for such time as is required for each to attain a capability for self-defence against regional threats. This may take a decade. The way in which this commitment itself is made has, however, the potential for destabilizing the recipient. This can be assisted by the USSR which argues that the Western commitment is not to the Arab peoples but to specific 'regimes' and that it is intended not to further orderly change but to suppress 'progressive forces' opposed to Israel.

Given the enormous difficulties for the outside powers in meeting the threats to regional security, and in the light of the problems associated with influencing or channelling rapid social change, it is scarcely surprising that other complementary means of bolstering regional order should be examined. Regional approaches to conflict-

145

limitation and management in particular are especially appealing in abstract. The emergence of harmony in regional politics would dampen the incentives for local conflict, reduce the opportunities for Soviet or radical exploitation, and diminish pressures on the US to assume a 'forward' position in the region's defence.

A regional security arrangement could be an important though partial solution to the problem of Gulf security. To be effective it would ideally be truly regional — in composition as well as inspiration. It would respond to common indigenous needs and in so doing address local priorities. At the present time it is difficult to envisage any but a partial arrangement emerging for Iran, preoccupied by its own problems and disruptive of regional order, cannot be involved. But the very fact of Iran's estrangement from her neighbours may provide the catalyst for greater co-operation among the Arab states.

The idea of a regional security arrangement in the Gulf is not new. Over the past decade it has been much discussed. Initially, after Britain's withdrawal, the US (and the UK) encouraged it as the primary means of meeting threats to the region. With the collapse of a pro-Western Iran and the emergence of a more pronounced Soviet threat, it became evident that a more direct Western military commitment would be necessary. A Gulf security arrangement thus became an adjunct to meet the lesser threats to the region and to provide for greater regional co-operation in general. The contribution that a regional arrangement might make to conflict-management in the Gulf has never been systematically examined. In this section I examine the general assumptions behind such an approach to conflict management — those held by the littoral states, by the US, and USSR, and those theoretically tenable. Second, I trace briefly the evolution of the various ideas involved in such an arrangement and their record over the past decade ending with an analysis of the limitations and potential of this approach to conflict management in the Gulf.

Assumptions

The local states

Though Gulf politics have been characterized by division, tension and distrust for much of the period since 1969, a sense of common interests has not been totally absent. This has been due to cross-cutting interests which have until recently prohibited polarization on Iran—Arab, or Republican—Monarchical lines.[1] Even during military hostilities co-

---

1 See S. Chubin, 'International Politics of the Persian Gulf', *British Journal of International Studies*, October 1976, pp. 216-30.

operation in certain areas has been maintained.[1] The element transcending the manifold differences among these states has been the perception of shared vulnerability, of diffuse insecurity which has manifested itself in a desire for more autonomy in regard to the superpowers. Despite different alignments, a fear of loss of control has been held in common. This has translated itself into support for the general proposition of a regional security arrangement, and the assertion that regional affairs are the concern of the local powers. The containment of local disputes is essential, in this view, to avoid the intrusion of the superpowers, whose entry would polarize the region. What is viewed by the outside powers as 'decoupling' regional from global disputes is seen from the region as 'not importing global tensions'. The threat posed by the superpowers is both one of unrestrained competition *and* a bilateral accommodation: either could pose a direct threat to the regional states' interests. Competition could spark counter-reactions and serve as a flashpoint for conflict or for sustained pressures on local states for bases, preferential treatment, and public diplomatic support. On the other hand a superpower concert would diminish an already limited margin for manoeuvre. The avoidance of polarization thus has two components: no direct association or alignment with the preferred superpower; and the opening of lines of indirect communication with the other. This does not detract from reliance on a particular superpower ally for ultimate protection, but it militates against the provision of bases or signing of pacts which could facilitate such protection.[2]

In brief, the regional states assume first that limited co-operation among themselves could erect norms to inhibit and reduce the risks of intervention, and second, that the most durable means of defusing conflicts are regionally based rather than through outside power management which creates other risks.

The United States

Washington's attitude toward a regional security arrangement has undergone considerable change since 1968, in part due to developments in the region itself;[3] and in part due to a better understanding of the region. The initial response to Britain's imminent withdrawal was to

1 This was true in the 1969–75 border incidents and the war in 1980 between Iran and Iraq, in OPEC affairs.

2 This may appear somewhat speculative. In my view it explains both Saudi and Iraqi reluctance *vis-à-vis* their respective superpowers, and accounts for the move each has made to meet the other in the centre away from sole reliance.

3 These are sketched below. This section deals with the current US approach, not with how it has evolved.

look to a NATO-type pact — a proposal made by Eugene Rostow in 1968 which was never pursued. By the end of 1980, Washington's conception of a regional arrangement was more subtle.[1] It now envisaged a variety of informal and formal relationships between the Gulf states, their neighbours, the US and Europe. The diversification of ties rather than a unilateral approach and the importance attached to non-military relations is testimony to this. Thus the security framework sought was explicitly not a replica of NATO and it would entail no permanent bases. It would be multi-levelled, seeking to defuse threats to the region in the political—economic as well as the military realms. It would encourage the wealthier regional states to provide their poorer neighbours with the means to resist external subversion, and would encourage the wealthier NATO allies to do the same for the poor but important states located near the Gulf — such as Turkey. As part of a diversification of roles and the sharing of responsibility which would diminish the visibility of any one power, Washington encouraged military co-operation among the states of the region as a whole. Thus Saudi—Pakistan in co-operation, or Jordanian co-operation with the Gulf states, or Egyptian offers of assistance to Oman and the Gulf states would be tacitly encouraged.

In 1979, with the fall of the Shah, the United States' approach to regional security in the Gulf underwent a remarkable transformation in three major respects. First Washington realized that it needed a greater military capability to meet threats in the region quickly and directly. Second, it recognized that threats to the region were not necessarily all military and it therefore looked to other means to shore up the political stability of the region. Third, it understood the political limitations on a direct unilateral presence in the region and sought to encourage a diversification of roles among local and external states interested in Gulf security. None of these detracted from the necessity for a greater military capability to meet threats to the region.

The United States' attitude toward regional security has thus been favourable, though with diminishing expectations. It has encouraged co-operation among pro-Western states as beneficial for regional security. It has seen in this a means for providing security for the smaller Gulf states which is more politically palatable. In the 1970s, in line with the tenet of self-reliance, it encouraged the assumption of defence responsibilities by local states. This was less burdensome in that it allowed the West to provide the means for security (arms and training) without a direct or formal involvement. Such involvement was not, however, excluded in the event of major threats.

1 The most authoritative description was by Z. Brzezinski, 'Building a Security Framework in the Persian Gulf', speech to Canadian Club of Montreal, 5 December 1980.

After 1979 the need for greater US responsibilities for the direct defence of the region became pressing for the regional buffers, the 'twin-pillars' had collapsed. Whereas between 1969 and 1979 the regional states had been assumed to be the first line of local defence, this was no longer tenable in the 1980s. Hereafter regional security arrangements would be encouraged but without illusions. They could meet minor threats, allow the improvement of each other's defence capabilities without the attendant political costs of external powers, and facilitate the co-ordination of policies to diminish local rivalries.

The USSR

Moscow has consistently opposed the concept of a regional security agreement in the Persian Gulf. In part this may be attributed to the persistent echoes it has had of a (revived) anti-Communist military pact. Eugene Rostow's comments in 1968 and the Shah's comments in Washington in May—June 1975 lent credence to the view that it was to be a substitute for a US military presence, a surrogate arrangement directed against the USSR. More important though is the USSR's refusal to accept a 'partial' arrangement in the Gulf without integrating it into the broader proposals she had herself made, namely the Asian Security plan and Brezhnev's proposal for the neutralization of the Gulf of December 1980. What the USSR seeks to achieve by the Asian Security formula has been discussed elsewhere.[1] It has been elaborated upon in the more recent five-point proposals. One of these is quite explicit in its provisions, namely that major powers should not try to draw Gulf states into 'military groupings'. This prohibition does not apparently refer solely to formal arrangements between local and outside powers. If Soviet declarations are indicative, it extends to regional arrangements among pro-Western states or bilateral co-operation between local states. Thus the Soviet Union has been exceedingly critical of military co-operation between Saudi Arabia and Pakistan, seeing in it a link in the 'structure of regional security', as part of a 'new aggressive military bloc', 'knocked together' by the US and as a substitute for the defunct CENTO.[2]

The Soviet Union has been equally critical of regional co-operation within the Gulf, which it sees as an old attempt by the US to form 'an aggressive military bloc in the Persian Gulf' to draw some of these

1 See S. Chubin, 'Soviet Policy towards Iran and the Gulf', *Adelphi Paper*, no.157, Spring 1980 (and citations therein).

2 See *inter alia*: Tass in Russian, 9 December 1980, SWB SU/6598/A4/1, 11 December 1980; Tass in English, 19 January 1981, SWB SU/6628/A4/3, 21 January 1981; and article in *Sovetskaya Rossiya*, Tass in English, 27 January 1981, in SWB SU/6634/A4/1, 28 January 1981.

states 'into the orbit of its hegemonist policy and to cause a split within the ranks of the Arab countries'.[1] Specifically this regional co-operation (it has argued) is being nurtured by Washington into a mutual security pact directed against the 'national liberation movement'. It has thus criticized plans by the Arab states of the Gulf announced in February 1981 to intensify their co-operation on internal security matters. It sees in this anxiety about the growth of these liberation movements rather than hostility toward the West's militarization of the region. The fact that the participants in this scheme — Saudi Arabia, Kuwait, Bahrain, Qatar, Oman and the UAE — are 'military clients of Western states' has not gone unremarked.[2]

Precisely what sort of regional arrangement would be acceptable to the USSR is as yet unclear. Presumably it would depend on the precise linkage between such attempts at insulating regions from outside rivalries and the broader strategic relationship. Issues such as the nature of the relationship between local and outside powers, in terms of pacts, access to facilities, military aid relationships and 'presence', would be involved. Arrangements between pro-Western states, particularly if they have any security content, are clearly unacceptable. Though silent on Iraq's call for the exclusion of the superpowers from Gulf affairs (February 1980), it is evident that the USSR wants assurances of co-management of the region rather than 'co-exclusion'. However it is also clear that, while rhetorically opposed to any equation with the other superpower, any proposal that gives them equal rights and imposes apparently equal constraints on them is in practice acceptable. This is so for two principal reasons:

1   Soviet geographical proximity facilitates its land based power projection capabilities and lengthens the shadow of its military power in the region. This advantage encourages Soviet officials to look for constraints on naval activities that will asymmetrically inhibit the US and her allies, while appearing 'equal'.

2   The dependency of the East on stability in the Persian Gulf is not yet as acute as that of the West. Disorderly change in the region does not therefore have similar connotations for the two blocs. The prospect is that it will (at least initially) prove disruptive of Western interests and influence, sweeping aside pro-Western regimes. The consequent 'loss of control' will have a quite dif-

1   See *Pravda*, 16 December 1980 (Rafail Moseyev). See also Dmitry Volsky, 'Time will not wait', *New Times* (51), 1980, pp. 7-8.

2   See Tass in English, 31 December 1980, in SWB SU/6613/A4/3, 3 January 1981. Moscow in Arabic, 6 February 1981 in SWB SU/6644/A4/2, 9 February 1981 and Vladimir Peresada, *Pravda*, broadcast by Tass, 10 February in SWB SU/6646/A4/2, 11 February 1981.

ferent impact on the two blocs, and it is for this reason that there exists a gap in the incentives of the two blocs to seek stability in the region.

The Soviet Union's attitude toward a regional security arrangement has certainly been consistent. During the Shah's day it sought with some success to frighten the Arab states with Iran's ultimate designs in seeking a collective security arrangement. Now it depicts Arab attempts at co-operation as an aggressive pact aimed *inter alia* at the overthrow of the Iranian Islamic Republic.[1] Since a primary aim of a regional arrangement is co-operation to maintain the stability of the region, Soviet support can only be expected when it is convinced that such stability is indeed in its interests.

The evolution of regional co-operation

The period prior to the UK's actual withdrawal from the Gulf (December 1971) was marked by increased contacts among the Gulf states and across the shores of the Gulf — in many cases the first contacts between sovereign states. In the Gulf sheikhdoms, Britain left behind security organizations to assist the governments, and Jordanian officers seconded to their armies remained in place. Iran and Saudi Arabia, encouraged by the West, improved their contacts, increased their military appropriations and succeeded in somewhat reducing mutual antipathies. Iran's offer in 1968 of formal military co-operation with the Gulf states was rebuffed. So too was Iraq's proposal in July 1970 for an 'Arab defence organization' but informal progress in concerting policies was achieved. There was general agreement that the peace of the area could best be achieved through regional means, and that co-ordination among local states could reduce the opportunities for external power intervention. There was a general willingness not to pursue territorial claims, even if these were not entirely dropped. Among the Arab states, Saudi Arabia played a leadership role while Iraq remained isolated and in conflict with Iran. It was under Saudi auspices that meetings were held in 1973 and 1974 to discuss co-ordinated action against subversion and the possibilities of joint defence.[2] Practical measures discussed included a plan for Kuwait to use airfields in Bahrain, Saudi Arabia, and Abu Dhabi for the dispersal

---

1 See National Voice of Iran (*Baku*), 16 January 1981 in SWB ME/6626/A/2, 19 January 1981.

2 See *Financial Times*, 25 June 1973 and *The Times*, 29 November 1974.

of its air force in the event of a threat to Kuwait's military airfield.[1] A measure of tacit co-operation was evident elsewhere. In the UAE, Jordanian officers took over Britain's training role while, in Oman, British officers remained in Salalah and Masirah to assist the government meet a secessionist threat. Iran's military assistance to Oman (1972–76) in combatting the PFLOAG (Patriotic Front for the Liberation of the Arabian Gulf) despite rhetoric to the contrary, 'won the grudging approbation of the Arab states of the Gulf, Iraq excepted'.[2] Iran's and Oman's joint naval patrols of the Straits of Hormuz after 1974 were another indication of limited regional co-operation in the defence area. Saudi leadership and example succeeded in settling several border disputes among the Gulf sheikhdoms, although those between Iraq–Kuwait and Iraq–Iran persisted.

The settlement of the latter in Algiers in March 1975 opened the door for more general regional co-operation. It removed an obstacle precluding co-operation between the Arab States and Iran. It ushered in an era of relative Iraqi moderation, reflected in Baghdad's acceptance of the principle of the non-export of subversion and it was followed by a period of intensified consultations among the Gulf states. For the first time, discussions revolved around a Gulf-wide 'security structure'. In the summer of 1975 and autumn of 1976, in conferences in Jiddah and Riyadh, various approaches were examined. The July 1975 Islamic Foreign Ministers' meeting in Jiddah reiterated the principle of the exclusion of outside powers and the inadmissibility of foreign bases, coupled with an assertion of the local states' responsibility for regional security. Nevertheless there was no unanimity on how to act together to that end, multilaterally or bilaterally, and little consensus on whether to seek an integrated defence arrangement or to settle merely for improved co-ordination among existing forces. The November 1976 conference of Gulf Foreign Ministers in Muscat was specifically convened to consider this issue. Six items were discussed:

1   Limitations on foreign powers' presence in the region.
2   A guarantee of the territorial integrity of states.
3   A non-aggression pact among the states.
4   Mutual assistance against subversion and co-operation in intelligence.
5   Measures to ensure freedom of navigation.
6   A territorial division of Gulf waters and establishment of the limits of the continental shelf.

---

1   See *The Washington Post*, 17 September 17 October 1974, and James Noyes *The Clouded Lens*, Hoover Institute, 1979, pp. 41, 125.

2   See Herman Eilts, 'Security Considerations in the Persian Gulf', *International Security*, vol.5, no.2, Fall 1980, p.96.

Representative of the difficulties in achieving agreement were the differences between Iran and Iraq on the type of defence arrangement sought and on the issue of navigation. Iran sought a unified, multilateral military force under a joint command to deal with both internal and external defence needs. Iran sought also the more restrictive legal regime of 'innocent passage' to govern transit through the Hormuz Straits. Baghdad preferred informal and bilateral arrangements for defence co-operation and the more permissive concept of 'free navigation' (or 'free transit') to govern access to the Straits. These issues need not detain us except to note that these positions reflected their proponents' assets. As the most powerful state with the longest coastline, Iran's interest was in dominating any defence arrangement and policing any suspicious activities in the Straits. Iran's attempts to proclaim the Gulf a semi-enclosed sea was, correctly, seen by the Arabs as an attempt to control traffic through the Gulf.[1] Less powerful, with only a few dozen miles of coastline on the Gulf and no prospect of naval influence in the southern Gulf, Iraq's position was also understandable. Saudi Arabia refused to be drawn into these differences and Kuwait's attempts at mediation failed.

Despite this set-back, considerable progress was made in less formal settings, especially in bilateral agreements, in the field of internal security. Consultations on this resulted in 1977 in agreements between Iran and Kuwait in June, Iran and Iraq in July—August and Iran and the UAE in November. Meanwhile Saudi Arabia intensified her discussions with the smaller Arab states. This trend toward an emphasis on co-ordination of internal security measures was given further impetus in October 1977 with the assassination of the UAE Minister of State for Foreign Affairs, Said al-Ghobash. Plans to form a Gulf organization to pool intelligence information and co-ordinate measures against sabotage and terrorism, were announced on 8 May, 1978. The principal aim was to share information among Iran, Saudi Arabia, Kuwait, Bahrain, the UAE and Oman.

The fall of the Shah created new problems in the quest for a regional security arrangement. While underscoring the need to buttress security throughout the area, the Iranian revolution set off new pressures making the achievement of an area-wide arrangement well-nigh impossible. At the same time in its militant nationalism it created problems for states in the region with close ties to the United States. By posing an acute security problem for both Iraq and Saudi Arabia, it served to catalyze their co-operation. On 9 February 1979 these two states signed

---

1 See Herman Eilts, 'Security Considerations in the Persian Gulf', *International Security*, vol.5, no.2, Fall 1980, p.96.

a 'security agreement' covering co-operation on internal security and extradition.[1] In the face of the common danger, both states loosened their ties with their respective superpower partners and moved toward the centre and a non-aligned posture, thus reducing their exposure to charges of being puppets or anti-Islamic.

Despite a reluctance to offend or provoke the new regime in Iran, the Arab states continued their consultations. In July 1979 the rulers and ministers of five states (Bahrain, Qatar, Kuwait, and the UAE under Saudi leadership) pursued their discussions on greater military co-operation, at a meeting in Khamis Mushait. In September 1979 Oman, which had aligned itself closely to the Shah's policies and which now found itself facing an unpredictable but unfriendly neighbour across the Gulf, offered a proposal for the defence of the Hormuz Straits. Aimed specifically at ensuring the freedom of navigation, the Oman proposal envisaged two levels of co-operation. The first, among the littoral states, would be to raise $100 million to purchase mine-sweepers, shore-based radar and patrol boats to protect the Straits. The second, related to outside powers, envisaged a multilateral naval force drawn from US, UK and the Federal Republic of Germany to provide a presence outside of the Gulf. The plan was doomed to failure because it contravened an article of faith of the adherents of regional arrange-ments — it made explicit provision for the inclusion not the exclusion of outside powers. It was interpreted, especially by Iraq, as a Western-inspired bid for a 'bloc' to replace CENTO.

By the Autumn of 1979 it was clear that Iran's revolutionary impulse would not be confined. Large-scale Iranian naval manoeuvres in the Gulf, border clashes with Iraq, and the revival of irredentist claims to Bahrain, combined with inflammatory radio broadcasts beamed to the Gulf, testified to this. Significant Shi'a minorities in Saudi Arabia, Kuwait and Bahrain were becoming restive, while Iraq, with the largest number, came under intense pressure. The common fear of Iran, and particularly of sectarian disturbances encouraged from that quarter, drove Riyadh and Baghdad closer. For Iraq, the gradual movement away from the Soviet bloc which has been taking place since 1975, and towards 'moderation' on Israel as evidenced in the 1978—79 Baghdad conferences, reflected a drive for influence in the Arab world. Saudi acquiescence if not support was essential for the achievement of this wider influence.

For the Saudis, Iraq had become an indispensable regional ally and buffer against Iran. In October both states extended assurances of

1 See *Le Monde*, 16 March; 6 April 1979.

assistance to Bahrain in the event of an Iranian attack.[1] In response to Shi'a disturbances in Bahrain, an Arab Foreign Ministers' conference was convened in Taif. Iraq's failure to attend reflected the now standard practice of Saudi leadership of the smaller states and bilateral co-ordination between Riyadh and Baghdad. The only public announcement was a reassertion that the defence of the Gulf was the responsibility of the littoral states, but the meeting testified to a habit of consultation that was becoming ingrained.

The Soviet invasion of Afghanistan in December 1979, followed by the espousal of the Carter Doctrine the following month, asserting a US vital interest in the Gulf region, together with the hostage crisis, which had stimulated a large US naval deployment in the Gulf of Oman, all testified to the difficulty of compartmentalizing into neat packages issues of security into 'internal' and 'external'. From the Iraqi perspective, these events underscored the danger of foreign interventions which would spark competitive or parallel interventions by the adversary bloc. Iraq's proclamation of an Arab National Charter on 8 February 1980[2] was intended as a counter to the right of foreign powers to intervene. It rejected all 'foreign' military forces or bases in the area, and threatened to boycott and ostracize any Arab regime which failed to adhere to this principle. It eschewed Arab involvement in international conflicts except against Zionism, and called for total neutrality and non-alignment toward any foreign party in the event of conflict. It called for a non-aggression pact among Arab states and, implicitly, for the resolution of all territorial disputes. The specific machinery envisaged for giving substance to common security interests was reminiscent of Iran's proposals of 1976. Its preference was for a collective security agreement encompassing the Arab states. A collective Arab security force,[3] drawn from the littoral states with a joint military command which would be autonomous with an independent budget, would provide the teeth for the arrangement. Financial contributions to the force would be according to resources but manpower commitments would be equal to avoid the domination of the force by any one state. In the event that these proposals were considered too ambitious, Iraq offered a fall-back position — bilateral agreements.

The Iraqi proposal, which essentially offered a third course between alignment with either bloc, obtained the 'endorsement' of the smaller

1 *Financial Times*, 2 October 1979. Egypt also offered its services if they were needed.

2 Text in *Survival*, July/August 1980, XXII, no.4, p.178.

3 This would supplement the Arab League Joint Defence Pact.

Gulf states but elicited no comment from Saudi Arabia. It was indeed an indirect challenge to Riyadh. The convergence of the states politically did not obscure the continuing lack of trust which was in part a reflection of differences of regimes and of alignment but also of disparities in power. A tactical partnership had not yet blossomed into a confident friendship and the Iran—Iraq war of 1980—81 was unlikely to convince the Saudis of the wisdom of exchanging American protection (with all its limitations) for a still more unproven and uncertain Iraqi umbrella.

The clashes between Iran and Iraq that escalated into major conflict in September 1980 increased the solidarity among the Gulf Arab states. Indeed it is possible that Saddam Hussein gained prior Saudi approval for his attack in his unprecedented visit to the Kingdom in the summer before the war. Certainly the Gulf states supported Iraq and intensified their consultations. At the Amman Arab Heads of State meeting in November discussions took place between Saudi Arabia and the other five Arab littoral states[1] and there were indications that, in the light of the war and its possible extension and prolongation, something approaching formal defence arrangements were contemplated. Initially this might take the form of bilateral security agreements between Saudi Arabia and Kuwait, Bahrain, Qatar, the UAE and Oman. While going beyond existing agreements to co-ordinate policies and share intelligence on internal security matters, it would not be intended as a 'defence pact' in the sense of a military alliance. However it would look remarkably like one in that it would be based on the assumption that a threat to one would be a threat to all, and in that it encouraged the attainment of improved defence capabilities.[2] Subsequent meetings in Taif and Riyadh in February 1981 bore testimony to Saudi interest in accelerating the movement toward a comprehensive political—defence arrangement with the other Arab Gulf states. Under the shadow of the continuing Gulf War, the Saudis took the initiative to propose a series of far-reaching measures integrating its neighbours more closely with the Kingdom.

1   Agreement was reached on forming a Council for Gulf Co-operation to pool resources to safeguard the stability of the region.
2   An organization consisting of a Council of Gulf Heads of State and another of Foreign Ministers was to be set up, with a secretariat, for regular meetings.

1   Still excepting Iraq.

2   See especially Patrick Seale's report in *The Observer*, 30 November 1980, and the document on Gulf security printed in *The Middle East*, January 1981; *The Times*, 9 March 1981.

3 A meeting in Abu Dhabi in May announced details of an agreement to get a secretariat and increase consultations but avoided mention of defence co-operation.[1]

The aim of these measures was to improve co-operation politically, economically and in security affairs. A form of loose political confederation appears to be under consideration to increase co-ordination in foreign affairs, to rationalize and streamline economic planning and so avoid wasteful duplication or harmful competition. Means for co-ordinating and eventually unifying military capabilities are also under study. An urgent priority here is co-operation to ensure the safety of oil installations and pipelines. Finally an arrangement encompassing the security of navigation through the Hormuz Straits is reportedly under consideration but, unlike the 1979 Oman proposal, it looks only to the littoral states' participation.[2] The role of outside powers in such a regional arrangement appears to be indirect: to provide the arms and technical assistance required for its realization.

The marked acceleration of movement toward a partial regional security arrangement is directly attributable to the advent of a revolutionary regime in Iran which threatens, in different ways, the security of its Arab neighbours. The deterioration of the international political environment and of relations between the superpowers, together with a marked devaluation of the United States' security connection, has increased Saudi Arabia's incentives to look for a regional substitute. Whether this politically less burdensome path constitutes a practical alternative remains to be seen. While the Gulf War has focused the minds of the sheikhs on security and eroded their reluctance to move quickly to practical measures of co-operation, it has also (with the dispatch of US AWACs aircraft to Saudi Arabia in October) underlined that even in regional conflicts there may still be no substitute for defence links with an outside power.

The scope and limits of a regional security arrangement

As a contribution to alleviating the security problems of the Gulf states, a regional arrangement — even loosely organized and partial in its composition — has value. Agreement on the proposition that superpower involvement in the region is likely to contribute to instability is widely

1 See *International Herald Tribune*, 26, 27 May 1980.

2 The preceding analysis is based on press reports which may prove inaccurate or at least premature. Useful sources include *Le Monde*, 6 February 1979; and Patrick Seale's reports in *The Observer*, 11 January, 15 February 1981.

shared. Decoupling the Gulf's conflicts from outside power rivalries by providing a modicum of local order has been a shared objective among the littoral states. The rhetorical genuflection accorded this proposition has not been totally without value. It has erected a norm which the local states themselves are bound to consider in their own policies and demonstrated a shared interest in regime survival, an awareness of exploitable domestic political weaknesses, and the exposure and vulnerability of oil installations to sabotage and attack. Therefore it has provided the littoral states with areas of common interest on which co-operation can be built.[1]

This co-operation has taken concrete shape in the past decade in the defusion, for example, of border conflicts and in the suspension of territorial claims especially among the Arab states. Where border disputes have flared into hostilities between Arab states, such as in the YAR—PDRY clashes in March 1979 which threatened to polarize the region between East and West (and to split the consensus of the Baghdad Front), the Iraqis played a major role in producing a cease-fire.[2] Here the Gulf states took advantage of the existence of the Arab League, a forum which can be used as a complement to any institution set up in the Gulf. Vulnerability to sectarian or minority disorders which the littoral states share has led to an agreement not to exacerbate each other's problems, most notably in the Iran—Iraq Accord of 1975. Not merely in defining the impermissible, but in co-ordinating policies in the face of the common threat of Iran's claims in 1979, the Gulf states have testified to their mutual security interests. The growth of co-operation in the security area covering intelligence, extradition and protection of oilfield installations similarly assists in meeting a concern — transnational terrorism — which affects them all. Finally, the Gulf states have real incentives for a regional approach in preventing divisive competition and in co-ordinating approaches to common problems such as pollution in the Gulf or strategies of industrial development. In this respect the harmonization of policies and the more rational distribution of resources and tasks makes political sense. Economic assistance by the richer to the less endowed states (for example from Saudi Arabia to Oman and the YAR and offers to the PDRY, or by Abu Dhabi to Ras al Khaimah) serve a security function in diminishing the incentives for alliances of convenience with outside powers.

1 This excludes revolutionary Iran which sees its interests as different from those of its neighbours.

2 In conflicts which can be settled by the provision of funds, the Saudis are usually available chequebook at hand to practice crisis management.

158

Co-operation among the Gulf states in security affairs has nevertheless been spasmodic. It was slow in the period 1969–75 when Iran–Iraq rivalry and distrust of both states impeded the other littoral states' co-operation. It moved faster in the period 1975–79 when real progress was made bilaterally in the field of internal security and it has moved faster still since the fall of the Shah. Co-operation soon may extend to the harder areas of defence.

The limits to the contribution that *any* regional security arrangement is likely to make to the overall security of the Gulf are clear. It will not be able to meet external threats to the region for the foreseeable future. It will not be able to deal with major inter-state wars within the region: conflicts between Iran, Iraq and Saudi Arabia could not be covered by such an arrangement.[1] As the Iran–Iraq War shows, not merely the Gulf but other *fora* such as the Islamic Conference, the Non-Aligned group, and the Arab League are paralysed in such cases. Only a partial arrangement, excluding Iran but (perhaps) co-ordinating with Iraq, is likely to emerge in the current political context. This has its value in that the threat posed by Iran concentrates the mind wonderfully and increases the prospect of real integration among the smaller states and the suspension of petty differences. But to the extent that it is oriented *solely* against Iran, it runs the risk of institutionalizing what may otherwise be a temporary polarization.

A second set of limits are intrinsic not to any regional arrangement but to the one likely to emerge in the Gulf. With respect to Saudi Arabia and the five countries discussing tighter political integration, there should be no serious problem in achieving substantial progress. Where difficulties will arise is in the precise relationship of such a grouping with Iraq, and especially in the area of establishing a common defence force. Despite Saudi–Iraqi political convergence since 1979, serious differences remain. Disparities in military power, different emphases in foreign orientation and radically contrasting domestic structures are the realities underlying the pious platitudes of Arab solidarity prevalent today. These have hampered the growth of trust and impeded co-operation in sensitive areas such as the exchange of intelligence, which could always be misused by the recipient. If real co-operation in the defence field were sought (such as the stationing of Iraqi troops in the Kingdom, or the establishment of a joint command, with the political contamination that might ensue from fraternization), these professions of solidarity may prove empty. Alternatively, should Saudi leadership of the other Arab Gulf states advance without a

---

1 This is inherent in the disparity in power among the littoral states.

parallelism in overall policies with Baghdad, the temptations for Iraq to play the spoiler in the unity arrangements may increase. So long as Iraq and Saudi Arabia agree on the overriding threat to the region posed by Iran, and on the importance of maintaining some distance from the two blocs, Iraq—Saudi co-operation in the Gulf will survive. Differences in response to crises in the Arab world, or in approaches to Israel, may however, crack whatever unity has been achieved in the Gulf, with the possible deterioration leading to a three-way split in the Gulf.

4 The Scope, Limits and Conditions of Influence

Arms transfer and influence

Western interests in the Persian Gulf include the traditional components of its denial to the USSR and securing access to the region but to these is added a dependency on the region's oil supplies that imparts to this interest a special dimension. The policies of regional governments and their attitude towards the West become extremely important. To cement a durable bond between the regional states and the West, a mutually advantageous bargain has had to be struck. This has entailed the exchange of oil at reasonable prices and levels of production, in return for assurances regarding security, the provision of technology, and a market for investments. By its very nature this compact is unequal; the commodities and services exchanged are not quantifiable or commensurable. Moreover the relationship is distorted: Western (and especially US) security assurances to Saudi Arabia are vague and hardly cast in concrete. By their very nature the threats to Saudi security are not easily susceptible to military guarantees. Furthermore the relationship with the Western superpower brings with it many problems for the Saudis — identification with the disruptive West (for the traditionalists) and support for the Zionists' ally (for the militant Left) — which give rise to problems both within Saudi Arabia and in the arena of Arab politics.

Western interests nonetheless dictate the cultivation of friendship with the major oil producing states. As we have seen, this has taken concrete form in various projects and particularly in arms sales and military modernization programmes. A narrow focus on arms transfers as a tool for supplier manipulation or leverage is mistaken. But, as one dimension of a broader relationship, the sensitive use of the arms supply component remains important for its symbolic aspect as well as for its practical military utility in the event of inter-state war. The question of the influence conferred by the transfer of arms was examined in depth in the first part of this study but it is worth summarizing the conclusions at this point.

For the supplier state the provision of arms holds several potential benefits: (a) it may serve as an entrée into the recipient's society and provide a key channel for influence; (b) it may serve as a visible symbol of its commitment to the recipient, act as a deterrent, and substitute for its own military involvement by bolstering a regional balance of power; (c) it may serve as a *quid pro quo* in the bilateral relationship creating an entangling dependency for the recipient and binding it closely to the supplier; and (d) it may provide a means for conflict management by restraining the recipient from certain actions and making it dependent on the supplier for new stocks.

Supplier influence derives in the first instance from the relevance of the supply of arms to the major security threats faced by the recipient and to the value attached to these arms by it. But the arms supplied are scarcely divorced from their political context. Influence is derived not from an arms relationship but from a *political* relationship, one tangible manifestation of which may be the supply of arms. This has important implications for the potential for supplier influence. The supplier is as much entangled as the recipient in a situation where arms are the product of a political relationship. For if arms are withheld or denied the political relationship will suffer, hurting both states. As a result of this deterioration, the arms tie will also inevitably be affected. A related issue is the degree to which the supplier can manipulate the arms relationship for influence in other areas. It would appear most difficult in the cases examined to document this. The arms supplied have largely been the reflection of shared interests (for example in the maintenance of a regional balance). Why this parallelism of interest should generate influence for the supplier (by threatening to renege on it) is not clear. In cases where arms are provided not as a 'favour' but for specific purposes, it is not self-evident that a refusal to furnish weapons would strengthen the supplier's influence. On the contrary it would suggest a redefinition of its interest and the recipient would draw the appropriate conclusions therefrom. A further complication surrounding supplier influence is the distinction between dependence and influence. The translation from a state of recipient dependency to one of supplier influence is by no means simple or inevitable. It is at least partially determined by the recipient's range of choice and his (subjective) response to this state of dependency. The record suggests that arms are more effective as inducements in relations than as coercive levers.[1] The Soviet Union has gained little influence from manipulating Iraq's arms supplies, and the US experience before and after Iran's revolution strengthens the proposition. No cases can be found where positions have been adopted (or changed) as a result of (explicit) pressure. More often positions taken can be plausibly explained by a parallelism of policy.

The conditions for maximal supplier influence are therefore:

1 If the recipient has overriding dependence on the supplier for arms and security and faces an imminent security threat.
2 If the recipient state has few options due to regional isolation, inadequate resources, or the absence of alternative suppliers.
3 If the recipient state is united both as to the priority of the security threat and on the appropriate response to it.

The relevance of arms to security requirements naturally affects the influence of the supplier. Where there is an overwhelming or imminent security threat, the value of this component of the relationship increases dramatically. Saudi insecurity regarding the PDRY lends special urgency to its military modernization programme, and the importance to it of the US connection. In Iran, where the US connection itself was a target of hostility, influence became impossible but that situation is not permanent. The perception of an aggressive neighbour or a malign proximate superpower could do much to revive Iran's traditional policy of seeking countervailing power from more distant states. An impending security problem might then well revive interest in Iran in a military connection with Europe and, in the short-run anyway, with the US. The durability of influence depends on the resilience of the political relationship. This requires: (a) a common 'language' (similar strategic perception and common values); (b) institutionalized, broad-based ties which can absorb differences of view and divergences; and (c) a sense that the alternatives for one or both parties are worse.

A related consideration is the weight of the two partners. It may well be the case that the most desirable relations are those involving near-equal or very markedly unequal partners. The oil-rich Gulf states are at neither extreme. Sensitive and insecure, they are acutely vulnerable to

---

1 Cf. Thomas R. Wheelock, 'Arms for Israel: the Limits of Leverage', *International Security*, vol.3, no.2, Fall 1978.

changes in political atmosphere and shifts in tone and nuance. For them the symbolic dimensions of the relationship assume great importance. Reassurance and 'hand-holding' are substantive issues. The denial of advanced aircraft to one but not to another state is seen as a political signal. The political implications of denial, or even delay, are greatly amplified in this setting and reverberate throughout the region. Because they are endowed with potent symbolism, arms are risky to manipulate and even more risky to deny. The desire to decide arms sales on 'specific evaluations of their concrete political and military contexts'[1] is understandable but these decisions cannot be divorced from either their domestic political setting or the overall relationship. When denial is a rebuff and a rejection, and supply is taken to mean approval and support, this reduces the ability of the supplier to manipulate the flow of supplies without risking the impairment of relations.

The utility of arms as a source of influence is further constrained in the following circumstances:

1   When they are no longer relevant to the major problems facing the recipient, as in a period of peacetime, or when arms supplied are marginal to defence capability.
2   When the risks associated with continued supply (or to adapting to the suppliers' pressure) are deemed to be higher than the alternatives (as in Iran after the revolution or in Iraq in 1980–81).
3   If the supplier is as equally entangled as the recipient in that he cannot refuse arms requests without disrupting relations.
4   If the recipient state's leadership is divided in its attitude toward the supplier, pressure may be counterproductive for supplier influence.
5   If the arms are the principal tie divorced from an overall relationship, or simply a commercial proposition, they will generate little influence for the supplier (as, perhaps, with the USSR in Iraq after 1975).

Supplier influence is also limited by considerations unrelated to the recipient. For example the supplier's interest in avoiding a regional arms race or provoking the other superpower may influence his policies. The supplier may also be unwilling to choose unequivocally or definitively between his regional partner and another (competing) regional state, thus setting limits on his influence with his partner.

1   Barry Blechman, *New York Times*, 2 April 1980.

Arms transfers are potentially more effective as levers in conflict than in peacetime. Experience in the Arab—Israeli Wars suggested that, while suppliers cannot prevent conflict, they can control its scope and duration and influence the mode and terms of its termination. This influence derived from the intensity of the conflict and the rapid need for extensive resupply which could be met only by the superpowers. In the Iran—Iraq War the intensity of the hostilities has not been such as to necessitate immediate reliance on the supplier. By limiting or severing supplies, the outside powers have prevented any major escalation of conflict — but even here personnel and other limitations have been equally operative as a constraint. Certainly it was the imbalance of arms in the region, in part a result of the strain in Iran—US relations, that furnished the conditions for the initiation of the conflict by Iraq. It is generally true that the supplier's influence will increase if (a) the protagonists decide to pursue the conflict as a priority and (b) if the war intensifies, requiring major resupply of the belligerents' inventories. While the supply of arms does not guarantee a continuing source of supplier influence, it does furnish the recipient with an incentive to maintain workable relations, unless that country is prepared to accept the consequences of a breakdown in relations. Iran in 1980—81 is illustrative of the proposition that advanced weapons require constant attention and maintenance, skills which recipients generally lack and can only attain gradually. Refusing to acknowledge its continuing need for the United States as a supplier has entailed high political and military costs. Iran in 1980—81 bears striking testimony less to the vulnerability of supplier influence than to the costs to the recipient of seeking to evade it.

The USSR and Iraq

Studies that focus predominantly on influence relationships in terms of access and leverage tend to ignore variations in the condition of the recipient. This is clearly illustrated in USSR—Iraq relations. Concentration on a range of variables would illustrate the more fluctuating and evolving context in which the supplier—recipient relationship takes place. These variables include:

1 The imminence of the security threat(s).
2 The degree of domestic support (unity, discord).
3 The capacity to otherwise defuse problems.

The latter in turn may be divided into component parts:

(a) Resources: alternative suppliers or means.
(b) Regional environment: the quality of relations with neighbours and the capacity to forge other alliances.

(c) Flexibility: the ability to adjust priorities tactically and to be nimble in the face of multiple challenges.

A focus on these factors would underscore the fact that 'influence', when identifiable, ebbs and flows, varying with many factors other than the supplier—recipient relationship itself.

Iraq's relationship with the USSR has been a function of the degree to which its interests (and priorities) have converged with those of Moscow, and of its capacity to achieve them elsewhere or by other means. The primary goal of Iraqi leadership has been regime security. In the initial period (1958—73), Iraq's alternatives were limited. Her ideology made the West largely unacceptable, her resources limited her choices and the imminence of problems (with the Kurds, Israel, Iran and Western oil companies) gave her little leeway.

In the second phase, (1974 to date) regime survival and independence were still the priorities but pragmatism and money made new choices possible. The willingness to assign priorities and to limit the multiple sources of insecurity, facilitated a reduced reliance. As the Soviet and Communist threat was seen to increase, a willingness to compromise on regional politics became evident. Emphasis on the Gulf replaced militance on Palestine and relations became less subject to doctrinal preferences. Domestically, while communists were suppressed, attempts at compromise with Kurds and Shi'a muslims were pursued and national elections were held in mid-1980. Iraq's aspiration to the role of defender of the Gulf's Arabism was not new but, in its anti-Soviet manifestation, it reflected a new component.

Seen from Soviet perspective, Iraq's evolution since 1974 must be testimony to the inherent unpredictability of ties with the Third World. As it has grown richer Iraq has become more independent and assertive, pursuing policies regionally divergent from the USSR and so posing for the USSR the usual dilemma — to deny arms or to maintain supplies (with caution) in the hope that things will improve?[1] Apart from the parallelism on policy with respect to certain areas (Palestine), Soviet arms have not generated anything resembling tangible or enduring influence. Strategic access has been limited and is unlikely to last in the light of Soviet policy during the 1980—81 War.

Iraq's current positions run counter to those of the USSR. Iraq is co-operating with conservatives in the Gulf, diverting energy away from

---

1 This may be illustrative of the proposition that 'gains in influence may be an illusory goal but anticipation of losses of influence is more compelling'. See the brilliant article by Richard Betts, 'The Tragicomedy of Arms Trade Control', *International Security*, vol.5, no.1, Summer 1980, fn.38.

Palestine, is at odds with Syria, and has suppressed Iraq's Communist Party. In some respects Iraq's continued dependency on the USSR for arms for the immediate future guarantees an Iraqi unwillingness to sever ties completely. This enables the USSR to cultivate the other power, Iran, which is intrinsically more important as a neighbour with a long coastline on the Gulf. Iran offers better opportunities also for domestic penetration and, in its anti-Westernism, it is more congenial. Its importance for an Afghanistan 'settlement' is an additional asset. As the War continues to sputter it is conceivable that there will arrive a moment of truth for the combatants, necessitating resupplies or a ceasefire. The Soviet Union's involvement on a small scale on both sides may enable it to retrieve some influence at that time.

The US and Iran

The United States' initial involvement in Iran after the Second World War was military. By the 1960s the relationship had expanded to encompass other areas, but the military aspect remained a symbol of US 'responsiveness' toward a friendly state. By the 1970s arms transfers were expected to increase as an element in the Nixon Doctrine. With Iran they indicated a US commitment and served, it was assumed, as an alternative to a direct involvement. The arms transfer relationship took on some of the attributes of a treaty relationship.

American expectations about the benefits of arms transfers as such can be exaggerated. The relationship developed on the assumption of a continuing overlap of interests. It was recognized that, in the 1970s, the relationship would be more equal, based often on unstated *quid pro quos*. The responsiveness of the US was considered important by the Iranian government and Iran's influence in the region could in turn be helpful to the US. It was assumed that the arms supplier would retain a measure of influence over the actual use of the arms supplied, particularly in an intense conflict[1] occurring before the arms were assimilated or stocks had built up. Finally the arms supplied to Iran were seen primarily in their regional and above all in their Soviet context. Foreign not domestic contingencies were seen as the appropriate basis for evaluating decisions on transfers.

In practice the United States found itself unable to check the pace or determine the content of the arms sold to Iran. Furthermore the scale of the sales necessitated initially an increased physical presence and

---

1 See Staff Report on *Arms Sales to Iran*, US Senate, Congress Washington DC (1976).

involvement. As a policy tool, arms transfers were not easily manipulable. Withholding would be seen as a change in policy with domestic political implications far broader than a purely technical decision would normally entail. At the same time the arms transfers constituted an implied commitment. Artful attempts at semantic camouflage could not make politically real distinctions between defence involvement and defence commitment.[1] The revolution in Iran demonstrated that several criticisms of the earlier arms sales programme had been largely erroneous. There was no automaticity of involvement in conflict due to a presence. The 'hostage' theory of US military advisers was an extrapolation of the Vietnam experience and little else. The dependency of the recipient in war for functioning on a day-to-day basis was seen in 1980–81 to be a matter of degree. For full utilization of its resources this may have been true but, with cannibalization and improvization and for sub-optimal use, Iranian resources were adequate.

Over the longer term, US influence will be dependent on the level of fighting which will condition the amount and type of arms needed and the emergence of a government which sees its interests as not threatened by renewed supplies. For the United States a commitment to Iran had been antecedent to the supply of arms and the arms supplied have been the consequence not the cause of that commitment. A willingness to continue to supply arms even in a period of revolutionary upheaval represented a belief in the persistence of this interest and in the efficacy of arms sales as an instrument in achieving them. The sustained efforts by the USSR to prevent such a *rapprochement* suggests that Moscow too believes that the arms relationship, while reflecting the political temperature, also has a life of its own.

The US and Saudi Arabia

The dependence of Saudi Arabia on the US for security is great. As the salience of external security threats grows, so will that of the US connection. It has been argued that the relevance of the outside power connection is limited insofar as it relates to other sources of instability, particularly domestic. But its importance, though limited, is nonetheless real:

1 As a deterrent against militant regional states (the PDRY).
2 As reassurance for the Saudi regime in Arab politics, which provides a tacit demonstration of the US stake in Saudi Arabia.

---

1 How else to explain the shattering of US credibility with the fall of the Shah? Note for example the illusory attempts of Richard Pranger and Dale Tahtinen, *American Policy Options in Iran and the Persian Gulf*, American Enterprise Institute, Washington DC, 1979, p.22.

3   As a favoured partner in the region (for technology, etc.).

The US connection through arms, security assurances, and skilful diplomacy, is capable of assisting in reducing the pressures and defusing the conflicts unsettling Saudi security. As a supplier of technology and knowledge, the US remains an important ally.

The contribution of the outside power to the local power's needs can thus be considerable but not total. The relevance of the outside power to the priorities of the local state will be critical. This will depend on a congruence of interest and a recognition of their respective roles, as well as on the policies pursued, and the outcome of politics within each state. For example, the US and Saudi Arabia share an interest in containing radicalism in the Persian Gulf. The US role may extend to deterring military adventures by radical states whereas Saudi Arabia's may be in shoring up moderate elements within those states, tempting their leadership with financial inducements, or isolating them in Arab councils. Policies in other areas affect both the stability of the relationship and the security of the two states. A Saudi action in OPEC that did not consider the impact on the world economy would result in basic Western reappraisals. Similarly a close alignment by Washington with Israel would raise similar incentives for readjustment by the Saudi leadership. The pattern of overlapping interest and reciprocal influence underscores that the issues rarely relate to raw leverage, but to adaptability and adjustment to divergences. Hence the *quality* of the relationship is as important as the relative power of either party on a specific issue. The degree of US 'influence' is not fully comprehended by reference to the provision of specific services. For the Saudi leadership, the US remains the only acceptable choice as a security partner. While this psychological dependence breeds excessive expectations which are doomed to occasional disappointment, the choices are stark and uninviting. Nonalignment or reinsurance with militants at this stage would severely limit her freedom for independent policies.[1]

Though not a 'balanced' partnership, the Saudi leadership has few alternatives. Other postures may remove some threats but not others (and may indeed create new threats). The relationship thus needs to be flexible to allow for divergences. For the US some of the policy instruments available may aggravate local problems. For example Saudi military modernization and conscription could undermine traditional sources of support for the Saudi dynasty. Industrialization may contribute to social problems of alienation and focus hostility on the

---

1 On the other hand, it is the inhospitable regional political environment that generates pressures for the US connection. The emergence of a security alternative for coping with regional threats (e.g. Egypt/Turkey) may generate greater freedom of action *vis-à-vis* the US.

US for disrupting age-old patterns of interaction.[1] US identification with the regime may as easily undermine as buttress it.[2] Sensitivity to Saudi concerns may dictate a more activist or acquiescent US regional policy than would otherwise be the case.

For the Saudis too, the relationship with the US requires flexibility. The Kingdom cannot be identified with US initiatives which are unpopular in the Arab world, such as Camp David. Under these circumstances Saudi silence or token opposition is inevitable. The Saudis cannot afford to look like a 'regional *gendarme*' or US 'agent' and so the Saudis must often be seen to take independent decisions divergent from that of the US. Military pacts or the provision of military bases are therefore refused. An obtrusive US military presence on Saudi soil is similarly avoided.[3] The Saudis must stress also their cultural identity and strength, and their distinctiveness. As Guardians of the Holy Places, the Saudi leadership places great emphasis on the future status of Jerusalem.

In short the US—Saudi relationship has had to accommodate divergent interests and priorities while maintaining essential links. The benefits have sometimes appeared uneven. The Saudis keep oil prices down or increase production while the US fails to meet their security concerns.[4] Yet the manner in which differences are reconciled testifies to the resilience of the relationship. Issue-by-issue bargaining or linkage is eschewed; and specific questions are not elevated into make-or-break tests of the relationship (as was sometimes true under the Shah). The style of the relationship is different. Saudi leaders prefer the use of the carrot to that of the stick (as was seen in 1976 and in 1979). Displeasure is indicated subtly: a trip is cancelled, or a rumour not denied.

The durability of a relationship in which the partners 'agree to differ' depends nevertheless on the persistence of a solid core of mutual

---

1 The relevance of economic development and large-scale industrialization to the needs of the populace will have to be clearly demonstrated in the light of Iran's reaction to a 'cardboard economy'.

2 Related to this is the narrowing of US policy choices by entanglement with regimes which may, or may not, be overthrown.

3 Saudi MAAG size was reduced from 133 to 80 between February 1974 and 1978. This understates the number of US military present which was as of March 1981, some 400. Semi-official assistance through the Vinnell Corporation, the Army Corps of Engineers and British Aerospace is still large at 2,000.

4 'You're asking too much. You're asking us to produce more oil, to keep the price down and to accept your inflation. Yet you didn't help us with our political problem in the region. It's not a balanced relationship' the Saudi Finance Minister Muhammad Aba al-Khayi has said. See *The Wall Street Journal*, 11 June 1979.

170

interest. This can change as a result of shifts in political values over time or with the preferences of a new ruling elite. The most durable relationship is a broad-based one in which the fruits of the partnership are seen to be reciprocally beneficial. In the Gulf states this must encompass the populations of the region and not just their leadership if it is to survive regime changes. Commercial relations in which economic 'white elephants' are visible or military sales which result in no observable improvement in defence capability,[1] will only undermine the relationship over time. The choices between short- and medium-term interests will need to be carefully weighed by the outside power. Short-term oil needs may dictate pressure on the regional partner to increase production, but this may expose it to domestic and regional criticism. Similarly the inclination to tighten leverage on the regional state may dictate encouragement of projects which increase its dependency while the longer-run optimum goal for both states might be a diversification of relations with outside powers, even at the cost of dilution of the leverage of the superpower partner.

Reference was made at the outset to the question of elite orientation in the regional states. None of the leaderships are truly monolithic or hold identical values. While there may be agreement on the need for regime stability, there is seldom unanimity on how this can be best achieved. This is clearly evident in the turmoil in Iran, but equally present in the Ba'ath leadership in Iraq and in divisions within the Royal Family in Saudi Arabia. Outside powers' policies can exacerbate factionalism and strengthen the hands of those arguing in Saudi Arabia, for example, for a more 'pro-Arab' rather than 'US' policy; for a more 'rejectionist' or more pro-Soviet stand in Iraq; or for greater balance in relations with superpowers in Iran.

These actions need not be deliberate; indeed often they are inadvertent. An insensitive public statement (such as the US search for 'bases' in Saudi Arabia) or public leaks about divisions within the Royal Family in Saudi Arabia (July 1979) can weaken the leadership in these states. Intrusive demands for statistics from ARAMCO by the US Treasury Department for anti-trust purposes (December 1979) lends ammunition to those in Saudi Arabia accusing the regime of being 'puppets' of the US. Particularly given the political atmosphere in the region in the aftermath of the Iranian revolution, much greater sensitivity is required by US policy makers. Improved co-ordination of policy machinery is essential if a smooth and consistent policy is to be sustained over time. Just as the Saudi leadership is vulnerable to

---

1 In which 'dependency' itself may come to be seen to be a 'cure' worse than the illness it seeks to combat, i.e. weakness.

political blackmail and intimidation through the threat of terrorism by its neighbours, so is it politically exposed to the charge of collusion with the West whether of acquiescence in Zionist policies, of weakening OPEC, or of indulging in anti-Arab, anti-Muslim or anti-National policies. It cannot afford to support firm US action *vis-à-vis* Iran although it may desire it and it must make ritual pronouncements against foreign military presence.

Improved co-ordination and greater sensitivity may be necessary but they will not be sufficient elements in US policy. A greater readiness to make quiet suggestions and to point out the manifold implications and interrelationships between the various strands of the development programmes under way is essential. Military modernization may require both foreign manpower and divert scarce skilled indigenous manpower away from the civilian sector. Some military weapons systems may be equally as effective as those being sought without such a major diversion. In such a case it may be necessary to make this clear to the Saudis. The cumulative impact of various programmes needs to be assessed for its effect on traditional social and power structures, on value systems and on the fabric of society. It is a delusion to believe that involvement in such an extensive development programme can be purely economic and that its political implications can be left to the host country. Oil has not yet brought with it the skilled human and organizational resources necessary for the producing state to make these studies and assess their implications. Unless they are made by the outside power they will not be made at all. The failure to anticipate the consequences and alternatives of current policies will then become extremely costly for both states. In short the outside power will have to steer carefully between the rocks of dictation and deference. It must eschew gratuitous and patronising advice but nonetheless must point out the full impact of decisions made in one sector on needs elsewhere, the interrelationship of decisions, the cumulative effect of small changes and the longer-run implications of decisions made today. To do this will require not only better knowledge about the region and more streamlined policy machinery, but also tact, consistency, commitment and a genuine involvement in the wellbeing of the regional partner. It may well be too much to ask.

Index

Carter, Pres. James (cont.)
Iran, 20-1; 'Doctrine' on Persian Gulf 1980, 136, 137, 141, 155; supplies aid to YAR, 59
CENTO, 7, 112, 149, 154
Central Intelligence Agency (CIA), 14: activities in Iran, 13n
Christopher, Warren, 25, 50
Church, Senator Frank, 11

Djibouti: French garrison, 139

Egypt, 80, 84, 143: French arms supplies, 79n; offers of assistance to Gulf States, 141; Soviet arms supplies, 78, 107n; supplies arms to Iraq 1981, 101n; US ally, 52-3; US arms sales to, 48, 53
Ethiopia, 39, 75, 90: conflict with Eritrea, 89; Soviet power in, 126

Fahd, Prince, 49, 50, 64
Faisal, King, of Saudi Arabia, 70
Faisal, Prince, 61
Ford, Pres. Gerald, 11, 12, 47
France: arms supplies and help to Saudi Arabia, 65, 66, 139; arms supplies to Egypt, 79n; arms supplies to Iraq, 81, 82, 99, 104; capacity to supply arms, 79n; troops in Djibouti, 139

Germany (FDR): relations with Saudi Arabia, 66, 67, 139-40
Ghashmi, Pres., of PDRY, 59
Gromyko, Anatoliy, 138

Habbash, Georges, 91
Harrison, Selig, 133
Hussein, Pres. Saddam, of Iraq, 80, 81, 83, 87, 101, 156: announces plan for Arab rejection of foreign forces 1980, 93-4, 155-6; on relations with Soviet Union 1980, 98, 104; on Soviet expansionism, 89n; visits Moscow 1978, 90
Huyser, General: mission to Iran, 15-16

India, 61
Iran, 6, 38, 39, 80, 81, 105, 115, 117, 133, 146, 153: Air Force destroys US rescue helicopters, 21n; destination of oil exports, 17n; Carter administration's policy towards Shah, 10-11, 34-5; differences with Iraq on regional security, 153; effect of US and Western sanctions on 1979-80, 22-3, 30, 165; instability and reduction of oil exports, 143; joint naval patrols with Oman 1974, 152; militant Shi'ism of revolutionaries, 95; military assistance to Oman 1972-76, 152; military build-up under Shah, 10-11, 34-5; offers military co-operation with Gulf states 1968, 151; outgrows US tutelage, 9; pact with USA undisturbed by oil price rises, 11; planned role of SAVAK security forces, 15n; post-revolutionary disintegration of armed forces,

Iran (cont.)
16, 165; post-revolutionary relations with USA, 16-19; post-revolutionary trouble with Kurds, 17, 18; regional problems created by revolution, 153-4, 158; relations with USA, 6-7, 9 *et seq.*, 163, 167-8; revolution 1978-9, 14-16, 50, 112, 113, 122, 129, 130, 141; seizes US hostages, 18, 19, 20, 129; Shatt al'Arab, 24, 86n; threat to play off Soviet against US arms, 23, 24, 34n; *Tudeh* (Communist Party), 92; US arms sales 1973-80, 5, 10, 13, 14, 17, 167; US hostages released, 26; US military-related personnel in 1976, 11

Iran-Iraqi War 1980-81, 95-101, 129, 142, 144, 159, 167: causes of conflict, 95; consequences of invasion in Iran, 24-34, 61, 102; failure of Iranian Air Force, 27, 30; Gulf states' support for Iraq, 156; Iran refuses US arms, 26-34, 35; Iranian search for spares, 28-30, 101; Iranian tank forces, 28n, 30; Iraqi invasion, 24; land fighting, 28; limits on 'influence' of arms supplier in, 102-3, 105, 165; powerlessness of superpowers, 95, 102, 135-6; reduction of oil exports, 143; reduction of Soviet arms to Iraq, 98-9, 100, 101; superpowers' fears about result, 136

Iran, Shah of, 4, 6, 9, 13n, 16n, 17, 35, 47, 56, 57, 85, 114, 148, 149, 153, 159: eager for

Iran, Shah of (cont.)
leading role in Middle East, 10; exiled by revolution, 14, 15, 16; relations with USA, 12-13, 71n; stabilising role in Gulf, 10-11

Iraq, 39, 60, 117, 118, 126, 150, 153: arms diversification, 82, 99, 100, 101, 107; arms relationship with Soviet Union and political divergences 1958-80, 6, 79, 84-9, 92-4, 106-9, 165-7; Ba'ath Party and government, 80, 81, 84, 85, 86, 88n, 89, 94, 100, 104, 105, 106, 171; background to military relationship with Soviet Union, 79-81; claims to Kuwait, 86n, 87; condemns Soviet invasion of Afghanistan, 93; Cuban and Chinese technicians in, 76n; differences with Iran on regional security, 153; disappointing results of Soviet connection regionally, 88n; failure of national coalition 1972, 86, 106; fears of Army infiltration by communists 1978-79, 92; French arms supplies, 81, 82, 99, 104; isolated in Arab world 1969, 85; military relationship with Soviet Union 1974-81, 81-3; moderates position on Palestine 1978, 88-9, 154, 167; negotiates for French arms, 80n; oil exports to USSR, 76; oil wealth, 76, 103n; opposes Soviet expansionism, 89, 94; plans for Pan-Arab rejection of foreign powers 1980, 93-4, 155-6; poor naval facilities, 86n, 153;

Nixon, Pres. Richard M. (cont.)
with Shah of Iran, 12
North Korea, 97

oil, Middle Eastern: dangers to flow of, 143; quintupling of prices 1973, 10; US perception of, 68; Western dependency on, 1, 116, 161
Oman, 94, 114, 122, 127, 150, 153, 156: British presence, 140, 152; Dhofari rebellion, 10, 14n, 117; military co-operation with Iran, 152; Saudi economic assistance, 158; unsuccessful proposal for defence of Straits of Hormuz 1979, 154, 157; US hostages rescue mission launched via, 61, 120n
OPEC, 11, 13, 68, 128, 132, 169, 172: influence of Saudi Arabia on, 36, 72n, 73

Packard, David, 5
Pakistan, 46, 61, 91, 133: assistance to Gulf sheikhdoms, 140; dismemberment, 10; relations with Saudi Arabia, 149; rumours of Pakistani 'Guard' for Saudi Royal Family, 141
Persian Gulf, 1, 103: aftermath of UK withdrawal from, 4, 112, 146, 151; approaches to conflict management in, 117, 118; arms sales and 'influence' in, 3-4, 126, 161-72; arms transfers and policy, 4-7; constraints on superpowers in, 119-20, 121; doctrine of local and regional responsibility for security, 4, 73, 130, 143-4, 146, 147,

Persian Gulf (cont.)
150; effects of Iranian revolution and Soviet invasion of Afghanistan on, 113-4, 116; era of British paramountcy, 111-2; evolution of regional co-operation, 151-7, 159; forms of conflict management in, 121-2, instability of, 113-5, 119-20, 163-4; Liberation Fronts, 88, 152; possible threats to flow of oil, 143; possibility of superpower co-management of, 132-5, 142; range of security problems today, 116-8, 119-20, 125; regional agreements 1977, 153; regional economic assistance 158; role of powers other than superpowers, 139-41; scope and limits of conflict management, 141-4; scope and limits of regional security arrangement, 157-60; security in Iran-Iraqi war, 62-3; Soviet assets in, 128-9; Soviet attitude to regional security arrangements, 149-51; Soviet 'collective solution' proposals, 135-9, 149; Soviet interests and policy in, 126-7, 131; Soviet vulnerabilities in, 129; Straits of Hormuz, 63, 119, 131, 143, 152, 154, 157; superpower relations and conflict management, 129-39; superpower roles in, 112-3, 115-6, 118, 119, 141-3, 145; US attitude to regional security arrangements, 147-9; US naval force, 58, 112, 123; US rapid deployment force, 122-6; US support of Shah of Iran as

Sisco, Joseph, 5
Somalia, 143: Iran prevented from arming by USA, 14; receives oil from Iraq, 89; Soviet aid, 75
South Korea: possible aid to Saudi Arabia, 139n
Sparkman, John, 51
Stanford Research Institute, 45
Sultan, Prince, 58
Syria, 80, 82, 97, 105, 126, 167: Soviet arms supplies, 78, 90, 107n

Taimur, Sultan, 111
Taiwan: possible aid to Saudi Arabia, 139n
Tucker, Robert, 11

Union of Soviet Socialist Republics (USSR), 11, 145: accepts subordination of Iraqi Communist Party, 85, 86, 105; aims of military aid, 74-5, 107, 108; arms relationship with Iraq and political divergences 1958-80, 6, 79, 84-9, 92-4, 106-9, 165-7; arms supplies for Iraq, 74-9, 80-3 *passim*, 87; assets and vulnerabilities in Persian Gulf, 128-9; background to military relationship with Iraq 1958-72, 79-81; capacity to supply arms, 79n; commercial reasons for arms sales, 75-6, 77, 107; importance of Iraq as ally, 78, 80, 84; interests and policy in Persian Gulf, 126-7; interests in Iraq, 103; military relationship with Iraq 1974-81, 81-3; policy towards Iran-Iraqi war, 96-7, 98, 100, 101;

Union of Soviet Socialist Republics (USSR) (cont.)
proposals for 'collective solution' in Persian Gulf, 135-9; supplies for Iran in Iraqi war, 29-30, 97; supports Iran over US hostages, 127; Treaty of Friendship with Iraq, 7, 10, 80-1, 86, 91, 95, 112, 126, 128
United Arab Emirates (UAE), 150, 153, 154, 156: Jordanian military assistance, 152
United Kingdom, 84: aftermath of withdrawal from Persian Gulf, 4, 112, 146, 151; era of paramountcy in Gulf, 43, 111-2; present contribution to Gulf security, 140
United States of America (USA), 6: agreement with USSR on neutrality in Iran-Iraqi war, 25; arms sales looked on as test of friendship, 14n, 35n; arms sales to Gulf states 1973-80, 5; Army Corps of Engineers, 43, 44, 170n; attempts to fulfil military agreements after Iranian revolution, 17-18; attitude to Iran-Iraqi war, 24-6; Carter administration's policy towards Shah of Iran, 13-14; commitment to support of Shah of Iran, 9-11, 12; failure to rescue hostages in Iran, 21, 61, 131; Joint Commissions with Saudi Arabia, 44; military-related personnel in Iran 1976, 11; military relationship with Saudi Arabia, 37, 38, 42-7, 58; misunderstandings with Saudi Arabia, 68-71; options

United States of America
(USA) (cont.)
during Iranian revolution,
14-16; pact with Iran un-
disturbed by oil price
increases, 11; policy to-
wards Persian Gulf
security, 4-5, 112; poor
co-ordination of govern-
ment agencies, 69, 70;
problem of freeing host-
ages in Iran, 18-26, 61;
question of supplying
F-15s to Saudi Arabia, 67;
rapid deployment force
for Persian Gulf, 122-6;
reaction to Soviet invasion
of Afghanistan, 61; re-
lations with post-
revolutionary Iran, 16-19;
relations with Saudi
Arabia, 6-7, 13, 14, 25,
36-42, 67-74, 161, 168-72;
sanctions against post-
revolutionary Iran, 20-1;
security guarantor role in
Saudi Arabia, 56-8, 63, 64,
145; support for Saudis in
Yemeni conflict, 59-60;

United States of America
(USA) (cont.)
tries rapprochement with
Iraq, 100n; willingness to
alienate allies, 75n

Vance, Cyrus, 50
Vinnell Corporation, 45,
170n

Yamani, Zaki, 54
Yazdi, Iranian Foreign
Minister, 20
Yemen, North (YAR), 43,
53n, 60, 93, 122, 144,
158: Saudi aid, 158;
Soviet aid, 126-7; US aid,
59
Yemen, South (PDRY), 10-
11, 38, 39, 53n, 57, 79,
89, 90, 92, 93, 117, 118,
122, 125, 126, 163: gives
sanctuary to Iraqi Commu-
nist Party, 94; invades
North Yemen 1979, 59,
60, 144, 158; Saudi offers
of aid, 158; Soviet aid,
75; Soviet power in, 126;
Soviet restraint on, 125